THE HUGUENOTS

HENRY OF NAVARRE

THE HUGUENOTS

AND

HENRY OF NAVARRE

BY

HENRY M. BAIRD

WITH MAPS

VOL. II.

AMS PRESS
NEW YORK

Reprinted from the edition of 1903, New York
First AMS EDITION published 1970
Manufactured in the United States of America

International Standard Book Number:
Complete Set 0-404-00540-3
Volume 2 ....0-404-00542-X

Library of Congress Catalog Card Number: 76-130987

AMS PRESS, INC.
NEW YORK, N.Y. 10003

CONTENTS

OF

VOLUME SECOND.

BOOK II.

CHAPTER VIII.

1588.

CHAPTER IX.

1588.

CHAPTER X.

1589.

CHAPTER XI.

1589–1590.

CHAPTER XII.

1591–1592.

CHAPTER XIII.

1592–1593.

CHAPTER XIV.

1593–1598.

CHAPTER XV.

1598–1610.

MAP.

BOOK SECOND.

FROM THE BATTLE OF COUTRAS (1587) TO THE DEATH
OF HENRY THE FOURTH (1610).

BOOK SECOND.

CHAPTER VIII.

THE BARRICADES, AND THE EDICT OF UNION.

"SAUL hath slain his thousands, and David his ten thousands." Such was the cry of the League. Its partisans, the clergy, the paid emissaries of the King of Spain, all were loud in their praise of the wonderful courage and address of the Duke of Guise, each man striving to outdo his neighbor in magnifying the number of German reiters and French Huguenots whom the favorite son of the Church had left killed or wounded on the scene of his engagements with the enemy. The king himself came in for scanty commendation or for positive censure, while the Duke of Epernon, his favorite, was all but overwhelmed with curses for interposing his army between the retreating foreigners and the avenging troops of Guise. Solemn Te Deums were indeed sung, by royal command, first, when the intimation was given that the Swiss mercenaries of the heretics, who had come supposing that they were to liberate the King of France, had been undeceived and had agreed to return home; and, again, when it was understood that the last of the reiters had passed

Guise gains the credit of routing the Germans.

the frontiers. Henry himself, when he returned to the capital, two days before Christmas, was received by the people with great demonstrations of joy. Loud cries of "Vive le Roi!" and "Noël!" to which he had long been a stranger, greeted him on all sides, as he rode, all booted and spurred, to the great church of Notre Dame, to render thanks to Almighty God. On the morrow the judges of parliament and the other judicial and municipal officers flocked to the palace to have the honor of kissing his hand.[1] Bonfires were lighted, and other demonstrations were ordered in the public squares, but the populace was at heart irresponsive to these suggestions of joy. Men murmured at the street corners against the compact made with the Germans. The queen mother herself encouraged the discontent, manifesting little gladness at her son's return, and telling everybody that, had he not interfered, the Duke of Guise would have routed the foreign army.[2] The preachers loudly maintained from the pulpit that, but for Guise, the ark of the Lord would have fallen into the hands of the Philistines. The theologians of the Sorbonne even went farther, and, in a session not so secretly held but that the king got wind of it, took occasion to declare the opinion that unfaithful or incompetent princes might be deprived of their government, just as suspected guardians could be removed from their positions of trust.[3]

---

[1] Lettres d'Étienne Pasquier (Edit. Feugère), ii. 303: "Le Roy y est arrivé fort applaudy du menu peuple, disant tout hault que les ligueurs ne faisoient que menacer, mais que le Roy avoit chassé les estrangers." Letter of Henry of Navarre, ubi infra.

[2] "La Royne-mère n'a monstré joye de son arrivée; ains dit partout que, sans le Roy, monsieur de Guyse les eust desfaicts." Henry of Navarre to the Duchess of Grammont, January 12, 1588, Lettres missives, ii. 331.

[3] "Et là dessus, la Sorbonne—c'est-à-dire trente ou quarante pédants et maistres ès ars crottés, qui après graces traictent des sceptres et des couronnes —firent un résultat secret, et non toutefois si secret qu'on soit adverti et le Roy des premiers, qu'on pouvoit oster le gouvernement aux princes qu'on ne trouvoit pas tels qu'il faloit, comme l'administration au tuteur qu'on avoit pour suspect. Ce sont les propres termes de l'arresté de la Sorbonne, fait en leur collége, le mercredi 16 du présent mois [Decembre] et an 1587." Lestoile, i. 233, 234. It will be seen that, in the course of events, the Roman Catholic theologians of Paris had come to adopt views, respecting the right of the people to depose

The most keen and dispassionate of observers were not slow, indeed, in coming to the conclusion that the capital had had a narrow escape from falling into the hands of the invading force, agreeing, however, that its deliverance was due, not to the generalship of Guise, but to the incredible folly of the German leaders. They recognized the fact that in the army of the reiters there was but one commander with mind so clear and will so firm and tenacious of its purpose, that, had his counsels been followed, victory must have perched on the standards of the Huguenots. That commander was Coligny's son. "If Châtillon had been obeyed," wrote the Tuscan ambassador, "we should to-day have been mourning where we are triumphant." And grave Étienne Pasquier echoed the same sentiment. "To tell the truth, had the reiters followed his advice and taken the road he pointed out to them, our affairs would not have turned out so well as they have done." [1]

François de Châtillon.

Meanwhile never had the king manifested more distinctly the inherent weakness of his character than he did at the present critical juncture. The machinations of the League produced in his mind indignation and excited a thirst for revenge which could never be slaked save by the blood of his enemies, yet they evoked no prompt and vigorous action on his part. He could storm and utter imprecations and dire threats, but he was afraid to take the risk of

The king fears to punish the seditious preachers.

vicious or incompetent kings, not very dissimilar to those which the Protestant Francis Hotman had propounded, a few years before, in his "Franco Gallia." The anti-monarchical tendencies of the League and its adherents have been treated at length by Labitte, De la démocratie chez les prédicateurs de la Ligue (Paris, 1841). Bayle, in his Dictionary, long since defended Hotman against the reproach of having furnished weapons for the enemy to turn against himself, and especially to the famous Louis d'Orléans, in his "Advertissement des Catholiques Anglois." "As long as the world will be a world," playfully observes Bayle, "there will be everywhere ambulatory doctrines, dependent on times and places; true transitory birds, which are in one country in the summer, and in another in the winter; wandering lights that, like the Cartesian comets, illuminate successively several vortices. Whoever pretends to set up for a censor upon this occasion, will be looked on as a morose critic, and a native of Plato's commonwealth."

[1] Letter of Cavriana, January 4, 1588, Négociations avec la Toscane, iv. 742; Lettres d'Étienne Pasquier (Edit. Feugère), ii. 303.

putting these threats into execution. Where the anger of his
grandfather, the first Francis, would scarcely have been satisfied without the decapitation of half-a-dozen of the most obnoxious of the theologians, the spite of Henry went no farther
than to induce him to summon Parliament and Sorbonne to the
Palace of the Louvre, to listen to a severe reprimand. But
neither for Parliament and Sorbonne, nor for seditious preachers like insolent Boucher, curate of Saint Benoît, the recipient
of the monarch's most terrible menaces, was punishment in
store. In point of fact, Boucher and his fellows were rather
the gainers by reason of the display of the king's impotent
fury; inasmuch as they obtained thereby a cheap notoriety,
and were held by the people to be confessors, if not martyrs,
in the cause of God, the Holy Virgin, and all the Saints. So,
too, when the Duchess of Montpensier was reported to have repeated the threat of the wife of Marshal Retz, and remarked
"that she carried in her belt the pair of scissors that would
give the third crown to friar Henry of Valois," the king merely
ordered her to leave Paris for this piece of impudence and for
her continual intrigues with the preachers, instead of consign-
ing her forthwith to a dungeon in the Bastile or the Castle of
Vincennes. Indeed, Henry had not given up the hope that he
might yet checkmate Guise by supplanting him and making
himself head of the party now so devotedly attached to the
Lorraine princes. His eyes were not opened even by rumors
that Guise had recently gone in disguise to Rome, where he
remained three days, and that the pope had sent to the young
chief of the League a sword blessed by himself, thus constituting him the champion of the Church.[1]

It would seem to have been for the purpose of proving his
unimpeachable catholicity, as well as attesting his dialectic
skill, that Henry of Valois about this time determined
He attempts
to convert   to try his hand at the conversion of heretics. Two
heretics.
young women, daughters of one Jacques Foucaud,
lately a procureur in the Parliament of Paris, had been thrown
into prison on the simple charge of being obstinate and heady

---

[1] See Lestoile, i. 235, 236, 244.

Huguenots. The younger was unmarried, the elder was the widow of one Jean Sureau, of Montargis, and the mother of three small children. One day, at the end of January, the king mustered up sufficient resolution to forego his ignoble pastimes and visit the Châtelet, where the two Huguenots were confined. The Foucaud When brought into his presence the women maintained their reputation for attachment to their creed, and for clear understanding of its articles. Though he talked long, Henry made no progress. To say the truth, his discourse amounted to little more than promises that if they would but consent to return to mass, they should instantly be set at liberty. When they excused themselves, on the ground of conscience, the king could endure it no longer, but exclaimed : " I see very well how the case stands : you are obstinate women who will be converted only by means of fire." The two priests, whom Henry had prudently brought with him, next plied the girls for a full hour with their arguments, but succeeded no better. The Huguenot prisoners knew the Holy Scriptures well, and could instantly answer the theologians by the apt quotation of particular passages.[1]

A more distinguished victim of religious intolerance was at the same time languishing behind the thick walls of the Bastile, Palissy, the and him, too, the king thought fit to honor with a visit. Potter. This was no other than Bernard Palissy, the Potter, now a man about seventy-eight years of age. Of humble and obscure parentage, he had, nearly fifty years before the time of which I am now treating, begun, in the city of Saintes, a series of remarkable experiments with the view of discovering a method of producing an enamel that would make of the rough pottery, with which alone he was acquainted, a proper material for the realization of his artistic thought. Undaunted by poverty and by frequent disappointments, the patient worker at last succeeded in his search. After fifteen years, during which he was treated by the educated as a visionary, and looked upon with suspicion by the ignorant as a cheat, and possibly a dealer in magical arts, Palissy found the way to fame and competence

---

[1] Ibid., i. 244, 245.

opening before him. Anne de Montmorency became his patron, and Catharine de' Medici, enchanted by the elegance of his designs, conferred upon him the singular title of "inventeur des rustiques figulines du roi," and employed him in decorating the gardens of the new palace of the Tuileries.   Meantime, Palissy had in Saintes received the doctrines of the Reformation at the hands of some obscure monks who suffered martyrdom in the last days of the reign of Francis the First.   The lowly potter was no trimmer in matters of religion, but used voice as well as pen in the dissemination of his new faith.   Twice had he consequently been in peril of his life.   Imprisoned as a heretic during the first civil war, he obtained his release through the intercession of the constable with the queen mother.   Ten years later, Catharine herself interposed to save him from death in the massacre of Saint Bartholomew's Day.   Now, for a third time, the artisan whom his contemporaries knew only as a worker in clay, but whom posterity has come to recognize as a marvellous thinker and a master of the French language excelled by few of his age, was menaced with death as a Protestant.

Henry visits him in the Bastile.

Henry condescended to visit him, and endeavor to persuade him to prolong a life, so useful to his royal master, by abjuring the religion of Calvin and Beza.

"My good fellow," said he, "for forty-five years you have been in the service of the queen my mother and in mine, and we have endured your living in your religion through fires and massacres.   But now I am so hard pressed by the Guises and my people, that I have been compelled, despite my own wishes, to throw you and these two poor women into prison.   They will be burned, and you also, if you do not suffer yourself to be converted."

To which the intrepid potter replied :

" Sire, Count Maulevrier came yesterday, and, in your name, promised the two sisters their lives on the most degrading condition.[1]   They answered that they would be martyrs for their own honor as well as for the honor of God.   You have told me several times that you pitied me, but it is I that pity you, who

---

[1] "Si elles vouloient vous donner chacune une nuit."

have uttered these words: ' I am compelled.' That was not speaking as a king. These girls and I, who have a portion in the kingdom of heaven, will teach you this royal speech, that neither the Guisards, nor all your people, nor you yourself can ever constrain a potter to bow the knee before images." [1]

Unfortunately, though Henry did not carry out his threat to bring his Huguenot captives at once to the stake, he lacked the magnanimity to release them. Palissy was left to languish and die in the Bastile, of old age and hard usage; while the two Huguenot women, after exchanging the royal custody for the tender mercies of the League, were brought out, four or five months later, to suffer death on the Place de Grève.

Martyrdom of the Foucaud sisters. On the twenty-eighth of June, 1588, the bloodthirsty mob of Paris again beheld a grateful sight to which it had for some time been a stranger. By sentence of the provost, confirmed by decree of parliament, the sisters were to be hung upon the gallows until dead, and their bodies to be consigned to the flames. They endured the ignominious punishment with exemplary constancy, refusing to recant, and testifying their faith until the gag, cruelly inserted in their mouths, prevented them from uttering words that might touch the hearts or convince the minds of those present. The sight of so much innocence and fortitude might have melted a savage to compassion; it only kindled the Parisian mob to fury. It was in-

---

[1] The fearless speech of Palissy rests upon the authority of Agrippa d'Aubigné, who tells the story in his Histoire universelle, iii. 216 (book 3, chap. 1), and more fully in his Confession catholique de Sancy (reprinted in the Mémoires de Henry III.), book 2, chap. 7, "De l'impudence des Huguenots," p. 122. Despite the attempt of M. Louis Audiat, in his inordinately long communications to the Bulletin de la Société de l'hist. du Prot français, for December, 1868, and January, 1869, I cannot but regard the speech as authentic, although not improbably somewhat affected in its form by the epigrammatic style of the narrator. D'Aubigné, it may be remarked, calls the girls Sureau, after the name of the husband of Radegonde, instead of Foucaud or Foucault, as they are designated by Lestoile and La Fosse. The illustrious Pierre du Moulin, in his autobiography, tells us that he arrived in Paris as a lad of twenty, shortly before the martyrdom, to which he refers in these words: " Monsieur de Guise, qui dominoit à Paris, fit pendre deux filles, qu'on nommoit les Suraut, qui estoient sœurs, pour la religion." Bulletin de la Société de l'hist. du Prot. français, vii. (1858) 177.

sufferable that Huguenots should be permitted to die so painless a death, defying, as it were, the impotent justice of the law. The younger of the two women had, indeed, speedily passed beyond the reach of human malice ; the noose had done its office well. The elder still lingered in the throes of death. Not a moment was to be lost. The rabble rushed forward ; the rope was cut, and the quivering form of the unfortunate woman was rescued from hanging, only to be thrown yet alive upon the fire prepared to receive her corpse.[1]

Meanwhile, if Henry of Valois had but poor success in the new part he undertook to act as a " converter of heretics," he Royal revels. showed himself as much of an adept as ever in his old character of master of the revels. Striving to drown the thought of the existence of League and Huguenot, of the discontent of men persecuted for their religion, of the murmuring of provinces borne down by the intolerable weight of excessive taxation, and of the ambitious designs of leaders determined never to lay aside their arms, he plunged from time to time, with all his old zest, in frivolous amusements and prodigal expenditures. In February, at the solicitation of some ladies of his court, he gave orders to have the fair of Saint Germain prolonged for six days beyond its usual term, and diverted himself and his minions by allowing them to indulge in coarse and insulting conduct toward the women in attendance, both young and old.[2] The Emperor Nero was not, in outward appearance at least, more unconcerned while Rome was burning, than the last Valois king sometimes seemed to be at a period when the flames of civil commotion had almost reached the throne itself.

Not so was it with the Duke of Guise and his cohort of conspirators against king and country. Their cause had made good progress these past months, and they were resolved that it should not now meet with any reverse. Peace could not for

---

[1] Lestoile, i. 258 ; Jehan de la Fosse, 219 ; Haag, France protestante, s. v. Foucault, v. 155. The " curé ligueur," who correctly places the execution "durant le temps que l'on parlementoit," is also careful to note that the sisters were put to death " for simply heresy, without being accused of any other crime."

[2] Lestoile, i. 245.

a moment be dreamed of ; and, fortunately for them, the cloak
of religion was conveniently near at hand. The garment was
too ragged from hard usage and too flimsy in its original text-
ure altogether to conceal their criminal designs, but it still
hung together sufficiently well to hide from the eyes of the un-
discriminating masses of the people the hideous nakedness of
projects needing only to be fully seen to be hated and loathed.
It was deemed a propitious time for a fresh proclamation. As
the fruit of a conference between the heads of the
League, held in the city of Nancy, late in January and
in the early part of the ensuing month, some " Articles " were given to the world, containing the demands to be
made of the king. Henry must more openly join the League
and remove from about him such objectionable officers of state
as shall be pointed out to him. He must establish the decrees
of the Council of Trent, and set on foot the Holy Inquisition,
at least in the chief cities. He must permit the ecclesiastics to
redeem their alienated property, put new places in the hands of
the League, furnish pay for troops to be maintained in Lorraine and thereabouts with the view of preventing the entrance
of a new army from Germany. In order to do all this, and
to continue the war already begun, the goods of all heretics
and their associates must be sold at the earliest moment, while
all persons reputed, since the year 1560, to have been guilty of
heresy must be required to pay yearly, for the maintenance of
the war, one-third, or at the least one-fourth, of their incomes.
A final demand respected the amenities of the war itself. " The
life of no prisoner shall be spared," it is truculently provided,
" save upon his giving valid assurance that he will be a good
Catholic, and paying the full value of his possessions, if these
have not already been sold. In case they have been sold, he
shall renounce all rights he might claim in them, and serve for
three years or more in whatever capacity it may be desired to
employ him." [1]

The League
agrees upon
the Articles
of Nancy.

---

[1] The articles of Nancy have been frequently printed. See Mémoires de la
Ligue, ii. 293; Mémoires de Nevers, i. 723 ; Agrippa d Aubigné, iii. 68 ; Recueil des choses mémorables, 657 ; De Thou, vii. (book 90) 172, etc.

The manifesto undoubtedly had its serious purpose, and that purpose it might possibly accomplish ; but some provisions were sufficiently absurd, as pamphleteers in the Huguenot interest were not slow to perceive. The memory of Coutras was yet fresh in men's minds, and it could be shown to be quite as probable that Roman Catholic prisoners might soon be pleading for clemency from Protestant captors, as that Protestants would have occasion to beg for their lives at the hands of Roman Catholics. As to the sale of the property of the Huguenots and their allies, the articles revealed a simplicity on the part of their authors which was well-nigh touching. What bidder would be sufficiently bold to offer to purchase the lands of so powerful a noble as the Duke of Montmorency ? Where would the unlucky officer of the law be found who would venture to undertake the execution of the mandate of confiscation upon the possessions of the Huguenots of Languedoc and Dauphiny and Guyenne, men who hitherto had set at defiance not sergeants and ushers, but forces of armed men ? [1]

Peace was quite out of the question, whether Henry of Valois should comply or refuse to comply with the League's demands.

The zeal of Guise satisfies the Spanish ambassador. Mendoza was well satisfied with his work, and wrote from Paris to his master in the Escorial, that it was clear that Mucius (Guise) and his friends were fully resolved to oppose the conclusion of a general peace, and equally determined to prevent the King of France from giving Philip the Second the slightest uneasiness. The Spanish ambassador felt himself secure in the saddle, and lightly held the reins. Guise and his fellows would go just where and just so fast as their master wished them to go. " I have had no need," he significantly wrote to Philip, " of making them feel the spur any farther." [2]

Don Bernardino must, indeed, have been very hard to satisfy

---

[1] See the running commentary, article by article, written, with his accustomed vivacity, by Duplessis Mornay, and put forth ostensibly by a Roman Catholic. Mémoires de Duplessis Mornay, iv. 168, etc. and Mémoires de la Ligue, ii. 293, etc.

[2] Mendoza to Philip II., February 25, 1588, De Croze, ii. 316.

had he not been pleased with Guise's docility. The secret correspondence, brought to light first in our times, which was kept up between the Spanish ambassador and his sovereign, and between the Spanish ambassador and Guise, shows that there was not a step taken by the French conspirators without consulting Mendoza, and scarcely a step that he had not himself dictated. Thus, when, as was customary at the close of wars, the Duke of Épernon was about to despatch the king's troops to quarters in Picardy, it was Mendoza that advised Guise to write in all diligence to the cities of that border province, instructing them to be on their guard, and by no means to admit the royal garrisons.[1]

Into the faithful ear of Philip's envoy, whom he trusted more than his own brother, as he trusted Philip more than his own lawful sovereign, Guise poured unreservedly the secrets which he shrank from confiding even to his ally, the Prince of Parma. The King of France, more and more alarmed at the progress of the plots daily brought to his notice, but reluctant to give himself over as a slave, bound hand and foot, by acceding to the terms dictated to him in the Articles of Nancy, made an effort to win Guise back by kindness and by promises. He sent Bellièvre and La Guiche to invite the duke to give him advice respecting the campaign against the Huguenots of Guyenne, and to assure him that if he would accompany his majesty in that direction he would receive the most flattering treatment. He took the same opportunity to strive to induce the head of the League to arrange matters in Picardy, and to consent to a reconciliation with the chief royal favorite, the Duke of Épernon. But, for all answer, the envoys of Henry received only empty promises that he would consult his confederates, without whose participation he could conclude nothing. Equally fruitless was the negotiation to break up the treasonable correspondence and intrigue outside of the kingdom. It only furnished occasion to Guise to write

The king labors fruitlessly to win back Guise.

---

[1] Compare Guise's "mémoire," sent to Mendoza with a letter dated February 8, 1588, and Mendoza's despatch to Philip II., of February 25, in De Croze, Documents, ii. 314, 317.

effusively to Philip's ambassador an epistle from which we learn that the author of a war that had brought bloodshed untold into France, and immeasurable misery into thousands of homes, could find a parallel for his trials nowhere save in those of the Blessed Redeemer. "They furthermore set forth," said he, "that if I would renounce all understandings in Spain as well as at Rome, the king would honor me with many benefits and charges worthy of my dignity, with a world of extraordinary offers throwing more light upon their artifices, which I liken to the temptation which the devil directed against our Lord on the mountain. And never shall I forsake the resolution that I have adopted to pursue with constancy the blessedness which it has pleased God to conduct happily up to this present hour; being well assured that I shall ever find good angels to bear me up and to avert the evil which my enemies would like to inflict upon me." [1]

Manifestly no hope was to be found in this direction. In fact, it can scarcely be supposed that Henry of Valois had ever been very sanguine of success with so perfidious a noble, the representa-

He turns to Queen Eliza-beth for help.

tative of a family which appeared to have renounced every tie of duty and loyalty to its liege lord in favor of his rival beyond the Pyrenees. Contemporane-ously with the mission of Bellièvre, therefore, or even a little before the interview of that able diplomatist with Guise, Henry had himself held a remarkable conference, in an obscure part of Paris, with the ambassador of the English queen.

To the king in his perplexity but one remedy for present and prospective evils seemed possible. Surrounded by faithless ad-visers, threatened by the insatiable ambition of the Guises with

Importance of converting Henry of Na-varre.

dangers almost too terrible to contemplate, sensible that by flagrant vices he had irretrievably forfeited the esteem and respect of all good men, and had alienated the loyalty of a people until now distinguished for devotion to the monarch, Henry of Valois turned, as a last resort, to a gallant prince who, if not free from conspicuous

---

[1] Mucius (Guise) to Mendoza, March 9, 1588, in De Croze, Documents, ii. 318, 319.

defects of character, was, at least, frank, courageous, and decided—a man who, whatever might be said to his disadvantage,
had never been accused of womanish fears. Could the King
of Navarre but be persuaded to renounce his infatuation for
"the religion" and forget that he was son of brave Jeanne
d'Albret—still better, could he bring with him in his change of
faith his perverse cousin, the Prince of Condé—the half, nay,
the whole of the troubles of the King of France would be over.
No objection could then be urged, no rebellion justified, because
of the heterodoxy of the prospective successor to the throne. The
present holder of that somewhat precarious possession would
then be left in peace to pass his remaining days in the congenial
society of his minions, collecting puppies or primers, according
to his preferences, revelling in filthy stories and still worse practices, and leaving the management of the affairs of state to hands
very willing to be intrusted with them—notably those of the indefatigable queen mother. But how to induce Henry of Navarre
to take the decided step—this was the difficult problem to solve.

Hitherto every attempt had proved unavailing—from the
time of Biron's mission in 1577 down to that of Lenoncourt in
1585, and that of M. de Sainte Colombe in this very year. To
every appeal the same answer was returned: "I cannot do violence to my conscience. A man does not change his religion as
he lays aside one coat or one shirt for another. However, I am
ready to listen to instruction, and shall submit to the decisions
of a council of the church, national or general, if lawfully convened." Here was just encouragement enough offered to lead
to the opinion that the King of Navarre might yet be won over.
In fact, though the Huguenots do not seem to have become
seriously alarmed, although staunch Protestants like Duplessis
Mornay—men beyond the suspicion of complicity in dishonest
intrigues—even drafted the sentences that now strike us as
wonderfully significant in the light of subsequent events, there
were not a few persons of the Roman Catholic party upon whom
the repeated allusions to a possible "instruction" made a profound impression.[1]

---

[1] See above, vol. i., chapter v., p. 342.

Knowing no better way of reaching the Béarnais, Henry of Valois had recourse, at this crisis, to Queen Elizabeth, and secretly begged the interposition of a princess whose offers of mediation between him and his Huguenot subjects he had, not long since, openly and somewhat ostentatiously declined.

One winter's night—it was late in the month of February—Sir Edward Stafford, the English ambassador, received from the king a request that he would at once accompany the messenger and come to see him on matters of importance. So pressing a summons could not be declined. Accordingly, conducted by the unknown person who had brought it, the English ambassador, after having been purposely led by a roundabout way through the tortuous streets of Paris, soon found himself in a strange house, where, although other voices were heard in the distance, he met his majesty alone. Of the interview Stafford informed the queen in a despatch of the most secret character.

The king holds a secret interview with Sir Edward Stafford.

Henry began by exacting of his guest the most solemn assurances that he would divulge to no living person save the queen herself what was now to be confided to his keeping. "I am about to deal plainly with you," he said, "and to lay my state more open to the queen than ever I did to any other person. I am well content, however, that the queen should take advice of any of her secret counsellors whom it may please her to consult ; for I know that her majesty has about her men respecting whom she may be sure that they will do nothing beyond her commandment. I would with all my heart that I might give of my own blood to have such counsellors myself—men that would depend upon no one else but upon my will. Then would not my affairs be trembling in the balance, as they are at present." After this preamble, not wanting in pathetic significance, he informed Stafford that his last message to Queen Elizabeth, sent through Secretary Pinart, had been such as it was because Catharine de' Medici and the whole council insisted that he should desire her majesty not to meddle in the affairs of France. And now he disclosed the purpose for which the audience had been granted. "I have sent for you," said the king, "in order that no one may suspect that I want anything of the queen, and through you to beseech her with all my heart to grant my request, without making it known to any one that it came from me; because the Huguenots can keep no secret. I beg her majesty to persuade the King of Navarre to have a care for his estate and to accommodate himself with me, in such sort that the League may have no pretext left to it for ruining France and me."

Upon this, an animated discussion arose. Stafford assured the king that Queen Elizabeth could as little attempt to influence Henry of Navarre to renounce Protestantism, as she had influenced him to adopt it. She could not meddle with his religion. If, however, Henry's own judgment were to lead him to take this step for the good of his estate, she would interfere neither with his conscience nor with his soul. "I will deal with you," replied the king, "as plainly as if you were my ghostly father. I am, in truth, so strongly attached to my religion that I would gladly have sacrificed a piece of my kingdom or a part of my blood that all the world, but especially all France, should belong to it. But I am not so much of a bigot [1] as to let my kingdom and myself go to ruin rather than grant both religious liberty and the exercise of Protestant worship, as I have already granted them and would willingly grant them again. But it is now out of my power to do this, or, indeed, to restore peace." From this Henry the Third proceeded to reveal a picture of his own most secret desires and purposes, respecting which we need not his majesty's asseverations to know beyond all controversy that he had never disclosed it before to mortal eye. "My last hope was to have secured peace by means of the reiters. If they had had either valor or discretion, they might have compelled the adherents of the League to fall on their knees and beg for the restoration of that which they had broken in arms. This was what I looked for and expected. This was the only reason that I did not avail myself of the many offers I received from the queen to arrest their coming. I gave them every oppor-

His hopes founded on the army of the reiters.

---

[1] "He was not so much a ' bigot,' as he termed it, which in English is ' over-superstitious.' "

tunity to accomplish their designs if they could only have embraced them, and to keep far away from me; as I remained far away from them, until they must needs come and seek me out, and by their mismanagement bring me to such a pass that the world almost pointed the finger at me. Had they ravaged Lorraine and those parts of Champagne and Burgundy that were devoted to the League, leaving none unspoiled that adhered to that party, my enemies would soon have been more glad to sue for peace than they had been to fight. Instead of which, the reiters came and sought me out, and permitted themselves to be brought so completely in my hands that I must either do as I did or give the League the advantage they desired to gain over me by appropriating the credit of the whole success." After which Henry went on to claim that he alone had been the instrument of saving the lives of those of the reiters that escaped, and to blame the stupidity of the leaders who had effectually precluded the possibility of making good use of any future armies that might come in from Germany.[1]

Again the king returned to the charge, and insisted that in the conversion of Henry of Navarre lay the only hope of overthrowing the League, and again did Queen Elizabeth's faithful ambassador oppose. He saw not, he said, how her majesty could open her mouth to Navarre on such a subject. Moreover, if she did, he saw not how Navarre could yield, for he had no power over the Prince of Condé; and, if both Navarre and Condé should yield, there were great numbers of Protestants and a great number of towns and strongholds over which Navarre would lose all control the moment he should forsake his faith. The pretext of religion would still remain for the League to make use of. "Not so," replied the king, "for the rest of the Protestants would more easily be brought to think upon

---

[1] When Stafford subsequently sounded the king to discover whether his majesty would be displeased should the reiters return and lay waste Lorraine, etc., but come no farther, Henry seemed not to be displeased at the suggestion; "for these were his very words, 'Le diable les emporte, qu'ils n'y ont demeuré dernierement, canaille qu'ils sont, et ne . . . chercher leur malheur, et [trouver ceux] qui ne les demandoient pas, sans faire ce qu'ils [debvoient] et pouvoient aizement faire.'"

their consciences and dispose themselves to submission. At any
rate, the popular fear based upon the fact that the next two
princes in the succession are Huguenots would cease, and the
League would be brought back to the same state that they were
in when the Duke of Anjou was alive. At that time they could
not find means to have this color (pretext) to put out their
horns, and now, if that cause ceased, they would be compelled
to pull in their horns, to their utter overthrow." To this specious argument Stafford promptly replied that, were he a member of the King of Navarre's council, and that prince were to
ask him to give his opinion without meddling with the matter
of his conscience, he would advise him to act as the King of
France desired; but that, were he a member of the council of
the King of France, he would rather be torn in pieces than advise the latter to desire Navarre's conversion. On the contrary,
he would do all in his power to prevent it. He would prefer
that his religion should remain a bar in the way of Navarre's
attempting anything to the king's disadvantage, rather than
that, this obstacle having been removed, the King of Navarre
should come forth from eclipse, like the sun rising clear to be
worshipped by all. Sir Edward Stafford's metaphors might be
somewhat mixed, but there was certainly some sound sense in
what he said. So Henry himself seems to have thought. "At
length, with thanks he told me," wrote the ambassador, "that
every one could rule a shrewd wife but he that had her, and
that he that had her could tell worse the way to rule her, and
that was his case; but that he had rather hazard the pulling
of them (the League) down with the King of Navarre, which
he saw a possibility in, and stand upon those hazards, than in
letting them have that color (pretext) still, to make it an impossible thing to pull them ever upon their knees, but to see
them strengthen in despite of him daily. . . . As for the
King of Navarre, having once the pretence of his religion and
then foregone it, the pretence of the Catholic religion would
never serve the King of Navarre to hurt him in his time."
    Such was the sorry condition in which Henry of Valois
portrayed himself before the eyes of the English ambassador
—a king reduced to ask, in the utmost confidence, the media-

tion of a foreign queen between himself and his subjects, a mediation opposed by his mother and all his council as " a thing unhonorable to him to desire it ; "—a king compelled to say of himself, " that his case, if it were well weighed, were both to be regarded, pitied, and helped ; that he had not many to trust to, when his nearest failed him, and they that with all kind of bonds were most tied to him." [1]

Not many days after the memorable interview just related, an event took place of much moment both to Huguenots and to Roman Catholics.   This event was the sudden death of the King of Navarre's cousin, Henry of Condé

In a preceding chapter it has been seen with what universal manifestations of joy the Protestants of the kingdom received the tidings of the marriage of the prince to an heiress profess- ing his own faith, Catharine Charlotte de la Trémouille.[2]   Not quite two years had elapsed, and now came the news that the bridegroom of so few months had been put out of the way by poison administered, it was stoutly main- tained, by instigation of the princess herself.   Accu- sations of this kind were indeed frequent in the sixteenth cen- tury, and in many cases they were wholly groundless.   Greater intelligence and a more profound knowledge of medicine than had then been attained, would, we must charitably believe, have

Death of the Prince of Condé, March 5, 1588.

---

[1] The long and important letter of Sir Edward Stafford to the queen, dated February 25, 158⅞, is given entire in Hardwick's State Papers (London, 1778), i. 251-264.   What Mr. Froude inserts in a note to his History of England, xii. 410-3, might be taken as intended for a copy of the letter taken from the MS. in the State Paper Office, but, in most places, is rather a condensation, not always accurate, of the original document.   Of more consequence, how- ever, are Mr. Froude's extraordinary statements in the text, where he says : " He [Henry III.] took the field himself to oppose them, deliberately giving them opportunities to defeat him.   When they would not use them, he fell back upon the Loire, leaving Lorraine and Burgundy open to them to overrun and destroy.   .   .   .   Unfortunately, they followed him into the heart of France," etc.   All this is just the opposite of what was really the case, and what the king stated to Stafford.   His majesty, instead of giving the reiters an opportunity to defeat him, studiously kept out of their way, never going near to the borders, and, of course, never " falling back upon the Loire."

[2] Supra; vol. i., chapter vi., p. 397.

accounted on natural grounds for many unexpected deaths for
which ignorance could find no explanation save in some de-
structive drug or perfume concocted and given by an enemy.
As a general thing, the accusation of poisoning is only less suspicious than the equally convenient charge of murder by the
use of incantation and witchcraft. Unfortunately, however,
the case now in question seems hardly to fall under the ordinary
conditions, and it is perhaps too great a stretch of scepticism to
doubt the guilt of the miserable wife. The rude post-mortem
examination which was made apparently establishes the fact that
the prince died neither from disease nor from the results of over-
exercise. The precipitate flight of two of his servants pointed
distinctly to the instruments employed, while the detection and
conviction of a superior officer of the household, who had supplied them money to make their escape, gave scarcely less unmistakable evidence of the source from which the blow was
struck.

However this may be, the unhappy Brillaut, from whom
confessions of complicity had been wrung by the tortures of the
rack, paid the penalty of his crime or his weakness by being
dragged on a hurdle through the streets of Saint Jean d'Angely,
and then torn asunder by four horses, on the great square of
that city. The princess herself barely escaped the most rigor-
ous treatment. Tried by commissioners appointed by the King
of Navarre, she was by their sentence to have been
questioned on the rack. Her pregnancy saved her
from being submitted to this indignity, by rendering it
necessary to adjourn the employment of torture until forty days
from her confinement should have elapsed. In the public joy
at the birth of a new prince of the blood, the harsh order was
never put into execution; but the princess remained six years
in close imprisonment. At length, long after the time of which
I am now writing, she obtained from the Parliament of Paris,
to which she had appealed as by marriage a princess of the
blood, a decision annulling all proceedings against her and setting her free. To so favorable an issue, her abjuration of Protestantism, and the desire of the judges to avoid throwing any
doubts upon the legitimacy of a boy whom events might yet

*Trial and im-
prisonment of
the princess.*

call to the throne of France, may well be supposed to have conduced.[1]

The death of Henry of Condé was to the Huguenots a loss of no ordinary magnitude. In a certain sense he could be styled the very heart of the party. Other leaders might be attached to it from motives of policy and interest; he belonged to it from conviction. As a military leader he was certainly not the equal of his cousin, though with a well-disciplined army he might have been well-nigh perfect. Brave to a fault, he did not so much bid his soldiers go, as himself lead the way. But he assumed too much for granted. When the command had been given, he took too little pains to see that it was obeyed. Lacking the keen insight into character that distinguished the King of Navarre, he gave credit to others for a probity which they did not possess. But if his ability to command was less conspicuous than that of the other Henry, the relative inferiority was, perhaps, compensated by other qualities. He was generous, liberal, and pious. If Navarre could on occasion make duty and conscience bend to considerations of safety, Condé was inflexible. Men who had little affection for him said that, besides being courageous, nurtured in the Huguenot faith, and highly esteemed by his party, he was firm and obstinate beyond those of his family and nation. "It seemed to us," wrote the Florentine Cavriana, on the receipt of the tidings of Condé's death, "that, were he removed from beside the King of Navarre, it would be an easier task to come to an agreement." And he added: "We shall now see whether the devil has found another temple wherein he may wish to be honored by a successor of the said prince."[2]

The prince's death an irreparable loss to the Huguenots.

---

[1] "Advertissement sur la mort de Monseigneur le Prince de Condé," in Mémoires de la Ligue, ii. 330–334, and reprinted in Cimber et Danjou, Archives curieuses, xi. 277–281. This contains the certificate of the physicians and surgeons. Recueil des choses mémorables, 660; De Thou, vii. (book 90), 179, etc.; Agrippa d'Aubigné, Lestoile, Cavriana, etc., ubi infra. See, also, the able article on Henry of Condé in Haag, La France Protestante, new edition, ii. 1077, etc. The child whose legitimacy was in question, it will be remembered, was grandfather of the great Condé, the victor of Rocroy.

[2] "Ora vedremo se il diavolo avrà trovato tempio nel quale voglia essere onorato per successore al detto principe."

'Others, who, though belonging to the party opposed to him, were more amiably disposed, magnified Condé's virtues and deplored only the adverse fates in accordance with which, all his life long, he seemed to have served as a shining mark for unfriendly darts. The Huguenots, on the other hand, and especially those of the number whom the lighter and more inconstant were wont to style the " Consistorial " faction, thought more of the prince's unswerving devotion to his religion, and never forgot that even the perils of Saint Bartholomew's Day had not prevented him from boldly testifying his Protestant faith. He might not be so prudent or so fortunate a general as Henry of Navarre, but at a moment that called for truer heroism than does the most desperate battle, while Navarre listened to the demand of Charles the Ninth—"the mass, or death " —" with countenance much moved and downcast," his cousin of Condé showed no perturbation of mind, and calmly professed his intention to remain constant in his religion, which he would, he said, always maintain to be the true religion, even should he be compelled to lay down his life for it.[1]

France could ill afford to part with such a man at this critical juncture. It is not safe to indulge in conjecture as to what the history of the kingdom would have been had he lived. It may, however, well be doubted whether the disgraceful record of a king's insincere abandonment of his religion, for the sake of a capital which he wished to secure, would have found a place there The crime that freed Henry of Navarre of a competitor in the good graces of the Huguenots, and of a rival in their affections, whom at times he viewed with suspicion akin to hatred, also removed the only kinsman who might have restrained him from the commission of the most signal error—shall I not say, the fatal blunder?—of his eventful life. But whether even that kinsman's arm would have proved strong enough to overcome in an ambitious monarch the promptings of his thirst

---

[1] See the Rise of the Huguenots, ii. 469. For the character of Henry of Condé compare Lestoile, i. 466, 467 ; De Thou, vii. 180 ; Agrippa d'Aubigné, iii. 72; Cavriana to Serguidi, February (read March) 11, 1588, in Négociations avec la Toscane, iv. 747.

for undisputed power, is a question I shall not undertake to answer.

Meanwhile the tidings of the untimely fate of Henry of Condé brought sincere grief to his cousin. The cold hand of death had obliterated the impulse of jealousy from Navarre's breast. He could now forget that Condé had sometimes shown too much independence to suit his kinsman's notions of his own dignity as the representative of the elder line. He could forget that the prince had often betrayed the feeling that, either because of his greater devotion to the good cause, or because of the year by which he was the senior of Navarre,[1] he was the truer exponent of Huguenot views and aims. He could forget the ambitious designs falsely ascribed to the prince, and the plans of aggrandizement which even Sully is not ashamed to lay to his charge.[2] At the present moment the Béarnais remembered only the cruel end of the poor prince, "poor—but not in heart,"[3] and the perplexities and dangers environing his own situation. In fact, never does Henry of Navarre's correspondence betray more disturbance of mind than he displayed about this time in his private letters to the Countess of Grammont. One day he jots down almost incoherently: "The devil is unchained. I am to be pitied, and it is a marvel that I do not succumb under the burden. If I were not a Huguenot, I should turn Turk. Oh, the violent trials by which my brain is harassed! I must needs soon become either a fool or a skilful man. This year will be my touchstone. Domestic misfortune is a very painful ill. All the tortures which a mind can experience are unintermittingly inflicted upon mine."[4] A day or two later, he writes of the new disaster of Condé's death, in which he sees the hand of the League: "I am at this hour

Depression of the King of Navarre.

---

[1] Henry of Condé was born at La Ferté sous Jouarre, December 29, 1552. Henry of Navarre was born at Pau, December 13, 1553.

[2] *E.g.*, in chapter xiii. of his Mémoires, "Ce prince fit lors des brigues et menées, pour former dans le party general de ceux de la Religion, quelque espece de party particulier, qui dépendist tout de luy," etc.

[3] "Ce pauvre prince (non de cœur)." Henry of Navarre to the Countess of Grammont, March 10, 1588, Lettres missives, ii. 343.

[4] Letter of March 8 (from Nérac), ibid., ii. 342.

the single target at which all the perfidious deeds of the mass
are aimed. They have poisoned him, the traitors! Yet is it
certain that God will remain master, and I, by His grace, shall
be the executor of His purposes." [1] Three days pass, and he
exclaims: "Recall to mind what I formerly told you (and I
am rarely mistaken in my judgments). A bad woman is a
dangerous beast. All these poisoners are papists." [2] In another letter, written on his way from Gascony to the town
where the prince had met with his untimely end: "The Romish preachers loudly proclaim through the towns about here,
that there is but one more person to be secured. They can-
onize this fine deed and him that executed it. They admonish
all good Catholics to take example from so Christian an enterprise. And you are of that religion!" [3] A miscreant was arrested, who was believed to have been hired to put Navarre out
of the way after the same fashion as his cousin; whereupon the
Huguenot king penned these lines to the Huguenot minister,
La Roche Chandieu, one of those who had prayed and had
fought by his side at Coutras: "Upon what a miserable time
are we fallen, and how incensed against us is God, that this
age produces such monsters, who, though they make a trade of
assassination and poisoning, yet wish to be esteemed men of
honor and virtue! I know that they can do nothing against
me, unless it be by the permission of God, upon whose providence I place my whole reliance, and am, well assured that,
though He may tarry, yet, in spite of all His enemies, He will
deliver His church. If He be not pleased to use me in this
matter, He has a plenty of other means in His hands to accomplish His designs." [4]

Entertaining such sentiments, the Navarrese king replied

---

[1] Letter of March 10, ibid., ii. 343.

[2] Letter of March 13, ibid., ii. 346.

[3] Letter of March 17, from Pons sur Saigne, in Saintonge, ibid., ii. 349.
The Béarnais used this as a text to urge his mistress not to defer her conversion to Protestantism. "Certes, mon cœur, c'est un beau subject et [que]
nostre misere, pour faire paroistre vostre pieté et vostre vertu. N'attendés
pas à une aultre fois à jeter ce froc aux orties."

[4] Lettres missives, ii. 351, 352.

with firmness to the advances made to him by a fresh envoy of
Henry the Third. He disclaimed any responsibility for the war
now raging, and thanked God for the French king's inclination
to peace. He promised his own co-operation in bringing about so blessed a state of things. But he did
not conceal his belief that his majesty would find it
impossible to secure a stable peace without satisfying the conscientious demands of his subjects. This was no newly discovered truth; it was the experience of all countries where religion had been brought into question, for the past thirty years.
As to himself, he repeated, as on so many other occasions, he
was not obstinate—obstinacy would be a very costly luxury
in his case—and he had always professed his willingness to
receive instruction in all proper ways.[1]

Firm answer to the advances of the King of France.

Meanwhile, Condé was scarcely dead before the enemies of
the Huguenots began to indulge in conjecture concerning a successor to the important place thus left vacant. The
question was not as to the prince's governorship of
the city of Saint Jean d'Angely. Disregarding the demands of the Guises, Henry of Valois had promptly
conferred that office upon the now loyal Duke of Nevers, and
not upon the Duke of Aumale. More important than the governorship of a single city was the position of Condé in the great
Huguenot party, second only to the position of Navarre himself. Who would take that? Upon this point the Tuscan
agent at the French capital enlarged much in his home correspondence, and his remarks are worthy of attention, both on
account of his wide acquaintance with the politics of the country of which he had long been a resident, and because they give
an admirable view of the cynical scepticism prevailing among
intelligent men as to the sincerity of the actors in the crusade
now waged against the Huguenots in the name of religion.

*Roman Catho-
lic conjectures
respecting
Condé's suc-
cessor.*

The most promising candidates for the succession, we are told,
are Châtillon and Turenne, both of whom the writer regards

---

[1] "Response du Roy de Navarre aux propositions du sieur de Saincte Colombe" (February, 1588)—written by Duplessis Mornay, and printed. in his
Mémoires, iv. 183-185.

as men of more firmness than the King of Navarre. Either one of these may become a Sertorius. Then there are the two brothers of Condé—the Count of Soissons and the Prince of Conty—who have the advantage of being of the blood royal. To this suggestion it may be objected that these two brothers cannot become leaders of the Huguenots because, being Catholics, they will not consent to change their religion, and because they cannot claim the confidence of Navarre's party. "I reply," says Cavriana, "that you gentlemen of Rome are very far removed from the state of the case. Men are not combating for the faith, nor for Christ, but solely for command. Everybody professes to believe in a king, wants one, and shouts for him; but all would like to strip him of his robes and his authority. Were a leader to be found more devout and Catholic than a Capuchin monk, who yet should promise the Huguenots to do what they do, he would be revered and adored by them. Moreover, there is to be considered the fact that men see that the most holy League wants to extirpate the family of Bourbon together with the royal family, having taken the Cardinal of Bourbon as its guide and general in the work of extinction. The Huguenots will always believe in the Bourbons sprung from the late Prince of Condé; be they of this or that sect, it makes no difference. And the old Frenchmen, bound by affection to their own nation, think it strange that Spain and Lorraine lay claim to the crown of the land of their birth. The Cardinal of Bourbon, an arch-Catholic, has shown marks of joy at Condé's death. I do not know whether, in his heart, he feels sorrow, as a man, for the loss of his nephew. Methinks, the old care little except for self-preservation, and when that demon, a desire to become king, has entered into a man, the removal of any obstacle will afford him subject for rejoicing."[1]

"Bellièvre and La Guiche have gone to Guise and are now

---

[1] Cardinal Bourbon, we learn from Lestoile, exclaimed to Henry III., when the tidings of his nephew's death first came: "See, Sire, what a thing it is to be excommunicated. As for myself, I attribute his death to nothing else than to the thunderbolt of excommunication by which he was struck." Mémoires de Henry III., 109.

expected back again.   But Guise will give them fair words and
nothing more, for he does not want peace on any conditions;
because, in the first place, so long as he is in arms he has power,
and because, secondly, Spain so advises, thanks to which he
manages barely to subsist in a manner that does not deserve to
be styled 'living;' for he can never secure enough
from that source to satisfy the gnawings of hunger,
so sparingly is he supplied with money. [1]   Consequently, this holy League eats on every side, and none the
less is very lean and emaciated.   If we lived as we should
live, the League would be undone within three months; but all
malcontents and lovers of novelty among us find a support in
it.   The League is set for the ruin of France, and, if God prevent not, for the ruin of the Catholic faith also.   You can see
that this is so.   Up to the present time ecclesiastical property
has been sold to the amount of two hundred thousand crowns
of yearly income, and yet the Huguenots are as strong and as
firm as at first.   Meanwhile the people are more and more completely ruined.   I have said that the League eats on every
side : Spain and Rome contribute to the Duke of Guise;
the churches of France and some individual persons do the
same, but a little more sparingly than used to be the case,
and the king makes great concessions.   Who, then, finding
himself so situated, would lay down his arms?   What so eloquent orator could persuade him ?   The Duke, young, florid,
ardent, with a numerous following of relations, all of them capable of bearing arms, cannot lose by waiting, and gains by every
mistake of the royal party.   Knowing its divisions, he bides his
time.   Men cry out against Épernon as the obstacle to the reconciliation of Guise and the king; but were Épernon to die,
another and yet another Épernon would arise to take his place.
Everybody wants to command.   You Italians are too far off to
hear our cries or to see our tears ; but, believe me, should this
kingdom be lost, which alone makes head against Spain, you
will see how little wisdom you displayed in assenting to the
League, and such a league as this, which purposely ruins the

The League
has no desire
for peace.

---

[1] This passage has already been referred to, vol. i., chapter iv. p. 268.

kingdom.   It is well to conserve the Catholic faith, but it must
be done by other means than these." [1]

It was a very shrewd and well-informed person who wrote
down these views of public affairs, and he was at the time just
where he might have been expected to enjoy the best opportunities for obtaining a clear insight into the course of events.
Yet even he did not know or suspect that the course of the
League was wholly dependent upon the will of Philip the Second, and that the next decided blow was to be timed
with exclusive reference to that enterprise against
England upon the execution of which the secret plot-
ter of the Escorial had long been concentrating his malignant
thoughts.   For the Duke of Guise must make his descent upon
Paris, and, by getting possession of the person of Henry of
Valois, put it out of that monarch's power to succor Queen
Elizabeth, and must make this move neither too early nor too
late—a fortnight or three weeks before the Invincible Armada
should set sail on its triumphant progress from the port of Lis-
bon. [2]   Thus would the same results be obtained as if the Duchess of Montpensier's plots had been successful, or those other
plots of humbler members of the League, who proposed to
waylay the king in the Rue Saint Antoine, on his return from
the Bois de Vincennes, and either murder him or shut him
up for the rest of his days in a monastery. [3]   Meanwhile, so

Philip the Second directs the League.

---

[1] Cavriana to Serguidi, February (March) 11, 1588, Négociations avec la
Toscane, iv. 747-752.

[2] The "Barricades" of Paris took place May 12 ; the Armada was to sail on
the 29th of the same month.   Michelet, La Ligue et Henri IV., c. 13, page
170.

[3] Such a plot seems to have been formed two years or thereabouts before, but
Poulain states his inability to fix the precise date.   "Procez Verbal d'un
nommé Nicolas Poulain," in Mémoires de Henri III., 155.   Although frustrated then, the scheme was now revived by the Duchess of Montpensier, and
again it was arranged that, on Thursday, May 5, 1588, just one week before
the Barricades, his majesty should be seized outside of the gate of Saint Antoine, and hurried off to Soissons.   It would then be given out that the Huguenots had abducted the king, and the populace would be stirred up to fall
upon and massacre every one suspected of belonging to the party of the Politiques.   Ibid., 183 ; De Thou, vii. (book 90) 184, 185.   Other conspiracies
betrayed by Poulain, as, for example, that on the day of "carême prenant,"

profoundly ignorant was the French monarch of Philip's common designs upon France and England, that he actually feared
lest some arrangement might be effected between Spain and
the latter country; and to prevent this result, he offered Queen
Elizabeth, should she be attacked by Philip, double the forces
which the treaty of 1574 bound him to furnish for her defence.[1]
Philip did not relax his precautions of secrecy as the time for
action approached, or cease to enjoin his agents to be careful.
Even when Mendoza wrote from Paris to inform him of Guise's
purpose to place his own son in the hands of the Duke of Parma
as a pledge of devotion to Spanish interests, his Catholic majesty
added his note of hesitation on the margin of the despatch: "I
do not know but that this would be to make too much of a disclosure."[2]

However, the work of deceptive negotiation did not intermit.
Guise, with the cardinals of Bourbon and of Vendôme and with
others of the party, had come nearer to Paris, and
were at Soissons—a city even more convenient as a
starting-point of military enterprises than as a place
of conference. It was also just in between the capital and the
province of Picardy, whose cities the duke protested to Mendoza and Parma he would under no circumstances allow the king
to garrison. He had taken his measures so well that, should
Henry of Valois start out in person for the refractory province,
he would soon rue it. "I hope," said Guise, with evident satisfaction, "to make him think about getting home again before
he shall have approached the Picards by a single day's journey."[3]
And what Guise only hinted, others understood well enough.
If the king should go against the Duke of Aumale, wrote Cavriana, he will accomplish nothing. Guise will help his cousin,
and the king will, for lack of money, have but a sorry following. Moreover, men will say that he is leaving the Huguenots

The Duke of Guise comes to Soissons.

---

or " mardi gras," need not be referred to in detail.   See Mémoires de Henry
III., 169 ; De Thou, vii. 182.

[1] Mignet, Marie Stuart, ii. (chapter 12) 396.

[2] Mendoza to Philip II., March 15, 1588, De Croze, Pièces justificatives,
ii. 321.

[3] Mucius (Guise) to Mendoza, March 31, 1588, ibid., ii. 324.

unmolested that he may pursue in arms the Catholics. "And who knows whether, if he leave Paris, the citizens, who hate the very name of Épernon, may not call in the Duke of Guise? *Undique angustiæ.*"[1] Only one thing was the Duke of Guise willing to do by way of throwing a sop to the enemy. "We shall be satisfied," said he, "with finding an expedient to permit the entrance, for a few days only, of a certain small number of men into two or three large cities where the superiority will remain on the side of the inhabitants, together with the power to put the troops out of doors whenever it shall seem good to them so to do."[2]

The mendacity of the Guises had become proverbial. Never were they less to be trusted than when their emotions seemed to have gained the upper hand. It was not, therefore, very strange that at the very moment when the duke was so unreservedly laying bare to the Spanish ambassador his treasonable designs against Henry of Valois, he was assuring Henry's envoy, Bellièvre, with tears in his eyes, of the falsity of the reports spread at Paris to his disadvantage, and begging the king to inquire into their authorship and inflict punishment upon the guilty. Not to be outdone in hypocrisy by the associates with whom he had cast in his lot, Cardinal Bourbon, with great grief depicted on his countenance, joined with Guise in complaining of the wrong done him and the manifest efforts to compass his ruin, but professed his belief that God would not permit them to succeed. As if this was not enough, the prelate had the effrontery to pretend that all the worthies gathered at Soissons, and the Duke of Guise more than all the rest, had been laboring hard to bring the Picards to reason.[3]

Under the circumstances there could be but one result. Guise had consented to the interview at Soissons solely to gain time and secure a good opportunity for going to Paris. "The king," wrote Mendoza to his master as early as the middle of April,

---

[1] Cavriana to Serguidi, March 1, 1588, Négociations avec la Toscane, iv. 763.

[2] Mucius (Guise) to Mendoza, April 19, 1588, in De Croze, ii. 332, 333.

[3] "Qu'ils ont icy travaillé et Monsieur de Guise plus que tous les aultres, pour ranger les Picards à quelque raison." Despatch of Bellièvre, April 26, 1588, De Croze, ii. 59, 60.

"would like to forego this journey, but he will not be able to oppose it, because the burghers of Paris are firmly resolved to carry out next week the project of which.I wrote to your majesty in my despatches of the month of July last. . .   If the project in question be put into execution, as I am assured, the king will have his hands so tied that it will be impossible for him, even in words, and much less by acts, to render assistance to the Queen of England.   It was with this end that I judged it best to have the execution deferred until his majesty's fleet should be ready to start." [1]

It was a dangerous step which Guise was about to take, but the duke was by no means deficient in a certain reckless courage. Did he know the man with whom he had to deal ? He thought so, and believed Henry of Valois to be an arrant coward. Mendoza appears to have thought so too, and he told his master that Guise maintained that he understood his French majesty even to the innermost folds of his character.[2] Moreover, though, according to his habit, slow and sparing of money and men, the Spaniard was lavish of promises. Parma had just sent to Guise the Commander Moreo to hold out the most flattering prospect of aid, to be rendered so soon as the duke should openly break with the Very Christian King. Philip would at once withdraw his ambassador from Paris and commission one instead to the united princes of the League. Meanwhile he would hold at the duke's disposal, upon the frontiers of France, five or six thousand foot soldiers and one thousand or twelve hundred lances, and furnish him with a sum of three hundred thousand crowns in money.[3]

The Leaguers in Paris were more and more urgent for Guise's immediate coming. The Swiss levies, posted by Épernon at Lagny on the Marne, seemed to threaten the unruly capital

---

[1] Mendoza to Philip II., Paris, April 14, 1588, second despatch, De Croze, ii. 329, 330.

[2] Same to same, March 15, 1588, ibid., ii. 321.

[3] Guise reminds Parma of this promise, and calls for a part of the proffered help in a paper entitled "Punctos de la instruccion del q' Mucio embio al duque de Parma," enclosed in a letter of the former, May 29 or 30, 1588, De Croze, ii. 341.

from above, while Épernon himself had gone to take possession of Rouen, the chief city of the province of Normandy,
The Parisians which had been committed to his charge, despite
beg him to Guise's opposition, after the death of Joyeuse. Should
hasten his
coming. Épernon secure Orleans also, Paris would be menaced from three different quarters.[1] In response to the appeals
of the Parisians and the urgency of the Spaniards, Henry of
Guise determined to wait no longer. He had, however, taken
good care to send into the city, as secretly as possible, a great
number of armed men who sympathized with his views, and these
had found shelter as well in the religious houses as in the homes
of noblemen belonging to the party of the League. This fact had
come to the knowledge of the king. Coupled with the evasive
answers returned by the duke to the reiterated requests or commands addressed to him that he should not come to the capital,
the incident excited his uneasiness to the highest degree. Indeed, a more pitiful object than Henry of Valois at this juncture it would be difficult to imagine. He did not, we are told,
appear to care much about the seizure of places about Paris
by the League—Meulan, Meaux, Château-Thierry, and the like
—and even now, when dismissing those who came to have an
audience with him, he gave them to understand that he wanted
peace and not war. No one could make out the meaning of
this constant reiteration ; whether it was that he hoped in time
to get the better of the League, or that his mind was inclined to
quiet on any terms. But more than ever before he found himself annoyed and perplexed by not knowing whom to trust
among the many recipients of past favors who stood convicted
of disloyalty to his interests. Averse as he was to trouble, he
was compelled to change his ordinary course of life, to write
his despatches with his own hand, to take counsel only with
himself. He feared treachery in every direction, and stood in
doubt of his own guards. Those who wished him well, sighed
to think that the cure of present complications was beyond
reach, because the remedy was nothing less than a change in
the king's own character. "If only the king, as he possesses

---

[1] Michelet, ubi supra, 173.

judgment and prudence, had also a trifle more courage than he displays "—so wrote Cavriana—" our affairs would go well. The rich, the good, the true Frenchmen are for the king; the others, who are fortune-hunters, follow the opposed party." " My good sir," he added to his correspondent, " this is one of the greatest revolts and rebellions ever heard of. I much fear that before a month shall have passed, I shall have to write of some very strange developments. Guise wants to reign, and the king has little ability to hinder him. In consequence he will be constrained to submit to the command of his subject." [1]

Now was Mendoza anxious in good earnest. He had succeeded in securing, by the treachery of Henry of Valois's trusty servants, a copy of the instructions given to the royal secretary sent to Constantinople to stir up the Grand Turk to make peace with Persia and attack the Spaniard. He had learned from Rouen that the partisans of the League in that city were fully prepared to seize the person of their archenemy, the Duke of Épernon. He had it on good authority that Henry's knavish secretary Villeroy, who seemed never more at home than when betraying his master's secrets, had given assurance to Guise, in a paper over his own signature, that he would rejoice at the murder of the king's haughty minion, and that the sentiment of gladness would be shared by most of the nobles not connected with the League. News had come that many of the gentlemen of the party were in the castles hard by Paris, and common soldiers in great numbers were already within the city. So eagerly did the Parisians long for Guise's arrival, that the duke's usual envoy, M. de Mayneville, sent by him with certain information which he deemed it imprudent to put down in writing, had been sent back by them, before he had even had an opportunity to deliver his message to Mendoza, to implore that champion of the Church to come instantly to the rescue. " From all this," wrote the Spanish ambassador, making use of a figure more forcible than refined, " from all this it is easy to conclude that the abscess will burst before long." [2]

---

[1] Cavriana to Serguidi, May 7, 1588, Négociations avec la Toscane, iv. 775.
[2] Mendoza to Philip II., May 7, 1588, De Croze, ii. 333–335.

One Monday morning in May—it was the ninth of the month
—Bellièvre was seen at the northern gates of Paris, on his way
back from Soissons. He had been despatched thith-
Guise unex-
pectedly
comes to the
capital. er, a few days before, with express orders to Guise to
adjourn his proposed visit to the capital. The duke
was told that, should he persist in his design, the king would
regard him as a criminal and hold him responsible for all the
troubles that might ensue. The envoy was sent back with an
evasive answer. It was toward nine o'clock when he entered
the Porte Saint Martin and directed his steps toward the palace
of the Louvre. Three hours had scarcely passed when a small
cavalcade—there may have been seven or eight gentlemen and
not over twice that number of horsemen all told—rode in from
the same quarter.[1] One of the party, and apparently the leader, wore his hat drawn far down over his face, as if to avoid
recognition. Suddenly, whether by a preconcerted plan or from
a mere love of sport, a bystander laid hold of the hat and,
raising it, disclosed the features of a man whom the Parisian
populace had come to adore as a god. The cry of "Vive
Guise" arose on all sides, and was repeated with far more enthusiasm than the cry of "Vive le Roi" had ever been caught
up within the memory of living man. And now the rebellious
subject who, taking his life in his hand, had come almost alone
to beard his sovereign in his very capital, was surrounded by a
throng, increasing at every step, until it was estimated that no
fewer than thirty thousand persons accompanied him before he
was half through the city. Never was ovation more complete.
Men and women rushed from work-room and from shop. There
was no act, there were no words too extravagant for the expression of the joy felt at the advent of him whom they greeted as
their savior from the worst of fates. Those fortunate persons
who could get near to him embraced him, or, failing in that,
kissed the very hem of his garments. Some drew out their

---

[1] "Y seroit arrivé en plein midy avec sept chevaux seulement," says the
"Copie des lettres que les habitants de Paris escrivirent aux villes du Royaume de France de la Religion Romaine, du dixhuitieme de May, 1588," in
the Mémoires de la Ligue, ii. 369.

rosaries and endeavored to add new sanctity to these aids to devotion by rubbing them against the body of him whom their
imaginations exalted into one of the company of the saints ;
whereupon they passionately pressed the beads to their lips,
their eyes, and their foreheads.   Those who could not get at the
duke for the press were fain to content themselves with expressive gestures and words of welcome.   The gentle sex from
their windows strewed flowers in his way, and loudly blessed
his coming.   Vitri, one of the queen's maids of honor, distinguished herself above the rest, by lowering the mask, behind
which it was the fashion for ladies of quality to conceal their
faces, and crying out : " Good prince, since thou art here, we
are all saved.   Shall I not die after having seen thee king ? "
No conqueror returning from a hardly contested field could have
desired a more splendid triumph.

The nobleman who was the object of their jubilant demonstrations accepted and returned the greetings of the people, hat
in hand, with the most conciliatory air.   After traversing a good
part of the Rue Saint Denis, without waiting to go to his own
stately house, he presented himself, all booted and spurred as
he was, to the queen mother, in her apartments in the Hôtel de
Soissons (or the Filles Répenties) hard by the church of Saint
Eustache.[1]

For shrewdness and fertility of device, Catharine de' Medici
had no superior, and few equals, among the women of her
He visits the   time.   If the ability to hoodwink the unsuspecting,
queen mother. to amuse half a dozen rivals for power by as many
false stories, and to deceive temporarily without reference to the
day of reckoning that is sure to come in the end—if this con-
stitutes the highest form of genius to which mankind should
aspire, then the Italian princess, who had spent close upon the
allotted threescore and ten years in such ignoble pursuits may
unquestionably be accorded the palm.   But never was there a
woman to whom, within the compass of a single brief life, a
greater number of humiliating experiences seemed to have been

---

[1] See, especially, Davila, book ix., 337 ; Agrippa d'Aubigné, iii. 73 (book i.,
chapter xix.).

reserved. On the present occasion she was both surprised and disconcerted. How should she defend herself against the reproaches of her son whom she had all along endeavored to quiet with assurances of the duke's good intentions? How prove to him that the nobleman, who, in direct defiance of the king's prohibition, had had the audacity to push on to Paris, was a faithful subject and entertained no sinister designs upon the royal authority? Catharine, when she received the duke, was pale, trembling, and almost dismayed. Her words were ambiguous and uncertain. She was glad, she said, to see him; but would have been much more glad to see him at another time. To which Guise replied with all appearance of respect, but almost angrily, that he was a faithful servant of the king, and that, having been informed of the calumnies circulated respecting himself, as well as of the mischievous designs set on foot against religion and against the honest and well-disposed citizens of Paris, he had come to clear himself and to avert these disasters, or else to lay down his life in the service of the Church and for the common weal.[1]

Embracing the first opportunity afforded, while the courteous duke was paying his respects to the ladies in waiting, Catharine de' Medici promptly despatched one of her gentlemen ushers, Luigi Davila, brother of the historian, to acquaint the king with Guise's arrival, and to tell him of her intention to bring him at once into his majesty's presence. If the unexpected turn of events had thrown Catharine into consternation, it quite unmanned her wretched son. The messenger found him closeted with Bellièvre, Villequier, and one or two others of his servants, discussing the present situation, on the supposition that Guise was full sixty miles distant, at Soissons. To find that the duke was actually within the walls of Paris, and about to visit him in the Louvre, was too much for the nerves of the Valois. He was almost crushed. He could scarcely hold up his head, but leaned it heavily upon

Surprise and dejection of the king.

---

[1] Davila, 338. The history of Enrico Cattarino Davila being at this point based upon the authority of his elder brother, Luigi, is of great weight, as virtually the narrative of an eye-witness of, and, to some extent, a participant in, the events related.

his hand till it well-nigh touched the table. After anxiously questioning Davila on every point, he dismissed him with the message to the queen mother to defer Guise's visit as long as possible. What should he do? Here was a fine opportunity for a good counsellor to come forward, had Henry possessed one. Such advice as was at command, however, was soon proffered. Alphonso Ornano, colonel of the Corsicans in his majesty's army, a soldier of tried valor and prompt resolution, advocated summary action, and volunteered his own services. Let the king receive the Duke of Guise in the very cabinet in which he now is seated, and his faithful servant promises speedily to put the rebellious nobleman out of the way. A churchman who held the same views, the Abbé d'Elbène, followed up the suggestion by quoting Scripture: "I will smite the shepherd, and the sheep shall be scattered." But the League was too well represented in the neighborhood of the king to permit so decided a measure to be adopted without remonstrance. The treacherous Villequier and the half-hearted Chancellor Birague, not to speak of Bellièyre, never a friend of extreme resorts, instantly opposed Ornano's suggestion. If Guise be assassinated, said they, the burghers of Paris will be moved to take immediate revenge, and the king's forces are inferior to those of the League. In their rage they might not spare the monarch himself, for whom the castle of the Louvre would furnish no safe retreat.

Between the two courses Henry of Valois found it difficult to decide. He was not allowed much time for deliberation. In the midst of his irresolution, Catharine de' Medici arrived, bringing with her the cause of all this anxiety. The queen, coming in her sedan, and the duke, on foot, left in the court of the Louvre the crowd of sympathizing citizens that had not forsaken Guise for a moment since he entered Paris, and passed in between close ranks of guards whose commanding officer showed the Lorraine chief scant courtesy. Grillon's sullen mien was a poor augury of a cordial welcome within. "I sent you word that you should not come," were the first words that greeted his ears, as he bowed low before Henry, and the abrupt speech was accompanied by an angry

The duke comes to the Louvre.

glance which only too clearly betrayed the conflict of passions
raging in the monarch's breast. The situation was ominous,
but it was too late to retreat. The duke controlled his natural
fears, and answered with greater deference than he had shown
to the queen. " I am come, Sire," said he, " to place myself
in the arms of your majesty's justice, in order to clear myself
of the calumnies heaped upon me by my enemies. Yet would
I never have come, had I been distinctly informed that your
majesty had commanded me to stay away." It was the beginning of a stormy interview. The king, full of passion, turned
to Bellièvre, and peremptorily demanded to know whether he
had not been instructed to warn Guise that, should he venture
to come to Paris, he would be accounted the author of all the
outbreaks that might ensue. Then, when Bellièvre was about
to answer, Henry bade him be silent, and turning to Guise exclaimed : " I know not that you have been calumniated by anybody ; but your innocence would have clearly appeared had
your coming produced no commotion, and had it not interrupted the quiet of the government, as it is likely to do." The
words were an open threat. The next thing might be a signal
to Colonel Alphonso to fulfil his pledge. But again Catharine
was at hand to sap her weak son's resolution, by whispering to
him hints of danger, and telling him what scenes she had witnessed in the streets. And the Duchess of Uzès was there, too,
to corroborate the queen's statements. Between the words of
the two women Henry's attention was diverted, if his anger
was not appeased, and Guise was permitted to avail himself of
the excuse of fatigue after his journey to bow himself out of
the king's presence and retire to his city house in the Rue Saint
Antoine. The duke had had a narrow escape. None felt it
more than he, unless it was Pope Sixtus, whose first exclamation, on receiving tidings of the duke's visit to the Louvre, is
said to have been : " Oh, the rash, the imprudent man, thus to
place himself in the hands of a prince whom he has treated with
such indignity ! " The pontiff's next utterance was of amazement at Henry's weakness : " Oh, the cowardly prince, the poor
prince, so to have suffered the opportunity to slip through his
fingers for ridding himself of a man who seems to have been

born for his ruin!" As for Guise, thankful to have escaped
so great a peril, he inwardly resolved never to expose himself
again. But to men constituted as he was, danger has a strange
fascination, especially if the danger be associated with wild
dreams of sovereignty. The flame may have singed them, and
the pain or the apprehension of future ruin may have wrought
wholesome but short-lived resolutions tending to greater prudence; but they are pretty certain in the end to return to the
scene of their first folly, and there to meet their fate in the all-
consuming fire.

Days of anxiety and ferment followed. The king, too late
discovering his mistake, endeavored to regain firm possession of
the capital which was fast slipping out of his grasp. The proclamation first issued, ordering all strangers not permanently
residing in Paris, or detained there by necessary business, to
depart at once, proved, like all similar proclamations, an empty
form scarce worth the paper on which it was printed. But
when, awaking to the importance of the crisis, Henry was persuaded by his advisers to introduce into the capital the Swiss
and French guards, hitherto posted in the neighborhood, the
real struggle began. The "sixteen," the leaders whom the populace had come to regard as the embodiment of Catholic orthodoxy and the conservators of the liberties of Paris, gave
the note of alarm, and instantly the whole city was in commotion. It was reported that the lives of Guise and of all true
friends of the faith were in danger. It was said that not the
humblest Catholic was safe. Nay, the wild story was repeated
from mouth to mouth that a threat had been dropped by a
leader of the royal forces that the honor of Parisian wives and
daughters should atone for the rebellion of their husbands and
fathers.

No other city in France, perhaps no other city of Christendom, could at this time boast a population so ready for revolt,
The populace robbery, and every form of violence as Paris. It was,
of Paris. in the view of a well-informed contemporary, the best
place for Guise "to execute his intended mischiefs, being a town
always affectioned to him, and swarming with multitudes of
poor artisans, porters, and peasants who, in hope of impunity

and reward, are ready at all times to attempt mutinies, murders, or any kind of villanies whatsoever, if they may but be egged on, encouraged, or countenanced by any man of authority or honor that in such actions will undertake to be their head and ringleader; as the miserable and more than barbarous massacre, most cruelly executed in that accursed town, upon the most renowned and worthy Admiral Châtillon and sundry nobles, gentlemen, students, and other men and women of all sorts, so they were suspected to be of the religion, may give sufficient testimony." [1]

The capital mistake of the king is said to have been that, in disposing his troops throughout the city, early in the morning of Thursday, the twelfth of May, the Place Maubert had been overlooked. Here, therefore, at a considerable distance from the Louvre, and in the very quarter where centred the most unruly elements, the populace had the advantage of position, and it was impossible to dislodge it. When the royal troops were sent to make the fruitless attempt, they found themselves suddenly confronted by a breastwork of such material as a great city could readily supply. To proceed was out of the question; to retreat was equally impracticable, for a similar barrier had risen in their rear. Nor was this all. As by magic, the system of defence improvised by M. de Bois Dauphin and the students of the University, had spread over all the chief streets of Paris. At intervals regularly marked out, of thirty paces each, The day of the the willing hands of men, women, and children had barricades. erected a succession of rude walls, in which barrels filled with earth, heavy timbers and logs, in short, whatever could be laid hold of to swell the size and add to the strength of the structure, had been hastily heaped together. Almost before they knew it, the Swiss guards found themselves shut up in the Cimitière des Innocents, the French guards on the bridges, at the Châtelet, at the Hôtel de Ville, and wherever

---

[1] " A brief discourse, containing the true and certain manner how the late Duke of Guise and the Cardinal of Lorraine, his brother, were put to death . . . for sundry conspiracies and treasons, etc. Written unto our late Queen Elizabeth, by Sir Edward Stafford, at that time her ambassador in the court of France." In Hardwick's State Papers, i. 274.

else they had been posted. To crown the insolent contempt of
royal authority, a barricade was thrown across the street under
the very noses of the king's own body-guard, and in sight of the
monarch's apartments in the Louvre. The Swiss, as foreigners and looked upon with greater suspicion by the people,
naturally fared worse than the other royal troops. Like these,
they had been prevented by the king's express orders from
using any violence. Now that it was too late, they found themselves imprisoned in a narrow place, at the mercy of the Parisians, and were forced to resort to prayer and entreaty. Shot at
with arquebuses, and struck by the ponderous stones that were
hurled upon their heads from neighboring windows, they could
only cry out in broken French: "Bonne France," "Miséricorde," "Vive Guise," and whatever other exclamations might
be expected to move the hard hearts of their enemies.

The moment had come for the duke to appear upon the scene
in his new character of the magnanimous hero. The plans he
had laid had succeeded to perfection. There was no need of a
resort to bloodshed, and the signal which was to have been
given, as a last resort, by stroke of the bell of the church of St.
Jacques de la Boucherie, was purposely withheld.[1] All the morning he had carefully remained within the barred gates of his
house, not far distant from the Bastile. There Luigi Davila, sent
by Catharine de' Medici, ostensibly to carry a complimentary
message, but in reality as a spy to ascertain what he was doing, on
being admitted by the wicket gate, found him, early that morning, pacing up and down between two long rows of armed gentlemen ; and Guise seemed to take gratification in satisfying his
visitor's curiosity. He led him by the hand into the adjoining
garden, and enabled him to obtain a good view of the great

---

[1] " De sorte qu'il prist une autre résolution d'essayer à faire faire barricades,
et, sy les choses luy succédoient, se gouverner doucement ; synon, avoit donné
signal que, au son de la cloche Saint Jacques de la Boucherie, ils missent tout
à feu et à sang. Toutesfois il n'en fut pas besoin, car tout leur rioit, ouvroit
les bras, détestoit le Roi et les siens, et ne parloit que de se saisir de sa personne ; ce qu'ils differoient au lendemain." Mémoires de Claude Groulart,
Premier Président du Parlement de Normandie (Collection Michaud et Poujoulat), 554.

quantity of weapons stacked there, as well as of the soldiers who swarmed in the lower rooms of the house. It was four o'clock when the duke, moved thereto, it is said, by the king's earnest prayer, conveyed to him by Marshal Biron, deigned to take notice that something like a revolution was actually in progress, and sallied forth from his peaceful home. He was dressed in a slashed doublet of white satin, and wore the large hat he so much affected; but he carried no arms, and somewhat ostentatiously held a short stick in his hand in lieu of a sword. The enthusiasm of preceding days was repeated when he appeared. Some were loud in proclaiming their desire to have him anointed king at once. "We must not trifle away the time any longer. We must take Monsieur to Rheims"[1]— was a significant cry that greeted his not unwilling ears, mingled with the universal "Vive Guise!" But the duke, thinking that his hour was not fully come, put on an air of displeasure, and said: "My friends, it is enough. Gentlemen, it is too much. Cry, rather, 'Vive le Roi! Long live the king!'"

Under such circumstances did Guise, now real master of Paris, go to the rescue of the French guards and of the unfortunate Swiss, whom he ordered to be escorted to the gates of the Louvre, and whose arms he restored to them.

Meanwhile, Catharine, to whom tears were about as natural as falsehood and intrigue, had scarcely dried her eyes all the time she sat at dinner.[2] Toward night, her old fondness for negotiation overcoming the pangs of gout, she set out to try her skill with Guise. It was out of the question to ride in her coach, so she went in a sedan; but it took two hours for her bearers to go the trifling distance that intervened between the palace and the rival establishment in the Rue Saint Antoine. At every barricade a halt must be made, and the citizen defenders positively refused to permit an

Catharine negotiates in vain.

---

[1] "Il ne faut plus lanterner; il faut mener Monsieur à Rheims." Lestoile, i. 250.

[2] "Bien les Roynes en furent elles grandement estonnées, et singulierement la Royne Mere, laquelle tout le long de son disner, ne fit que pleurer à grosses larmes." Amplification des particularitez, etc., in Mémoires de la Ligue, ii. 347.

opening larger than would barely allow the sedan to pass through. The queen mother found Guise elated with success, full of complaints against the king, exorbitant in his demands. He must be appointed lieutenant-general of the kingdom, with as ample powers as his father had enjoyed after the Tumult of Amboise. The appointment must be confirmed in a session of the states general to be called in the city of Paris. Henry of Navarre and the Bourbon princes that adhered to him must, as heretics, be declared incapable of succeeding to the crown. The taxes must be reduced. Épernon and his brother La Valette, Marshals Retz and Biron, Monsieur d'O, and Alphonso Ornano, must lose their offices and be dismissed from the court. The king must give up his famous body-guard of the " Forty-five" gentlemen. The Duke of Aumale must be governor of Picardy, the Duke of Nemours of Lyons, the Duke of Elbeuf of Normandy. Mayenne must become admiral. La Chastre must have Biron's place as marshal. Six cities, to be named by the chief men of the League, must be given them for their security. Such were some of the modest requests of Henry of Guise.

The queen mother argued and remonstrated, but did not absolutely reject; then returned to the Louvre in the same tedious manner in which she had come. The next day, Friday, the thirteenth of May, after a sleepless night taken up with a protracted discussion between the advocates of concession and of resistance in the royal council, the indefatigable queen mother was again at the duke's house. She displayed no impatience, but went over the same subject, taking up item after item of the League's alleged grievances and demands. Never had she seemed to be less in a hurry, or less irritated by the duke's increasing obstinacy. Unfortunately the quiet conversation was interrupted by the abrupt entrance of M. de Mayneville, a gentleman who, as we have seen, had had much experience in carrying messages for the League. Leaning over Guise's shoulder, he whispered the fatal news that the King of France, whose affairs the duke and the queen mother were now discussing, believing him to be a captive in the hands of his enemies, had quietly slipped out of Paris, and had full two

hours' start on the way to the city of Chartres.   Never had escape been more neatly effected.   The Duke of Guise, prepared
for almost everything else, was quite unprepared for this.   The
queen mother was, to all appearance, equally surprised, protesting that her son had not said a word to her of any intention to
flee.   " Ah, Madam," said Guise, with a loud voice, " I am altogether undone!   While your majesty has been detaining me
here, the king has gone away to effect my ruin."

The tidings were well founded.   Henry of Valois had left
the castle of the Louvre under the pretext of taking a little
walk, as he was accustomed to do, in the neighboring garden of
Henry of   the Tuileries.   On the present occasion, however, he
Valois escapes   had not tarried to expend any inopportune admira-
from his capi-
tal.   tion upon the rustic works and grottoes so skilfully
constructed by the art of Palissy the potter.   He had, instead,
hastily donned a riding suit, and mounted a horse standing
ready saddled for him.   A minute more, and he had cantered
out of the new gate of the gardens, accompanied by sixteen
horsemen and followed by twelve footmen.   It was the only
outlet of Paris which the Duke of Guise had left unprotected.

Pursuit was useless.   By the time the vigilant guards of the
Louvre learned of their prisoner's escape, he had crossed the
bridge of Saint Cloud, and was out of harm's reach.   That
night he slept at Rambouillet, and the next day in Chartres.
The king had saved the heads of the League the trouble of
carrying into effect their threat of going to get Friar Henry in
his Louvre and carrying him off to the monastery.[1]   It was
evident that this was not exactly what Mendoza and his fellow-
conspirators—French and Spanish—had anticipated.   The pressure of the Parisians had brought Guise to the city before matters were quite ripe for the execution of his plans both as to
Épernon's assassination and as to Henry's arrest and virtual de-
thronement.

Meantime Guise, desirous of giving dignity to his newly acquired lordship of Paris in the eyes of foreign powers, bethought

---

[1] "Ne tenoient autre langage (*i.e.*, the preachers and the Count of Brissac)
si non qu'il faloit aller querir frère Henri dans son Louvre." Lestoile, i. 251.

him of no better way than to proffer his kind offices to the
ambassador of Queen Elizabeth.   This was none other than
Sir Edward Stafford, a high-spirited gentleman and a staunch
Staunch Prot- Protestant.   How keenly sensitive he was in both
estantism of capacities, is seen from an incident that had hap-
the English
ambassador. pened about four years before the events now referred
to.   In 1584, as Corpus Christi approached, he was determined
that the English Embassy should display no drapery in honor
of a day consecrated to the exaltation of the Roman Catholic
doctrine of Transubstantiation.   " I have had somewhat to do
this ' Fête Dieu,' " he wrote to the queen's secretary, " for the
keeping of my house unhanged, as this bearer can tell you;
but at the length I had the victory, and would not permit them
to hang an inch of anything that belonged to me." [1]   It turned
out in a few days, however, that the ambassador was mistaken
in supposing that the French had renounced their purpose.   In
vain did Stafford protest that for the king to insist was deroga-
tory to the queen's dignity and " a breach of the privilege of
her ambassador; "   the curt reply was " that *within*, the house
is free, *without*, the house is the king's."   It was a time for
prompt action.   Not to be forced in his dignity or his conscience, Stafford, the day before the occurrence of the church
festival, " gave over the house " to the owner, and removed his
quarters to " a little lodging in a garden," where no conformity
with the hateful practice could be exacted of him, meanwhile
declaring, " Never will I come into the other again, that they
may not say they have hung the English ambassador's house
while I am in it, which is all I can do till I know her majesty's
pleasure." [2]   Such was the man with whom the Duke of Guise
determined, if possible, to ingratiate himself.

In the duke's name Count Brissac presented himself at Sir
Edward Stafford's house, and requested him to give himself no
uneasiness at what occurred outside, but by no means to go into
the streets, and promised him the duke's gracious protection.

---

[1] Sir Edward Stafford to the secretary, May 23, 1584, Murdin's State Papers,
402.

[2] Same to same, May 29, 1584, ibid., 404, 405.

" If," replied Stafford, " I were a private individual, I should at once go and throw myself at Guise's feet, humbly thanking him for his courtesy. But being here, at the king's court, in behalf of the queen my mistress, I neither can nor will have other safeguard than the king's."

Sir Edward Stafford declines the protection of the Duke of Guise.

"The Duke of Guise," continued Brissac, " did not come to Paris to execute any enterprise against the king his master. He is simply acting on the defensive. There was a great conspiracy on foot against him and the city of Paris. The Hôtel de Ville and other buildings are full of gallows on which the king intended to hang great numbers of the citizens and others. The duke begs you inform the queen your mistress of all these things, in order that everybody may understand them."

" I shall be glad," replied Sir Edward, " to believe it so. To speak frankly, what is now occurring in Paris will be thought very strange and very ill by all the princes of Christendom. No cloak, be it never so gaudily worked, could conceal the deformity of a revolt against one's sovereign. If there were so many gallows prepared, we shall more easily believe the fact when the gallows are placed upon exhibition. But granted the truth of the assertion, it is a hateful and insufferable presumption for a subject to seek by force to stand in the way of his sovereign's administration of justice. I shall notify the queen as promptly as possible of everything you tell me, but it is no part of my commission to convey to her the views of the Duke of Guise. The queen my mistress is wiser than I am, and will believe and judge as may seem good to her."

Losing his temper the count began to bluster. " The people of Paris bear you ill-will," said he, " because of the cruelty which the Queen of England exercised against the Queen of Scotland." Here the ambassador, as in duty bound, interrupted. " Stop there, sir, at the word ' cruelty.' An act of merited justice is never properly called cruelty. Moreover, I do not believe that the people have any spite against me, as you say. Why should they ? I am here in a public capacity, and have never wronged any one."

" But have you not arms ? " said Brissac.

" If you asked me as having formerly been an intimate

friend of your uncle, Marshal Cossé, perhaps I might tell you, but being what I am I shall tell you nothing about it."

" You will be visited by and by, for it is believed that you have arms, and there is danger that force will be used."

" I have two doors to this house," replied Stafford. "I shall close and defend them so long as I shall have the ability; that, at least, I may show the whole world that the law of nations has been unjustly violated in my person."

" But tell me, as a friend, have you arms ? "

" Since you ask me as a friend, I will tell you as a friend. If I were here as a private man, I should have them; but being an ambassador, I have no other arms than right and public faith."

" I beg that you will have your doors closed," said Brissac in conclusion.

" I must not do it," was Stafford's final rejoinder. "The house of an ambassador must be open to all comers. Besides, I am not in France to sojourn in Paris alone, but near the king, wherever he may be." [1]

There was no disguising the fact that the abrupt flight of Henry of Valois had seriously disarranged the League's plans. Once away from the dangerous capital, he had a fresh opportunity to assert his authority. Great was the disappointment of the Parisians, who spared no pains to stigmatize his majesty's departure as the disgraceful sequel of the conspiracy of the Duke of Épernon and other secret par-

The League entrenches itself in Paris.

---

[1] " L'ambassadeur, personnage eloquent et doué de grande prudence, fit à Brissac et à Ligue la leçon qui leur appartenoit," etc., says the author of the Recueil des choses mémorables. See the conversation reproduced at length in the Mémoires de la Ligue, ii. 350, 351. On the affair of the Barricades consult Davila (book ix.), 336–347 ; De Thou, vii. (book 90), 185–195 ; Agrippa d'Aubigné, iii. 72–75 ; Lestoile, i. 249–252 ; Lettres d'Étienne Pasquier (Edit. Feugère), ii. 304–310; Mémoires de la Ligue, ii. 337, 338, and 346–350 ; Journal d'un curé ligueur (Jehan de la Fosse), 211–214 ; Recueil des choses mémorables, 660–2 ; Histoire de la journée des Barricades de Paris (written by a member of the League), MS. printed in Cimber et Danjou, Archives curieuses, xi. 365–410 ; Histoire très véritable de ce qui est advenu en ceste ville de Paris depuis le vii. May, 1588, etc. (ascribed to Sainct-Yon, an " échevin" of Paris), reprinted, ibid., xi. 325–350 ; Cavriana to Serguidi, May 13, 1588, in Négociations avec la Toscane, iv. 780, 781.

tisans of the heretical Henry of Navarre. " In order to cast
the king quite down from the height of his reputation, they
have counselled him to betake himself shamefully to flight, and
to forsake his palace under color of going to the Tuileries." [1]
So wrote the seditious burghers of Paris in letters that were
intended to excite everywhere throughout France a revolt
similar to their own. Meanwhile they took good care, under
Guise's skilful direction, to entrench themselves well against
any possible attack. The Swiss guards had been permitted to
follow the king, and the city was placed under charge of men
in whom the League could safely trust. The coffers of the
royal exchequer were carefully sealed up—so said Stafford—
after their contents had been no less carefully appropriated. [2]
On Saturday, the day subsequent to the king's flight, the Bastile, after a brief show of resistance made by the officers in command, surrendered at discretion. Two or three days later the
strong castle of Vincennes imitated its example. Some of the
municipal officers, too loyal to join in the general revolt, made
their escape. The highest of their number, the " prévôt des
marchands," fell into the hands of the Leaguers at the capture
of the Bastile, and was reserved to be tried for treason. On
the following Wednesday these magistrates, together with the
" procureur de ville," atoned for their attachment to their lawful sovereign by being solemnly deposed from office. An
assembly of the citizens proceeded at once to fill their places
with men of an entirely different stripe. [3] Paris was firmly
under control of the League, whose sway—whether beneficent
or otherwise, time would show—was to last full five years.

It is not necessary here to relate in detail the events that
succeeded—events disgraceful in themselves and having no im-

---

[1] "Afin de jetter le Roy du haut en bas de sa reputation, ils l'auroient con-
seillé de s'enfuir honteusement," etc. Letter of the Parisians, above quoted,
of May 18, 1588, Mémoires de la Ligue, ii. 370.

[2] The Duke of Guise " sealed up the king's coffers of his exchequer, but
took out the money first." A brief discourse, etc., written unto our late
Queen Elizabeth, by Sir Edward Stafford ; in Hardwick's State Papers, i. 276.

[3] See the contemporary pamphlet "Histoire très véritable de ce qui est
advenu en ceste ville de Paris," in Cimber et Danjou, Archives curieuses,
xi. 350.

mediate bearing upon the fortunes of the Huguenots. Merry-hearted Henry of Navarre, with anxieties enough resting upon him to crush a man of a less sanguine temperament, received in far distant Guyenne the news of the Barricades and the sorry plight of his cousin, Henry of Valois.

Henry of Na-varre's satis-faction.

For a few moments he said nothing, startled by the strange turn of affairs, and possibly musing upon the effect which the king's mishap might have upon the unequal contest in which the Huguenots were engaged. Then he sprang up gayly from the grass where he had been lying, and gave expression to his pent-up feelings in the cheery exclamation: " They have not yet caught the Béarnais." [1] It may well be that some secret satisfaction mingled with Navarre's compassion. His opponent, and the relentless enemy of Protestantism, a prince more wedded to Catholicism than any one of the adherents of the League, had received at the hands of that highly orthodox and professedly holy association such treatment as was ordinarily reserved for Huguenots alone. Surely it would seem that the irony of fate could no further go. [2]

If Guise and Mendoza felt deep chagrin when they found that the opportunity to seize the king's person had escaped them, Henry of Valois himself was doomed to equal disappointment at Chartres. He had confidently counted upon a revulsion in his favor. The Parisians, he imagined, could not fail to repent of their misdeeds, and would speedily be suing for pardon at his hands. Instead of which, the heads of the League had no trouble in making them believe more implicitly than ever the story that the king had intended first to garrison and then to sack the city. Finding that Henry was not stirred up to manly action even by the indignities of which he had of late been the recipient, Guise and his party quickly recovered their courage. A king too senseless or too cowardly to resent an insult could be braved with impunity.

---

[1] " Ils ne tiennent pas encore le Béarnois." Lestoile, i. 252.

[2] " L'entreprinse que la Ligue a voulu, ces jours passez, faire sur le Roy, qui est plus catholique que pas un d'icelle. Toutesfois vous voyez si on a laissé de le traicter en huguenot." Henry of Navarre to Madame de Fontevrault, May, 1588, Lettres missives, ii. 378, 379.

Intelligent foreigners versed in history, looking dispassion-
ately at the actual situation of France, were, indeed, at no loss
to suggest different methods by which Henry could,
How Paris might be punished. as they thought, easily bring his rebellious capital to
its knees. He might remove from Paris to some
other place the court of parliament, the chamber of accounts,
and the great body of financial officers through whose hands
passed the tribute of the provinces. It was calculated that he
would thus destroy the means of support of more than eighty
thousand persons who were directly dependent for their daily
bread upon these three classes of magistrates.[1] He might pronounce invalid all decisions of legal tribunals, save those of the
parliament thus transferred. He might declare Guise and all
his followers to be rebels. He might besiege Paris, and compel it to return to its allegiance by cutting off the supply of
food that came down on the rivers Seine and Marne.[2]

But Henry of Valois had as yet formed no manly resolution.
He still fancied that he could regain his much-coveted ease without a resort to extremities. So when the Parliament
The king's weak protest. of Paris deputed some of its members to proffer excuses for what had been done at the capital, his tone was that
of a whining child rather than that of a man. He prated about
the fondness he had shown for the city, and the great benefits
it had derived from his residence there, which had been more
protracted than that of any one of the last ten occupants of the
throne of France. He actually entered into a justification of
his actions and purposes, treating the calumnies of Guise as if
they had been the true motives of the revolt. He did, it is
true, mildly suggest the damage he might do to the trade of
Paris by taking away the courts of judicature and the university ;
reminding them of the disastrous consequences which had resulted in the year 1579—the year of the great plague—from the
absence of the king and the suspension of parliament. So

---

[1] " Perche da questi tre magistrati sono nodriti e mantenuti in Parigi più
che ottanta mila personi." I do not vouch for the accuracy of Cavriana's
calculation.

[2] Cavriana to Serguidi, May 13, 1588, Négociations avec la Toscane, iv. 782.

utterly prostrate was business at that time that men played at quoits in the streets of the capital. He had something to say also of irritated patience turning into fury, and of what a king offended may do. But he soon relapsed into his apologetic attitude. He had ever used mildness and not severity. "I am no usurper," said he, "but a legitimate king descended from a race that has always ruled by gentleness. And as to making an excuse of religion, that is a mere fable. Some other path than that must be taken. There is not in the world a more Catholic prince than I am, nor one who so strongly desires the extirpation of heresy. My actions and my life have sufficiently testified this to my people. I would that it had cost me an arm, so that the last heretic were here in a painting upon the walls of this room." [1]

His undiminished hatred of heresy.

The delegation of parliament had been sent through the persuasions of Catharine de' Medici, who, remaining in Paris after her son's flight, seemed to have discovered too late that her intrigues had gone too far, and that she must lend her support to Henry of Valois unless she wished to see his complete overthrow. But the language of the king to others was as deficient in force as his address to the friendly judges. It was a just recompense of his timidity that the very acts by means of which he strove to curry favor with the people were interpreted as additional proofs of pusillanimity and only gave strength to his enemies. Thus, under guise of affording relief to the greatly burdened people, Henry revoked on a single day thirty-six of the edicts of preceding years imposing extraordinary taxes. He gained nothing thereby but the reputation of a poltroon who has not the courage to maintain the ground he has taken.

The success of Guise was a foregone conclusion. The loyal servants of the crown, who would have been strong enough un-

---

[1] " C'est un compte (conte) de parler de religion, il faut prendre un autre chemin. Il n'y a au monde prince plus Catholique, ni qui desire tant l'extirpation de l'heresie que moy : mes actions et ma vie l'ont assez tesmoigné à mon peuple. Je voudrois qu'il m'eust cousté un bras, et que le dernier heretique feust en peinture en ceste chambre." Mémoires de la Ligue, ii. 398 ; Recueil des choses mémorables, 667 ; De Thou, vii. (bk. 91) 211, 212.

der other circumstances to secure a brilliant victory over the League, were at too great a disadvantage. The royal commis-

Discourage-
ment of the
king's loyal
subjects.

sioners sent out to counteract the efforts of the conspirators in the provinces met with some success. Among them the historian De Thou, who visited Normandy, did good service. But the weakness of the king ruined everything. He had not even the moral force to stand by his old favorite Épernon, and Épernon's brother La Valette, whose inordinate influence at court had been, and was still, one of the chief grounds of complaint. He made no great opposition when Épernon, perceiving that the royal support could not be counted upon, exhibited some spirit and promptly resigned the governorship of the province of Normandy. He did, indeed, accede to the duke's condition that the post should not be given to any of his enemies, and instantly granted it to the loyal Montpensier before any of the Lorraine princes, never over-modest in their requests, had a chance to ask for it. But he willingly permitted Épernon to leave court and go to entrench himself in Saintonge and Angoumois.[1] Thus while cities and towns were passing over to the League, and nobles, even those most closely bound to him by considerations of gratitude, were playing into the hands of his enemies, Henry of Valois was impotent to adopt a decided policy. It was clear that true courage was, in his case, out of the question. Some cowardly and treacherous deed, some reminiscence of St. Bartholomew's Day, might emanate from his mean and contemptible nature, but no open and valorous act. His perplexity, however, was patent to all beholders. Every one knew that he had nobody to turn to. His mother had more than once played him false.

Treachery of
the royal
council.

Of his council two-thirds were the pensioners of those who sought his crown, and possibly his life.[2] Not a word was spoken around the board but it was straightway reported to Guise, and Guise made good use of his intelligence.

---

[1] See, besides the tracts in the Mémoires de la Ligue, etc., the brief account in De Thou, vii. 223.

[2] Agrippa d'Aubigné seems to be justified in stigmatizing the king's official advisers as "un conseil desquels les deux tiers tiroient pension de l'autre parti." Histoire universelle, iii. 77.

He had been secretly advised by one of the leading statesmen at court that his majesty was so terrified that he was resolved to have peace on any terms, and he had been counselled by the same honorable personage not to abate a tittle of his demands. So when Villeroy, the royal envoy, tried, or made a feint of trying, to extort from him some concessions in favor of the king, Guise could assume an insolent air and browbeat him. "'S death!" said he, "I know very well what you have been commissioned to agree to. If, then, you do not do your duty, you will repent of it."[1] It was no wonder that the poor king, a miserable object enough under any circumstances, but now doubly miserable, distrusted everybody, concealed his true designs from all his court, and undertook to do everything himself. No wonder, too, that he was forced to yield on every point to the League; for the longer he waited the more embarrassed was he, hearing daily some new and signal act of perfidy.[2]

It was a proud day for the ambitious Duke of Guise when, after the news of the Parisian Barricades reached Rome, Pope

Guise and Pope Sixtus.

Sixtus the Fifth sent him a congratulatory letter, in which the pontiff likened him to the most valiant of the Maccabees; and when the Duke of Parma, in his delight at the triumph of the rebellious subject of the Very Christian King, ordered all the chief cities of Flanders to be illuminated in honor of the event, and, as a token of friendship and admiration, sent to Guise his own armor.[3] But it was a still prouder day when he compelled the unhappy Henry of Valois, against his will and better judgment, to affix his signature to the docu-

---

[1] Dr. Cavriana, writing in Italian, has inserted Guise's very words in his letter of June, 1588, to the secretary of the Grand Duke of Florence: "Mortdieu! je sçay bien ce que vous avez eu en charge d'accorder; parquoy, si vous ne le faites, vous vous repentirez." Négociations avec la Toscane, iv. 793.

[2] The words in the text are little more than a paraphrase of the lugubrious account of Cavriana (ubi supra), who instances the events at Havre de Grâce, whither a relation of the late Duke of Joyeuse had lately been sent, who had promised to open the gates of the town to the king, but, having been bribed by the other side, admitted the king's enemies.

[3] Lestoile, i. 269; Agrippa d'Aubigné, iii. 80, 82.

ment that has come down to posterity under the name of the "Edict of Union."

The importance of this document in its bearing upon the history of the Huguenots during the next ten years requires that we should look in detail at its provisions respecting the exclusive toleration of the Roman Catholic religion.

In the preamble, Henry, by the grace of God, King of France and Poland, was made to recognize his infinite obligation to the Almighty for having trusted him with the sceptre of the most noble realm in the world, a realm wherein the faith of our Lord and Saviour had been sacredly taught from the time of the Apostles, and had been religiously preserved in the hearts of kings and subjects by reason of the zeal and devotion they had entertained for the Holy Cathlic, Apostolic, and Roman religion. In defence of this religion the king had himself exposed his life when yet a mere lad; and his resolution had grown with years, so that it was now, and ever would be, more dear than royalty and long life. In order, therefore, that when called to appear in the presence of God, his conscience should not accuse him of any neglect to provide, as far as it was possible for the human intellect so to do, against any change or alteration in the matter of religion that might ensue in France after his decease, his majesty had determined to unite all his Catholic subjects with himself for the prosecution of the sacred undertaking in which they were engaged. To this end, after long consideration, and by advice of the queen, his mother, and of the princes and lords of his council, he proclaimed the following articles, ten in number, which he commanded to be held as "an inviolable and fundamental law" of his kingdom.

The king forced to sign the Edict of Union, July, 1588.

In the first article Henry renewed the oath taken at his coronation to live and die in the Roman Catholic and Apostolic religion, and honestly ("de bonne foi") to devote his means and even his life to the extirpation of all schemes and heresies condemned by the holy councils, and especially by the Council of Trent; and engaged never to make peace or truce with the heretics, or to issue any edict in their favor. The second article imposed upon all the king's subjects, of whatsoever

Its intolerant provisions.

rank, the duty of uniting and taking a similar oath for the extermination of the heretics.   The third prescribed that they
should also swear that, after the death of the present monarch
without issue, they would recognize as king no prince who was
himself a heretic, or a favorer of heresy.   By the fourth, Henry
engaged to give no military charge to anyone but a Roman
Catholic, and forbade that any person be admitted to a judicial
or financial office without due attestation of his orthodoxy by
his bishop, or, at least, by a curate supported by the testimony
of ten other persons of standing and above suspicion.   In the
fifth article provision was made for the safety of the adherents
of the League, whom the king pledged himself to protect
against the violence of the heretics equally with those who had
fought by his command.   In the next three articles the monarch's subjects were enjoined to swear mutual protection, loyalty
to the crown, and renunciation of all unions, leagues, and associations, whether within or without the kingdom, contrary to the
present union and hostile to the royal person and authority.
The ninth article declared all persons who should refuse to sign
the union, or, having signed it, should renounce it, to be guilty
of treason, and threatened disobedient cities with the loss of all
privileges heretofore granted to them.   Finally, in a long and
carefully worded article, the king was made to pardon and con-
sign to oblivion all the recent acts of the adherents of the League;
especially such as had occurred on the twelfth and thirteenth
days of May; on the ground that he had been informed that
those acts had been caused by nothing else than zeal for the
conservation and maintenance of the Catholic religion.   For
this reason no punishment was ever to be exacted for the levy
of troops and other hostile practices, and the officers of justice
were strictly enjoined from holding the participants in the late
troubles to an account for such sums of the royal revenues as
had been expended without warrant of law.[1]

---

[1] The text of the Edict of Union, Rouen, July, 1588, is given in the Mémoires de la Ligue, ii. 402–407, in Agrippa d'Aubigné, iii. 101–105, and in
Isambert, Recueil des anciennes lois françaises, xiv. 616–622.   There are
summaries in the Recueil des choses mémorables, 667, 668, in De Thou, vii.
237, etc.

Nor did the public edict contain all the humiliation of which Henry was forced to taste. In the secret articles previously agreed upon by the queen mother, on the one hand, and Cardinal Bourbon and the Duke of Guise, on the other, there were some important points of which shame or policy dictated the omission in the more formal document given to the world. Henry of Valois was pledged to prosecute the work of extirpating the Protestants, by sending two "good and strong" armies against them. It was stipulated that the command of that army which was to march into Dauphiny should be intrusted to Guise's brother, the Duke of Mayenne. His majesty was very graciously permitted to select the general who should lead the second army into Poitou and Saintonge. It may have been intended as an equivalent for this sorry concession to the royal prerogative, that the term for which certain cities had been confided to the princes of the League, by the secret articles of Nemours, in 1585,[1] was lengthened by four years; so that they were to be restored in 1594, instead of 1590. Not content with this, the League secured the uninterrupted control of such prominent places as Orleans and Bourges, by a provision that gave to its leaders the nomination of the governors in case of the death of the present incumbents. A sop was even thrown to the pope, by a paragraph which somewhat vaguely and incoherently prescribed that the decrees of the Council of Trent should be published at the earliest moment, but added that this should be "without prejudice to the rights and authority of the king, and the liberties of the Gallican Church, which shall, within three months, be more amply specified and elucidated by an assembly of certain prelates and officers of parliament, and others whom his majesty shall depute for this purpose."[2]

Henry of Valois signed his name to the Edict of Union, in the city of Rouen, with tears in his eyes, and bewailing his

The secret articles.

---

[1] See above, vol. i., chapter v., p. 346.

[2] "Articles secrets de l'union de l'an 1588," Mémoires de Nevers, t. 725–729. Also, in Matthieu, Histoire des derniers troubles de France, liv. iii., fols. 99–101.

misfortune in being constrained, while he secured his own personal safety, to endanger his estate.[1] At the capital there was

Tears of the king, and joy of the Parisians.

great glee, and lively congratulations were interchanged over the reconciliation of the king and the "Catholic" princes. Paris, ever gay and ever bloodthirsty, had lately been diverting itself with a harmless bonfire and with a real auto da fé, both at the expense of the Protestants. It had long been a custom, on the eve of Saint John's day, to heap up on one of the public squares a huge pile of wood, to which the king himself, if present, or otherwise some prince of the blood, set fire with great ceremony. This year, in default of anyone more suitable, the prévôt des marchands kindled the pyre, over which, suspended from a mast, hung the image of a woman, clothed in armor, with a bloody right arm. A sword was in her right hand, a book in her left, and from her head dangled serpents instead of tresses of hair. The personage represented was unmistakable. The burgesses congratulated themselves, and loudly expressed their satisfaction at having burned the English Jezebel, at least in effigy, on the streets of the orthodox capital of France.[2] Quite different from this puerile diversion was the horrible immolation of the two Huguenot women, to which reference was made on a preceding page.[3]

On the twenty-first of July, the edict was brought to parliament, and was promptly approved and registered. The same day—the eve of the feast of Saint Mary Magdalene—the heralds did their office and made proclamation of it by sound of the trumpet. Catharine de' Medici and the younger queen, both of whom had remained in Paris from the day of Henry's flight, took part in the public demonstrations of joy, and were present at the singing of a grand Te Deum in the cathedral of Notre Dame. Salvos of artillery were fired on the Place de Grève, the scene of many a martyr's death, an appropriate spot for the commemoration of the passage of an intolerant law.[4]

---

[1] Lestoile, i. 260.

[2] Mendoza, in a letter to Philip II., dated June 26, 1588, is my authority for this incident. De Croze, ii. 348.   [3] See above, page 9.

[4] Journal d'un curé ligueur (Jehan de la Fosse), 219.

No one was more delighted at the publication of the Edict of Union than was Bernardino de Mendoza. That careful ambassador had a keen appreciation of the importance of times and seasons. After long urging Guise forward in his rebellious course, he had, some months since, informed his royal master, as we have already seen, that the duke no longer needed the spur. Of late, if he had done anything, he had restrained the Frenchman's excessive ardor. "We do not press Mucius to break with his Very Christian Majesty," Mendoza wrote to Philip, a fortnight or so before the conclusion of the terms of reconciliation, " because in that case it would be necessary to pay him the balance of three hundred thousand crowns, and your majesty would be involved in the embarrassment of a fresh war, which would not only be ill-timed but prejudicial to the interests of Mucius himself." [1] Indeed, as it was, the penurious envoy of Spain found his ingenuity taxed to the utmost. It was difficult to frame specious excuses for not satisfying Guise's demand for the sum just named. It was difficult to induce him to be content with the seventy thousand crowns which he had already received. The duke complained, not without reason, of the enormous expenses in which the present contest had involved him. He would have found it quite impossible to meet them, but for a loan of two hundred thousand crowns, for which he was still indebted to the merchants and burgesses of Paris. As for himself, he soon betrayed to Mendoza, by tone as well as by word, that he had begun too late to regret that he had not given the rein to the populace on the day of the Barricades, and permitted the execution of projects long since formed. [2]

Meantime the Parisians daily flocked to the Palais de Justice to sign their names to the Union which was expected to seal the fate of the Huguenots in France. [3]

(marginal note: Satisfaction of Bernardino de Mendoza.)

---

[1] Mendoza to Philip II., June 26, 1588, De Croze, ii. 346.

[2] Mendoza to Philip II., July 24, 1588, De Croze, ii. 350, 351.

[3] Cavriana to Serguidi, August 8, 1588, Négociations avec la Toscane, iv. 806, 810.

CHAPTER IX.

THE ASSEMBLY OF LA ROCHELLE, AND THE SECOND STATES OF BLOIS.

So far as the Huguenots as a religious body were concerned, it cannot be said that the Edict of Union seriously affected their standing before the law. The Edict of Nemours, promulgated three years before, had already placed them outside of the body politic. It abrogated every provision made for their protection, forbade their solemn worship of God on pain of death, allowed their ministers but a single month to escape from the kingdom, and gave such of the laity as refused to abjure but half a year before they too must go into exile. To this severe legislation the Edict of Union could add little. It could band the Roman Catholics of France more closely together in the work of extirpating heresy, by imposing it as a duty upon all classes, from the king down to the humblest citizen, and by making apathy or refusal on the part of anyone a crime of the nature of treason. It could make the tenure of office to depend on direct proof of unimpeachable Catholicity, rather than on the absence of proof of Protestantism. It could exact an oath from the monarch that he would conclude neither peace nor truce with the Huguenots. But this was all. I dismiss, for the moment, the matter of the succession, a question upon which, indeed, the later edict gave no uncertain voice, by declaring all heretics and favorers of heresy to be incapable of inheriting the crown.

Taken together, the two edicts of 1585 and 1588 constituted the proscriptive legislation for the enactment of which the intolerant party, with the Roman Catholic clergy at its head, had for years been longing, and which it now hailed as the true and proper fundamental law, to be maintained at any cost.

The Huguenots, on the contrary, had, from this time forward, but one object in view: they would compel the repeal of these inimical ordinances.   What should be substituted was not so clear.   The more sanguine insisted upon the perfect freedom offered on paper by the Edict of 1576, as the only basis on which the permanent structure of peace could be reared.   But the great majority saw in the present or prospective situation of affairs little chance of securing so ideal a liberty, and were consequently content to claim the privilege of other edicts less liberal in theory, but practically more valuable in their concessions.   Only two royal enactments met the requirements of the case.   The Edict of 1577, which introduced the Peace of Bergerac, had in its favor the circumstance that it had been generally accepted as a " modus vivendi " —if not the best that could be imagined, yet the only one which had been tried and found feasible.   With some of its features modified by the Conference of Nérac and the Peace of Fleix, it had for a time bid fair to enjoy a permanence unusual in the fluctuating code of French law.   But the greater number of the Protestants looked with peculiar affection upon an older enactment—the Edict of the seventeenth of January, 1562.   The reasons for this preference are clearly set forth in a remarkable petition presented, a few months later, to Henry the Third at the second states of Blois.   " We very humbly beg your majesty," said the Protestants, "since you aim at restoring everything in your kingdom to such tranquillity that your memory may be for ever happy and blessed of all, that it may please you to restore to us the liberty of the first edict, made for our relief so soon as it was discovered that we were altogether different persons, both in the matter of religion and in questions of state, from what we had previously been calumniously declared to be—the edict which, from the name of the month in which it was published, has been called the Edict of January.   We do not, however, ask for that edict in particular because in it more was granted to us than in all the others—although this must cause us so much the more earnestly to desire it—but rather because that edict has features that should render it agreeable to your majesty and to all men, and to us,

Huguenot demand for the edict of January, 1562.

above all the rest. For all the other enactments, bearing the title
of edicts of pacification, are marked with the stamp of troubles
and of civil war, the memory of which, whereas it ought to be
wholly abolished, is hereby preserved. To this we must add,
that to many persons it has seemed that these edicts were
not granted by your majesties of right good will, but rather
snatched from your hands by the violence of arms. But the
Edict of January had no other foundation than an inquiry into
the situation, which was at that time peaceable and friendly,
when in a full assembly, of such a character as we have already
set forth, it pleased your majesties to assign to us places where
we might, under your protection, serve God according to our
conscience and belief. And everybody, Sire, can recall that
this Edict of January had so satisfied both parties, that it would
have lasted until this moment, had not the turbulent audacity
of the predecessors of our present enemies broken it with all violence and cruelty, and thus laid the foundation of the troubles
which have afflicted us and your entire realm of France." [1]

Indignant as the Huguenots were at the continued persecution of which they were the victims, it can scarcely be said that
they were surprised or disappointed at the publication
of the Edict of Union. The character of Henry of
Valois was no new subject of study. If the Duke of
Guise believed himself to be familiar with it to its inmost re-
cesses, there were others, and the King of Navarre was of
the number, upon whom the opportunities they had enjoyed
for watching him closely had not been thrown away. They
were not taken at unawares by the king's imbecility, and
were, therefore, but little discouraged when they learned that
he had yielded to all the League's demands. Meanwhile they
were resolved to continue without abatement the desperate
struggle against the united forces of the monarch and the unruly subjects whom he had just united to himself. A few
Huguenot nobles and gentlemen, it is said, found in the new

*The Protes-
tants not dis-
heartened.*

---

[1] " Remonstrance et requeste tres-humble adressée au Roy en l'assemblée
des Estats, par les François exilez pour la Religion, ses tres-humbles et tres-
obeissans subjects." Reprinted in Mémoires de la Ligue, iii. 149, 150.

edict an occasion for abandoning what appeared to them to be a
forlorn hope ; but the number of such persons was insignificant
in comparison with the steadfast, or even with those who had
yielded after the Edict of Nemours.

Incidents in themselves trifling have frequently an important
influence at critical junctures in the world's history, and serve
to encourage or dishearten men in a degree quite disproportion-
ate to the intrinsic magnitude of the occurrences. So it was
that the news of a success gained by Henry of Navarre, not far
from La Rochelle, accomplished the important end of infusing
new strength into the hearts of the Huguenots, while it dis
pelled the illusions of such courtiers as had taken for granted
that all was now over with the son of Jeanne d'Albret, and
that the Protestant stronghold would easily be reduced by
siege. At any other time the engagement might have been
viewed as unworthy of special mention.

Of the two rivers which bear the name of Sèvre, and jointly
give name to a department of the present republic of France,
The "Île de   that which flows by the city of Niort—the Sèvre
Marans."   niortaise—presents the unusual phenomenon of losing
in breadth and depth the farther it proceeds from its source.
The same river which at Maillé is a respectable stream, three
hundred feet wide, contracts before reaching the ocean into a
narrow channel hardly more than one-fifth as broad. The very
considerable mass of water collected from an extensive basin
seems to lose itself in marshes, or to be diverted into minor
conduits. These have made of much of the vicinity of the
Sèvre, from the village of Coulon, not far from Niort, down to
the town of Marans, scarcely two leagues from the mouth of
the river, a morass difficult to cross in the rainy season, both
because of the uncertain footing offered by the wet soil, and
because of the ditches and canals intersecting it.[1] From time
to time tracts of dry and fertile land are met, as one descends
the Sèvre, which, from the circumstance that they are thus cut
off from the mainland, are known as " islands." The most im-

---

[1] See the "Description chorographique de l'Aunis" prefixed to Arcère, Histoire de la ville de la Rochelle, i. 165, 166.

portant of these in the sixteenth century, and perhaps even at
the present day, is the so-called "Île de Marans," a long and
narrow tract lying between the river itself, on the north, and
the Canal de la Brune, or of Saint Michael, on the south.   The
little domain, which had a story of its own running back through
a good part of the Middle Ages, was considered of sufficient
value by its possessors to be provided with not less than six
forts commanding the approaches both from the land side and
from the mouth of the river.[1]

The Île de Marans was at all times a favorite stopping-place
of Henry of Navarre, to whom, amid the harassing cares of a
life of unrest and anxiety, the occasional glimpse of its quiet
and placid existence seemed doubly sweet.   So it was that,
two years before the adventure which I am about to narrate, he
sketched, in a letter from La Rochelle to the Countess of Grammont, a charming picture of its beauties, such as can scarcely
be found elsewhere in his voluminous correspondence.   Not
the fabulous island of Calypso was painted in more glowing
colors by the father of epic poetry, than was this attractive
spot by the enthusiastic pen of the Huguenot prince.

"I arrived here last night from Marans," writes Henry, "having visited the place in order to make provision for its safety.
O, how much I longed for you!   It is the place most suited to
your fancy that I have ever seen.   For that reason alone I am
about to secure it by exchange.   It is an island shut in by marshy
groves, in which, at every hundred paces, there are channels by
which one can go by boat in quest of wood.   The water is
limpid and has a gentle flow ; the channels are of all breadths,
the boats of all sizes.   Amid this wilderness there are a thousand gardens that can be reached only by boat.   A stream passes
by the foot of the castle walls, in the midst of the town, which
affords as good lodging as Pau.   There are few houses from the
door of which one cannot step into one's little boat.   This stream
extends in two arms which not only float large boats, but permit the passage of ships of fifty tons.   The distance is but two

---

[1] Ibid., i. 137.   The detailed map of Aunis prefixed to the first volume of
Arcère will be found very useful to a clear understanding of the geography.

leagues to the sea; it is, in fact, a channel, not a river. Up stream, large boats go as far as to Niort, twelve leagues distant. There are countless mills and isolated farms. Countless, too, are the kinds of singing birds that frequent the sea. I send you some of their feathers. Of fish, the quantity, the size, and the price are a marvel—a large carp is sold for three sous, and five sous are paid for a pike. It is a place of great traffic, and all by boat. The land is full of wheat of a very fine quality. One can live there agreeably in time of peace, and securely in time of war. One can delight one's self there with the object of one's love, or bewail its absence. O, how pleasant it is to sing there!"[1]

Such was the spot which Henry of Navarre selected, late in the month of June, and while the preliminary negotiations were still in progress relative to the Edict of Union, for an exploit which should show that the Huguenots were yet no contemptible foes. Marans, which had formerly been in friendly hands, had, not long since, fallen into the hands of the enemy. It was of importance to prevent them from obtaining a secure foothold in the province of Aunis and within little more than a dozen miles of La Rochelle. Provided with a goodly number of portable bridges, Henry set foot upon the neighboring island of Charron, on the morning of Friday, the twenty-fourth of June, and aided by two light galiots which he had brought up the stream, attacked the small fort known as Le Braut, both from the front and from the rear. The surrender of Le Braut was closely followed by that of the only other redoubt upon the island, and the next day the King of Navarre was able to approach the Île de Marans itself. But it was no easy matter to cross. The channel was wide and deep. On the opposite side stood two forts, distant about six hundred paces from each other, commanding with their cannon the open ground where the Huguenots must prepare the materials for their bridge. A redoubt, newly constructed between the forts, covered the very spot where the stream must be spanned. But the king did not relinquish his venturesome undertaking. The

Its capture undertaken by Henry of Navarre.

---

[1] "Ha! qu'il y faict bon chanter!" Henry of Navarre to the Countess of Grammont, June 17, 1586. Lettres missives, ii. 224, 225.

whole of Saturday was spent in discharging the rude artillery
carried by the galiots against the forts, and in skirmishes with
the enemy. At evening the boats were ordered to drop down
toward the sea, while the Huguenot troops retired from sight.
If, however, the enemy imagined that the attack was abandoned,
they were quickly undeceived. It was scarcely three o'clock on
Sunday morning before the Huguenots returned. Before the
sun was well up they might be seen busily preparing their
bridge, bringing forward their mantelet, or movable shield, under cover of which they made ready to advance, and dragging
their boats into position to facilitate the crossing. Henry of Navarre was himself conspicuous at the head of his troops, arranging the infantry in battle array, and marshalling his cavalry
to give the foot-soldiers proper support. The enemy in vain
disputed the paggage.   "At eleven o'clock," says the chronicler,
who appears to have been an eye-witness and a par-

The soldiers
pray and sing
psalms.

ticipant in the action, "prayer having been offered
up to God, and psalms having been sung by all these
regiments and troops of cavalry, and all having received orders
as to what they were to do, the army began to force the crossing,
which was guarded, on the opposite bank, by the regiment of
M. du Cluseau and the company of light horse of the Sieur de
la Tremblaye, and which was flanked by two forts and defended
in front by a third fort and by a trench." The struggle was
stubborn on both sides. The King of Navarre, ever watchful
and ever exposing himself with reckless imprudence, led the way,
riding with head bare and without armor, apparently intent
only upon encouraging his followers to press on to victory. Although most of the Roman Catholics fought well, some of them

Consternation
of the Roman
Catholic
troops.

had entered the battle with serious misgivings, and
some were panic-stricken. There were those who,
when they saw the Huguenots kneel upon the ground
before the action began, exclaimed one to another in consternation : "They are praying to God ! They will beat us as they
did at Coutras!" [1] Suffice it to say that, before the sun set,

---

[1] The fullest account of this affair is the "Discours de la reprise de l'Isle,
forts et Chasteau de Marans, faite par le Roy de Navarre, au mois de Juin,

the Roman Catholic force was routed and the forts were in the possession of the Huguenots. Within three days every remaining stronghold of the enemy upon the island, even to the castle of Marans itself, had fallen into their hands.

Nor was this the only exploit of the restless King of Navarre. While the grand army of the west tarried, which, under the

Other successes of the King of Navarre.

Duke of Nevers, was expected to reduce the Protestants of Poitou and Guyenne, the Huguenot prince put his leisure to good use. From the walls of La Rochelle northward to the river Loire he made himself virtually master of the districts bordering upon the sea. Although the names of Montaigu, of Beauvoir-sur-mer, and of the other places which he captured may be obscure, and although the Protestant gains may seem inconsiderable, no slight advantage was secured. It was something that, in the months immediately succeeding the publication of the Edict of Union, when men were predicting the speedy overthrow of the Protestant

---

1588," reprinted in Mémoires de la Ligue, ii. 411–416. A more general reference is made in the "Discours sommaire des choses plus mémorables qui se sont passees, és sieges, surprises et reprises de l'isle de Marans en Onix (Aunis), és annees 1585, 86, 87 et 88," ibid., ii. 53–84. Respecting the last incident mentioned in the text, the former says, p. 413 : "Aucuns d'eux ont dit depuis, que plusieurs d'entr'eux, voyans les regimens le genouil en terre, commencerent à dire: Ils prient Dieu ; ils nous battront comme à Coutras." The language of the other account, which appears to be not free from a tinge of exaggeration, is even stronger (p. 83): "Lesquels (par leur rapport mesme) s'estans preparez à la resistance, et voyans les trouppes du Roy de Navarre, qui faisoyent la pointe, s'estre mises le genouil en terre, pour (à leur coustume) faire leur priere, avant que d'aller au combat, se ressouvenans des prieres qui avoyent aussi esté faites à Coutras, entrerent en tel effroy qu'ils ne tendirent quasi aucun combat, seulement adviserent au moyen de se sauver. Aucuns furent tuez en l'ardeur de la charge, plusieurs se sauverent par les marais." See, also, De Thou, Agrippa d'Aubigné, Recueil des choses mémorables, etc. The magical influence which the sight of Huguenot soldiers kneeling before the engagement exerted over their Roman Catholic opponents, appears to have connected itself, over a hundred years later, in the time of Jean Cavalier, with the sound of the favorite battle-psalm of the Protestants— the 68th. So, at least, an officer who had fought against them informed the author of the anonymous Histoire des Camisards (London, 1754), i. 244. "Quand," said he, "ces diables-là se mettoient à chanter leur B. de chanson 'Que Dieu se montre,' nous ne pouvions plus être les maîtres de nos gens: ils fuyoient comme si tous les diables avoient été à leurs trousses."

faith in France, Henry of Navarre, often with a paltry following of a hundred horse and a few companies of foot, should be
able to compel the Duke of Mercœur to abandon the siege
of Huguenot towns and seek safety in the walls of the city of
Nantes. The circumstance that the prince whom the Spanish
ambassador and his allies of the League still affected to despise
as the " Béarnais," had skirmished with the troops of the royal
governor of Brittany, had carried off eight standards, had captured four hundred and fifty prisoners, had taken a great number of horses and baggage-wagons, within two leagues of Pirmil,
a suburb of the great provincial capital, produced a moral effect,
both on friends and on enemies, not much inferior to that
which might, at another time, have followed the winning of a
great pitched battle.[1]

Before the completion of the military movement just referred
to, the states general of the kingdom, called by Henry the
Third some months previously, met in the city of Blois.[2] The
shameful and sanguinary history of this national gathering,
eclipsing in tragic interest the more dignified representative
body which sat in the same place, twelve years earlier, must
necessarily occupy us further on. But before attending to a theme
whose consideration is germane to the subject of this history
only so far as it affected the external relations of the Huguenots,
let us glance at a congress which met about the same time, and
whose connection with the inner spiritual and political life of
Protestantism was far more close.

More than four years had elapsed since the last political assembly of the Huguenots was held in the city of Montauban.[3]
During that long and eventful period neither political assembly
nor national synod was possible. In fact, six years of tumult

---

[1] The account of Henry's successes in lower Poitou and on the borders of
Brittany may be read in detail in the Mémoires de la Ligue, ii. 555, seq.; as
well as in De Thou, vii. 304–6, the Recueil des choses mémorables, 678–680,
Agrippa d'Aubigné, iii. 129–132, and Matthieu, Histoire des derniers troubles,
fol. 108.

[2] The royal " mandement " for the convocation of the States of Blois, dated
Chartres, May 31, 1588, is given by Isambert, Recueil des anciennes lois
françaises, xiv. 613–616.

[3] In August and September, 1584. See above, vol. i., chapter v., p. 290.

and confusion were yet to pass before the churches could again send their ministers and elders to confer together respecting matters of religious doctrine and practice. Meanwhile, however, the political situation admitted of no such delay. More than one question of practical importance in the conduct of the war pressed for an answer. Twice had the attempt been made to bring together in a political assembly the representatives of all portions of Protestant France, but the expense, the difficulties of the way, or the supineness of some of the more distant provinces, had interfered with the realization of the plan. Now, however, so considerable a number of delegates came together in the city of La Rochelle, that on Monday, the fourteenth of November, 1588, the assembly was formally opened. Great hopes had been entertained of it in advance. " It will heal many public sores and many private ones," Duplessis Mornay had written.[1] It was a body sufficiently large and sufficiently dignified to assume the place which circumstances beyond its control compelled it to occupy, of the Protestant counterpart of the Roman Catholic states general of Blois. In actual numbers, indeed, it could not bear comparison, but the delegates represented both the nobility and the third estate of the kingdom, and came from every province in which the Reformed faith could boast of adherents. From Picardy, on the north, to the Protestant districts at the base of the Pyrenees, on the south ; from Brittany, on the west, to the principality of Orange and to Dauphiny, on the east, there was scarcely an important bailiwick or sénéchaussée that had not its deputy. Besides the thirty-seven representatives of the nobles and the towns, the King of Navarre was permitted to have nine deputies of his own. This concession, however, was distinctly understood to furnish no precedent for future assemblies. The meeting was held in the spacious common hall of the " échevinage " of La Rochelle. From the ceiling hung a great number of standards taken from the enemy—trophies of the recent successes of the Huguenots. The king himself presided at the opening exercises, supported

Huguenot political assembly at La Rochelle, November.

---

[1] Duplessis Mornay to Buzanval, October 18, 1588, Mémoires, iv. 271.

by Viscount Turenne, his lieutenant-general for the province of Guyenne, by La Trémouille, colonel of his light infantry, and by many other lords, barons, viscounts and gentlemen, as well as by the members of his council.[1]

Two days later, on Wednesday, the sixteenth of November, after the customary invocation of God's name, the King of Navarre delivered a long speech, setting forth the chief causes for which the assembly had been summoned. Although addresses of this kind do not ordinarily call for more than a passing allusion, I cannot avoid noticing a discourse which throws no little light upon the attitude of the Huguenot protector, and is interesting in view of the events culminating in his abjuration, still almost five years distant.

"Long have I desired the convocation of this assembly," said Henry; "but it seems that God has been reserving it until now, in order that He might oppose it to the conspiracy[2] of the assembly at Blois. The necessities of the times ought to impel everyone to institute a strenuous opposition against the enemy, whose aim must be clear to all, directed, as it is, both at the ruin of the king and at the overthrow of the entire state. As for myself, I have, until now, spared neither property nor life in so holy a cause. Of this my past actions can bear witness. You cannot raise your eyes," he added, glancing upward, "without seeing the proofs. If the difficulties go on increasing, I also feel that my courage is redoubled of God to persevere in the determination I long since formed, which is, to expend, in defence of the churches, the last drop of my blood and the last fragment of my possessions. Hereunto I feel myself called by the Almighty. I desire solely that the world may discern in this resolution my upright intentions. Herein I have ever walked soundly, truly, sincerely, and in the sight of God; and thus I desire, more than ever, to do in future. I regret, in-

Address of the King of Navarre.

---

[1] Mémoires de la Ligue, ii. 576.

[2] The obsolete sense of the word which Henry employed—"monopole" (Latin, "monopolium")— is explained by Du Cange, Glossarium ad scriptores mediæ et infimæ Latinitatis, s.v. : "Hinc denique eadem vox ad quasvis illicitas confœderationes fluxit."

deed, that there are those by whom my labors have not been recognized, and by whom my actions have been misrepresented. Yet daily do I pray to God that He may grant me the grace to lead His people through so many horrors and such fearful deserts to a safe and blessed rest—even should I not myself be permitted to partake of it, even should it be at the price of my own life. The length of the war and the license of arms have, to my great regret, introduced many disorders, for which I desire that provision be made in the best manner possible, to the glory of God, and the advantage of the king, the state, and every individual person in the realm. To the consideration of this subject I beg every member of this assembly to bring an unbiassed mind, zealous for the public good. This being so, I am confident that God will bless your deliberations, and enable you all to gather their fruit, for His own glory and the deliverance of His children."

Next the King of Navarre proceeded to portray the happy results that would flow, in so holy a cause as that in which the Huguenots were engaged, from an indissoluble union, and from mutual agreement, for the firm establishment of every form of good order. In this he exhorted them all to persevere as heretofore; so much the more as the innovations and changes introduced by the malice of the enemy seemed more imperatively to demand it. Especially did he ask them to make provision for that which most concerned the glory and service of God— the order, government, and discipline of the Church.

" And," he added, " that the wrath of God be not further provoked by the oaths, blasphemies, abductions, lewdness, thefts, forbidden games, and other excesses that have, by the misfortune of war, found their way into the practice of some, I require that the ordinances made to this end be strictly enforced by all governors and magistrates, and be observed without any dissimulation or respect of persons. And I enjoin upon the same magistrates, under severe penalties, that they see to it that the discipline of the Church have its due weight and authority."

The king closed with a plea that proper provision should be made for the wants of the poor, and that care should be exercised in the selection of competent men for all public offices.[1]

The Huguenot assembly replied to Navarre's address in words as cordial as his own. The delegates humbly thanked him both for the care his majesty had been pleased to exercise over their churches, as their true and lawful protector, and for the interest he had displayed in the common weal. They pledged their persons, their lives, and their estates to his service, and begged that God would continue to extend to him His blessing and favor, for His own glory, the preservation of His Church, and the public prosperity and peace.[2]

Cordial response of the delegates.

The King of Navarre's speech was an excellent one, full of noble thoughts and high aspirations such as his Majesty knew well how to frame in language, even without the help of the great heart and ready pen of Duplessis Mornay. And in some sense the speaker was not merely playing a part when he uttered them. His higher and better nature indorsed them in every particular. But the exhortations to a careful application of the ecclesiastical and civil laws against the various forms of vice and uncleanness, have a strange sound in our ears as they come from the lips of the royal orator. We are each moment tempted to ask ourselves whether his auditors were able to banish from their minds the name of the Countess of Grammont and the memory of that fatal delay after Coutras; whether the grave deputies

The Protestant prince's inconsistencies.

---

[1] The accounts of Henry's speech differ considerably from one another, and I have found it by no means easy to bring them into complete harmony. I have followed in the text chiefly the authority of the Mémoires de la Ligue (ii. 577, 578), of which the preface to the second volume bears the date of May 16, 1589, or precisely six months after the delivery of the speech; but I have had under my eyes, and have made use of the brief statement of the Histoire de la vie de Messire Philippes de Mornay (Leyden, 1647), 119, 120; the longer "Proposition du roy de Navarre en l'assemblée teneue à La Rochelle," in Mémoires de Duplessis Mornay, iv. 272–5; Cayet, Chronologie novenaire, 68, 69; De Thou, vii. 306, 307; Agrippa d'Aubigné, iii. 133; Anquez, 39; Von Polenz, iv. 571, etc.; and Stähelin, 189, etc., who inadvertently speaks of the assembly as a "Synod."

[2] Mémoires de la Ligue, ii. 578.

could suppress the feeling that the man who spoke so eloquently in favor of purity, while his private life was not above reproach, was but playing a part.

Henry of Navarre's associates in the great struggle for religious liberty now in progress were no cowards. Not even the strong conviction that his assistance in the desperate struggle Frank remonstrances. was indispensable to the success of the good cause, was potent enough to seal their lips. In this very crisis there were found deputies bold and candid enough to remonstrate with him on his present course. His faults and his blunders, his prodigal gifts to the unworthy and his neglect of the deserving, his favors extended to members of the League in the vain hope of winning them over, his amours and the great expense they entailed, at a time when faithful servants of his crown were dying of hunger—these and other things were told him to his face with wonderful frankness. He learned much of what upright men thought of his course from the ministers of the gospel, whom, in the parlance of the times, he had not yet succeeded in "civilizing." Jean Gardesi, a prominent pastor of Montauban, enjoys the honor of being described by Agrippa d'Aubigné as "the most severe Nathan" among them all.[1]

It is worthy of note that Henry of Navarre bore all this sound advice and rebuke with a patience for which few would have given him credit.[2] As he had not been offended by the Henry hears them patiently. plainness of speech of Theodore Beza, and even thanked the aged reformer for his Christian candor, so he took the counsels of Gardesi and others in the best part. Was this because he was callous to appeals of the kind now addressed to him, but was content, from motives of policy, to allow them to be uttered and then to be dismissed unheeded? I cannot believe it was so, at least at this stage of his history. A careful examination leads rather to the view that, while by no means ready to renounce his sinful pleasures, the

[1] Histoire universelle, iii. 133.

[2] "Il supporta le tout avec merveilleuse patience," says Agrippa d'Aubigné, iii. 133.

king still cherished the memory of the virtuous example and the wise precepts of his mother. If disinclined to conform his life to the strict code of Huguenot morals, he was, nevertheless, frank enough to admit, in effect if not by words, that the code in question had the full approval of his conscience. The Huguenot minister who rebuked him had only discharged his duty. Henry of Navarre was not disposed to find fault with him for being consistent. Whether he would alter his own conduct in consequence, was another question.

But the prince so wonderfully patient of censure in matters pertaining to his private life, was quite a different personage when the political situation was touched upon. He was greatly displeased, and showed no reluctance to testify his annoyance, at the opposition exhibited by some of the deputies to what the provinces styled the "protectoral tyranny." Any measures proposed with the view of re-establishing the former order of things and taking new precautions vexed him. The fact was that in his eyes the political rank to which he aspired, with the prospective succession to the crown of France upon the death of the present possessor of the throne, seemed of far greater consequence than any question of religious faith or practice. He forgot that others might not take the same view ; and, it is said, ventured to sound the assembly at La Rochelle as to the propriety of that body's petitioning the states general of Blois for the " instruction" of the King of Navarre by means of a Council ! When he found that the sturdy Protestant delegates would hearken to no such suggestion, he did not abandon the idea, but himself sent to ask for " instruction." The ridicule with which his petition was received by the adherents of the League at Blois was only equalled by the indignation felt by the " consistorial," or more thoroughly religious party among his fellow Protestants.[1]

He is intolerant of political opposition.

His petition for "instruction."

Of the results of the deliberations of the Assembly of La Rochelle, much as they present that would be of interest to a

---

[1] Agrippa d'Aubigné, iii. 133, 148 ; Stähelin, Uebertritt König Heinrichs des Vierten, 191.

student of the political antiquities of the Huguenot party, but little can, in the very nature of the case, be said here.[1] It provided, first of all, for an oath to be assumed by all the leaders, without distinction of rank, to remain faithful to the Confession of Faith promulgated by the first Synod of the Church, and to uphold an indissoluble union among themselves. Henry of Navarre, as Protector of the Cause, pledged his word to devote himself unreservedly to the maintenance of good laws, and to be guided by the advice of the council[2] that should be given him. The deputies in turn, while distinctly protesting their undiminished allegiance to the King of France, swore submission to the authority of Henry of Navarre and support of his arms against those who, through hatred of Protestantism, should resist his will. It defined the constitution of the council—a representative body, five of whose members were to be deputed by as many provincial assemblies, and five more to be chosen by the national assembly itself. One member was to be chosen by the city of La Rochelle. All the princes of the blood and peers of France that should espouse the Protestant side, as well as noblemen of tried valor such as La Noue, Turenne, Montmorency, La Trémouille, Châtillon, and Lesdiguières, were also permitted to have a seat.

Organization of the Huguenot party.

The Protector's council.

The minute regulations as to the convocation of annual provincial assemblies, the levy of troops, the management of the common funds, and the administration of justice, need not detain us.[3] More interesting, from our point of observation, is the

---

[1] See the very full statements in Anquez, Histoire des assemblées politiques des Réformés de France, 40–50.

[2] "Le tout par protestation expresse de ne nous départir de la naturelle sujétion que nous devons au roi, notre souverain seigneur, auquel nous jurons et protestons devant Dieu vouloir rendre toute obéissance et fidélité dues, l'empire souverain de Dieu demeurant en son entier." Anquez, 40.

[3] It may, however, be noted that provision was made for a very complete system of courts of justice. These included the "sovereign court" already existing for Dauphiny, and several new courts—one "mi-partie," or composed of an equal number of Protestants and Roman Catholics, at Montpellier in Languedoc ; others, composed exclusively of Protestants, at Saint Jean d'Angely, Bergerac, and Nérac ; and a seneschal's court at Castres. The letters

solicitude exhibited, even in the midst of a desperate struggle for very existence, for the maintenance of a body of religious teachers, and for the promotion of higher learning. With the former of

Provision for religious teaching and for education. these two objects in view, a portion of the ecclesiastical revenues which the Huguenots might seize was to be applied to the support of the Protestant pastors, and, in case of their death, to that of their needy widows and children. To accomplish the second object, it was arranged that a university should be founded at La Rochelle. Its income was to be derived from the Romish ecclesiastical revenues. The faculty was to consist of one professor and one doctor of theology, and several professors of humanities. The first two were provided with salaries of eight hundred livres each, the others were to have six hundred. Forty-six scholars were to be admitted. Languedoc and the larger Protestant provinces had each the privilege of sending eight scholars; the smaller could send but two or four. Every student was allowed a sum of money for his support; but the grant to the student of theology was four times as great as that given to the student of humanities. All the matriculants, excepting the sons of deceased ministers, were required to enter into a formal engagement to pursue a systematic course of study; and no one was to be admitted to the institution under the age of seven years.[1]

An assembly so solicitous for the advancement of religion and sound learning may well be pardoned, even if it showed some lack of confidence in the "Protector" of the Reformed Churches, and was not quite so careful as it might have been not to wound his ambition or his vanity. As it was, when the convocation closed, on Sunday, the seventeenth of December, with preaching, the administration of the Lord's Supper, and public prayers, and with a ceremonial not inferior in dignity to that

---

patent for the institution of a "sovereign court" at Saint Jean d'Angely were issued in the name of the assembly, December, 22, 1588, and were verified by that court in the following spring (March 28, 1589), "without prejudice to the rights of the king." This court was suppressed by Henry IV. a month after his accession. See Anquez, 129, and Soulier, Histoire des édits de pacification, 175, 176.

[1] Anquez, Appendice, 454, 455.

which characterized the opening, the King of Navarre was more delighted than any one else. The month of its sessions had brought him face to face with unpleasant truths. "You thought me relieved because I had retired into our garrisoned towns," he wrote to the Countess of Grammont. "In truth, were there to be another assembly, I should go stark mad. All is finished, and well finished, thank God!"[1]

Meantime, his anxiety to get rid of the troublesome assembly had not induced Henry to neglect his interests. Before the delegates dispersed, he had taken pains to seek out and become reconciled with every one of those who, as he had learned by his secret agents, had spoken ill of him.[2]

It would be neither altogether fair to Henry of Navarre, nor in strict accordance with truth, to deny that some members of the Assembly of La Rochelle had given the king abundant reason for annoyance. Like many of their constituents, the delegates belonging to the "consistorial" party occasionally erred in the direction of extreme suspicion respecting everything done at the Protestant court. Democratic tendencies asserted themselves. Little account was made of Navarre's services, and his mistakes were magnified.[3] There had long been talk of electing John Casimir, the tried ally of the Huguenots, Protector in place of Henry; now, some were in favor of the appointment of distinct protectors for each province. The management of the common funds was, as usual, a fruitful source of complaint. But, fortunately

The consistorial party suspicious.

---

[1] Henry of Navarre to the Countess of Grammont, December 22, 1588, Lettres missives, ii. 411.

[2] Agrippa d'Aubigné, iii. 134.

[3] If we might believe Anquez, Histoire des Assemblées Politiques, 39, some one had the audacity to say in Henry's very presence, at La Rochelle: "Here is the time to make slaves and serfs of kings." This usually accurate historian, however, has here made a mistake. Charlotte Arbaleste, wife of Duplessis Mornay, to whose Mémoires, 166, he refers, does not record the obnoxious remark. But the editor of the Mémoires recalls, in a note, an incident doubtless drawn from Cayet (Chronologie Novenaire, 68), who says: "Les beaux et gentils esprits qui estoient avec le roy de Navarre, et qui avoient des nouvelles de ce qui se passoit à Blois, disoient: 'Voicy le temps que l'on veult rendre les princes serfs et esclaves,'" which is an entirely different thing.

for the king, he had confided the supreme administration to Duplessis Mornay, and that pure and scrupulous statesman and financier was able to satisfy the most captious, and to convince impartial men that they ought rather to be surprised at the great results that had been attained with such slender means, than to wonder at the magnitude of the sums expended.[1]

The Huguenot deputies had worked ably, as well as faithfully, during their four weeks' sojourn at La Rochelle. This the completeness of their organization amply testified. The assiduity with which they subsequently applied themselves to the task of securing the strict enforcement of the plan adopted produced, on thinking men among their opponents, the impression that the Protestants were prepared to wage eternal war, unless a peace on suitable terms were conceded to them.[2]

The convocation of the states general, after an interval of eleven years during which the popular voice had been silent, was one of the important points in the compact between the king and the League. Both Henry of Valois and his namesake of Guise counted much upon the support of the people, the former hoping to recover the authority he had thrown away, the latter confident of his ability to consolidate, by means of the influence of his partisans, the structure of usurped power which he had long been rearing.

The second states general of Blois.

Outwardly, indeed, the triumph of the aspiring duke appeared complete. He was already Grand Master of France ; he now received the appointment of Lieutenant-General of the kingdom.[3] The patent that made him commander-in-chief of the armies in the king's absence, incidentally conferred such extensive powers upon him,

Guise made lieutenant-general.

---

[1] See the summary of Duplessis Mornay's speech in Histoire de la vie de Messire Philippes de Mornay (Leyden, 1647), 120, 121. "Ne demandés poinct," Duplessis had written to Buzanval, October 18, 1588, "comme plusieurs, pourquoi ne faisons nous ceci ou cela? mais admirés plustost comment, depuis quattre ans, nous pouvons faire ce que nous faisons, et priés Dieu qu'il assiste le prince, qui, certes, si son zele, sa diligence, son industrie estoient secondés de moyens, ne manqueroit de vertu pour plus grandes choses." Mémoires, iv. 272.   [2] So says Cayet, introduction, 68, 69.

[3] See the document, dated August 4, 1588, in Mémoires de Nevers, i. 729, 730, well characterized by the editor (in the table of contents) as a " Commis-

that it almost seemed as if his majesty had resigned into
his hands the entire administration of the affairs of state.
With perhaps as much sincerity as is ordinarily contained in
such requests, the duke at first took care to beg that he might
be excused from accepting this new honor and responsibility;
but, upon the king's insisting, his obedient subject yielded.[1]
There is often significance in a comparison of dates. The very
day Henry the Third signed the suicidal decree in favor of
Guise, the "Invincible Armada" was off the Isle of Wight,
fully equipped for the work of the reduction of heretical England, to accomplish which it had been despatched by Philip
the Second with all imaginable papal blessings.[2] Fear of the
Spaniard had undoubtedly had much to do with the cowardly
surrender of the Valois to the League. But now that he had
made his choice, the king was resolved to act his part to perfection. In fact, he outdid the expectations of his enemies,
and excited suspicion by the very effusiveness of his
demonstrations of amity. It was not enough to welcome the envoys of the city of Paris, the Archbishop
of Bourges, and other violent adherents of the League, as though
they were personal friends; he must greet them and the Guises
as his liberators. "I was a captive in body and mind," said
he, "so possessed by those about me as not to be able to call
myself my own master or your king. Now, thank God, I am
free, and I recognize this fact to be owing to your goodness
and the goodness of my cousins of Guise. Henceforth I mean
to be controlled by their advice and that of the other princes,
and to govern my kingdom with their counsel."[3] The farce
was kept up when the king and the duke met at Chartres, for
the first time after the day of the Barricades. His Very Christian Majesty could not have been more affectionate to a dearly
loved brother. It was noticeable, however, that neither of the
actors was quite at his ease. Guise was "red as fire;" Henry

Hypocrisy of Henry of Valois.

sion du Roy Henry III. en faveur du Duc de Guise, par laquelle il luy octroye,
non seulement la Lieutenance generale de ses armées, mais la conduite de
l'Estat."

[1] De Thou, vii. 239, 240. [2] Motley, United Netherlands, ii. 481.
[3] Cavriana to Serguidi, July 26, 1588, Négociations avec la Toscane, iv. 798.

of Valois was pale and livid when, after sundry embraces, he courteously invited his guest into his cabinet.[1] Even the wily Lorraine prince was perplexed what to make of the situation. Was the king insincere? The dissimulation was greater than Frenchmen knew how to practise. Was his "conversion" genuine? The change of intention was so marvellous as to baffle belief. It was a veritable new creation.[2] Yet, had Guise been by nature the most unsuspicious of men, the warnings that reached him from every quarter must have occasioned him some misgivings. Bernardino de Mendoza, in particular, did not keep silence. That prudent ambassador, who had been remonstrating till he was weary at the inconsiderateness with which his French allies, far from concealing, even boasted to the whole world of the help derived from Philip, met Guise by night and with the utmost secrecy, and urged him to be on his guard. But Guise was determined to go to the royal court, and to be on hand at the meeting of the states general. He would brave the danger, he said, rather than incur the charge of pusillanimity. Besides, he would have a following that would make him stronger than the king.[3] "The only real danger I shall have to run," said the duke, with almost prophetic apprehension of his coming fate, " may possibly be in the king's cabinet, into which a man is only admitted by himself, and where that prince has every facility for attacking and killing me by means of ten or twenty men that might be posted there for the purpose. But even this danger is little to be feared. It would scarcely be possible to make all the arrangements for the execution of such a project but something must transpire, and certainly if a conspiracy existed I should be informed of it by the personal friends I have about the king." The ambassador was not convinced, but, seeing Guise's determination, he forebore farther remon-

Imprudence of Guise and fears of his friends.

---

[1] Cavriana to Serguidi, August 8, 1588, Négociationes avec la Toscane iv. 804.

[2] "Bref, nous ne pouvons de ce qui se pense en crédence que en juger ou une extrème disimulacion et plus grande que les espris françois ne la peuvent couvrir, ou bien une merveilleuse mutacion de volontez et come un nouveau monde." Guise to Mendoza, August 6, 1588, De Croze, ii. 353, 354.

[3] Mendoza to Philip II., August 9, 1588, De Croze, ii. 355, 356.

strance. The duke, he saw, derived his confidence mostly from the fact that he had in Villeroy, the king's secretary, a friend who would reveal everything to him; partly, also, from the devotion to his interests of the younger queen, who was an excellent Christian, living exemplarily, going to confession and communing every Sunday, and possibly cherishing some resentment against her unfaithful husband.[1] Six weeks later, when the time for the opening of the states was approaching, Guise had lost none of his defiance and contempt of danger. "We are not lacking in warnings from all sides," he wrote to Mendoza, "that an attempt is intended upon my life. Against it I have, thank God, made such provision, as well by the accumulation of a goodly number of my friends, as by gaining over by presents and money a part of those whom it is the intention to use in this execution, that, if the other side make a beginning, I shall make an end of it more roughly than I did at Paris."[2]

If, in the concessions made to Guise and to the League, the king had taken counsel of his fears, he was not without the hope of being able to regain his ascendency by means of the states general. For this purpose he endeavored to secure the election of delegates of undoubted loyalty, and when the states met he spared none of the arts of the demagogue. Each member was accosted by the king's agents, and was courteously invited to call upon his majesty in the castle.[3] But if Henry of Valois hoped thus to gain the

The king fails to secure a majority of the delegates.

---

[1] Mendoza to Philip II., August 9, 1588, De Croze, ii. 356, 357. The representations of the Florentine agent at the court of France agree well with those of Mendoza; but the former emphasizes the fear of a general massacre. "Quelli del duca di Guise, cioè della Lega," writes Cavriana, October 13, 1588, "temono molto, che, essendo egli rinchiuso nel castello, il Re gli faccia una burla al tempo della notte; e, avendolo levato dinnanzi, faccia un simil Vespro Siciliano sui suoi, che sono più di trecento gentiluomini, e Madonna Santa Lega con questo artifizio se ne vada a spasso." Négociations avec la Toscane, iv. 829.

[2] "Que si l'on comance (commence), j'achèveray plus rudement que je n'ay fait à Paris." Mucius (Guise) to Mendoza, September 21, 1588, De Croze, ii. 361.

[3] Agrippa d'Aubigné, iii. 120.

support of a majority of the delegates, he was destined to be speedily undeceived. Guise had, as usual, anticipated him. Into every province, to every bailiwick and sénéchaussée, the duke had sent men in whom he could repose implicit confidence. More than a month before the formal opening of the sessions, he already felt sure that he had a majority of the delegates devoted to his cause.[1] The blandishments of the king had no effect in changing the determination of the members, whether representing church, noblesse, or third estate, to uphold the cause of the Holy League and make no peace with heretics.

Meanwhile Henry of Valois had but one consolation: the Invincible Armada had been utterly ruined, and, with it, the The Invincible adventurous hopes of the conquest of England, which Armada. Philip the Second had founded upon the expedition, disappeared forever. The Very Christian monarch took no pains to conceal the joy he felt at the discomfiture of his brother, the Catholic king. "You would not believe," wrote the Duke of Guise, at Blois, to Bernardino de Mendoza, at Paris, "you would not believe the artifices here resorted to for the purpose of hindering the affairs of the King of Spain, nor how open is the joy expressed over the little effect produced by his naval expedition."[2] And Frenchmen at court and elsewhere told one another, with great glee, how that on Pasquin's statue in Rome itself the following notice, purporting to come from the Vatican, had been found attached:

"If any man or woman have tidings of the army from Spain, lost at sea within the past three weeks or thereabouts, and can give information as to what has become of it, let that person come and reveal the matter, applying at the palace of Saint Peter's, where the Holy Father will see that his wine be given to him."[3]

The solemn opening of the states general took place on the

---

[1] Mucius (Guise) to Mendoza, September 5, 1588, De Croze, ii. 360.

[2] Mucius (Guise) to Mendoza, September 21, 1588, De Croze, ii. 361. See, also, Motley, United Netherlands, ii. 530, 531.

[3] Lestoile, i. 263.

sixteenth of October. Against a convocation which he scarcely knew whether to fear, as tending to restrict the absolute
authority claimed by the crown of France, or to hail with
delight, as likely to offer some escape from the intolerable en-
croachments of the League, Henry of Valois had made preparations as best he might. For some time had he been importuned
to bring new men to his council-board, and Guise had suggested
as a candidate for the office of keeper of the seals the
Archbishop of Lyons, his own most intimate adviser
among churchmen. With a shrewdness which, in
spite of his ordinary fatuity, his majesty was occasionally capable of displaying, the king anticipated the complaints sure to
greet his ears when the deputies should come together by suddenly dismissing the responsible members of his council, good
and bad—Chancellor Chiverny, brother-in-law of the historian
De Thou, trusty Bellièvre, treacherous Villeroy, Pinart, and all.
For them he substituted other men, respecting whom little was
known, and who certainly were not tools of his opponents. It
would, at all events, be convenient to be able to cast all the sins
of the past upon the shoulders of the disgraced ministers, and
to present to the states a body of secretaries against whom no
misdemeanors in office could be alleged. The court was startled
at the unexpected blow; the poor secretaries were in despair.
The first intimation of it which Villeroy and his colleagues received was contained in a note addressed to each one in the
king's own handwriting, after this model:

"Villeroy, I am very well satisfied with your service; do
not, however, fail to go away to your house, where you will
remain until I send for you. Inquire not into the cause of
this my writing, but obey me." [1]

In vain did Bellièvre weep, and Pinart bemoan his cruel lot
in words much like the lament of Cardinal Wolsey.[2] The die
was cast. The king had called, from the Parliament of Paris,

*Henry ap-
points new
counsellors.*

---

[1] Cavriana to Serguidi, September 13, 1588, Négociations avec la Toscane,
iv. 822 ; Cayet, Chronologie novenaire, 67.

[2] " Se io avessi così bene servito Dio come ho il Re, mi troverei il più fedele
(felice ?) uomo del mondo." Cavriana, ubi supra.

Montholon, a simple advocate, on whom he had never laid his eyes, but whose reputation for integrity and ability as a barrister had reached him, and had, on the sixth of September, committed the seals to his keeping.   Beaulieu-Ruzé and Revol had succeeded to the places of Villeroy, Pinart, and Bruslart.[1]

Contemporary writers have described at great length the magnificence of the scene when Henry entered the grand hall of the castle of Blois in which were gathered the depu-

Opening of the states general.

ties of the three orders of the kingdom.   One hundred and thirty-four ecclesiastics, including four archbishops and twenty-one bishops, stood before him on the right, clothed in rochet and surplice.   They were the representatives of the powerful Roman Catholic Church.   One hundred and eighty noblemen in velvet caps and cloaks were on his majesty's left hand; while, posted between the other two orders and farther back, were the one hundred and ninety-one delegates of the tiers état.   The members of the judiciary wore long gowns and square caps.   The provosts, and other royal officers were distinguishable by their short gowns and small caps; and the rest were in merchant's dress.   It was twelve years since an assemblage of equal dignity had convened in the same spacious room.[2]

Of all France, only the Huguenots, with their faithful ally Marshal Montmorency, were unrepresented in this august gathering.   They had wasted few words upon the convocation of Blois.   Too prudent to forfeit any advantages that might ac-

---

[1] Cayet and Cavriana, ubi supra ; Agrippa d'Aubigné, iii. 115, 116 ; De Thou, vii. 270–273 ; Mendoza to Philip II., October (September ?) 24, 1588 ; De Croze, ii. 370, 371.   See, also, Picot, Histoire des États Généraux, iii. 91. The letters patent appointing François de Montholon "garde des sceaux" were dated Blois, September 6, 1588.   See Isambert, Recueil des anciennes lois françaises, xiv. 623.

[2] Matthieu, Histoire des derniers troubles de France, fols. 115–117, gives the most minute account of the arrangements, and states the order in which the deputies were called.   See, also, Cayet, 69, 70, and Isambert, xiv. 623–628. The plan accompanying L. Vitet's Les États de Blois gives a good idea of the castle, of which the room still known as the " Grand'salle des États " is at the northeastern angle.   The chambers occupied by the king were near the northwestern corner, and communicated with the hall of the states general by the " Gallerie des Cerfs."

crue to them from its sessions by condemning it beforehand, they reserved to themselves the right of rejecting its conclusions as null and void because the Protestants had not been invited to take part in the deliberations.[1]

The king's address was a prolix but not unskilful production. The strong professions of singleness of purpose, of devotion to the interests of his subjects, of sorrow over the past misfortunes of the people, and of a firm determination to remedy prevailing disorders, were those which might have been expected from a prince as hypocritical as he was selfish. Nor was it strange that such a son should lavish praise upon the mother, now tottering on the verge of the grave, from whom he had inherited the character that has rendered him odious for all time. More important for our present purpose are those expressions which cannot be suspected of insincerity, wherein Henry gave utterance to his sentiments respecting the toleration of the Huguenots and their religion.

The king's renewed expressions of hostility to the Huguenots.

" Favor, I pray you, my good subjects," he said, " my upright intention, which tends only to cause the glory of God and of our holy Catholic, Apostolic, and Roman religion to shine forth more resplendent, to extirpate heresy from all the provinces of this kingdom, to re-establish good order, to relieve my poor people now so greatly oppressed, and to raise up my own authority now so unjustly abased."

To the same topic he again adverted. " The evidence is sufficiently well known and can be given even by some of you who have honored yourselves in assisting me therein, both before and since I became your king, as to the zeal and steadfastness with which I have ever proceeded to the extirpation of heresy and of the heretics. In this work I shall more than ever expose my life, even to a certain death, if that be necessary, for the defence and protection of our holy Catholic, Apostolic, and Roman faith. The proudest tomb in which I could be buried would be amid the ruins of heresy."

---

[1] See Duplessis Mornay's reasons for refusing to write against the states general, as reported in Mémoires de Charlotte Arbaleste sur la vie de Duplessis Mornay son mari (Paris, 1824), 166.

"Not only," continued Henry, "are the battles which I have gained a sufficient proof, but that great army of the reiters, whose glory the Divine goodness chose me to humble, to the honor of God's holy name and of His Church. Of this thing the trophies and the spoils remain in the sight of all men. Will there be found, then, minds so incapable of cherishing the truth as to credit the statement that any one else is more inflamed with the desire to compass the final extirpation of the heretics, whereas no more certain effects have resulted than those that have flowed from my efforts? Even if the honor of God, which is dearer to me than my own life, were of less importance than it is in my esteem—whose is the patrimony which the heretics seize and dissipate? Whose revenues are they exhausting? Whose subjects do they alienate? Whose obedience do they despise? Whose respect, authority, and dignity do they violate? And should not I desire their ruin at least as much as any one else?

"The reuniting of all my Catholic subjects, by means of the holy Edict which I have made within a few months, has borne sufficient testimony to this, and has proved that I have nothing more at heart than to see God alone honored, revered, and served in my kingdom. And this I should have continued to show, as I shall always do, at the risk of my life, had it not been for this division among Catholics, which has been productive of incredible advantage to the party of the heretics, inasmuch as it has prevented me from marching into Poitou, where I believe that good fortune would not have forsaken me any more than in other places from which, thanks be to God, my state has drawn the desired and necessary benefit."

Nor did Henry of Valois forget the popular apprehension of a possible Huguenot succession. "The just fear," said he, "which you may have of falling, after my death, under the rule of a heretical king, should God so determine as not to give me issue, is not more rooted in your hearts than in mine. And I protest before God, that I am not more desirous of my salvation than I am to remove the fear and the reality of this consummation. It is for this reason principally, and for the purpose of abolish-

The fear of a Huguenot successor.

ing this damnable heresy, that I enacted my holy Edict of Union." [1]

In such unmistakable terms did the king, even now, and after a bitter experience of the conspiracy of the League, abetted by a goodly part of the Roman Catholic clergy, signify his relentless hatred of the Reformed faith and its professors. Certainly the ringleader in the massacre of Saint Bartholomew's Day showed no signs of amiable weakness for the Protestants, victims of a quarter of a century of persecution. The war for their extermination must be carried on to its bitter end.

The royal speech, in addition to all its orthodox professions, contained a distinct invitation to the members of the states general to join with his majesty, on the succeeding Tuesday, in a solemn renewal of the pledge to maintain the intolerant Edict. As if the process of heaping oath upon oath could add to the inviolable character of the disgraceful statute, of which it was proposed to make a fundamental law of the kingdom, this new device was resorted to for the purpose of making an impression upon the people. Wise men only doubted the more what the issue would be.[2] And this all the more, because it was no secret that only under dire compulsion had Henry consented to the step of repeating the oath he had taken at Rouen; a step humiliating to his self-respect, and shameful in one pretending to be a free monarch. At first he had positively refused. He even answered the deputies that came to him "with words sufficiently sharp."[3] He yielded only on learning that the states general were determined to break up, rather than yield the point.[4]

Renewal of the oath to the Edict of Union proposed.

---

[1] The king's speech is given in full by Matthieu, Histoire des derniers troubles, fols. 119–124; more correctly by the Mémoires de la Ligue, ii. 524–535. Synopses are given by De Thou, Agrippa d'Aubigné, etc.

[2] "Il y en eut qui trouvoient cette reiteration de mauvaise grace, comme ne se perdant la virginité de la foi qu'un coup seulement." Agrippa d'Aubigné, iii. 123.

[3] "Paroles assez aygres."

[4] It is Guise that gives us this information in two postscripts, under date of October 16th, to his letter of October 13, 1588, to Bernardino de Mendoza, De Croze, ii. 370, 371. He chuckles over his success in having so handled

Henry having concluded, Montholon, Keeper of the Seals, who sat in front of his majesty, proceeded to deliver an oration intended to set forth more fully his master's purpose. It cer-

Speech of Montholon, Keeper of the Seals. tainly could not be alleged that the new head of the judiciary of France was deficient in classic or in sacred learning; for in urging the utility of the institution of the states general, the speaker took occasion to draw his illustrations indiscriminately from every quarter. Good King Asa, Saint Paul, Childebert, Clotaire the Second and Dagobert the First, Pepin, Charlemagne, and Saint Louis figured side by side with the Assyrian and Persian monarchs and Saint Augustine.

Nor did the Archbishop of Bourges, the representative of the clergy, who spoke next, prove unequal to the demands of the occasion. He appealed to Henry of Valois—pos-

Speech of the Archbishop of Bourges. sessed, as was that prince, of the sagacity of Ulysses as well as of the grave eloquence of Nestor, and assisted by the prudence of that so virtuous and renowned princess, his mother, who might well be styled Irene, lady of peace and tranquillity—to raise up France, now lying prostrate after twenty-eight years of disastrous war. Thus would he acquire all the glorious titles lavished by grateful antiquity upon Hercules, Theseus, and other heroes and demi-gods who freed the world from giants, monsters, and other enemies of God and of the human race. Having taken good care to master his subject, the good prelate was not satisfied until he had expended upon his devoted hearers all his erudition, purchased, doubtless, at the cost of many nights of assiduous research. Unfortunate, indeed, was the eastern king, or the Roman emperor, whose name was not dragged into the discussion, to meet the ravenous appetite of the age for pedantic allusion. The archbishop extolled the wisdom displayed by the king in dissipating the army of German reiters and Swiss pikemen, so lately come into France. He expressed the confident hope that, under so good and great a king as Henry, the audacious heretics would

---

(manié) the states, and adds: "Les estatz persistent en leur résolucion, et plus tost de rompre que d'en rabatre."

find themselves repressed, and brought under the yoke of God, the Catholic Church, and the king. Then would peace return and universal security. Then would every man sit under his own vine and fig-tree. Then would the demolished churches be rebuilt. Then would the cities be freed from the sound of arquebuse and drum ; then would the temple of war be closed.

Was it intentional irony, or was the speaker carried away by his eloquence, when, in his peroration, he exclaimed, with much apparent unction : " O king, may you live forever ! May you live here below the years of Nestor—nay, the years of Arganthonius of Gades, who lived ninescore years ! [1] Live, represented by the succession of a long posterity ! Live here below by your name, and the glory of your virtue, which shall never die ! At the last, live above in the skies, not as an earthly king, but as a partaker and fellow-heir of the kingdom of God, whither He calls all those who have governed well His subjects here below ! "

The addresses of the Baron of Sennecey and of the Prévôt des Marchands of Paris, in behalf of the nobility and the people, echoed the sentiments expressed by the delegate of the clergy, and lauded the monarch's determination to expel heresy, and to restore the supremacy of the Roman Catholic Church. Both orders pledged themselves to expose their lives to every peril, and to pour out the very last drop of blood to secure the success of this meritorious undertaking.

Speeches of Baron Sennecey and the Prévôt des Marchands.

This much for Sunday's work. When, two days later, the states general assembled a second time, not only did Henry and the three orders again solemnly swear to maintain the Edict of Union,[2] but his majesty caused a fresh royal declaration, upon the same subject, to be read aloud by one of his secretaries, proclaiming the edict to be henceforth a fundamental and irrevocable law of the king-

The Edict of Union again sworn to, October 18, 1588.

---

[1] " Vivez Roy," disoit-il, " vivez eternellement ! Vivez ça bas les ans de Nestor, voire ceux d'Arganthonius, Roy de Gadar, qui vescut neuf vingts ans ! "

[2] "Mettant par les ecclesiastiques, les mains à la poictrine, et tous les autres, levans les mains au ciel." Mémoires de la Ligue, ii. 553.

dom.[1] After which, the whole body of those present, including
the king, the queens—his mother and wife—with princes, cardinals, and other dignitaries, proceeded to the Church of the
Holy Saviour, there to listen to the chanting of a solemn
Te Deum.   The people accompanied the king as he went with
loud cries of " Vive le Roy ! " and displayed, we are told, extreme joy and gladness.[2]

There were those, however, to whom the royal speech at the
opening of the states general was not a source of unmingled satisfaction.   A sentence or two had dropped from Hen-
ry's lips betraying the deep resentment he cherished
against the authors of the present disturbed condition of the
kingdom.   He went out of his way to say that, had he not been
anticipated and hindered by the inordinate ambition of some of
his subjects, he felt sure that the new religion would by this
time have been altogether exterminated from France.[3]   He cast
a slur upon the intriguing authors of the Roman Catholic con-
federacy at the very moment when he ostentatiously pardoned
their offences.   " Certain great personages of my kingdom," said
he, " have entered into leagues and associations, but, evidencing
my accustomed goodness, I tread under my feet, in this respect,
all that is past." [4]   The reference to Guise and his followers
was unmistakable.   The insult was insupportable.   To be held
up to the world's gaze as guilty of treason, even if the treason
was condoned, and this, too, in the very hour of triumph, was
more than the proud spirit of an aspirant to the throne could
brook.   The Archbishop of Lyons, pliant tool of the conspirators, was sent to remonstrate with the king, to threaten and
bluster in the royal cabinet, until the weak Valois, rendered

Annoyance of the Guises.

---

[1] " Declaration du Roy sur son Edit de l'union de tous ses subjets Catholiques," Blois, October 18, 1588, in Mémoires de la Ligue, ii. 545–571, and in
Isambert, xiv. 629, 630.

[2] Mémoires de la Ligue, ii. 554, 555.

[3] " Que s'il n'eust esté prevenu et empeché par l'ambition démesurée de
quelques siens subjects, il s'assuroit que la religion nouvelle eust esté lors tout
à fait exterminée de la France."   See Pasquier, apud Lestoile, i. 264.

[4] " Aucuns grands de mon royaume ont faict des ligues et associations;
mais, tesmoignant ma bonté accoustumée, je mets sous le pied, pour ce regard,
tout le passé."   Cayet, Chronologie Novenaire, 72.

still weaker by the persuasions of a mother who always sided with the enemy, consented to permit the obnoxious phrases to be erased from the report of his speech already printed and ready for publication.[1] Henry's reluctant acquiescence in so humiliating a change has been regarded as a strong proof that he had already formed a deliberate plan of the tragic events which occurred a little more than two months later. But the very boldness he displayed in affronting Guise at the opening of the states general, before an assembly in which the duke's sympathizers were known to be in the majority, would seem to indicate, on the contrary, that he had as yet adopted no definite scheme which might be thwarted by an untimely display of ill-will.[2] It seems more than probable that—despite his intense and inextinguishable hatred of Guise, despite, too, his settled and sullen determination to be avenged on him, for the gross insults he had received at his hands, when the best moment for striking a blow with safety to himself should have arrived— Henry had not yet mustered the courage, much less elaborated the details, necessary for the execution of his sanguinary projects. The kings of the sixteenth century, no less than the ruling statesmen of our own times, frequently received credit for greater foresight and larger plans than they were actually entitled to.[3]

---

[1] Lestoile and Cayet, ubi supra ; De Thou, vii. (book 92) 286, 287. Strange to say, the historian Davila (book 9, p. 359) maintains that the statement that Henry, yielding to the archbishop's importunity, omitted many things from his printed speech which he had uttered in the public meeting of the states, is altogether incorrect. He affirms that he was himself present, and so near to his majesty that he heard every word ; that he is certain that as much was printed as was spoken ; and that the king's " expressions, being quickened by the efficacy of his action and the tone of his voice, were much more sharp and moving than when they came forth in print, wanting that life and spirit with which they were delivered."   [2] De Thou, vii. 322.

[3] Agrippa d'Aubigné's remarks upon this point (iii. 114) are, as the remarks of this forcible writer will so frequently be found, well worthy of quotation : " Le Roi emploioit le temps, les ruses et les finances à endormir ses ennemis, soit (comme quelques uns ont estimé) avec dessein arresté de les empoigner à la pipée des Estats, soit (comme autres ont jugé) que ce fust pour rouler au jour la journée, dessein sans dessein, et pensée plus coutumière aux Rois que ne cuident ceux qui en vivent esloignez."

Meantime, while there were some humiliating concessions which Henry was willing to make—striking out the allusions to the Guises from his printed speech, as we have just seen, and submitting to the indignity of being required to repeat his oath to observe the Edict of Union, as though he might take it into his head to violate the oath to the same effect more privately taken three months before at Rouen—he was less inclined to yield to certain other demands. The clergy, early in November, took the initiative against the King of Navarre, whom it pronounced to be a relapsed heretic, and declared to have forfeited the succession to the throne. The other orders followed the lead of the clergy, and the Archbishop of Embrun, a noted Leaguer, was commissioned to carry the common decisions of the three estates to the king for approval. But for such action, even against a prince upon whom he wasted little love, Henry was by no means ready. He objected with good reason that the forms of judicial procedure had not been observed; nay, that it was out of the question to condemn as a heretic one who professed himself ready to receive instruction. And so, although the churchmen continued to urge their point, the king put off all decisive action in the matter.[1]

The clergy seeks to have Navarre declared incapable of succeeding.

It must not be supposed that the course of Guise was altogether plain and easy. The States of Blois, devoted as they were to the duke, whom in most things they regarded as their champion, had well-defined views of their own on some points, and neither he nor his brother, the cardinal, could move them. The tiers état proposed that the king be requested to diminish the hateful load of taxation that ground the miserable people to the earth, and called for the institution of a new tribunal which should compel the plethoric farmers of the public revenues to disgorge their ill-gotten wealth. The clergy and the nobles promptly supported the demand. In vain did Catharine de' Medici send for some of the most prominent deputies and remonstrate with them on their course. In vain did her son fume, and fret, and ply one

The tiers état demands the diminution of the taxes.

---

[1] De Thou, vii. 310, 311.

and another of the refractory commoners with threats and with promises. Neither the king, nor Guise, who, fearful of the ulterior consequences, besought them to modify their project, nor the cardinal, who declared that they would ruin France, could move them. So, finally, his majesty, making a virtue of necessity, gracefully yielded the point. " I grant your requests," he suddenly exclaimed ; but when the surprise, and the rapturous applause, and the loud cries of " Long life to the king ! " had ceased, and quiet was restored, he took good care to add that he made the concession on condition that the states should provide for the crown's necessities and for the prosecution of the war, according to their own promises. Meanwhile he was profuse in his expressions of the trust he reposed in the representatives of his people. He would have the money-chest containing the funds to carry on the war against the heretics to be made secure with two locks. The states should have the one key and he the other. He swore that without their consent he would impose no burden upon his people. He told them, confidentially, that some members of his council objected to all this, and warned him that he was fashioning France after the republic of Venice, and hampering himself till he might become another doge, and his kingdom be transformed into a state half-democratic. " But," said he, very magnanimously, " I shall do it." His tone, however, changed very materially when the states failed to redeem their promise to supply his pressing needs ; apparently unmoved by the pathetic picture he drew of his purveyor refusing to provide food for the royal table, and of the choristers of his chapel leaving his service for lack of wages.[1]

More embarrassing, however, than the indocility of Guise's own party at home was the clumsiness of his allies abroad. The Duke of Savoy invades the Marquisate of Saluzzo. The very moment when it was important for the purposes of the League that nothing should occur to distract the popular attention, much less by any accident to kindle into flame the long dormant fire of patriotism,

---

[1] See Picot, Histoire des États Généraux, iii. 117–133. This writer has ably, though, perhaps, somewhat too strongly painted the picture of the courage of the states general and their manly independence even of the Duke of Guise.

was chosen by the Duke of Savoy for an ill-timed invasion of
the Marquisate of Saluzzo or Saluces.   This district, which had
for many years been in the possession of the French, had long
been regarded with covetous eyes by Charles Emmanuel, because of its situation on the Italian slope of the Maritime
Alps and Monte Viso, and because of its tempting proximity
to Turin.   When the duke suddenly entered it, the King of
France was easily persuaded that the blow at the integrity of
his realm had been struck through the instigation of Henry
of Guise.   His council, the loyal party throughout France,
above all, the Huguenots, were confident that they saw in the
act only another of the stealthy moves of the calculating
League.   The more Guise and his followers protested their
innocence, the more fully was the world persuaded of their
complicity.   One thing was sure, and that was that for a few
days it seemed probable that this act of aggression from without would lead to a restoration of peace within the kingdom.
" It will be time enough to cross swords with the Huguenots
when we shall have driven the insolent invader from our soil."
Such was the cry of the best part of France, and, apparently, of
no inconsiderable part of the deputies at Blois.   Henry of Valois
for a moment imagined that this would be the prevailing sentiment of the states general.   But no!   The Guises resisted
with all their might and prevailed.   " We must first make provision," said they, " for the heart of the kingdom, and remove
the heresy which now afflicts it; afterward we shall easily
drive off the foreigners who have made attempts upon the
frontiers."   And the duke himself called upon his majesty to
secure to the pious French the fruits they had expected to
gain from the oath of the holy Union, volunteering the promise
that, when once the Huguenots should be extirpated, he would
himself be the first to cross the Alps and compel the Savoyard
to make restitution, should the king be pleased to honor him
with a commission.'   As the Huguenots had held out already
almost a full generation, the contingency referred to did not
appear a very near one to his royal auditor, nor was he likely
to be profuse in his thanks.

---

[1] Cayet, Chronologie novenaire, 74.

It is interesting, however, to note at this point that Henry of Valois, the patriots, and the Huguenots were mistaken; and that the mendacious Duke of Guise spoke the truth. The correspondence he maintained with the Spanish ambassador—

The Duke of Guise not privy to the enterprise.

a correspondence whose publication the duke would have been the very last to desire—demonstrates his innocence of any understanding that Charles Emmanuel should invade Saluzzo at this juncture. Indeed, it reveals instead the fact that Guise was greatly annoyed at the unexpected news which reached him, and sought in every practicable manner to have the blunder retrieved. When the first tidings were received, he wrote, in great anxiety, to Philip's ambassador: "I fear that this accident of Carmagnola may defeat all my intentions and plans, and that the king may seize the opportunity to come to an agreement with the heretics, so as to make war with the Duke of Savoy. This would kindle a fire which it would not be easy to extinguish, and would undoubtedly bring the ruin of Christendom and the overthrow of our religion. I beg you to consider this matter, and see whether there be any means of pacifying the Duke of Savoy, in order that we may follow out the course we are here pursuing." [1] "Everything was going well," the duke despondingly exclaimed, a few days later. "We should have obtained a fresh confirmation of the edict, the oath of the king, open war with the heretics to their utter destruction. Soon even the heretics of England and Germany would have been ruined. To-day our plans are so frustrated that a great number of the deputies are in favor of a general peace with the Huguenots, for the purpose of uniting with them; which thing will lead to the utter desolation of religion. All good people would be infinitely obliged to the Catholic King, if, before it be too late, he should bring about an accommodation." [2]

But if Henry of Valois and his more faithful counsellors, as well as the greater number of historians who have since touched

---

[1] Mucius (Guise) to Mendoza, October 9, 1588, De Croze, ii. 366.

[2] Same to same, October 13, 1588 ; ibid., ii. 369, 370. It will be noticed that this was written before the king's opening speech.

upon the matter, were mistaken in believing that the invasion of Saluzzo was an act of the Duke of Savoy, instigated by the
The king re-
solves upon
the murder
of Guise. Duke of Guise, and intended to further the success of the ambitious designs of the latter in his struggle with the crown, there can be no doubt about this — that no other belief was more potent in determining his majesty to hesitate no longer to rid himself of his turbulent and disloyal subject. It may well be (if we are to give so faithless and contemptible a personage as Henry the Third credit for entertaining any conscientious scruples) that the king fancied himself fully released from every oath he had taken in favor of the duke, by Guise's continued violation of his own equally solemn engagements, and by the intrigues at home and abroad in which his hand was ever discovered or suspected.[1] For the sake of securing undisturbed tranquillity, a monarch, indolent beyond others, might have overlooked, even could he not forget, past insults; but here was a subject who, so long as he was alive, would not allow his master to indulge the faintest hope of future quiet. There was no help for it. Such a restless conspirator must be summarily put out of the way, the most sacred promises, made upon the holy sacrament, to the contrary notwithstanding. In the expressive words of a contemporary historian, whom no writer of his own day, and few writers of a later day, have excelled in nervous vigor of diction, the Duke of Guise, absolved of past offences, was condemned to death for the crimes he was about to commit.[2]

Of warnings the king had had no lack. Unless Charles of Mayenne be a much maligned man, Henry of Valois had received accusations of Guise's ambition even from
Mayenne is
said to have
warned the
king. Guise's own brother. I would fain believe, with the generous historian to whom reference has just been made, that the story was afterward discovered to be an invention;[3] certain is it, however, that not only did writers of tried

---

[1] Cayet, Chronologie novenaire, 75.

[2] "Le duc de Guise, absous des offenses passées, fut condamné à mort pour les crimes à venir." Agrippa d'Aubigné, iii. 150.

[3] "Quelques uns ont mis le duc de Maienne au nombre des avertisseurs, mais après une bonne perquisition on a trouvé que non." Ibid., iii. 149.

impartiality, like De Thou, but sceptical diplomatists, like the
envoys of Florence and of Philip the Second, give full credence
to it. " Receiving advices," says Cavriana, " almost every day
from the Duke of Mayenne, brother of the deceased, and this
by the medium of Alphonso, colonel of the Corsicans, the king
was compelled to secure himself and his states."[1] According
to Mendoza's statement in a despatch to his royal master at
Madrid, Henry called upon the colonel in the presence of the
council itself, saying : " Seigneur Alphonso, repeat to the council what the Duke of Mayenne instructed you to tell me."
Whereupon Alphonso came forward and declared that the Duke
of Mayenne had accused his brother of having resolved upon a
resort to the last extremities against the king, with the intention of taking his crown from him.[2]

Henry of Valois himself positively asserted the fact that he
received a direct warning from Mayenne, and that, too, in the
very " Declaration " which he issued, two months later, enjoining that the duke be proceeded against as a traitor, and pretended to give the substance, if not the very words, of the message that was sent to him.[3]

Guise, on his side, had had an abundance of prudent advice,
which had shared the ordinary fate of such sensible counsel.
Conference respecting Guise's move- ments. A conference had even been held by the heads of the
League to decide whether it were not better for him
to retire from Blois. But the Archbishop of Lyons
had opposed this step, and had pointed out the disastrous results that might follow. The duke would be accused of being
a disturber of the public peace. Besides, he reminded his

---

[1] Cavriana to Serguidi, Blois, December 31, 1588 ; Négociations avec la
Toscane, iv. 848.

[2] Mendoza to Philip II., Saint Dié, December 27, 1588, De Croze, ii. 386.
Compare De Thou, vii. 322–5 ; and Lestoile, i. 266, 267.

[3] " Peu de jours auparavant sa mort [sc. de Guise], icelui duc de Mayenne,
entr'autres choses, nous manda par un chevalier d'honneur qu'il nous envoya
exprès, que ce n'étoit pas assez à son frère de porter des patenôtres au col, mais
qu'il falloit avoir une ame et une conscience ; que nous prissions bien garde
à nous . . . et que le terme étoit si brief, et que s'il ne se hâtoit, il étoit
bien à craindre qu'il n'arriveroit pas assez à temps." Declaration against the
Dukes of Mayenne and Aumale, Blois, February, 1589, Isambert, xiv. 638.

hearers, the common saying is that he who gives up the game
loses it.   Thus fortified in his resolve, Guise declared that he
would rather die a hundred deaths than be the cause of dis-
organizing such an assembly as was the gathering of the states
general.   Moreover, had he a hundred lives, he would freely
sacrifice them to be the means of giving some rest to the poor
people of France, so grievously afflicted.   " And, in addition to
this," said he, " I shall never believe that the king, who is so
good a prince, has any wish to execute so cowardly a design
against those who have never offended him and have never
been other than his faithful servants." [1]   We may smile at the
simplicity or the effrontery with which the duke uttered such
professions of consideration for a people whom he would not
permit to enjoy the blessings of peace guaranteed to them by
repeated edicts of pacification, and such assurances of loyalty
to a sovereign whose ruin he had nearly compassed, expecting his words to be accepted as unalloyed truth.   But we
can scarcely be surprised that he was slow to believe that the
king meditated so deadly a thrust at the " Holy League " in
the person of its foremost leader.   Had not his majesty summoned some of the principal deputies to him, on the ninth
day of December, the morrow of the great feast of
the Conception of our Lady, and had he not, after
confessing himself, and with his eyes fixed upon the
consecrated wafer, uttered such words as these, the Duke and
the Cardinal of Guise being present: " I have sent for you
all to come here in order to tell you and to swear on the Body
of my God, which I am about to receive in your presence, that
I again take an oath to support the holy Union, and again
unite myself with you all in such wise that never will I depart
therefrom until I shall have wholly extirpated heresy and the
heretics from my kingdom.   I call upon you all to help me in
this matter as you have promised to do; and, on my side, I

*The king
again swears
to persevere
in the Union.*

---

[1] MS. Relation of Jehan Patte, a burgess of Amiens, respecting the assassination of the Duke and Cardinal of Guise, printed for the first time in the Bulletin de la Société de l'Histoire de France (Documents historiques originaux),
i. 79. See, also, the very similar views, expressed a month or two earlier, as
reported by Cavriana, Négociations avec la Toscane, iv. 830.

protest on this holy sacrament to fulfil my engagements; or, may this reception be to my damage, ruin, and entire confusion! Were I to have a hundred daggers at my throat, never would I desist from this holy enterprise."[1]

The story of the king's preparations for the stealthy blow he was about to strike has been told often and well. It will be sufficient for my present purpose to touch lightly upon the incidents of the bloody deed which has given to the castle of Blois those gloomy associations that will outlast even the massive walls of the building itself.

It was very early on Friday, the twenty-third of December, that a meeting of the royal council was called. The king, so he said, wished to expedite business, that he might go and spend Christmas, but two days distant, at Notre Dame de Cléry. The morning of the shortest day in the year was rendered more gloomy by a cold, wintry storm. The rain fell steadily. Never had such dreary weather been known.[2] Guise had been summoned from his room in the western wing of the castle, by message upon message from the king. After a hurried toilet and with customary prayers unsaid, he presented himself at the stairs leading up from the courtyard to the royal apartment.[3] An unwonted

The assassination of the Duke of Guise.

---

[1] Relation of Jehan Patte, ubi supra, i. 78. According to Lestoile, i. 266, it was on Sunday, the 4th of December, that the king swore perfect reconciliation and friendship with Guise.

[2] Péricaud, Guise's secretary, states in his deposition that but few of the duke's retainers were at his rooms that morning, "à cause du mauvais temps qu'il faisoit, comme à la vérité c'estoit le plus obscur, ténébreux et pluvieux qui fut jamais." See "Information faicte par P. Michon et J. Courtin, conseillers en la cour de Parlement, pour raison des massacres commis à Blois ès personnes des duc et cardinal de Guise" (an inquest made at the request of the Duchess of Guise), Cimber et Danjou, Archives curieuses, xii. 194.

[3] Very obedient to the king's commands, "comme ung pauvre Isacq." On leaving his room he had exclaimed: "Je n'ay jamais accoustumez de sortir de ma chambre sans premierement avoir pryé Dieu, dont j'ay ung extraime regret d'estre ainsy pressé." Relation de Jehan Patte, ubi supra, i. 79. The northern part of the castle of Blois, where the king lodged, was built by his grandfather, Francis I. The eastern portion, including the portal, over which stands, or lately stood, an equestrian statue of Louis XII., was erected by this monarch, the father of Renée of France, Guise's grandmother. See the plan in Vitet, Les États de Blois (Paris, 1827). The coincidence is of interest.

sight met his eyes; the royal guard of archers lined the ascent;
for the king had been resolved that his prey should not this
time escape him.   But if the duke's suspicions were aroused by
the signs that pointed to some plot against his person, they
were quickly allayed by the assurance of the officer in command,
that the guards had come to beg his majesty to pay them their
wages, long overdue, and to tell him that otherwise they would
be compelled to sell even their horses, to procure themselves
the necessaries of life.   So, after promising to support the
archers' reasonable request with all his influence, Guise entered
the council-chamber, where his brother the cardinal, the Archbishop of Lyons, and a few others of the king's advisers were
already assembled.   In the light of a great catastrophe, even
the most insignificant of circumstances—circumstances that at
other times would have been deemed unworthy of a second
thought—assume a fantastic importance, and are told by the
curious in all their details, as if having an essential bearing
upon subsequent events.   Long years after the time of the
scenes here described, the partisans and the enemies of Guise
alike, never tired of relating how the valiant duke was overtaken, as he stood near the fire, by a sudden feeling of faint-
ness, and must needs send for some preserved fruit to stay his
stomach; or, how the eye so nearly lost by that honorable
wound which had procured him the surname of " Le Balafré,"
began to weep, and he was constrained to despatch a servant,
whom the guards, according to the strict orders they had received, refused to let pass, for the handkerchief which in his
haste he had forgotten to bring with him.   Such incidents,
however, whether simply fortuitous or bearing some resem-
blance to the premonitions of danger affecting a bold nature
until now but little influenced by warnings received from others,
are of little moment.   A false security still blinded Guise to
the deadly net into whose meshes he had thrust himself.   Had
he not informed the Spanish ambassador with the utmost positiveness that he knew the cowardly king to the very core?
He must, therefore, persuade himself, as he had more than once
maintained to others whose apprehensions he wished to allay,
that the king would not dare to attack him.   " Il n'oserait ! "

were the confident words he scribbled down as an answer to
one of the last of the warnings mysteriously conveyed to him.

Revol, one of the secretaries of state, now appeared at the
door of the council chamber, and announced to Guise that his
majesty desired his presence. Instantly the duke arose, and,
after courteously bidding his associates good-by, prepared to
follow the messenger. He had thrown his cloak about his left
arm, and held gloves and comfit-box in his hand. At his knock
the door of the royal bedchamber, through which he must pass,
was opened, and his eyes rested, not upon the monarch, but
upon six or eight of Henry of Valois's famous band of the
" Forty-five " gentlemen. At the farther end of the room a
heavy velvet curtain fell over the doorway leading to the king's
new cabinet. The game had indeed fallen into the toils; for,
beyond that tapestry, in the " old " cabinet, overlooking the
castle yard, lurked another dozen of the " Forty-five," ready to
spring from their lair upon the unfortunate nobleman, should
he by any chance penetrate so far. With them, or hard by, the
king himself, anxiously awaiting the success of his cowardly
plot; in his oratory, just across a narrow entry, Henry's chaplain, engaged in prayers which he had been charged to offer
to heaven for the success of the king's project. The gentlemen
posted in the bedchamber returned the duke's salute with a
semblance of courtesy. There was something, however, in the
expression of their faces, or in their bearing, as they moved
to accompany him, that aroused his curiosity or his alarm; for,
having reached the portière, and while in the act of raising it,
he turned his head to take a second look at them. The in-
stinctive act was understood as a preparation for retreat or for
self-defence. In a moment the assassins were upon him. Mont-
ferry, who was nearest, close to the fireplace, was the first to
seize him, and plunged a poniard in his breast, crying: " Ha!
traitor, thou shalt die! " Effranats entangled his legs; Saint
Malines dealt him a cruel thrust close to the throat; Lognac
struck him with his sword in the loins. Thus, overwhelmed by
numbers and taken at unawares, impeded by his cloak, with the
blood gushing from many a wound, the Duke of Guise exerted
his prodigious strength to no purpose, but yet had vigor and

resolution enough to drag himself and the assailants who had fastened upon him the full length of the room, where he fell at the very foot of the king's bed. It was but a moment before all was over. The few words that escaped him were remembered by the assassins: "Ha! my friends," several times repeated. "Mercy!" "My God, have pity on me!"

There was no need of the assistance of the king's reserved force. Henry of Valois himself, mustering up courage, now that his enemy was breathing his last, pushed aside the curtain and came upon the scene. His satisfaction was unconcealed. He ordered the body of Guise to be searched for further evidence of his treasonable designs. Besides a few gold crowns, a bit of paper was brought to light with the words: "To carry on the war in France, seven hundred thousand livres are necessary every month." In his exultation over the dead, Henry is even said to have kicked the Duke of Guise in the face. So the Duke of Guise himself kicked the corpse of Admiral Gaspard de Coligny, fifteen years before, in the court-yard of a house in the little Rue de Béthisy.

It was not the Huguenots alone that saw marks of retributive justice in the similarity between the death of the Duke of Guise and that of Admiral Coligny. "This tragedy," wrote the Florentine Cavriana, "is very similar to that of the death of the admiral on Saint Bartholomew's Day; since he who so eagerly sought the admiral's death, he who wished to see his enemy dead and thrown out the window, he who arranged that the body should remain for some days unburied, after having been dragged through the public streets, he who insulted it, and who contrived his enemy's death by lying in wait—this same man fell into the snare, in the self-same manner. It looks like a divine judgment against which there is neither wisdom nor counsel." [1]

In the council chamber the Cardinal of Guise heard the noise of the struggle going on in the adjoining room. "Ha!" he exclaims, as he springs to his feet, "they are killing my

---

[1] Cavriana to Serguidi, December 31, 1588, Négociations avec la Toscane, iv. 849.

brother." But Marshal d'Aumont, who is in the secret, is at
the cardinal's side in an instant with drawn sword. " Stir not,
sir," he cries, with an oath, " the king has to do with you." At
this Guise's fellow-conspirators, at the council board resign themselves to their fate; the Archbishop of Lyons, in abject fear,
ejaculating, " Our lives are in the hands of God and of the
king."

The king's first intention had been merely to imprison the
brother of his arch-enemy. Cardinal Guise's own words and
actions, when hurried away to the lower room of
the castle, for safe keeping made him change his
purpose. Even there the defiant spirit of the Lorraine prince could not consult prudence. " I hope that I may
not die," he was reported to Henry as saying, " before I shall
hold the head of that tyrant between my knees, and make him
a crown with the point of a dagger." True or false, the words
cost the prelate his life. The next day, the eve of the day
commemorating Christ's birth, the cardinal was drawn from his
cell, only to be speedily despatched. The bodies of the two
brothers were then placed in the care of the grand provost of
France, M. de Richelieu, father of the famous cardinal of that
name. Whether they were burned by fire in a room of the
castle, adjacent to the gate, as some said, or destroyed by quick-
lime, as others reported, certain it is that no vestige of the
body of either brother was spared to become an object of the
idolatrous worship of the Parisian populace. The same Loire
that had carried past Blois the bodies of the unfortunate victims of the father's vengeance, after the failure of the Tumult of Amboise, now sluggishly bore along to the ocean the
indistinguishable ashes of the sons.[1]

How will the murder of the Duke of Guise affect the policy
of the King of France in respect to his long-persecuted subjects
the Huguenots, is the inquiry which most nearly concerns us at

Murder of Cardinal Guise.

---

[1] Cavriana, however, gives a different account. " È pianto in segreto sola-
mente, ma il corpo suo posto in un lenzuolo è seppellitto in luogo sacro senza
alcun onore di mortorio, e in un villaggio separato dal mondo, insieme col car-
dinale, suo fratello ; e ciò si sa da pochissimi." Négociations avec la Toscane,
iv. 847.

this juncture. Will the monarch who has just been despatching
a troublesome nobleman, through whose machinations the "Holy

Henry's pol-
icy toward the
Huguenots.
Catholic League " has forced upon him a war of extermination to be waged against the Protestants, assume a conciliatory attitude now that the pressure
seems likely to be removed ?   Happily we are not left to conjecture the thoughts which were passing through the mind of
Henry of Valois.

There was a woman in the same castle of Blois without
whose participation little of importance had been done in
France for the past thirty years, or thereabouts. Catharine
de' Medici's apartments were on the story below those of the
king, but corresponding, room for room, with his. While the
Duke of Guise was falling under the daggers of assassins, the
queen mother lay in the room precisely beneath, dangerously
ill, and completely ignorant of her son's designs. Now, however, that the deed was done, Henry felt himself impelled by
an uncontrollable impulse to communicate the tidings of his
triumph to a mother who had reigned so many years under the
name of her weak sons.

In the corner of the king's bedroom, not over two or three
yards from where yet lay the inanimate form of the duke, a
narrow, spiral staircase, hidden in the wall, led to the bedroom
of Catharine de' Medici. Down this the king made his way.
It lacked yet some time of sunrise. Of what happened, and
particularly of what Henry said on this occasion, we are informed in a letter of Dr. Filippo Cavriana, Catharine's own
physician (who was also the secret agent of the Grand Duke of
Florence), written within twenty-four hours of the events described, and from the castle of Blois itself.

" Yesterday," says Cavriana, " which was the day before
Christmas eve, and the twenty-third of December, about eight

The king's
account giv-
en to Catha-
rine de' Med-
ici.
o'clock in the morning (that is, according to the Italian fashion of counting, about half-past one o'clock),
the Duke of Guise was stabbed to death, in the room
of the king, by those gentlemen that are perpetually
on guard about him (who from their number are called the
Forty-five), assigned to him, three years ago, by Épernon, Joy-

euse, and La Valette, when they were governing the world at
their will.   The manner of the death I shall relate to you as
I heard it recounted by the king himself to the queen, his
mother, I being present and very close to him when he narrated
the incident.

"So soon as the king saw the competitor and rival of his
command to be dead, he descended to the room of the queen
mother, and asked me particularly how she was.   I replied,
that she was doing well, and that she had taken a little medicine.   He then approached her and said, with a countenance
the most steady and assured in the world:

"'Good-morning, madam.   I beg you to excuse me.   Monsieur de Guise is dead, and will be talked of no more.   I have
had him killed, having anticipated him in what he designed to
do to me.   I could no longer tolerate his insolence, despite my·
resolution to endure it, that I might not imbrue my hands in
his blood, and despite my forgetfulness of the insult received
on the thirteenth of May (which was a Friday, the day on which
he was compelled to flee from Paris).   I had also cast into
oblivion his frequent attempts to offend me in life, honor,
and kingdom.   Nevertheless, discovering, and proving it every
hour, that he was anew sapping and mining'—these were his
very words—'my authority, life, and state, I resolved upon this
enterprise, which long perplexed my mind, as I disputed within
myself whether I ought to execute it or not.   However, seeing
that my patience was resulting in damage and shame to myself,
and that every day I was irritated and offended by new plots
of his, at last God inspired and aided me, to whom I am now
going to render thanks in church at the sacrifice of the mass.
If any man henceforth speaks of belonging to the League, I will
do to him as much as I have done to Monsieur de Guise.   I
mean to remove the burdens from my people ; I mean to hold
the states ; but I mean also that they shall speak according to
their station, and not after the fashion of kings, as they have
done until now.   To the family and property of the deceased
I intend no injury whatever.   I will favor, embrace, and aid
his relatives, as the Dukes of Lorraine, Nemours, and Elbeuf,
and Madame de Nemours, whom I know to be faithful and

affectionate toward me. But I mean to be the king and no longer a captive and slave, as I have been since the thirteenth of May until this hour. Now I begin afresh to be the king and the master. I have also placed guards over the Prince of Joinville, over Nemours, Elbeuf, and Madame de Nemours, not to do them harm, but because I wish to secure myself. I have done the same to the Cardinal of Guise and the Archbishop of Lyons, and, for the same reason, to my uncle, the Cardinal of Bourbon, who will receive no harm at my hands. I shall, however, place him in a position where he will be well off, and where I cannot be harmed by him. I shall prosecute with more boldness and ardor the war against the Huguenots, whom I intend by every means to exterminate from my kingdom.' [1]

The Huguenots still to be persecuted.

"Having said this with the same steadiness with which he came and began, he retired in nowise disturbed in countenance or in thought, a thing which to me, who was present, appeared marvellous. Afterward I began to consider with myself that such is the sweetness of revenge that it gives new vigor and life to the mind, and clears up the countenance. This example will serve to deter others from making attempts upon their prince; for, as he then said very wisely, not a case has been known where a person has rebelled against his master and natural lord that he has not been punished sooner or later." [2]

What Catharine de' Medici, startled by the sudden intelligence, answered her son, Cavriana has not recorded; but we know from other sources that she confined herself to the expression of the hope that Henry had prepared himself against future contingencies. When he declared that he had done so, she said she prayed that God would grant that the issue might prove advantageous. [3]

---

[1] "Seguirò più ardita e ardentamente la guerra contro gli ugonotti, i quali vuo' ad ogni modo estirpare dal mio regno."

[2] Cavriana to Serguidi, Blois, December 24, 1588, Négociations avec la Toscane, iv. 842, 843.

[3] Jehan Patte will have it that the queen mother did more : " laquelle luy dist plusieurs injures, et s'il avoit bien donné hordes (ordre) à ses affaires, pour ce que M. de Guise avoit beaucoup d'amis." This is highly improbable.

That very morning, after despatching Richelieu to announce to the tiers-état, assembled in the Hôtel de Ville, that he desired them to continue their deliberations, despite a conspiracy which he said that he had discovered to stab him in his room, his majesty proceeded to hear mass, as much exhilarated over his exploit—so the spectators said—as if he had conquered the whole world.[1]

Thus perished, in the flower of his age, a prince of fine presence and of no mean abilities, before whose eyes the prospect of a brilliant future seemed to be spread.[2] The Huguenots, who had experienced the effects of his military prowess and skill, never doubted his capacity, however much they might deplore the perversion of high natural endowments to the support of an evil cause. Shrewd in counsel, prompt and vigorous in execution, he united great boldness in planning a campaign to signal personal courage, verging upon recklessness. His claim to have been the prime author of the repulse of the Army of the Reiters might be successfully disputed ; but no one could challenge his bravery or the brilliancy of his charges at Vimory and at Auneau. His was just the character to conciliate favor and to fit him to be the idol of

The character of the Duke of Guise.

---

[1] For the incidents of the death of the Duke of Guise and his brother, see De Thou, vii. 338–347 ; Mémoires de la Ligue, iii. 155–162 ; Recueil des choses mémorables, 676 ; Agrippa d'Aubigné, iii. 151, 152 ; Étienne Pasquier's letter of December 27, 1588 (Œuvres, Edit. Feugère), ii. 316–321 ; Davila, 370, 371 ; Lestoile, i. 267, 268 ; Jehan de la Fosse, 221; Mendoza to Philip II., Saint Dié, December 27, 1588, De Croze, ii. 381–4 ; Cavriana, ubi supra, iv. 842–845 ; Relation de Jehan Patte, in the Bulletin de la Société de l'Histoire de France, i., doc. hist., 77–86 ; Le martyre des deux frères, a virulent pamphlet printed in 1589, reprinted in Cimber et Danjou, Archives curieuses, xii. 57–107 ; Relation de la mort de Messieurs les Duc et Cardinal de Guise (written probably by Miron), ibid., xii. 109–138 ; Information faicte par P. Michon et J. Courtin, conseillers en la cour de Parlement, etc., containing the depositions of Péricaud, of Olphan de Gast, one of the king's guards, of Étienne Dourgain, the king's chaplain, sent for by Henry III. to pray for his success, of Michel Marteau, prévôt des marchands, of the Archbishop of Lyons, etc., ibid., xii. 189–221.

[2] According to Cavriana, Guise had all the elements of greatness : " bellezza, grandezza, forza, dolcezza, ardire, prudenza, pazienza, dissimulazione, segrezza ; ci mancava la fede, per la quale sarebbe poco meno che re." Négociations avec la Toscane, iv. 847.

the Roman Catholic multitude in Paris and, indeed, throughout all France.   In the race for popular applause he had, from the start, this signal advantage over every competitor, that he was the son and successor of a father whom the Church had exalted to the high dignity of a martyr for the faith.   His private morals were not, indeed, above the low standard of the courtiers of his day.   Of conjugal fidelity he knew nothing; and it was characteristic that the last night of his life had been spent in the society of Madame de Sauve,[1] one of those ladies of easy conscience and more than doubtful reputation for whose smiles not only Henry of Valois and the late Duke of Anjou, but Henry of Navarre himself had been successful suitors.   None the less was the claim to Catholic orthodoxy an inalienable possession, inherited along with many family traits.   More polished in address than his father, he seemed to have derived from his uncle, the great cardinal, his full portion of the prelate's untruthfulness, without one particle of the prelate's notorious cowardice.   Men who knew the two brothers intimately, contrasted Henry of Guise and Charles of Mayenne to the disadvantage of the former.   Henry was rash, Charles was prudent.   Henry's word could not be depended upon; Charles was straightforward and veracious.   Henry spent lavishly, involving his private finances in hopeless indebtedness, and giving himself little concern so long as he could borrow enough to meet the most pressing claims; Charles managed his affairs with rigid economy.   It remained to be seen whether the cooler head of the younger brother would prove more successful than the impulsive nature of the elder, in rearing the perilous edifice of the League.

Of one thing there could be no doubt: the inordinate ambition of Henry of Guise sealed his fate.   Not content with

---

[1] " Une des plus belles dames de la cour." Miron's relation, ubi supra, xii. 199.   The portrait of Madame de Sauve (Catharine de Beaune) is given in Niel, Personnages françois du XVIe, siècle, tome ii., from a contemporary crayon sketch.   It affords little evidence of the strange fascination which this famous beauty is said to have possessed.   After the death of M. de Sauve, his widow had married the Marquis de Noirmoutier, October 18, 1584.   She continued, however, to be known by the name of her first husband.

the office of lieutenant-general, he aspired to absolute military
command.   Should the king confer upon the duke the rank of
high constable of France, in addition to the powers
His ambition. already wrung from his majesty's unwilling hands,
the first step to the throne would be conceded to his enemy.
Therefore it was that the assassination of Guise was ordered at
the very moment when the draft of the patent for his promotion was under the hands of the duke's secretary.[1] The Duke
of Guise had not displayed even ordinary caution.   Only the
day before his assassination, while walking with the king, after
mass, in the garden of the castle, he indulged in loud complaints of his majesty's continued resentment, and declared his
purpose to resign his office of lieutenant-general and retire to
the province of which he was governor.   Henry of Valois understood the meaning of the threat: Guise would give up the
inferior dignity only that he might receive the higher office at
the hands of the states general, according to their promise, and
owe no obligation for it to the monarch.[2] In fact, what with
the Duke of Guise's prospective military authority and the
remodelled council which the states general urged the king to

---

[1] " A l'heure que M. de Guise y minute ses lettres de connestable, et la degradation du roy de Navarre, contre le jugement d'ung chacung, le roy le faict
tuer en sa chambre." Mémoires de Madame Duplessis Mornay, 165.   Jean
Péricaud, Guise's secretary, in his deposition, stated that the king having arrested him, after the duke's death, examined him narrowly as to his master's
intentions, threatening "to make him wed a rope within a quarter of an
hour," in case he did not tell the truth.   One question was, whether Guise
did not intend to carry his majesty off by force to Paris.   A second was,
whether Guise did not wish to be made constable, to seize the royal power and
to reduce the king to a cipher (" un O en chiffre ").   Of course, the secretary
denied everything ; but Henry declared that Madame d'Aumale had warned
him of Guise's intention to take him forcibly to Paris, more than a week before.   See Péricaud's testimony in the Information faicte par P. Michon et
J. Courtin, etc., printed in Cimber et Danjou, Archives curieuses, xiii. 176.

[2] According to the Relation, ascribed to Henry III.'s physician, Miron,
the king when ill, a few days later, so explained his conversation with Guise
to the Duchess of Angoulême, who had come to visit him.   The writer was
present.   " ' Il me vouloit rendre cette charge pour ce que les estats lui avoient
promis de le faire connestable, et ne m'en vouloit pas avoir l'obligation.'
Voilà les propres termes du Roy."   Cimber et Danjou, Archives curieuses, xii.
125-127.

institute, with powers absolute and without appeal, his majesty bade fair soon to find himself, so far as all influence in the state was concerned, as naked as he had come into the world.[1]

The assassination of the Duke of Guise and of the Cardinal his brother was followed, within a few days, by another death, which, at an earlier date, might have shaken France and made an important change in its fortunes, but which, at this juncture, produced not the faintest ripple on the surface of the waters. Catharine de' Medici, lying grievously ill in the castle, had been deeply affected by the intelligence of the duke's murder, but she experienced a still greater shock when, on the succeeding New-Year's Day, by her son's request, she visited the captive Cardinal of Bourbon. The weather was unpropitious. The cold was intense and the winds were high. Her physicians warned her in vain of the risk she was running. But the exposure to which she was subjected, while carried from her bedchamber to the room wherein the prelate was confined, had less effect upon her enfeebled constitution than the harsh words with which he greeted her: "Madam, if you had not deceived us and brought us hither by fine words and under no security, the two brothers would not be dead, and I should be a free man."[2] As it was, the humiliated queen mother returned to her bedchamber in deep dejection, and only to succumb speedily to the disease which had already fastened upon her. She died on the fifth of January, 1589.[3] Had she lived but three months and a few days more, she would have completed her

Illness and death of Catharine de' Medici—January 5, 1589.

---

[1] "Il quale protesto vuole inferire di lassarlo *infantem nudum.*" So writes Orazio Rucellai, the great Florentine banker, to the Grand Duke's first secretary, Blois, December 19, 1588. Négociations avec la Toscane, iv. 877, 878. See, also, Picot, Histoire des États Généraux, iii. 136.

[2] Cavriana to Serguidi, Blois, January 5, 1589, Négociations avec la Toscane, iv. 853, 854. See Lestoile, i. 278.

[3] "Ieri, che fu il v di gennaio e la vigilia dei Re, a un' ora e mezzo dopo mezzodì, la Reina, gran madre dei re, passò a miglior vita di un male di costato, il quale era passato a un altro, detto peripneumonia, che tanto importa quanto infiammazione dei polmoni." Cavriana to Serguidi, January 6, 1589, ibid., iv. 853.

seventieth year.[1] It was over fifty-five years since she came, as the bride of Henry the Second, to the country with whose fortunes her connection was so disastrous.

It would be a superfluous task here to discuss the character of the remarkable woman who now passed off the stage of action, her demise, to use the homely simile of a contemporary, creating no greater sensation than would the death of a paltry goat.[2] The history of the age in which she lived has been read to little purpose if the personal lineaments of the widow of Henry the Second, the mother of Francis the Second, Charles the Ninth, Henry the Third, and Francis of Alençon and Anjou, and the chief author of the Massacre of St. Bartholomew's Day, be not clearly impressed upon the mind—not the strongly marked and not ungracious features of her face, the prominent eyes, the long nose and sensual lips of her extant portraits—but the more clearly defined and unmistakable outlines of her mental and moral constitution. Pope Clement had the credit with the world, at an early date, of having cleverly tricked Francis the First into consenting to mate his second son with an obscure Italian girl; and this Italian girl had apparently deemed it her duty ever since to keep up the traditions of the Medici family by endeavoring to cheat every one with whom she came into contact. How it all ended, what had been gained by falsehood and double dealing and wars and massacres, was now seen in the disgust expressed by Cardinal Bourbon, and still more manifestly in the contempt with which her death was summarily dismissed by those who deigned to record the event at all.

The Florentines in Paris were, perhaps, the most sincere mourners, although we can hardly read their words without

---

[1] We have already seen that Catharine was born at Florence, April 13, 1519. Her mother, Madeleine de la Tour d'Auvergne, died of fever on the 25th of the same month, and her father, Lorenzo de' Medici, on the 4th of May following, scarcely twenty-eight years old.

[2] "On ne parla non plus d'elle que d'une chevre morte." Recueil des choses mémorables, 688. See De Thou, vii. 366 ; Mémoires de la Ligue, iii. 184, 185 ; Lettres d' Étienne Pasquier, ii. 322, etc. ; Lestoile, i. 278 ; Jehan de la Fosse, 223 ; Agrippa d'Aubigné, iii. 153.

suspicion. Was not the banker Rucellai indulging in a little
quiet irony when he wrote down this pious prayer in her behalf ? " May it please His Divine Majesty to have given her a
place in heaven, as her entire life and the departure which she
has so holily made give us a firm hope of the same ! " [1] Her
worthy son-in-law, the King of Navarre, did not pretend to
mourn. On Christmas Day he wrote to Ségur: " I have seen
letters brought by a courier in which the writer stated that he
had left the queen mother, who was dying. I will speak as a
Christian : God's will be done concerning her ! " [2] A week
later, having heard of the circumstance that Henry the Third,
after the assassination of the Lorraine princes, had sent to
Lyons to arrest their brother, the Duke of Mayenne, the gay
monarch wrote to another correspondent, in playful allusion to
Catharine's illness and to the efforts of the pope and the League
to deprive him of his ancestral throne : " I am only awaiting
the good fortune of hearing that they have sent and strangled
the *late* Queen of Navarre. This, with the death of her mother,
would certainly make me sing the song of Simeon ! " [3] His New-
Year's Day wishes were every way as humane as his Christmas
resignation had been Christian.

---

[1] " Piaccia a Sua Divina Maestà avergli dato luogo in cielo, sì come ne danno
ferma speranza tutta la vita che ella ha trapassata, e la partita che così santa-
mente ell' ha fatta ! " Négociations avec la Toscane, iv. 877, 878.

[2] " Je parleray en chrestien : Dieu en fasse sa volonté." Navarre to Ségur,
St. Jean d'Angely, December 25, 1588, Lettres missives, ii. 412.

[3] " Je n'attends que l'heure (l'heur) de ouïr dire que l'on aura envoyé
estrangler la feu reyne de Navarre. Cela, avec la mort de sa mere, me fairoit
bien chanter le cantique de Simeon." Navarre to the Countess of Grammont, January 1, 1589, ibid., ii. 418.

CHAPTER X.

OPEN REBELLION OF THE LEAGUE, AND UNION OF THE TWO KINGS.

VARIOUS were the emotions awakened in the breasts of the Huguenots by the intelligence that reached them from Blois.

The Hugue-nots breathe more freely on the death of Henry of Guise, The very essence of the unjust persecution of which they had so long been the victims seemed to have been embodied in the elder of the two brothers who had just met an unexpected death at the hands of an offended king. Not more truly had it been said of Francis of Guise, a quarter of a century before, that he was the chief enemy of the Protestant churches of the kingdom, than the same charge could now be brought against the son who had succeeded at once to his name and to his prejudices. How could the adherents of the Reformed faith be expected to feel no joy that Heaven had deigned to interfere in their behalf by the removal of the most determined foe of their doctrines, the sworn advocate of their extermination? Accordingly, the first impulse, at the court of Henry of Navarre and in the city of La Rochelle, was to indulge in public manifestations of joy and to offer thanksgiving to Almighty God. But wiser and more humane counsels prevailed. If the result was a pros-

but abstain from unseemly rejoicing. pect of relief from the violence of the most relentless of foes, the means by which that result had been reached deserved only the reprobation, as they awakened the disgust, of every honorable man. The Huguenots, indeed, breathed more freely, now that the Duke of Guise was no more; but they could not forget that his death had been compassed by treachery. As for the contemptible being that occupied the throne of France, although destitute of every heroic virtue which is commonly supposed to stamp the proper candidate for royalty, he had succeeded in proving to the entire world that he was not only a weakling and a coward too timid to resent insults in a manly fashion, but a perjurer whom not the most solemn oath taken on the very wafer in the holiest of sacraments could bind, a dastardly assassin without a spark of knightly honor in his breast. The picture of the effeminate voluptuary, given over in secret to loathsome vice, save when in well-simulated devotion he walked barefooted to some shrine to implore the long-denied boon of a son and heir, became more repulsive as the popular imagination essayed to add the traits of the poltroon, crouching in his innermost closet while the daggers of his guards were despatching in his bedchamber the nobleman who had been enticed thither by protestations of affection and confidence.

So the bonfires were not lighted in the streets of La Rochelle, and the cannon were not fired in token of joy, and the worthy burghers re-echoed the sentiments which Duplessis Mornay so decidedly expressed in their Hôtel de Ville : " Let it not be said that the adherents of the Reformed religion have by a solemn act approved a deed of too doubtful a character ! " [1] None the less was there fervent gratitude to Heaven for the wonderful manner in which retribution had again been visited upon their adversaries. " Sire," wrote Duplessis Mornay to the King of Navarre, on the first receipt of the intelligence, "we have reason to praise God. His judgments are great, and the favor He has shown to us is not small, that you have been avenged of your enemies without defiling your hands with their blood." [2] Still more feelingly did the same great man write to the aged reformer of Geneva, Theodore Beza, in allusion both to the death of Guise and to Huguenot successes which will soon occupy our attention : " Sir, God smites with hard blows whenever it pleases Him. Of such a character is this stroke, so much the greater in itself as it was

Duplessis Mornay's words on the event.

---

[1] " Qu'il ne fust point dit, que ceux de la religion approuvassent par un acte solemnel une action trop ambigue." Vie de Duplessis Mornay, 125. See, also, Agrippa d'Aubigné, iii. 154.

[2] Duplessis Mornay to the King of Navarre, December 26, 1588, Mémoires, iv. 277–279.

neither hoped for nor dreaded ; and so much the greater for us,
as neither our souls nor our hands were concerned in it. At
the same time, He has also blessed our arms in the taking of
Niort. So many benedictions make me afraid! Let us pray
that He will grant us the grace to render Him thanks for
them ! " [1]

It must not, however, be imagined that the Huguenots suffered themselves to be deceived respecting the conflict in which
The struggle they were engaged. So far from anticipating a
not ended. speedy reconciliation between the Kings of France
and of Navarre, and a cessation of the proscriptive measures
against Protestantism, statesmen saw that Henry of Valois
would be compelled to vindicate his claims to orthodoxy by
continuing the war against reputed heretics with undiminished,
if not, indeed, with increased, activity. Only after months
should have elapsed could it be hoped that necessity or expediency might lead him to renounce a struggle forced upon him
by the enemies of his crown, and might induce him to call in
the assistance of Henry of Navarre and his followers, the most
sincere and trustworthy of his subjects.[2]

The city of Niort, situated about midway between La Rochelle and Poitiers, had long been a thorn in the side of the
Huguenots. Strong in their fancied security, the inhabitants
(most of them strong partisans of the League) had not con-

---

[1] "Pryons-le qu'il nous donne la grace de lui en rendre graces." Letter of
December 30, 1588, Mémoires de Duplessis Mornay, iv. 284. In a letter
dated a day earlier a sentence occurs which well merits to be reproduced
here : "Or voyons nous que c'est de se fier en Dieu, qui sçait abreger les
desseings des hommes comme il lui plaist, et confondre les entreprises d'ung
siecle en une matinee." Letter to Pujolz, ibid., iv. 283. So, too, he wrote
to La Noue, "Bras-de-fer:" "Certes, autrefois nous avons esté accablés
des fleaux de Dieu ; maintenant nous le sommes de ses graces," Ibid., iv.
291.

[2] Duplessis Mornay's views were thus expressed : "Que pour ceste muta-
tion il [le roy de Navarre] n'avoit rien à changer en la conduite de ses affaires
ny dedans ny dehors; par ce que le roy se sentira à tant plus obligé à faire le
bon catholique, et n'ozera de plusieurs mois traicter de paix avec luy ; au
contraire luy jettra tant plustost ses forces sur les braz—plus foibles, neantmoins, par ce que le Duc de Mayenne, qui sur ceste douleur redoublera ses
effortz, les pourra distraire." Vie de Duplessis Mornay, 124.

tented themselves with laying in an immense store of provisions
and a good quantity of munitions of war ; but, by their raids in

Capture of
Niort by the
Huguenots. every direction, they had made it impossible for any
one suspected of being a Protestant to inhabit the
open country.   Their insolence had of late become so
great that, having killed a grand provost of the King of Navarre in a combat just outside of the walls, they had subsequently amused themselves by dragging his dead body ignominiously through the streets of the city, and then hanging it upon
the gallows.   It was therefore with special satisfaction that the
Huguenot prince permitted Duplessis Mornay to arrange a plan
for the capture of the place.   The execution was committed to
other chiefs, and especially to Monsieur de Saint Gelais, who,
as the patrimonial estates which gave him his territorial designation were not far from the northern gate of Niort, might be
supposed to feel more than ordinary interest in the undertaking.   Right well did he discharge himself of his trust, with
the help of his brave associates.   The moon was bright on the
night chosen for the attack, but the Huguenots waited in the
neighborhood until it had fully set.   Then, leaving their horses
in charge of grooms—for they had ridden hard to reach the
rendezvous—they applied themselves to their task without delay.   Two parties placed their ladders against the walls, and
hastened to scale the enemy's defences.   A third detachment affixed a petard to the gate and attempted to blow it in, but succeeded only in making an opening large enough to admit them
man by man.   The noise of the explosion awoke the inhabitants
from their sleep.   But, although they made a stout resistance,
the citizens were no match for the valor and skill of the Huguenots.   In a few hours Niort was in the hands of the officers of the
King of Navarre, and when that prince himself arrived on the
scene, from St. Jean d'Angely, the castle promptly capitulated at
his summons.   To its governor—no other than Jean de Chourses,
Sieur de Malicorne, the nobleman to whom Renée de France
had, at Montargis, twenty-five years before, returned a defiant
answer well becoming a daughter of Louis the Twelfth [1]—

---

[1] See the Rise of the Huguenots, ii. 111.

were accorded favorable terms of surrender, and he was permitted to retire to a friendly refuge. Never, in fact, did the difference between the Huguenot mode of warfare and the conduct approved and practised by the League show itself more distinctly than in the surprise of Niort. True, it cannot be asserted that the ideal excellence of discipline and of morality enjoined by the ordinances of Admiral Coligny, in the first civil war, had been maintained intact throughout an entire generation of almost continuous hostilities, and among men embittered by the recollection of relentless persecution and cowardly massacres. But there were some outrages they scarcely ever committed. They certainly plundered the unfortunate townsmen of Niort without stint, and probably with but little compunction. The capture of a city whose granaries contained provision enough to sustain an army of twenty thousand men for two years was not an every-day occurrence, and the opportunity was well improved. Indeed, so determinedly did the Huguenots pillage as to prove that they were moved less by cupidity than by a thirst for revenge.[1] But not a single man was murdered in cold blood; and not a single one of the feebler sex, usually the victims of the lustful passions of a successful soldiery, suffered any dishonor. The Huguenots, at Niort as elsewhere, showed by their actions that they might wage a warfare whose code was stern and bloody enough, but that they were neither assassins nor enemies of the purity of woman. One wealthy citizen, indeed, was ordered to be hanged for past treasonable language respecting the King of Navarre and other members of the royal house of France ; and the dead body of the author of the inhuman treatment visited upon the grand provost of the King of Navarre, having

Contrast between Huguenot warfare and that of the League.

___

[1] " À la pointe du jour le soldat se mit à piller le ville ; et il le fit avec tant d'acharnement, qu'on s'appercevoit aisément qu'il étoit moins animé par l'avarice, que par la vengeance." De Thou, vii. 362. The writer of the narrative given in the Mémoires de la Ligue (iii. 158) makes the Huguenot soldiers more moderate than they might have been expected to be in their treatment of a city so conspicuously in the interest of their enemies. A tradesman having in his house merchandise to the value of ten or fifteen thousand livres did well to come off with a payment of two or three hundred crowns, a sum equal to thrice as many livres.

been discovered, was itself suspended for a while to the very
gibbet upon which the corpse of the provost had been exposed
to the eyes of the populace. But of real atrocities there was
no instance. None the less, however, was a pamphlet published in Paris purporting to give a full account of
the execrable conduct of the Huguenots at the taking
of Niort. The Roman Catholic historian De Thou,
than whom we have no more trustworthy guide in the intricate maze of a period abounding in contradictory statements
of facts, affirms, from personal investigation, that the whole
story was a baseless fabrication of those who considered it a
meritorious act to tell falsehoods to the disadvantage of heretics.[1]

Fictitious stories of Huguenot atrocities.

The arms of the Huguenots were not always so fortunate.
La Ganache, a small but strongly fortified place, two or three
leagues from the ocean, on the confines of Poitou and
Brittany, after long detaining the royal army under
the command of the Duke of Nevers, finally surrendered. Yet
even here the disastrous result was due less to military superiority than to an apparently fortuitous circumstance. The Huguenot garrison had entered into an engagement to evacuate
the place unless reinforcements should arrive within a fixed
number of days. But Henry of Navarre, hastening to their
relief, had fallen dangerously ill by the way, and was compelled
to give up the undertaking; while La Rochefoucault, La Trémouille, and Châtillon, whom he sent on in his stead, were
misled by their guides, themselves either bribed to go astray
or ignorant of the country. At all events, La Ganache had

Failure at La Ganache.

---

[1] " Ceux qui écrivoient alors à Paris, gens sans honneur et sans jugement,
font une relation affreuse des meurtres et des excès commis par les Protestans
à la prise de cette place. Mais en passant par-là quelques mois après, je re-
connus par moi-méme la fausseté de ces calomnies." De Thou, vii. 363.
Upon this siege see, also, Recueil des choses mémorables, 682, 683 ; Agrippa
d'Aubigné, iii. 154–158; Cavriana's letters of December 31, 1588, and January 16, 1589 ; Négociations avec la Toscane, iv. 852, 855 ; Mémoires de la
Ligue, iii. 162–172. The last-named authority, which also enters into details,
gives us (p. 170) the title of the pamphlet printed at Paris (" Les cruautez ex-
ecrables commises par les Heretiques contre les Catholiques de la ville de Niort
en Poitou ") and the specific accusations it contained.

already fallen when the Huguenot troops came in sight of the walls.[1]

The very circumstance that the historian is called upon to note the capture of so insignificant a place by the royal troops is a sufficient proof of the futility of the undertaking to conquer the Huguenots, and to carry into effect the stipulations of the Edict of Union. The court itself and foreign ambassadors recognized the fact that the loss, in the very heart of Poitou, of so strong and wealthy a city as Niort, together with the capitulation of the neighboring town of St. Maixent, which at once submitted to the Protestants of its own accord, was of far greater moment than the capture of a paltry stronghold like La Ganache amid the snow and rain of lower Poitou.[2] But if anything more was needed to show the hopeless character of the crusade for the extermination of Protestantism, to which Henry of Valois had pledged himself anew after the death of the Duke of Guise, it was found in the rapid dissipation of the army of the Duke of Nevers. The news of the bloody tragedy of Blois had reached the besiegers before the advent of the new year, but it was not until after the surrender of La Ganache that it suddenly bore fruit. Men knew not what to think or to do. Not a nobleman but was restless and either asked leave to retire, or showed that he would retire without the consent of the commanding general. The partisans of the League were unwilling to battle for the

Dissipation of the army of Nevers.

---

[1] Mémoires de la Ligue, ii. 585–603 ; De Thou, vii. 315, 316, 363–365 ; Recueil des choses mémorables, 681, 684. The siege of La Ganache seems, however, to be entitled to some honorable distinction, because, first, of the humanity of the Huguenot garrison, on the 4th of January, in bringing into the walls and carefully nursing the wounded left by the royalists in the ditch after an unsuccessful assault ; secondly, because of the kindly return for this on the part of Nevers and his army at the time of the surrender ; and, thirdly, because of the good faith of the Huguenot governor of the place, Duplessis-Gecté, in carrying out in good faith his promise to surrender La Ganache, although he had heard the signal guns of the approaching relief under Châtillon and La Trémouille. The siege lasted from Friday, December 16, 1588, to Saturday, January 14, 1589.

[2] The contrast is drawn by Cavriana, in his letter to Serguidi of Blois, January 16, 1589, Négociations avec la Toscane, iv. 855. He styles (ibid., iv. 852) Niort "fortissima e richissima terra."

assassin of their favorite chief, the idol of the ultra-Catholic faction. Those who wavered between the two parties were anxious to gain time for consideration. Trimmers desired to be where they might better observe the drift of affairs. The Duke of Nevers himself was half-hearted and quite willing to lead back what troops could be held together to the city of Blois, whence he shortly retired to his own estates on the upper Loire. To tell the story in the fewest words, the formidable expedition of the king, which was to have reduced all Guyenne, disappeared from before men's eyes in a manner quite incomprehensible to all save those who understand the slight degree of cohesion that existed in the armies of the sixteenth century—an inherited weakness of the preceding period. Noblemen following the king, much in the fashion of the feudatories of the middle ages, at their own charges for the support of themselves and their retainers, claimed, and certainly exercised, the privilege of coming and going according as the fancy seized them ; while the mercenary troops, when their wages were withheld or paid only at irregular intervals, were wont to take matters into their own hands, and abandon with little ceremony an unprofitable service. The most powerful army was capable of melting away like a mist. As for that of the Duke of Nevers, the grateful Huguenots saw, in the unexpected manner in which it vanished from sight, nothing less than a sign that the finger of God had touched the fabric, and it had instantly crumbled to pieces.[1]

Meanwhile the fortunes of France were trembling in the balance. In the castle of an obscure village, Henry of Navarre,

Illness of Henry of Navarre. ill of pleurisy—as many thought, beyond hope of recovery—seemed likely to pay with his life the penalty of too reckless exposure in severe wintry weather while hastening to the relief of his fellow Protestants.[2] The

---

[1] " En un moment ceste grande et furieuse armee s'en alla en pieces, comme frappee du doigt de Dieu." Memoires de la Ligue, ii. 603. See Recueil des choses mémorables, 684 ; De Thou, vii. 365.

[2] " Le roi de Navarre s'acheminant à la Ganache, le 9 de ce mois, tomba malade d'une forte pleuresie au costé gauche, sans medecin, en ung village. Nous l'avons veu en danger extresme." Duplessis Mornay to Morlas, January 21, 1589, Mémoires, iv. 310.

Huguenots of independent La Rochelle, not less than the
Huguenots of more exposed districts, wept over the danger
impending, and prayed earnestly to heaven that it might be
averted. "The news was brought to La Rochelle,"
wrote a contemporary and apparently a participant in
the events he describes, "about nightfall on the thirteenth of January, 1589, which might be the fourth day of the
king's illness. At once the entire population was summoned,
by the ringing of the bells, to assemble in the churches for
prayer. It was about seven o'clock in the evening, an unusual
hour for such convocations. Yet, necessity requiring it, and
everybody being informed of the cause, never was there seen
in that city such a concourse of people in the churches. All
the inhabitants without distinction, even to the children and
the servants, left their houses to run thither. So great was the
concourse that many, not being able to enter the churches,
which were full to overflowing, returned home very sad, but,
nevertheless, engaged in private prayers, answering to the public prayers that were at that time offered, with great mourning
and many tears. Few persons were ignorant of the greatness
of the affliction for all France in general, had God, at a season
so full of trouble and confusion, removed this first prince of
the blood, endowed with so many graces. The extraordinary
prayers were continued for several days, until the certain news
of his recovery was received." [1]

General anxiety at La Rochelle.

Nor, if we may credit the accounts that come to us, was
the subject of so much solicitude himself insensible to the danger of his situation or to the claims of piety. He
professed patient submission to the will of God. He
was ready to die, if that were the pleasure of the
Almighty. His only regret was the need of his presence which
the Church in France might experience, the loss of his fidelity
which the entire kingdom would feel. In the midst of his
sufferings, however, we are told that he never intermitted his
care of the military concerns of the Huguenot cause.

Henry's religious professions.

Such was the anxiety of the Huguenots respecting the life of

---

[1] Mémoires de la Ligue, ii. 602.

the prince upon whom they had conferred the proud title of Protector of their churches. Such were the religious sentiments which that prince himself professed to entertain when apprehensive that he might be on his death-bed. That these sentiments stand in marked contrast with the tenor of his life in times of health is only another strange phenomenon in a character full of inconsistencies and contradictions.[1]

Meanwhile it is necessary once more to turn northward and inquire how affairs were proceeding at Blois and in the capital of the kingdom.

Henry of Valois had slain his arch-enemy, and had not spared the brother of his victim, whose every thought, word, and action had been war and bloodshed.[2] Other heads of the League had been thrown into prison, and hourly expected a like fate. Up to this moment, the measures taken had been prompt and decided. In continued promptness and decision lay the sole chance of success. Sagacious men recognized the fact instantly. Dr. Cavriana, on the morrow of the duke's assassination and on the very day of the execution of the cardinal, wrote home that the present occurrence would serve to deter others from conspiring against their princes; for, as the king had sensibly remarked, no one had ever been known to rebel against his natural lord but he had sooner or later paid the penalty. Six or seven of the authors of the revolt, intimate associates of Guise, had been apprehended, and would shortly be executed. The king had despatched Alphonso Ornano, better known as the " Corsican Alphonso," to Lyons. His object was to make sure of the Duke of Mayenne and persuade him to remain faithful in his allegiance, despite the death of his brothers. His majesty had taken other precautionary measures. But Henry could not stop. He must

First measures of the King of France.

---

[1] Mémoires de la Ligue, ii. 601; Recueil des choses mémorables, 684; Agrippa d'Aubigné, iii. 160. Madame Duplessis Mornay, in her Mémoires, 169, confirms the statements of others: "Il n'avoit consolation en son mal que de faire chanter des psalmes, et parler de sainctz et bons propos."

[2] "Telle fut la fin du cardinal, qui ne souffloit que la guerre, ne ronfloit que massacres, et ne haletoit que sang, lequel porté par terre par un juste jugement de Dieu, se sentist ce jour veautré dans son propre sang." Lestoile, i. 269.

either shed more blood, or, if he should pardon the rebels, he must be forever in fear of his life, through the lying in wait of the many great and brave members of the family of Guise. These would never forgive the monarch for what he had done, and certainly few men would be found to trust him after breaking his word confirmed by so many oaths.[1]

A week had scarcely passed, however, before every man of ordinary sense began to exclaim at the sluggishness of the king. He apparently thought that everything was done at the very moment when an energetic person would have thought that nothing was as yet accomplished, and would have set himself with relentless determination about the task which he had commenced. " Now at last I am king!" he exclaimed after despatching Guise; yet never had he been less a king than he was then and from that time forward. He failed to make instant provision for securing the cities of Paris and Orleans, both of which he might have gained in the first surprise and consternation resulting from the news of the duke's assassination. Above all, he neglected to recall Nevers and his army at once from Poitou—a step urged by Marshal d'Aumont and other patriotic advisers. He preferred to believe the treacherous Duke of Retz and the cardinal, his brother, who, it is true, conceded the advantage of having about the king's person the large accession of strength which Nevers would bring, but maintained that, should Henry recall that general, when warring against the heretics, for the purpose of fighting against Catholics, he would run the risk of being himself blamed as a heretic and, indeed, an infidel. In short, he was told that thus he would completely alienate the people, already incensed with him both on account of the intolerable burdens under which they groaned and by reason of the murder of Guise.[2] It was not the first time that courtiers

He soon relapses into sluggishness.

---

[1] " But in truth," added the Florentine, apologetically, " his majesty was in very great danger of being irretrievably ruined before the close of the states general "—" di lasciarvi la pelle." Letter of Cavriana, Blois, December 24, 1588, Négociations avec la Toscane, iv. 844, 845.

[2] " Così," says Cavriana, " vinsero la risoluzione del Re." Letter of February 9, 1589, Négociations avec la Toscane, iv. 859. See, too, De Thou, vii. 352, 353.

preferred the public ruin to the sacrifice of their private interests. So long as Nevers remained where he was, the large
possessions of Retz and his brother in lower Poitou were com-
paratively safe; should he withdraw, the Huguenots would in-
fallibly capture them all.[1]

Nothing could surpass the fury of the clergy and of the people of Paris, when the tidings of the tragedy of Blois reached
The fury of   the banks of the Seine. The crime of laying violent
the Parisians. hands upon the cardinal, upon whose head the sacred
oil had been poured, was, in one aspect of the case, more unpardonable than the assassination of his brother, because it
partook of the character of sacrilege. But, after all, it was the
murder of their favorite hero, the duke, that stirred the Parisians to madness. The miserable prince who had perpetrated it,
hitherto more a subject of contempt and loathing than of hatred, at once became in their eyes the incarnation of evil. There
was not a secret story of orgies, celebrated in the Louvre or
elsewhere by the monarch and his minions, that was not now
dragged to the light and repeated with fresh additions and ex-
aggerations. The charges of atheism and sorcery were boldly
advanced against one whose devotion to the Roman Catholic
Church had been his chief recommendation to the popular favor. Wits discovered that they could, from the words "Henri
de Valois," by a simple transposition of the letters, exactly make
"Vilain Herodes;" and the anagram, connecting the martyrs
of Blois with the innocent babes slaughtered at Bethlehem,
mightily pleased the fancy of an age over-fond of such con-
ceits. Even Catharine de' Medici came in for her share in the
prevailing denunciation. Men would not believe her to have
been free of complicity in the treachery of her son. The services she had rendered the Papal Church on Saint Bartholomew's Day were forgotten. So, when the news came that she
was actually dead, while one fervid preacher exclaimed in Script-

---

[1] Cavriana, ubi supra. It must be noted that the Duchy of Retz comprised
a considerable territory in Poitou (within the part of the modern Department
of Loire Inférieure that lies south of the Loire). Its capital town was Mache-
coul, situated on the little river Falleron a short distance above its mouth.

ural language, with reference to Guise : " O holy and glorious
martyr of God, blessed is the womb that bare thee and the
paps that thou hast sucked ! " another from a neighboring pulpit gave expression to his own uncertainty regarding the claims
of Pope Clement VII.'s niece to a share in the pious intercessions of the faithful.   He thought it doubtful, he said, whether
or not they were called upon to pray for the repose of the soul
of a woman who had done much good, but accompanied by
much ill, and probably more of the latter than of the former.
On the whole, however, he advised his hearers to take the risk
of giving her a Pater Noster and an Ave Maria, and letting her
get what advantage from them she might.   At any rate, there
would not be much lost.[1]

I need not speak at length respecting the tumult and confusion that ensued.   It seems well established that a little more
vigor on the part of the government, and a little more
concert among the best-disposed citizens, would have
spared the capital its shameful fate of subjection, for
the next four years and over, to the power of the League—a
great part of the time to the irresponsible sway of a self-constituted body unknown to the law.   As it was, the " Sixteen,"
promptly recovering from their momentary discouragement,
seized upon the reins of government.   The chief municipal
officers—the prévôt des marchands and the échevins—were
prisoners at Blois.   Had the parliament received the earliest
intelligence, the judges would have taken possession of the city
in the king's interest.   But the " Sixteen " were so fortunate as
to be first informed, and it was to them, said the League, that
the salvation of Paris was due.[2]   At their instigation, and contrary to the will of the better class of the citizens, the Duke of
Aumale, the only chief of note then within the walls of the
capital, was elected governor.   The most august judicial body
in France was not safe from the insults of the new usurpers.
The Parliament of Paris had early sent to petition the king for

The "Seize" save Paris for the League.

---

[1] Lestoile, i. 279.

[2] Dialogue du Maheustre et du Manant (reprinted in the Ratisbon edition of
the Satyre Menippée, Preuves, iii. 446–449).   Mémoires de la Ligue, v. 649,
650.

the release of the prévôt des marchands and his companions
in captivity, employing as envoy one of its most distinguished
members, President Le Maistre. Instead of securing the boon
sought for, Le Maistre brought back letters patent from his
majesty, which were to be recorded and published by parliament, extending pardon to his subjects—as though the people
had offended him—and justifying the execution of the duke
and cardinal, and the incarceration of the prévôt des marchands
and others. As it was believed that parliament was plotting
the king's restoration to power in the capital, three of the "Sixteen" were now deputed to arrest ten or twelve of the most
prominent of the members. But when their spokesman, the

Dignified at-
titude of the
Parliament
of Paris.
notorious Bussy, made his appearance in the "chambre dorée" where the suspected persons sat, a striking
scene took place. Parliament could still, on occasion,
muster up its ancient dignity. No sooner had Bussy pronounced
the name of the first president, as one of those whom he was
commanded to apprehend, than the entire body of presidents
and councillors rose as one man, and declared their purpose to
accompany him and partake of his perils. In the streets of
Paris, crossing the bridge from the "Île de la cité," threading
the narrow lanes to the Grande Rue Saint Antoine, and marching
down that great thoroughfare, might be seen a procession of
grave and venerable judges, walking, two and two, amid the
jeers of the populace, from the Palais de Justice to voluntary
imprisonment in the dungeons of the Bastile.[1] With the insult offered to law in the persons of its most august representatives, Paris seemed also to have laid aside all respect for de-

"Naked pro-
cessions"
through the
streets of
Paris.
cency and common morality. The priests and monks
who had accompanied and emboldened Bussy in his
invasion of parliament set on foot other processions
of a less decorous character. In connection with extraordinary public prayers offered in the churches to implore
the favor of Heaven, a motley crowd of men and women, boys
and girls, paraded the streets of Paris to worship at some fa-

---

[1] January 16, 1589. Dialogue du Maheustre et du Manant, ubi supra, iii.
450, 451 ; Mémoires de la Ligue, v. 651 ; Lestoile, i. 280.

vored shrine. It was well that the time selected was the night, for the attire of the participants in the singular devotion was so scanty—a simple shirt—that the eye-witness and chronicler makes bold to style them nude. Misdirected zeal, pluming itself with the name of religion, has at times assumed strange forms; but no forms perhaps have been more strange or revolting than the "naked processions" of Paris in the dead of the winter of the year of grace 1589.[1]

Nor were prayers and processions the only means employed to kindle zeal and compass desired ends. We have it upon the authority of one of the most trustworthy of contemporaries, whose diary places us as nearly as possible in the position of spectators of the times in which he wrote, that strange arts were resorted to. Upon some, at least, of the altars of the city waxen images moulded to represent Henry of Valois were placed at the beginning of the forty hours of special devotion. As each successive psalm was repeated the image was pricked with a sharp instrument. But when the fortieth psalm was reached a savage thrust in the region of the heart was inflicted, accompanied by words of magical import, intended to prefigure and render certain the death of the king.[2]

Resort to magic.

Meanwhile, both in Paris and elsewhere throughout the kingdom, the League took prompt measures for strengthening itself. All persons suspected of being either Huguenots or Politiques were put under arrest. Charenton and Saint Cloud were garrisoned. The artillery was drawn out to reduce the castle of the Bois de Vincennes to obedience. The king's seals were solemnly broken, in token of

Arrests and revolutionary acts.

---

[1] It is but fair to note that a few curates are said to have condemned "ces processions nocturnes, pour ce que, pour en parler franchement, tout y estoit de quaresmeprenant, et que hommes et femmes, filles et garsons marchoient pesle mesle tout nuds, et engendroient des fruits autres que ceux pour la fin desquels elles avoient esté instituées." Lestoile, i. 284. "En chemise et pieds nuds," was the customary fashion, despite the extreme cold. See Lestoile, i. 282, who enters into particulars respecting the demoralizing effect produced.

[2] So, too, in the processions, tapers properly compounded were successively put out, with magical formulas. Lestoile, i. 282, 283.

the renunciation of his authority, and new seals were engraved bearing simple reference to the kingdom of France.[1] Presently Bernardino de Mendoza, in order to be near the fire which he desired to kindle to a brighter flame, left Blois and the king's vicinity without condescending to ask for leave, and came to Paris. His house had ever been the hotbed of sedition ; but from this time forward the malevolence and hostility of the Spanish ambassador and of his master became open and undisguised.[2] In the theologians of Paris he found ready and efficient allies. As early as on the seventh of January, the Sorbonne met to give spiritual advice respecting the present crisis. Two questions were submitted for the adjudication of the masters in theology gathered to the number of some threescore and ten : First, whether the people of the kingdom of France could be freed from their oath of loyalty to Henry the Third ; and, second, whether the same people could, with an assured conscience, take up arms and collect money and contributions for the defence of the Catholic, Apostolic, and Roman religion against the nefarious designs and attempts of that king, and against his violation of the public faith committed at Blois, to the detriment of the said religion, of the Edict of Union, and of the natural liberty of the convocation of the three orders of the realm. To each of these questions the theological faculty, through its dean, gave an unqualified answer in the affirmative.[3]

The Sorbonne declares the people free from its oaths of loyalty.

But even this gracious indorsement of the rebellion did not suffice the chiefs of the League. The authority of the same parliament which had recently made so striking a display of magnanimity was essential to their success ; and, just a fortnight subsequent to the dramatic march to the Bastile, a document was procured from it fully committing the highest court of judicature in France to the

Declaration of the parliament.

---

[1] Mendoza to Philip II., Blois, January 5, 1589, St. Victor, February 1, 1589, etc., De Croze, ii. 390–398.

[2] De Thou, vii. (book 94) 373 ; Davila (book 10), 390.

[3] Recueil des choses mémorables, 686 ; De Thou, vii. 374 ; the articles themselves in Mémoires de la Ligue, iii. 192–194, and Cimber et Danjou, Archives curieuses, xii. 349–353.

new crusade against royalty. Henry the Third was not, it is
true, mentioned by name, but the massacre of Blois was stigmatized as a breach of public faith and of the liberties of the
Estates. The officers—from the presidents, princes, and peers
of France down to the humblest notary connected with the
body—swore by Almighty God, by His glorious Mother, by
the angels, and by all the saints, male and female, of paradise,
that they would live and die in the Roman Catholic religion,
and that they would not spare even to the last drop of their
blood in its defence. They furthermore engaged to stand by
Paris and all the cities of the Union, and to bring to justice the
authors of the murder of the Duke and the Cardinal of Guise.
It was significant that the declaration expressly stated that no
one was excepted from the provisions of the paper, whatever
might be his dignity or quality.[1]

It may be charitably hoped that many of the intelligent and
upright members of parliament were purposely absent on the
occasion. This we know to have been the case with some, including the virtuous De Thou. But unless the records of the
court itself are falsified, not less than one hundred and twenty-
six persons took part in the proceedings. Some signed the
declaration with alacrity. One judge—and the same was true
of more than one, if we take the words of the register literally
—opened a vein of his arm, and wrote his name in his own
blood.[2]

It did not take long for the anti-monarchical government to
acquire form and consistency. The Duke of Mayenne, having
escaped the clutches of those sent to arrest him, and having
reached Paris in safety, assumed supreme command, with the

---

[1] "Extrait des registres du parlement," January 30, 1589, in Mémoires de la
Ligue, iii. 189-191, and in Cimber et Danjou, Archives curieuses, xii. 327-
329.

[2] De Thou, vii. 378, gives a wretch by the name of Baston the doubtful
honor of this act; but the parliament records imply that others shared it
with him: "A esté leue la presente Declaration en forme de serment, pour
l'entretenement de l'union qui fut hier arrestee, laquelle tous lesdits Seigneurs
ont juree sur le tableau, et signee aucuns de leur sang." The number of persons present I have stated as it is given in Cimber et Danjou, "six-vingt six,"
but the Mémoires de la Ligue make it three hundred and twenty-six.

title of " Lieutenant-General of the Royal Estate." His hands
were upheld by a Council of Forty, composed of three bishops,
The Duke of
Mayenne
made lieuten-
ant-general. five curates, seven gentlemen, and various presidents
and councillors of parliament and burgesses of Paris,[1]
whose only regret seems to have been that the " Sixteen" declined to resign in their favor an authority grown
doubly dear with the lapse of time.[2]

The royal cause, in truth, appeared to be well nigh hopeless.
From all quarters came the news that cities, and even whole
Accessions to
the League. districts, had gone over to the League. In the north,
such places as Amiens, Abbeville, and Senlis ; on
the lower Seine, Rouen ; in the northeast, Laon ; in the central
parts of France, Orleans, Melun, Sens, Mans, Chartres, and
Bourges ; Rennes, with a great part of Brittany ; most of the
province of Auvergne ; and toward the southeast the great
city of Lyons—such were some of the conquests of the League.[3]

The incidents of the revolt at Toulouse were invested with an
aspect of barbarity peculiarly in keeping with the reputation of
the populace of that place as the most blood-thirsty in France.
The two principal victims on the present occasion were the
first president of parliament and the advocate-general of the
Murder of
President
Duranti at
Toulouse. same body. Never did popular fury show itself more
blind and unthinking. President Jean Estienne Du-
ranti, a man reputed to be of sterling integrity of
character and an impartial judge, was not only far removed
from all suspicion of so-called heretical proclivities, but a determined enemy of Protestantism and a zealous Roman Catholic. A great admirer of the monastic orders, he had been instrumental in founding at Toulouse not less than two religious
confraternities; of which the one, bearing the name of the
Confraternity of the Holy Ghost, had for its object the marriage of portionless girls, while the other, known as the Confraternity of Pity, devoted its energies to the relief of poor
prisoners. It was he that had introduced the Jesuits into the

---

[1] Recueil des choses mémorables, 687 ; De Thou, vii. 385.

[2] Journal d'un curé ligueur (Jehan de la Fosse), 223.

[3] The complete list included many other towns. See Davila, 380.

city ; it was he that had brought thither members of the Capuchin Order from Italy, and that had even braved the opposition
of many of his associates by carrying through the plan of in-
stituting an association of the despised Penitents at Toulouse.
Not only so, but he had warmly advocated the persecution of
the Huguenots, and had shown little or no disgust at the intelligence of the bloody matins of Paris. He even took an active
part in extending the massacre that began on St. Bartholomew's
Day to the city of Toulouse. Soon after the tidings came of
the murderous work done at the capital, the unfortunate Protestants of Toulouse were thrown into the various convents and
jails of the city. A few weeks later they were transferred to
the conciergerie, or prison, attached to the parliament house.
Some days passed, and the command was brought by Delpeuch
and Madron, special messengers from Paris, that if the massacre had not yet been consummated, it should at once be put into
execution. The judges of parliament were convened to deliberate with the " capitouls " of the city respecting the course
which was to be pursued. The majority of the members present drew back in horror from the proposal to perpetrate so foul
a crime as that to which they were invited. Some were outspoken in favor of clemency. Others, more timid, shrugged
their shoulders and kept their eyes upon the ground. But
Duranti knew no compunction. Rising, he exclaimed to his
more tolerant colleagues : "You will do what you please, and
say what may seem good to you. As for myself, I am going to
execute, in the king's name, what my charge and my duty require of me." Abruptly leaving the company, he at once issued
the necessary orders. How well he was obeyed appeared on
the morrow, when two unworthy scholars of the university,
with a following of seven or eight wretches of the like sanguinary type, forced their way into the conciergerie, armed with
cutlasses and axes. Summoned one by one into their presence,
the prisoners were successively butchered at the foot of the
stairs, to the number of three hundred or more.[1] Surely Du-

---

[1] Mémoires de Jacques Gaches sur les guerres de religion à Castres et dans
le Languedoc, 1555–1610, 118–120. See Rise of the Huguenots, ii. 521, 522.

ranti was a follower of Mother Holy Church whose past exploits
might well have earned for him immunity from suspicion of
disloyalty to her creed, or to its supporters.

Yet the very moment that Duranti displayed his intention to
frustrate, if possible, the attempts made to bring the city into
revolt against the king's authority, from an idol of the people
he became an object of hatred. The mob pursued him as he
returned from the session of parliament, and riddled his carriage
with thrusts of their swords. Thrown into prison by his enemies, he was afterward sought for in the Dominican convent
which served as his place of imprisonment, and mercilessly
slain. One of the very guards to whose keeping he had been
trusted brought him out to the mob with only too much willingness, and turned him over to their hands with the impious
exclamation, " Behold the man ! " Not content with simply
killing him, the mob dragged him ignominiously through the
streets ; then, finding no gallows at hand from which he might
be hung, placed the corpse upon its feet and tied it to an iron
gate immediately in front of a portrait of the king contemptuously dangling from a stake. " Thou hast so loved thy king ;
now enjoy the sight of him at thine ease, and die with him "—
were the words of the inscription, more honorable than its
authors intended, with which the remains of the loyal first president were left for a whole day exposed to the gaze of men.[1]

Meantime, if the royal authority was maintained in some

---

[1] "Advertissement particulier et véritable de tout ce qui s'est passé en la
ville de Tholose, depuis le massacre et assassinat commis en la personne des
Princes Catholiques, touchant l'emprisonnement et mort du premier Président et
Advocat du Roy d'icelle, etc.," Paris, 1589. Reprinted in Cimber et Danjou,
Archives curieuses, xii. 283–302 ; De Thou, vii. (book 95), 412–417 ; Agrippa
d'Aubigné, iii. 166. The Duke of Nevers, in his Traité des causes et des
raisons de la prise des armes, first printed in 1590, eulogizes Duranti as "le
plus homme de bien de justice qui fût de nostre age," and says of him and his
fellow-victim : "Ils avoient tous deux tout le temps de leur vie esté fort con-
traires aux Huguenots, et courru de grandes fortunes pour telle occasion."
Mémoires de Nevers, ii. 50. See, also, Mémoires de Jacques Gaches, 379–383,
who adds this touch to the barbarous treatment received by President Duranti's
corpse : "Les charretiers, en passant, se destournoint pour luy aller bailler
des coups de fouet avec injures et exécrations, au grand estonnement des gens
de bien."

important cities, such, for example, as Bordeaux, it was owing
to the fidelity and decision of men like Marshal Matignon,
much rather than to any manly action on the part of Henry of
Valois himself that was fitted to strengthen the hands of his
adherents. On the contrary, his feebleness was such as to disgust even those who would have preferred, perhaps, to remain
in his service. Marshal Retz, feigning illness, deserted the
Desertion of court under pretext of going for the benefit of his
Marshal Retz
and the Duke health to the Baths of Lucca. The Duke of Mer-
of Merœur. cœur, the king's own brother-in-law—they had both
married daughters of the same Count of Vaudemont-Lorraine
—with signal ingratitude, allowed himself to be elected by an
ecclesiastical assembly of Brittany, a province of which he was
governor by royal appointment, to the novel office of Protector
of the Roman Catholic Church.[1]

The first aim of Henry himself was to demonstrate that he
was a good Catholic, and that no latent spark of pity or love
                for Protestantism lurked in his breast. On the last
Henry re-en-
acts the Edict day of the year 1588, just a week after the execution
of Union.
                of the Cardinal of Guise, he sent to all the parlia-
ments of the kingdom a declaration forgiving all past contra-
ventions of the Edict of Union of the preceding July, but reaffirming his own purpose to enforce that edict as a fundamental
law of the realm. "We have from all time," said Henry,
" and especially since our edict of the month of July last, endeavored, by every means in our power, to unite all our good
Catholic subjects in concord and good intelligence under our
authority ; in order, from that union and the strength thence
derived, to secure the fruit to which we have always aspired
and tended, that is to say, to purge this kingdom of ours from
                heresies, and fully to re-establish our holy faith and
and releases
many prison- the Catholic, Apostolic, and Roman religion." [2] The
ers.
                re-enactment of the Edict of Union at such a junc-
ture was puerile enough, and a manifest sign of weakness ; but
the release of many of the most important personages whom

---

[1] De Thou, vii. 383, 384 ; Agrippa d'Aubigné, iii. 164.
[2] Declaration du Roy (December 31, 1588), Mémoires de la Ligue, iii. 181–184.

the king had arrested at the time of the assassination of Guise
and his brother was equally childish, and still more likely
to expose the King of France to contempt. True, the persons upon whom this unexpected mercy was lavished promised to abstain from all acts of hostility toward his majesty;
but it will be readily understood how little value attached to
such engagements, when there were ecclesiastics ready to pronounce them void because exacted under moral or physical
compulsion.[1]

Amid the frenzy which had taken possession of men's minds,
and which moved the preachers of the kingdom to the utterance of the most violent denunciations of the monarch and of
all that continued to adhere to him, one ecclesiastic of
high rank preserved his self-possession and watched
calmly the drift of the present movement. Cardinal Morosini, the papal legate, was at Blois when the duke
and his brother were murdered. He remained with the king
even when the Spanish ambassador and others saw fit to vindicate their attachment to the Roman Catholic religion by withdrawing from Henry, as from an accursed and contaminate person. In the minds of many devotees his actions occasioned
surprise and disgust. But the prelate was sagacious and prudent. Left to himself, the king might be compelled to make
common cause with the Huguenots. The legate could hope at
least to delay, and possibly to avert, so deplorable a result.
Receiving the unexpected intelligence of the duke's murder,
Morosini at once exerted himself to save the life of his brother,
the cardinal. Foiled in this, he directed his energies to dis-
suade his majesty from entering the sacred precincts of the
Church, and succeeded in inducing him to send to Rome to obtain the papal absolution. Better than all, he prevented Henry
of Valois from coming to an agreement with the heretical King
of Navarre, and from forming an alliance that might have
widened until it should embrace not only these two rulers, but

*Cardinal Mo-
rosini, the leg-
ate, remains
at court.*

---

[1] " Car depuis que les prédicateurs et les confesseurs avoient gâté l'esprit du
peuple," remarks De Thou (vii. 353), " on ne se faisoit plus un scrupule de
violer, sous prétexte de religion, les sermens les plus solemnels."

the Protestant princes of the German Empire and Queen Elizabeth of England. By Cardinal Morosini's self-control and patience the court of Rome gained a substantial advantage, even if its astute legate exposed himself to some obloquy. Of what consequence was it that he was accused of acting from fear where boldness was called for ? To have placed Henry of Valois under an interdict would have driven to desperation a king already standing on the verge of a precipice. The drug too hastily administered as a medicine, to use the legate's own figure, would have been likely to prove a poison and carry off the patient.[1]

However, the king in his isolation could not hope to maintain himself long without Protestant aid. The Sorbonne had declared his Roman Catholic subjects absolved of *Henry tardily turns to Germany and Switzerland for help.* their oaths of allegiance, and had given them full freedom to levy war against him; and these subjects, instigated by preachers who from the pulpit applied to him such names as tyrant, murderer, perjurer, and atheist, were forsaking him almost in a body. The Huguenots, on the contrary, had shown no signs of disloyalty. Persecuted, the victims of a barbarous legislation that denied them the common rights of citizens, compelled to stand armed to repel the assaults of the enemies of their lives and the plunderers of their possessions, they nevertheless waited only for the word that should summon them to the king's side. Still that word came not yet, though everything pointed to the near approach of the time when it must be spoken. Marshal Retz and other counsellors of doubtful loyalty had no great difficulty in persuading Henry to reject the propositions of M. de Sancy, who had acted as French ambassador to Switzerland, and who, early in the year, represented to his majesty the great advantage to be derived from an alliance such as could at this time be concluded with the four great Protestant cantons of Berne, Zurich, Basle,

---

[1] " Ed io potrei rispondere che l'accelerare questa medicina era un convertirla in veleno." The exculpatory letter of Giovanni Francesco Morosini written to an unknown correspondent, is published in the Négociations avec la Toscáne, iv. 868–871, from the Medicean Archives. It is here dated January, 1589. See Agrippa d'Aubigné, iii. 154, for a different representation.

and Schaffhausen.[1] But a few weeks later, when the prospect became more gloomy, when the king found himself compelled to issue fresh edicts against the insurgents, and to send out his summons to every part of the kingdom, commanding, in old feudal fashion, all his principal noblemen and gentlemen by name to come to him, before the twelfth of March, at the head of their men-at-arms[2]—Henry perceived his mistake, and despatched Sancy to Switzerland and Germany to carry out the plan he had previously rejected. The prodigal and impecunious monarch could furnish the messenger with no money, and he wisely left all the details of the negotiation to the discretion of one whom experience in former enterprises abundantly qualified for the responsible trust. Sancy's success more than realized Henry's anticipations.[3]

Once more restored to health, Henry of Navarre had again taken the field, and, full of his accustomed energy, was resolved
Henry of Navarre advances to the Loire. to show mankind that he had no intention of remaining a passive spectator of the conflict waged by the League against the crown of France. With his recent gains of the cities of Niort and St. Maixent, he felt himself strong enough to make an advance toward the river Loire. At his approach, towns of great importance made haste to open their gates and offer their service—Loudun, L'Isle Bouchard on the Vienne, Châtellerault farther up the same river, Mirebeau, and Vivonne above Poitiers on the Clain; all gladly admitted the Huguenot prince, whose clemency was not less signally displayed than was his courage and determination. For, at a time when the adherents of the League, pretending

---

[1] De Thou, vii. 352.

[2] See the documents, "Declaration du roy sur l'attentat, felonnie et rebellion du Duc de Mayenne, Duc et chevalier d'Aumale et ceux qui les assisteront," dated February, 1589, Mémoires de la Ligue, iii. 215–224; "Declation du roy sur l'attentat, felonnie et rebellion des villes de Paris, Orleans, Amiens, et Abbeville, et autres leurs adherans," ibid., iii. 224–228; "Lettres patentes du roy sur le mandement de sa gendarmerie," dated February 6, 1589, ibid., iii. 231, etc. The latter was addressed to one hundred and two noblemen whose names are given.

[3] De Thou, vii. 373. Sancy left Blois about the beginning of February, and reached Geneva on the fourteenth of the same month.

to act in the name of religion, did not hesitate to indulge in indiscriminate murder and pillage and in the foulest of outrages, Henry of Navarre not only threw a shield about the lives and honor of the conquered, but freely granted them the undisturbed exercise of their religion. He simply stipulated that the Huguenot inhabitants who had been expelled, or deprived of their right to worship God according to the dictates of their conscience, should be granted the unimpeded enjoyment of their civil and religious privileges. Next, crossing the boundary line separating Poitou from Berry, the central province of France, by one of those sudden movements, executed with a small body of horse and foot, by means of which he was wont to gain most of his signal advantages, the King of Navarre made himself master of Argenton, an important point in the midst of a hostile district. Thence returning to Châtellerault, he gave to the world another of those remarkable papers whose ability may be said to have accomplished for the cause of the valiant prince almost as much as the skill with which he wielded the sword.

The appeal of Henry of Navarre on this occasion to the three orders of the kingdom was a plea for the immediate restoration of peace as the sole remedy for the maladies of France. He deplored the unhappy circumstance that he who was in reality the lover of his country's prosperity should serve to the wicked as a pretext, should be regarded by the ignorant as the cause, and should be, in his own eyes, the occasion of the woes at present afflicting his native land. He expressed his regret that it had not seemed good to the king, and to those whom he addressed, to invite him to the late assembly of Blois. His suggestions might have proved beneficial; for there is no physician so good as the one that loves the patient. He called attention to the utter futility of all the efforts made for his overthow.

Navarre's appeal to the three orders.

"I should play the braggart soldier," said he, "were I to tell you, one by one, what armies have been sent against me these past four years. You would think that I wished to recount my deeds of prowess. That is not my intention. Would God that I had never been a captain, since my apprenticeship must be made at such an expense! It would be a much shorter task to inquire of you what leaders France has still remaining, after those that have marched against me. In four years I have seen ten armies, ten royal lieutenants, having behind them the forces and the support of the foremost kingdom of Christendom. You think that this elates me? Far from it. I will tell you, for the purpose of removing this impression, that of these ten armies I have, in point of fact, had to do with only one, which I fought and defeated. In that single one God was pleased specially to make use of me as an instrument for its ruin. But in the case of all the others I had scarcely any trouble; they almost melted away before reaching me, and I heard of their dissipation as soon as I learned their approach. The angel of God, the rod of God, took away from them the means of injuring me. Not unto me belongs the glory of this; I hardly contributed anything of my own to the achievement of the result."

And of the outcome, what could be said? The lives of countless men had been lost, a mine of gold had been squandered, the people of France had been ruined; but the objects of the war were no nearer their accomplishment.

Turning next to the proposition, which had so generally been inserted in the petitions presented at Blois, that a kingdom should have but one religion, and that the foundation of a state is piety, which cannot exist everywhere if God be worshipped in diverse ways, Henry declared his adherence to that view. "It is so," said he; "but to my great regret I see an abundance of people that bewail the fact, and only a few who are willing to apply the remedy. Now, I have always been open to conviction, and I am so still. Let the methods that are customary in such cases be taken. If there are any extraordinary ones, let them be searched out. Both I myself and the members of the Reformed religion will always submit to the decisions that may be adopted by a free council. That is the true path. It is the only one that has been followed in all time. But to believe that this can be obtained from us by blows of the sword I esteem before God to be an impossibility. And, in point of fact, the event abundantly proves that it is so. . . . I have often

He declares himself open to conviction.

been summoned to change religion ; but how ? With the dagger at my throat ! Had I no respect for my conscience, yet respect for my honor would have prevented me from changing. . . . What would those persons say who are most devoted to the Catholic religion, if, after I had lived in one fashion up to thirty years of age,[1] they were to see me suddenly changing my religion under hope of a kingdom? What would those say who have seen and experienced my courage, should I, through fear, shamefully abandon the manner in which I have served God from the day of my birth ? These are reasons that touch worldly honor. But, at bottom, what a conscience should I have ! To have been nurtured, instructed, and brought up in one profession of faith, and then, without hearing and without speaking, all of a sudden, to throw myself on the other side ! No, gentlemen, it will never be the King of Navarre that will so act, were there thirty crowns to be gained. Far be it from him to conceive a desire for such a thing through hope of a single crown. Instruct me ; I am not opinionated. Take the road of instruction ; you will derive infinite profit therefrom. For if you show me another truth than that which I believe, I will yield to it. I will do more ; for I am persuaded that I shall leave no one of my party who will not submit to it with me."

Next Henry of Navarre repelled the suspicion, which was possibly entertained by some, that, unless converted to Roman Catholicism, he might one day undertake to use constraint toward them. His course, particularly in respect to the cities that had recently submitted to him, proved the contrary. Moreover, there was no probability that a handful of persons of his religion would be able to constrain an infinite number of Catholics to a thing to which that infinite number had not been able to constrain this handful.

Again the Huguenot prince returned to his plea for peace, and entreated all three orders—and not least of these the clergy—to exert themselves for its recovery, and to esteem as enemies those, and only those, who should stand in the way of obtaining it. As for himself, gladly as he would welcome a summons from the

---

[1] More accurately speaking, Henry of Navarre was in his thirty-sixth year.

king to come to his help, he declared his purpose from this time
forth to apply himself to the restoration of the royal authority
in all places where he might have the ability.   " To this end,"
said he, " I take under my protection and safeguard all those,
He takes all   of whatsoever quality, religion, or condition they may
patriots under be, whether of the nobles of the cities or of the peo-
his protection. ple, who shall unite with me in this good resolution.
And although, more than anybody else, I regret to see the differences in religion, and, more than anybody else, I desire to
heal them, yet clearly recognizing that it is from God alone and
not from arms and violence that the cure must be expected, I
protest before Him—and to this protestation I pledge my faith
and honor, which, by His grace, I have until now kept untar-
nished—that, just as I have been unable to suffer my own conscience to be constrained, so also I shall not suffer or ever permit the Catholics to be constrained in their conscience or in the
free exercise of their religion.   Furthermore, I declare that in
the cities that shall unite with me in this determination, and
shall place themselves under the obedience of my lord the king,
and of myself, I shall permit no innovation either in government
or in the church, unless in so far as may concern the liberty of
each individual person.   Again, I take both the persons and the
property of the Catholics, and even of the ecclesiastics, under my
protection and safeguard.   For I have long since learned that
the true and only means of uniting nations in the service of
God, and of establishing piety in a state, is gentleness, peace,
and good examples; not war nor disorders, whence are born
into the world all forms of vice and wickedness."

So closed a memorable appeal to the candid judgment and
patriotism of all true Frenchmen—an appeal which, although
in its form and impressive eloquence betraying the masterly intellect and practised pen of Duplessis Mornay, yet unmistakably
reflected the true sentiments of the Huguenot prince by whose
inspiration he wrote.[1]   Elevated in tone, full of considerations

---

[1] The text of the document, dated Châtellerault, March 4, 1589, is given in
full in the Mémoires de la Ligue, iii. 244–258, and in the Mémoires de Duplessis
Mornay, iv. 322–340.

addressing themselves to the highest and noblest of human
motives, and exhibiting a thorough grasp of the situation of the
wretched country, so long a prey to civil dissension, the paper
nevertheless held forth a hope, as its predecessors had done, of
a possible reconciliation of religious parties by the conversion of
Henry of Navarre to Roman Catholicism.   Still the
conversion to which it pointed was as yet sketched
only as a change based upon rational instruction, in
connection with or consequent upon a free council—a conversion so genuine as to involve the conversion of great numbers,
if not of all the Huguenot followers of the prince.   Into the
secret thoughts and intentions of men it is not permitted us to
look with clear vision.   All that we can hope to attain in the
search is a probable approximation to truth.   Whether at this
time Henry of Navarre contemplated a change of his religion,
as a political necessity likely to confront him in the near future,
may be doubted.   Henry of Valois still lived, with constitution
enfeebled, it is true, by excesses, and little likely to leave behind him a son to inherit the crown, but yet a young man,
scarcely twenty-seven months the senior of his cousin of Navarre,
and lacking more than two years of being forty years of age.
Under all the circumstances of the case, while the King of Navarre may very well be suspected of foreseeing a contingency
in which he might be desirous of finding some plausible pretext for deserting the religion of the "handful" of the French
people in favor of that of the "infinite number," we hesitate
to admit that the idea of any such indecorous apostasy as that
which was to take place four years later had as yet ever entered his brain, or, if it had been conceived, was not dismissed
with some degree of honest scorn.

"I cannot believe that the king will be willing to make use
of us," wrote a Huguenot, about the middle of February; "and
yet I see no other resource for him in his difficulties."[1]   Yet it was only a month later when the
same person that penned this sentence was in the
city of Tours—whither Henry of Valois had not only re-

The hope of a conversion held forth.

The king and Henry of Navarre enter upon negotiations.

---

[1] Duplessis Mornay to Morlas, February 11, 1589, Mémoires, iv. 313.

moved his own residence, but transferred the loyal portion of
the Parliament of Paris[1]—engaged in active treaty for the
purpose of effecting a reconciliation between the monarch and
his loyal subjects the Huguenots.[2] He found the king, despite
his passionate hatred of Protestantism and his ostentatious devotion to the Roman Catholic Church, not altogether averse
to an arrangement which might tend to rescue him from his
present straits.   Even now, it is true, Henry of Valois could
not conceal the reluctance with which, under constraint, he de-
parted from the traditions of the past.   We have it upon the
word of the historian De Thou that the king still hoped against
hope that some tardy accommodation with the League might
come in to free him from the distasteful necessity of making
common cause with the Huguenots.   Even after he had solemnly appended his signature to the treaty, of which I am
about to speak, with the King of Navarre, in the presence of
that monarch's envoy, Duplessis Mornay, the Very Christian
King had the effrontery to ask for a delay of a fortnight in
transmitting the document, hoping that within that time he
might secure from Mayenne either peace or a suspension of
arms; in which case he purposed to push hostilities against the
Protestants more vigorously than ever.[3]

The new compact established a truce between the Kings of
France and of Navarre for the term of a year dating from the
third day of April, and included in its provisions not
only all the Huguenots and other loyal subjects of
the crown, but, as a particular mark of favor to the
pope, the inhabitants of Avignon and the Comtât Venaissin.
The King of Navarre engaged for himself and his followers to
carry on no military enterprise without the command or consent
of the King of France, and especially to make no changes, so
far as the Roman Catholic religion and its adherents were con-

The truce be-
tween the two
kings.

---

[1] "Edit du Roy, par lequel sa Cour de Parlement, qui souloit seoir à Paris,
est transferee à Tours, et aussi sa Chambre de Comptes," Blois, February,
1589, in Mémoires de la Ligue, iii. 239–241.

[2] Duplessis Mornay to Henry of Navarre, Blois, March, 1589, Mémoires,
iv. 343–346.

[3] De Thou, vii. (book 95) 430, 431.

cerned, in any cities that might fall into his hands during the course of the war. The King of France in turn pledged himself that the Protestants should have undisturbed enjoyment of all their possessions.[1] Such were the points given to the world in the formal publications of the two monarchs. The agreement as signed, however, stipulated further that the King of Navarre should receive a city and bridge on the river Loire, and that the Huguenot prince should cross that stream and proceed against the Duke of Mayenne. While all cities that he might take were to be placed at the disposal of the King of France, it was provided that Henry of Navarre should be permitted to retain one place in every bailiwick and sénéchaussée as security for the expenses incurred by him. It was furthermore agreed, and noted as a distinct appendix to the articles of the truce, that Protestants were no longer to be proceeded against, but were to enjoy the free exercise of their religion in all cities through which Navarre and his army might pass. Exception for the term of four months was made of the city situated on the Loire which was to be confided to his safe-keeping.[2] This city, according to the agreement, should have been the insignificant Ponts-de-Cé, near Angers; but when the governor of the paltry castle flatly refused to make the surrender without receiving in lieu an extravagant recompense, the much more convenient city of Saumur was substituted. It was characteristic of the inflexible rectitude of Duplessis Mornay, in whose care, as governor, the city was now placed, that for the stipulated term he refused to permit his own fellow-believers to celebrate any other than private worship within town or castle.[3]

---

[1] " Declaration du Roy sur la trefve accordee par sa Majesté au Roy de Navarre, contenant les causes et preignantes raisons, qui l'ont meu à ce faire," Blois, April 26, 1589, in Mémoires de la Ligue, iii. 315–321. Also, the similar declaration of Henry of Navarre, Saumur, April 24, 1589, ibid., iii. 321–324. Both documents are also inserted entire in Agrippa d'Aubigné, iii. 207–212, 212-214.

[2] " Articles du traicté de la trefve negotiée par M. Duplessis, de la part du Roy de Navarre, avec le Roy Henry III." Signed by Henry and his secretary Revol, Tours, April 3, 1589. Mémoires de Duplessis Mornay, iv. 351–355. Vie de Duplessis Mornay, 129, 130.

[3] Vie de Duplessis Mornay, 131. Agrippa d'Aubigné, iii. 167.

So it was that the Huguenots crossed the Loire! The day was a memorable one. Four years before, the king and the majority of the people of France had banded together for the destruction of Protestantism. Proscribed by the law, the Huguenots found no refuge save on the shores of the ocean about La Rochelle, or beyond the Garonne and in the province of Languedoc. The few adherents of the Reformed doctrines in Paris and scattered throughout Central and Northern France lived only by sufferance, and mostly escaped notice by reason of their prudence and the comparative insignificance of their numbers. It was long since Protestant preaching had been heard by devout multitudes on the northern side of the Loire, and he would have been esteemed by the Huguenots of Guyenne a rash prophet who should have foretold to them the near approach of the day when such a privilege would be enjoyed. An enthusiastic minister—the same Gabriel d'Amours who stood by Navarre and implored the aid of Heaven on the battle-field of Coutras [1]—had, indeed, encouraged his master with the prediction, in the very darkest hour of the war, when tidings came from Blois of the decision of the states general declaring the Huguenot prince an apostate incapable of succeeding to the throne of France. Addressing the despondent king, in a public discourse delivered in the market-house of Saint Jean d'Angely, he had exclaimed: " Sire, men will not be able to strip you of what God has conferred upon you in virtue of your birth. Very soon you will cause us to preach beyond the Loire, and will reestablish the churches in that region." But his words had fallen on incredulous ears. It was not until still stranger news

The Hugue-nots cross the Loire.

Gabriel d'Amours' prophecy.

---

[1] Among the strange vicissitudes of his life, Gabriel d'Amours, having had the imprudence to visit Paris, in March, 1589, was discovered and thrown into the Bastile. It was generally agreed that the brave minister would never come out alive ; but, strange to say, Bussy le Clerc, who, violent and bloodthirsty Leaguer as he was, yet entertained an unaffected admiration for D'Amours' character, seems to have taken him under his special protection, and, in the end, to have secured his release He swore that, Huguenot as he was, D'Amours was worth more than all the hypocritical presidents and councillors of parliament put together. Lestoile, i. 289.

came from the north that the King of Navarre recalled and believed the bold prediction. "Well, D'Amours," said he, meeting his chaplain at the conclusion of another sermon in the
same place; "well, D'Amours, we shall preach beyond the
Loire! The Duke of Guise is dead!"[1]

And now the prophecy had actually come to pass. Not only
so, but the hand of Almighty God was seen, to the amazement
of all beholders, employing the very monarch that had driven
forth the King of Navarre and his followers into exile to bring

The League
an instrument
of God in
bringing Na-
varre to the
throne.

them back again to their inheritance. It was no
wonder that thoughtful men of all shades of religious
opinion, however much they might differ on other
matters, were equally impressed at the sight of so
singular a coincidence and alike ascribed it to the design of a
higher Being who presides over the destinies of the human
race. Thus the fair-minded Lestoile, curious collector of all
that was most singular and deserving of preservation for the benefit of subsequent ages, jotted down in his invaluable journal:
"The king who, carried away by the times, had so long waged
war against Navarre, and had even been constrained to furnish
the League both men and means for waging it, was he that led
this prince, as it were, by the hand, in order afterward to es-

---

[1] This interesting incident is preserved in a remarkable letter of the Huguenot minister, of which I have already made use, and to which I shall again
have occasion to refer. " Peu de jours avant que feu monsieur de Guise fust
tué et qu'aux estaz de Bloys on avoit prononcé sentence contre vous, vous con-
solant en ung presche je vous dys en la hasle de St. Jehan: ' Les hommes ne
vous sauroyent oster ce que Dieu vous a donné de nature; vous nous ferès
bien tost prescher delà la Loyre et y redresserès les églises.' Monsieur de
Guyse fut tué peu de jours après et me dictes en la hasle après un presche de
Mons. de Lacroix: ' Eh bien, Damours, nous prescherons delà la Loyre; Mons.
de Guyse est mort!' " Bulletin de la Société de l'histoire du Protestantisme
français, i. 281. It was a graceful thing in Henry of Navarre to select the
minister who had been the first to predict from the open pulpit the re-establishment, under his authority, of the Protestant churches north of the Loire
to deliver the first sermon after the crossing at Saumur. And it was appropriate in D'Amours himself to take the themes of his discourses on this occasion from the mighty deliverances of Israel by the hand of Joshua—"car,"
said he, " vous estiès le Josué du Seigneur des armées pour nous faire passer
le Jordain et nous mestre en possession de la terre de Canaan." Ibid., i. 282.

tablish him in the heritage which God had promised him by so
many pledges of His blessings; and this by means altogether
unknown to men, and more miraculous than can be imagined.
For it was the pope, it was the Spaniard, it was the Lorraine
princes, it was the Savoyard, it was the League, it was the 'Sixteen;' in short, it was his greatest enemies that bore him on
their shoulders to a seat upon the royal throne.   A miracle of
miracles in truth, yet a miracle which we have seen with our
own eyes!"[1]   And Davila, a writer as different from Lestoile
as Italy in the sixteenth century was different from France,
took the very same view.   "Truly," he exclaims, "it was a
thing worthy of very great wonder, and one of the secret mys-
teries of God's divine wisdom, that the King of Navarre, being
weak and forsaken of all, reduced into a narrow corner of the
kingdom, and for the most part in want of things necessary for
his own maintenance, so that he was fain to live more like a
soldier of fortune than a great prince; his enemies, by too
much eagerness in pursuing him, and by too ardent a desire to
see him utterly ruined, should labor to plot so many ways, to
raise so many wars, to treat so many leagues, to make so many
conspiracies and practise so many arts, from all which resulting
to his advantage, his greatness and exaltation did, as it were,
miraculously succeed.   For there was no man versed in the
affairs of France, and far from the passions of both parties,
who saw not clearly that, if the king had been suffered to live
and rule as peaceably as he ought to have done, the King of
Navarre would by little and little have been destroyed and
brought to nothing; for peace and length of time would absolutely have dissolved that little union which was among the
Huguenots, and, by those occasions and necessities which length
of time would have produced, the obstinacy of the Rochellers,
wherein the sum of affairs consisted, would finally have been
overthrown and broken, and the king, a most bitter enemy to
heresy, would in a manner insensibly, by divers arts, have
rooted it out and destroyed it.   Whereas, on the contrary, the
revolution of the wars and factions did not only foment the

---

[1] Lestoile, i. 291.

stubbornness of the Huguenots (who were so much the more hardened to resist by how much they thought they were wrongfully persecuted), but also in the end made way for the King of Navarre's reconciliation with the king and with the French nobility, furnished him with arms and power, and, at last, contrary to his own expectation and the natural course of things, opened him a passage to attain unto the crown." [1]

Nothing remained, for the more perfect exhibition of the new union between Henry of Valois and Henry of Navarre,

Meeting of Henry of Valois and Henry of Navarre. except that they should again meet after their long separation. Accordingly, on Sunday, the thirtieth of April, they were brought face to face under the trees of the park of Plessis lès Tours. Great was the crowd of spectators anxious to behold the unlooked-for scene of the reconciliation of the king and his brother-in-law. Great were the demonstrations of joy on every side. For full a quarter of an hour, if we are to believe the chronicles of the day, did the two princes strive in vain to cleave the press, that they might reach each other. For so long did deafening shouts fill the air of " Long life to the king! Long life to the King of Navarre! Long life to the kings! " And when at last they came together, when they embraced one another with effusive affection, when tears " as big as peas " rolled down Navarre's cheeks, when Henry of Valois, not permitting his Huguenot cousin to throw himself at his feet, walked with him in friendly converse to the town—the enthusiasm of all who saw them knew no bounds. [2] Truth to say, however, Navarre breathed somewhat more freely when he returned to the quarters of his troops. He had received an abundance of warnings from his faithful followers, and he was not himself ignorant of the French king's past acts of treachery. Nothing seemed more possible than that the Valois might take a fancy to send the heretic's head to the Parisians—a grateful pledge of peace. [3] In proportion as his

---

[1] Davila (book 10), 391, 392. I have followed the somewhat quaint old English of the London translation published in 1678.

[2] Lestoile, i. 291 ; Davila, 397 ; De Thou, vii. 450, etc.

[3] Lestoile, ubi supra.

own apprehension had been great, his expressions of relief were hearty. " Monsieur Duplessis," he wrote, in a note despatched the very evening of the interview, " the ice is broken, not but that I received a great number of warnings that if I went thither I was a dead man. I have crossed the water, commending myself to God, who in His goodness has not only preserved me, but caused indications of extreme joy to appear upon the king's countenance, and made the people indulge in unparalleled applause. They even cried, ' Vivent les Rois ! '—a thing that displeased me much." [1]

And now the outcast, whom the King of France had so long been endeavoring to annihilate, became at one stroke that monarch's most trusty adviser and the right arm of his strength. Exasperated beyond endurance at the treachery of the Duke of Mercœur, Henry of Valois could scarcely renounce the idea of marching in person into Brittany to bring him to his knees. But Navarre by his firmness prevented him from taking so suicidal a course. "If the king go to Brittany," he had written, a month or two earlier, to Duplessis, " he is lost. It will look like a flight before the Duke of Mayenne. On the simple announcement of it Meung, Beaugency, Blois, Tours, and Saumur will revolt." [2] And later, hearing that the project had been revived, he wrote in haste to the king himself : " I fell into a rage about it, for to regain your realm you must pass over the bridges of Paris. Whoever shall counsel you to take another path is no good guide." [3] He therefore begged the king not to divide his forces, but to gather them all into one great army against which the enemy could not stand.

It was not long before the new Huguenot allies were able to do effective service for their late persecutor. Scarcely had a week elapsed since the interview at Plessis lès Tours when the Duke of Mayenne, who had advanced with an army to a short

---

[1] Henry of Navarre to Duplessis Mornay, dated from the suburbs of Tours, April 30, 1589; in Mémoires de Duplessis Mornay, iv. 355, and Lettres missives de Henri IV., ii. 477.

[2] Henry of Navarre to Duplessis Mornay, March, 1589, Mémoires, iv. 349.

[3] Same to Henry III., June 6, 1589, Lettres missives, ii. 499.

distance north of the city of Tours, with the apparent intention
of pushing westward to Angers and the river Maine, suddenly
Mayenne's at- turned and presented himself on the banks of the
tack upon the
suburbs of Loire. The city of Tours, built on the left bank of
Tours.   the river, was united by a bridge to the suburb of
Saint Symphorien, occupying the opposite shore. To get possession of the suburb was Mayenne's first object, and in this,
after a long and severe struggle, he was successful. Nor, indeed, did it seem improbable that he would go farther, and that
Tours itself would fall into his hands. Fortunately Navarre, to
whom the king in his distress sent, imploring assistance, although
too far distant to bring up his whole forces in time, was able,
nevertheless, to send in advance his arquebusiers, under command of François de Châtillon. Never was help more timely
or effective. With the support of the Huguenots, the loyal
Roman Catholics turned the tide of battle, and the night fell
leaving the bridge still in the hands of the king's troops.

Nor was Henry of Valois altogether insensible of the great
service which the Protestants, lately hunted down with relentless hatred, had rendered him. He even testified his appreciation of their valor by ostentatiously throwing the white scarf
of the Bourbon prince over his own shoulders, to the no small
disgust of such bigoted and intolerant followers as Monsieur
d'O, Clermont d'Entragues, and Châteauvieux, while sensible
Roman Catholics like Marshal Aumont applauded the act.

The soldiers of the League were not less complimentary than
the king; for, recognizing among their opponents the champions of that religion which they were sworn to exterminate,
they had, notwithstanding, paid an almost involuntary tribute
to their valor. " Withdraw, wearers of the white scarf! " they
cried. " Withdraw, brave Huguenots, honorable men! Withdraw, Châtillon! It is not with you we have to do, but with
that perjurer, the murderer of your father! " [1] It seemed to
men a strange freak of fortune that threw in the way of Admiral Coligny's son the opportunity to defend against the as-

---

[1] The words are given, with slight variations, by Lestoile, i. 294, by Agrippa
d'Aubigné, iii. 169, etc.

sault of one of the Guisards the life of a king who had countenanced Henry of Guise in his dastardly plot to butcher the
great Huguenot captain in the Rue de Béthisy.[1] That night
the suburb of Saint Symphorien remained in the power of the
army of the League. Of the deeds of horror that were per-
Excesses of   petrated contemporary chronicles have left us ac-
the army of   counts whose authenticity is but too well attested.
the League at
Tours,   Men, claiming to be enlisted in the defence of religion,
boldly avowed the principle that the champions of so holy a
cause were justified in disregarding every precept of the divine
law, and might properly give the rein to every unholy passion.
Not a woman that fell into their hands was spared the most
extreme indignities. Drawn from their hiding-places, all were
alike made to minister to the lust of a soldiery that showed no
respect for things human or divine. Even the church of Saint
Symphorien, which gave its name to the suburb, afforded no
safe refuge to the miserable fugitives. Maid and matron were
outraged in the holy precincts, and before the eyes of fathers,
brothers, and husbands, compelled, at the point of the sword,
to look on, but impotent to render assistance. It was a practical demonstration of the hypocrisy of the League's pretence
of warring against its lawful king in behalf of the orthodox
Christian faith, that Roman Catholics inflicted this violence not
upon heretics, but upon their fellow Roman Catholics. The
coffers of the church and the instruments of its most sacred
rites were not too holy to be plundered. Two chalices having
been discovered, of which the one was of silver and the other of
pewter, the pious robbers found it a good occasion for the display of their grim humor. The pewter chalice was inconti-
nently declared to belong to the " Union," and could not be
touched with a clear conscience ; but the silver was " royal "
and " heretical," and, consequently, a lawful prize.[2]

---

[1] " Mr. de Chastillon, à la teste des troupes de ceux de la religion, fit mer-
veille de bien combattre pour le roy qui avoit assisté de sa présence le duc de
Guise lorsqu'il fit massacrer laschement l'amiral son père, pendant le règne
de feu son frère Charles neuviesme." Mémoires de Jacques Gaches, 388.

[2] See the loyalist pamphlet, "Conseil salutaire d'un bon François aux
Parisiens . . . avec un discours veritable des actes plus mémorables de

Had the incidents of the treatment of the faubourg Saint
Symphorien stood alone, there would be little occasion for remark.   The best of causes may sometimes be unfortunate in
and else-   the persons of its advocates.   But the conduct of the
where.   soldiers of the League at Tours did not constitute a
solitary exception.   It was the rule of what happened throughout France.   Where, as at Arquenay, near Laval, credulous
Roman Catholic burghers submitted to troops professing the
same religious tenets, with little fear of suffering wrong, they
were speedily undeceived.   Their own lives, the honor of their
wives, the treasures of their churches—all were sacrificed.
Sometimes, in mere wantonness, the Leaguers took delight in
defiling baptismal fonts with filth, or dressed the camp-follow-
ers, by way of derision, in the vestures of the priests, or paro-
died the service of the mass and gave the consecrated wafer to
the dogs, or trampled it under foot.   Now and then, it is said,
they pretended to evidence both their scrupulous determination
to observe the church's appointed fasts, and their belief in the
virtue of the sacraments when administered by an ecclesiastic properly ordained.   Setting before a curate, or his vicar, a
plentiful supply of meat, they compelled him, with the dagger at his throat, to go through the ritual of Holy Baptism.
When veal, pork, mutton, chickens, and capon had been duly
christened by the names of pike, carp, soles, turbot, and herring,
the mailed champions of the papacy, pledged to the utter extermination of the Huguenots, did not hesitate to partake of the
most sumptuous banquet on the days of strict abstinence.[1]   In

---

la Ligue, depuis la journee des Barricades, jusques à la fin de May, 1589," reprinted in Mémoires de la Ligue, iii. 446, 447, and, in part, in Cimber et
Danjou, Archives curieuses, xii. 312–348.   Recueil des choses mémorables,
693 ; Lestoile, i. 293, 294 ; De Thou, vii. 456.

[1] The author of the " Conseil salutaire," above cited, himself evidently a
Roman Catholic as well as a loyalist, expressly declares, with respect to this
particular form of sacrilege, that it had occurred more than once : " Cela ne
s'est pas fait en un lieu seul, ne (ni) par une seule troupe, ni une seule fois ; vous
ne le pouvez ignorer, comme aussi ne pouvez-vous l'endurer, que vous ne par-
ticipiez à cest atheisme, pour lequel sans doute Dieu les confondra bien tost et
vous aussi."   Ubi supra, iii. 439.   See, also, Recueil des choses mémorables,
694 ; Lestoile, i. 298.   The curious reader may compare with this occurrence,
thus vouched for, the story of Boccaccio (to which Mr. Creighton has referred

short, to such a pass had matters come, that a royalist could bit-
terly exclaim, and others caught up the remark and gave it
their indorsement: "At the present day, to plunder one's
neighbor; to murder one's brother, uncle, cousin; to rob altars;
to profane churches; to levy upon Catholics—this is the ordinary exercise of a Leaguer. To have the mass and religion
always on the lips, and atheism in the heart and in the actions;
in a word, to violate laws, divine and human, is the infallible
mark of a 'zealous Catholic.'"[1]

The insolence of the League at Tours was short-lived. As
soon as night was over, Mayenne, fearing to attempt to hold
the suburb, or to renew his attempt upon the town, since the
King of Navarre had come to the help of the King of France,
hastily withdrew the attacking force. And now, indeed,
The fortunes strengthened by the accession of the Huguenots,
of Henry of
Valois im- whom he had once driven forth from his presence,
prove. Henry of Valois seemed to have passed the apogee of
his unfortunate reign. The capital might rave in its fury
against the monarch who had added to the crime of assassinating the "good Catholic princes" the yet more heinous offence
of making common cause with an excommunicated heretic; the
doctors of the Sorbonne might stand by their rebellious opinions, adding, on the fifth of April, a fresh resolution, to the effect that the petition for Henry of Valois should henceforth be
dropped from the canon of the Mass, and prescribing a form
of prayers which the clergy might use for those in authority,

---

in his History of the Papacy, i. 110), of the bishop who, not having fish at hand
for his dinner on Friday, eats a partridge and explains the act thus to his
scandalized servant: "You know that by means of words I and all the other
priests make of a wafer, which is nothing but wheat and water, the precious
body of Jesus Christ. Can I not then much more by words cause these partridges, which are flesh, to be converted into fish, albeit they may still retain
the form of partridges?"
[1] "Conseil salutaire," in Mémoires de la Ligue, iii. 447, 448. (The expression is repeated in almost the same words by Lestoile, i. 290, 291.) Elsewhere the anonymous writer uses equally strong words to describe the prowess
of the Leaguer: "Aussi les violemens des femmes et filles de tous ages,
mesmes ès temples saincts, les sacrileges des autels, cela n'est que jeu parmi
eux, c'est vaillantise et galanterie, c'est une forme essentiel d'un bon
ligueur." Ubi supra, iii. 439.

without leading the incautious people to mistake the celebrant's intention and suppose that he was interceding for the hated monarch ;[1] the pope might fulminate a " Monitory," excommunicating the King of France, unless, within ten days, he should release the Cardinal of Bourbon and the Archbishop of Lyons from the unjust imprisonment in which they were detained, and summoning him and his accomplices to appear at Rome, within sixty days, to give account for the murder of the Cardinal of Guise.[2] But neither the wrath of the Parisians, nor the denunciations of the Sorbonne, nor the ecclesiastical thunders of Sixtus the Fifth could check the progress of the two kings. It is true that the poor commons of France, burdened almost beyond endurance, were in no mood to lend very enthusiastic support ; but the rebellion of the " Gautiers "—armed peasants of Normandy—had been suppressed,[3] and there was the prospect that the patient tiers état might continue for a while longer to afford to the rest of Christendom the edifying spectacle of a people crushed to the earth, but making little or no effort to free itself from the intolerable load of taxation, and of other forms of oppression which monarch, church, and nobles had united in heaping upon it.

Defeated near Bonneval, in Beauce, by the Huguenot François de Châtillon, and before the walls of Senlis, on the opposite side of Paris, by the troops of the Duke of Longueville, the boastful League saw steadily approaching the army which might soon bring the capital to sue for peace. The mission of Schomberg and De Thou to Germany had met with a favorable response, and Sancy had been still more successful in Switzerland. By midsummer a force of ten thousand Swiss, with two thousand lansquenets and fifteen hundred reiters, had penetrated the kingdom and were hastening to the king's assistance. Meanwhile Henry of Va-

The king advances toward the capital.

---

[1] " Arrests et resolution des docteurs de la Faculté de Paris, sur la question, sçavoir s'il faloit prier pour le Roy au Canon de la Messe. A laquelle sont adjoustees avec licence des superieurs deux oraisons colligees pour la conservation des Princes Catholiques, et pour obtenir la victoire encontre les ennemis." Mémoires de la Ligue, iii. 567–570. [2] De Thou, vii. 442, 443. [3] Ibid., vii. 438, 439. Agrippa d'Aubigné, iii. 170.

lois, approaching Paris from the south, had come from Tours
to Jargeaux and Pithiviers, had taken Étampes, hanging the
magistrates of the town as a warning to others that might venture to defy his authority, and had struck the Seine below the
capital. Poissy, scene of the famous colloquy, offered but faint
resistance, and, by means of its broad bridge, permitted the
royal forces to press on to the siege of Pontoise.[1] The time
required for the reduction of this place was well spent; for
with Pontoise in his possession, and with a tight grasp upon
the lower Seine, the king effectually cut off all possibility of
victualling Paris from the direction of Normandy, whether by
land or water. At this auspicious moment the Swiss made
their appearance, in company with Tavannes, who had gone to
meet them on the confines of Burgundy, and with Longueville
and La Noue, whose troops had acted as their convoy from the
province of Champagne. It was a proud day for the royal
cause, lately so depressed, when, in company with his cousin of
Navarre and his kinsman, the Duke of Montpensier, Henry of
Valois reviewed an army now numbering forty-two, or, according to other accounts, forty-five thousand men.

If the royalists were elated, the League was correspondingly depressed. The Duke of Mayenne had been able to do
nothing to hinder the junction of the foreign auxiliaries with
the king's main force. He now saw his small army daily
shrinking by the desertion of the French troops, and threatened with the loss of all the foreigners, who loudly talked of
going over in a body to the enemy's side. Only a blow at the
person of the king himself could save Paris from falling into
his hands, and that blow was now struck.

A weak-headed monk of the Dominican order, a mere boy
of twenty-two or twenty-three years, with mind possessed by
The monk
Jacques Clé-
ment. the idea incessantly proclaimed by the preachers of
Paris, that Henry of Valois was not only a tyrant,
but a perfidious enemy of the church, whose existence
upon the earth ought no longer to be endured—such was the

---

[1] See the " Discours du siége de Pontoise," in Le Charpentier, La Ligue à
Pontoise.

puny instrument that was to cut the thread of the sovereign's life in the very hour of approaching victory. Such was the man who was to bring to its end a royal house which had reigned for the space of two hundred and sixty-one years, and had given to France no fewer than thirteen successive monarchs. Such was the man who was to introduce to the throne a Huguenot prince, in the person of the first Bourbon king of France. Friar Jacques Clément seems to have meditated the murderous act for a considerable time, but his threats, uttered when Henry of Valois was still distant from Paris, were regarded by those who heard them as idle boasts, such as weak men often indulge in with the hope of making themselves appear important. Davila, the historian, tells us that he remembered well to have seen the future assassin's fellow-monks making sport of an enthusiast whom they regarded as master of but half his wits, and derisively styled "Captain Clément." But now, with Henry of Valois hovering over Paris, ready to pounce upon the devoted city, the League felt that the critical moment had arrived. Now, too, the friar's menaces became offers, and these offers fell upon not unwilling ears. Clément's confessor did, indeed, refer him to his superior, the prior, and both of the ecclesiastics advised him to fast and pray, with the view of obtaining certainty that his design was no instigation of the devil, but a true inspiration from Heaven. But when, as might have been anticipated, the hot-headed youth returned with the assurance that he had followed their suggestions, and that he found himself only the more impelled to his undertaking, his ghostly counsellors themselves became the advocates of regicide. They depicted in glowing colors the preferment he should have, if he escaped death, and held forth to him the prospect of the martyr's crown, in case he should perish. They introduced him to the "holy widow," as she was called, the Duchess of Mont-

He is encouraged by the Duchess of Montpensier.

pensier, sister of the murdered Guises, and that frenzied devotee of the League encouraged him yet more to persevere in his project. She received him hospitably at her house, and plied him with all the persuasive arts which the members of the Society of Jesus, then active in the capital, were able to exercise. If the duchess be not greatly maligned, she even stimulated his courage by dishonorable favors accorded or promised.[1]

Thus it was that, on the last day of July, the clownish monk, having been provided by an unsuspecting royalist lately taken prisoner by the Parisians with a letter of introduction to his friends in the king's army, commending him as a man who had important intelligence to give to Henry in person, found his way to the village of St. Cloud, where the monarch had taken up his quarters in the castle not long since erected by Gondy. Clément came none too soon. The king's troops already invested the northern suburbs of Paris—St. Honoré, Montmartre, and St. Denis; while Henry of Navarre, with his quarters at Meudon, kept the southern suburbs of St. Germain and St. Marcel well shut in. A general assault on the enemy's works had been determined upon for the second day of August. Early on the morning of Tuesday, the first day of that month, the monk was admitted to an audience by the king, who had just risen and was partially dressed. Henry of Valois, upon whose mind, as he was wont to tell his courtiers, the sight of the monastic cowl made an impression as pleasurable as the most delicate bodily sensation,[2] had readily consented to see Clément. As readily did he now direct his attendant noblemen to retire to a distant part of the room, that he alone might hear the friar's confidential disclosure. Clément had handed to the seated monarch a letter, with the request that he should peruse it, when he saw that the expected opportunity was his. Quickly drawing from his sleeve a knife which he had kept there con-

Clément comes to St. Cloud.

He wounds the king.

---

[1] " Ils ajoutent," says the historian De Thou (vii. 488), who never fails to be as charitable as the circumstances of the case will permit him to be, " que, pour achever de le déterminer, elle en étoit venue jusqu'à lui accorder sur l'heure ce qu'il y avoit de plus capable de tenter un moine débauché ; ce que je ne puis cependant croire, à moins qu'on dise que l'ardeur de la vengeance, qui avoit déja aveuglé cette femme violente jusqu'à lui faire commettre tant d'autres crimes, l'engagea encore, pour assouvir sa rage, à fermer les yeux sur l'infamie de celui-ci."

[2] " Je lui ai moi-même souvent entendu dire, que leur vue [sc. des moines] produisoit le même effet sur son âme, que le chatouillement le plus délicat sur le corps." De Thou, vii. 486.

cealed, he instantly plunged it up to the handle in the body of
the unprotected man before him, making a deep gash on the
left side of the abdomen. In another moment Henry had
drawn the weapon out, still further enlarging the wound, and
with it had struck Clément on the forehead. At the noise of
the scuffle, and at the sound of the king's exclamation, " Ah!
the wicked monk ! " the noblemen in attendance rushed to the
king's side. One of them ran Clément through with his sword,
thus despatching the murderer, and saving him from the lingering tortures which would otherwise have been his fate. In another moment the infuriated courtiers had precipitated the body
of the assassin from the window to the ground below, there to
be torn in pieces and burned. The ashes were ultimately cast
into the Seine.[1]

The first opinion of his physicians was favorable to the king's
recovery. Letters were accordingly written in his name to the
Count of Montbéliard and other allied princes abroad, as well
as to Duplessis Mornay, and to other officers and governors
throughout the kingdom, full of hopeful prognostications. His
perfidious enemies, Henry was made to say, in despair of succeeding by other means, had taken advantage of the zeal he
bore to his religion, and the free access and audience he was
accustomed to give to all religious persons, poor churchmen,
that desired to talk with him, and had violated all divine laws
by sending a Dominican monk to assassinate him. But God
had disappointed his damnable design, by causing the knife to
slip; so that, if it pleased Him, no damage would ensue, and
in a few days he would recover his former health.[2] But the
joy of fancied deliverance from peril was short-lived. A hem-
orrhage, unnoticed at first, showed that the wound of the royal
patient was mortal. Nor did Henry of Valois, when he learned

---

[1] The composers of anagrams were unusually fortunate in the case of the
assassin's name. They found that " Frère Jacques Clément " was convertible
into " C'est l'enfer qui m'a créé "—" It was hell that created me." The discovery was altogether so satisfactory as to discourage any further attempts.

[2] Henry III. to the Count of Montbéliard, Bridge of St. Cloud, August 1,
1589, in Mémoires de la Ligue, iii. 590, 591. The same to Duplessis Mornay,
same date, in Mémoires de Duplessis Mornay, iv. 379–381.

the fact, exhibit any lack of courage. In fact, if the manner of
dying were as satisfactory a test of character as the manner of
living, we might easily be misled by the calm deportment and
pious words of a prince who until now had merited little else
of the world than loathing and contempt. But while we may
charitably pass by without comment the religious professions of
the king, we must note his political injunctions, and particularly
his views of the treatment of the Huguenots. Instead of the
prosecution of a plan for the extermination of heresy such as he
had ostentatiously proposed for himself after the murder of the
Duke of Guise, he counselled his assembled noblemen to defer
the settlement of differences in matters of religion until the
convocation of the states general of the realm. Meanwhile he
conjured them to remain united, and never to lay down their
arms until they should have utterly cleansed France of those who
now disturbed its peace. Above all, he called upon them to
give their loyal support to his successor, Henry of Navarre, who,
on receiving the news of the monk's dastardly attack, had
hastily ridden over from Meudon, and at that moment stood
in the midst of the group of his sorrowing attendants. "I pray
you as my friends, and I command you as your king," said he,
" to recognize after my death my brother who stands there." [1]

The customary mass was celebrated; the customary litanies
were repeated. The solemn words of the " Miserere " were upon
the dying king's lips as he followed the voice of the
officiating priest, when, just as he reached the petition,
" *Redde mihi lætitiam salutis tui* "—" Restore unto
me the joy of thy salvation "—speech failed him.[2] It was early
on the morning of the second of August, 1589, that he expired. Though he had reigned more than fifteen years, he was
but a little more than thirty-six years of age.[3]

Death of
Henry of Va-
lois, August
2, 1589.

---

[1] Mémoires du Duc d'Angoulême (Collection Petitot), 532. See, also, the
reported speech in the contemporary publication, " L'assassinat et parricide
commis en la personne du tres-chrestien et tres-illustre Roy de France et de
Pologne, Henri troisiesme du nom," in Mémoires de la Ligue, iii. 587–590.

[2] Davila, 406.

[3] For the incidents connected with the death of Henry III., the following,
among others, may be consulted : Pasquier, Lettres, ii. 333–335 ; Lestoile, i.

One of the last of Henry of Valois' reported speeches is said
to have been a suggestion to his namesake of Navarre to abjure
his present religious faith: "Brother, I assure you," he is said
to have exclaimed twice, as he embraced him, "you will never
be King of France if you turn not Catholic, and if you humble
not yourself to the church." [1] Yet, even with respect to the
deceased himself, so difficult and doubtful was the
question whether he did not die excommunicated, that
the answer could only be reached by an arithmetical
process. His enemies, indeed, maintained that the monitory of
Sixtus settled the point; for the Very Christian King had
neither liberated the imprisoned prelates nor done penance for
the murder of the Cardinal of Guise. But his advocate, the
Duke of Nevers, had an unanswerable argument to offer in rejoinder. The papal monitory itself had allowed thirty days for
the release of the Cardinal of Bourbon and the Archbishop of
Lyons, dating from the formal publication of the document
within the kingdom. Now, that publication took place in the
city of Chartres on the ninth day of July. Since Jacques Clément struck the blow of which the king died within twenty-four
days, or on the first of August, it was evident, not only that
Henry the Third died free of the censures of the church, but

Did he die excommunicated?

301, etc. ; Davila, ubi supra ; Agrippa d'Aubigné, iii. 182–185 ; De Thou, vii.
486–489 ; Recueil des choses mémorables, 702 ; Journal d'un curé ligueur
(Jehan de la Fosse), 225, 226 ; Mémoires du Duc d'Angoulême, 529, etc. ;
L'assassinat et parricide commis en la personne du très-chrestien et très-illustre
Roy de France et de Pologne, Henri troisiesme du nom, in Mémoires de la Ligue,
iii. 587, etc.; Discours véritable de l'estrange et subite mort de Henri de Valois,
ibid., iv. 9, etc., and other pieces of the times reprinted in the same collection,
and in Cimber et Danjou, Archives curieuses, vol. xii., such as "Le martyre
de Frère Jacques Clément," etc.

[1] Davila, ubi supra. According to the Duke of Angoulême (ubi supra, 530),
who was present, his words were : "La justice, de laquelle j'ay tousjours esté
le protecteur, veut que vous succediez après moy à ce royaume, dans lequel
vous aurez beaucoup de traverses si vous ne vous resolvez à changer de religion.
Je vous y exhorte autant pour le salut de vostre ame que pour l'avantage du
bien que je vous souhaite." It will be remembered that the writer of these
Mémoires was Charles, Count of Auvergne, natural son of Charles IX. by Marie
Touchet, a lad of fifteen or sixteen at the time of his uncle's death. He subsequently became Duke of Angoulême.

that he had actually a respectable number of days of grace—
nine, according to the duke's liberal computation.[1]

However this might be, of one thing there was no doubt:
the King of France, a Roman Catholic, had been murdered by
the hand of a Roman Catholic—indeed, of a monk of
the Roman Catholic Church. It was no persecuted
Huguenot, maddened by the remembrance of past
wrongs done by Henry or his predecessors, that had
avenged the injuries of his fellow-believers. It was no fanatical Protestant, intoxicated by the prospect of securing a monarch of his own faith and party, that had opened the way to
the throne for Henry of Navarre by violently thrusting aside
the only obstacle remaining in the way. The Protestants of
France, the hated Huguenots, had added yet another proof that
they were no regicides, by abstaining, through the long years
of oppression under a fifth persecuting king, from the slightest
attempt to play the part of self-constituted agents of divine
retribution. In an age in which assassination was so common,
they were fairly entitled to this proud distinction; and it is
noteworthy that a member of the "Sacred College," a Roman
cardinal, voluntarily accorded them this unsolicited homage in
a secret interview which he held, some years later, with the
pope's principal representative. It was on Sunday, the twenty-
second of January, 1595, that the eminent Cardinal Ossat sought
and obtained an interview with Cardinal Aldobrandini, nephew of Pope Clement the Eighth. The news of the attempt
made upon the life of Henry the Fourth, now a Roman Catholic, by Jean Chastel, had reached Rome only the preceding

The murderous deed emanates from a Roman Catholic.

---

[1] "Traité des causes et des raisons de la prise des armes," Mémoires de
Nevers, ii. 47. Nevers reckons only to July 31st, when Jacques Clément de-
parted from Paris, after having celebrated the mass, on his mission of assassination. Cardinal Ossat will have it that the term was but of ten days, at the
most, between the publication of the monitory and Henry's death; so that
there were full twenty days to spare. "Raisons et moyens pour montrer que
le Roy Henri III. n'est mort excommunié," in Mémoires du Cardinal d'Ossat,
i. 29–32. Unfortunately, even such high dignitaries as the members of the
"Sacred College" have occasionally been known to yield to the temptation of
tampering with facts in the interest of those whom they desired to favor.

Thursday. In reference to this great crime the French cardinal had much to say. "From such outrages," remarked Ossat,
" as you have very wisely and holily said, no good can come.
In the case of a prince converted to the Catholic religion,
who ought to be strengthened and built up in every way,
it is calculated to put a great stumbling-block in his path,
and to disgust him with the Catholics, when those who style
themselves the support of the Catholic religion thus seek to
assassinate him. If there were any occasion for such murderous plots, it would be the part of the heretics to contrive and
execute them—the heretics whom he has left and forsaken, and who might have reason to fear him. And,
nevertheless, they have attempted nothing of the
kind, either against him or against any of the five
kings, his predecessors, whatever butchery their majesties may
have made of the aforesaid Huguenots." [1]

The Hugue-
nots never
plot against
the kings of
France.

No, it was not a Huguenot hand that had despatched Henry
the Third—an inveterate hater of Protestantism and everything
Protestant, a prince who, in his last moments, was overheard,
at the moment when his almoner, Boulogne, was offering mass
in his behalf, to address the Almighty in these words: " Thou
knowest, my Lord and my God, that nothing is so dear to me
as the maintenance of the true Catholic, Apostolic, and Roman
religion, of which I have ever made profession." [2] It was the
hand of a Dominican monk that had done the deed. It was
by Roman Catholics professedly the most zealous for their faith
that the assassination had been instigated, and it was they who
now, in their savage delight over the success of their miserable
agent, indulged in such mad demonstrations as Paris has witnessed only once since then, when a revolutionary mob held
high carnival over the corpses of Louis the Sixteenth and Marie

---

[1] Cardinal d'Ossat to M. de Villeroy, Rome, January 25, 1595, Lettres du
Cardinal d'Ossat, i. 108. " Là où s'il y avoit aucun lieu de tels assassinats, ce
seroit aux Heretiques à les pourchasser, ou executer, eux qu'il a quitez et
abandonnez, et qui auroient à se craindre de lui. Et toutefois, ils n'ont rien
attenté de tel, ni contre lui, ni contre aucun de cinq Rois, ses predecesseurs,
quelque boucherie que leurs Majestez ayent faite desdits Huguenots."

[2] Mémoires du Duc d'Angoulême, 529.

Antoinette. And it was the Roman pontiff, Pope Sixtus the
Fifth, who, transcending the bounds of ordinary prudence, as
well as of what is esteemed decent in civilized countries, declared to his cardinals, in an allocution carefully prepared beforehand, that the action of Jacques
Clément was an enterprise so surprising, and so admirable, that
he did not fear to compare it to the work of the Incarnation of
the Word, and to the mystery of the Resurrection of our Lord.
It was the same reputed head of the Roman Catholic Church
that pronounced a eulogy upon the courage, constancy, and zeal
of the depraved monk who had ended his dissolute life after
murdering the Very Christian King, and exalted the monk
himself to a position superior to that occupied in history by
Judith and Eleazer.[1] No wonder, then, that laymen like Mendoza, the Spanish ambassador, found nothing else but the hand
of the Almighty himself to which the "happy event" could
be ascribed; or, like young Maximilian, of Bavaria, were full
of joy that the King of France had been despatched.[2]

The expression of Pope Sixtus the Fifth.

The day was yet distant when the church was to feel shame
for the deed which Sixtus had lauded, and when the Dominican
order would show some desire to disclaim connection
with the assassin of Henry the Third. That day had
come when, in the following century, an over-zealous member
of the order gravely undertook to demonstrate that it was not
the real Jacques Clément, but possibly a disguised Huguenot,
who plunged the fatal knife into the body of the last Valois
king of France. The world, however, was not convinced, and
the curious will probably long continue to peruse the Dominican
apology, much as the "Historic Doubts relative to Napoleon

A literary curiosity.

---

[1] Ranke, History of the Popes (Amer. edit.), 211. De Thou, who gives a
pretty full account of the papal allocution in the consistory of September 11,
1589 (vii. 495), is unable to repress his honest indignation at words "so unworthy of the common father of all the faithful." After which, it is not
surprising either that his magnificent work, the most precious historical production of the sixteenth century, was censured at Rome, or that its title occurs in the Index Librorum Prohibitorum (I have before me the edition of
Rome, 1841) as condemned by the decrees of November 9, 1609, and May 10,
1757.

[2] Ranke, ubi supra.

Buonaparte" and similar works of delicate irony are read, with little expectation, indeed, that the established belief will be reversed, but with unbounded admiration for the author's ingenuity.[1]

So did a monarch, whom few loved, whom none sincerely respected, end his reign. Of pleasing appearance and easy address, endowed by nature with no little power over men by means of a conciliatory oratory, he threw away every advantage and perverted every faculty of mind and body in a blind and reckless pursuit of pleasure. With aims as unstable as the caprice of the moment, he degraded life to the level of an ignoble sensual existence, from which not even the extreme peril of his position could supply him motives powerful enough to extricate him. For the most part, he wished only to be left undisturbed in those low enjoyments which he esteemed happiness. The very importunity of favorites soliciting offices at his hands irritated him, from time to time, beyond endurance. Certainly, among feeble or indolent monarchs, the king may fairly be deemed to have carried off the palm who issued his solemn edict declaring guilty of treason and enemies of the public quiet all persons who, by memorial or by petition, should ask of him the re-establishment of certain offices which he had determined should be left vacant upon the resignation or death of the present incumbents.[2]

A determined enemy of the Huguenots, Henry of Valois had left them little peace during the fifteen years of his troubled reign. If we might credit the assertions of the Duke of Angoulême, he had, by his kindness, so gained the good will of the Protestant chiefs that most of them were already resolved to forsake their party and their religion.[3] Others, like the Florentine Cavriana, four years earlier, anticipated that, but for

Character of Henry of Valois.

---

[1] The opuscule "La Fatalité de S. Cloud près Paris," ascribed by some to Père Nicolai, a Dominican of Paris, by others to Père de la Haye, a member of the same order, of Lille, originally appeared in 1672. It is reprinted in the second volume of the Ratisbon edition of the Satyre Ménippée, pp. 435–515.

[2] Edict of November, 1584, Isambert, Recueil des anciennes lois françaises, xiv. 591–593.

[3] Mémoires du Duc d'Angoulême, 522.

the war then forced upon him by the League, Henry the Third would soon have compassed the utter extinction of Protestantism in France. The same results had again and again been predicted as certain to flow from the severities of Henry the Second and his eldest son, had not their lives been suddenly cut off. But the Huguenots had survived both persecution and cajolery; and now a Huguenot prince had succeeded to the throne of France.

CHAPTER XI.

ARQUES, IVRY, AND THE SIEGE OF PARIS.

THE accession of a king professing their own faith to the throne of a country in which they constituted but a small mi-
Accession of a Huguenot king. nority of the population marks an important epoch in the history of the Huguenots. A contingency remote enough, according to human prognostication, a few years since—a contingency, however, which, improbable as it seemed, had appeared so dreadful as to excite the fears of many bigoted adherents of Rome—had actually become a reality, and that, too, hastened by the hands of the very persons who most feared and dreaded it. He would have been esteemed a madman who should have ventured to prophesy that the Protestant head of the Bourbon family would be placed in possession of the French crown by the hand of a fanatical monk ; or that the secret plots and intrigues of Madame de Montpensier and her fellow-conspirators would transmute the elected " Protector " of the Reformed Churches into the monarch of the whole country. Yet this was precisely what the hatred of the ultra Roman Catholic party effected ; and history can produce few more instructive examples whereby to illustrate the tendency of blind human passion to overreach itself than the assassination of the last Valois king, a devoted adherent of Roman Catholicism, by those who found even his zeal too cold to satisfy their own hatred of Protestantism.

Yet must it be confessed that rarely has a monarch ascended a throne under more trying circumstances than did Henry
Difficulties of his position. the Fourth. True, of the legitimacy of his claim there could be no honest doubt. None but the most prejudiced mind could call in question the right of the Bourbons, as descended from Robert, younger son of Saint Louis, to

follow the Valois family, descended from Philip the Third, St. Louis' elder son; or doubt that, among the Bourbon princes, Henry of Navarre, as son of Antoine, was nearer to the throne than Cardinal Charles, Antoine's younger brother. Had not religious considerations intervened, no dispute would have arisen upon this point. Unfortunately for Henry, however, as well as for the peace of France, royalty had sought and had obtained the sanction of the church. The king claimed to be king by the grace of God—not, it was held, merely in the sense in which all the powers that be, or the established order of government in general, may be said to be ordained of Him—but in a peculiar, mystical, and sacramental sense. The grace, moreover, was not conferred by the very fact of hereditary succession, but chiefly, if not solely, so far as France, at least, was concerned, in connection with the rite of unction at Rheims, celebrated by priestly hands, with oil taken from the sacred vial known as "La sainte ampoule." In addition to this, the kings of France had accepted, and they still continued to cherish, as their proudest prerogative, the title of "Very Christian" conferred upon them by a pope. If the church threw its mantle over royalty, was it too much to ask that royalty should be in full accord with the church? Was it too much to require that the king, if not of irreproachable morals, should, at any rate, be of immaculate orthodoxy? How could the people be expected to submit to the authority of a king upon whose head no anointing oil had been poured, and who thus broke in upon a custom sanctioned by the example of the long line of his predecessors? Could a Protestant, on the other hand, be permitted to receive this sacred unction? Applied to him, the title "Very Christian" would, in the estimation of the majority of the nation, be solemn mockery; while, as to the distribution of ecclesiastical benefices and preferments, archbishoprics, bishoprics, and the like, which the Concordat of Leo the Tenth with Francis the First had made the richest source of income of the crown, to intrust this to the hands of a heretic would be flagrant impiety.

Moreover, Henry of Navarre was, according to the views adopted by the majority of churchmen, not only a heretic, but

an apostate condemned by the highest ecclesiastical authority, and expressly declared by Pope Sixtus the Fifth, in advance of
His relations the death of Henry of Valois, to be a child of wrath,
to the pope. excommunicated, and incapable of inheriting any
principality or kingdom, and especially the kingdom of France. The idea that a foreign potentate could interfere in the domestic concerns of France had, indeed, been repudiated with honest scorn by the best and most patriotic part of the nation, and the pope's bull had excited more indignation among Roman Catholics than dismay among Protestants. Yet many, even of those who resented the pontiff's unwarranted interference, confessed their reluctance to acknowledge the authority, and their unwillingness to serve in arms under the banner of a Protestant king.

It has just been stated that the adherents of Henry's religion formed a small minority of the population of France. What added particularly to the difficulty of the situation was the geographical distribution of this minority. The Huguenot strength lay in the south. Much has been said of late of the adapt-
The Hugue- edness of Roman Catholicism and Protestantism re-
not strength spectively to the southern or Latin races, and to the
in the south
of France. northern or Teutonic; and the attempt has been
made to account in this way, by innate or congenital proclivities, for the reception of the Reformed doctrines by one large portion of Christendom, and for the rejection of the same doctrines by another and numerically more considerable portion. The explanation, if true, should apply with still greater accuracy of territorial demarcation to France, and should throw light upon the cause of the unequal diffusion of Protestantism among the provinces into which that kingdom was formerly divided. Instead of this, however, the criterion is found to be so utterly incorrect that the result of its application is the very opposite of the true state of the case. In the northern prov-
Religion not inces, in which the admixture of German blood was
determined the greatest, and where the success of the doctrines
by race or
climate. preached by Luther and Calvin should consequently
have been the most complete, Roman Catholicism continued to reign supreme. In the south, on the contrary, where the physi-

ognomy of the people, no less than the peculiarities of the dia-
lects they speak, betray the fact that they belong distinctively
to the Latin race, the protest against the errors of the Church
of Rome has never been intermitted, from the age of the Albi-
genses, through ages of bloody crusades and persecutions, down
to our own times.   Paris has never shown any marked hospi-

Paris and   tality for the Reformed doctrines, but Nismes, "the
Nismes.   city of antiquities," where the traveller may stumble
at any turn upon a temple, an amphitheatre, a fountain, or a
tower built by the Romans—Nismes, whose archæological remains have been said to be surpassed by those of no other city
of Western Europe save Rome itself, retains a distinctively
Protestant type which not even the Revocation of the Edict of
Nantes, with its enforced interruption of the authorized exercise of Reformed worship for more than a century, has been
able to efface.

It cannot be denied that the circumstance that the French
capital was so far distant from the Protestant strongholds of
Languedoc, Gascony, and Dauphiny multiplied the obstacles in
the way of the new king.

But there were other facts which rendered his position a per-
plexing one, and which must be understood by him who would
comprehend the fatal influences hurrying the new monarch
onward to the great catastrophe of his life in the hypocritical
renunciation of his religious faith.

Certainly Henry of Navarre had long looked and longed for
the possession of the crown of France ; but if his impatience

Attitude of   had ever been great, his regret was now still greater
the late ad-   that the object of his hopes had come so soon.   At
herents of
Henry the   the tidings of the death of Henry the Third, he
Third.   hastily took horse and rode over from Meudon to St.
Cloud ; but the sights and sounds that awaited him in the room
where lay the body of his predecessor were such as might have
daunted even a more courageous heart than his.   At the feet
of the corpse two friars, with lighted candles, were mournfully
chanting the litany of the dead ; around was a scene of unre-
strained grief and confusion.   No cries of "Long life to the
king !" greeted the arrival of the Huguenot prince; but only

murmurs of displeasure were heard, curses, imprecations. In place of respectful homage, he saw Roman Catholic leaders—such men as the Sieur d'O, his brother, Manou, Entragues, and the like—draw down their hats over their eyes in a manner that boded no good, while pledging themselves to die a thousand deaths, or to submit to any one in the world, rather than suffer a Huguenot king to rule over them. It was a trying time, and for a moment even Henry, who hardly knew what it was to fear an enemy upon the battle-field, was in danger of quailing.[1] Happily, among his little company of Huguenot lords, and among the still smaller band of really disinterested and patriotic noblemen professing the Roman Catholic faith, he had those who could speak a word, who could act, in due season. Agrippa d'Aubigné nerved the arm of the king, by showing him the folly of betraying any marks of timidity or irresolution to his wavering subjects. Guitry induced him to abandon as suicidal a plan hastily formed of falling back upon the Loire. He showed him that, while he might thereby secure possession of Tours, Blois, and Angers, he would forfeit the advantage of the hold which Henry the Third had regained upon the Seine, the Oise, and the Marne, and virtually surrender Northern France to the enemy. But of all the friends of the Bourbon, in this emergency, none was able to confer upon him so signal a service as Sancy, the able negotiator who to the credit he won, ten years before, in connection with the Treaty of Soleure and the protectorate of Geneva, had, as we have seen, just added fresh laurels by securing for Henry of Valois a large auxiliary force of Swiss mercenaries. It was Sancy who, by his prompt action, and by his convincing presentation of the case, induced the Swiss colonels to transfer their commands from the service of the Roman Catholic Valois to that of the Protestant Bourbon. It was Sancy who wrought what the men of his time esteemed almost a miracle, by persuading a body of mercenaries, intent only upon gain, not merely to

Good service rendered by D'Aubigné, Sancy, and others.

---

[1] Agrippa d'Aubigné's description is in the best vein of that graphic writer. Histoire universelle, iii. 183, etc.

continue to follow a penniless king, but actually to take an oath to serve him for three months without pay—a thing the like of which, as the negotiator himself observed with pardonable complacency, was perhaps never seen among the Swiss pikemen and the German reiters.[1] But Sancy was not alone in rendering essential help. Even before he had had time to bring to Henry the welcome intelligence of the fidelity of the Swiss, Givry had come to announce that he might count upon the support of the nobles of the Île de France, and Humières and Aumont had been the bearers of equally encouraging assurances from two hundred lords and gentlemen of Picardy, and from the powerful leaders of the province of Auvergne.

Meanwhile, if the expedition of these faithful servants placed the king out of danger of immediate violence, the war of intrigue still went on. Some of the most loyal of the late king's followers, like M. d'Espeisses, president of the parliament sitting at Tours, were so appalled by the gravity of the situation, as actually to propose, as a means of reconciling Roman Catholics and Huguenots, that Cardinal Bourbon should be associated with his nephew in royal authority, alleging the instances of joint possession of the imperial office among the Romans.[2] The majority of the great Roman Catholic followers Selfishness and intrigue. of Henry of Valois, taken completely by surprise at their master's sudden demise, talked violently, and were agreed only upon one point—that they would derive all the private advantage possible from the present needs of the monarch. Some, like the dissolute Monsieur d'O, pronounced themselves in favor of excluding the heretical claimant from the throne, or compelling him to abjure upon the instant.

---

[1] " Chose qui ne s'estoit veue peutestre jamais parmy les Suisses et les Reistres." Extrait d'un discours d'estat de M. de Sancy, Général de l'armée estrangere qu'il amena au Roy Henry III. en l'armée 1589, printed in Mémoires de Nevers, ii. 590–594. The whole account of Sancy is extremely valuable, affording, as it does, with that given by Agrippa d'Aubigné, the most authentic statements respecting this critical period. See, also, Auguste Poirson, Histoire du règne de Henri IV., i. 22, etc.

[2] Mémoires de Madame de Mornay (Edition of the French Historical Society), 182, 183 ; Vie de Duplessis Mornay, 139.

Others, of whom Marshal Biron was spokesman, affected greater moderation, but were not less dangerous, for they advocated delay. The cities of the realm, as well as the camp itself, they said, were divided between Roman Catholics and Huguenots. The Roman Catholics themselves were split into two factions, the royalists and the League. All the great cities and the lowest part of the populace belonged to the League. Should the action of the Roman Catholics in the camp cut off all hope of future reunion, these would at once throw themselves into the arms of Spain. He counselled, therefore, that Henry of Navarre, until his conversion, be not recognized as King of France, but simply as Captain-General, and as such receive the oaths of the loyal nobility there present. To all which, the reply made by Sancy, as spokesman of the patriotic party, was cogent. Henry of Bourbon, as nearest prince of the blood, was already king, having succeeded to the throne the instant his predecessor died; for France, being a monarchical state, could no more be without a king than a body could exist without a head. One could not well render the crown worse service than by following the marshal's advice. What hope would there be of inducing others to recognize Henry as king, if his very followers should deny him any higher title than that of captain-general. Better would it be that those who were determined upon such a course should retire to their homes than that they should refuse him the designation of king until such time as he might embrace Roman Catholicism.

These were good, sound arguments, but Biron needed something more convincing. He drew Sancy aside from the conference of nobles, in the midst of which he had spoken, and said: "Until the present moment I deemed you a man of sense, but now I begin to lose that opinion. Do you not see that if, before we have settled our matters with the King of Navarre, we establish his affairs altogether, he will no longer know or care for us? The day has come for us to attend to our own interests. If we lose the opportunity we shall never recover it, but rue our error all our lives." No one could mistake the drift of the marshal's speech. Honest Sancy, although he could not help expressing his own

Marshal Biron's demands.

judgment that it would be full time to look after private interests when France should have been rescued from present anarchy, delicately proffered his own services to carry to the king the intimation of what Biron thought that he ought to receive as the guerdon of his fidelity. The offer was promptly accepted. Henry the Fourth was in a chamber overhead, awaiting the issue of the conference; Sancy laid before him Biron's demand, and in a few minutes returned with his majesty's gracious promise that the marshal should be rewarded with the County of Perigord.[1]

So early did Henry of Navarre learn the lesson of worldly wisdom that, if he would become undisputed king of France, he must buy his way to the throne by concessions of money, The purchase rank, or principle. Was there no path that would of loyalty. have led him to the same destination save this ignoble one ? The question is by no means simple. I shall not undertake to answer it decidedly, nor shall I venture to affirm that the manly course of Christian integrity would have been rewarded with so complete a success as that which crowned a policy, consistently pursued, of pliant and opportune yielding to circumstances. A man that should have endeavored to convince the ambitious prince of the propriety of clinging to principle, come what might, would doubtless have lost his pains. To him who has fixed his mind upon the attainment of his purpose as the supreme object of life, considerations of morality have lost the power they possess over souls of higher aspirations. Thus much may, however, be asserted without fear of contradiction: the system of purchase, upon which Henry the Fourth now entered, contained within it the seeds of its own perpetuation. The success of one aspirant was the encouragement of a second. The whole administration of government became venal. Military achievements which would have secured prompt submission to a prince made of sterner stuff lost much of their immediate effect; for the unsuccessful opponent, if not completely vanquished, still had the hope of exacting large sums of money as the price of ultimate surrender. The more protracted and

---

[1] See Sancy's own account, Mémoires de Nevers, ii. 592, 593.

persistent the haggling, the better the prospect of securing favorable terms. So it was that, almost before he knew it, Henry found himself launched upon a sea of perplexity from which only the most lavish grants of money could extricate him —money, which with him was a scarce commodity, to be obtained only by burdening yet more a wretched people. From the purchase of Biron's loyalty, on the first day of Henry's reign, to the day, nearly nine years later,[1] when the Duke of Mercœur, last of the Leaguers, secured a favorable edict, with the retention of all his honors, as a reward for the obstinacy with which he had held out, the historian is compelled to chronicle a long series of discreditable compacts, made in the interest of rebellious princes, nobles, and cities—not to speak of the royal abjuration itself, the most immoral concession of them all. Of the consequent taxes which the monarch was compelled to lay upon the unfortunate people of France, the contemporary De Thou informs us that they were exacted with unprecedented rigor, ruining not only the lower classes, but even the most honorable families, whose incomes were altogether cut off by the abject poverty into which the common people were plunged.[2]

When, shortly after his arrival at St. Cloud, Henry heard d'O's insolent demand that he should instantly abjure Protestantism as an indispensable condition to recognition as king, the Huguenot prince replied firmly and frankly. He remonstrated against the attempt of those who would seize him by the throat as he took the first step to the throne, and compel him to adopt a course to which it had been found impossible to force so many plain persons, simply because they knew how to die. "From whom could you expect such a change in religious faith but from one who had no faith? Would you prefer a godless king? Would

Henry refuses to abjure instantly.

---

[1] The edict in favor of the Duke of Mercœur was accorded at Angers, March, 1598, in the ninth year of Henry's reign. It forms the last of the documents of the kind contained in a volume of nearly three hundred pages, entitled : "Recueil des edicts et articles accordez par le Roy Henry IV. pour la réunion de ses subjets. Imprimé l'an de grace, 1604."

[2] De Thou, viii. 743, 744.

you rely upon the troth of an atheist? You know how that with my mother's milk I imbibed the teachings of a religion wherein I have been nurtured and brought up. You know that I have incurred all imaginable dangers to maintain myself in it, believing that I could in conscience have no other. But as from childhood I have been instructed in it, now that I have reached a more advanced age and am consequently more open to conviction, if you will show me that I have more error than truth, inasmuch as there is nothing I hold dearer than my salvation, I shall receive instruction in this matter with more readiness than I have hitherto maintained constancy therein." [1]

Meanwhile, the king's decision and the wise counsels of the better part of his Roman Catholic followers bore fruit in the adoption and publication of a document, which, it has been remarked,[2] must be regarded, not as a contract beween the Protestant monarch and his subjects of another religion, but rather as a mutual recognition of rights.

In the Declaration of St. Cloud, signed two days after his accession, Henry the Fourth pledged his faith and his royal word to maintain and conserve in its integrity, throughout his kingdom, the Catholic, Apostolic, and Roman religion, and to introduce no innovations or changes in its worship or government. He renewed the statement, made in his public declaration before the death of his predecessor, that he desired above all things to be instructed by a good, legitimate, and free council, and that he would abide by its conclusions. He promised, therefore, within six months, or earlier, if possible, to convene such a council; and meanwhile to permit no exercises of any other religion than the Roman Catholic beyond the places where they were now held, in accordance with the articles of the truce granted by Henry the Third in the month of April past, until it might be otherwise

The Declaration of St. Cloud.

---

[1] Agrippa d'Aubigné and the Duke of Angoulême (at this time as yet only Count of Auvergne—see above, chapter x., p. 159, note), seem both to have been present. I combine their accounts of Henry's speech. Histoire universelle, iii. 186 ; Mémoires du Duc d'Angoulesme, Petitot Collection, 541.

[2] By M. Auguste Poirson.

determined in a general pacification of the kingdom, or by the
states general to be held within the ensuing six months. He
engaged to intrust to the hands of Roman Catholics all the
places that might be captured, save as his predecessor had reserved for the Protestants one town in each bailiwick and sénéchaussée. He agreed to fill vacancies with adherents of the
established church, to maintain in office all the present incumbents, and to visit upon the guilty exemplary punishment for
the murder of the late king.

This document was followed by a second declaration on the
part of the princes and other noblemen and gentlemen, faithful servants of Henry the Third, " whom may God absolve,"
formally recognizing Henry the Fourth as King of France and
Navarre, and pledging him their service and obedience, upon
the promise and oath by him above written. Besides which,
they humbly begged his majesty to permit them to send an
envoy to Rome, to explain to the pope the motives that actuated them in entering into these engagements, and to obtain
his advice.

The first document bore the signature of Henry, authenticated by that of his secretary, Ruzé ; the other was signed by
the Prince of Conty, by the Dukes of Montpensier, Longueville,
Piney, and Montbazon, by Marshals Biron and Aumont, and
by many others.[1]

The joint paper was admirably suited to accomplish the object in view. Whatever doubts might previously have existed
in the mind of any candid and dispassionate Roman
Catholic respecting Henry's intentions, there was no
longer room for uncertainty. He had distinctly repeated the assurances given, a few months earlier, in his solemn
appeal, issued at Châtellerault, to the three orders of the kingdom. He fulfilled the engagement there entered into, to take
the Roman Catholic religion under his protection. He even

Ample guarantees for the Roman Catholic religion.

---

[1] Déclaration du roy Henry IV., St. Cloud, August 4, 1589. Text in Mémoires de Duplessis Mornay, iv. 381–383, and Lettres missives, viii. 357–359.
See, also, De Thou, vii. 534 ; Davila, 410 ; Recueil des choses mémorables,
705 ; Lestoile, ii. 6.

consented that the exercises of the Protestant worship should
be restricted to the places in which they were authorized by the
terms of the truce made by Henry the Third.   Nay, more, he
repeated his offer, so frequently made in the past, to receive
instruction from a council of the church duly convened, and to
submit to its decisions.   What more could any reasonable man
ask in the way of guarantees for the protection and free action
of the Roman Catholic Church?   Nothing, certainly.   And accordingly every impartial adherent of that church, from Henry's contemporaries down to his latest historian in our own
times, has regarded the Declaration of St. Cloud as removing
the last vestige of excuse from those who, under color of conscientious scruples, still persisted in their refusal to acknowledge
the authority of the new occupant of the throne.   It is true
that one great nobleman of Henry the Third's suite, his former

*Discontent of
the Duke of
Épernon.*

minion, the Duke of Épernon, refused to append his
signature to the declaration, and weakened the royal
army, at this inopportune moment, by withdrawing
from the camp to Angoulême, followed by his retainers, a body
of twelve hundred horse and six thousand foot, and by assuming in the province of which he was governor a sort of armed
neutrality.   But, although the duke had religion upon his lips,
men needed not to be informed that the true motive was disappointed ambition.   He had not been permitted to sign the
document before the marshals, and it was not likely that he
would fare better in the matter of precedence upon the field of
battle.[1]

Whatever disapproval the Declaration of St. Cloud might
incur would naturally have been expected to come from the

*Advice of
Duplessis
Mornay.*

king's former companions in arms, the Huguenots.
The document was not, like so many of the most important papers to which Henry's signature was affixed,
from the pen of Duplessis Mornay.   That skilful writer and
judicious counsellor was, at the time, lying ill in the city of
Saumur.   But how fully the declaration must have commended
itself to him, and to all the more prudent and sensible among

---

[1] De Thou, vii. 537.

the Protestants, appears from a long memorial which he wrote to Henry the Fourth immediately upon hearing of the fatal effect of Jacques Clément's blow. In view of the natural alarm of the Roman Catholics at the accession of a Huguenot to the throne of France, Duplessis Mornay recommended Henry to publish just such a declaration as, in point of fact, his majesty had sent forth before the receipt of this communication, assuring them that no innovation would be made to the disadvantage of the Roman Catholic religion. At the same time the king must be careful not to displease the Protestants by following the practice of his predecessors in designating them as "ceux de la religion prétendue réformée." Let the name be rather "la religion que nous disons réformée," or, "dicte réformée." If, as is reasonable, the Protestants ask for greater liberty, let it be by petition of the chief men in each province, founding the demand upon preceding royal edicts that have been contravened through the violence of the League. Meanwhile, let the king write to all the churches, and to the governors of places now in Protestant hands, urging upon them both to exercise greater moderation than ever, and to restrain the popular insolence ; and let the regulations heretofore adopted for the protection of churches, relics, and public worship be more scrupulously observed than in the past.[1]

It must, nevertheless, be noticed that the moderation of Henry the Fourth, however perfectly it might commend itself

Many of the Huguenots are dissatisfied.

to the independent judgment of Duplessis Mornay, by no means satisfied a very considerable part—perhaps constituting a majority of the Huguenot population of France. The publication of the declaration was the signal for the departure of not a few of Henry's own followers. The loss was a sensible one, even if we abate somewhat from the statement of the Duke of Angoulême that the Protestant deserters were as numerous as the Roman Catholic.[2] And as

---

[1] "Memoire des affaires generaulx pour le service de sa majesté, tant dedans que dehors le royaume, qui lui feut envoyé par M. Duplessis après la mort du roy Henry III.," in Mémoires de Duplessis Mornay, iv. 393–398.

[2] Mémoires du Duc d'Angoulesme, 542.

time passed on, and as rumors were circulated of secret assurances given by the king conflicting somewhat with his public
announcements,[1] the discontent became wide-spread throughout Protestant France. In Poitou and Saintonge the murmurs
were particularly loud. The Huguenots complained that, in
gaining a king, they had lost their "protector;" that Henry
in his very "Declaration" had lapsed into the use of a distinctively Romish formula, having employed after the name of
Henry the Third the words "que Dieu absolve;" that he seemed
to have lost all remembrance of the churches of his own faith;
that in divers places Protestants were left to endure the same
annoyances and oppression as before; in a word, that their
condition was no better than under the previous king, if, indeed, it was not actually worse.

Such were some of the grievances alleged by the Huguenots,
as reported in the correspondence of Duplessis Mornay with
his royal master. It may not, therefore, be amiss to
anticipate somewhat the order of events, and, in justice to the monarch, to glance at the vindication of his course
which, about three months later than the events now under
consideration, he wrote with his own hand in the form of an
open letter to his trusty Protestant servant.

*Henry vindi-
cates himself.*

"For a month past," says Henry, "there have been rumors
of a movement set on foot, in a colloquy held at St. Jean
d'Angely, tending to the election of a new protector of our
churches. The movement was based on an alleged uncertainty
with regard to my perseverance in the Protestant religion.
There are malcontents who make use of every artifice in their
power to seduce our churches of these parts. You know what
a plot was concocted underhand in the last assembly held at
La Rochelle. These men think that they have now found the
right opportunity, by an examination of my actions, to accuse
me of inconstancy and, under this pretext, to attain their ends.
I write not because you have not heard of these matters, but I
beg you, as one acquainted with the past, and able to vouch for
my determination as fully as any one else, to notify the churches

---

[1] See Agrippa d'Aubigné, iii. 217.

and all others whom you may, that such proceedings are unlawful, and full of calumny and falsehood."

After this exordium, here somewhat abridged, Henry proceeded to the history of the declaration, in which he had had for his counsellors such men as Châtillon, La Noue, Beauvoir la Nocle, and Guitry. He declared that he had himself erased from the original draft of the document the objectionable words, "que Dieu absolve," and that he was not responsible for their reinsertion in any copies. Then, after noticing the other accusations brought against him, as a ground for the attempt to choose in his place a new protector of the Protestant churches, he expressed his curiosity to know the person that could be found for that office who had exposed to danger his life, his property, and the fruits of his toil, so often as had Henry of Navarre. As to a change of religion, he thanked God that thus far he had remained steadfast in the faith. "I have never intermitted the exercise of the Protestant religion," said he, "in any place where I have been. To such a degree is this true, that there were single weeks in the course of which seven sermons were delivered at Dieppe by Monsieur d'Amours. Was this to give any indication of my purpose to change my religion?"[1]

Meantime, the joy that filled the hearts of the adherents of the League in Paris, in consequence of the success of the murderous scheme of Madame de Montpensier and Jacques Clément, exceeded all bounds. The assassin himself was exalted to the position of a martyr in the cause of religion. But a day or two passed before his portrait was to be found, painted or in relief, adorning the walls of private houses, and even of the churches. Those fortunate

The memory of Jacques Clément honored at Paris.

---

[1] " N'ai poinct intermis l'exercise de la relligion partout où j'ai esté, tellement que telle sepmaine sept presches se sont faicts à Dieppe par le sieur d'Amours. Est-ce de là donner argument ou indice de changement ? " Henry IV. to Duplessis Mornay, Étampes, November 7, 1589, in Mémoires de Duplessis Mornay, iv. 426–430, and Lettres missives, iii. 70–73. It is only fair to state that the editor of the latter collection, M. Berger de Xivrey, was unable to discover any copy of the royal Declaration of St. Cloud containing the words, " que Dieu absolve." Ibid., iii. 71, note.

persons who could show that they were his kinsmen became
the surprised recipients of public contributions of money.[1]
The League threw off its habiliments of mourning, worn since
Guise's death, and decked itself in bright colors, as a token of
rejoicing at the death of the tyrant. The Duke of Mayenne,
though pressed to assume the crown, was shrewd enough to see

that his hour had not yet come, and declined an

Cardinal
Bourbon pro-
claimed king.
empty honor which would have cost him the friendship and support of Spain. He was content to have
the old Cardinal of Bourbon proclaimed king of France, under
the title of Charles the Tenth, and, since the prelate was a
prisoner, carefully guarded, by his royal nephew's orders, in the
castle of Chinon,[2] himself to discharge the real functions of sovereignty, in the capacity of Lieutenant-General of the State and
Crown of France.[3] Nor did the adherents of the League in some
other parts of the country suffer the capital to outdo them in
ferocious glee. The Parliament of Toulouse, in particular, dis-

tinguished itself by issuing an order calling upon all

Decree of the
Parliament
of Toulouse.
persons, of whatsoever station, to render thanks in
their respective churches for the favor shown by the
Almighty to France in the deliverance of Paris and the cities
of the realm; and, lest there should be any misapprehension of
its meaning, proceeded to command that every year, on the
first day of August, processions and public prayers be made
in token of gratitude for the benefits received upon that day.[4]

---

[1] Matthieu, Histoire des derniers troubles, ii. fol. 9.

[2] Duplessis Mornay, shortly after this, succeeded in persuading M. and
Madame de Chavigny, in whose care the captive had been placed by Henry
III., to surrender the prelate into his hands. Cardinal Bourbon was then
transferred to the keeping of La Boulaye and Parabère, who conducted the
prelate to Maillezais, and thence to Fontenay le Comte, in Poitou. The receipt of the new jailers for the cardinal's person is given in the Mémoires de
Duplessis Mornay, iv. 408, 409. It is dated September 4, 1589. Cardinal
Bourbon did not long survive, since he died at Fontenay, May 8, 1590. Lestoile, ii. 16.

[3] Matthieu, Histoire des derniers troubles, ubi supra; Lestoile, ii. 10.

[4] Arrest de la Court de Parlement de Tholose, contre Henri de Bourbon, pretendu Roy de Navarre, et ses adherans, August 22, 1589. Mémoires de la
Ligue, iv. 51.

The judges renewed their declaration that Henry of Bourbon was incapable of succeeding to the throne of France.

Altogether different was the attitude of the less bigoted Parliament of Bordeaux, under the prudent suggestions of Marshal Matignon. It did not go to the length of recognizing the authority of Henry the Fourth, and, in fact, enjoined the strict observance of the so-called Edicts of Union; but instead of testifying their joy at the murder of Henry the Third as "miraculous," after the fashion of Toulouse, the judges of Bordeaux deplored it as "sad and lamentable," and exhorted all the ecclesiastics, from the archbishop down, to offer prayers to God for the soul of the deceased monarch.[1]

The Parliament of Bordeaux.

Meanwhile, with forces much diminished by defections both of Roman Catholics and Protestants, Henry the Fourth found himself impotent to carry the siege of Paris to a successful termination. The lack of men was not his sole difficulty. Of ammunition he had a scanty store; of ready money he was almost destitute. Therefore, making a virtue of necessity, he granted leave of absence to the nobles of Guyenne, Poitou, and other distant quarters, who, even before the catastrophe of St. Cloud, had requested permission to revisit their homes. Meantime, he despatched the Duke of Longueville to Picardy, and Marshal d'Aumont to Champagne, with what troops he could spare, and with injunctions to rally as speedily as possible such cavaliers as could be induced to return to the field. He himself took another direction. The duty of escorting the remains of Henry of Valois to Compiègne—the Parisians would not have tolerated the interment of the "tyrant" in the crypt of the abbey church of St. Denis—afforded a decent excuse for the withdrawal of the royal army from the neighborhood of the capital. From Compiègne Henry directed his course toward Normandy, expecting on the shores of the British Channel to welcome the force which Queen Elizabeth had

Henry's straits for money and ammunition.

Henry marches into Normandy.

---

[1] Arrest de la Court de Parlement de Bourdeaux, August 19, 1589. Ibid., iv. 49.

promised to send to his relief. His following amounted barely
to twelve hundred horse, three thousand French foot-soldiers,
and two regiments of Swiss. So scanty an army, though it
might lead Pont de l'Arche to surrender, Dieppe to open its
gates, and the Huguenots of Caen to assume new courage, could
scarcely be expected to perform any notable action, and itself
offered a tempting object of attack to the enemy. So at least
thought the Duke of Mayenne, who, at the urgent call of the
burghers of Rouen, fearful for their own safety, issued from
the capital at the head of three thousand horse and fifteen
thousand foot. He had assured the credulous Parisians that
he would, at one stroke, put an end to the war ; that soon they
would see him returning in triumph, with the Béarnais for his
prisoner, tied hand and foot.[1]

The undertaking was not, however, so easy as the lively imagination of the duke had pictured it. On learning the ap-
The conflicts proach of his enemy, Henry had taken an advantage-
at Arques. ous position on the banks of the little river Béthune,
with the friendly town of Dieppe two leagues in his rear. He
seized the village of Arques, and employed his men to such
good purpose that in three days his position was everywhere
protected by a ditch at no place less than seven or eight feet in
depth. In vain did the duke, with superior forces, attempt to
dislodge him. Although the point of attack was more than
once changed, and the mode of warfare varied from the simple
use of artillery to the more exciting and perilous encounter in
hand-to-hand combat, the Huguenots did not flinch. Nor were
the Swiss less brave. It was the fortune of the mountaineers
of the Alps, on this occasion as on others, to be represented by
their soldiers on the side of the Protestant king as well as in
the army of his opponents ; but the men of the Roman Catholic canton of Soleure, fighting under the banners of Henry,
had the reputation of surpassing in valor their countrymen who

---

[1] "Vray et sommaire discours de ce qui s'est passé en l'armée conduite par
sa Majesté Treschrestienne, depuis son advenement à la Couronne jusques à
la fin de l'an 1589," in Mémoires de la Ligue, iv. 53–79 ; Recueil des choses
mémorables, 707 ; Agrippa d'Aubigné, iii. 217.

fought in the ranks of the League. The Germans earned few laurels. A body of reiters in the service of the Duke of Mayenne not only played the traitors by making overtures to pass over to the royalist side, but, subsequently, thinking that they had committed a blunder, and that the king was likely, after all, to prove the poorer master, betrayed him in turn, and went back to the service of the Duke of Mayenne. Three standards which they captured were the only trophies won by Mayenne. Even this small number, however, was turned to good account. Accompanied by fifteen or more banners of the same general appearance, hastily prepared to order by the direction of the Duchess of Montpensier, the flags were soon after displayed at Paris, where they served the purpose of convincing the populace of that city that if Henry had thus far neither been driven into the sea nor captured, he yet had experienced an overwhelming defeat. The fraud was so successful that it was destined to be repeated on other occasions, though it may be doubted whether the results in the end paid for the misdirected ingenuity displayed. However this may be, after a series of engagements, lasting through more than ten days from first to last, the Duke of Mayenne drew off his army in the direction of Picardy, ostensibly with the view of seizing certains towns which he was bound by treaty to place in the hands of the Spaniard.[1]

Upon the Huguenot king the repulse of so greatly superior an army conferred all the advantages that would have been derived from a victory in the open field. Henry was, Henry returns however, not content with the glory of the action, but toward Paris. resolved to strike a blow that might undeceive the credulous denizens of the capital. So it was that, late in the month of October, having called in the divisions of the Duke of Longueville and Marshal d'Aumont, and with an army re-enforced by

---

[1] See the detailed "Vray et sommaire discours," ubi supra; Recueil des choses mémorables, 708–710; Mémoires de Sully, c. 28; Agrippa d'Aubigné, Davila, etc. The Duke of Mayenne brought his forces before Arques on Wednesday, September 13th, and broke up his camp at midnight on Sunday, the 24th of the same month. It was only, however, to make a circuit and return to the attack at another point, nearer Dieppe, on Tuesday, the 26th. He finally retreated on Thursday, October 5th. De Thou, vii. 550.

the addition of four thousand Englishmen sent to him by Queen Elizabeth, under the command of Lord Willoughby,[1] the king again turned his face toward the heart of the realm. From Dieppe to Meulan his course lay north of the Seine, but no enemy dared oppose his progress. Then crossing the river, he pushed on to the vicinity of Paris. The last day of the month saw him in possession of the little village of Bagneux, scarcely more than a league south of the walls of Paris, while his troops were quartered in the neighboring villages of Montrouge, Gentilly, Issy, and Vaugirard—places which the great metropolis, in its rapid extension, has, within our own times, either actually absorbed within the network of its almost endless streets, or, at least, environed with its frowning forts. The same prince who, a little over two months before, had left St. Cloud and Meudon penniless, and with a diminutive army, was back again, flushed with success, accompanied by a respectable force, and able to pay his way. Thanks to the generosity of Queen Elizabeth, Henry, who never remembered to have had a full exchequer, could boast the possession of over twenty

---

[1] De Thou (vii. 551) makes the commander to have been Roger Williams; but Hume (History of England, chapter xliii.) is correct in stating that it was Lord Willoughby. In the "Mémoires des sommes de deniers que la Reyne d'Angleterre a prestez ou desboursez pour le Roy Treschrestien," submitted to Henry's council, May 21, 1599, O. S., is the item: "1589. Desboursé pour la despense et transport des soldatz envoyez au secours du Roy subs la conduicte du Baron de Willoughby. Lib. Sterl. 6,000. Scud. Franc. 20,000." Edmund Sawyer, Memorials of Affairs of State, i. 29. It will be seen that the French écu, or crown, is here reckoned as the equivalent of six shillings sterling. As the livre was, at this time, worth one-third of the écu, its equivalent was two shillings. The debasement of the circulating medium, it is well known, was much greater in France than in England. In the early part of the Middle Ages, a pound or livre, in both countries, represented a full pound's weight of pure silver. In England, by the time of Queen Elizabeth, a pound of silver had come to be coined into just three pounds sterling, or sixty shillings. Since Elizabeth's reign, the further decline has been very slight, the same quantity of the precious metal now producing a trifle over sixty-six shillings. But in France, at the outbreak of the Revolution, seventy-eight livres, or nominal pounds of account, were coined from a single pound of silver! The depreciation of the currency had not advanced quite so far as this in the sixteenth century ; for a livre of the reign of Charles IX. was worth nearly three of the livres of Louis XVI.

thousand pounds sterling. It was, he said, a greater sum than
he had ever before seen.[1]

And now was the king able to deal a blow that filled the
hearts of his enemies with terror. Early the next morning,
under cover of a thick fog that seemed to have come
up purposely to conceal the advance of the royalists,
the Parisians learned, to their surprise, that Henry
was assaulting the faubourgs or suburbs of their city with irre-
sistible fury. Each of the three divisions into which the king
had divided his army carried consternation before it; but it
was the corps under François de la Noue and Coligny's son
that distinguished itself most by its valor, and executed the
greatest carnage. The Huguenot soldiers, as they approached
the scene of the treacherous massacre that had cost the lives of
some of the noblest men of whom France had ever boasted,
forgot that full seventeen years had elapsed since the ill-fated
Sunday of August, and that they were fighting under the banner, not of the great admiral himself, but of his eldest son.
They only remembered that it was a Châtillon who led them,
and that their battle-cry was "Saint Bartholomew!" So it
was that they drove the enemy to the very gate, and nearly followed in with the crowd of fugitives. Nor did the hero of the
Iron Arm fail to make good his reputation for impetuous courage. On the river's bank, near the spot where now stands the
Institut de France, the southern circuit of the walls ended in
the strong Tour de Nesle. Here, intent only upon penetrating
into the city, La Noue threw himself into the water, disdaining
even to send a single soldier before him, and was recalled from
his hazardous undertaking only by the express command of the
king. As it was, what with the strength of the current and
the little use to which his iron arm could be put in swimming,
the Huguenot captain incurred as much danger of his life as
he had encountered in a score of battle-fields.

Marginal note: *Successful attack upon the southern suburbs.*

---

[1] Hume, History of England, ubi supra. The prudent queen took good care
to have security for her money. The " Mémoire " above quoted has the entry
of a loan of £22,350, made September 7, 1589, " presté sur l'obligation de
Messieurs Beauvoir, Buhy, et Buzenval."

After all, however, the destruction of some hundreds or thousands of lives; the plundering of a host of houses, involving the ruin of many a guiltless family—this was all the king accomplished. Even Sully could exclaim on this occasion: "I am weary of striking; I cannot bring myself to kill any more people that do not defend themselves." Possibly a little more expedition on the part of the royalists in following up Sully and an adventurous party of fifteen or twenty that had actually pushed their way within the gate of Nesle, or greater promptness in bringing up the cannon to batter down the gates elsewhere, might have enabled the king to master a part, or the whole, of the city. However, Henry was spared the perilous venture of forcing his way in. The Duke of Mayenne, hastening to the relief of the endangered capital, entered the city from the north; and the king, having at least succeeded in making a diversion in favor of the loyal Picard nobles, drew off with an army laden with plunder.[1] He had taken good care, in the midst of the attack made upon Paris on All Saints' Day, to protect the Roman Catholic churches and monasteries from insult. If we may credit the accounts that have come down to us, the ordinary services of one of the great ecclesiastical festivals not only proceeded unmolested in the midst of the confusion of an army engaged in pillage, but were attended by great numbers of captains and soldiers.[2] It was a part of Henry's policy to demonstrate his honest intention to guarantee the undisturbed exercise of the worship of the great majority of his subjects. In no better way could he exhibit the unreasonable character of the fears entertained by the adherents of the League.

There were those to whom the failure to make a vigorous attempt upon Paris was a serious disappointment. Henry's faithful Huguenot chaplain was of the number of these. Ga-

---

[1] Mémoires de Sully, c. 29; Recueil des choses mémorables, 710, 711; Mémoires de la Ligue, iv. 76, 77; Lestoile, ii. 7; Davila, 424, 425, De Thou, vii. 551, 552; Agrippa d'Aubigné, iii. 223–225; Histoire des derniers troubles, ii. fol. 13.

[2] Davila, De Thou, etc., ubi supra.

briel d'Amours, for a full year before the battle of Ivry, was
the king's constant attendant and spiritual adviser, encouraging
and admonishing him with all the boldness and fidelity of some
Hebrew seer of the olden time.   When the monarch and his
army were besieged at Dieppe, twice did D'Amours visit him,
early in the morning, before he was risen from bed, and exhort
him to put his trust in God.   " You will yet come forth from
this tomb," said he, " and you will give me an opportunity to
sing, in the faubourgs of Paris, the song of Simeon : ' Lord,
now lettest thou thy servant depart in peace.'"   But when the
faubourgs were taken, while the king remembered distinctly
enough the encouraging prediction, D'Amours saw plainly that
for some reason his master was not inclined to pursue his advantage and capture the city now apparently within his grasp.
" Sire, all things are possible to God, and nothing is impossible to the believer," said D'Amours.   " I do what I can," was
the only reply he could elicit from Henry.   " Sire," exclaimed
Gabriel, in the first sermon he preached, in the presence of all
the gathered Huguenots, " you would not take Paris when God
gave it to you ; one day you will wish to take it and God will
not give it to you.   The fine army of French gentlemen which
you would not use will melt away." [1]

While the Huguenot king, by word and by still more impressive acts, endeavored to dispel all sincere apprehension that
License of   might be cherished respecting his intentions, and while
the League.   he gave to his old associates in arms, it must be confessed, just ground for complaint that the Roman Catholics were
everywhere permitted to enjoy privileges denied, or grudgingly
conceded, to the Protestants, no pretence of such moderation
was exhibited upon the other side.   The League and its follow-

---

[1] " Le premier presche que je fis apres, je vous dis devant tous, ' Vous ne
l'avez voulu prendre quand Dieu la vous a donnee, vous la vouldrez prendre
ung jour et il ne la vous donnera pas.'   N'aviez-vous pas quatre mil gentils-
hommes françois devant Paris, une si belle et puissante armee laquelle vous
fustes contraint licencier apres la venue du duc de Parme ; ce que je vous
avoy predit en preschant vous advint."   Gabriel d'Amours to Henry IV.,
June 20, 1593, Bulletin de la Société de l'histoire du Protestantisme français, i. 283.

ers raved not only against Protestantism, but against the royal
authority, and even against every form of law and decency.
All seemed intent to prove to the world the truth of the assertion made years before by the keen-sighted pope, now in the last
year of his pontificate, that there was not a man among them
who was moved by a sincere desire for the glory of God and
the promotion of the true faith.[1] The personal jealousies between the leaders were notorious. The followers of each narrowly and enviously watched the possible successes of all other
and rival candidates for the first place. The mere circumstance that Sixtus the Fifth, in the brief which he sent by the
hands of Cajetan, the new papal legate, made no mention of
the Cardinal of Bourbon, was sufficient to alienate many of the
partisans of that prelate.[2] As if the claimants of the throne
within the kingdom, with Philip of Spain outside of it, were
not enough, and more than enough, for poor France, the Duke
of Savoy deemed the proper moment to have arrived for him

The Duke of
Savoy's pre-
tensions upon
the French
crown.

to put forward his pretensions. Accordingly he lost
no time in sending a trusty servant with a message
to the Parliament of Dauphiny, signifying his request to be recognized as King of France. The letter making this modest suggestion contained an abundance of
expressions of sorrow over the untimely death of Henry the
Third, and set forth, in detail, the advantages which the good
Catholics of France would reap from the accession of one, not
only piously affected, but able, because of the proximity of his
dominions and his military resources, supplemented, if need be,
by the resources of his father-in-law, the King of Spain, to
make good his claim by force of arms. Naturally, the duke
did not fail to note the fact that, as a first cousin of Henry
the Third, on his mother's side, he was justly entitled to the
throne; that monarch's nearest relatives having forfeited their
rights by obstinate persistence in heresy, or by favoring here-

---

[1] See above, vol. i. chapter v. p. 305.

[2] De Thou, vii. 567, 568. The pope's missive was dated October 7, 1589,
but the legate did not actually reach Paris until about the beginning of the
next year.

tics.   The duke had hoped for a kindly hearing on the part of
the judges, because of the strong attachment of many of their
number to the ancient faith, and because of the devotion of the
city of Grenoble, where the parliament held its sessions, to the
League.   But these sensible magistrates, while thanking him profusely for his offers, referred the decision of so important a matter to the approaching
states general.   Meanwhile, they begged him not to think of
entering their province, lest his coming might lead to the
abrupt termination of a truce recently concluded between
Ornano and Lesdiguières, on behalf of the Roman Catholics
and the Protestants respectively.[1]

We have seen the gentleness with which Henry the Fourth
treated the Roman Catholics.   What usage the Huguenots
might have received at the hands of Charles Emmanuel, had he succeeded in persuading the Parliament of
Dauphiny and the rest of the Romanists of France
to receive him, appears from the warfare which he
suffered his troops to wage against the city of Geneva in the
months of August and September, and to renew in the month
of May of the following year.   Of the ravages of war, in towns
and villages plundered and then consigned to the flames, in
human lives wantonly destroyed, history can give the statistics ;
but there are details the knowledge of which is absolutely
necessary for a full understanding of the course of events, but
which are too horrible to be recorded.   Forced to choose between leaving his readers in partial ignorance of the enormity
of the sins committed against God in the persons of the beings
created in His image, and defiling his pages by a disgusting
catalogue of crime, the historian feels himself instinctively compelled to prefer silence to a truthful but repulsive narration.
Let those that will satisfy their curiosity on the subject and
read for themselves the names of the unfortunate victims of
cruelty and lust, peruse the contemporary treatises in which
they are set forth with painful minuteness.   Suffice it, for our
purposes, to say that in the fourscore villages that fell beneath

Opposition of the Parliament of Grenoble.

Outrages perpetrated by the duke's troops about Geneva.

---

[1] De Thou, vii. 579, 580.

the power of the Duke of Savoy, neither age nor sex was respected, and that in the light of the magnitude of the atrocities perpetrated, death itself seemed the most tolerable of misfortunes.[1]

And what the Duke of Savoy's troops did about Geneva, other troops in the service of the League did in France itself. The lansquenets who escorted Cardinal Cajetan from Dijon to Paris thought themselves, by reason of that very fact, relieved of all moral obligations. "It is impossible to express the excesses they committed along the whole way," writes the Roman Catholic De Thou. "The very churches were not sheltered from their insults. Although it was Lenten-tide, they did not hesitate openly to eat meat. They made a jest of the matter, saying that they could do so with a clear conscience, since they were bringing with them the Pope's legate. The cardinal, as they travelled, gave them absolution every day, and opened to them the treasuries of Heaven."[2] In fact, so far as the armies of the League were concerned, to use the words of the same impartial historian, "all the profligate wretches that could be found, all the persons who had reason to fear the rigor of justice, threw themselves into the party of the League, in the hope of the impunity which the preachers liberally promised them in their sermons."[3]

Insults offered by the legate's escort.

Meanwhile, the fortunes of the Huguenot prince who, with so small a part of France decidedly supporting his rightful claims to the throne, never despaired of ultimate success, were visibly improving. In distant Provence, Bernard Nogaret de Valette secured for him two or three important places. Among these the castle of Toulon

Singular surprise of the castle of Toulon.

---

[1] De Thou, vii. 581–584, has given a brief account of this shocking episode of European history ; but the reader must examine for himself the "Discours sommaire de la guerre du duc de Savoye contre Genève," in the Mémoires de la Ligue, iv. 732–743, and, especially, the "Bref et vrai recueil des horribles carnages perpetrés de froid sang par les troupes du duc de Savoye, à leurs entrees tant du balliage de Gez, que du mandement de Gaillard," etc., ibid., iv. 743–762. M. Gaberel, in his excellent Histoire de l'Église de Genève, has reprinted these accounts in great part.

[2] De Thou, vii. 598.   [3] Ibid., vii. 587.

was taken by one of the most singular of the many remarkable devices resorted to in this treacherous period of civil war. The castle was held for the Duke of Savoy, but the unsuspecting commandant not only cultivated the acquaintance of his neighbor, La Valette, but had shown him over the entire fortifications. This courtesy emboldened La Valette to request permission, which was readily granted, for a friend, one Montault, to enjoy the same privilege. Accordingly, Montault presented himself at the gate, accompanied by a score of men with weapons well concealed beneath their clothes. This escort he left just without the entrance, ostensibly to await his return ; but he had himself gone only a few steps into the castle, when, feigning a sudden illness, he fell at full length upon the ground. At the sight of a man apparently in the last agonies of death, the castle guards forsook their post and ran to his assistance. It was the expected signal. The band of royalists rushed in. Montault aroused himself from his assumed stupor, and drew out his sword. In a few moments all was over. The guards, paralyzed with astonishment, were easily overpowered, and paid with their lives the penalty of their too great humanity. La Valette, who was lurking in the vicinity, was admitted with his troops. The castle was won.[1]

Happily, the more essential gains were made by Henry himself and in less reprehensible ways. The king could now afford to leave for a time the immediate vicinity of the capital, where he had proved himself to be no despicable foe, and labor to strengthen his cause elsewhere. Turning southward and westward, he successively made himself master of Étampes, of Chateaudun, and of Vendôme, and entered Tours, the seat of the loyal parliament transferred from Paris, amid demonstrations of universal joy. As at Chateaudun he had received the deputies of the Swiss cantons, coming to renew their league with the French crown, so at Tours he gave audience to Mocenigo, the Venetian ambassador, bringing him the first recognition on the part of a foreign state of Henry's authority as King of France. Then passing to the north, the

Substantial fruits of Henry's first campaign.

---

[1] De Thou, vii. 584, 585.

important cities of Alençon, Argentan, Domfront, Falaise, Lisieux, Pont-Audemer, Pont-l'Evêque, Bayeux, and Honfleur opened their gates, without very serious opposition, to his triumphant advance. Before many weeks, Henry had added to his actual domain several of the provinces of central France and a good part of Normandy.[1]

A clear and vigorous writer, whose history of the reign of Henry the Fourth throws fresh light upon this important period—Auguste Poirson—has made an approximate estimate of the ground the Huguenot king had gained during the few months that had elapsed since his accession. When the last Valois prince had been put out of the way by the dagger of Jacques Clément, his successor's claims to the throne were recognized by barely one-sixth part of France. It is true that it would be a mistake to suppose that all the remainder held for the League. Yet, even with the addition of such neutral cities and territories as Bordeaux and Guyenne, which still affected to use the name and the seal of the deceased monarch as in an interregnum, only about one-half of the population and one-half of the territory of the kingdom opposed the schemes of Mayenne and Philip the Second. It was, however, Henry's good fortune to hold effectually in his grasp the river Loire, which divides France in two; for of all the bridges and crossings which must be used in passing between the northern and southern banks, only the city of Orleans was in the possession of the opposite party.[2] But now, the victories at Arques, followed by the successful march of six hundred miles, had confirmed the king's authority in eight contiguous and powerful prov-

Division of France between Henry and the League.

---

[1] De Thou, vii. 585–588; Recueil des choses mémorables, 714, 715; Mémoires de la Ligue, iv. 188, etc.

[2] "Que cette ville (Orleans) seule servoit de passage à ceux de la Ligue sur la riviere de Loire, qui traversoit, voire divisoit presque tout le royaume de France, tous les autres ponts et passages qui estoient sur ladite riviere jusques à Nantes, estans en l'obeissance de sa Majesté. De sorte que ceux de la Ligue n'avoient que le pont seul d'Orleans pour traverser d'une part à l'autre de la France, qui estoit peu et beaucoup incommode, pour se secourir les uns les autres quand le besoin le requereroit." Mémoires de Nevers, ii. 408.

inces,[1] and—which was equally important to the necessitous prince—had made him master of resources that would bring him in two million crowns a year. It was not less significant of future success, that the clemency and toleration avowed and The high practised by Henry had won over to his side the ecclesiastics great majority of the higher ecclesiastics of the Ro- support the king. man Catholic Church itself. While the curates, for the most part, and the monks, with few exceptions, were ardent and fanatical adherents of the League, one hundred out of the one hundred and eighteen bishops and archbishops of the king- dom espoused the monarch's side within the three months fol- lowing his accession.[2] No stronger proof could be advanced of the amplitude of the guarantees given by Henry the Fourth to the Roman Catholic Church, and the faithfulness with which those guarantees were observed by him.

Meantime Paris had been a theatre of discord. The " Six- teen " had in the first instance taken advantage of the losses Contention sustained by the Duke of Mayenne about Arques and between the Dieppe to strengthen their own faction. Parliament " Sixteen " and Mayenne. was again invaded by insolent men, and its authority reduced to naught. Scenes of robbery and assassination were again witnessed. In the " Council of the Union," preparations were on foot to make a virtual surrender of France to Philip the Second, but the plan was cleverly thwarted by Mayenne when he secured the solemn recognition of Cardinal Bourbon as king under the title of " Charles the Tenth," and of himself as the phantom king's lieutenant-general. To exclude Spanish

---

[1] Île de France, Picardy, Champagne, Normandy, Orleanois, Touraine, Maine and Anjou.

[2] Poirson, Histoire du règne de Henri IV., i. 50, 51, 148, 157, 158. " Car s'il faut esplucher les choses," wrote a pamphleteer about the close of the year, " de cent ou six vingts evesques et archevesques qui sont au royaume de France, il n'y en a pas la dixiesme qui approuve les conseils de l'Union." Response à un avis qui conseille aux François de se rendre sous la protection du roy d'Espagne, printed in Mémoires de la Ligue, iv. 199. The Dialogue du Manant et du Maheustre, published about three or four years later, more distinctly states the royalist prelates as consisting of 11 archbishops and 89 bishops, and the opposite party as composed of 3 archbishops and 15 bishops, " encore des moindres."

pretensions still more completely, the pope was declared sole protector of France, and the very " Council of the Union " was replaced by a " State Council " attached to the duke's person.[1]

Upon one point, however, the adherents of the League seemed at this time to be almost unanimous—Henry the Fourth must not be permitted in any way to obtain a decent excuse for becoming a Roman Catholic, or be recognized as king, even should he simulate conversion. Villeroy, alone, gave Mayenne some sound advice—which the duke took good care not to follow— and held up to him the imperishable glory he would acquire by becoming the author of a blessed peace throughout France.[2]

The legate forbids the bishops from assembling at Tours.
But the papal legate, Cardinal Cajetan, effectually precluded the possibility of a consummation devoutly prayed for by honest men on both sides. Henry the Fourth had ordered the convocation of the states general to take place at Tours in the coming month of March, with a special view to the conference of the archbishops and bishops in a national council, to deliberate respecting the means of the king's conversion. But the legate, on the first day of the month that should have witnessed their gathering, addressed to each of the French prelates a letter in which he not only protested against the validity of a meeting called by a prince unauthorized to perform such an act, but declared in advance any decisions it might reach to be null and void. If Henry of Bourbon, " self-styled King of France," was sincerely desirous of returning to the Catholic faith, there were sufficient of doctors and preachers in Paris competent to instruct him without putting so many bishops to the trouble of coming together. If, on the other hand, it was contemplated to enter into a discussion on points of controversy between the Romish Church and the synagogue of Calvin, this was but giving the advantage to heretics and making a mock of religion. He, consequently, forbade

---

[1] For these events I must refer the reader to the admirably clear narrative of M. Poirson.

[2] See "Advis de M. de Villeroy à M. le duc de Mayenne," an important paper appended to the Mémoires de Villeroy (Collection Michaud et Poujoulat), 225. It was written and handed to Mayenne about the close of the year 1589. Ibid., 147.

the prelates from going to Tours, and, in the name of his master, proclaimed all that should persist in proceeding thither to be excommunicated and deposed.[1]

The audacious act of the presuming foreigner effectually prevented the assembly of Tours, and indefinitely postponed the pacification of France. As pontifical legate he had claimed, in the document just referred to, the exclusive right of calling together the French prelates at his good pleasure. In fact, his whole course of conduct testified to an overweening estimate of his importance. It was characteristic of the man's arrogance that, on the occasion of his formal reception by the parliament, he proceeded straightway to the corner of the hall always reserved for royalty, and was about to take possession of the king's place, when the patriotic and somewhat indignant first president laid forcible hands upon him, and compelled him to accept a more humble seat by his own side.[2] It was the same impetuosity that led Cajetan to go far beyond his instructions and throw in his lot distinctly with the League. Sixtus the Fifth had certainly contemplated no such thing. Anxious only to side with that party which should prove the stronger,[3] he was resolved that his legate should act with the utmost circumspection. As it was, some thought it a fortunate circumstance for Cajetan that Sixtus was dead by the time the returning legate again reached Rome; else the pope would have had him beheaded for kindling the fire of sedition, contrary to his express commands.[4]

Audacity of Cardinal Cajetan.

Henry, after his successful march through Normandy, again began to approach Paris. Early in the month of March, 1590, having relieved the garrison of Meulan, bravely defended for many days against a superior attacking force, the king found himself near the spot where, about twenty-seven years before, the Huguenots under Condé and Coligny had fought their first pitched battle with the Roman Catholics, commanded by Constable Montmorency, Francis of

Henry lays siege to Dreux.

[1] Lestoile, ii. 12 ; De Thou, vii. (liv. 98) 605, 606.
[2] Lestoile, ii. 11 ; De Thou, vii. 602.
[3] De Thou, vii. 601.   [4] Lestoile, ii. 35.

Guise, and Marshal Saint André.[1] In laying siege to the city
of Dreux, it was Henry's purpose to cut off one of the principal
sources of supply for the capital, whose inhabitants were already
chafing under the interruption of their communications with the
upper Seine and Marne. The Duke of Mayenne found himself
compelled by the urgency of the Parisians to go to the rescue.
On his approach, the king, who desired nothing better than an
opportunity to meet his enemies on the open field, promptly
raised the siege and prepared for a conflict which he hoped
might prove decisive.

The battle of Ivry, fought on Wednesday, the fourteenth of
March, 1590, is one of those great days in the history of the
world whose occurrences, even to the smallest details,
are of interest, and have been frequently told. There
is perhaps no military engagement, within the bounds
of the sixteenth century, a careful examination of which will better repay the student of the art of war. The disparity between
the armies was considerable. Mayenne's troops numbered sixteen thousand men, of whom twelve thousand were foot soldiers
and four thousand cavalry. Henry had but eight thousand foot
soldiers and two thousand two hundred cavalry, or a little over
ten thousand men in all. Of this number a part had but just
reached him the day before the battle, and a part came up
when the forces were already drawn out on the field. Even
thus, however, Henry commanded not far from twice the number he had led, two years and a half before, at Coutras ; while
Mayenne's forces exceeded by almost a half the whole assemblage of men engaged on both sides upon that eventful day.

Each of the two armies had its own advantages. The body
of horse brought by Count Egmont from the Netherlands was
a formidable detachment. That their leader, degenerate son of
a noble father, was fighting under the banners of the assassin of
that father, detracted neither from his courage nor from theirs.
Fifteen hundred of his followers were armed with the lance, a
weapon before which scarcely anything could stand when there
was sufficient room for a deliberate charge. On the other hand,

*The battle of
Ivry, March
14, 1590.*

---

[1] See Rise of the Huguenots, ii. 93.

the two thousand French horsemen serving under their king presented a sight that called forth admiration from friend and from foe. Composed of the picked nobility of the realm, and armed cap-a-pie, they had no counterpart in the opposed ranks. If with Mayenne's cavalry there was more gold and glitter, with Henry's knights there was more steel. To the former it was of the utmost consequence that there should be ample space between the armies; to the latter, who had long since discarded the lance and relied upon the pistol and the sword as their weapons of offence, it was of equal importance to come into close quarters, where the arms of their opponents, after the force of the first onset was spent, were well-nigh useless.

On the side of the Huguenot king there was brave Gabriel d'Amours, a preacher who knew how to fight as well as how to exhort, and a favorite minister of his majesty. His prayer before the charge at Coutras had, as we have seen, deeply impressed both Protestant and Roman Catholic, and one nobleman who had been in the opposite ranks, but was now about to fight for Henry, had, on the eve of the battle of Ivry, begged the king for the ministrations, in the sight of the two armies, of that Huguenot pastor who was believed to have cast a potent spell over the army of Joyeuse at Coutras, and the army of Mayenne at Arques.[1] The League, too, had its supposed magician—a monk, who, we are told, was put forward by the Walloon troops of Egmont, clothed in priestly robes, and holding a St. Andrew's cross. He had promised his compatriots to curse the heretics so effectually that they would turn to flight without striking a blow. But, at the first sign of a charge on the part of the enemy, the poor ecclesiastic threw down his cross upon the ground, and fled in abject fear.[2] However it may have been with his opponents, Henry of Navarre was not content to delegate to another the duty of offering supplications in his behalf. If we may believe one who must speak from personal knowledge, the Bourbon prince, strange compound of devotion and of worldliness, spent almost

---

[1] See above, volume i. chapter vii. p. 432.
[2] Agrippa d'Aubigné, iii. 230.

the whole of the night preceding an engagement, which he rightly judged likely to prove of critical importance to his fortunes, in prayers—not merely prayers offered in his presence, but offered by himself.[1] Such of his followers as could not join in such worship he cheerfully permitted to go to their priests, or to implore the favor of Heaven upon his arms in whatever way they might prefer.

And now his opportunity was come. The field had been carefully explored, the position of each corps in the coming conflict precisely defined. The royal line was but slightly curved. The extreme left was occupied by a squadron of three hundred horse, under Marshal d'Aumont, flanked on either side by a body of French infantry. At a very brief interval came the second squadron of three hundred horse, under the Duke of Montpensier, with a body of five hundred lansquenets on the left and a Swiss regiment on the right, and these again flanked by French infantry. This formed the left wing of the main line. Some fifty paces in advance of this was thrown forward the squadron of two hundred and fifty horse, under command of the Baron Biron, son of the aged marshal of that name, to whom, as will be seen, an important trust was confided elsewhere upon the field. He was supported by eight hundred infantry. On the same line was drawn up the fourth squadron, composed of two bodies of two hundred light horsemen each, under the young Count Givry and the young Count of Auvergne respectively. Between this squadron and that of Baron Biron had been posted the effective artillery of the king, consisting of four larger pieces and two culverins. Henry himself commanded the fifth squadron, occupying the centre of the main line, and composed of six hundred horsemen—the very flower of the Huguenots and of the French noblesse. Like the other squadrons, it had a support of infantry on either side—first, two regiments of Swiss, and, beyond these, two regiments of French soldiers. The sixth squadron was that under command of old

---

[1] " Presque toute la nuict le Roi, apprehendant cette bataille, fut en prières, lesquelles il faisoit lui-mesmes, et envoioit ceux qui n'y vouloient pas assister," etc. Agrippa d'Aubigné, iii. 229.

Marshal Biron, the father, two hundred and fifty horse strong, and with a Swiss regiment on either flank; but Biron had been purposely thrown somewhat to the rear, and was instructed to abstain from the engagement until his reserve force might be needed to decide the fortunes of the day. The two hundred and fifty German horse of Count Schomberg constituted the seventh squadron, and occupied the extreme right.

In no great battle of the sixteenth century, perhaps—certainly in no battle wherein the Huguenots took part—had more care been displayed in arranging the troops to the utmost advantage. The different divisions, while offering no dangerous gaps for attacks, were yet sufficiently far apart to allow freedom of action. The horsemen were marshalled, not in the dense columns which experience had found unserviceable, but in five ranks. The cannon had been assigned a position from which they could strike terror and create confusion. Everything that human foresight could provide had been disposed, even to the injunction given to the soldiers that, in case of separation from their comrades, they should instantly make their way to the rallying-point, for the locality of which three pear-trees, standing out conspicuous upon the plain, on the right, were to serve as the convenient indication.

The army of the League, of which the Duke of Nemours commanded the right wing, and the Chevalier d'Aumale the left, with the Duke of Mayenne himself in the centre, was drawn up somewhat after the same fashion, so far as the distribution of the infantry was concerned; but the line was made decidedly a crescent, and the imperfect vision of the near-sighted Viscount of Tavannes, upon whom the task of arranging the horse upon the field of battle had devolved, led him to commit the fatal blunder of crowding the different corps. Not only were there no open spaces for the execution of contemplated manœuvres, but the slightest divergence to right or left compelled horse and foot to jostle and interfere with each other.

The superior skill displayed in the arrangement of the Huguenot king's army certainly contributed quite as much as the valor of his followers to the subsequent victory. Nor did the caution which was as much a characteristic of Henry's mode of warfare as his reckless courage in the actual conflict, forsake him when on the very eve of engaging the foe. As he advanced his forces a hundred and fifty paces or so, to bring them nearer to the lines of the reluctant enemy, he also shifted his position, so as to relieve his men of the glare of the sun in their eyes, and prevent the smoke from rolling back upon them.

The battle began with a furious cannonade from the king's artillery, so prompt that nine rounds of shot had been fired before the enemy were ready to reply, so well directed that great havoc was made in the opposing lines. Next, the light horse of M. de Rosne, upon the extreme right of the Leaguers, made a dash upon Marshal d'Aumont, but were valiantly received. Their example was followed by the German reiters, who threw themselves upon the defenders of the king's artillery and upon the light horse of Aumont, who came to their relief; then, after their customary fashion, wheeled around, expecting to pass easily through the gaps between the friendly corps of Mayenne and Egmont and to reload their firearms at their leisure in the rear, by way of preparation for a second charge. Owing to the blunder of Tavannes, however, they met a serried line of horse, where they looked for an open field, and the Walloon cavalry found themselves compelled to set their lances in threatening position to ward off the dangerous onset of their retreating allies. Another charge, made by a squadron of the Walloon lancers themselves, was bravely met by Baron Biron. His example was imitated by the Duke of Montpensier farther down the field. Although the one leader was twice wounded and the other had his horse killed under him, both ultimately succeeded in repulsing the enemy.

It was about this time that the main body of Henry's horse became engaged with the gallant array of cavalry in their front. Mayenne had placed upon the left of his squadron a body of four hundred mounted carabineers. These, advancing first, rode rapidly toward the king's line, took aim, and discharged their weapons with deadly effect within twenty-five paces. Immediately afterward the main force of eighteen hundred lancers presented themselves. The king had fastened a great white plume to his helmet, and had adorned his horse's head with another equally conspicuous. " Comrades ! " he now exclaimed to those about him, " Comrades ! God is for us ! There are His enemies and ours ! If you lose sight of your standards, rally to my white plume ; you will find it on the road to victory and to honor." The Huguenots had knelt after their fashion ; again Gabriel d'Amours had offered for them a prayer to the God of battles ; but no Joyeuse dreamed of suspecting that they were meditating surrender or flight. The king, with the brave Huguenot minister's prediction of victory still ringing in his ears,[1] plunged into the thickest of the fight, two horses' length ahead of his companions. That moment he forgot that he was King of France and general-in-chief, both in one, and fought as if he were a private soldier. It was, indeed, a bold venture. True, the enemy, partly because of the confusion induced by the reiters, partly from the rapidity of the king's movements, had lost in some measure the advantage they should have derived from their lances, and were compelled to rely mainly upon their swords as against the firearms of their opponents. Still, they outnumbered the knights of the king's squadron more than as two to one. No wonder that some of the latter flinched and actually turned back ;[2] especially when the standard-bearer of the king, receiving a deadly wound in the face, lost control of his horse, and went riding aimlessly about the field, still grasping the banner in grim desperation. But the greater number emulated the courage of their leader. The white plume kept them in the road to victory and to honor. Yet even this beacon seemed at one moment to fail them. Another cavalier, who had ostentatiously decorated his helmet much after the same fashion as the king, was slain in the hand-to-hand conflict, and some,

---

[1] " A la bataille d'Ivry vous me fistes faire la priere. Je vous dys que Dieu vous donneroit la victoire." D'Amours to Henry IV., June 20, 1593, Bulletin de la Société de l'histoire du Protestantisme français, i. 283.

[2] "Vous donnastes dans un gros de douse ou quinse cents lances mal suivi des vostres, car plusieurs de vostre gros tournerent visage." Ibid., ubi supra. So Sully's secretaries write: " Plusieurs de l'escadron du Roy s'enfuirent, et quasi toute la main gauche d'iceluy." Mémoires de Sully, c. 30.

both of the Huguenots and of their enemies, for a time supposed the great Protestant champion himself to have fallen.

But, although fiercely contested, the conflict was not long. The troopers of Mayenne wavered, and finally fled. Henry of Navarre emerged from the confusion, to the great relief of his anxious followers, safe and sound, covered with dust and blood not his own. More than once he had been in great personal peril. On his return from the mêlée, he halted, with a handful of companions, under the pear-trees indicated beforehand as a rallying-point, when he was descried and attacked by three bands of Walloon horse that had not yet engaged in the fight. Only his own valor and the timely arrival of some of his troops saved the imprudent monarch from death or captivity.

The rout of Mayenne's principal corps was quickly followed by the disintegration of his entire army. The Swiss auxiliaries of the League, though compelled to surrender their flags, were, as ancient allies of the crown, admitted to honorable terms of capitulation. To the French who fell into the king's hands he was equally clement. Indeed, he spared no efforts to save their lives.[1] But it was otherwise with the German lansquenets. Their treachery at Arques, where they had pretended to come over to the royal side only to turn upon those who had believed their protestations and welcomed them to their ranks, was yet fresh in the memory of all. They received no mercy at the king's hands.[2]

Gathering his available forces together, and strengthened by the accession of old Marshal Biron, who had been compelled,

---

[1] " Et est une chose digne vraiment de notre roi, que dedans la mêlée il avait cette parole souvent en la bouche, que l'on épargnât le sang des Français le plus qu'il serait possible." Lettres d'Étienne Pasquier (Ed. Feugère), ii. 343. According to the same writer, an officious valet having next day brought out the sword Henry had used in the battle, still bloody and dented, with particles of flesh and hair yet clinging to it, the prince at once commanded him to take out of his sight so palpable a mark of the horrors of war.

[2] Among many others, Gabriel d'Amours refers to this circumstance : " Je vous dys au champ de bataille, les Suisses n'estant encor rendus, lors qu'on tuoit des lansquenetz au coing d'ung boys pource qu'ils nous avoyent trahi à Arques." Bulletin de la Société de l'histoire du Protestantisme français, i. 283.

much against his will, to remain a passive spectator while others fought, Henry pursued the remnants of the army of the League many a mile to Mantes and the banks of the Seine.[1] If their defeat by a greatly inferior force had been little to the credit of either the generals or the troops of the League, their precipitate flight was still less decorous. The much-vaunted Flemish lancers distinguished themselves, it was said, by not pausing until they found safety beyond the borders of France, and Mayenne, never renowned for courage, emulated or surpassed them in the eagerness he displayed, on reaching the little town from which the battle took its name, to put as many leagues as possible between himself and his pursuers. "The enemy thus ran away," says the Englishman William Lyly, who was an eye-witness of the battle ; " Mayenne to Ivry, where the Walloons and reiters followed so fast that there standing, hasting to draw breath, and not able to speak, he was constrained to draw his sword to strike the flyers to make place for his own flight. "[2]

---

[1] The most full and accurate account of the battle of Ivry is undoubtedly the " Discours véritable de la victoire obtenue par le Roy en la bataille donne pres le village d'Yri (Yvry), le quatorziesme jour de Mars 1590 " (Mémoires de la Ligue, iv. 254–271), an official paper written, it is known, by one of the king's secretaries, M. de Fresne, sieur de Forget, for immediate publication. It is the " discours " referred to by Henry himself in his letter of March 25th, to M. de Luxembourg (Lettres missives, iii. 183, 184), as prepared by his orders and accompanying his letter. The descriptions in the Recueil des choses mémorables (Histoire des cinq rois), 716–720, and in Matthieu, Histoire des derniers troubles, liv. 5, fols. 16–20, are mere abridgments of the same, in great part reproducing the very words. Duplessis Mornay's Mémoire was written on the 16th of March, and contains general impressions of great value (Mémoires, iv. 473–477). Henry the Fourth's own letters, of March 14th and 25th, are of prime importance (Lettres missives, iii. 162 and 183). The letter of Longueville to Nevers, of March 17th (Mémoires de Nevers, ii. pref.), contains some particulars which an official account would scarcely be expected to insert. See, also, Mémoires de Sully, c. 30 ; De Thou, vii. 609–619 ; Agrippa d'Aubigné, iii. 228–233 ; Davila, 443–449 ; and Marshal Biron's letter to M. du Haillan, written from Mantes, March 24, 1590, printed in Daniel, Histoire de France, xi. 587–591. In this he remarks: " L'on me met de ceux qui ont part à la victoire, encores que je n'aye combattu."

[2] I am indebted for this quotation to Mr. Motley (United Netherlands, iii. 56), whose narrative of the battle is a beautiful example of the great historian's characteristic brilliancy of description. Among the conflicting state-

The battle had been a short one. Between ten and eleven
o'clock the first attack was made; in less than an hour the army
Brilliant suc- of the League was routed.[1] It had been a glorious
cess of Henry. action for the king and his old Huguenots, and not
less for the loyal Roman Catholics who clung to him. None
seemed discontented but old Marshal Biron, who, when he met
the king coming out of the fray with battered armor and blunted
sword, could not help contrasting the opportunity his majesty
had enjoyed to distinguish himself with his own enforced in-
activity,[2] and exclaimed: " Sire, this is not right! You have
to-day done what Biron ought to have done, and he has done
what the king should have done."[3] But even Biron was unable
to deny that the success of the royal arms surpassed all expectation, and deserved to rank among the wonders of history.
The preponderance of the enemy in numbers had been great.
There was no question that the impetuous attacks of their cavalry upon the left wing of the king were for a time almost
successful. The official accounts might conveniently be silent
upon the point, but the truth could not be disguised that at
the moment Henry plunged into battle a part of his line was
grievously shaken, a part was in full retreat, and the prospect
was dark enough. Some of his immediate followers, indeed,
at this time turned countenance and were disposed to flee, whereupon he recalled them to their duty with the words: " Look
this way, in order that, if you will not fight, at least you may

---

ments that have come down to us respecting the incidents of a somewhat
intricate engagement, it is not strange that Mr. Motley seems to have fallen
into a few mistakes. I need only refer here to the confusion of the names of
Baron Biron and his father. When the writer says that the heavy troopers of
Flanders and Hainault dashed upon old Marshal Biron, routing his cavalry,
charging clean up to the Huguenot guns and sabring the cannoneers, he for-
gets that that veteran officer was in reality on a distant part of the field, chafing
under the orders that forbade him from bringing his reserves into the action.

[1] Henry IV. to the Mayor of Langres, March 14, 1590, Mémoires de la Ligue,
iv. 274.

[2] " J'oubliois à vous dire qu'il y a eu beaucoup de cavalerie, où commandoit
M. le Mareschal de Biron, qui ne combattit point." Letter of M. de Longueville,
ubi supra. " Le Mareschal de Biron avec deux cents hommes de reserve
n'avoit point combatu." Agrippa d'Aubigné, iii. 232.

[3] Péréfixe, 118.

see me die." [1] But the steady and determined courage of the
king, well seconded by soldiers not less brave, turned the tide
of battle. "The enemy took flight," says the devout Duplessis
Mornay, "terrified rather by God than by men; for it is certain that the one side was not less shaken than the other." [2]
And with the flight of the cavalry, Mayenne's infantry, constituting, as has been seen, three-fourths of his entire army, gave
up the day as lost, without striking a blow for the cause they
had come to support. How many men the army of the League
lost in killed and wounded it is difficult to say. The Prince of
Parma reported to his master the loss of two hundred and seventy of the Flemish lancers, together with their commander, the
Count of Egmont. The historian De Thou estimates the entire
number of deaths on the side of the League, including the
combatants that fell in the battle and the fugitives drowned at
the crossing of the river Eure, by Ivry, at eight hundred. The
official account, on the other hand, agrees with Marshal Biron
in stating that of the cavalry alone more than fifteen hundred
died, and adds that four hundred were taken prisoners; while
Davila swells the total of the slain to the incredible sum of upward of six thousand men. [3]

Resting his pursuit at Rosny for the night, Henry retired,
with a very few of his followers, into a private chamber and
rendered thanks to God Almighty for so signal a victory.
"What think you of our work?" he asked his faithful Duplessis Mornay. "You have done the bravest act of folly that ever
was," replied the secretary; "for you have risked your kingdom on a throw of dice. But you have had the opportunity to

---

[1] Étienne Pasquier, Lettres (Œuvres choisies), ii. 342. M. de Longueville
is even more candid. He represents the king, at the moment of charging
Mayenne, as having seen "toute son avant-garde ébranslée." Mémoires de
Nevers, ubi supra. According to the military nomenclature of the times, the left
wing, under Montpensier, etc., constituted the "avant-garde," the centre and
right wing, the "bataille." Pierre Corneio says of the forces of the League :
"Dieu rabaissa tellement en un instant leur esperance, qu'en un quart d'heure
ils furent quasi maistres du champ, et en demi-quart d'heure depuis mis en
route et vaincus." Mémoires de la Ligue, iv. 297.

[2] Mémoires de Duplessis Mornay, iv. 475.

[3] Motley, De Thou, Discours véritable, Davila, Biron, etc., ubi supra.

learn that the lot is in God's hands, and the results must in
very deed be devoted to Him. Meantime, we all swear to fight
for your preservation; but we demand of you another oath to
secure our own safety—that henceforth you promise never to
fight in person." [1]

That very evening the Béarnais wrote an account of his exploit to the faithful Mayor of Langres. "It has pleased God,"
he said, "to grant me what most I desired—the opportunity to offer battle to my enemies, being confident that he would give me the victory, as has happened to-day.
. . . A battle has taken place, in which God has been pleased
to make known that His protection is ever on the side of right;
for in less than an hour after the enemy vented upon me their
wrath, in two or three charges made and sustained by them, all
their cavalry began to despair, abandoning their entire infantry, which was very numerous. Seeing this their Swiss had
recourse to my mercy and surrendered—colonels, captains, soldiers, and all their standards. The lansquenets and French
footmen had no leisure to come to this resolution; for there
were cut to pieces more than twelve hundred of each, while the
rest were taken prisoners or driven into the woods at the mercy
of the peasantry. Of their cavalry nine hundred to a thousand
were killed, and four or five hundred unhorsed or made prisoners, without reckoning their valets, who are in great numbers,
or those that were drowned at the crossing of the river Eure.
. . . The white ensign [the standard of the commanding
general] has fallen into my hands, together with the officer who
carried it; also, twelve or fifteen other colors of cavalry and
twice that number of colors of infantry, all the artillery and
countless lords taken prisoners. . . . It is a miraculous
work of God, who preserved me, and vouchsafed to give me this
resolution to attack them, and then the grace to be able to carry
it out so happily. His alone is the glory, while that part which
by permission may belong to men, is due to the princes, officers
of the crown, lords and captains of all the noblesse that flocked

Henry's own account.

---

[1] Mémoires de Madame de Mornay (Edition of the Historical Society of
France), 192.

hither with such eagerness, and deported themselves so successfully that their ancestors have left no more beautiful examples
of heroism than they will leave to their posterity." [1]

Had Henry and his victorious army pushed on at once to
the capital, instead of pausing at Mantes, as they did, for a
whole fortnight, there is every reason to believe that
Paris would have opened its gates at their approach,
and the war would have been virtually ended. [2]   The
League was overwhelmed with terror; the army was either destroyed or utterly demoralized.   No prompt assistance could be
expected from any quarter.   The disaster which had befallen
the Flemish auxiliaries, with the death of their young and arrogant leader, discredited for the time even the ability of Spain
to rescue its French allies.   The secret partisans of Henry
were as much elated as the " Sixteen " and their adherents were
dispirited.   A vigorous advance on the part of the king might
have given them the courage to assert themselves boldly.   La
Noue of the Iron Arm, than whom a better adviser could not
be found, warmly recommended that Henry should ride on at
the same pace with which he had come to Mantes, until he
should reach the gates of Paris.   Must the blame for the failure to carry out this plan be laid to the account of Henry himself ?   Must the blunder be classed with the examples of supineness and inability to reap the fruit of victories, which he had
given after the battle of Coutras and after the capture of the
faubourgs of Paris ?   Not primarily, nor altogether.   It was the
misfortune of Henry to have in his council Roman Catholics of
ability and influence, men who had hazarded life in his service
even in this last battle, men who were therefore really desirous
of his ultimate success, but would have been disappointed had
the Huguenot king been able, before the conversion of which

The king fails
to push his
victory.

---

[1] Henry IV. to Roussart, Mayor of Langres, Rosny, March 14, 1590, Mémoires
de la Ligue, iv. 273-276.

[2] Lestoile and Pierre Corneio, both of whom were well qualified to express
an opinion, agree on this point.   The former says that Henry could and should
have taken Paris ; the latter regards his delay, the result of intoxication with
success in the battle of Ivry, as a mark of the Divine intervention for the
salvation of Paris.   Mémoires de la Ligue, iv. 297, 298.

he held forth hopes, to obtain an easy and complete triumph over the last vestiges of the League. Religion gave a superficial coloring to their motives, but private interest was at the bottom the controlling power. Two names have come down to us of such disloyal advisers—old Marshal Biron and Monsieur d'O. The former knew that with the return of peace his own authority as chief military counsellor would be at an end; the royal pupil would be fully emancipated from the master's ferule. The latter, as superintendent of the finances, preferred that Paris should be taken by force rather than by peaceable means, for he looked with covetous eyes upon the probable confiscation of the municipal revenues. While the doughty old warrior dissuaded the king by raising up imaginary difficulties, the wily and unscrupulous treasurer had a hundred ways of presenting very real and insurmountable obstacles, in the form of an absolute deficiency of money to meet the demands of mercenary troops always clamorous at the most inopportune time.[1]

Marshal Biron and Monsieur d'O hinder the siege of Paris.

And so the golden opportunity was missed to conclude the struggle virtually at one blow. How much of disaster to France, of dishonor to the king himself, depended upon the die now cast, the world will never know. Three years later, Henry, wearied of protracted war, was told, and he believed the statement, that Paris was certainly worth a mass. If, by promptly following up his victory at Ivry, the son of Jeanne d'Albret had now gained possession of his capital, its later purchase at so heavy a price would have been unnecessary. It is, at any rate, doubtful whether the memory of the most chivalric

---

[1] Sully, in two passages (chapter 30 of the first part, and chapter 50 of the second part of his Œconomies royales), charges the delay upon a concerted plot of the "financiers," and in one of them particularizes Monsieur d'O. The second passage occurs in a letter written by Sully to Henry IV. in 1605, where he distinctly reminded his majesty that when Henry was anxious to proceed to the capture of Paris, "the men of your council and their followers made your army immovable, by causing it to be deficient of all things." Mézéray (Abrégé chronologique, vi. 26) inculpates both Biron and d'O, the former "parce qu'il craignoit que le Roy, lequel il traitoit comme son disciple, ne sortît, s'il faut ainsi parler, de dessous sa ferule," etc.

prince of the sixteenth century would have been tarnished by
the record of an insincere abjuration.

If by his delay the king hoped to give an opportunity to
Mayenne and the Parisians to return to a better mind, he was
greatly deceived.   The duke made use of the respite to write
to Philip and to the pope imploring aid.   In both his letters he cast the entire blame for the recent defeat upon the

The duke of
Mayenne im-
plores help of
Philip and
the pope.

German reiters, whom a few discharges of cannon
and a few arquebuse shots so terrified that they
promptly fled, and throwing themselves upon the
duke's own cavalry caused irremediable confusion.[1]
The tone of the letter to Philip was of abject supplication.
"Sire," wrote this very patriotic Frenchman to the king of a
rival country, "I protest that, whether strong or weak, I shall
never make default in any duty, and shall finish my days with
the fulfilment of the oath which I made and which I again
repeated in the letters I wrote to your majesty, on the departure of M. Tassis, which is that I shall rather die than be false
to it."   In return for which, he begged for money to raise
troops—money, the lack of which he said drove him to despair.[2]
To the pope Mayenne assumed the air of injured innocence,
and boldly reproached his holiness with having abandoned him
when engaged in the service of God.   And he did not conceal
his disgust that the head of the faithful should allow himself
to be swayed by purely human considerations, selfishly hoarding
up his treasures, shunning all expense, and remaining an idle and
uninterested spectator of the public calamities of Christendom.[3]

For, strange to say, the League had come to regard itself as
more Catholic than the pope himself, and, encouraged by the

Altered views
of Sixtus V.

example of Spain, looked at Sixtus as little better
than a favorer of heretics.   In truth, Sixtus had so
greatly changed his views respecting Henry the Fourth since he
despatched Cardinal Cajetan to France, that he appeared to be

---

[1] "La vraye cause de notre mal fust, que nos reistres estonnez de quelques
coups de canons et harquebuzes qui donnèrent parmi eux, s'enfuirent aussy-
tost en groz et se vindrent renverser sur ma cornette et trouppe." Mayenne
to Philip II., Soissons, March 22, 1590, De Croze, ii. 403.

[2] Ibid., ii. 405.   [3] Summary in De Thou, vii. 621.

acting at cross purposes with his legate, when this legate was merely following out his original instructions.   Sixtus the Fifth had from the commencement conceived for the chivalric prince an admiration which was heightened, rather than abated, by the undaunted boldness of Henry's attitude in respect to the papal bull of excommunication of 1585.   Recently his leanings in this direction had become more evident.   The Roman Catholic princes of the blood and great nobles of France who had espoused Henry's interests had sent Monseigneur de Luxembourg to Rome, and, in January, 1590, Sixtus had gone so far as to grant him an audience, despite the remonstrances of the Spanish party.   Nay, instead of closing his ears, the pope had listened with undisguised pleasure to the description Luxembourg gave of Henry's courage, goodness, and greatness of soul. "Now, truly," broke in the admiring pontiff, "I grieve that I have excommunicated him."   And when the envoy expressed the confident hope of the king's speedy conversion, Sixtus unhesitatingly declared that, in that case, he would embrace and comfort him.[1]

To say that the League and its ally, Philip of Spain, were annoyed is but to express half the truth.   They were indignant, they were enraged.   In Paris Sixtus was denounced as a miser that wanted only to enrich his relations at the expense of the public treasure.[2]   In Spain a Jesuit preacher from the pulpit declared, that not only the republic of Venice but the pope himself countenanced the heretics.   At Rome, upon the very day on which Mayenne indited

He is denounced as a miser and an encourager of heresy.

---

[1] Ranke, History of the Popes, 222.

[2] Nevers, in a letter to Sixtus V., prefixed to his "Traité des causes et des raisons de la prise des armes," boldly tells him of some of the accusations laid to his charge, as, for example, that he winked at the Duke of Savoy's designs on Provence, because he hoped either to annex a part of it to the Comtât Venaissin, or, at least, to induce the duke to hold it from the pope as lord paramount.   Respecting his accumulated wealth he remarks: "On a publié que quelqu'un se plaignant du peu de secours que V. S. donnoit, au prejudice de la promesse que Monsieur le Cardinal de Montalto avoit faite de vostre part à MM. du Conseil General de l'union estably à Paris, on luy avoit respondu que les cinq millions d'or qui sont le sang et la moëlle de vos sujets, n'avoient pas esté ramassez dans le chasteau Sainct Ange [San Angelo] pour les employer

his two letters to Philip and to Sixtus, the Spanish ambassador undertook to lodge with the irascible pontiff a formal protest in his master's name against that pontiff's behavior. Six-

Philip protests against his conduct.

tus was furious, interrupted, upbraided, threatened, blustered; but, after all, the ambassador succeeded in telling the pope on bended knee all the unpalatable things he had come to utter. More zealous for the faith than the so-called Vicar of Jesus Christ, Philip, by the mouth of his ambassador, demanded that Sixtus should declare all " Navarre's " adherents indiscriminately excommunicate, and pronounce " Navarre" himself incapable of holding the crown of France under all circumstances and forever. "If not," said the ambassador, " the Catholic king will renounce his allegiance to your holiness; for he cannot suffer the cause of Christ to be ruined." [1]

Meantime, quite indifferent to the change that had taken place in Sixtus, his legate, Cardinal Cajetan, now at a safe distance, pursued his old way undisturbed, and urged the Parisians to persist in relentless hostility to the Huguenot king.

That king, having lost the chance of taking his capital by a single blow, tardily moved to the south of the city and took

Henry lays siege to Paris.

Corbeil and Melun on the upper Seine, and Lagny on the Marne, together with some more distant points— Crécy-en-Brie, Montereau, Provins. It was evident that Henry had not idly placed his hand upon the sources of supply of hungry Paris, and that but a slight tightening of his grasp would be necessary to make the citizens feel their folly in neglecting betimes to provide themselves with a good store of the necessaries of life. The assurances of speedy victory with which Mayenne and the preachers had fed the credulous populace had had the effect of leading them to forego the most ordinary precautions. The moment, however, the citizens saw the hated

---

à soustenir la cause de Dieu, mais bien pour enrichir vos parents, et donner moyen à ceux qui espouseront Mesdames vos niepces, d'acquitter leurs debtes." As the letter is dated August, 1590, Sixtus probably died before it reached Rome. It is printed at the head of the second volume of the Mémoires de Nevers.

[1] Ranke, History of the Popes, 222-224.

prince calmly settling down at the bridge of Charenton, close to the confluence of the principal rivers, they awoke from their dream of fancied security. " Paris is a great body that cannot long endure the inconveniences of a siege," Mayenne wrote to Philip the Second, only eight days after the battle of Ivry, and the truth of the statement was now to be put to the test of experience.[1]

The Parisians made good use of the short respite allowed them by Henry's tardiness. They elected the Duke of Nemours governor of the city. Provisions were hastily brought in from the neighborhood. It was perhaps characteristic of the times and of the country that over against three thousand hogsheads of wheat, oats and other grain thus introduced, there figured in the account more than ten thousand hogsheads of wine. The fortifications, too, were not forgotten. Walls, in places so ruinous that the people were in the habit of clambering over them in preference to going around by the gates, were repaired and strengthened. All the cannon that had graced the ramparts, with the exception of a single one, had been taken away to be used in recent battles, and had fallen into the hands of the enemy. The Parisians set themselves so vigorously to work that, before many weeks, they mustered sixty-five pieces of the rude kind in use toward the close of the sixteenth century. The display of devotion to the cause of the League was great. The poor labored at the public works, the rich contributed of their means. On all sides it was agreed that Paris should never submit to a heretical king. A frenzy took possession of all classes. The preachers were especially distinguished for their zeal, thundering from the pulpit against Henry of Bourbon—that was the most courteous designation they ever applied to him—and extolling the piety of resistance to his claims. Neither in church nor in street did any one dare contradict them—a circumstance that creates no surprise in view of the fact that more than a score of persons had been summarily put to death without judge or form of trial, or had been

Active preparations of the Parisians.

---

[1] " C'est un gros corps qui ne peult supporter longtemps les incommoditéz d'un siége." Mayenne to Philip II., March 22, 1590, De Croze, ii. 405.

thrown into the Seine, for the mere suggestion that it would be better to make peace with the victor of Ivry.

On the seventh day of May the Sorbonne—the "sacred faculty of theology," as it loved to be styled—on being consulted by the municipal officers as to whether, should "Charles the Tenth" die, or resign in favor of "Henry of Bourbon," the latter ought to be recognized as legitimate king, rendered a long decision in the negative. That very day Henry of Bourbon encamped before the city, from the Porte Saint Antoine and the Bastile, to the Porte Montmartre, and the next day "Charles the Tenth"—otherwise called Cardinal Bourbon, expired at Fontenay-le-Comte, in Poitou. The former fact interested the Parisians, at present, more than did the latter; for the "heretical king" promptly burned every windmill on the hills about the capital, and reduced the citizens to the dreary use of mills worked by hand or turned by horses, and the horses were presently needed for other purposes.

The Sorbonne decides against Henry of Bourbon.

Death of old Cardinal Bourbon.

It was not long before a serious problem confronted those in authority. How long would the existing provisions hold out? A careful census was made—more accurate, we may believe, than any previous attempt at enumerating the population. The largest city of France, some said of Christendom, was found to contain two hundred and twenty thousand souls.[1] At a pound of bread a day, the supply of grain might last a month from date, that is, from the twenty-sixth of May. Paris was no place for beggars and useless persons. Thirty thousand such had been ordered to leave the city, but the order had been negligently executed; and now, when the supernumeraries attempted to go they were driven back by the besiegers.

It was all-important to keep up the enthusiasm of the people: so their piety and their worldly hopes were in turn appealed to. One day it was a grand ecclesiastical procession that showed itself, with Rose, bishop of Senlis, at its head as commander-in-chief, and monks and friars, from grave Carthusian to sordid

---

[1] So says Lestoile, ii. 16, but Pierre Corneio makes the number only a round 200,000.   Mémoires de la Ligue, iv. 303.

Franciscan, walking four abreast, each order marshalled by its own prior. A halbert or an arquebuse in one hand, a crucifix in the other, the members of this "church militant," as its admirers called it, passing in review before the papal legate, presented a singular mixture of the churchman and the soldier; for though the gown was trussed up and the cowl thrown back, the color of the dress betrayed the wearer's profession, despite helmet and breastplate. The only mishap that marred the scenic effect was the result of the awkwardness of one of the good fathers in handling his gun, and Cardinal Cajetan, having had his almoner shot dead at his side, might certainly be pardoned for requesting that no more salutes should be fired in his presence. Meanwhile the people were fed on the constant assurance that help was on its way, that Philip would soon have an army at their gates; and in proof of the truth of the assertion, the empty farce of sending and receiving pretended messengers to and from Parma in the Netherlands was sedulously kept up for the popular benefit.

But enthusiastic preaching—even that of Father Pierre Cristin, likened for his eloquence to Demosthenes himself—
Progress of the famine. could not feed empty stomachs. Food became more and more scarce. The rich, renouncing unattainable luxuries, were reduced to oaten bread, and to the flesh of asses, mules and horses. The poor could not even afford these viands, for they had not the opportunity to earn even a liard, and articles of food once cheap, or even rejected with disdain, now commanded extravagant prices. An uninviting porridge made of bran was all they could procure for themselves. Even the scanty alms in money occasionally doled out seemed an empty mockery. The Spanish ambassador, one day, as he passed by the parliament house in company with the Archbishop of Lyons, met a crowd of poor people crying for hunger, and bade his attendants throw them handfuls of halfpence coined
Visitation of the religious houses. with the Spanish arms. But the multitude hardly took the trouble to pick them up. "Ah, sir," they piteously exclaimed, "throw us bread, for we are dying of hunger." The incident had one good effect; it led to an enforced visitation of the monastic and other great estab-

lishments. The rector of the Jesuits tried to beg off; but the prévôt des marchands administered a severe rebuke. "Your prayer, master rector," said he, "is neither civil nor Christian. Has it not been found necessary that all that have grain should offer it for sale, in order to meet the public need? Why should you be exempted from this visitation? Is your life of greater price than ours?" When the abashed rector reluctantly admitted the officers into the Jesuit house, they found that the prudent members had a store of wheat and hay, of biscuit and salt meat, that would have lasted them a full year. Others had been scarcely less provident. The members of the Capuchin order, an order at that time not over sixty-five years old, seemed to have forgotten the stringent vows of poverty distinguishing them even from the parent order of St. Francis. The people who had understood that the Capuchins lived only upon daily alms and distributed whatever remained over night to the poor, were scandalized when they discovered their house well furnished with food. The result of the investigation was that the monks were forced to share their supplies with the destitute. An enumeration of the dwellings of the poor revealed the fact that there were twelve thousand three hundred houses coming under this designation. In seven thousand and three hundred a little money was still to be found; the inmates of five thousand had neither bread nor money. Thereupon it was ordered that, for the space of a fortnight, the ecclesiastics should give to the extremely poor gratis, and to the others on presentation of a token stamped with the municipal arms, a pound of bread a day for each person. The appointed term over, famine pressed with redoubled force. Prayers and litanies, eight days' devotions, processions multiplied. Vows were made. The citizens gathered in the Hôtel de Ville, voted to send a lamp and a boat of silver to Our Lady of Loretto, in case of deliverance. Still the price of food steadily advanced. Nothing was cheap any longer, Lestoile tells us, but sermons.

In the village that clustered around the neighboring abbey church of Saint Denis, matters were even worse. The populace were reduced to rations of four ounces of bread a day. Happily

Saint Denis capitulated on the ninth of July, and the Parisians had only themselves to think about.[1]

And now men bethought them of Sancerre and its marvellous experiences of seventeen years before; and doubtless Jean de Léry's story of the famine became a very serviceable "cookery book for the besieged." The Roman Catholics of Paris learned from the Huguenots of Sancerre the art of making the very refuse of the city a means of sustaining human life. Dogs, cats, rats and mice were eagerly sought for and devoured. Decoctions of herbs took the place of wine, and were sold on the squares which but a few weeks ago had echoed to the cry of good Malmsey. Presently recourse was had to the skins of animals, first rendered soft by being soaked and boiled in water. Money would hardly buy for the rich, when ill, the most essential delicacies. A man was lucky if a crown of silver would secure a pound of bread. A pound of butter, usually worth four sous, commanded thirty times that sum. For a single egg more was asked than the amount of a laboring man's wages for a day. Men, women and children were dying in the streets—one hundred and fifty or two hundred every twenty-four hours. "I have seen the poor eating dead dogs all raw in the streets," says Pierre Corneio. "I have seen others devouring the entrails that had been cast into the gutter; others mice and rats that had been similarly thrown away." Expedients still more revolting were resorted to. In a company, at an earlier time in the siege, Don Bernardino, much to the disgust of some present, recounted how that in a city besieged by the Persians, bread had been manufactured of

The besieged have recourse to strange food.

---

[1] While in Saint Denis, Henry the Fourth took occasion to enter the abbey church, and inspect the sepulchres of the kings and queens of France. Standing near the tomb of Henry the Second, he noticed with particular satisfaction that since his last visit Catharine de' Medici had been laid at rest beside her husband. Doubtless remembering well the time of the Conference of Nérac, when the late queen mother waged war against him " as a lioness," the years when she would neither rest quietly in her own bed nor permit him to rest in his, the king observed to himself, but in tones quite audible to those about him, that it was just the best place for her—" O qu'elle est bien là ! " Lestoile, ii. 23.

human bones reduced to powder. Now the abominable experiment was tried in Paris with remains disinterred from the Cimetière des Innocents. The people made a grim jest of it and called it Madame de Montpensier's bread, but all that tasted of it died. The horrible story is no fiction. "I saw it with my own eyes," writes Corneio; while Lestoile informs us that he long kept a piece of the duchess's bread among his curious relics. In one instance at least, a wretched mother is said to have subsisted for some days upon the salted flesh of her own dead children. These children had died of hunger; but there were other children whom the German lansquenets, maddened by privation, hunted down like dogs in the streets, and killed and ate.[1]

Meanwhile Mendoza and Cajetan, with the cohort of preachers, endeavored to keep up the people's courage, giving freely of their money and of such food as they could dispense. What was lacking the legate made up with indulgences, assuring every one that death in so holy a cause was a sure passport to paradise. But the growing restiveness of the populace, more and more distinctly clamoring for bread or peace, could not be repressed. At last a council, to which the leading nobles, the parliament, and the chief burghers were invited, found it necessary to yield so far to a movement now becoming formidable, as to depute Cardinal Gondy, Bishop of Paris, and the Archbishop of Lyons to visit Henry of Bourbon, and ascertain whether some universal peace for the entire kingdom could not be secured. Now, as

Cardinal Gondy and the Archbishop of Lyons sent to the king.

---

[1] The two best and fullest narratives are that of Lestoile (Edition Michaud and Poujoulat), ii. 15–30, and that of Pierre Corneio, entitled "Discours bref et veritable des choses plus notables arrivees au siege memorable de la renommee ville de Paris, et defense d'icelle par monseigneur le Duc de Nemours, contre le Roy de Navarre," in Mémoires de la Ligue, iv. 296–325. The Leaguer Corneio's story must be read in connection with two other relations, written by loyalists, inserted in the same collection (iv. 326–337, and 337–340), one of which, "Brief traité des misères de la ville de Paris," is particularly valuable. The accounts given by De Thou and other historians are derived from these sources almost exclusively. M. Alfred Franklin has republished (Paris, 1876) an interesting contemporary French translation of an Italian relation, from a MS. in the Mazarin Library, under the title, "Journal du siége de Paris en 1590, redigé par un des assiégés."

this same Henry of Bourbon was the prince whom the pope
had expressly excommunicated, as not only a heretic but a
relapsed heretic, declaring him incapable of succeeding to the
throne of France, the two prelates were naturally solicitous ,lest
in undertaking the negotiations with him they should bring
upon themselves the censures of the church.   They applied to
the legate for a full discharge, but Cajetan would not grant one
until he had obtained from three doctors of theology a favorable reply to the questions he submitted to them.[1]   The envoys
next sought a safe-conduct from the king, to meet him at Saint
Denis; but Henry graciously granted them an audience nearer
the capital, in the old abbey of Saint Antoine des Champs,
whither he himself rode, with a goodly retinue of a thousand or
twelve hundred gentlemen.   The venerable ecclesiastical establishment where the meeting took place stood about two-thirds
of a mile from the Bastile and from the gate to which it gave its
name, on the road to the Bois de Vincennes.   The city has long
since taken the abbey—now transformed into a hospital—and
its spacious gardens, into its ever-widening embrace.

It was between noon and one o'clock that the envoys entered
the cloisters.   To their respectful greeting the king returned a
kindly welcome, and conducted them to an upper room, to hear
the message they brought.   Meantime the Huguenot gentlemen
of Henry's suite crowded close upon their monarch and his
guests, in a manner that somewhat excited the surprise of the
latter.   But the Béarnais's native wit readily found an excuse

---

[1] The doctors consulted were Panigarole, Tirius, rector of the Jesuits, and
Robert Bellarmin, the most celebrated controversialist the Roman Catholic
Church has ever produced, whom Sixtus had sent with his legate into France.
The points submitted were : "Whether persons surrendering a city to an
heretical prince, by reason of the necessity of famine, are excommunicated ?
Whether in going to an heretical prince in order to convert him, or in order
to better the condition of the Catholic Church, they incur the excommunication pronounced by the bull of Sixtus the Fifth ?"   The doctors replied :
" _Negativé_, quod non incurrunt."   Recueil de ce qui s'est passé en la conference des Sieurs Cardinal de Gondi et Archevesque de Lion avec le Roy,
reprinted in Mémoires de la Ligue, iv. 340–347.   This account was written,
as appears from its statement, on the 7th of August, the next day after the
conference.

for the apparent want of decorum, in the circumstance that his fearless braves were more used to the mêlée of the scene of conflict than to the nice etiquette of court receptions. " Be not astonished," said he to the prelates, " if I am so hard pressed ; I am still more hard pressed when I enter into battle." [1]   A word from their master, following this flattering speech, made the attendants part and leave a clear passage.

The cardinal-bishop was chief spokesman on the side of the League. He depicted in lively colors the miserable condition of France, which had induced the Parisians to send the present deputation to his majesty to beg him to apply a remedy, and, that the peace might be general, to permit them to go and confer with the Duke of Mayenne. Moreover, to enforce his request, he warned the king that Paris might imitate the desperate courage of the city of Ghent, or the endurance which little Sancerre had displayed, in defence of life and religion. Henry heard him out very patiently ; he even made no positive objection to recognizing their credentials, though but a simple determination of sundry deputies held in the Chambre Saint Louis, wherein he was styled merely King of Navarre. But he absolutely refused to have his city of Paris undertake the office of mediator. " I would gladly give a finger to have a battle; I would give two fingers for a general peace; but I can-

Henry's re-
ply to the   not grant what you ask." Besides, he objected on the
envoys.
              score of humanity to the delay entailed by negotiations for a general peace. The number of deaths was already great ; but if the famine must continue eight or ten days longer, ten or twenty thousand lives more might be sacrificed. " I am the true father of my people," Henry exclaimed, " I am like the true mother whom Solomon judged. I would almost rather have no Paris, than have it all in ruins after the destruction of so many poor people. Not so with the partisans of the League. No wonder ; they are all Spaniards or Hispaniolized." He touched upon the daily loss incurred by the faubourgs of Paris,

---

[1] " Ne trouvez estrange si je suis ainsi pressé, encores davantage aux batailles." Recueil de ce qui s'est passé en la conference des Sieurs Cardinal de Gondi et Archevesque de Lion avec le Roy. Mémoires de la Ligue, iv. 340.

and addressing himself to Gondy individually, he said: "You, cardinal, ought to have compassion. These are the sheep of your fold; for the smallest drop of their blood you will have to give an account before God. And so will you, too, Archbishop of Lyons, who occupy the rank of primate over all the other bishops. I am not much of a theologian, but I know enough to tell you that. God does not expect you thus to treat the poor people whom He has intrusted to your care, especially for the sake of gratifying the King of Spain, Bernardino Mendoza, and the legate. You will have your feet well scorched for it in the other world. How do you expect to convert me to your religion, if you make so little account of the lives and salvation of your flock? It is giving me poor proof of your sanctity!"

The archbishop did not relish the imputation of being turned into a Spaniard; but he must have been somewhat confounded Philip's claim to Paris. when the king produced, in evidence of the disloyalty of the League, an intercepted letter of Philip the Second wherein the writer had the effrontery to recommend that measures be taken to preserve for him "his city of Paris," inasmuch as, should he lose it, his prosperity would be seriously affected.[1]

The cardinal undertook to make an insincere apology for the attempt to treat for a general peace. Should Paris yield and admit the king, its doom would be sealed. It would at once be besieged by the united forces of the King of Spain and the Duke of Mayenne, and most probably be captured; at any rate, three-fourths of its population would desert it. Thereupon the king's anger took fire. He looked proudly round upon his nobles and said: "Let the King of Spain come with all his allies! By God, we shall beat them thoroughly and show them clearly that the French noblesse knows how to defend itself." Then correcting himself: "I have sworn, contrary to my custom; but I tell you again that, by the living God, we will not endure that disgrace." The gentlemen who stood by emulously took the

---

[1] "Au surplus, je vous monstrerai une lettre, par laquelle le Roy d'Espagne mande qu'on lui conserve sa ville de Paris; car, s'il la perd, ses affaires vont tres mal." Ibid., iv. 343.

oath each for himself, while Henry proceeded to inform the prelates that, should Paris be deserted by a few bad citizens, he would himself speedily repeople it with one hundred thousand trusty men, both rich and loyal.   In fact, wherever he went he would make his Paris.

The interview was long and animated.   While Henry refused the request of the prelates, he offered Paris free forgiveness, if its citizens would pledge themselves to surrender the place—unless it were succored, or a general peace were made—within eight days.   "If they accept this condition," said he, "in eight days they will be in quiet.   If they expect to wait to capitulate when they shall have but one day's provisions, I shall let them dine and sup that day, on the morrow they will have to give themselves up with the halter—*corde*—about their necks, instead of the mercy—*miséricorde*—which I offer them.   I shall take away the wretchedness—*misère*—and they will have the *corde*." Nor did Henry fail, before he concluded, to take exception to the comparison the cardinal had instituted between the Parisians, on the one hand, and the Protestant inhabitants of Sancerre and the determined burghers of Ghent, on the other.   The people of Sancerre subjected themselves to unheard-of privations, because they were threatened with the loss of their lives, their property, and their faith ; whereas their rightful monarch was only desirous of restoring to the Parisians the lives that Mendoza, the Spaniard, was taking away from them by famine. As to religion, all the Roman Catholic princes and gentlemen present could abundantly testify what treatment they received, and whether their consciences were constrained or their freedom of worship was interfered with in the slightest degree.   So also was it with regard to their possessions.   The illustration drawn from Ghent was equally bad.   "The Parisians," said Henry, "have sufficiently shown what amount of courage they have, in allowing their suburbs to be taken.   I have five thousand gentlemen here that will not suffer themselves to be treated in Ghentish fashion." [1]

---

[1] I have followed in the text the account above referred to, "Recueil de ce qui s'est passé," etc., upon which the narratives of De Thou and others are

Whatever might be said of the patient endurance of the Parisians, the facts of the case certainly seemed fully to bear out the charge of pusillanimity and cowardice brought against them by the king. The besieging force, though considerably increased during the progress of the siege, never approached the total number of twenty thousand men—perhaps did not exceed, at any one time, fifteen thousand. [1] The Duke of Nemours, on the other hand, had within the city some eight Pusillanimity thousand mercenary troops; while of the citizens of the capital. themselves fully fifty thousand were men in the prime of life, one-third of them possessed of some military training, all of them furnished with arms, all raised to the highest pitch of enthusiasm by the ardent declamations of their preachers. Yet no sortie of any magnitude was ever attempted. After the seizure of the faubourgs the royal army was, of necessity, so distributed that only a small detachment—not over twelve or thirteen hundred men—could be spared to blockade each gate. Against any one of these a fearless and skilful leader of brave troops could, at any moment, have hurled an overwhelming mass of twenty thousand men, and these, in all human probability, must have been victorious before the half-hour or more had expired which would have been needed to bring reinforcements from the neighboring gates. But the Parisians made no such

chiefly based. Motley (United Netherlands, iii. 66–68) gives some interesting particulars respecting the interview derived from a letter of W. Lyly to Sir E. Stafford, despatched the day after that on which the "Recueil" was written.

[1] De Thou, vii. 649, makes it consist, on its arrival before Paris, of 10,000 foot and 3,000 horse, but states that it received large accessions, especially the 4,000 foot and 1,000 horse brought from Guyenne by Viscount Turenne. The Recueil des choses mémorables, p. 721, and Corneio, Mémoires de la Ligue, iv. 304, make the original numbers 12,000 foot and 3,000 horse; Corneio swells these subsequently, ibid., iv. 320, to 12,000 or 13,000 foot and 3,500 horse. Agrippa d'Aubigné, iii. 233, says 14,000 foot and 2,500 horse. But Henry IV. himself, in a letter to Montmorency, dated St. Denis, July 22, 1590, speaking of his army as containing "la plus belle troupe de noblesse ensemble qu'il y eut peut-estre de trente ans en France," makes it consist of rather over than under 3,000 gentlemen serving on horseback, 6,000 Swiss and German lansquenets, and more than 6,000 French foot soldiers. Lettres missives, iii. 228.

dash. They preferred to see themselves hemmed in by an inferior number of Huguenots and royalists, to making a single desperate venture. Thirteen thousand persons—some said
thirty thousand persons—died of actual starvation, or of the
diseases engendered by want; still the besieged did not move
from the fatal spot, with arms in their hands, determined to
free themselves of the besiegers or die in the attempt.[1]

The loss of life would have been still greater had it not been
for the humanity of Henry the Fourth. In their desperation,
many of the besieged let themselves down over the walls, into
the ditch, and made their way to the royal outposts.
Tenderheart-
edness of the The cries and the tears of these poor persons accom-
king.
plished with his majesty what entreaty had been unable to effect earlier in the siege. He granted permission to
the number they asked—three thousand, it is said—to pass
through his lines; but, in point of fact, more than four thousand took advantage of the opportunity to gain the open country.[2] The Duke of Nemours was glad to have them go; for he
was relieved of the necessity of trying to find food for so many
famishing men. But there were others who condemned Henry's
mercy as ill-timed, and prejudicial to his own interests. In
fact, we are admitted just here to a very instructive view of
Queen Eliza- the contrast between the characters of two of the
beth finds fault. principal actors upon the stage of history in the sixteenth century. Queen Elizabeth, now fifty-seven years of age,
was so far from showing any feminine compassion for the per-

---

[1] Agrippa d'Aubigné, iii. 233–236, discusses the matter in a very forcible
manner.

[2] Brief traité des misères de la ville de Paris, in Mémoires de la Ligue, iv.
331. "En fin son bon naturel rompit la barriere des loix militaires. Il ac-
corda premierement passeport pour toutes les femmes et filles et enfans; et
pour tous les escoliers qui voudroyent sortir; il augmenta depuis pour les
religieux et gens d'église. Il passa à la fin jusques à ceux qui avoyent esté ses
plus cruels ennemis, et eut soin que sortans ils fussent humainement recueillis
et receus en toutes ses villes où ils se sont voulus retirer." Sommaire discours de ce qui est advenu en l'armee du roy, depuis que le duc de Parme s'est
joinct à celle des ennemis jusques au quinziesme de ce mois de Septembre, in
Mémoires de la Ligue, iv. 351. This last document was prepared for despatch
to all royal governors, etc.

ishing men, women, and children of Paris, that she scolded her
ally roundly for his folly in letting so many persons go out of
the city, whose presence would have compelled its surrender.
"If God, in His merciful favor, shall grant you victory," she
wrote to him, "I swear to you (if I dare say so) it will be
more than by your carelessness you deserve."[1]   And Henry
the Fourth, more than a score of years her junior, was com-

Henry defends pelled to justify himself, and endeavor to prove that
his conduct.   he had in no wise contributed to lengthen out the
siege. The Duchess of Montpensier and her partisans would
have remorselessly allowed the poor refugees, if driven back,
to perish before their eyes, as so many others had died. He
asserted, moreover, that, even had the royal permission been
denied, the fugitives would have contrived to pass the lines.
The most stony heart, among the soldiers, must have melted
at the sight of so much wretchedness.[2]

It was not the only time that the nature of Henry of Bourbon, full of humane feeling, stood in advantageous relief over
against the unsympathetic and calculating character of the daughter of Henry Tudor.

By the close of August it seemed that the supply of food was
almost absolutely exhausted, and that in two or three days the
city must certainly fall into the hands of the king. At this critical moment, however, the coming of the Prince of Parma was
announced. Reluctantly yielding to the importunity of Mayenne
and to the positive orders of Philip the Second, Alexander Far-

Opportune   nese had passed the northern borders of France, and,
approach of   by an almost direct march, marching through Guise,
the Duke of
Parma.   Soissons and La Ferté-Milon, had reached Meaux, on
the Marne, twenty-eight miles east of Paris. He brought with
him from Flanders a force almost precisely as large as that with
which Henry had begun the siege of his capital—three thousand
horse and twelve thousand foot; but, including the troops of

---

[1] "Si Dieu vous donne la victoire de sa grace misericordieuse, je vous jure que
ce sera plus que (si je l'ose dire) par vostre nonchaillance, pourrés meriter."
Queen Elizabeth to Henry IV. (without date), in Lettres missives, iii. 285.

[2] Henry IV. to Beauvoir, October, 1590, Lettres missives, iii. 285, 286.

Mayenne, with whom he now formed a junction, he had at his command an army numbering five thousand horse and eighteen thousand foot.[1] His object was evident. He had not come so much to fight the battles of the League as to relieve Paris of the sore famine that was crushing it, and his first blow must be struck at Lagny and Corbeil, which prevented the supplies from the upper Marne and Seine from entering the city.

Opinions differed much among the counsellors of the king as to the course to be adopted. Should Henry continue the siege, or, abandoning the fruits of so many months' labor, should he go out and meet Parma upon the open field? It was a grave question, and it was to be decided at once. Perplexity of the king. Henry had sent forward a detachment of cavalry as far as to Claye, within ten miles of Meaux, and these had driven in the outposts of the enemy. La Noue, with the experience of a lifetime to guide him, advocated the plan of retaining a portion of the royal army in its present position about Paris, and continuing the siege without intermission. The rest he would have thrown forward to Claye, where, in a narrow place, with the Biberonne, a little tributary of the Marne, in front, and woods and a marsh in close proximity, even an inferior force would enjoy many advantages for holding at bay or defeating a larger one. At any rate, it could delay the enemy's progress, until in an emergency the whole body of the royalist army might be collected together.[2] Others held that, in view of the cowardice shown by the Parisians, a very trifling band of Huguenots would be sufficient to keep the present positions, so as to allow most of the army to make the advance. Duplessis Mornay regarded three thousand men as all-sufficient to hold the Université, or southern half of Paris, in a state of siege; and this was the only side from which provisions could be introduced during the king's advance.[3] Viscount Turenne reaching the royal camp

---

[1] Motley, United Netherlands, iii. 74-76.

[2] Agrippa d'Aubigné, iii. 238; Mémoires de Villeroy (Edition Michaud-Poujoulat), 160. See Davila, 475.

[3] Mémoires de Madame de Mornay (Edition of the Historical Society of France) 197.

just at this juncture, indeed, offered to guard the posts which the
king's troops might leave, with the three or four thousand arquebusiers and the few hundred horsemen he had brought from
Guyenne.[1]   But Marshal Biron thought, or pretended to think,
otherwise. He magnified the danger of a general sortie of a score of thousand armed men from the walls
of Paris upon the handful of royalists left to keep
them in.   He ridiculed the idea that a French detachment at
Claye could find the opportunity to inflict damage upon the
well-disciplined Spaniards under Parma's command.   He urged
the advantage arising from the courage which a general advance
would inspire in the breasts of the king's followers.   It is needless, perhaps, to inquire whether the marshal erred in judgment,
or, as is more probable, purposely chose to lengthen out the war
in revenge for the king's failure to confer upon him, according
to promise, the sovereignty of the county of Périgord.[2]   Such
charges of disloyalty might be dismissed with incredulity and
treated with contempt, were it not but too certain that a very
considerable party among the Roman Catholics of the royal
army were impatient of the delay in the monarch's promised instruction, and would prefer that Paris should be relieved rather
than see it fall into the hands of a Huguenot king.   It was
notorious that breadstuffs found their way into the capital, from
time to time, through the connivance of officials in Henry's employ, whose lukewarmness was equalled only by the readiness
they displayed to receive bribes at the hands of the besieged.[3]

Unfortunately the marshal's advice coincided but too fully

[1] Agrippa d'Aubigné, iii. 238.

[2] Ibid., ubi supra ; Mémoires de Sully, c. 31.—M. Poirson (Histoire du règne
de Henri IV., i. 251) does not hesitate to style Marshal Biron " the true author
of the deliverance of Paris."

[3] " Plus vous vous souviendrez," says Sully in his remarkable letter of
reminder to Henry IV., " comme quelque temps après vous voulustes essayer
d'affamer Paris, mais vous fustes si mal servy par tous ceux qui ne vouloient
point de roy huguenot dans Paris, que tous les gouverneurs des places voisines
laissans passer les vivres à puissance, et les chefs des troupes assiegeantes les
laissans entrer librement dans Paris, pour de l'argent et des babioles, ils leur
donnerent moyen et loisir d'attendre un secours, pour estre fournis de vivres."
Mémoires de Sully, chap. 49 of part ii. (vol. iv. pp. 265, 266, ed. of 1663.)

with Henry's inclinations. Siege operations were less to his taste than the prospect of a battle which might once for all decide the issue of the war. Not but that, the night before he withdrew his troops from before Paris, his anxiety was great. And his anxiety, as was so often the case with this strangely inconsistent prince, displayed itself in professions of deep sorrow for his sins and earnest supplications for the divine mercy, which struck the sole bystander as utterances of genuine feeling. When Duplessis Mornay, returning from the discharge of a commission intrusted to him by his majesty, entered Henry's chamber at Saint Denis, he found him wakeful and with mind and heart interested in religious matters. He rose from his bed, and, calling for the Huguenot psalter, read several of Marot's and Beza's translations, apposite, as he thought, to the circumstances; then requested Duplessis Mornay to offer up a prayer. The king's devotion was evidently sincere · it was, to all appearance, very superficial and evanescent.[1]

The story may be apocryphal that, having once made up his mind to follow Biron's advice, the gay monarch laughingly charged La Noue with having given a contrary suggestion through fear that he might again fall a prisoner into the hands of the enemy, and be obliged to endure another captivity in Flemish dungeons.[2] However this may be, on the thirtieth of August Parma learned, greatly to his relief, that the King of France had withdrawn all his troops from before Paris; and that, instead of holding the strong position of Claye, he had drawn up his army, as though for battle, full ten miles nearer Paris, on the plain of Bondy. As Parma did not make his appearance, Henry advanced the next day to the village of Chelles, confident that now at length he would have an opportunity to cross swords with the only living

Henry withdraws from Paris. August 30, 1590.

---

[1] "Revenant à St. Denis, il trouva le roy tout seul en son lict, qui l'entendant, se leva en robe de nuict, s'enquit ce qu'il avoit faict, puis luy demanda ses Psalmes, en leut quelques uns à propos de ce qui se présentoit, et luy commanda de faire la priere ; et est certain que le roy estoit en anxiété et monstroit un cœur douloureux de ses fautes et avoit un grand recours à la miséricorde de Dieu." Mémoires de Madame de Mornay (Edition of the Historical Society of France), 198.			[2] Lestoile, ii. 31.

man whose military reputation equalled or surpassed his own. In this hope, however, he was doomed to disappointment. Parma had no name to make; his exploits elsewhere had earned him sufficient renown. Least of all was he disposed to risk an unnecessary engagement. It is said—and we have no reason to doubt the truth of the assertion—that, at sight of the French army he was surprised, almost alarmed, and reproached May-enne for having deceived him as to the foe whom he was to meet. Certainly all accounts agree that so goodly an array of soldiery as that which stood ready to fight under Henry's standards had rarely, if ever, been seen. The number did not, indeed, greatly differ from that of Parma's own army—there were five or six thousand horsemen and eighteen thousand foot soldiers—but, with four thousand French nobles and gentlemen of the best houses in the realm, with six princes, two marshals of France, and, as the patriotic chronicler assures us, more captains and experienced chiefs than all the rest of Christendom could afford, the Huguenot king's army presented an appearance such as Parma could best appreciate.[1] Nor were the Protestant soldiers and their Roman Catholic comrades in the king's army less remarkable for their loyalty than for their fine appearance. Any man among them would have deemed it a privilege to die for his sovereign and "the good cause." If all had not the

Brave M. de Canisy.

wit, many had the zeal of that grand Huguenot, M. de Canisy, mentioned by Henry the Fourth in one of his letters, who took part in a furious attack upon Vique, in Lower Normandy. "It would have been a complete triumph," writes the monarch, "had it not cost Canisy a second wound in the mouth. This does not, however, stop his brave talk. 'Do not pity me,' said he to La Noue, 'for I have still enough to cry "Long life to the king!" when we shall have gotten into Paris.'"[2]

In vain did Henry, in the spirit of a chivalry now quite out

---

[1] Compare the statements of the "Sommaire Discours," in the Mémoires de la Ligue, iv. 354, with the eulogistic phrases of Sir Edward Stafford in a letter to Lord Burleigh, as quoted by Motley, United Netherlands, iii. 79.

[2] "Mais bien disoit-il à la Noue de ne le plaindre point, puisqu'il lui en restoit assez pour crier 'Vive le Roy' quand nous serons dedans Paris." Henry IV. to the Countess de Grammont, April 5, 1590, Lettres missives, iii. 187.

of vogue, send to his enemy a challenge in due form, and invite him to decide the present disputes in set battle. Parma, who had strongly entrenched himself, quietly made answer to the effect that he would fight or abstain from fighting precisely as it might suit his interests.¹ It evidently suited him better just now not to fight. So for an entire week the Spanish general kept Henry and his Huguenots chafing under their disappointment at being unable to cross swords with their opponents, and then, after bringing out a part of his army as though for battle, quietly but rapidly shifted the main body and brought it opposite to the town of Lagny, which lay a little to his rear, separated only by the stream of the Marne. Important as was

Parma takes Lagny. Lagny, the fortifications were of the old style and such as not to be capable of withstanding even the primitive kind of artillery then in use. A bridge of boats had been provided while the Flemish army lay apparently inactive, and the troops that crossed upon it were ready to rush in and take possession of the place, the moment that a practicable breach had been made by the cannon. With the capture of Lagny and the butchery of its garrison, Parma accomplished one part of his mission. The Marne was once more open. Meantime Henry seems not to have guessed his adversary's design until it was half executed. The distance was considerable, there was, we are assured, a dense fog, and a strong wind from the southwest prevented him from hearing the detonation of the cannon. Even when made aware of what was going on, he was powerless to hinder it. A marsh lay between him and Lagny upon the right bank of the river, not to speak of the part of Parma's forces that had been left to oppose his advance ; while, had he been able promptly to transfer his army to the left bank of the Marne, not only would he have reached Lagny too late to avert

---

¹ Parma's answer to Henry's herald, according to Corneio, was this : " Tell your master that I have come to France by the command of the king my master, in order to put an end to and extirpate the heresies of this kingdom ; which thing I hope to accomplish, with the grace of God, before I leave. And if I find that the shortest road to this end is to give battle, I shall give it and compel him to accept it, or else I shall do whatever may seem to me to be for the best." Mémoires de la Ligue, iv. 323.

the catastrophe, but he would have left the road to Paris clear to the enemy.[1]

Annoyed at the mistake he had committed, and vexed that his rival in arms had so easily gained a signal advantage under his very eyes, Henry undertook, two days later, to re-trieve his fortunes by a nocturnal attempt upon Paris. Ladders had been provided, and that portion of the walls was chosen for the escalade which was farthest distant from the scene of the recent movements of the two armies. It was believed that, if any part of the walls would be negligently guarded at such a time, it would be the space between the gates of Saint Germain and Saint Jacques, on the southwest of the city. And so it proved. Indeed, had it not been for the vigi-lance of the Jesuits of the college hard by the Porte Saint Jac-ques, the escalade would have been successful. As it was, the first man who reached the top received so vigorous a blow from an old halberd in the hands of one of the fathers, that he fell back into the ditch, and it fared no better with the others who followed his example. The ladders were too few and too short for the purpose, and before a sufficient number of men could be placed upon the walls to make a stand, the citizens had heard the alarm and flocked to the spot in overwhelming numbers. The night was dark, but great quantities of lighted hay were thrown down into the dry moat, and the assailants, who were thus seen to number some two thousand men, finding their enterprise frustrated, at once withdrew.[2]

Failure of a nocturnal at-tack on Paris.

---

[1] Corneio, Discours bref et veritable, in Mémoires de la Ligue, iv. 323 ; Som-maire Discours, ibid., iv. 353–355 ; Recueil des choses mémorables, 730, 731 ; De Thou, vii. 659–663 ; Agrippa d'Aubigné, iii. 240, 241 ; Davila, 470–474.

[2] Pierre Corneio, in his account of the siege to which we are indebted for so many valuable details, gives a circumstantial narrative of the escalade (Mé-moires de la Ligue, iv. 323-325). The official circular sent out to the governors, etc., barely refers to it (ibid., iv. 355). There is a slight discrepancy of dates, the former making the capture of Lagny to have occurred on Friday, Sept. 7th (" le vendredi, veille de Nostre Dame de Septembre "—sc. Nativity of the Holy Virgin), and the escalade on Monday morning, Sept. 10th, and the latter placing each event one day later. Motley, however (United Netherlands, iii. 81), is certainly as incorrect in assigning the date of Sept. 15th to the assault on Lagny, as is De Thou (vii. 663) in giving it that of Sept. 6th.

Meantime, the moment the king went off to meet Parma, provisions had poured into the city. The famishing citizens,

Paris provisioned. but a few hours ago reduced to the utmost verge of despair, again beheld the welcome sight of bread. The poor could now buy freely what had been beyond the reach of all except the very richest. The fall in the price of grain was well-nigh as sudden and as unexpected as that which followed the famine of Samaria. A sceptical Parisian might well have exclaimed, on the eve of Parma's approach: "Behold, if the Lord would make windows in heaven, might this thing be?" —had a prophet foretold that the "setier" of wheat, which then could scarcely be bought for one hundred and twenty crowns, would be sold within a few days for three or four.[1]

The fall of Lagny was followed, in October, by the capture of Corbeil. Before he once more turned his face northward, the

Capture of Corbeil by Parma. Prince of Parma had freed the Seine, as well as the Marne, from the deadly grasp of Henry. It is true that Alexander Farnese was scarcely gone before Givry, one of the king's most active generals, recovered both Corbeil and Lagny, and began once more to distress the capital. None the less was it but too apparent that from Henry's magnificent victory at Ivry, and from his persevering siege of Paris, he had reaped the most meagre harvest. The battle had indeed exalted his military fame and given him an unquestioned place among the most brilliant commanders of his time, but, instead of securing for him the possession of his capital, it had been merely the prelude to a tedious siege. The siege itself, after leading him to the very threshold of success, had left him apparently as far from ultimate triumph as ever. For these rebuffs the lukewarmness or actual disloyalty of a considerable body of his counsellors and officers was responsible. At Mantes, Marshal Biron

Unfaithfulness of governors of cities. and Monsieur d'O compelled him to fritter away a precious fortnight, whose opportunities could never be recovered. During the siege, governors of adjacent places and officers who would have been sorry to see his majesty in full possession of his realm before he should have renounced the

---

[1] Corneio, ubi supra, iv. 325.

Huguenot faith, were induced, by paltry bribes of finery and bawbles, to suffer just enough food to be smuggled into the city to enable it to drag out an existence until the tardy approach of Parma.   In the last hours of the siege the baneful influence of Biron again came in to cause the king to abandon an advantageous position, and to prefer the plain of Chelles to the more favorable pass of Claye.

Immediately after the fall of Lagny, and some weeks before the loss of Corbeil, Henry took the extraordinary step of disbanding the greater part of the magnificent army which, but a few days before, had kindled the admiration of Alexander Farnese and of Sir Edward Stafford.   Strange, as this course may seem to us, it had had a parallel on more than one occasion during the previous wars.   The pretext was that the country about Paris was thoroughly exhausted and could furnish no adequate supply for so large a body of troops; while the gentlemen, serving at their own charges, had long since come to the end of the little outfit they had brought with them.   The statement was not unfounded; yet the common voice of the people was not far wrong when it contrasted with this inconstancy the generous endurance of the city of Paris, and exalted the steadfastness of a promiscuous rabble of men, women, and children, greatly to the disadvantage of a noblesse that could not bring itself longer to put up patiently with the temporary loss of a few of the ordinary comforts of life.[1]

Henry gives a furlough to his troops.

Putting, therefore, good garrisons in various cities of the neighborhood of Paris, and despatching the Prince of Conty into Maine, Montpensier into Normandy, Longueville into Picardy, Nevers into Champagne, and Aumont into Burgundy, to watch over the interests of the crown in these provinces, Henry once more addressed himself, with the small body of troops he retained about his person, to an adventurous warfare.[2]

When Alexander Farnese, having finished, after a masterly

---

[1] De Thou, vii. 664–665.
[2] De Thou, ubi supra.

fashion, the task he had unwillingly taken upon himself, prepared to return to Flanders, the king promptly determined to Henry follows accompany him so far as the borders. " Our Spanthe duke in his retreat iards," he playfully wrote to Montmorency, " are from France. much honester people than those you have to do with ; for they are not willing to put their host to any farther annoyance and talk of withdrawing. They have done me so little harm that I regard myself obliged to do them the honor of escorting them home." [1] Accordingly, such was the pertinacity with which he attached himself to the retiring columns, and such injury was he able to inflict, that Parma's movement assumed the form of a retreat, and Henry, by his apparent pursuit, gained so much credit with the Picards that not a few castles and towns came over to his side. [2]

Meantime, in other parts of France the arms of the Huguenots had, during the past year, met with some signal successes, The war in beginning with an important victory gained in the provinces. Auvergne upon the very day of the battle of Ivry. [3] But these advantages were counterbalanced by serious losses. It was difficult to determine whether the fortunes of the king or those of the League were on the whole predominant in Brittany. If the able Lesdiguières performed remarkable exploits in Provence and Dauphiny, and even made his way across the Alps and defeated some troops of the Duke of Savoy not far from Susa, the duke amply made up for this by invading the French territory and making a pompous entrance into the city of Aix, where, to their shame, not only the municipal magistrates, but the presidents and members of the Parliament of Provence came, each in the order of seniority and rank, to kiss his hand and to swear fidelity to him as protector and governor-general of the province. [4]

Marshal Matignon obtained, by peaceable methods, a more substantial triumph for the king in the great province of Guy-

---

[1] Henry IV. to Montmorency, Escouy, Nov. 4, 1590, Lettres missives, iii. 289,290.

[2] Agrippa d'Aubigné, iii. 244 ; De Thou, vii. 673, etc.

[3] De Thou, vii. 623–7.   [4] De Thou, vii. 681–7.

enne ; for he persuaded the Parliament of Bordeaux, which had until now absurdly retained the name of the deceased Henry the Third upon its official seal, to recognize the authority of Henry the Fourth, and to issue its documents in his name. Yet even this concession was not made without an equivalent on Henry's part. If not actually purchased, the favor of the Bordelois was rewarded by a solemn declaration of the king, given

Henry abolishes the three Protestant courts. at Mantes, on the tenth of November, whereby he abolished the courts of justice at Saint-Jean-d'Angely, Bergerac and Montauban, which, though established by the Huguenot political assembly held at La Rochelle contemporaneously with the second states of Blois, had been recognized by Henry of Valois at the time of his reconciliation with Henry of Navarre.[1]

Thus it was that the Huguenot monarch of France showed himself quite ready, whenever the occasion required, to sacrifice the interests or even the safety of the men who had fought under his standards and elected him protector of their churches. True, of words and kind assurances Henry showed no lack. Less than a week before the edict was signed whereby he deprived the southern Huguenots of those judicial bodies without which, in the excited state of the public feeling, they could hope for no justice, he wrote to the "ministers of the churches of Languedoc," expressing full satisfaction with their entire conduct, and begging them to persevere in their "devout prayers and supplications." Spiritual weapons, he thought, would be more effectual than temporal in removing the evils at present afflicting France ; for it was very certain that, should God's anger be appeased, He would cause the arms to fall from the hands of the enemy.[2] But when any measure was proposed for the relief of the Protestants, there was a strange apathy, amounting to positive reluctance. Of this a clear proof was given in the very month in which this letter was written.

---

[1] Anquez, Histoire des assemblées politiques des réformés de France, 129 ; De Thou, vii. 680, 681.

[2] Henry IV. to the Protestant ministers of Languedoc, Cerny, November 4, 1590. Lettres missives, iii. 292, 293.

Keenly alive to the injustice to which his fellow-Protestants were exposed, Duplessis Mornay, with the king's consent, drew up the form of an edict, to be signed by him, with the view of adjusting present differences. His majesty was made to reiterate his promise to hold, within a year, a council to which all Christian princes should be invited, or, in case this should be impossible, a national council or, at least, an assembly of holy and learned men. His hope was to prove, " by the docility, attention, and facility he would bring to his instruction, that he had continued until now steadfast in his religion, not through vanity or obstinacy, but solely from fear of offending God." It was ordered that all Roman Catholics, save such as were notorious rebels, should be restored to their rights ; and that, while the exercises of the Romish religion were everywhere restored, those of the Protestant religion should be maintained wherever this was guaranteed by the truce between the late king and the King of Navarre. But the cardinal articles of the proposed edict were two, which defined the rights of the Protestants more distinctly. The one declared the edicts of 1577 and of 1580, together with the interpretative articles of Nérac and the so-called secret articles, to be in force. The other distinctly repealed the pretended " edicts of re-union " which the League had violently extorted from the late king in the months of July, 1585 and 1588.[1]

Duplessis Mornay draws up a bill for the relief of the Protestants.

The efforts of Duplessis Mornay to secure the consent of the royal council to the measure were crowned with success. The chancellor, Biron, Aumont, O, and all who were present, pronounced it eminently just and equitable. The document received the king's signature. Duplessis Mornay and Chancellor Chiverny were commissioned to proceed at once to the city of Tours, and use their influence to obtain the prompt approval and registration of the edict by the loyal Parliament there in session. But before they had reached their destination—in fact they had gotten no farther

Henry at first approves, but afterward recalls the edict.

---

[1] " Formulaire de la declaration pour la revocation de l'edict de juillet, faict par M. Duplessis," Pont St. Pierre, November, 1590, in Mémoires de Duplessis Mornay, iv. 492-504.

than Anet—the chancellor received a hastily scrawled letter of four lines from Henry, bidding him return and defer the business until some future occasion. The opponents of the Protestants had secretly thwarted a scheme of such manifest justice that they were ashamed to oppose it openly.[1]

But the Huguenots were not inclined to acquiesce in this delay ; least of all was the able author of the proposed edict so disposed. His remonstrance addressed to Henry has come down to us. "The revocation of the two edicts of July (1585 and 1588) ought," he remarks, "to meet with no opposition. These edicts were extorted from the crown by violence, they have engendered the extreme calamities at present subsisting, they assassinated the late king, they have dishonored the nation, and confounded the state. It is disgraceful to have tolerated them so long, seeing they declare the reigning monarch incapable of holding the sceptre, degrade the princes of the blood, and render all that recognize Henry the Fourth liable to impeachment. On the other hand, the edict of pacification of 1577 was enacted with great solemnity. All the princes of the blood took part. France fared well in consequence of it. All the king's subjects were satisfied. The Roman Catholic religion was maintained in its dignity, while provision was made for the needs of the Protestant religion. In sum, the matter was regarded as settled and not to be reopened.

A remonstrance against further delay.

"An adjustment of the rightful claims of the Huguenots," continues Duplessis Mornay, "cannot longer be deferred. God has given the king extraordinary tokens of His favor, and He must be recognized. The difficulties are all on man's side; they will disappear, if we invoke and serve God. It was much farther from the proscriptive ordinance laid down as a fundamental law of the realm to the royal court, than it is from the edict

---

[1] "Et par là nos adversaires traversèrent ce qu'ils eussent eu honte de renverser." Vie de Duplessis Mornay, 154, 155, where a full account of the matter is given. Pont St. Pierre, where the edict was signed, is about midway between Rouen and Les Andelys ; Anet, where the commissioners were overtaken, lies only a few miles beyond the battlefield of Ivry.

of the truce to the edict of pacification of 1577. Since God
brought us the former distance, we cannot refuse or delay to
take the last step.[1]

"We are told, 'Let the Huguenots have patience!' They have
patiently endured for fifty years and more ; they will be patient
still in the king's service, for they are his subjects and
do not waver in their affection. But it is not for the
good of his service to condemn them to patience in such a matter. If they were willing, the king ought not to permit it. It
is his duty to enkindle religious zeal. Religion is extinguished
in men, if it be not fostered. Of private men God requires only
that they be religious themselves ; of those born for the good
of others, He demands that they cause their subjects to serve
Him.

Huguenot patience.

"Some say, 'Matters will be adjusted with the Protestants,
when we shall come to treat with the partisans of the League.'
This is iniquitous. The latter have warred against the king and
require peace ; the former need only to be delivered from the
oppression to which their consciences have been subjected.
Besides, what patience can there be in such affairs ? Every day
children are born, men and women are married, some one dies.
Shall our children die without baptism, shall marriages not be
solemnized, shall dead bodies lie unburied? To pray to God
for the king's prosperity in a gathering of three families, to sing
a psalm in one's shop, to sell a Testament or a French Bible—
these things are reckoned crimes by the judges, and every day
sentences are pronounced because of them. The judges allege
that they are bound by the last laws. They weigh in the same
scale the unobtrusive offering of prayer to God in a private
room for the king's prosperity, and seditious preaching from
the pulpit against his person and welfare.

"A foreign auxiliary army, composed of Protestants, will soon
be coming. Foreign princes will beg his majesty to restore to
his subjects their religion. It will be little to the credit of one

---

[1] "Il y avoit trop plus loing de la loi fondamentale jusques à la cour, qu'il
n'y a par de l'edict de la trefve jusques à l'edict de 77 ; et si Dieu a faict l'ung
pour nous, nous ne lui pouvons ni desnier ni dilayer l'autre."

that is ' Very Christian ' to be asked to do his duty and entreated
to satisfy God's honor.   The princes will request of him more
than it is in his power to give.   If he grant the request, it will
be to recall his concession later, and to afford the Roman Catholics reason to think that the concession was extorted.

"It is occasion for thanksgiving that his majesty honors God,
whereas his predecessors blasphemed His name.   But should
the king's subjects behold him growing cold or apathetic in his
religion, should they see him living less scrupulously than that
religion enjoins, their respect for him will diminish.   They will
say : ' If it is a religion, why does he not make more
account of it ?   If it is no religion, why does he not
give us quietness by changing it ?' " [1]

The king's inconsistency.

Such was the manly remonstrance of one of the clearest
thinkers of the period, one of the purest souls upon the earth.

Henry's Roman Catholic subjects might well have remembered these pregnant expressions, and, two years later, after the
abjuration so lightly made, have required Henry to make answer to just this inquiry : If your Protestant faith amounted to
anything more than a mere pretence, why did you not hold to
it more stoutly, and practise it more consistently ?   If it was so
empty and insincere as it would now seem to have been, why
not have spared us these long and terrible years of war, rapine,
and disgrace ?

Meanwhile the position of the Huguenots, even in the loyal
portions of the kingdom, and under a king professing their own
faith, was not devoid of anxiety.   In the confused state of legislation it was doubtful what their civil rights really were.   Of
the edicts of Henry the Third only those that proscribed the
Protestant religion were in force.   The edicts of pacification, of
which it was remembered with a smile that each of them had
successively been enacted with solemnity and declared to be irrevocable and perpetual, had long since been abrogated and an-
nulled.   The lot of the Protestants had, it is true, been tem-

---

[1] " Discours envoyé au roy en mars 1591, sur ce que sa majesté retardoit la
publication de la declaration ci-dessus, faicte par M. Duplessis," in Mémoires
de Duplessis Mornay, v. 36–41.

porarily bettered by the truce between the late king and the King of Navarre; but the duration of the truce was expressly limited, and the term had expired. No wonder, then, that ill-disposed persons pretended to deny the Huguenots even the slightest relaxation of the severities to which they had been exposed for years. At Caen, where the loyal Parliament of Normandy sat, despite the impotent wrath of the rival court at Rouen, priests and monks were provoked almost beyond endurance by what they styled the audacity of the heretics. The hated "prêche" was frequented with little attempt at secrecy.

The Parliament of Normandy and the Protestants.
The familiar sound of Marot's psalms was again heard in the streets and lanes. It was even apprehended that on the coming feast of Corpus Christi the Protestant householders would decline to drape their doors and windows in honor of the holy sacrament. The provocation was enough to set preaching friars at their old work of denunciation from the pulpits of all the churches. The judges, quite at a loss how to act under the circumstances, applied to the king for instructions as to what it was his good pleasure to command respecting the exercise of the Reformed religion. Obtaining no answer in season, they calmly proceeded to draw up an order prescribing, under penalty of ten crowns for disobedience, that all houses be draped, all shops be closed, and all labor be suspended on the day of the coming festival. When this extraordinary action of the provincial parliament was reported to the monarch, together with sundry other acts of petty annoyance to which the Norman Protestants were subjected, Henry at once wrote directing that the provisions of the truce granted by his predecessor be regarded as still in force, until such time as he might have the opportunity to convene an assembly of princes and other competent persons to settle the questions pertaining to the general peace of France. Not even so, however, were the judges content to acquiesce in a system of toleration. They did, indeed, go through the form of resolving to send a deputation to the king to explain their motives; but none the less did they repeat their order the next year, in advance of the recurrence of Corpus Christi Day. Nay, they summoned to their bar one Beaulard, a counsellor in

the presidial court, to answer for his insubordination in daring to refuse to hang tapestry before his residence. In vain did the brave lawyer allege his faith and his religious scruples. He was soundly berated for the bad example which, as judge and counsellor, he had set to the other inhabitants, and was informed that parliament might, if it so pleased, have inflicted a severe fine upon him. As it was, he escaped with the payment of twenty crowns. But, while willing to gratify the churchmen of Caen by such defiant disobedience of the royal commands, there were some acts of priestly insolence which the Parliament of Normandy saw fit to rebuke. Thus, when the curates and their vicars undertook to draw up careful and complete lists of all the Huguenots who had abstained from draping their houses, the prosecuting officer of the crown received a peremptory order from the supreme court to take no account of the lists, and to regard the priests as interested parties whose unsupported testimony could not be received against their adversaries. The judges would allow none to be condemned on the testimony of others; though quite willing that a few of the more prominent offenders be made examples of, should they admit their own misdemeanor.[1]

Any historical investigator who has perplexed himself in the vain endeavor to find a particular statement which, though really in plain sight, has seemed maliciously to elude all his efforts to discover it, may derive comfort from the experience of Von Polenz in his description of the battle of Ivry.

The story of Henry's white plume at Ivry.

The incident respecting the white plume of Henry of Navarre, according to Von Polenz (iv. 666), lies outside the domain of criticism, being as much a historical embellishment as the stories in which the cane of Frederick the Great and the hat of the first Napoleon figure. As to the king's speech to his soldiers which I have given in the text, he declares that it is found in no original historian. Anquetil, he asserts, took it from Bishop Péréfixe's panegyrical biography of Henry IV., and in this had the support of a popular tradition nearly two hundred years old.

_____

[1] See the account in Floquet, Histoire du Parlement de Normandie, iii. 548–556, based upon the secret registers; and the letter of Henry IV., of October 8, 1590. The first action of the parliament, as to the draping of houses on Corpus Christi Day, was taken June 20, 1590; the second, June 12, 1591. It was three days after this last date that the priestly denunciation received a rebuke.

In a note Von Polenz informs us that Sismondi, it is true, cites D'Aubigné as authority for the king's spirited address, but adds that he does not find it in D'Aubigné's history.   "It is remarkable," he proceeds to say, "that the address is not given by De Thou."—Now it happens that the white plume is as well authenticated as any point pertaining to the battle.   The official account of the minister of state Forget—" Discours véritable " (Mémoires de la Ligue, iv. 265)—expressly says that Henry was "assez remarquable par un grand panache blanc qu'il avoit à son acoustrement de teste, et un autre que portoit son cheval "—a statement which is, as usual, repeated almost or quite word for word by the careful " Recueil des choses mémorables," page 718, and by Matthieu, Histoire des derniers troubles, liv. 5, fol. 18.   Moreover, the king's address *is* to be found in Agrippa d'Aubigné, iii. 231 ; and if De Thou does not insert in his history the very words of the king, he gives their substance (vii. 617): "Il est vrai que le Roi . . . avoit fait mettre ce jour-là sur son casque une aigrette blanche, afin d'être reconnu de plus loin ; et il avertit en même temps, qu'au cas que son drapeau fût abattu, comme il arrive assez souvent, on prît garde à l'aigrette blanche et qu'on la suivit."

CHAPTER XII.

GROWTH OF THE TIERS PARTI, AND HENRY'S DIFFICULT POSITION.

A YEAR and a half had elapsed since the accession of Henry to the throne of France, but he seemed to be about as far as ever from the undisputed possession of his kingdom. His very victories were robbed of their fruit by the conspiracy of his disloyal captains. His rebellious capital, when at the point of starvation, had been enabled to hold out, through the negligence or connivance of unfaithful guardians of places that nominally held for him. His armies were full of those who avowed the purpose never to acquiesce in the domination of a Protestant prince, should that prince defer too long to be "instructed." In the court itself the religion still professed by the king was regarded an insuperable bar to promotion. One day—it must have been early in March[1]—the council was sitting in the village of Saint Denis, when a gentleman was introduced who came from southern France. It was M. de Saint Julien, a man short in stature, secretary of Lesdiguières, and commissioned by his master to bring the tidings of the exploit in the mountains of Dauphiny mentioned in the last chapter. At the same time he was directed to request the council to confer upon the Huguenot general the government of Grenoble. The petition was not an unreasonable one. It was not every day in the week that a servant of the king was able to report the capture of a city the most important in its province and the seat of a sovereign court of the realm. So probably thought Henry himself, as he stood in another part of the council chamber conversing with Soissons and Givry, but

The secretary of Lesdiguières in the royal council.

---

[1] Grenoble was taken by Lesdiguières, March 1, 1591, De Thou, viii. 15.

listening to what was said around the board more attentively than he pretended. Not so thought the gentlemen who transacted his affairs. No sooner had the despatches of Lesdiguières been read and Saint Julien been permitted to explain the object of his mission, than Monsieur d'O started to his feet, furious that an adherent of the Reformed religion should have the audacity to ask for so important a trust. Other members supported his violent remarks, and it devolved upon Marshal Biron to signify to the secretary the impossibility which the council found in acceding to the wishes of Lesdiguières. Truth to say, the marshal was at heart inclined to give a different answer to a gallant soldier, whose daring he admired; none the less did he discharge his official duty without faltering. In a somewhat prolix address, he set forth to Saint Julien the great obligations under which Lesdiguières had laid his majesty and the whole realm, as well as the desire which all felt to recognize his services suitably. It was, however, quite out of the question to place a city which was the seat of one of the parliaments of France in the hands of a Protestant.

The king listened, and his brow lowered. Saint Julien also listened most respectfully, and, at the conclusion of the harangue, retired with a very humble bow. A moment or two afterward, however, a knock was heard at the door, and once more the little secretary presented himself with profuse apologies for again intruding upon the scene. "Gentlemen," he said, "your unexpected decision made me quite forget a single point more which I should have mentioned. It is, may it please you, that since your great caution has led you to refuse the city of Grenoble to my master, you will do well to deliberate also as to the means of taking it away from him." This said, he withdrew without further ado. "The little man tells you the truth," exclaimed the marshal cheerily; "we must consider the point." The light-hearted king, toward whom he cast a furtive glance, answered with a laugh full of enjoyment of the incident. Lesdiguières received the appointment, and Saint Julien was the bearer of the official announcement.[1]

---

[1] Agrippa d'Aubigné, iii. 281, 282.

Meanwhile, despite half-hearted adherents and resolute enemies, the war against the League went on, though not with uniform success. It is true that an attempt made by the Parisians to surprise Saint Denis, a point essential both to their comfort and to their security, disastrously failed, and their leader, the Chevalier d'Aumale, paid the penalty of his rashness with his life. But it was only a few days after, that Henry himself was equally unsuccessful in an enterprise having for its object the capture of Paris. Unfortunately the massing of troops in the vicinity of the city had not been so secret as to escape the notice of the enemy. Apprehending an attack from the west, they had, in particular, blocked up the gate of Saint Honoré, which then spanned the street of the same name, not far from the present site of the Palais Royal. Now it was by this gate the royalists had intended entering, disguised as peasants, with working clothes over their cuirasses. As the provisions that found their way into the beleaguered capital generally came at night, no great surprise was felt when, about three o'clock on the morning of Sunday, the twentieth of January, ten or a dozen men, each driving before him a horse or donkey laden with sacks of flour, presented themselves at the gate. It was not suspected that the pretended countrymen were experienced officers, nor that a stronger detachment of soldiers in similar costume lurked about the grounds of the Convent of the Capuchins (where now the Treasury Buildings face the gardens of the Tuileries), ready to bring up wagons wherewith to prevent the closing of the gate when once it should have been opened. But the information received by the forerunners, that they must either go down to the water's edge and suffer their provisions to be brought in by boat, or make the circuit of the fortifications to the Porte Saint Denis, disconcerted the well-laid plan. Henry himself, who, with a strong body of men, was abiding his time, hidden from view on the other side of the hill of Montmartre, was reluctantly compelled to interpret the noise which soon after arose in the city as a proof that his project was discovered, and gave the signal for retreat. If his disappointment was great, the delight of the Parisians far exceeded it in intensity. The superstitious popu-

"Le jour des farines," January 20, 1591.

lace had felt no little chagrin at the previous rebuff experienced at Saint Denis. The time had been carefully chosen by the priests to insure the favor of Heaven—it was the eve of Saint Geneviève's day, a holy season when it might reasonably be expected that the patron of the city would see to it that the arms of her devotees should prevail over those of the heretics who refused her intercession.[1] As a result, Saint Geneviève fell into disrepute. She was accused of having treacherously passed over to the enemy's camp. Now, however, the Parisian League was jubilant. Not satisfied with having lately added to their calendar three days of annual thanksgiving, to commemorate the flight of Henry the Third, the raising of the siege by his successor, and the failure of the escalade, the municipal authorities proceeded to enjoin the observance of a fourth celebration—destined to as short-lived favor as all the rest—to be held on the twentieth of January every year, and known as the " Day of the Flour "—"le jour des farines."[2]

It is one of the paradoxes of history that the death of the very pope who had excommunicated him, and who absolved his subjects from their oaths of allegiance, was a misfortune for Henry the Fourth. Sixtus the Fifth died on the twenty-seventh of August, 1590, just at the close of the siege of Paris, hated by Philip the Second and the Spaniards, whose ambitious plans he understood and opposed, equally detested by the League, against whom his coffers were resolutely locked. The preachers in Paris did not spare him. They denounced him from the pulpit as a heretic. Lestoile tells us that he himself heard the curate of St. André's church preach a sermon in which he rejoiced over the death of the pontiff as a miracle of divine goodness. " God," said he, has delivered us from a wicked pope ! "[3] The Spaniards and Italians went

Unpopularity and death of Sixtus V.

---

[1] The festival of Saint Geneviève, as observed by the Roman Catholic Church, falls upon January 3d.

[2] For the attempts upon Saint Denis and Paris, see Mémoires de la Ligue, iv. 362, and 364-371 (a contemporary letter by a partisan of the League), Recueil des choses mémorables, 734, Agrippa d'Aubigné, iii. 247, Lestoile, ii. 42, De Thou, vii. 770, etc. Lestoile records later the celebration of the first anniversary of the " fête des farines," ii. 81.　　　　　[3] Lestoile, ii. 34.

farther, and gave out that his holiness had been carried off by
the devil, in pursuance of a bargain made long before between
Sixtus and the prince of evil. Some said, indeed, that he had
bought his elevation to the pontifical chair at the price of his
soul.[1] So it was that the same pope who had expressed grave
fears lest the soul of his predecessor might be enduring the sufferings of another world, in atonement for the bloodshed occasioned by the favor he had shown the League,[2] was himself
supposed to have passed to a place of torment. It was even
asserted that Sixtus had been promised by Satan the possession
of Peter's chair for a period of six years. When, after the
expiration of five only, the infernal messenger was sent to
summon him, he complained loudly of the breach of faith. But
the envoy soon silenced his remonstrance by reminding him of
an incident that had occurred early in his pontificate. The
friends of a youth sentenced to death for some slight offence—
some said it was for mere resistance to the pope's soldiers, who
were taking away his ass—pleaded in his behalf that he lacked
yet a year of the lowest age at which the laws permitted a man
to be executed. The angry pope, resolved to put him out of the
way, thereupon exclaimed : "Very well, then, I give him one of
my years," and ordered the sentence to be carried into effect.
That year, the Satanic messenger intimated to the dying Sixtus,
was the missing sixth year of his pontificate.[3]

Sixtus was succeeded by Urban the Seventh, a creature of
the King of Spain, but Urban died after enjoying his elevation
less than a fortnight. Next Cardinal Sfondrato was chosen, and
took the name of Gregory the Fourteenth. It would have been
strange had the new pope not been well pleasing to
Philip the Second ; for his Catholic Majesty had made
up beforehand a list of seven cardinals, and demanded
that the conclave should elect one of them to the papal see.[4] Accordingly Gregory, upon whom the choice fell, was as decided

Pope Gregory
XIV. supports
the League.

---

[1] Ranke, History of the Popes, 225.   [2] Above, vol. i. 305.

[3] The strange story seems to have enjoyed wide currency among the superstitious. See Agrippa d'Aubigné, iii. 236, De Thou, vii. 724, 725, and Ranke,
142.   [4] Ranke, ubi supra, 226.

in support of the League as Sixtus had been determined in condemnation of it, and detested Henry the Fourth as much as
Sixtus admired him.   And now the treasure which had been so
carefully hoarded was quickly expended.   Surprise has frequently been expressed that Sixtus was able in five years to ac-
cumulate the sum of four and a half million scudi or dollars;[1] but
none, so far as I know, at Gregory's success in making away with
the whole in a pontificate of ten months and ten days.   The late
pope, who from his earliest days had experienced the keenest
gratification in the practice of economy and saving, did, indeed,
undertake to bind his successors in office to reserve the fund
which he left laid up in the castle of San Angelo sacredly for certain purposes, under pain of the wrath of Almighty God and of
the holy apostles St. Peter and St. Paul.   It was to be used
only in the event of war for the reconquest of the Holy Land or
of a general war against the Turks, to relieve famine or pestilence, to avert manifest danger of the loss of a province of Catholic Christendom, to repel invasion of the States of the Church,
or to recover a city belonging to the papal see.[2]   But Gregory
was scarcely seated upon the throne, which he ascended on the
fifth of December, 1590, before he began to lay out the money
for purposes quite repugnant to the designs of Sixtus.   One of
his first acts was to write a brief to the Parisians praising them
for their past conduct and exhorting them to persevere to the
end.   He enforced his words by the promise of a monthly sub-
sidy of fifteen thousand crowns, and by sending Marcellino Landriano as papal nuncio to France, to second the efforts

Landriano
sent as papal
nuncio.

of his legate, the Bishop of Piacenza, who had, some
time since, taken the place of Sixtus's disobedient
envoy, Cardinal Cajetan.   Meantime a force consisting of six
thousand Swiss, two thousand foot soldiers, and fifteen hundred
horsemen, was to proceed as speedily as possible to the relief
of the League, under command of the pope's nephew, Ercole
Sfondrato, newly created Duke of Montemarciano.   The outrages which the pope's auxiliary army perpetrated in the friendly

---

[1] See Ranke's discussion of the financial system of Sixtus V., in his History
of the Popes, 146–148.   [2] Ibid., 146.

Milanese, before leaving Italy, were a presage of the damage
that might be expected at its hands when once France should
have been reached.[1] Nor was this all. In a solemn bull, under
date of the first of March, Gregory warned the clergy of France
that he suspended and excommunicated them, unless within

New bulls issued against Henry IV.

fifteen days they should renounce the obedience of
Henry of Bourbon. In case a further period of fifteen days should elapse, they were to be deprived of
all their possessions and dignities. Under the same date, he addressed a second bull to the nobles, judges, and tiers état, wherein he called upon them to abandon the king, under pain of transforming Gregory's pontifical goodness and paternal piety into
judicial severity. Moreover, he declared the said Henry of
Bourbon to be excommunicated and to have forfeited all his
kingdoms and seigniories, as a relapsed heretic.[2]

The papal bulls were promptly answered by a spirited decree
of the Parliament of Châlons, and the insulting language of

The Parliament of Châlons orders them to be burned.

Gregory was hurled back in defiance. The judges
ordered the bulls to be publicly burned by the hangman on the principal square of the city. They declared
the pope's documents of excommunication to be null
and void, " as abusive, scandalous, seditious, full of imposture,
and drawn up contrary to the holy decrees, canonic constitutions, approved councils, and the rights and liberties

And the nuncio to be arrested.

of the Gallican Church." They ordered the arrest
of Landriano, " pretended nuncio, who had clandestinely entered the kingdom without leave of the king," and
offered a reward of ten thousand livres to the person who

---

[1] Letter of Gregory XIV. to the Council of the "Seize," Rome, May 12,
1591, in Cayet, Chronologie novenaire (Ed. Michaud et Poujoulat), 278, 279 ;
De Thou, vii. 774–777 ; Mémoires de la Ligue, iv. 371 ; Recueil des choses mémorables, 733, 734 ; Ranke, ubi supra, 226.

[2] Summary in the contemporaneous " Response aux commonitoires et excommunications de Gregoire XIV. jettees contre tres-illustre, tres-victorieux,
et tres-auguste Prince Henri de Bourbon, Roy tres-Chrestien de France et de
Navarre," reprinted in Mémoires de la Ligue, iv. 410–654, a long and exhaustive treatise, in which the rights of kings and of the Gallican Church are
vindicated with marked ability and no little display of erudition.

should capture him and deliver him to the authorities for trial. They pronounced sentence of forfeiture of all benefices held by them in France upon the Roman cardinals and ecclesiastics who had counselled and signed the bulls, and who had approved "the very inhuman, very abominable, and very detestable parricide committed on the person of the late Very Catholic king." They strictly prohibited all sending of money to Rome for bulls, dispensations, or other such ends.[1]

The bulls of Gregory the Fourteenth were fraught with more important consequences than might perhaps have been anticipated. We have it upon the authority of Cayet[2] that it was these documents that first introduced division into the royalist *The bulls in-* party, hitherto a unit, and led to the institution of a *troduce divi-* political faction which arrogated to itself the title of *sion in the* *royalist party.* the "tiers parti." This was a very different body, and with quite diverse principles and aims, from that which, in the reigns of Charles the Ninth and Henry the Third, had been known sometimes by this name and sometimes as the party of the "politiques" or malcontents. The designation now covered a considerable fraction of the Roman Catholic adherents of Henry of Bourbon whom the monitory bulls and the renewed excommunication of the pope suddenly awakened to a sense of their peril, as the followers of a prince solemnly deposed by the highest ecclesiastical authority, and as themselves incurring, by their failure to renounce his allegiance, the gravest censures of their church. Such men had before this felt no little reluctance to serve an "heretical" king, while biding the time when he should see fit to submit to the long-deferred "instruction." They now began to clamor for the speedy fulfilment of his promise, for his prompt abjuration, as an indispensable condi-

---

[1] The decree of the Parliament of Châlons, of June 10, 1591, is reproduced in Mémoires de la Ligue, iv. 395–396.

[2] Chronologie novenaire (Ed. Michaud et Poujoulat), 295 : "Bref, il y avoit en ce party bien du desordre et de la confusion, au contraire du party du Roy qui estoit sans aucune division : ce qui fut entretenu jusques au temps de la publication des bulles monitoires du pape Gregoire XIV. que d'aucuns voulurent engendrer un tiers-party, et le former des catholiques qui estoient dans le party royal."

tion of continued support.   An aspiring prelate saw in the un-
certain state of the affairs of France a possible chance for asserting a claim of his own to the throne.   Charles of Bourbon,
Ambition of   Archbishop of Rouen, was one of the three surviving
Cardinal   sons of Louis, Prince of Condé, who fell at Jarnac,
Charles of
Bourbon.   twenty-two years before the time of which I am now
writing.   He was the same prelate that had addressed his cousin,
Henry of Navarre, in 1583, an ill-considered demand that he
should become a Roman Catholic, as a means of acquiring the
support of the nobles, and had in reply received some useful
information as to what the nature of sincere religion is.[1]   The
eight intervening years, however, do not seem to have had any
effect in impressing upon his mind the lesson then inculcated,
that religion is not an article of which a man can divest himself with as much ease as he changes one shirt for another.
At any rate, he had resolved to obtain what advantage he could
from Henry's reluctance to abjure Protestantism under manifest compulsion.   It is true that the claim which he could advance to be regarded as the first prince of the blood was a very
shadowy one.   The young Cardinal of Bourbon—he had been
known as Cardinal of Vendôme until lately but had assumed
the former designation upon the death of his uncle, the phantom king of the League—had an older brother, the Prince of
Conty, not to speak of his young nephew, the son of the late
Prince Henry of Condé.   But Charles affected to despise the
latter as of more than doubtful birth, while he esteemed his
brother's physical defects as sufficient to exclude him from the
succession.   As the cardinal, though a member of the papal
consistory, had never been ordained, no dispensation would be
necessary to enable him to enter upon the duties of a secular
monarch.   The pope, indeed, whom he sounded upon the point,
was careful to give him no encouragement in his ambitious designs ;[2] but popes were short-lived, and Gregory's successor
might prove more gracious.

The new party deemed the moment propitious for a demon-

---

[1] See above, vol. i., page 271.
[2] De Thou, vii. (book 101), 778–781.

stration, and resolved, under cover of a call upon Henry to
gratify his Roman Catholic subjects by embracing their relig-
The tiers parti ious faith, to address an appeal to the people.   The
calls upon
Henry to ab- paper that was drawn up came to be known, from the
jure. place of its surreptitious printing, as "the Remonstrance of Angers."   The circumstance that nowhere else are
the motives more clearly set forth by which Henry was plied
to abjure Protestantism will justify a somewhat minute examination of its contents.

"The Supplication and Advice to the King to make himself
a Catholic," contained the four cardinal propositions, that this
The Remon- course would be holy, that it would be honorable,
strance of that it would be advantageous, and that it was a bso-
Angers. lutely necessary.   Let it not be supposed, however,
that under the first head there was any calm discussion of the
religious, or even the purely moral, aspects of the case.   For such
a discussion we shall look in vain from the beginning to the end
of the document.   Nowhere was a single high motive appealed
to.   The king was informed that the title of "Catholic" had,
from almost the very beginning, been a badge as distinct as the
designation "Christian," and that there was, and could be, but
one church, which continued to subsist while every form of
heresy had successively disappeared before it.   The private individuals who had undertaken to reform the church, had done
so without any warrant.   That right belonged to the king.
"Come into our church and cleanse it so thoroughly and carefully that all pretext for a division shall be taken away.   You
are the eldest son of the church and entitled to command ; but
you will be obeyed only when you issue your mandates from
within.   Rather be instructed by the multitude of learned men
in the church than by a few reformers.   Let not the conduct
of one pope or more be a stumbling-block ; go back to the time
when the Roman pontiffs were also martyrs.   The reformers
themselves do not claim to be perfect ; if that is so, they will
need to be reformed by others, and these last by still others.
In ten years there will be as many schisms and quarrels.   Nothing is permanent and enduring.   After all, it is ceremonial, not
doctrine, that is chiefly in dispute.   Do not imperil your soul's

salvation for such trifles. You were baptized in the Catholic Church ; you ought to live and die in it."

The writer had no difficulty in proving, to his own satisfaction, that Henry would consult his honor by abjuring Protestantism. All his predecessors were Catholics. Saint Louis was canonized, not in Geneva, but in Rome. " Sire," said the writer, "the first rank which you hold among kings you have received for the service of the Christian religion. Who will preserve it for you—the Church of Geneva or the Catholic Church ? In the councils of the so-called Reformed, the kings of England, Scotland, and Denmark will have the precedence over you, since you came in later than they did ; while in the assemblies of the Catholic Church you will have no standing, because you have separated yourself from it. Your nobles will follow you into battle, for they recognize you as their natural head and their lord by the grace of God ; but will it conduce to your dignity to have them forsake you at the door of your " temple " (Protestant church) ? Will it be of advantage to your authority to have all the princes of the blood and all the officers of state gathered in one spot, while you are with a few private persons in another place ? Is it becoming that any one of your subjects should have a greater following anywhere than you have ? And when it comes to your coronation (for I have no expectation that you will despise a solemnity so ancient and venerable), with what honor, with what majesty, with what pomp and ceremonies will you celebrate it, if you are to be anointed in a church whose foundation-stone is yet to be laid—if popes, cardinals, archbishops, and bishops take no part therein ? Will you take at the hands of the Reformed clergy the oath to maintain the Roman Catholic and Apostolic Church in all its rights ? And when it comes to dying (for the great must think of this as well as the small), will it seem good to you that you cannot be buried in the old royal crypts at Saint Denis, where the church can never receive you ? "

The profitableness of the change of religion was made equally manifest. Henry would gain over all his Roman Catholic subjects. Even the adherents of the League would gradually submit. The cities, tired of war and ready to catch at any pretext,

would open their gates. The church would help by subventions
of money. The king would increase his alliances with Roman
Catholic princes abroad and lose none of his Protestant allies.
His Huguenot subjects would in part follow his example ;
those who did not would at least prefer him to their former
persecutors. Let his majesty not fear lest he should be exchanging a certainty for an uncertainty—the Roman Catholics
would stand by him, while as for the Huguenots, if they were
obedient to the late king, they would with much greater reason
obey the present monarch.[1]

When the absolute necessity of the abjuration came up, the
writer almost waxed eloquent. Were the king to refuse to be
converted, he would drag his Roman Catholic followers with
him to destruction. France, said he, is already a prey to neighboring princes, each one of whom wishes to appropriate a portion for himself. His majesty lacks men, money, arms, provisions. The country, now resembling a den of robbers and
murderers, rather than a kingdom, must have peace, and it can
have it only if Henry becomes a Roman Catholic. All the
three orders of the state are of the Catholic religion ; there are
not enough Protestants in France, all told, to make a fourth
division. To please his subjects the king must be of their
religion. If the affections of the Greeks for Alexander the
Great were chilled by his merely adopting the Persian dress,
much more will the French be alienated by a gulf existing between their monarch and them that reaches down to the depths
of the heart. For Frenchmen can tolerate a Turk better than
they can a heretic. Even the nobles may tire of the endless
struggle, and waver in their devotion ; but, if they should not,
what can they do against the united clergy and people ? Julius
Cæsar, with the help of the people alone, triumphed over Pom-
pey, though the latter had the senate and the equestrian order
at his back. It is true that Henry has done nothing to the disadvantage of Roman Catholicism as yet, but the popular anxi-

---

[1] "Et quant aux huguenots, s'ils ont obéi au défunt roi, ils vous obéiront à
plus forte raison." It is instructive to notice another of these numerous,
almost unconscious, tributes to the unwavering loyalty of the Huguenots.

ety pictures the evil he may do, when once his power shall be unrestricted. That anxiety can be allayed by a single word from the king. Let that word come as an inspiration of God, rather than a suggestion of man. Let it be prompted by gratitude to Heaven, which has brought the king to Saint Denis, where lies buried the good bishop who first brought Christianity to France, where are his relics, where is his church! It is a fitting place for exchanging the "white scarf" for the "white cross." The people's voice is God's voice. If Henry were simple Duke of Vendôme, he might suit himself in the matter. As King of France he must consult the interests of his realm. Let Henry be prevailed upon. He is not implored to become an idolater, a superstitious devotee, a hypocrite, nor to turn Jew, Turk, or heathen; but, in the divided condition of Christendom, to attach himself to the more numerous party without becoming an enemy of other parts. Thus only can he reconcile divisions, secure his own position, and strike the death-blow at the designs of the Spaniard.

Such were the lofty motives wherewith Henry of Navarre was to be determined, such the most disinterested grounds that could justify his abandonment of the religion which, to use his own expression, he had imbibed with his mother's milk! Not a word as to deep-seated convictions of duty, no attempt to refute the close logic by means of which reformers had fortified their positions, no pretence of demonstrating the truth of the doctrine of transubstantiation, the efficacy of the mass as a sacrifice for the living and the dead, the existence of purgatory, the utility of good works, as the means of supplementing the work of Jesus Christ in the justification of the believer, the authority of tradition as equal with the authority of revelation, the lawfulness of worshipping saints and angels, the mediation of the Virgin Mary, the claim of the Bishop of Rome to a universal episcopate and to the dignity and attributes of a vicar of God on the earth. All these and similar matters were jauntily set aside with the general observation that, after all, it was not the doctrinal tenets of the Roman Catholic Church to which the Protestant ministers were so obstinately opposed, but merely ceremonies and traditions,

An appeal to low considerations.

and these might be changed ! No wonder, then, that in the mind of one who took so conveniently superficial a survey, the whole matter virtually resolved itself into this proposition—that the king's position could never be anything else than one of extreme discomfort so long as he deferred the politic step of professing the Roman Catholic religion.

That these were practically the views of the Roman Catholics of Henry's party, that the considerations set forth in the paper were essentially those that influenced Henry himself to take the important step at Saint Denis, two years later, there seems not to be room to doubt. It was quite another thing, however, for an anonymous writer to divulge the state of the matter to the world. And so the authorities, at once upon its appearance, took strenuous measures to prevent the accomplishment of those ulterior ends at which this untimely publication apparently aimed. Any further printing or sale of it was forbidden on pain of death. As to the two hundred copies which had already issued from the press, so thorough and so successful was the search instituted for them, so remorseless the destruction, that not a single one, so far as is known, has come down to our times.[1] Nor was this all. Lest any copies of the pestilent treatise should have escaped, and in order to counteract the pernicious influence which such sentiments as were there expressed might exercise, the production of the "tiers parti" was subjected to candid but merciless criticism in several contemporary pamphlets. One of the ablest of these answers, preserved by the discriminating care of the editor of that invaluable collection, the "Mémoires de la Ligue," well de-

The Remonstrance suppressed.

---

[1] See De Thou, vii. (book 101) 778, 781, and Cayet, Chronologie novenaire (Ed. Michaud et Poujoulat), 295. Happily, although, according to Cayet, but two hundred copies were printed, and these seem all to have been destroyed, two manuscript copies have been preserved at Paris, the one in the Library of the Arsenal, vol. 176, with which Ranke was acquainted (see the summary in "Civil Wars and Monarchy in France," Amer. édit., pp. 473, 474), and the other in the National Library, Dupuy Coll., 337. Stâhelin has inserted a translation of this in his Uebertritt König Heinrichs IV., 301–309, which I have used in the text. See also pages 298-300, and 319 of the work last mentioned. From the answer to which reference is made below, it appears that the author of the "Advis" took the "nom de plume" of Juste, or Justus.

serves to be read as an illustration of the usual superiority of
the Protestant controversial papers of the sixteenth century
over the corresponding works of their opponents.[1]

Meantime the king, while keeping his eyes and ears open to
the suspicious deportment of Cardinal Bourbon and the new
"tiers parti," did not think it necessary to employ against so
weak a personage as the prelate any more severe
weapon than his keen mother-wit. When Bourbon,
overcome with shame that the secret of his intrigues
at Rome and their disastrous failure had gotten abroad, fell sick,
Henry, who had in his hands the proofs of the cardinal's treachery in writing, did not hesitate to visit him and administer such
comfort as his bantering words were calculated to impart.
" Take courage, cousin," said he, with a cheery laugh ; " it is true
that you are not yet king, but it is possible that you will be,
after me." [2]

The king's jeer at the cardinal's pretensions.

The Declaration of Saint Cloud, made on the fourth of
August, 1589, immediately after the accession of Henry the
Fourth, contained, it will be remembered, a petition on the part
of his Roman Catholic nobles that his majesty would allow them
to send to Rome an envoy, who might explain to the pope the
motives that had actuated them in their recognition of the new
king, and might obtain the pontiff's advice in return.[3] We have
seen how courteously Sixtus granted an audience to Monsieur de
Luxembourg, Duke of Piney, whom the nobles sent in accordance with the king's permission.[4] But Luxembourg was able to
effect little or nothing, and returned to France.[5] Even then,

---

[1] It bears the title " Response à l'instance et proposition que plusieurs font,
que pour avoir une paix generale et bien establie en France, il faut que le Roy
change de Religion et se renge à celle de l'Eglise Romaine." Mémoires de la
Ligue, iv. 700-732.

[2] " Mon cousin, prenez bon courage ; il est vrai que vous n'étes pas encore
roi ; mais le serez possible après moi." Biographie universelle (Paris, 1812), v.
348, 349, article Bourbon, Charles de.

[3] See above, chapter xi., p. 175.

[4] Above, chapter xi., p. 210.

[5] " Olivarez [the Spanish ambassador at Rome] obliged the pope to send
away Luxembourg, though it were only under the pretext of a pilgrimage to
Loretto." Ranke, History of the Popes, 224. Yet, according to the Instruc-

however, he had not given up all hope, but had written, immediately after reaching home, a very full paper to the college of cardinals. Hearing that the opposition of some enemies of his mission had prevented this communication from being laid before the conclave, he even wrote a farther letter to the prelate who might be chosen pope. The person whom he had intrusted with the duty of delivering this missive reported that Gregory the Fourteenth not only received it kindly, but gave him to understand that he would answer it and make such provision as he might deem most advisable.[1] These assurances the pope fulfilled by sending his nuncio to the Parisians with exhortations to persevere in their rebellion, with pledges of monthly'remittances of money, and promises of the speedy advent of a large auxiliary force; and, not least of all, with the two bulls which not only declared the French king to be an excommunicated heretic, but threatened with ecclesiastical censures and all the severity of an offended judge the entire body of Henry's adherents, of whatsoever rank or profession, churchmen and laymen, nobles or roturiers!

The pope incites Paris to persevere in rebellion.

Who could have believed that those thus menaced and condemned would, notwithstanding, renew the proposals so contemptuously rejected, or that the king who had been repelled and abused would himself deign to take part in the negotiations?[2]

Yet this is what actually came to pass. In the first place, Luxembourg, swallowing his pride as best he might, addressed the new pope a letter from the royal camp before Chartres, on

tions given by the French nobles to Luxembourg, July 7, 1591, when next requested to go to Italy, he accomplished at least one thing: "Tant s'en faut qu'elle [Sixtus V.] condamnast les susdits princes . . . qui avoient reconnu et suivoient le roy, que par un sien brief sur ce à eux despesché, elle leur donnoit sa benediction, louant ce qu'ils avoient fait entendre de leurs bonnes intentions en ce qu'ils avoient fait à l'entretenement de la religion Catholique, Apostolique et Romaine." Mémoires de Nevers, ii. 515.

[1] "Copie des lettres missives envoyées de la part du Seigneur Duc de Luxembourg au Pape," dated "au Camp devant Chartres," April 8, 1591, in Mémoires de la Ligue, iv. 374-378, and Mémoires de Nevers, ii. 529-532.

[2] This pertinent question I take from E. Stähelin, Uebertritt König Heinrichs IV., 267, who justly remarks that Henry's conduct on this occasion is significant of his inner views and plan.

the eighth of April, to accompany a more formal congratulatory address sent in the name of such of the nobles as were there present, felicitating him upon his assumption of the tiara.

M. de Luxembourg's letter to the pope.

Conveniently feigning incredulity as to the report that Gregory had promised aid to the rebellious Parisians, and expressing the hope that the nuncio now sent might act a better part than the envoys who had preceded him, Luxembourg reminded the pontiff of the notable change which had come over the mind of Sixtus the Fifth. Deceived, at the commencement of his pontificate, by the artifices of the enemies of France, this pope began to espouse the interests of the League in good earnest; but subsequently discovering his mistake, he applied himself to appeasing the civil dissensions of the kingdom. The writer stated that he had been assured from various quarters that Gregory had yielded to the persuasions of the ministers and pensioners of Spain, but that he had steadily refused to give any credit to these stories; for he remembered that, having, on his return from Italy, met his holiness, then Cardinal Sfondrato, near Torniceri, in Tuscany, the latter, who was on his way to take part in the election of a successor to Sixtus the Fifth, had, among other things, made this remark: "It is necessary that the King of France be King of France, and the King of Spain be King of Spain; for the greatness of the one will serve as a barrier to the ambition of the other." He warned the pope that the true Frenchmen, should they not only be abandoned but openly persecuted by the Holy See, might be forced to resort to strange alliances, alliances from which religion might be exposed to new perils. The princes of the blood, dukes, peers, marshals, officers of the crown, and the entire nobility of France—indeed, all good Frenchmen—had no other intention than to remain always very Catholic; and they hoped to be able by their services to oblige their king to recognize the truth of the Roman Catholic and Apostolic religion, and to make profession of it after the example of all his predecessors.[1]

---

[1] Mémoires de la Ligue, and Mémoires de Nevers, ubi supra. De Thou, vii. 786–788.

Nor was this all; the Roman Catholic nobles of Henry's court resolved, two months later, to repeat the experiment of sending Luxembourg himself to endeavor to treat with the pope. Indeed, Henry the Fourth at one time was strongly inclined to write in his own name to Gregory. He thought it best, however, first to consult Duplessis Mornay on the propriety of the action, and the reply he received was strongly adverse. It is of great importance to please the pope, said the Huguenot counsellor, but the favor of God is of still greater moment. The mere writing of a letter is a trifling matter—one can write to anybody—but the king must make use of the customary forms, or he will only give displeasure. He must call the pope his " very holy father ; " he must humbly kiss his feet and do him homage, and so doing he will recognize him as the head of the Christian Church. Report will exaggerate the action and make it still worse. Far better were it to let the French cardinals and those of their belief address Gregory. Let them complain of Sixtus for having sent Cardinal Cajetan, and of the present legate (the Bishop of Piacenza) for conspiring with the Spanish ambassador to overturn the kingdom, and for consorting with rebels against the authority of the lawful sovereign.[1]

Duplessis Mornay dissuades the king from writing to Gregory.

But if Duplessis Mornay succeeded by his remonstrances in dissuading the Huguenot king from addressing an undignified and fruitless appeal to the chief ecclesiastic of a system which he still professed to regard as corrupt, if not anti-Christian, he did not prevent him from taking such a part in the proposed mission of Luxembourg that the official instructions drawn up for his guidance bore this attestation of his majesty's approval : " Done at Mantes, the king being present, by deliberation of the aforesaid princes, as well of the blood as others, of the dukes, peers, chancellor, marshals of France, and other officers of the crown, archbishops, bishops, prelates, and lords of the council assembled for this purpose, I, the undersigned, secretary

---

[1] " Advis sur la formalité d'escrire par le roi au pape, envoyé à sa majesté, en 1591, après le siége de Chartres," in Mémoires de Duplessis Mornay, v. 42–48.

of state, being in attendance by their command and by the authority of the king, the seventh day of July, 1591." [1]

It is unnecessary here to rehearse all the arguments by which Luxembourg was to ply the pontiff, or the complaints he was to

Instructions prepared for M. de Luxembourg.

lodge against a nuncio who, upon his arrival, had gone straight to the Duke of Mayenne at Rheims, thus from the start renouncing the character of a judge and assuming the attitude of a party to the quarrel. [2] On one or two points, however, the explanations to be given to Gregory are worthy of attention. He was to be informed that it was no fault of Henry, that he had been prevented by the constant war waged against him from holding the assembly which he had promised to convene within six months after his accession to the throne. And Luxembourg, if questioned respecting the king's disposition to be converted, was ordered to make reply that his Roman Catholic nobles had none but good hopes; yet he was to add: " His majesty will never give to those that cover themselves with this pretext in their unjust uprising, the advantage of being able to boast that they have compelled him to do anything by force. If peace be restored to the realm, there will be an opportunity to propose to him the instruction to which he has shown a willingness to submit, not without hope of some good results. For he is not obstinate by nature." [3] Respecting the repeal of the proscriptive edicts of 1585 and 1588, Luxembourg was directed not only to plead the necessity of such an arrangement, that Roman Catholics and Protestants might live together without distrust, but to

---

[1] " Instruction à Monsieur de Luxembourg, allant à Rome," in Mémoires de Nevers, ii. 512–524.

[2] It is worthy of notice that the very first thing of which the pope was to be assured was, " that the aforesaid lords and princes, as well ecclesiastics as others, hold it as altogether certain and determined that outside of the Catholic, Apostolic and Roman Church there is no salvation."

[3] " Mais il ne donnera jamais cet advantage à ceux qui se couvrent de ce pretexte en leur injuste soûtenement, de se pouvoir vanter de luy avoir fait faire quelque chose par force ; et que si la paix estoit en ce royaume, il y auroit lieu de luy proposer l'instruction à laquelle il a monstré vouloir se soûmettre, non sans esperer quelque bon effet. Car il n'est point de naturel opiniastre." Ibid., ii. 520.

point to the fact that, under the edicts of pacification which those proscriptive edicts had displaced, Henry the Third was able, by the judicious use of his patronage, to sap the very existence of the Huguenots. If we may believe the writers, "most of them were withdrawing from the party, or were bringing up their children in the Catholic religion, in order not to be deprived of the honors and dignities of the kingdom, of which they saw that they could not otherwise have a share; so that it is evident that a few more years of patience would have brought them all back to the Catholic religion." [1]

Nor did the Roman Catholic princes and nobles forget to throw out a vague hint that papal obstinacy, in rejecting their just requests, might bring about in France results as disastrous as those that had been witnessed in Germany, England, and elsewhere. "Despair," they significantly remarked, "often urges men on to actions of which, but for it, they would not have entertained a thought." [2]

I have given this notice of Luxembourg's instructions, not that they were ever of practical moment, but simply to indicate the drift of thought with the nobles who, though Roman Catholics, were faithful to the king, and more particularly the tendencies, still latent, which were speedily to develop in the mind of Henry the Fourth himself. For, as a matter of fact, Luxembourg, although he had been selected for the mission, and although letters were written in various directions to secure for him all possible support, [3] did not set out for Italy. The incongruity was too great between the conciliatory attitude which the French nobles were attempting to assume toward the pope and the defiant attitude of the highest courts of law, staunch supporters of Henry's claims, which called Gregory " soi-disant," " self-styled," pope, pronounced his bulls to be abusive and null and void, and offered a reward of ten thousand livres for the arrest

---

[1] Ibid., ii. 521.   [2] Ibid., ii. 522.

[3] Five letters, addressed by the French nobles to the pope's nephew, to several cardinals, to the French ambassador, to the Republic of Venice, and to the Grand Duke of Tuscany, respectively, are given in the Mémoires de Nevers, ii. 526–528. Henry IV. himself wrote in advance, July 7, 1591, to the Duke of Retz, respecting Luxembourg's expected coming. Lettres missives, iii. 417.

of his nuncio, Landriano. "The royalist parliament," says De
Thou, "opposed this embassy, on the ground that the decrees
that forbade sending to Rome, and that declared
Gregory the Fourteenth an enemy of the realm, were
too recent. The Duke of Piney (Luxembourg) himself declined to fulfil this commission; and accordingly the
matter was deferred until, the aspect of affairs having changed,
Cardinal Pierre de Gondy and Jean de Vivonne, Marquis of
Pisany, went on an embassy to Rome."[1]

*Parliament ob-
jects to his
mission.*

Meantime the course of events had at length convinced the
king that he must grant to the Protestants that tardy justice
for which Duplessis Mornay and other representative men had
long been clamoring. It was at Mantes, on the banks
of the Seine, and early in the month of July, 1591,
that he announced his purpose to the royal council.
And first, in order to disarm prejudice, and to defeat,
so far as might be, the designs of the pope and his mischief-mak-
ing nuncio, Henry made a declaration, intended not merely for
the persons present, but for publication as a solemn edict, "concerning the intention which he has to maintain the
Roman Catholic and Apostolic Church and Religion
in this realm, together with the rights and ancient
liberties of the Gallican Church." He again referred to the
first acts after his accession, especially to his declaration of
Saint Cloud, that there was nothing he more heartily desired
than the convocation of a holy and free council for the settlement of the points in dispute; that for himself he had no obstinacy or presumption, but intended more willingly than ever
to receive all good instruction that might be given him; and
that, should God do him the favor to show him if he were in
error, he purposed embracing what he might see to be commanded of God and for his own salvation. At the same time he
had pledged his word and his oath neither himself to make, nor
to suffer to be made by others, any change or innovations respecting the Roman Catholic Church, but, on the contrary, to

*Henry an-
nounces his
purpose of
doing justice
to the Protes-
tants.*

*The declara-
tion of Man-
tes, July,
1591.*

---

[1] De Thou, vii. (book 101), 802. Stähelin (Uebertritt König Heinrichs IV.
273) seems to suppose that Luxembourg actually went on this mission.

conserve and maintain all its authority and privileges.   This declaration must have satisfied all who had taken up arms ostensibly for the defence of their faith, had they not in reality been animated by a desire to aggrandize themselves—as was sufficiently indicated by the compacts into which they had entered for the invasion of the kingdom in conjunction with the King of Spain and the dukes of Savoy and Lorraine.   Sixtus the Fifth, after having at first been imposed upon, learned, before his death, to see through their designs; but the present pope, a man of an entirely different character, had, upon the simple assertion of the French rebels that the king was conspiring against the Catholic religion, and that he rejected all instruction, held him to be incapable of receiving that instruction.   Moreover, he had sent a nuncio, who had entered France without the king's knowledge or consent, the bearer of bulls fulminated against the monarch as well as against the loyal princes, ecclesiastics, and officers.   In view of these facts, Henry reiterated his desire to be instructed by a free council, and renewed his oath for the maintenance of the established church; enjoining it upon the parliaments and the prelates of the kingdom, as being their proper and legitimate function, that they should take cognizance of the offence committed by the nuncio, and should adopt appropriate measures for the maintenance of the recognized privileges of the Gallican Church.[1]

The king followed this declaration with a long and forcible address, intended to convince any members of his council who might be ignorant, of the absolute necessity of an edict in behalf of the Protestants.

"Every one knows," said he, "under what fatal auspices my predecessor revoked the edict of 1577, at the solicitation of the authors of the present troubles, who had extorted from him by force edicts on other subjects also.   What disasters did not this revocation entail!   At length, to escape imminent ruin, Henry the Third was constrained to unite with

Henry's forcible address.

---

[1] "Lettres patentes du roy, contenans declaration de l'intention qu'il a pour maintenir l'église et religion catholique," etc.   Mantes, July 4, 1591, in Mémoires de la Ligue, iv. 387–392 ; De Thou, vii. 791, 792.

those very Protestants whom the rebels wished to destroy and annihilate. And he entered into a truce with them, solely for the purpose of effecting this union, which was so greatly desired, and of which the event demonstrated the utility, without, however, repealing the edicts issued against my person and my adherents.

"These prospective edicts have been condemned and abolished, as it were, by common consent. In fact, if they retained the force of law, I, to whom you show such marks of attachment and fidelity as lawful heir of the crown, should have forfeited my rights to the throne; the Protestants would merit no favor; you yourselves would deserve punishment as traitors, since, by your courage and your exertions you have opposed the progress of those who base their pretensions on these edicts and have prevented their success. These men must therefore be resisted by means of other edicts, and of an ancient law, to annul the new law; in order that our royal dignity and our rights be not contested, that the Protestants may enjoy the rights possessed by our Catholic subjects, and, finally, that you yourselves may be able to render us the obedience which is our due, and live in peace with the Protestants, who, under the eyes and with the consent of all men not blinded by party hatred, claim these same rights despite the edicts—it is not proper that such a state of things should any longer be tolerated. In fact, nothing is more pernicious in a state than to suffer the existence of factions, the inexhaustible source of disturbance; especially when he who ought to administer justice impartially, allows himself to be drawn in the one or the other direction, by prejudice or favor. Is it not better for us to lay down the law for the Huguenots, than to have it laid down by them? It is to be feared that there may arise among them a party leader, such as formerly was Admiral Coligny, who, by presenting a petition to the king in the name of all, earned the title of Protector of the Protestants—a title which he retained throughout his life. But since the laws of the realm have called us alone to the royal dignity, our glory demands that we should not tolerate the presence of a number of kings in France; for party leaders are kings, so to speak. Public security and the quietness of the state demand that all our subjects, being united under a single prince and under the authority of his officers, should together obey the laws they administer.

"We have," he added, "still more urgent reasons for conceding this edict to the Protestants. You are not ignorant of the fact that the Queen of England and the princes of the Empire, soon to arrive at the head of an auxiliary army, will not fail to make exorbitant demands, in order to obtain conditions favorable for the French Protestants. How far will they not carry their claims, should this matter at their coming remain in its present state? What shall we be able to refuse them with propriety, especially under circumstances in which their prayers, supported by the presence of a large army, will in some fashion be commands? It is for our interest not to have these foreign troops for enemies. We must therefore anticipate their requests; we must abolish and annul those violent and bloody edicts which have done so much damage, in order to revive that salutary edict which our predecessor of glorious memory used to call peculiarly his own edict. We ardently desire, therefore, that you should concur with us in so necessary a plan as this. It is the sole means of parrying the extraordinary requests which the Protestant princes are ready to make of us. Nothing can be more conformable to justice and reason. Those who think otherwise must condemn the war in which we are engaged for the defence of the state. They seek only an opportunity to sow divisions among you." [1]

The gathering of nobles whom Henry addressed was a large and imposing one, including not merely his ordinary council, but also a considerable body of ecclesiastics of the highest rank, and many of the most influential lords and statesmen. The Huguenot king was gratified to find that his remarks were received on all sides with respectful silence and evident approval. The young Cardinal Bourbon

Cardinal Bourbon alone objects.

---

[1] De Thou, vii. (book 101) 792–793. The historian, who took a leading part in carrying out this measure, and was, as he tells us, present when the king made his address, is an unimpeachable authority for the words and sentiments uttered on the occasion.

was the solitary exception. He seemed to feel himself called upon to espouse the cause of intolerance, evidently expecting that others would follow his lead. He loudly exclaimed that a Very Christian kingdom could not stand this motley crew of religious sects. These new doctrines, he said, were a poison, and France would never cease to be convulsed so long as she harbored them. A good deal more he added, making up in the warmth of his expressions for his lack of eloquence. Then he rose as if to leave the room. To his surprise not a man stirred —neither the Archbishop of Bourges, nor the Bishops of Nantes, of Maillezais and of Bayeux. As a demonstration in favor of the tiers parti, Cardinal Bourbon's angry speech was a failure, complete and almost ludicrous. His royal cousin contemptuously bade him resume his seat, and the discomfited prelate was forced to be a witness to the enactment of a law in favor of the Protestants which he was powerless to prevent.[1]

In the edict that was next read and approved, the words "Huguenot," "Reformed," "Protestant," "those of the religion," and their equivalents were conspicuously absent.

Henry abrogates the "edicts of July," Henry simply abrogated the pernicious edicts of July, 1585, and July, 1588, and restored to their full vigor the edicts of pacification previously existing—that is to say, the Edict of Poitiers, of September, 1577, as modified in some of its provisions by the secret articles of Bergerac and the conference of Nérac, and virtually re-enacted at the peace

And restores the edicts of pacification. of Fleix. There was not a syllable in the document to give offence to the most sensitive conscience of a loyal Roman Catholic. Henry dealt with self-evident truths— the quiet and fair prospects of the kingdom under the previous legislation, the foreign conspiracy for its overthrow, the unscrupulous methods pursued by the enemies of the crown to compel Henry to repeal his edicts of pacification, the disasters flowing from the intolerant Edict of Nemours, the unmixed evil for which the Edict of Union was accountable, culminating in the execrable assassination of Henry of Valois. It was an obvious inference, from the mere mention of these events, that

---

[1] Ibid., ubi supra; Mézeray, iii. 968, in Stähelin, 291; Davila, 498.

the repeal of the laws which had occasioned all this misery was not only proper but necessary. Their very memory ought to be consigned to everlasting oblivion. Henry would have been false to the traditions of the period, had he failed to style "irrevocable" his revocatory edict itself, but this designation was limited, in point of fact, by a sentence inserted at the suggestion of the historian De Thou, as he informs us, and couched in the following terms: "All this provisionally, until that it may please God to give us the grace to reunite our subjects by the establishment of a good peace in our kingdom, and to provide for the matter of religion, in pursuance of the promise which we made at our accession to the crown."[1]

The Protestants might have had somewhat to find fault with in an edict wherein the king, their professed fellow-believer, seemed to figure altogether as a stranger to their faith, making no reference, from beginning to end, to their common religion, while on the other hand he did not hesitate to speak of "the Catholic, Apostolic and Roman religion," quite as though he were one of its adherents. But the Protestants were already well used to such cavalier treatment at the hands of the king for whom they had fought and bled, and the coming Abjuration was already throwing distinct and unmistakable shadows before it. The eloquent La Roche Chandieu, companion of Henry and of D'Amours at Coutras, foresaw the approaching catastrophe, and the faithful Huguenot minister, it is said, died of grief at the melancholy prospect.[2]

Henry's attitude.

La Roche Chandieu dies of grief.

---

[1] "Edit du roy, contenant restablissement des edits de pacification, faitz par le deffunct roy Henri troisiesme sur les troubles de ce royaume," Mantes, July 1591, in Mémoires de la Ligue, iv. 383-6. See Recueil des choses mémorables, 738; De Thou, vii. 793, 794.

[2] "Voilà le roi à la messe nouvelle," writes Agrippa d'Aubigné (iii. book iv. c. 10, p. 363) referring to the events of the abjuration in 1593, "qui fut moins estrange, comme preveue par plusieurs, et entr'autres par la Roche-Chandieu, qui en mourut de desplaisir."—This eminent Huguenot minister— "ce grand personage," as Beza styles him—died greatly regretted February 23, 1591, as we learn from a very interesting MS. letter of Beza to Viscount Turenne, dated Geneva, March 9 (O. S.), 1591, first printed in the Bulletin de la Société de l'histoire du Protestantisme français, i. 277-279.

Meantime, thankful at least to be freed from the legal penalties which, though unexecuted, still hung over their heads, the Protestants welcomed with delight an edict which definitely proclaimed the most loyal part of the nation to be no longer outcasts.[1]

Jacques Auguste de Thou was intrusted with the honorable and important duty of securing the registration of the king's two edicts by the loyal court that claimed to be the true Parliament of Paris, although now sitting at Tours, and obtaining a declaration from this body respecting the actions of the pope and his intrusive nuncio similar to that made by the judges at Châlons. In both respects he was successful. Not only did the individual members of the Parliament of Tours declaim with learning and eloquence against papal aggression, recalling more than one historical event to support their rhetoric, but they jointly rendered a decree, on the fifth of August, in which, going even farther than their brethren of Châlons, they declared "Gregory, self-styled pope, fourteenth of the name, to be an enemy of peace, of the unity of the Roman Catholic and Apostolic religion, of the king and his estate;" and, moreover, "an adherent of the conspiracy of Spain, an abettor of rebels, guilty of the very cruel, inhuman and detestable parricide treacherously perpetrated on the person of Henry the Third, king of very blessed memory, Very Christian and Very Catholic." The next day the edict in favor of the Protestants was registered. The same formality had been observed at Châlons about a fortnight earlier.[2]

The Parliament of Tours denounces the pope, and registers the edict.

It must not, however, be supposed that the Parliament of Paris, now completely overawed by the League, suffered these and other similar decrees of courts whose legal existence it denied, to pass unnoticed. A war of retaliatory decisions arose. As the Châlons judges had ordered the burning of the pope's bulls, so the Paris judges directed the public executioner to tear in pieces and burn publicly

Retaliatory action of the rebel parliament at Paris.

---

[1] "Je loue Dieu," wrote Duplessis Mornay to his friend De Thou, July 18, 1591, "qu'elle ait esté mise en vos mains pour l'apporter à Tours." Mémoires, v. 64.

[2] See "Arrest de la cour de parlement seante à Tours," August 5, 1591, in Mémoires de la Ligue, iv. 393–395, De Thou, vii. 794–799, and Davila, 503.

an order upon which they heaped every opprobrious epithet,
and which they forbade all men from obeying.[1]

The Protestants had at length gained some part of their
rights, though far less than they had good reason to expect
under a king of their own faith. The edict in their favor was
provisional. The mixed courts to secure justice for
Protestants in their suits with Roman Catholics, were
not again instituted as under the Edict of Bergerac.

Scanty justice
done to the
Huguenots.

The Parliament of Tours openly maintained that the practice
of Henry the Third—who, while pledging the Huguenots by his
edict equal admission with Roman Catholics to all offices and
dignities, had taken good care never to appoint them to such
offices and dignities—must serve as the rule under his successor
as well. In short, the inferiority in the eye of the law to
which the adherents of the Reformed doctrines had been condemned was apparently to be maintained indefinitely.[2]

A convocation of the French hierarchy at Chartres followed
the example set by the laity, and, two months later, solemnly
pronounced the bulls of the pope, who was "badly informed,"
to be null and void; but concluded the declaration with an exhortation to all the faithful that their prayers should
ascend to Almighty God that He would deign to induce Henry to become a Roman Catholic, "as, from
the time of his accession to the crown, he gave us reason to
hope that he would do."[3]

Declaration of
the clergy at
Chartres.

Not content, however, with making this declaration, and thus
fulfilling the sole object for which they had been convened by
the king, the clergy undertook some other matters which but too
clearly revealed the hand of Cardinal Bourbon and the intriguing "tiers parti." They begged permission of his majesty to
write and send an envoy to the very pope whose bulls they had
just condemned, whom the Parliaments of Tours and Châlons

[1] De Thou, vii. 799. See also a later "arrêt" of December 22, 1591, in
Mémoires de la Ligue, iii. 397–399.

[2] Duplessis Mornay to Turenne, October 3, 1591, Mémoires, v. 84; Benoist,
i. 80, 81; Stähelin, 293, 294.

[3] "Declaration du clergé de France," Chartres, September 21, 1591, in
Mémoires de Duplessis Mornay, v. 72–75.

had pronounced an enemy of peace and an abettor of the assassins of the late king, and on the head of whose legate a price
had been set. They resolved to defer to some future time the
consideration of the order to be established for the provision of
benefices throughout the kingdom—the very thing to which,
above all others, they ought to have applied themselves in the
present anomalous state of the ecclesiastical relations of France.
They had the audacity to propose that parliament be forbidden
to take cognizance of any disturbances in the religious relations
of the realm, thus robbing the supreme court of one of its immemorial rights. All this was but prefatory to the request
that Henry would allow himself to be instructed and become a
Roman Catholic, and that he would look with favor upon the
undertaking of the clergy to make peace—"as if," wrote the
indignant Duplessis Mornay, "as if the king were not striving
for that very thing, and had not declared that for every step
taken by others toward him, he was ready to take four steps
toward them!" [1] The action of the assembled prelates effected nothing but to exhibit more clearly the
trouble which the clergy stood ready to give on occasion. Parliament justly resented the assembly's attempt to
usurp the functions of the most august tribunal of the realm.
Henry was firm in rejecting the proposal to confer upon ecclesiastics the office of umpires in settling the terms of peace. But
although the convocation of the clergy at Chartres was so bar-
ren of practical results, it ought not to be forgotten that one
remarkable suggestion was made and considered during the
sessions. Excommunicated as were the prelates by the terms
of Gregory's monitorial bulls, for not having renounced their
fealty to the king within fifteen days after the papal notifica-

Parliament resents their usurpation.

---

[1] The principal authority for the articles of the assembly of Chartres is the
"Depesche envoyée de Tours par M. Duplessis au Roy, le 3 Octobre 1591,"
in the Mémoires de Duplessis Mornay, v. 85, etc., together with the memorial
sent by the same person to the Parliament of Tours to set forth the assault
made upon its authority (ibid., v. 89–94). The service thus rendered to the
supreme court won for him the thanks of the judges and an invitation to confer with them at Tours. See also the Vie de Duplessis Mornay (Leyden,
1647), 161.

tion, and precluded as they were by decree of parliament from
sending to Rome for any of those purposes for which the authority of the See of St. Peter was supposed to be necessary, it
was gravely proposed that the French Church should cut loose
from Italy by recognizing as its head a Patriarch of its own.

The institu-
tion of a
French patri-
arch proposed.
We are assured that the single great obstacle that
prevented the realization of the plan was the inability of Cardinal Bourbon, who had never received
priestly orders, to obtain the coveted dignity. The Archbishop
of Bourges, upon whom the choice would naturally have fallen[1]
as the highest of the ecclesiastical dignitaries who had espoused
the royal side, and as the only French prelate already enjoying
the titular rank of Patriarch, not only would have been glad to
accept the rank, but exerted all his influence to secure it. Bourbon, however, would not permit his brother archbishop to get
the prize which he himself could not attain.[2]

Meantime the royal arms had been far from unsuccessful.
After a long siege, lasting from February to April, Henry himself had captured Chartres, a city of great importance

Henry takes
Chartres and
Noyon.
in the present crisis. For Paris was still pressed for
want of the necessaries of life. Corbeil and Lagny,
again in their opponents' hands, cut off from the inhabitants of the
capital their sources of supply along the upper Seine, but hith-

---

[1] Strictly speaking, the title of primate was regarded as belonging either to
the Archbishop of Sens or to the Archbishop of Lyons. The claim of the
former seems to have been the best, and he was "Primat des Gaules et de
Germanie;" the archbishop of the larger and more populous city, however,
gradually made good his claim throughout the greater part of the kingdom
(see Rise of the Huguenots, i. 118). But the Archbishop of Bourges alone
had the advantage of being styled Patriarch. "Les ennemis de ce prélat,
qui étoit déja Patriarche—dignité qui n'apartient en France qu'au seul Arché-
vêque de Bourges—disoient," etc., De Thou, viii. (book 103), 78.

[2] "Et peut-estre que le cardinal y eust consenty, s'il eust eu les qualités
requises pour l'estre luy mesme ; mais comme il n'estoit pas prêtre, et qu'ainsi
il eust esté contrainct de ceder cet honneur à un autre, il rejetta cet expedient et traita mal de paroles l'Archevêque de Bourges, qui dans l'imagination
qu'il avoit, que cette dignité luy appartenoit à cause du titre de Primat attaché
à son siège, briguoit de toutes ses forces de le faire agréer à l'assemblée."
Mézeray, Histoire de France, iii. 968, apud Stähelin, 328.

erto the rich "pays chartrain" had somewhat made up the deficiency. The preachers endeavored to quiet the popular alarm at the tidings that the granary of Paris was threatened, by assuring them that Henry would not accomplish his undertaking. An Italian monk, in a Lenten address on Shrove Tuesday, in the Sainte Chapelle, pledged his soul's salvation that Chartres would never be captured.[1] The denizens of Chartres were almost equally assured of a favorable issue; for was not their city the only one in Christendom that could boast of being the fortunate possessor of the ancient Druidical image upon which was the prophetical inscription, carved long before the advent of Christ, or, indeed, the birth of the Virgin Mary, foretelling the miraculous Incarnation?[2] And was not the virtue emanating from the image so potent that, according to the popular belief, a soldier's shirt which had been placed upon it became instantly proof against the deadliest blows of the enemy, nay, even against cannon-balls—in attestation of the truth of which, numerous garments supposed to have saved their owners' lives were hung, in lieu of tapestry, on the walls of the shrine?[3] But the "Virgo paritura" of Chartres seemed to be as deaf to the supplications of her devotees, as Sainte Geneviève had been to the litanies of the Parisians on occasion of the attack upon Saint Denis. On the nineteenth of April, just ten days after the Italian's venturesome assertion, Chartres surrendered to the royal army,[4] and the preachers had to content themselves with venting their impotent wrath in threats and imprecations. The "Politiques," as usual, came in for their full share of denunciation. Boucher said that they must all be killed; Rose,

---

[1] Lestoile, ii. 50.

[2] See Rise of the Huguenots, i. 59. De Thou, vii. 777.

[3] "Les gens de guerre, craignant les coups, ont accoutumé de vêtir cette image d'une chemise de toile, laquelle puis après ils portent en guerre, les uns dessus, les autres dessous leur harnois, ayant cette opinion, que les coups de canon même ne les sauroient offenser. Et de fait, plusieurs ayant par hazard échappé de grands coups, y ont fait des tapisseries de leurs chemises ; mais," adds the writer, with quiet sarcasm, "celles qui sont percées demeurent en chemin." Bèze, Histoire ecclésiastique des Églises Reformées, i. 103.

[4] Recueil des choses mémorables, 735–737 ; Agrippa d'Aubigné, iii. 244, etc.; De Thou, vii. 777–782 ; Davila, 494–496.

that a blood-letting after the fashion of Saint Bartholomew's
Day was needed, and that the throat of the disease must be
cut; Commolet, that the death of the Politiques was the life of
the Catholics. St. André offered to lead to the slaughter in
person, while the truculent curate of St. Germain l'Auxerrois,
apparently in disgust that his words excited derision rather than
enthusiasm in the hearers, made bold to assert that all who
laughed were Politiques, and that the men that hung about the
street-corners waiting for news ought to be dragged to the
banks of the Seine and drowned.[1]

The capture of Noyon followed that of Chartres—Noyon,
that small city of northern France which, far from honoring
the memory of John Calvin, has from that time to this appeared to experience deep shame at having given birth to one
of the greatest minds of our modern civilization. But on the
coast new perils threatened France. Philip of Spain had at
length begun to send troops as well as money for the conquest
of a country he hoped soon to call his own. His first venture
was in the west, where, in the month of October, 1590, his fleet
landed a body of five thousand Spanish soldiers in the commodious harbor of Blavet, where they were soon strong enough,
with the assistance of the Duke of Mercœur, to assault and take
the town of Hennebon.[2] The selection of the point of attack
was not without a plan. Philip claimed to have inherited the rights of his deceased wife, Isabella or
Elizabeth of France, who was a great-granddaughter
of that Anne de Bretagne who had brought to Louis the
Twelfth the magnificent dowry of one of the great provinces of
France. In the kingdom at large the Salic law might be, or
might not be, what some Spaniards asserted it was, a mere legal
fiction; but there was no question that Brittany was a female
fief, and could be held and transmitted by a woman. The royalists of France maintained, indeed, that the ancient duchy had
been incorporated in the kingdom and could not be separated
from it; none the less was it a standing menace to Henry that,

A Spanish force lands in Brittany.

---

[1] Lestoile, ii. 50.
[2] De Thou, vii. (book 99), 678, 679.

for a year, his arch-enemy had been entrenched on French soil.

But more inauspicious for the king than the Spanish foothold gained in southern Brittany, and quite effacing any success which his troops might lately have gained over Mercœur in that province, was the death of one Huguenot soldier, fatally injured in the siege of the little town of Lamballe.   François de

Death of François de la Noue, and François de Châtillon.

la Noue was, it is true, a man of three-score, and it was many years since he had first made his courage to be respected by friend and foe alike in the wars of the Low Countries.   But the hero of so many battles, through which his iron arm had stood him in good stead, was as ardent and almost as strong as ever.   Indeed, his devotion to the cause which, at great pecuniary expense and the cost of toils, wounds, and repeated imprisonments, he had maintained without flinching, had rather grown than diminished.   A Huguenot from deep conviction, his last hours reflected the serenity of a Christian to whom death has no terrors.   So long as he was able, he listened with attention to one of his friends who, at his request, read to him those precious psalms which, whether in peace or in war, in the closet or on the battlefield, in sickness or in health, were never far from the thoughts or the lips of the Huguenots, at any time between the Reformation of the sixteenth century and the days of the Revocation and the "Desert."   What had supplied enthusiasm to so many at the charge of Coutras or Ivry, now administered comfort to La Noue at the close of life. When failing utterance gave him premonition of the near approach of death, he directed his attendant to read him the words of Job respecting the resurrection, and when asked whether he believed this article of faith, he replied, with eyes upturned toward heaven, that as he had lived, so he now died in the hope that he would rise again from the dead.[1]   What rendered the king's loss still greater was that the death of François de la Noue, on the fourth of August, was followed, on the eighth of

---

[1] De Thou, a Roman Catholic, may serve as our voucher that the accounts of the peaceable end of La Noue given by Protestant writers are not exaggerated.   Histoire universelle, viii. (book 102) 7, 8.

October, by the death of François de Châtillon, the son of Admiral Coligny.[1] Henry could, at this critical period of his course, as little spare the young man in the dawn of a military career of extraordinary promise, as the veteran counsellor.

Henry retained, however, some brave and successful captains, upon whose shoulders the mantle of La Noue and Châtillon might worthily rest. Chief among these, doubtless, was Lesdi-guières, who, not satisfied with the capture of Grenoble, never grew tired of roaming through the higher Alps, transporting his forces with the greatest celerity over roads so rough as almost to deter the peasant when he threaded his way on the sides of precipices with his sure-footed mule, and penetrating with apparent ease the mountain passes where the traveller, despite grand roads laid out by the highest engineering skill of our times, is once and again tempted to turn back through fear or fatigue. One day he dashed down from the dizzy heights upon the plains of the Viennois and the banks of the Rhône, striking terror among the adherents of the League and encouraging the friends of the king. The next day he was on his way toward Provence, following up the steep course of the Drac to its springs, only to descend on the other side of the mountains by the sinuous Beuch and Durance. Effecting a junction with the forces of La Valette in the lower lands of Provence, he was soon afterward seen defeating the

Exploits of Lesdiguières.

---

[1] François de Châtillon was only thirty-four years old when he died in his castle of Châtillon-sur-Loing. Some of his exploits have been chronicled in these pages. He was an adept in military science, and had already made great attainments in mathematics and mechanics. According to De Thou, he contributed greatly to the capture of Chartres, and, at the time of his death, he was engaged in equipping vessels for the Indies. Henry the Fourth had appointed him Admiral of Guyenne, and the monarch showed his appreciation of his great merits by conferring the office upon his children. "He had," says the historian just referred to, "acquired so great a reputation, that men had no difficulty in believing that he would one day have surpassed the reputation of his father and grandfather in the profession of arms, had not death prevented it." Histoire universelle, viii. (book 102) 46. See the account of his life in Haag, France protestante (new ed.), iv. 215–223, and especially Count Jules Delaborde's recent monograph, a model of conscientious and appreciative biography.

troops of the Duke of Savoy near Esparron, at the foot of the
hills appropriately named "la chaîne de Sainte Victoire," and
pushing on for the relief of beleaguered Berre, under the very
walls of disloyal Aix, to Marignane and the shores of the Mediterranean Sea.   He was almost as much at home on the eastern,
as on the western slopes of the Alps.   When he had succored
the French garrison of Exilles, in the Italian valley of the Dora
Riparia, he returned with equal expedition to Grenoble, in order
that he might be in time to dispute the passage of the troops of
the Duke of Savoy, reinforced by the mercenaries sent, at the
pope's expense, from Rome and the Milanese.   The beautiful
stretch of the Grésivaudan, through which the Isère makes its
way before issuing into the broader fields of Dauphiny, is said
to have been celebrated for the extraordinary number of nobles
Battle of
Pontcharra,
September 19,
1591. who inhabited it.[1] The remarkable engagement, which
now took place in the vicinity of the village of Pont-
charra, occurred at the very foot of the castle Bayard,
the former home of the great general of Francis the First.   Men
thought that the spot had been purposely selected ; certain it
was that the manes of the brave Pierre du Terrail, the knight
without fear and without reproach, were placated by a slaughter
of the enemies of France so complete as almost to baffle belief.[2]
On the day of the battle—the nineteenth of September—two
thousand five hundred Savoyards were killed, while three hundred horsemen and almost all the colonels and captains were
taken prisoners.   On the morrow, two thousand men more, of
the pope's forces, unable to make their way home, surrendered
unconditionally.   Five hundred were butchered by the pitiless
soldiers before they could be stopped by the officers; the rest
were sent back to Italy, having promised never again to bear
arms against the King of France.   The booty was immense—
chains and collars of precious metal, money, and the like—to

---

[1] "La vallée de Grésivaudan, célèbre par la quantité de noblesse qui
l'habite." De Thou, viii. (book 102) 18.

[2] "Comme si on avoit eu dessein de les immoler aux manes du brave Pierre
du Terrail, surnommé Bayard, du nom de ce château qu'il avoit fait bâtir."
Ibid., viii. 21.

the value, it was estimated, of two hundred thousand crowns of gold. The French maintained that they themselves lost but four men killed and had but two men wounded.[1] The jealousies that had long subsisted among the adherents of the League at Paris now broke out into an open flame. It was well known that the mischievous legate of the pope, Sega, Bishop of Piacenza, recently created a cardinal, co-operating with the Spanish ambassador, Don Diego de Ibarra, was as anxious to further the designs of Philip the Second upon the crown of of France as was the ambitious Duke of Mayenne to thwart them and to secure the prize for himself. Early in November the legate set on foot a conspiracy which bore fruit about the middle of the month in a sanguinary tragedy intended to manifest to the world the impotence of the leader of the French portion of the League. To the success of the Spanish designs the Parliament of Paris constituted the most formidable obstacle. Judges who had not been loyal enough to forsake the capital and take their seats at Tours, in accordance with the command of Henry the Third, were nevertheless too patriotic to countenance a deliberate attempt to betray the country to a foreigner, and that foreigner one who had been an undisguised rival of Henry the Second and his sons. The seditious "Seize," who from being representatives of the sixteen quarters of Paris had come to aspire to figure as petty kings, and to manage the affairs of the nation, readily yielded to the legate's suggestions. Private resentment somewhat shaped the particular direction of the blow they struck. On his way to the parliament house, Bar-

Murder of President Brisson by the "Seize." nabé Brisson, the first president of the highest judicial body in France, was suddenly arrested by agents appointed for the purpose, and hurried off to the prison of the "Petit Châtelet." Cromé, one of the "Sixteen" and the president's sworn enemy, soon presented himself and read to the

---

[1] "Discours de la desfaicte de l'armee du duc de Savoye, faicte par le seigneur Les-diguieres en la plaine de Pontcharra, pres le chasteau de Bayard, vallee de Graisivodan, le 18 [19] jour du mois de Septembre 1591," in Mémoires de la Ligue, iv. 666-671. Recueil des choses mémorables, 742. De Thou, viii. (book 102) 15-25.

astonished magistrate a formal sentence, which condemned him
to death as guilty of treason against God and man. Inquiries
as to his judges, and the evidence whereon the writ was based,
elicited sneers and expressions of amusement at Brisson's simplicity. The bystanders vouchsafed him only the advice that
he should at once prepare to die, for his time was short. Indeed, scarcely had the unfortunate man the opportunity to
make his confession to a priest, before he was hanged upon a
ladder which served him in lieu of gallows. Two other judges,
Larcher and Tardif—the former a councillor of parliament, the
latter a councillor in the châtelet—shared Brisson's fate. Next
day the three corpses were suspended in front of the Hôtel de
Ville, upon the fatal Place de Grève, with appropriate labels
descriptive of their alleged crimes, and were exposed to the
jeers and insults of the populace.[1]

Having by this exploit, as they fancied, humbled beyond
measure both parliament and that portion of the League which
still "had the lilies of France engraven on their
hearts," the Sixteen turned to Spain with more confidence than ever that their treasonable purposes might be
carried into effect. On the twentieth of November, 1591,
five days after the murder of President Brisson, they signed
and despatched, by the hands of Father Matthieu, a joint letter addressed to Philip the Second. The Jesuit had enjoyed
rare experience in delicate matters of the kind ; happily for the
world, however, he was detected by the governor of Bourbon-

Disloyalty of the "Seize."

---

[1] "Discours sur la mort de Monsieur le président Brisson, ensemble les arrests donnez à l'encontre des assassinateurs, Paris, 1595." Reprinted in Cimber et Danjou, Archives curieuses, xiii. 319–331. The learned Étienne Pasquier has devoted two long letters (Œuvres, edit. Feugère, ii. 349–366), to the
conspiracy against Brisson and the execution. Both papers are full of interesting details, and will repay a careful perusal. It was regarded as in some
degree a just retribution that the first president, who had been too timid or
too ambitious to espouse the side of the king, should have been described, in
great capitals, as "Barnabé Brisson, chief of the heretics and politiques."
One of his companions was stigmatized as "favorer of the heretics," the other
as "an enemy of the holy League and the Catholic princes." See, also, De
Thou, viii. (book 102) 36–41 ; Recueil des choses mémorables, 743, 744 ; Lestoile, ii. 67, 68, etc.

nais, while passing through that province, and his precious document fell under other eyes than those for which it was intended. Never had there been such a revelation of the baseness of the ignoble junto which had usurped the reins at Paris and now undertook to dispose of the fortunes of the whole realm.

The " Sixteen " began with profuse expressions of the obligations incurred by France toward Philip—obligations so great that to repay them would be impossible, so intimate that they must regard any Frenchman who did not own himself to be for all time the most obliged servant of the Catholic king, and that king's posterity, as an enemy of God, of religion, of the quiet and public peace of the state, nay, of all Christendom. Next, they deplored the general affliction of the house of God, the pollution of churches, the discontinuance of the mass, the persecution of the clergy, the loss of souls by reason of heresy, the city, as it were, deserted, the fair colleges empty, the university forsaken. Only the Faculty of Theology continued to be well attended, that school which, both in Paris and throughout the kingdom, had, by its divine admonitions and exhortations, drawn closer the bonds of the holy union between the Catholic princes, lords, and people.[1] They dwelt in particular upon the wretchedness to which Paris was reduced, and to which it must succumb unless relieved by his majesty of Spain. Over against great discouragements the writers set two signal blessings, vouchsafed by Heaven, of which the glad tidings had come to refresh their drooping spirits. The first was the new zeal displayed by Philip himself, and by him enkindled in the Roman pontiff; the second was the deliverance from captivity, in which he had languished ever since the tragedy of Blois, " of that young prince of Guise, son of the first martyr of his quality, in this kingdom, since these present persecutions excited against the Church." From Guise they affirmed that, in view of his long and unmerited sufferings

Their letter to Philip of Spain, November 20, 1591.

---

[1] Among the ills enumerated is an allusion to the misdeeds of Henry the Fourth, which may be quoted as a sample of the amenities of the original. The " Sixteen " speak of " les sainctes vierges à Dieu sacrées, corrompues et violées par ce puant bouc et les siens."

and his persecuted innocence, they entertained the highest expectations that God would bless his efforts to the consummation of His work in the good cause " under the shadow, favor,
and aid of his Catholic majesty." Both of these items of good
news had come in August, a month which, for a number of
years past, they declared, God had, according to the meaning of
the designation, rendered propitious to the cause of religion.
It was in August, 1572, that Admiral Châtillon's conspiracies
being discovered, "he was ignominiously treated according to
his demerits, and this realm and the states of your Catholic
majesty in Belgian Gaul and Lower Germany were delivered
from the invasion which the heretics contemplated making."
It was in the same month, two years since, that besieged Paris
was miraculously delivered by the strange and unlooked-for
death of him who had been recognized as king, but, for his acts
of perfidy toward God and man, had been rejected. And it
was again in August, 1590, that the capital was rescued from
the peril in which it stood, from traitors within and enemies
without, by the opportune arrival of the Duke of Parma at a
time when a delay of but three or four days more would have
compelled surrender on the most miserable terms.

But Paris was poor and exhausted. She had spent five million crowns of gold and over. For more than three years she
had gathered nothing from her usual sources of income, from
her lands and inheritances; her officers had received no wages,
and her merchants had had no trade. For upward of a year
and a half she had been beset on all sides by an enemy who
watched her so closely that nothing could come in save by accident or force of arms, an enemy who would have ventured
upon more decided measures but for the garrison which the
King of Spain had been pleased to give to Paris. One thing,
however, remained to be secured. France must have a monarch crowned with the accustomed rites, and for this monarch
she looked to Philip's help. Indeed, according to the Sixteen,
France wanted no other person than the occupant of the Escorial to be her master. "We can certainly assure your Catholic Majesty," say they, "that it is the prayer and desire of
all the Catholics to see your Catholic Majesty hold the scep-

tre of this crown and reign over us—accordingly we cast ourselves very gladly into your arms, as into those of our father
—or else that you should here establish some one of your
posterity. If it be more agreeable to you to give us another
than yourself, let your majesty choose a son-in-law whom we
shall receive as king and obey with all our best affections,
with all the devotion and obedience a good and faithful people
can render. For thus much do we hope from the blessing of
God upon this marriage, that what we once received from that
great and very Christian princess, Blanche of Castile, mother
of our Christian and religious king Saint Louis, we shall receive—nay, the double of it—from that great and virtuous
princess, daughter of your Catholic Majesty, who for her rare
virtues attracts to her the eyes of us all. " [1]

By such words and more to the same effect did the Sixteen
lay the crown of France, so far as their words and acts could
lay it, at the feet of Philip, and give him very clearly to understand that it would please them marvellously well should he
condescend to give both that crown and the hand of the Infanta
to the young Duke of Guise.

There was one, however, who, though closely connected with
Guise, did not participate in these views. It was notorious that
the Duke of Mayenne had no desire to see the crown transferred
either to Philip or to Philip's son-in-law, even should that son-
in-law be Guise himself. But it was presumed that the blow
struck at parliament would terrify him, or, at the very least,
compel him to acquiesce. Instead of this, one day he
made his appearance in the city, having suddenly left
Soissons and deferred the junction which he was about
to make with Parma and his auxiliary forces. Evidently he
deemed it of more pressing importance to crush the sedition in

Mayenne avenges President Brisson.

---

[1] The original of the letter of the "Sixteen" is found among the MSS. of the
National Library at Paris (Fonds de Béthune, coté 9137). It was first published in 1830 by M. Paulin Paris in his Monumens inédits de l'histoire de
France, in connection with the Correspondence of Charles IX. and Mandelot.
De Thou, Lestoile, and the authors of the Satyre Ménippée, while referring to
this important document and quoting some of its most insulting expressions,
were not, according to M. Paris, acquainted with the text itself.

the capital than even to defeat the king himself. In vain did
the Spanish ambassador intercede for the culprits, and from
intercessions pass to open menaces; the duke, having placed a
faithful officer in command of the Bastile, proceeded to arrest the
most obnoxious of the Sixteen, and, on the fourth of December,
one of the lower rooms of the Louvre witnessed the exemplary
punishment of four men—two of them members of the council
of the Sixteen, and the other two as deeply implicated in their
bloody deeds—hanged to expiate the murder of President Brisson and his companions.[1] The council of the Sixteen henceforth ceased to be a power in the state. Parliament was able
to reassert itself. The time when an illegally constituted commission could demand of the municipality
of Paris the institution of a "chambre ardente" to make short
work of heretics, and could secure the right to designate the
members of the bloody tribunal, was passed.[2] Reason had begun to be heard in the councils of the League.

Fall of the "Seize."

Meanwhile the king, having recently obtained important accessions of strength in answer to his appeals to Germany and to
England, had resolved to complete the reduction of Normandy,

---

[1] See Pasquier's letters above referred to, and De Thou, viii. 42-44. Ame-
line and Louchard were put to death on this occasion, who, just two weeks before, had signed their names to the joint letter of the Sixteen. Henry IV.,
on hearing that Mayenne had put out of the way four of the "Seize," remarked that his cousin, the duke, had done well, but ought to have gone four
degrees further (*i.e.*, destroyed one-half of the council). Lestoile, ii. 75. See,
also, the " edict" given on the subject by Mayenne, December 10, 1591, under the title of "Abolition du duc de Mayenne de ce qui s'est faict à Paris, sur
la mort ignominieuse du President Brisson, les conseillers Larcher et Tardif,"
in the Mémoires de la Ligue, v. 74-77.

[2] Among the "Articles sur lesquelz les Catholiques de Paris desirent leur
estre presentement et promptement pourveu," presented by the " Sixteen " to
the prévot des marchands et échevins, November 15, 1591, the first was:
" Qu'il soict promptement estably une chambre ardente de douze personnes
qualifiez et grandes, d'ung president et ung substitut du procureur general et
ung greffier, qui soient notoirement de la Sainte Ligue, pour fé [faire] les pro-
ces aux heretiques, thraistres, leurs fauteurs et adherans, et qui seront nom-
mez par le conseil des seize quartiers de ceste ville." To which the answer
was: " Accordé que la nomination sera faicte par le bureau de la ville et de
leur consentement." Loutchitzky, Documents inédits pour servir à l'histoire
de la Réforme et de la Ligue, 279-281.

the richest province of Northern France, if not indeed of the entire realm. Rouen having once been wrested from the grasp of the League, the entire course of the Seine would be in the hands of the royalists, from Paris to the broad estuary through which Rouen besieged. the river empties into the English Channel. Havre and Honfleur, on either side of the entrance of the estuary, would not then be long in making their peace with the king. This is not the place to relate in all its details the remarkable siege that followed. The royal army was amply strong enough for the undertaking. Henry had received, near Vouziers, on the upper Aisne, the fourteen thousand Germans brought by Turenne; and to these were soon added six thousand English and as many more Swiss, not to speak of four thousand French troops, the remains of old regiments of foot. The united force thus numbered fully thirty thousand men, chiefly Protestants, who, as they served for pay, were pretty sure not to desert the monarch, when most he needed their services, on the plea offered by the gentleman serving at his own cost, that long neglected affairs at home must receive attention. The royal treasury, too, was in a far better condition than ever before, thanks in part to the sale which Henry had effected of portions of his own private domain and of crown property in Béarn and Normandy, in part, also, to loans of money from abroad.[1] But unfortunately the king had other obstacles to confront than those interposed by the besieged. Marshal Biron, having new grievances to complain of, thought himself justified in new measures to thwart his master. Intrusted by Henry with the task of beginning the siege, he turned his attention to assaulting the strong Fort Saint Catharine, which commanded Rouen upon the east, instead of following the sensible advice of directing his main attack against the city itself, whose position was lower and whose walls were in places very weak. In vain was the obstinate veteran remind-

---

[1] See Poirson, Règne de Henri IV., i. 300, 301. The considerable sums lent by Queen Elizabeth about this time appear in the "Mémoire des sommes de deniers que la Reyne d'Angleterre a prestez ou desboursez pour le Roy Treschrestien," in Sawyer's Memorials of Affairs of State (from Sir Ralph Winwood's papers), i. 29.

ed of the old military adage, "Ville prise, château rendu;" in vain was it suggested to him that when once Rouen was taken the fort could not long hold out. His comrades in arms soon came to the conclusion that the marshal, having been refused the post of governor, which Henry had previously promised the Duke of Montpensier to confer, when the place should be taken, upon Monsieur de Hallot, had fully made up his mind to do everything that was necessary to prevent the success of the army he commanded.[1]

The siege began on the eleventh of November, 1591. On the first day of the succeeding month Henry addressed the citizens, from the town of Vernon on the Seine, a conciliatory letter, assuring them of his friendly disposition toward them, and citing the treatment received by all the cities that had submitted to him, in proof of the sincerity of his purpose to protect and maintain the privileges of the Roman Catholic Church. But these kindly advances were received with scorn. The herald who brought the king's letter was told to inform his master that God had not been so lavish of His favor to Henry but that He had reserved a portion for His Catholic people; nor would He suffer the city where the extirpation of the heretics had been sworn in the Edict of Union to fall into the power of the heretics. The Rouennais were resolved to die rather than recognize a heretic as king of France.[2]

Answer of the Rouennais to Henry's summons.

---

[1] The secretaries of Sully tell us that their master strongly censured Biron's plan: "lequel dessein nous vous ouismes grandement blasmer, ayant tousjours eu la fantasie qu'il falloit attaquer la ville de Rouen, que vous disiez estre fort foible en de certains endroits, et par consequent fort facile à prendre, au lieu de s'amuser à attaquer une teste si estroite," etc. Of the motive they add: "Plusieurs vindrent à croire, et le bruit n'en estoit pas sourd, que le vieil Mareschal de Biron mal content de ce qu'ayant demandé le gouvernement de Rouen au Roy, il lui avoit respondu qu'il en estoit engagé de parole à Monsieur de Montpensier, pour Monsieur de Hallot; il faisoit toutes choses par despit, et ne vouloit nullement que la ville se prist." Mémoires de Sully, c. 33 (Ed. of 1663, i. 284).

[2] The "Bref discours des choses plus memorables advenues en la ville de Rouen, durant le siege mis devant icelle par Henry de Bourbon, pretendu Roy de Navarre" (Mémoires de la Ligue, v. 103-121), contains both the letter of Henry IV. and the city's answer.

Not content, however, with brave words, the citizens, under
the skilful leadership of Monsieur de Villars,[1] than whom
besieged city has scarcely ever boasted of a better governor,
applied themselves to the means of defence.   Not least curious
among the incidents of the time was a solemn service, instituted
on Sunday, the eighth of December.   Leaving the magnificent
cathedral of Notre Dame at the early hour of seven in the
morning, the procession moved successively to the churches of
St. Ouen, Notre Dame de Bonnes Nouvelles and the Capuchins,
Litanies and where in every case the host was exposed upon the
processions. grand altar amid all the splendors which ecclesiastical ingenuity could devise.   It would be tiresome to enumerate
all the dignitaries of church and state, from the governor down,
that were present.   The inclement season of the year did not
prevent three hundred merchants of the city, all of them walking with bare feet under the standard of the crucifix, from
heading the pompous array.   Every reliquary of which Rouen
could boast was there, from that of St. Romain to that which
contained some fragments of the bones of the eleven thousand
virgins.   It was in the stately church of St. Ouen that the
chief solemnities were observed.   There the Bishop of Bayeux
said mass, and there Monsieur Jean d'André, a doctor of theology and penitentiary of Rouen, delivered the sermon, from a
scriptural text never before, it may be believed, applied in such
a manner.   "*Nolite jugum ducere cum infidelibus*"—"Be not
unequally yoked together with unbelievers"—according to the
new exegesis here propounded, signified that the Roman Catholics should not and could not receive a heretic to be king of
France, and that death endured in so good a cause as that in
which Rouen was engaged was holy and enjoined of God.   The
discourse closed with an appeal to all who were present to raise
their hands and swear to prefer the loss of life to a recognition
of Henry of Bourbon, and with an injunction that every one
should fast on bread and water during Wednesday, Friday, and

---

[1] André de Villars-Brancas, governor of Havre de Grace, who had been
brought in the capacity of lieutenant to supply the inexperience of Duke
Henry d'Aiguillon, the young son of the Duke of Mayenne.

Saturday of the current week, with a view to the reception, on the ensuing Lord's day, of "the holy Sacrament of the altar—true and assured weapon against the heretics."[1]

Despite, however, all the resolution of the citizens and all the ability of Villars, despite processions and desperate sorties,

The Duke of Parma invades France. Rouen must fall if not speedily relieved. Again the Duke of Parma was urged to make no delay in coming to the relief of the orthodox of France. Already Philip had a foothold in Brittany, and Spanish war vessels swept the shores of France, sailed to and fro in the estuary of the Seine, and kept the communication open between the Norman capital and the sea. Now a new concession was demanded before Alexander Farnese would enter France, and Mayenne was compelled reluctantly to suffer a Spanish garrison to be placed in the town of La Fère, on the upper Oise, and near the Flemish borders.

At the approach of the Duke of Parma the king advanced to meet him with his mounted gentlemen and a few arquebusiers,

Henry wounded at Aumale. leaving the conduct of the siege during his absence to Marshal Biron. But his first encounter with the invader, a little beyond Aumale, on the borders of Normandy and Picardy, was not a success; his troops were driven back in considerable disorder, and Henry himself received a slight wound in the loins from a half-spent ball. Too weak in men to dispute the duke's advance, the king was compelled to permit the capture of Neufchâtel in Bray, and could only hang on the sides of the Spaniards, ready to take advantage of every mistake committed by his antagonist.[2] Parma was consequently forced to make short marches, and every evening to throw up intrenchments for the purpose of protecting himself from surprises at the hands of a vigilant and active foe.

---

[1] "Bref discours" in the Mémoires de la Ligue, v. 112, 113.

[2] It was in one of the minor engagements of this time that poor Chicot, the well-known clown of the king, was fortunate enough, though himself mortally wounded, to take prisoner the Count of Chaligny, a nobleman of the princely house of Lorraine, and actually in command as a general officer of one of the divisions of the present expedition. It is almost needless to say that the count was overwhelmed with chagrin at being captured by such an antagonist.

The king's repulse at Aumale and his wound were the least of his causes for annoyance. One day, when sitting at the Protestant preaching service in his camp, he received a messenger from Rouen who brought most unwelcome tidings. Villars had watched his opportunity, and, on the morning of the twenty-sixth of February, had made a sortie not less determined than unexpected. Pushing on to the enemy's position at Darnetal, and meeting little resistance, he had made himself master of Biron's cannon, carrying off some and spiking the rest; had turned the trenches, and had slaughtered the besiegers when, tardily and just awaking from sleep, they hurried to defend them. Not to speak of the damage to the works, the butchery of three or four hundred faithful soldiers, some of them men of bravery and eminence, was enough to discourage a less sanguine monarch than Henry. But the actual loss was not the most depressing circumstance. Again Marshal Biron had been culpably, inexcusably negligent, and such was the state of affairs, civil and political, that the king dared not take him to task. It was, indeed, more than suspected that, if the marshal had not purposely invited the murderous attack, with the view of further avenging his disappointment upon the monarch, he was, at any rate, not at all sorry that fresh disasters should befall the king who persisted in his heresy. And Biron had many counterparts among the Roman Catholics of Henry's suite. The king might make light of the reverse he had met with, and observe that the gain of another battle would make everything right; but all his fine speeches, as Sully informs us, could not restore the equanimity of the " malignants," nor prevent them from manifesting, by their sorrowful faces, by their melancholy looks, by shrugging their shoulders, by rolling their eyes upward toward heaven, by low whispers in the ear, and by predictions of all kinds of ill-success so long as the king should continue to be a Huguenot, the annoyance and displeasure with which they endured the rule of a king of the Protestant religion, and their hatred of its professors. This hatred, indeed, exhibited itself, in the army before Rouen, in a very tangible form. The victims of the late sortie had been

A successful sortie from Rouen.

Lukewarmness of Biron and others.

buried in ditches hastily dug in the nearest church-yards, and among the ten or twelve corpses consigned to each grave no attempt had been made to discriminate between orthodox and heretic. Such impartiality did not suit the prejudices of the more bigoted. They began to demand that the ground should be reopened, and the bodies of those whose presence desecrated the holy spot should be cast to the wolves and the crows. What with the difficulty of ascertaining the religious sentiments of each of the deceased and the indignation and threats of the Huguenots, who constituted two-thirds of the army, the atrocious proposal was not carried into execution. But like many other incidents trifling in appearance, but deeply significant of the implacable rancor of religious partisanship, it was another proof to a king already weak of purpose that he could never be secure of his crown until he should have renounced his mother's faith.[1]

Meantime, Villars at Rouen and Mayenne in the field were even more apprehensive that they might be too much indebted to the Duke of Parma for deliverance than afraid of the arms of Henry. The former hastily sent word to the Spaniard that Rouen could now take care of itself;

Parma's help dispensed with.

while Mayenne, in reply to the duke's very natural suggestion that the best thing to be done was certainly to press forward and at once make an end of all trouble by breaking up Biron's operations, politely informed Parma that he had come so far only to bring succor to the besieged. Now that fortune had effected this without the intervention of either the duke or of himself, his duty was to lead the army back to a place of safety. "Were I a private soldier," said he, "I should be happy to follow you anywhere; but, as Lieutenant General of the Crown of France, I cannot consent to make any rash and useless ventures."[2]

Nothing remained for Parma to do but to yield to the bad counsels of the leaders who had been so earnest in soliciting

---

[1] Mémoires de Sully, chap. 35 (vol. i. 308–310). M. Poirson takes the most unfavorable view of Marshal Biron's action at Rouen.

[2] De Thou, viii. 61.

his presence, and who now made it a point of pride to oppose him at every point. But scarcely had he crossed the river Somme, on his way back to the Netherlands, before Villars began to repent his self-sufficiency. The king had taken matters into his own hands, for Marshal Biron was still disabled in consequence of a wound received on the occasion of the disaster of the great sortie. Rouen was hard pressed, and the citizens, worn out by their incessant labors and prostrated by diseases incident to their situation, were driven to the verge of despair. Again Villars had unwilling recourse to Farnese, warning him that, unless relieved before the twentieth of April, he would have to capitulate with the king. His appeal was more promptly heard than it deserved to be. By one of those marvellous efforts of which Parma was capable, within six days, he

He is again begged to return.

traversed the space which Henry thought, from his own experience, could hardly be accomplished in less than twenty. In fact, the king was not only surprised, but in some peril; for in his fancied security he had given a brief leave of absence to his nobles, the infantry alone being deemed essential to the prosecution of the siege. Happily he had taken the precaution to provide for summoning the absentees in an emergency, and not many days elapsed before he again found himself formidable, with three thousand French horse, an equal number of German reiters, and twelve thousand foot. But he was not able to maintain the siege of Rouen, nor to prevent the fruit of the labors of four or five months from being

The siege abandoned.

snatched from his hands. It was, indeed, only the jealousy entertained by Mayenne of any plan proposed by Parma which shielded Henry from assault until the arrival of his re-enforcements. The Frenchman insisted that the king would easily be able to effect a retreat across the Seine, and that it was far better to turn the army's attention to the Dutch cruisers who had come to dispute with the Spanish vessels the command of the outlet to the sea. He recommended an attack upon Caudebec, a fortified place lying on the second fold of the sinuous river below Rouen, and again the Spaniard was constrained to yield to the superior authority of the "Lieutenant General of the Crown." Nor was this all. After the fall of

Caudebec, Parma, having been dangerously wounded in the arm while approaching too near the works, was not only compelled to take to his bed, but reduced to the necessity of seeing his wise counsels a third time overruled by the persistent opposition of the Lorraine prince.   Alarmed at the rapid growth of Henry's army, the duke was in favor of abandoning the newly acquired prize, and counselled a retreat westward to Lillebonne, where he might draw an abundance of provisions for his troops from friendly Havre, in his rear.   But Mayenne insisted upon retaining a position which might, he said, enable him to relieve Rouen from a renewal of the trial to which that city had recently been subjected.   How injudicious the latter plan was soon appeared, when the army of the League found itself confronted by a force larger than its own, and when, in a district desolated by war, the necessaries of life, even to water itself, became scarce and dear.   To the king's eager attempt to bring on a general engagement, the enemy's generals, now at last united in counsel by the common danger that menaced their destruction, gave no heed, but gradually shifted the camp from Yvetot, once famous for its claim to have been an independent kingdom, to the banks of the Seine.[1]   Retreat indeed seemed to be cut off. Not a bridge spanned the river at any point below Rouen.   But for nothing was Farnese more remarkable than for the fertility of his mind in devices to elude an adversary and to extricate himself from desperate straits.   Having secretly ordered the construction of pontoons in the Norman capital, he directed them to drop down the stream to the neighborhood of Caudebec.   With beams already prepared, a

Masterly retreat of the Duke of Parma.

---

[1] De Thou (viii. 68, 69) seriously discusses the merits of the story of the origin of the "royaume d'Yvetot," but, while inclined to concede its substantial truth, sees difficulties hard to be overcome in the statement that Gualtier, lord of Yvetot, was on his way home from a crusade against the Saracens, when sacrilegiously slain in a chapel at Soissons, on Good Friday, by King Clothaire.   As this was about 534 A.D., or between thirty and forty years before the birth of Mohammed, it must be confessed that the historian's perplexities are well founded.   Clothaire is said to have been threatened with excommunication by Pope Agapetus, unless he should make satisfaction to the widow and children of the murdered nobleman.   This he did by giving them the sovereignty of the fief which Gualtier had previously held of him.

floating bridge was quickly made, and almost before Henry suspected his intention, a great part of the Spanish army and of its
French allies was on the left bank of the Seine. By the skilful
management of Parma's son, young Ranuccio, the rest was safely brought across, and the French royalists had the mortification
of seeing the troops which, but a day before, they had supposed
to be hemmed in by a wide expanse of water, making their way
without hinderance toward the friendly refuge of Paris. The
brilliancy of Parma's movement was equalled only by the blunder of his opponents, who, on the announcement of his escape,
neglected even to send forward a portion of their well-appointed
cavalry to the nearest bridge in their possession, the Pont de
l'Arche, to harass, if not cut off, the retreat of Parma.¹

The fault, however, lay not with Henry, but with his treacherous council, and particularly with Marshal Biron, author of so
many disasters and disappointments. Only a few days
before, this doughty warrior gave a fresh proof of his
half-heartedness. During not less than five engagements between the twenty-eighth of April and the
tenth of May, the combined forces of Parma and Mayenne had
been roughly handled; and, during their retreat from Yvetot to
Rançon, near Caudebec, only a little more vigor on the part of
the marshal would have turned their flight into a rout. It was
at this juncture that the younger Biron applied to his father for

¹ De Thou has given a good description of the siege of Rouen, and of the
second campaign of Parma in France, in the 102d and 103d books of his admirable history (viii. 46–73). See, also, Agrippa d'Aubigné, iii. 257, etc.; Recueil des choses mémorables, 743–748 ; "Bref discours des choses plus memorables advenues en la ville de Rouen," in the Mémoires de la Ligue, v. 103–121,
already referred to ; "Bref discours de l'heureuse victoire qu'il a pleu à Dieu
envoyer au Roy contre la Ligue, et ses principaux chefs, és mois d'Avril et de
May, 1592," reprinted in the Mémoires de la Ligue, v. 155–157 ; "Avis du camp
de Fescamp, le iii May, 1592," ibid., v. 157. The last two documents, composed at the time by loyalists, must be read with caution. The "Bref discours"
makes the loss of Parma during his campaign to have amounted to between
six and seven thousand men. The "Avis" was written at a time when it was
confidently believed that the enemy's forces were so shut in that their destruction or dispersion was inevitable. Henry's dismissal of his nobles and others
is here represented as a feint to entice the enemy.

five hundred horse, a number quite sufficient to accomplish the end proposed.   But the marshal gruffly denied the request. To have granted it might be to bring the war to a close, and, with the war, the occupation and importance of military men. " What, knave," said he, " do you wish, then, to send us to home to plant cabbages at Biron ? " [1]   The young man went away muttering, it is said, that, were he king, he would have the marshal's head cut off.[2]   Now the same disloyal servant of the French crown used his predominant influence in the royal council to check Henry's impatience and cover Parma's retreat. And he was not alone.   In assigning the causes of the failure of the royalists, Sully puts Biron's selfishness only in the second place, and mentions as first of all, and principal, the opposition of the most zealous among the prominent Roman Catholic noblemen.   Again the fear that Henry might triumph over his enemies and establish himself firmly upon the throne before the fulfilment of his promise to be " instructed," and the insuperable aversion to the sight of a Huguenot seated upon the throne of France, postponed the hope of peace already long deferred.   Again the disloyal treasurer found it convenient to have no funds at hand wherewith to pay Swiss and German mercenaries, who chose this very opportunity to protest that they would not take a single step before their wages should be forthcoming.[3]

---

[1] " Quoy donc, maraut, nous veux-tu envoyer planter des choux à Biron ? " Péréfixe, Histoire de Henry le Grand, 160.

[2] " On disoit, et mesme son propre fils le luy reprocha, que s'il eust alors poussé vivement, il eust aisément deffait toute l'armée, mais qu'il arresta son bonheur, parce qu'il craignit qu'un si grand coup ne mist fin à la guerre et à son employ."   Mézeray, Abrégé chron., vi. 73.   " Ils ajoutent que si le maréchal de Biron n'eût point arrêté l'infanterie du roy, qui dejà avoit défait deux régimens des ennemis, la victoire auroit été entiere."   Lestoile, ii. 87.   See Poirson, i. 315.

[3] " Le pire conseil fut suivy pour quatre causes et raisons, dont la premiere et principale provient des plus zelez et qualifiez Seigneurs Catholiques, desquels vous sçavez bien les noms sans que nous les disions, car il y en avoit de vos plus proches et de vos intimes amis.   .   .   .   La quatriesme, que ceux des Finances, pour reduire les choses où ils desiroient, firent manquer l'argent que l'on avoit promis aux Suisses et Reistres," etc.   Mémoires de Sully, chap. 35 (Ed. of 1663, i. 320, 321).

The bridge of Saint Cloud had been broken down by the Leaguers of Paris. As the inhabitants of the capital had no inclination to admit their Spanish allies into the city by the Pont Notre Dame, a bridge of boats was hastily constructed for their accommodation. Having remained in the vicinity of Paris long enough to receive the congratulations of Madame de Montpensier and her coterie, Parma proceeded to Château-Thierry, and thence, after giving some rest to his exhausted army, to the Netherlands. It was the last time that able general ever set foot in France. On the second of December, worn by fatigue, prostrated by illness, and suffering from his recent wound, he died at the city of Arras, when about to undertake a third invasion of France in the interests of the League.[1] He was preceded to the grave by Marshal Biron, whose head was carried away by a cannon-ball as he was imprudently inspecting the fortifications of Épernay, recently captured by Mayenne, but soon after retaken by the king.[2] It may be questioned whether Henry gained more by the death of his gallant enemy in arms than by the removal of his own general, whose great military abilities had so often been exerted to restrain the king's victorious arms and to render fruitless his most strenuous efforts.

Death of the Duke of Parma.

---

[1] Mémoires de la Ligue, v. 201; Recueil des choses mémorables, 758; De Thou, viii. 131.

[2] De Thou, viii. 74, 75.

CHAPTER XIII.

THE ABJURATION.

THE siege of Rouen was not the only event of the year from which Henry and the Huguenots, who had so faithfully clung to his fortunes, derived little satisfaction.   Three years had passed since the assassination of the last of the Valois, yet his successor was even now engaged in a conflict with his enemies, of which the issue was still doubtful; three years had passed since a Huguenot had ascended the throne, yet were his fellow-believers no nearer the realization of the dream of complete religious liberty which had sustained their courage through an entire generation of struggles, massacres, and pitiless warfare.   In scarcely a year of the last quarter of a century had the general results of their military operations been more indecisive, even when they fought under the banners of noblemen of inferior degree, than in 1592, when they possessed the signal advantage of having royalty upon their side.   True, in the northeast of the kingdom, success attended the arms of Henri de la Tour d'Auvergne, Viscount of Turenne, whom, a year before, the king had rewarded for his devotion and loyalty by honoring him with the hand of Charlotte, sole heiress of the great house of De la Marck, and by conferring upon him the dignity and the ample domains of the Duchy of Bouillon.[1]   But the gains in the neighborhood of Sedan were more than balanced by the

Various fort-unes of war.

Successes near Sedan.

---

[1] De Thou, viii. (bk. 102) 44, 45.   See, for the victory of the Duke of Bouillon, ibid., viii. 101, 102, or more in detail, a contemporary document entitled, "Brief discours de ce qui est advenu en la prise de la ville de Dun, sur le duc de Lorraine, par le duc de Bouillon, au commencement de decembre 1592," reprinted in Mémoires de la Ligue, v. 191–194.

losses sustained by the royalists in the provinces of Anjou and
Maine, where the cities of Château-Gontier and Laval opened
their gates to the Duke of Mercœur and the League,
Losses in
Anjou and   after the defeat experienced by the Prince of Dom-
Maine.
bes, eldest son of the Duke of Montpensier, in his
retreat from the fruitless siege of Craon.[1] So, too, in the south,
a conspiracy to betray to Philip the city of Bayonne, the key
of the Spanish entrance on the shores of the Bay of
Bayonne.
Biscay, signally failed; but, farther to the east, the
younger Joyeuse, brother of the favorite of Henry the Third
who lost his life in the battle of Coutras, greatly advanced the
cause of the disloyal party in Quercy and the adjacent region.
The important city of Carcassonne had fallen into his hands
toward the end of the previous year, and the whole of upper
Languedoc seemed likely to share in the fate of Carcassonne.[2]
Antoine Scipion de Joyeuse, however, was himself destined to be
a victim to the strange mutations of fortune which were characteristic of this period. At the close of his brilliant career
Defeat and   of almost uninterrupted success, the ambitious young
death of An-
toine Scipion general, after having ravaged the vicinity of Monde Joyeuse.   tauban, and captured Montbartier, Monbequin, and
other places of minor importance, proceeded to lay siege to the
city of Villemur, lying about midway between Montauban and
Toulouse. It was a venturesome undertaking, of a kind against
which his father had warned him with his last breath. " Be
careful," said Duke William of Joyeuse to his son, " not to lay
siege to towns belonging to the adherents of the Protestant
religion, since they fight with desperation in defence of their
property, their religion, and their lives. Attack, if you will, the
' Politiques,' who, being of the same religion with ourselves, are
more ready to enter into some composition, after having made
sufficient resistance to vindicate their honor."[3] Not only did the

---

[1] May 24th. De Thou, viii. 94-98; Agrippa d'Aubigné, iii. 271-274.
[2] See the Mémoires de Jacques Gaches, 418, 419.
[3] " Au mépris des dernières instructions du feu duc son père, décédé quelque
temps auparavant [in January, 1592], qui luy avoit recommandé de prendre
garde à n'entreprendre point de siége des villes de ceux de la religion, qui se

garrison of Villemur institute a determined resistance to their
assailants, but a resolute force of Huguenots gathered from all
quarters to its relief. Antoine Scipion de Joyeuse was himself attacked in the intrenchments which he had thrown up
around his army. Surprised by the suddenness and fury of the
assault, the Leaguers, at the first discharge, abandoned their
outermost works to take refuge within a second line of breast-
works. A half-hour of hard fighting ensued, when the Huguenot captain, impatient at the delay, commanded his nephew,
who carried the colors of the regiment, to hurl them within the
enemy's ramparts. "Let us see," cried he at the same time to
his soldiers; "let us see whether our men will be so cowardly
as to abandon the flag to the foe!"[1] At the word the royalists rushed forward, and, before their opponents had realized
their situation, the works were carried. In a few minutes
the forces of Joyeuse, superior in numbers, were flying pre-
cipitately in the direction of the river Tarn and the friendly
city of Toulouse. In vain did the duke endeavor to check the
panic of his troops; they would listen to no remonstrance,
and he was fain to follow their example. Unfortunately the
bridge across the Tarn had been broken down, and, in the attempt to save themselves by swimming, the fugitives, in great
numbers, perished in its waters. Among them was the young
duke himself, who, plunging in clad in full armor, was drowned,
with the curses called forth by his ill-success still fresh upon
his lips.[2]

---

défendent en desespérés pour leurs biens, pour leur religion, et pour leurs vies;
mais de s'en prendre aux politiques qui, estans de mesme religion qu'eux, sont
plus faciles à composer, après quelque résistance pour leur honneur. Il en-
treprit ce siége sans se souvenir de tous ces advis." Mémoires de Jacques
Gaches, 432.

[1] "Voyons un peu sy on sera sy lasche d'abandonner le drapeau aux ennemis." Ibid., 437.

[2] " Le pont qu'il avoit basti estant coupé, causa la mort de presque tous ceux
qui avoyent quitté la terre pour se refugier à l'eau. Lui forcenant de despit
et aboyant le ciel, 'A Dieu mes canons,' dit-il, 'ha je renie Dieu, je cours
aujourd'hui grand' fortune.' De ce pas il s'achemine au Tar [Tarn], pour
se rendre comparsonnier au malheur de ceux qui alloyent en l'eau, pour
souffrir la juste peine des maux que sous sa conduite, ils avoyent fait par

It was not otherwise in Dauphiny and Provence. There, too, victory perched sometimes upon the standards of the Duke of Savoy, at others upon those of Lesdiguières. Into the hands of the former fell the small but highly fortified port of Antibes, on the Mediterranean coast; and the ancient Roman town of Vienne, on the bank of the river Rhône, was gotten through treachery by the Duke of Nemours; while their Huguenot rival in the art of war pursued a course of almost uninterrupted success in the high Alps, where no other military leader of the day seemed so much at home. Rocky defiles possessed no terrors for this indomitable general. The enemy were amazed both at the hardihood and at the expedition of a commander who revelled in the accomplishment of what to others appeared impossible. Early in the year, summoned by the earnest entreaties of the inhabitants of Provence, he left the city of Gap, and rapidly descending the narrow valley of the Beuch, threw himself upon the towns of the Durance and of the more distant seaboard which held for the League. A long list might be made of the places that yielded to his arms or opened their gates in terror at his approach.[1] After carrying consternation

The gains of the Duke of Savoy.

Achievements of Lesdiguières among the Alps,

---

le feu. . . . Le Tar, par la violence de son randon, le ravit d'entre les mains de ceux qui le tenoyent; et comme executeur de la justice divine, mit fin à son orgueil, sa cruauté, et ses blasphemes." Copie d'une lettre contenant le vrai et entier discours tant du siege de Villemur, que de la defaicte de Monsieur le Duc de Joyeuse, in Mémoires de la Ligue, v. 178, 179 —a long and valuable communication signed by Claude de la Grange, of Montauban, styled by the author of the Recueil des choses mémorables (p. 750), "excellent historien, et tres eloquent entre les eloquens de nostre temps." The royalists lost but ten men; the League two thousand men in dead, and only forty-three prisoners. Neither the Mémoires de Jacques Gaches (pp. 436-438) nor the Mémoires du baron d'Ambres (apud Mémoires de la famille de Portal, 353, 354), both of which are contemporary authorities and do ample justice to the bravery of Joyeuse, make any reference to the alleged blasphemous words of the unfortunate young man. See, also, Recueil des choses mémorables, 752, 753 ; De Thou, etc.

[1] Among the more important may be noticed upon the map the names of Peyrolles, Jouques, and St. Paul, on the Durance ; Castellane, on the Verdon ; Aups, Barjols, Cotignac, and Muy, on or near the Argens ; La Cadière, near Toulon, etc.

to the citizens of Nice, he turned westward and was so successful in the region beyond Toulon that the inhabitants of Mar-
seilles were glad to redeem from pillage a number of towns in
their vicinity by the payment of twenty thousand crowns of
gold.[1] In the autumn Lesdiguières carried out a cherished plan
and in Pied- of invading the ancestral estates of the Duke of Savoy.
mont.   Crossing Mont Genèvre from Briançon, with a force
of six hundred horse and three thousand five hundred foot, he
ravaged with one part of his army the vicinity of Susa, in the valley of the Dora Riparia, but meanwhile directed the other part
to the neighboring Val Pragelas, descending into the lower valley
of Perouse, and advancing to the walls of the city of Pignerol
itself. His ladders proved too short to enable him to capture
this stronghold, but Luserne and Cavour, farther to the south,
fell into his hands. At the entrance of the valley of Luserne
he constructed the powerful fortification of Briqueras.[2] Here,
among the Italian Waldenses, the Huguenot soldiers of Lesdiguières—many of them doubtless descendants from the same
stock, Waldenses or Vaudois from the valleys of Freissinières
and Queyras among the mountains of Upper Dauphiny, or from
Mérindol and Cabrières on the Lower Durance—found themselves in the midst of a people of the same faith. Loyalty to
their prince struggled in the breasts of their hosts with religious
sympathy and the sense of a community of interests: If we
may credit the French historians, the Waldenses testified in
their countenances their delight at the coming of the French,
wrought with zeal on the works of Briqueras, and took without
reluctance the oath of allegiance to Henry the Fourth, which
was required of them. Their own historians give a different account of the matter, and insist that the Waldenses at first refused
to take the oath, and only complied with the repeated demand
after having received from Turin the secret consent of the
Duchess of Savoy—her husband was absent in Provence—and
of her council. Their assertion does not appear to be ground-

---

[1] "Brief recit des exploits de guerre du sieur des Diguieres," etc., in Mémoires de la Ligue, v. 781, 782 ; De Thou, viii. 110, 111.

[2] De Thou, viii. 113-119.

less, if, as is said, at the end of the two years of French occupation the Waldenses were able to convince the duke's council —certainly not prejudiced in their favor—of the integrity and loyalty of their conduct.[1]

There could be little doubt that, in estimating accurately the relative importance of the gains and losses of the king during the year 1592, the balance would be found to be somewhat in favor of his majesty. He had rather advanced than receded in his struggle for universal recognition. Yet the inquiry naturally forced itself upon the minds of the worldly-wise—How long will it require, at so slow a rate, to secure ultimate success? Evidently the moment was rapidly approaching when Henry, if he were not firm in his religious convictions, would see no other way to the attainment of his hopes than by a renunciation of the faith in which he had been brought up—a moment when, too, he would not lack for prudent advisers to suggest to him the necessity of no longer hesitating to give France peace by the sacrifice of his personal preferences.

Outside of the kingdom the prospect was dark. The great ally of the League was deeply interested in its success, profuse in promises, and lavish of men and treasure; the nearest and most natural ally of the king was capricious, at times indifferent. "Our neighbors," wrote Duplessis Mornay on one occasion—and his words clearly pointed to Queen Elizabeth of England—"give us succor only out of season and peevishly, while the King of Spain neglects everything else that he may attack us, denies himself everything that he may be able to supply our enemies. He esteems the affairs of France to be more his own affairs than those which immediately concern him; whereas our neighbors of whom I have spoken are nettled if one merely suggest to them that they too have interests at stake. These are the reasons that lead us to look about us for the best means of reaching a peace."[2] Nor was the Huguenot diplomatist overstating the case with re-

Supineness of the king's allies.

---

[1] See Monastier, Histoire de l'église vaudoise depuis son origine, et des Vaudois du Piedmont, i. 303, 304.

[2] Duplessis Mornay to Buzenval, April 18, 1592, Mémoires, v. 303.

spect to the great Protestant queen. When, some three or four
months before the time at which he wrote, Duplessis Mornay
was sent to England to solicit help for the king his master,
he found Elizabeth boiling with anger against Henry for his
dilatoriness, against the Earl of Essex for not bringing back
the troops she had sent to France—in short, against every one
concerned. In a second interview she did indeed treat Duplessis Mornay and his fellow-envoy with a little more
courtesy, and, after reading a memorial handed in by
them, actually consented that they should have two
thousand pikemen and one thousand musketeers ; but in the
brief space of two hours she changed her mind again, and was
furious in her reproaches against her own counsellors, whom she
openly accused of collusion with the Frenchmen. In short,
Queen Elizabeth dismissed Duplessis Mornay and Beauvoir
with the assurance that henceforth she would content herself
with "praying" for the King of France. To which the Huguenots very naturally replied that her majesty must pardon
them for saying, that to pray to God in the king's behalf was
indeed a woman's succor, but not the aid to be expected of a
queen and powerful princess such as she was, who to her prayers
ought to add of her means. It was characteristic of the fickle
Elizabeth that scarcely had Essex regained the shores of Great
Britain before she despatched to Henry a re-enforcement of two
thousand men—one-half of what he had asked for—with an
intimation that she did so in consequence of the reasons ad-
duced by the late envoys.[1] So fitful and uncertain were the
breezes that came across the Channel as compared with the
strong and steady currents of help from Spain!

The marginal note, beside the paragraph:

*Queen Eliza-
beth's capri-
ciousness.*

The spasmodic and uncertain support, which was all that he
could hope to obtain from his Protestant allies, led Henry to
consider the quickest means of securing peace, and this consideration prompted the secret negotiations into which Du-

---

[1] See at great length the "Negotiation de M. Duplessis en Angleterre, en
janvier 1592," in the Mémoires, v. 152–188 ; and the instructions of the
envoy signed by Henry IV. in camp before Rouen, December, 1591, ibid.,
v. 129–137.

plessis Mornay entered, on behalf of his majesty, with Villeroy, representing Mayenne and the League. This was during the siege of Rouen (March and April, 1592). The time had at last come when the leaders of the rebellion were, with few exceptions, ready to throw off the mask of religion, and make such terms as their prolonged resistance to the king's arms seemed to entitle them to dictate. No talk now of the crime of treating with an heretical prince, excommunicated by Mother Holy Church. Those hitherto so fiery in their zeal were quite ready to lay down their arms if only their private interests might be duly considered. The Duke of Mayenne, now hopeless of securing the crown of France for himself, at heart preferred to see that bawble resting upon the head of Henry rather than gracing the brow either of the decrepit Philip the Second or of the Infanta, his daughter. Even the Duchess of Nemours and the Duke of Montpensier were reported to be for peace and reconciliation. Only Madame de Guise was opposed, because she still hoped to see her son upon the throne as husband of the Infanta, and Monsieur de Rosne, by reason of the two thousand crowns he drew monthly from Spain.[1]

Negotiation between Duplessis Mornay and Villeroy.

It was the private conditions demanded by the leaders which Duplessis Mornay was most anxious to ascertain. What use was there in treating of the religious question, of the king's " instruction " and prospective " reunion " with the " Catholic Church," which were but excuses, so long as the price at which each one of the noblemen now loud in professions of zeal was ready to sell out his opposition had not been definitely stated? The Huguenot declined to begin serious discussion until the envoy of the League should have produced his instructions upon this point. Villeroy, however, protested with great solemnity that he had no documents of the kind about him. His master was too disinterested, forsooth, to suffer any selfish purposes of his own to interfere with the advancement of the common weal. But Duplessis Mornay had too

Mayenne's secret expectations.

---

[1] Mémoire sent by Duplessis Mornay to the king, March 28, 1592, ibid., v. 247, 248.

large an experience in the arts of diplomacy to give much credit
to such asseverations. By and by his companion is seen to
change countenance; he hesitates, his denials become more
faint, and finally, not without many indications of the shame
he feels to be engaged in such ignoble work, he draws out of
his pocket the desired paper. There it is in black and white.
Over against each name, beginning with that of Mayenne himself, stands the precise sum, in honors, offices, and filthy lucre,
at which the submission of the owner of the name can be
bought. Villeroy, under promise of strict secrecy, produces the
key to the cipher, and puts Duplessis Mornay in possession of
the precious facts: The Duke of Mayenne demands the government of the province of Burgundy in perpetuity for himself
and for his heirs after him; the royal domain of the same province as a pledge for some notable sum; the right to dispose of
all civil offices and churchly benefices in the same province; a
large amount of ready money to pay his debts; and a dignity
that shall elevate him above all other subjects of the French
crown. The Dukes of Mercœur, Nemours, Guise, and Joyeuse
are a little more modest in their claims. Each must have the
government he now possesses assured to him, together with the
right to nominate the governors of the included cities and
towns.

Duplessis Mornay had come prepared for extravagant demands; he had certainly expected no such exorbitant demands
as these. Glad as he was to come at the truth—especially glad
to possess the proof that the leaders were ready for a sale—he
threatened at once to break off the negotiations. He

A virtual dis-
memberment
of France.
informed Villeroy that what was proposed was nothing
less than the dismemberment and ruin of France. A
man might, under certain circumstances, be willing to cut off
an arm to save his life; he would never consent to part with
one to destroy his life. It might be reasonable to advise the
king to sacrifice Burgundy for the purpose of preserving the
rest of his realm; but the example would be disastrous, inasmuch as five or six chieftains, over whom the authority of
Mayenne was but slight, would each want his share of the kingdom—the princes of the blood with better reasons than the rest.

As to the duke's demand for a rank superior to all others, it meant nothing else than that the ambitious prince should be constituted a mayor of the palace or a lieutenant general of France.[1]

Irrespective of the greed of the nobles of the League, the difficulties confronting Duplessis Mornay in the negotiation were

<small>Duplessis Mornay's diffi-cult position.</small> great. He was fully aware of the pressure brought to bear upon the king by his own adherents. "Our Catholics," he wrote, "desire peace at all hazards; they blame us and say that everything depends on the king, that for the sake of an opinion he is losing the state; and thereupon, one after another, they enter into private truces which go so far that one of these days the king will be sustaining the war alone."[2] Henry himself had long been proclaiming his willingness to be "instructed," and declaring that he would not be found to be "obstinate." If the instruction had not yet taken place, it was no fault of his, but rather the fault of the papal legate and of other ecclesiastics who had absolutely forbidden the required conference. The Roman Catholics who adhered to the king's party, and likewise the better-disposed part of those not yet united with him, understood this instruction to be only another name for conversion, and were urgent that Henry should at once declare his intention to be reconciled with the Romish Church within a certain prescribed term. That his master was fully resolved to barter the faith in which he had been brought up for the crown—if indeed Henry was fully resolved at this time—Duplessis Mornay did not as yet know. That faithful Protestant had but one object in view—to secure quiet for his native land without the sacrifice of principle. "We are engaged in treating for peace," he wrote on one occasion, "but nothing will be done to the prejudice of the glory of God."[3] Yet in the same letter he did not disguise his apprehension of danger. "These men with whom we are treating

---

[1] See the graphic account in the Mémoires de Charlotte Arbaleste sur la vie de Duplessis Mornay, i. 218–220.

[2] Duplessis Mornay to Buzenval, April 18, 1592, Mémoires, v. 303.

[3] Duplessis Mornay to M. de la Fontaine, May 16, 1592, Mémoires, v. 334.

demand much, but we must come out with boldness.   They and we are like two combatants on the edge of a precipice, each uncertain who shall throw his fellow, each in danger, even when pushing, of himself falling in.   Pray to God for us!"[1]

As the result of much discussion, a memorandum was virtually adopted for submission to Henry, under the heading, "The expedient proposed."   It ran as follows: "The king shall promise his instruction within a definite period, with desire and intention to unite himself to and join the Catholic Church, by means of the said instruction, conducted as comports with his dignity.

"He shall permit the Catholics who accompany him to send to the pope, to be aided by his counsel and authority to facilitate and effect the said instruction, as is becoming.

"And, meantime, consideration shall forthwith be secretly given to the most appropriate means of affording safety to religion and to the private individuals who have an interest in the cause, whether to be employed after the conversion, or, if need be, before it, so as to relieve the kingdom of the burden of war by a suspension of hostilities or otherwise."[2]

Here were articles sufficiently vague and indefinite, articles, moreover, which, if not positively menacing to the Protestant interests, were certainly not free from suspicious phraseology.   To understand the attitude of the Huguenot diplomatist in advocating the adoption of this basis of settlement, the articles must be read in connection with his private comments intended only for the king's eye—comments respecting which the writer was so anxious that he begged his majesty to return the despatch to the bearer in order that it might not go astray.[3]

"The intention is," says Duplessis Mornay, "that if the enemy approve this expedient, we shall settle with M. de Villeroy upon two kinds of articles; the one to take effect when

---

[1] Duplessis Mornay to M. de la Fontaine, May 16, 1592, Mémoirés, v. 335.

[2] The three articles appear in a minute sent to the king, accompanying a letter of Duplessis Mornay, dated Mantes, April 4, 1592, and entitled "L'expedient proposé."   Ibid., v. 270, 271.

[3] "Je supplie vostre majesté de rendre la presente despeche au porteur, afin qu'elle ne s'esgare."

the conversion may have come about, the other before its occurrence.[1] In which matter we must have this dexterity, to make the latter kind so good that they shall cause men to neglect the former, and consequently insist less upon the pretended conversion. For, when interests shall have been removed out of the way and personal desires shall have been satisfied, the bare pretext remaining will have no great weight in their case; and it may be that, without waiting to hear from the pope, they will pass on either to a peace or to a long truce which will detach them from Spain."[2]

We must not be misled, by our knowledge of what actually occurred at a subsequent time, into supposing that, in penning

The Huguenot view of the king's "instruction." these lines, Duplessis Mornay—zealous Protestant that he was—had in his mind's eye any such "instruction" or "conversion" as that which, in point of fact, preceded the abjuration of Saint Denis. Duplessis Mornay looked forward, indeed, to an instruction as unavoidable. It had been promised by the king, and it was not in itself undesirable. But it was to be no mock-fight. Much rather was the world to witness an orderly marshalling of forces, Protestant and Roman Catholic, to discuss, in the august presence of the monarch, the points of doctrine, government, and practice regarding which the two systems differed—a sort of grander and more equitable "Colloquy of Poissy," to which the theologians on both sides should come fully equipped ; where no arrogant Cardinal of Lorraine would be allowed to prescribe terms of subscription, because the contest would be presided over, not by a timid and time-serving queen-mother, nor by a feeble boy-king, but by a quick-witted and chivalric monarch who had faced the cannon's mouth, and could therefore be expected to despise the puny artillery of bigots. If, after such a conflict of learning and ability, the king should be " converted "—a supposition hardly possible—let the conversion come. The Huguenot statesman gave Henry of Navarre credit, notwithstanding all his faults, sensual and of other sorts—and no one knew the king's faults

---

[1] " Deux sortes d'articles : les ungs pour avoir lieu avenant la conversion, les aultres avant icelle." [2] Ibid., ubi supra.

better than did Duplessis Mornay, though the king had paid
him this high tribute of respect that he never had made him
the confidant of his amours [1]—at least, for the intention to afford a respectful and equal hearing to the representatives of
his own religious views, men who had been his companions in
council and upon the battle-field.   The Protestants would, Duplessis Mornay was assured, enjoy the fullest opportunity of
setting forth their own views and of combating those of their
opponents.   "His majesty promises to submit to instruction,"
he wrote.   "This may engender a conference, perhaps within
six or seven months.   We must make preparations for it, and I
have therefore persuaded him to agree that I should bring together at Saumur seven or eight of the most distinguished ministers of France, so that they may fortify themselves beforehand.
I promise myself that, by a method which I have proposed to
M. de Beaulieu, and which he adopts heartily, great advantage
will result.   You know his good judgment.   I have nominated
you, among others, to the king, and have obtained his consent.
I beg you to let me know whether you will be able to come to
Saumur.   Try by every means in your power to do so ; for it is
a decisive move.   It may, at latest, be in two months.   His majesty will meet all the expenses." [2]

Not content with merely sketching the general outlines of
this preparatory conference of Protestant theologians, Duplessis Mornay even elaborated the details.   Be it a formal council
of all France, or a simple colloquy, which should result from
the promise of instruction, the fruits must not be lost by want
of timely attention to some minute point of controversy.   The little band of Protestant theologians were
not only to be well provided with lodging and food,
but to have within reach every convenience, and especially to
enjoy access to the best books.   They were to refresh their mem-

A full and
fair discus-
sion.

---

[1] "Continuant en la façon dont il avoit tousjours vescu auparavant avec M.
Duplessis, auquel, nonobstant quelconques privautez, il n'avoit jamais parlé de
ses amours, le tenant suspect en tous telz affaires." Mémoires de Charlotte
Arbaleste sur la vie de Duplessis Mornay, i. 347.

[2] Duplessis Mornay to M. de la Fontaine, May 16, 1592, Mémoires, v. 335.

ories as to the ancient Christian writers, and especially as to the scholastics. Each would have his special portion to study, and each would take notes of what he read. Thus would it be distinctly seen for how long a time purity of doctrine had been maintained in the church, when and how abuses had crept in, by what means they had grown, and who were those who opposed them at each successive stage of their development. Men thus equipped for their work, entering into a dispute in the presence of a king whose single word would effectually check all extravagance of discussion, might reasonably expect both to strengthen his majesty's religious convictions and to prove to the most ignorant and malevolent of Roman Catholics that the Protestant system of doctrines rested on a firm foundation of truth and reason.

Moreover, it was a part of the Huguenot statesman's plan that Henry should order a list to be drawn up of the Roman Catholic ecclesiastics most distinguished for learning, excellence of life, and zeal for the restoration of the church to its pristine purity. From this roll all vacancies in the hierarchy must be filled, in order that, when the council should assemble, it might be found that the soundest part of the Gallican clergy was represented. Similar lists of the nobles and the judiciary were to be made. From their joint labors a greater glory would accrue to Henry the Fourth than had fallen to the lot of any or all princes during the last millennium.[1]

Unfortunately, the bright vision of Duplessis Mornay shared the fate of many another sanguine anticipation of the reformers of the sixteenth century and their immediate successors. The king listened with attention, with apparent approval, but never took the necessary measures to insure success.

The negotiations of Duplessis Mornay and Villeroy came to nothing. The publicity which had unintentionally been given to them rendered it advisable that the interviews between the agents should be intermitted. But they had served the incidental purpose of revealing inclinations toward peace which had hitherto been concealed or denied, and

The negotiation ends.

---

[1] Mémoires de Charlotte Arbaleste sur la vie de Duplessis Mornay, i. 238–241.

of pointing out the terms of private advantage upon which the leaders, who prated loudly of their incorruptible integrity and unassailable disinterestedness, were at any moment prepared to betray and abandon their dupes.

Upon Henry himself the suggestions of Villeroy and the pressure of the Roman Catholic nobles about him had one notable effect. He resolved to attempt a more direct effort than he had ever before made to gain over the pontifical See. Death had of late been very busy with the occupants of the papal throne. Gregory the Fourteenth, the great prop of the League, died in the month of October, 1591. His successor, Innocent the Ninth, bade fair to follow in Gregory's footsteps, and had engaged to contribute fifty thousand crowns monthly from the revenues of the church to the support of the French rebels, when his pontificate was abruptly ended by his decease, within two months after his elevation. A third pope now came upon the scene, in the person of Cardinal Aldobrandini, who assumed the designation of Clement the Eighth. Though a former partisan of Sixtus, and, like his master, no friend of the Spaniard, the new pontiff was too shrewd to fall into the mistake committed by Sixtus, and incur the suspicion or hatred of the powerful party of zealots at Rome by withholding contributions to the maintenance of the French League, or by recalling from France that fiery legate, the Bishop of Piacenza.[1] On the contrary, he deemed it prudent, before three months had elapsed, to issue, on the fifteenth of April, a brief addressed to that legate, providing for the election of a new and Catholic king of France. The document had the usual fate of papal bulls about this time. It was duly registered by the Leaguer Parliament of Paris, while the royalist Parliament at Châlons forbade its publication, uttered threats against any person who should presume to retain a copy in his possession, denounced the men who were desirous of introducing "the Spanish barbarians" into the kingdom, and cited the legate to appear at the bar of the court. The Parliament of Paris re-

Henry tries to make a friend of Clement the Eighth.

Clement's brief for the election of a new and Catholic king.

---

[1] Ranke, History of the Popes, 230.

torted by ordering the decree of the Châlons judges to be publicly burned at the foot of the great staircase of the Palais de
Justice, in the presence of the Duke of Mayenne.[1]

Not deterred by Clement's hostile demonstrations, Henry the
Fourth resolved to send an embassy to Rome, with the view of
paving the way to a reconciliation. The event was of more
than ordinary significance. Ostensibly, the Cardinal
of Gondy set out for Italy merely in the capacity
of a member of the papal consistory ; the Marquis of
Pisany, solely to visit his wife and his family connec-
tions. In reality, the marquis was the bearer of the messages of
the Roman Catholic princes of the court; while with the cardinal Duplessis Mornay had, by royal command, held long conferences, and had fully instructed him as to the arguments he
should employ in order to convince Clement of the absurdity of
the pretext of religion alleged by the League. He was to assure
the pope that those who now endeavored to make capital of the
"heresy" of Henry had not scrupled to make advances to secure Henry's favor. He was to tell him that this was equally
true of Philip himself, who had sought to induce him to rebel
against Henry of Valois, by the offer of great treasure and by
the promise not to desert him until he should have placed the
French crown upon his head, and of the Duke of Mayenne, who
had secretly solicited his alliance at the very moment when he
was himself in command of an army for the extermination of
the heretics. Gondy was to warn Clement, at the same time, of
the impolicy of promoting the ambitious plans of Spain, which,
if successful, would degrade the pope to the position of a private
chaplain of the great king, and the cardinals to be the surpliced
clerks of the royal chapel. He was to lay before him the danger
of provoking to an open schism a country like France, which
had of late been compelled to take decisive steps to curb ultramontane insolence, whose parliaments had forbidden the faithful to send money to Rome, had burned papal bulls, and had

*Cardinal
Gondy and
Marquis Pisa-
ny sent to
Italy.*

---

[1] See De Thou, viii. (book 103) 87–89; Recueil des choses mémorables, 755–
757 ; and, for the text of the arrêt of the Parliament of Châlons, Mémoires
de la Ligue, v. 188–190.

made systematic arrangements for the supply of vacant benefices by recurring to the metropolitans, archbishops, and bishops of the kingdom, independently of the pontifical curia.[1]

There was one document wherewith the ambassadors went provided which was not from the pen of Duplessis Mornay, author of most of the other despatches. This was a letter of Henry the Fourth himself to Clement. As often as the matter had been broached, Duplessis Mornay had dissuaded his master from writing to the pope. "Your majesty," said he, "cannot in good conscience write to him in the form used by your predecessors; to write otherwise would be more damaging than useful."[2] The letter which Henry actually sent is, therefore, the more interesting, as an indication of the complete submission to papal authority here foreshadowed.

Henry's letter to the pope.

"Most holy Father," said the still professedly Protestant king to the head of the Roman Catholic Church, "as we are resolved to cause to be proffered in our name, and to render during our entire life, the obedience which we owe to your Holiness and to the Apostolic See, we desire also to resume and to observe in all things the same means that have been held and employed by the Very Christian kings, our predecessors, in the observance of the honor and respect due to the Holy Father and the Holy See; and this for the purpose of entertaining, together with the filial devotion and reverence that belong to it, the good and perfect intelligence which is requisite between the Holy See and the kings and the kingdom of France, for the universal weal of Christendom and the maintenance therein of the holy Catholic church and religion." Hence his majesty was desirous of having an ordinary ambassador at Rome, and sent the Marquis of Pisany, who had served in this capacity under his predecessor, Henry the Third, "que Dieu absolve"—"whom may God pardon."[3]

---

[1] Mémoires de Charlotte Arbaleste sur la vie de Duplessis Mornay, i. 225–228. See De Thou, viii. 85.

[2] Mémoires de Charlotte Arbaleste, i. 230. One would infer from Madame Duplessis Mornay's words that she was ignorant of the fact that the king wrote to Clement despite her husband's advice.

[3] Henry IV. to the pope, October 8, 1592, Lettres missives, iii. 674, 675.

It might be little that the king deliberately inserted the objectionable formula which had so scandalized his old companions in arms and his Protestant fellow-believers at the time of his accession to the throne: it was of more consequence that the entire tone of this letter, as of a letter to the Duke of Tuscany sent by the same hands, betrayed a readiness to renounce Protestantism and to submit tó the Romish church, quite irrespectively of any "instruction," whether by council, conference, or otherwise.

And yet the pope was not reády to welcome the prodigal son who showed symptoms of a disposition to return ! Great was the joy, both in Rome and at Paris, when it was learned that the pope had shown such anger at the news of Gondy's approach, that he actually sent a Dominican monk to meet him at Florence and forbid

Clement forbids Gondy to enter the States of the Church.

him to set foot within the States of the Church. In order to add insult to injury, the friar delivered the message to the cardinal in the presence of the grand duke, and just when the latter was giving in marriage one of his nieces to a prince of the house of Sforza.[1]

Will it be believed that, while sending Gondy and Pisany to Italy in order to prepare the way for a recognition by the pope based upon his approaching abjuration, Henry the Fourth was despatching another envoy, the Sieur du Maurier, across the British Channel, for the express purpose of deceiving Queen Elizabeth respecting his intentions ? It was,

Henry tries to deceive Queen Elizabeth.

of course, beyond the range of possibility that his old and faithful ally should not speedily learn, from her agents in France and in Italy, the departure of Gondy and Pisany, and obtain a tolerably distinct idea of the contents of their instructions. To lose English Protestant support before making sure

---

[1] "Et le meilleur est," gleefully writes a prominent sympathizer of the League at Rome to a friend in Paris, " que cette ambassade s'est faicte sans aucun respect du lieu où se trouvoit lors ledit cardinal, mesmes on n'en parla aucunement audit grand duc, qui est le plus grand affront que l'on lui pouvoit faire." It is almost needless to say that the League took good care to circulate the letter from which this sentence is taken, dated Rome, October 26, 1592, widely throughout France. It thus found its way into the Mémoires de la Ligue, v. 183–5. See also De Thou, viii. 85–87 ; Lestoile, ii. 98.

of the support of equally powerful Roman Catholic allies, would
indeed be both a misfortune and a blunder.   With unparalleled
audacity Henry set himself to the task of deliberately misin-
forming his "dear sister" and "best friend."   It was a sorry
piece of business for the victor of Coutras and Ivry to be engaged in, and one that reveals, perhaps, better than any other
incident the fearful decadence of his moral nature.

Henry did not deny the embassy to the pope, but explained
it, and asked for the queen's counsel.   The zeal of his partisans,
he said, had grown somewhat cool through the length of the
war, while the pressure of his enemies was ever increasing and
well-nigh overpowered him.   Division had entered his own
party.   The ecclesiastics, in particular, already lukewarm in
their devotion because of his religious profession, had shown
their ill will to such a degree that it almost seemed as though
they had secretly consented to the choice of another Catholic
king, for which his enemies were just now making preparations.
In these circumstances the king found himself compelled to
resume negotiations, and to promise to allow himself to be instructed in the Catholic religion; the more so, as the Grand
Duke of Tuscany, the Senate of Venice, and other allied princes
had notified him that they would no longer support him, as they
desired to do, should he not become a Catholic.   He had therefore requested Cardinal Gondy to proceed to Rome, and had
impressed upon him his own ardent desire to see the present
unhappy war ended, and to be instructed in the Catholic religion.   He had not, however, concealed the fact that a change
of religion could not be effected in an instant, since his present
faith had been implanted and nurtured within him from
his youth up.   Bouillon, Pisany, Schomberg, and Revol had
conferred with the cardinal, and it had been agreed that the
latter should assure the pope, as of his own motion and not
empowered by the king, that Henry was ready to be instructed,
if only the necessary time were granted and no force

His intention
to remain
constant.

were exerted.   "Meanwhile," proceeds the document,
with unblushing effrontery, " the queen is to be notified that it is the king's intention not to forsake the religion of
which he has always made, as he now still makes, profession;

and that, in order to protract this negotiation, the cardinal will
be followed by the Marquis of Pisany, who is deputed by
the nobles of the kingdom.[1] . . . The king thinks that the
path which he intends following is that which is best adapted to
enable him to take time to consider and provide for his preservation. On this point he will beg the queen to give him her
counsel, being well assured that she will not refuse it to him,
and, moreover, that she would not advise him to change his
religion, or to do anything contrary to his conscience."[2]

After these barefaced falsehoods the envoy was instructed to
inform the queen of the king's intention to assemble those prelates and ecclesiastics of his realm who were most reasonable and
best affected to his service, and to notify them of his intention
to be instructed, " being sure that, by fine promises, words, or
otherwise, he will protract this affair as much as he may wish ;
so that, even if they should make little progress in their design,
nevertheless they will content foreign princes, the ecclesiastics,
and the people, whose ears the rumor hereof shall reach, with
the hope they will conceive of success in gaining over the king.[3]
Meanwhile his majesty will gather about him at this time some
of the most learned ministers of his realm, for the purpose of
inducing them to confer together in a friendly way respecting

---

[1] " Cependant ladicte Dame sera advertye que l'intention dudict Seigneur
Roy est de ne se departir de la religion de laquelle il a tousjours faict, comme
il faict encores profession, et que pour faire traisner ceste negotiation en
longueur ledict Sieur Cardinal seroyt [suivy] du Sieur Marquis de Pizany,
lequel de la part de la Noblesse de ce Roiaulme doibt supplier respectueuse-
ment le Pere commun de trouver bon," etc.

[2] "Il a pensé que la voye de laquelle il se voulloit servir estoyt la plus
propre, pour cependant adviser et pourvoyer à sa conservation ; à quoy il sup-
pliera ladicte Dame de luy donner son advis, s'asseurant qu'elle ne le luy re-
fusera et ne luy voudroit aussy conseiller de changer de religion ny de rien
faire contre sa conscience."

[3] "Leur faire entendre que sa resolution est de se faire instruire en la religion catholicque, s'asseurant que par belles promesses, parolles ou aultrement
faire traisner en telle longueur qu'il voudra, *leur faisant bon visage ou leur
faisant dons*, de sorte qu'encor qu'ils advancent peu en leur desseing, neant-
moings ils contenteront les princes estrangers," etc. The characteristic clause
which I have italicized is omitted by Stähelin, but has every appearance of
authenticity.

such difficulties as may arise. By means of such conferences he
will be able in time to gain something from both parties, and
by gentleness he will reconcile minds alienated by reason of
wars." [1]

Whether purposely or by accident, Henry, in his attempt to
deceive his English ally, sketched an alluring prospect much
resembling that which Duplessis Mornay had been fruitlessly
endeavoring to realize, but he did it only to conceal his true
intentions. Nor is it astonishing that Duplessis Mornay should
have been duped as to his master's designs, in view of the fact
that the quick-witted Queen of England, more remote from the
scene of action and therefore better situated for taking a calm
and dispassionate view, was completely hoodwinked.[2] The
envoy was in fact surprised at his own success in convincing
Queen Elizabeth. " She felt great pleasure," he noted down at
a subsequent time, " when I explained to her what I had been
commissioned to tell her. Only," he adds, with pardonable bit-
terness, " something occurred, a year thereafter, which made
me appear to be a liar, to be sure through no fault of my own." [3]

Meanwhile the clamor of the French people for peace became
loud and could not be suppressed. It found an utterance in
The Parisians a proposition, made in a general municipal meeting,
for peace. held in the Hôtel de Ville of the capital on the
twenty-sixth of October, to send a deputation to the " King of
Navarre " to treat with him the terms of an arrangement of

---

[1] MS. in Collection Dupuy, National Library at Paris, t. 152, entitled " Mémoire au Sieur du Maurier, despesché par le Roy vers la Reyne d'Angleterre
et le sieur de Lomenie, son ambassadeur près d'elle." This important document has been printed by Prince Galitzin, Lettres inédites de Henri IV. (Paris,
1860), 94–98, and by D'Ouvré among the pièces justificatives appended to his
life of Du Maurier. Dr Stähelin gives a summary and some extracts, Uebertritt König Heinrichs des Vierten, 484–6.

[2] The remark is that of Dr. Stähelin. Ibid., 487.

[3] D'Ouvré, apud Stähelin, 487.—This seems to prove that Prince Galitzin is
quite wrong in placing the " Instruction " (which, unfortunately, is not dated
in the manuscript) so late as May, 1593. Although the editor of the supplementary volumes of the Lettres missives de Henri IV. evidently intended to
insert the document (see ix. 155, note), I have looked in vain for it in his
pages.

some sort. For such a negotiation, however, the Duke of Mayenne was not yet ready. It suited his purpose better to await the convocation of the states general which had been summoned, in the interests of the League, to meet in the city of Paris; for he cherished the vain hope that after all the ambition of the Spaniard might be disappointed, and the coveted crown might yet be placed upon his own head. Consequently he rebuked the city for having ventured, in his absence, to entertain a motion diametrically opposed to the oath that had been taken, and advised the impatient burghers to await the issue of the approaching conference between the representatives of the whole nation.[1] Plucking up courage, he even made use of this event as an occasion for endeavoring to seduce the Roman Catholic followers of Henry from their allegiance. The lengthy appeal which the duke put forth in the month of December, 1592, was followed, on the fifteenth of the next month, by an equally prolix "Exhortation" to the same effect, emanating from the Cardinal Legate of Piacenza, who, on more than one occasion, had proved himself no unworthy successor of Pope Sixtus's rebellious envoy, Cardinal Cajetan.[2] Neither the layman nor the ecclesiastic spared the piety of Roman Catholics, who, while they professed subjection to the pope, continued, in defiance of his anathemas, to follow the fortunes of the heretic. The legate, indeed, waxed hot in his denunciations, not respecting in his inconsiderate passion even those immemorial liberties 'of the French ecclesiastical system which, on the northern side of the Alps, were regarded as the very stronghold of defence against papal usurpation. "By your discord and connivance," he exclaimed, "you have suffered heresy to gain such foothold that it no longer asks, as heretofore, the favor of enjoying impunity, but

Mayenne and the legate appeal to the loyal Roman Catholics.

---

[1] " Response faicte par le duc de Mayenne en l'assemblee generale tenue en la maison de ville de Paris, le jeudi 6 Novembre, sur la proposition de paix conclue en son absence, et depuis ce 26 Octobre ;" reprinted in Mémoires de la Ligue, v. 187.

[2] Any one curious to plod through these documents may peruse them in the Mémoires de la Ligue—the "Declaration" of the Duke of Mayenne, v. 283-294, and the "Exhortation" of the legate, v. 312-323.

begins to punish, how cruelly every one knows, those who, being
more solicitous for their salvation, refuse to submit to its yoke.
Strange and unfortunate change, that makes you detest as an
extreme vice what you yourselves have taught others to be an
excellent virtue, and, on the other hand, makes you crown the
same crime which you ought still to-day to condemn to the fire,
as you did in the past.   Such is the power of the deadly poison
of heresy, whose contagion has engendered those many absurd-
ities and contradictions which, if you will but lay your hand
upon your conscience, you dare not deny prevail among you.
For, to venture to maintain that the privileges and liberties of
the Gallican Church extend so far as to permit one to recognise
as king a relapsed heretic, who has been cut off from the body
of the Church Universal, is a frenzied dream proceeding from
no other source than from heretical contagion." [1]

It was in these circumstances that a thought presented itself
to the minds of two of the king's most sincere and trusty servants, which was destined in the end to bring the present critical
condition of affairs to an unexpected issue.   The Duke of Mayenne had invited the princes and nobles who followed the
king's fortunes to confer with those who had thrown in their
lot with the League, at the meeting of the pretended states
general in the city of Paris.   Why not take advantage of the
professed willingness to discuss the matters in dispute ?   Why
not respond by a counter-invitation, which the duke and his
partisans could not decline without clearly exposing themselves
to the charge of insincerity ?   The time had come when the
danger menacing France no longer came from the League, but
from the Spaniard.   That danger must be conjured, peace must
be restored by the united efforts of both parties.   So

Schomberg
and De Thou   thought Gaspard de Schomberg and his bosom friend,
propose a
peace con-   the future historian Jacques Auguste de Thou.   They
ference.
consequently requested the king to lend his sanction
to a conference, to be held in some neutral place outside of Paris, where the royalist nobles might ask their brethren in the
other camp to meet them.   Their words were eloquent, their

---

[1] Mémoires de la Ligue, v. 316.

plea for peace was forcible and coincident with the desires of their royal auditor. There could be no doubt whither their arguments tended; for a conference that offered to the king's rebellious subjects no guarantees of an approaching renunciation of Protestantism would have been worse than futile. But Henry of Bourbon did not draw back from the meeting at which the bargain must be sealed. He had, indeed, some words to say in reply about his faith and his convictions, words much like those he had uttered many times before, and accompanied by the usual profession of a teachable mind. " Men reproach me with my religion," he said ; " but you know that I am not obstinately attached to it. If I am in error, let those who attack me with so much fury instruct me and show me the path of safety." [1]

The invitation sent by " the princes, prelates, officers of the crown, and chief Catholic lords, as well of the council of the king as others being near his majesty," has come down to us, and is an instructive document. Adopted in the presence of Henry in the city of Chartres, on the twenty-seventh of January, 1593, it was carried the next day to Paris by a royal herald. The writer skilfully took advantage of the situation. He made the princes express their hearty accord with the Duke of Mayenne in the sentiments he had uttered in his recent declaration, respecting the disastrous results sure to flow from the continuation of the war, not only to the material interests of the kingdom, but to the Catholic religion itself. Only the restoration of peace would repair the losses sustained by the cities, re-establish commerce and the arts and trades by which the people are nourished, give fresh life to

Invitation of the royalist nobles.

---

[1] " On m'objecte ma religion ; mais vous sçavez que je n'y suis pas attaché avec obstination. Si je suis dans l'erreur, que ceux qui m'attaquent avec tant de fureur, m'instruisent, et me montrent la voye du salut." De Thou (who is our best authority), viii. 212. See however, also, Davila, 587, 588, who gives as one of the reasons why a plan looking so directly toward abjuration came to be adopted by Henry, the significant circumstance that " the Sieur du Plessis [Mornay] was far off, who, with his reasons, partly theological, partly political, was wont to withhold him and put scruples in his mind, to the end he might not change his religion."

the universities and the other schools of learning, formerly so
flourishing and a source of splendor and renown to the realm,
but now in a languishing and moribund condition ; only the return of peace would secure cultivation for the fields which, instead of yielding, as of old, fruits meet for the sustenance of
man, lay fallow or were covered with a hideous growth of thorns
and thistles.   The princes therefore accepted the proposition of
the duke, and signified their willingness to confer, by means of
deputies, with such " good and worthy personages " as the adherents of the League might be pleased to select.   They suggested, however, that the place for the colloquy, instead of the
capital, should be some spot between Paris and Saint Denis.
But if the advances now made should be rejected, if the way of
conciliation should be rejected and other ways pernicious to religion and to the state should be chosen, and if France should,
in consequence, be brought to the extremity of ruin and misery,
a prey to the greed and covetousness of the Spaniards and a
monument of the triumph of their insolence—if all these disasters should be brought about by the hands and the blind
passions of men bearing the name of Frenchmen, degenerate
sons of honorable ancestors, they protested that the blame must
not rest upon the royalists, but upon those whose refusal would
prove that they preferred the measures that might serve to advance their own greatness and selfish ambition above the means
for the promotion of God's honor and the salvation of the realm.[1]

Two days after the publication of the " Proposition " of the
princes, Henry put forth his own answer to the Duke of

Henry's an-
swer to May-
enne's mani-
festo.

Mayenne's manifesto, with the intention of strengthening the courage of that growing party within the
League which, with daily increasing distinctness, was
declaring itself favorable to reconciliation and peace.[2]   On the
one hand, his majesty denounced the League as nothing else

---

[1] " Proposition des Princes, Prelats, Officiers de la Couronne et principaux
Seigneurs Catholiques, tant du Conseil du Roy, qu'autres estans pres sa Majesté,"
reprinted in Mémoires de la Ligue, v. 304–307, and in Cayet, Chronologie
novenaire, 423, 424.   Also in Davila (book 13), 585, 586.

[2] " Declaration du Roy sur les impostures et fausses inductions contenues en
un escrit publié sous le nom du Duc de Mayenne," dated Chartres, January

than a plot against the royal authority, and ridiculed the pretension that the fundamental law had been changed by Henry the Third's declaration at the States of Blois, in 1588. "It is the province of the laws," said he, "and not of kings to fix the succession to the throne; not to mention that the states themselves acted, not with free deliberation, but as open conspirators, and that Henry the Third's declaration was extorted from him by violence." On the other hand, the monarch reiterated, with more emphasis than ever before, his intention to gratify the expectations of his Roman Catholic subjects in the matter of religion. The most careless reader could see the word "abjuration" written under such expressions as these: "We shall never fail to make known that we have no obstinacy, and that we are quite prepared to receive all good instruction and to submit ourselves to what God shall counsel us as being for our welfare and salvation." Yet, even when about to perform so immoral an act as the insincere renunciation of the religious creed in which he had been educated from his earliest years, Henry could not allow the opportunity to pass without indulging in a phrase or two of lofty sentiment. And thus it happens that, in the light of the farce enacted, less than six months later, at Mantes and Saint Denis, under the title of a conversion, the king's own words constitute the most bitter censure of his unprincipled deed, and a prophecy of the harvest of hypocrisy and scepticism sown by that act in the courtiers whom he induced to copy his example. "It must not be deemed

His view of a heartless conversion.   strange by all our Catholic subjects, if, having been nurtured in the religion we now hold, we are unwilling to abandon it without first having been instructed, and before it has been proved to us that the religion which they desire in us is the better and the more certain religion. This instruction in good form is the more necessary in us, as the example of our conversion would conduce much to influence others. Moreover, it would be to err in the first principles of religion and to

---

29, 1593. Text in Mémoires de la Ligue, v. 295–304, and Cayet, 425–429. See also Recueil des choses mémorables, 759, 760, Lestoile, ii. 115, De Thou, viii. 213–218.

show that we had no religion, were we to consent, in answer to a simple summons, to change ours, with so precious a matter at stake as the answer to the question, Whereupon must a man found his hope of salvation ? " [1]

Great was the consternation of the leaders at Paris.   Great was their embarrassment in deciding how to deal with the proposal of the loyal Roman Catholics.[2]   The more extreme were in favor of taking no notice of it whatever.   The legate distinguished himself by his intemperate conduct.   He

Embarrassment of the League.

rose up in great anger, exclaiming that the princes' proposition was full of heresies, and those were heretics that should take it into consideration.   It was therefore fitting, he maintained, that no answer should be returned.   Cardinal Pellevé and Ibarra, the Spanish ambassador, were of the same opinion.   Not so, however, with the rest.   Villeroy and President Jeannin insisted that a message brought to the representatives of the three orders could not be rejected without a reference to the states general.   The Duke of Mayenne, whom the recent conduct both of Philip the Second and of the pope had not been calculated to conciliate, was quite willing to thwart the purposes of the Spanish and pontifical envoys, while he still retained the external semblance of deference to the wishes of his august allies.   Nor was his good humor restored by the visit which he thought fit to make to the Duke of Feria and

Dispute between Mayenne and the Duke of Feria.

Inigo de Mendoza, at Soissons.   For the ambassadors insisted much upon the necessity of at once electing the Infanta queen of France, but had no authority to assist the cause of the League with more than the paltry sum of twenty-five thousand ducats; while the troops brought by Count Charles of Mansfelt amounted to only four thousand foot and

---

[1] " Ce seroit aussi errer aux principes de religion, et montrer n'en avoir point, que de vouloir, sous une simple semonce, nous faire changer la nostre, y allant de chose si precieuse, que de ce en quoi il faut fonder l'esperance de salut."

[2] De Thou gives a brief statement of the arguments employed on both sides. Davila's account of the scene when the letter of the royalist princes was brought to the small council summoned by the Duke of Mayenne, then ill, to his bedroom to hear it, is animated and interesting, book 13, 585, 588, etc.

one thousand horse. To make up for the meagreness of the present support, the Spaniards dwelt at length upon the future munificence of Philip, who, when once his daughter should be well seated on the throne, would give her fifty thousand foot and ten thousand horse, and lavish all the treasure of his kingdom to secure her success. When Mayenne urged the necessity of coating that bitter pill, the violation of the Salic law, to render it palatable to the French states general, Mendoza had the effrontery to declare that it was notorious that all the deputies would not only accept the Infanta, but would beg Philip to grant her to be their queen; indeed, that Mayenne was the only person who opposed the universal desire. This was too much for the pride of the ambitious Frenchman. He informed Mendoza, for all reply, that he knew nothing about the affairs of France if he supposed that the Spaniards could manage its deputies as they were accustomed to govern the senseless Indians. The debate soon degenerated into an unseemly altercation, Feria telling Mayenne that the Spaniards would assume the command of the army and intrust it to the Duke of Guise; while Mayenne, in a towering rage, declared that he had it in his power to turn all France against the Spaniards, and, if he pleased, to shut them out of the kingdom in a single week. Feria and Mendoza, he said, were playing the parts rather of ambassadors of "the King of Navarre" than of the Catholic King, and could not have done Henry better service, had they been paid by him. As for himself, he was not yet their subject, and, judging from the usage he had received at their hands, it was very unlikely he ever would be such.[1] However, Mayenne was too valuable an ally to the Spaniards, and the Spaniards were likely to be too indispensable to Mayenne, that the two parties should so abruptly part company. By the next morning the duke had thought better of the matter, and with the help of skilful intermediaries a hollow reconciliation was effected.[2] In return for his solemn promise, to secure, by all honorable means in his power, the election of the Infanta Doña

Mayenne's terms with Spain.

---

[1] Davila (book 13), 591–594.
[2] Ibid., 597; De Thou, viii. 220.

Isabella by the states general, Mayenne, than whom there was no negotiator of the period more proficient in the art of providing for future emergencies, stipulated for, and obtained from Feria, terms as large as the demands with which he had, a year before, startled Duplessis Mornay. The Spanish ambassador engaged, in the name of his master, that the Duke of Mayenne should receive the Duchy of Burgundy, with all its revenues, as an hereditary possession to be transmitted in the male line to his descendants, the crown reserving for itself only a claim to bare sovereignty. He was to have an income of two hundred thousand crowns from the revenues of other provinces, to be put in possession of the government of Normandy, to obtain the discharge of all the debts he had contracted in the service of France and its new queen, to derive another sum of two hundred thousand crowns from Philip's funds, a third sum of twice that amount from the Infanta, to be lieutenant-general until the coming of the princess, and, after that event, one of the greatest dignitaries of state. On these conditions, with no less than two additional provisions for the further replenishment of his insatiate pocket, the Duke of Mayenne declared himself forever satisfied. It must be confessed that he would have been hard to please had he required more.[1]

The discussion of the proposition of the princes of Henry's party by the states general of the League soon showed the temper of the people. Had the deputies themselves been lukewarm, the Parliament of Paris would have aroused them by a protest ; had neither states nor parliament been attentive to the signs of the times, the miserable inhabitants of the capital, harassed by a state of partial siege that had already lasted three years, would have broken out in open revolt. Even the legate was brought to recognize the necessity of yielding to the overwhelming force of public sentiment, which already condemned him for inordinate deference to

The League reluctantly agrees to the conference.

----

[1] "Copie de la Promesse que le Duc de Feria a faite au Duc de Mayenne relativement aux intérêts particuliers de celui-ci et Promesse du Duc de Mayenne," Soissons, February, 1593, in De Croze, Les Guises, les Valois et Philippe II., ii. 410–414.

the Spaniard. Finally an answer was drawn up, on the fourth of March, in the name of Mayenne, and of the princes, prelates, and deputies. Montmartre, St. Maur, and the queen's house at Chaillot were suggested as places at any one of which royalist and Leaguer might meet for a consideration of the present unhappy state of France.[1] In the end, none of these localities was chosen, but the quiet village of Suresnes, on the other bank of the Seine, was selected, and the month of April was appointed as the time.[2]

Meanwhile the states general summoned by the League, with the full approval of the Papal See, had been for several months nominally sitting in the castle of the Louvre. Opened on the twenty-sixth of January, with an attendance of deputies contrasting very disadvantageously with previous assemblies held under royal sanction, this body, on account of Mayenne's absence from the city, deferred its second formal session until the second of April. It is not within the province of this history to detail the acts of a well-known convocation, whose most salient features have been held up to immortal ridicule in the wonderfully acute descriptions of the "Satyre Menippée." The Spaniards had anticipated an easy triumph by means of this assembly, convened in imitation of the ancient representative bodies of the French people. In the second session the Duke of Feria extolled to the skies the disinterestedness of his master, from whom he presented a letter addressed to the states themselves; but he went no farther than to express the hope entertained by Philip, that a king would be elected both zealous in the matter of religion and sufficiently powerful to secure France from her enemies. Cardinal Pellevé replied in a prolix speech still more laudatory of the Catholic king and of his achievements. In the peroration he pictured

The states general of the League.

---

[1] Text of the answer in Mémoires de la Ligue, v. 308–312, and Davila, 597–599. See Recueil des choses mémorables, 760; De Thou, viii. 220–222.

[2] Montmartre, on the north, and Chaillot, on the west, have, within the present generation, been absorbed in the City of Paris. St. Maur lies beyond Charenton, in a curve of the Marne. Suresnes is situated on the left bank of the Seine, just west of the capital, opposite the Bois de Boulogne and Longchamps, and barely two miles north of St. Cloud.

Philip, at the close of his mortal course, rewarded for his virtues and enjoying the beatific vision of God, in company with the spirits of the blessed. "Into whose tabernacles, when he shall have been raised by the hand of God, the Rewarder of the pains and labors he has undergone for religion's sake, not only will there come to meet him a thousand of thousands of angels, who wait upon and serve the King of kings; but, in addition, an infinite number of people whom he has rescued, some from the thick darkness of infidelity, others from the obstinacy and wickedness of their heresies, will present themselves to him with gladness, bearing in their hands crowns which will add fresh lustre to the crown prepared for him by God." [1]

But when it came to practical results, the Spaniards, as well as the legate, had disappointment in store for them. A spark of the old spirit of national feeling still burned in the breasts of the deputies. A commission, appointed by the states to examine into the decrees of the Council of Trent, whose reception in France was again pressed by the pope, reported that they found them to be in conflict with the laws and usages of the kingdom, and with the prescriptions of the Pragmatic Sanction and the liberties of the Gallican Church. It was a significant circumstance that, of the two commissioners who drew up a document fatal to the pretensions of Rome, one was the first president of the Parliament of Paris, Jean Le Maistre, who had been elevated to office by the Duke of Mayenne himself. [2] A month later, the same spirit of opposition to foreign interference exhibited itself in another and very unexpected quarter. A conference was held at the palace of the papal legate, to which none but persons of unquestioned zeal for the League were invited. Each of the three orders was represented by two delegates. The Archbishop of Lyons and Rose, Bishop of Senlis, were there for the clergy.

The decrees of Trent under discussion.

---

[1] The Duke of Feria's speech is given in the Mémoires de la Ligue, v. 341–345, Philip the Second's letter, ibid., v. 345, 346, and Cardinal Pellevé's reply, ibid., v. 346–353.

[2] De Thou, viii. (book 105) 231–236.

In this select company the Duke of Feria made bold to propose openly the election of the Infanta, daughter of Elizabeth of France, and granddaughter of Henry the Second and Catharine de' Medici. He declared that his master, who had already spent six million gold crowns in defence of Roman Catholicism in France, would send in the early autumn, in addition to the army of ten thousand men now on the frontier, a second force of equal size, not to speak of subsidies for French troops. It was then that, to the amazement of all present, the Bishop of Senlis broke out upon the Duke of Feria with rough words. "The Politiques," said he, "were right in maintaining that your ambition was covered by the cloak of religion. In conjunction with the other preachers, animated by a true zeal for the Holy Union, I have been trying to refute their statements. Now I learn, from what you have just advanced, that what I took to be calumnies invented by the sectaries are the true sentiments and views of the Spaniards. For twelve hundred years the Salic law has been in force in France. If this venerable law be infringed by placing a woman upon the throne, must we not fear that the sceptre may through her pass into the hands of a stranger, and that a monarchy which owes its glory and power to an inviolable law may in the sequel be brought to nothingness?"[1] The states general did not go so far as this, for if they declined the proposition of the Spaniards to elect the Archduke Ernest of Austria king of France, with the Infanta as his consort, and warned them that the French nobles would never accept a foreigner as their monarch, they formally requested that the Infanta marry a French prince, who should thereupon be elected to the vacant throne.[2] But the Parliament of Paris grew daily more outspoken in its resistance to Spain and to Spain's ambitious designs. Finally, on the twenty-eighth of June, it published a formal resolution declaring null and void any treaty or convention, made or to be made, contrary to the Salic law, or for the election of a foreign prince

The Bishop of Senlis on Spanish ambition.

President Le Maistre's manly protest.

---

[1] De Thou, viii. 265. The conference took place May 20, 1593.
[2] Ibid., 275, 276.

or princess.   Nor did President Le Maistre, whom the judges
deputed to carry the paper to the Duke of Mayenne, fail to
fortify their position by pertinent reference to former mishaps
to France arising from female domination—to the seditions
and civil wars caused, under the first race of kings, by Frede-
gonde and Brunehaut; to the troubles occasioned, under the
second race, by Judith, wife of Louis le Débonnaire; to the dis-
quiet of the regency of Blanche, mother of Saint Louis.   " Finally," said he, " we still remember with horror the bloody
tragedies of which France was the theatre under Catharine de'
Medici." [1]   When subsequently summoned by the Duke of Mayenne, and reproached with ingratitude to the benefactor to whom
he owed his present exalted position, Le Maistre defended himself and the parliament with firmness and dignity, and he was
rewarded by the unanimous endorsement of the court over
which he presided. [2]   Not otherwise than parliament thought
the people, who insulted the legate, hooted at the Duke of
Feria when he came out into the streets, and even threw stones
at him as he passed. [3]

The eventful Conference of Suresnes has become a part of
the general history of France.   Happily, among the deputies
on the royal side was the historian Jacques Auguste
De Thou, who has devoted the greater part of the one
hundred and sixth book of his immortal work to a
narrative of the successive sessions, than which nothing can be
more authentic, and in which those anxious to follow the tortu-

---

[1] "Arrest donné en la Cour de Parlement à Paris, le 28. jour de Juin, 1593,"
in Mémoires de la Ligue, v. 397.   See De Thou, viii. 280, etc.; Lestoile, ii.
147.

[2] "Ledit Sieur le Maistre lui fit response, que s'il entendoit parler de lui,
que à la verité il avoit receu beaucoup d'honneur de lui, estant pourveu d'un
Estat de President en icelle, mais neantmoins qu'il s'estoit tousjours conservé
la liberté de parler franchement, principalement des choses qui concernent
l'honneur de Dieu, la justice, et le soulagement du peuple, n'ayant rapporté
autre fruict de cest Estat en son particulier que de la peine et du travail beaucoup, lequel estoit cause de la ruine de sa maison, et que lui estoit exposé à la
calomnie de tous les meschans de la ville."   Account of the interview of June
30, in Mémoires de la Ligue, v. 399.   De Thou, viii. 285.

[3] Lestoile, ii. 145.

ous paths of the negotiation can easily trace it. One significant fact, however, is not mentioned by De Thou, which deserves to be referred to here. When the royalist deputies, with the Archbishop of Bourges at their head, were about to start for the appointed place of meeting, a desire was felt to know with greater definiteness, and from the lips of the monarch himself, what Henry the Fourth's intentions really were ; and Monsieur d'O was chosen to put the question bluntly to his majesty. It was no time for doubtful or ambiguous assurances, and Henry gave none. Not even in his letters to the pope and to the Grand Duke of Tuscany had he spoken so distinctly. He informed d'O that he had contemplated going over to the Roman Catho-

Henry's intimation of his intended conversion.
lic Church from the very moment of his accession to the throne, and that he was in earnest when he promised to submit to instruction within six months.

Circumstances beyond his control had prevented the fulfilment of his engagement—the obstacles thrown in the way by successive popes; the probability or certainty that the Protestants, abandoned by him, would elect another Protector in his stead ; the power of the League yet unbroken ; the avidity of the people for a war whose hardships they had not yet experienced. In such conditions, his conversion would have failed to secure peace to France. Not so at present. "For," said he, with easy frankness, " I have taken measures to make sure of and to summon to me all those of the [Reformed] religion who might create a disturbance. As for the heads of the League, they have not at present forces enough to resist me without the help of the Spaniard. As to the people of that party, I know that the annoyance they have experienced from the war makes them desire peace. Having, therefore, secured those of the [Reformed] religion who might make a disturbance, I am resolved to ruin the ' tiers parti' entirely by means of my conversion to the Roman Catholic religion. This conversion I hope to execute through the instruction to be given me by the French prelates, whom I shall convene within three months at farthest. There will then remain only the adherents of the League, and with them, I hope, by the instrumentality of the conference agreed upon (should the deputies deport themselves properly), to bestow upon my people the peace which they so much need. Inform the Archbishop of Bourges of my intention, and let him manage this affair according to his prudence." [1]

Delighted with the possession of a weapon whose importance they could scarcely over-estimate, the Archbishop of Bourges The first dis- and his associates boldly engaged the deputies of the cussion. League. Of these the most prominent were the Archbishop of Lyons, President Jeannin of the Parliament of Dijon, and Villars, the brave defender of Rouen, recently rewarded for his services by Mayenne with the post of high admiral, once held by Gaspard de Coligny. The discussion became from the start a tilt between the two archbishops. The prelate of Bourges extolled the prospective benefits of peace, and demonstrated that through submission to the king alone could the attainment of peace be hoped for. The prelate of Lyons maintained, on the contrary, that provision must first be made for the safety of religion. The former set forth the claims of the ruling monarch, a descendant of Saint Louis, no idolater, or Mohammedan, but a prince who had received Christian baptism, who professed to hold the same creed as the Roman Catholic Church, and who, if not entirely free from error, had always offered to submit to instruction. The latter ransacked history, both sacred and profane, to prove the extreme danger of obeying a heretical prince. The Archbishop of Bourges showed that neither under the old nor under the new Dispensation were subjects permitted to revolt against their prince upon the pretext of religion. The Jews were indeed forbidden to elect a foreign king lest he lead them into idolatry; yet, on the one hand, Jeconiah having, in obedience to the prophet Jeremiah's injunctions, submitted to Nebuchadnezzar, saved his own life and the lives of his wife and children, and, on the other hand, Zedekiah, who refused to submit, saw his children slain before his face, and was then himself deprived of his eyes, while Jerusalem was

---

[1] Cayet, Chronologie novenaire (Edition Michaud et Poujoulat), 445. I concur with Dr. Stähelin, Uebertritt Heinrich des Vierten, 521, 522, that the absence of reference to this interview with Monsieur d'O by any writer except Cayet is not sufficient ground for scepticism as to its occurrence.

laid waste, the temple burned, and the people carried away into
captivity.   The Archbishop of Lyons declared that Heresy is a
crime of treason against God, annihilates all privileges, and de-
grades all who are its followers.   An heretical king is so much
the more criminal, as he is, by virtue of his office, specially
bound to defend religion, and as his example is more dangerous
than that of a private person.

Others took part in the debate.   The royalists alleged the
immemorial right exercised by the French to defend themselves
against papal aggression.   The Leaguers denied the so-called
Gallican Liberties.   They maintained that these privileges were
pure fictions of the imagination.   The friends of Henry pressed
the other party to set forth clearly the terms upon which they
would conclude a peace which they affected so ardently to desire.   His opponents, through their old spokesman, declared
that they must wait to hear from the pope, whose commands
they were ever ready to obey.[1]

So passed the first three sessions, held at intervals during the
latter part of April and the beginning of May.   Toward reconciliation little or no progress had been made.   The moment had
come when something decisive must be done.   The fourth
session took place on the seventeenth of May.   The royalist
deputies Schomberg and Revol were bearers of an important
announcement.   His majesty had written letters to all the principal prelates of his realm, in which he declared that the regret he felt at the misery into which France had been
Henry invites
the bishops to plunged under pretext of religion, and his desire to
Mantes.
testify to his good Catholic subjects his sense of their
fidelity and affection, had determined him, in order that he
might leave them, if possible, no scruple based on the diversity
of his religion, to receive at the earliest moment instruction on
the differences whence proceeded the schism existing in the
Church.   For this purpose he invited them to meet him at
Mantes, on the fifteenth day of the ensuing month of July.
He assured them "that they would find him well disposed and
teachable in all those matters which ought to influence a Very

---

[1] De Thou, viii. (book 106) 238–258.

Christian King, a monarch having nothing more deeply graven on his heart than zeal for the service of God and the maintenance of His true Church."[1]   Similar letters had been sent to the chief nobles of the kingdom, to secure their presence on the august occasion.[2]

The secret of the king's intention had been well kept; the surprise of the Archbishop of Lyons and his associates was Opposition of correspondingly great.   Yet the virtual promise con-the League. tained in the royal letters produced upon the professed advocates of the Roman Catholic Church no such immediate effects as might have been anticipated.   Instead of hastening to welcome the royal convert, they lost no time in making his way more difficult, and in attempting to rob him of any advantage which his conversion might procure him.   Then it was that, as we have seen, the Infanta's election was pressed upon the reluctant states; then it was that, as an answer to the king's declaration, the deputies of the League wrote letters for general circulation, in some of which they confined themselves to the expression of incredulity respecting the proposed conversion of one who had not yet intermitted the public exercises of a worship which he was beginning to blame, nor dismissed its ministers, and who was notoriously the same in words and in deeds that he always had been;[3] then it was that others undertook to prove that a heretic can never be sincerely converted.   Sooner might the Ethiopian change his skin, or the leopard his spots, than a sectary return to the bosom of the Church.   The thing might occur, but it would be by a very extraordinary grace of Heaven.[4]   New sessions of the conference took place, it is true, first at La Roquette, not far from the Porte Saint Antoine and the Bastile, and subsequently at La Villette, on the road to Saint Denis; but the deputies, acting under instructions from Paris, were obstinate, and would not even consent to a three months'

---

[1] One of the royal letters is printed in the Mémoires de la Ligue, v. 380. "Copie de Lettre du Roy à l'Evesque de Chartres."   The date is Mantes, May 18, 1593.   Also, in Lettres missives, iii. 771.

[2] These letters were also of a stereotype form.   See Lettres missives, iii. 773.

[3] In the Mémoires de la Ligue, v. 381-385.

[4] De Thou, viii. 267.

truce. The nobles and the people were, as usual, more moderate than the clergy, who received their orders from the legate. The suffering populace, in their indignation at the conduct of the foreign prelate, were ready for a riot. They trooped to the gates of the city, once and again, when the deputies set out for Suresnes, uttering loud cries of "Peace! Peace! Blessed be they that seek and procure it! Cursed be those who do otherwise; may all the devils take them!"[1] Parliament evidently sympathized with the discontent of the people.[2] Meanwhile Henry the Fourth took ample revenge for the refusal of the League to consent to an armistice, by besieging and capturing Dreux, the only place of importance which had continued to hold for the League in the vicinity of the capital."[3]

The deed was virtually done. After long delay, after an appearance of hesitation which was probably more feigned than real, the son of Jeanne d'Albret had at length committed himself fully. He would renounce the religion which he had imbibed, as he had been fond of reiterating, with his mother's milk, this coming July. He would embrace the Romish mass, of which that mother had said that, sooner than attend it, had she her kingdom and her son in her hand, she would cast them both into the depth of the sea.[4] It was currently reported that he even made the cynical observation that Paris was certainly worth a mass.[5] The story was perhaps apocryphal, but it expressed a sentiment which he felt, if he did not utter.

It must not be supposed that the Huguenots had seen with unconcern or observed without remonstrance the progress of the drama whose catastrophe was now approaching. They would

---

[1] Lestoile, ii. 127. [2] De Thou, viii. 268–278.
[3] De Thou, viii. 287–291. [4] Rise of the Huguenots, ii. 10.
[5] The Recueil des choses mémorables (2d edition, 1598), 761, 762, ascribes the expression, somewhat modified, to the royalists when urging Henry to embrace Roman Catholicism. "Le sommaire de leurs sollicitations estoit . . . que tandis que le Roy adhereroit ouvertement à son acoustumee Religion, ceux du parti contraire (cent fois en plus grand nombre) suivroyent la maison de Guise et les autres chefs Ligueurs, qui par le moyen de l'Espagnol et du Pape sçauroyent bien trouver le moyen de maintenir et augmenter l'embrasement par tous les coins et au milieu de son Royaume, lequel valoit bien une Messe ; et ne faloit le laisser perdre pour des ceremonies," etc.

have been not only untrue to their own instincts, but false
to their own history and to their proverbial boldness, had they
The Hugue-
nots remon-
strate. suffered any motives of policy to silence their earnest protest against a crime affecting, not so much the
moral character of one man as the public conscience
of Christendom. With Henry's promise to submit to instruction they could not indeed be offended; for the crafty monarch
had quietly taken every advantage of his old companions in
arms, and had turned their innocence and simplicity to good
account. What objection could the Protestants consistently
urge against the interview at Mantes, when Duplessis Mornay,
of all their diplomatists and statesmen the most incorruptible
and sincere, had taken pains to make of the king's instruction a
cardinal article in the terms discussed with Villeroy?[1]   Thus
had the Huguenot governor of Saumur earned the life-long regret that he had been made the unconscious, but none the less
efficient, instrument of furthering a plan which he loathed from
his inmost soul.

When, in the early spring, certain Protestant ministers sounded Henry respecting the current rumors of his apostasy, his
Henry's as-
surances. majesty bade them give no credit to the story, and be
well assured that he would never change his religion;
for he had always acted intelligently and conscientiously.[2]   And
when they came again, a month or two later, with their more
distinct remonstrances, he denied, but with less positiveness,
that he intended to become a Roman Catholic. " You know,"
said he, " what I have always told you."   Then he added:
"Yet, were I to do it, you have no reason to be alarmed thereat,
nor to take it amiss. On the contrary, I am entering the house,
not to live in it, but to cleanse it. I promise you, it is so.
And as for yourselves, I shall not give you any worse treatment

---

[1] The remark is that of Benoist, Histoire de l'Édit de Nantes, i. 90, to
which Dr. Stähelin has called attention : "Les Catholiques gagnerent nean-
moins cecy à ces conferences qu'ils delivrerent le Roy de la crainte d'offenser
les Reformez, en prenant des mesures pour se faire instruire, puis que celuy
de tous les Reformez, qui étoit le moins suspect en matiere de Religion, vouloit bien faire de cette instruction un article du Traitté de paix."
[2] "Par science et par conscience." Lestoile, ii. 127.

than I have always given you, up to the present day. Pray
God for me, and I shall love you." [1] The last sentence need
occasion no surprise.. Henry of Navarre was at all times prodigal of pious references to the Divine power and to his depend-
ence upon heavenly aid. He had even the assurance to inform
his correspondents that he hoped, during the approaching instruction, that God would grant him the assistance of His Holy
Spirit in the plan he had adopted, whose sole object was to
choose and follow the true way of salvation. [2] We naturally ask
ourselves whether Henry was thinking of these utterances
when, as will be seen later, upon a remarkable occasion, during
his own severe illness, he anxiously pressed Agrippa d'Aubigné
for an answer to the inquiry, whether he thought that his king
had committed the unpardonable sin against the Holy Ghost. [3]

Nor was it only by delegations that the Huguenot ministers
endeavored to deter the king. One of their number, preaching
before him at Mantes, boldly warned him from the pulpit of
the judgments of the Almighty, should he apostatize. When
they heard of it, Cardinal Bourbon and Monsieur d'O were full
of indignation, and, going to his majesty, begged him to punish the minister's insolence. But Henry, bowing his head, for
all answer only said: "What would you have me do? He
has freely told me my faults." [4]

Those of the leading Huguenot ministers who were away
from court used their pens, and some of the most eloquent let-

---

[1] Lestoile, ii. 138.

[2] "Esperant que Dieu assistera de sa grace par son Sainct-Esprit ceste
mienne resolution selon le sainct zele que j'y apporte ; qui ne tend qu'à em-
brasser et suivre la vraye voie de mon salut." Henry IV. to the Grand Duke
of Tuscany, May 30, 1593, Lettres missives, iii. 783. Henry, about this time,
indulged in many expressions of the kind. President Groulart reports him as
stating to the magistrates and officers whom he assembled, on the 24th of July,
the day before the abjuration, that he had been brought up in a contrary belief to theirs, but that "by the grace of the Holy Ghost," he began to "relish "
the arguments for the Roman Catholic religion which had been alleged to him.
Mémoires de Claude Groulart (Edition Michaud et Poujoulat), 560.

[3] Mémoires d'Agrippa d'Aubigné (Edition Panthéon), 503.

[4] "Que voulés-vous ? Il m'a dit mes verites." Lestoile, ii. 133. The preacher is said by Lestoile to have been D'Amours.

ters that have come down to us from the end of the sixteenth
century were their unavailing pleas with Henry to vindicate his
better nature and do justice to his convictions of right and
truth.   From Geneva came a vigorous epistle from the aged

Letters of
Beza, Jean
de l'Espine,
and others. reformer, Theodore Beza, opportunely brought to
light in our own days to relieve his memory from the
strange misapprehension or calumny that he acqui-
esced in the advisability of Henry's abjuration.[1]   From other
quarters came the scarcely less noteworthy appeals of Jean de
l'Espine, and another whose name, could it be ascertained, would
well deserve to be held in lasting remembrance.[2]   From St.
Jean d'Angely came a masterpiece of eloquent and affectionate
remonstrance, to which I have had frequent occasion to refer,
and which will ever place Gabriel d'Amours among the most
pleasing personages of an age not deficient in well-defined
characters.   He it was who laid bare the king's weakness, and
warned him of the insidious influence of that fair Gabrielle
d'Estrées, now Duchess of Beaufort, who, seeing that the only
hope of securing her royal lover's divorce from Margaret of
Valois and his marriage to herself lay in the favor of the pope,
was employing every seductive art to persuade Henry to enter
the Church of Rome.[3]

---

[1] The discovery of the letter written by Theodore Beza to Henry IV., in
June, 1593, among the treasures of the Library of Geneva, is one of the most
interesting of the many discoveries of M. Jules Bonnet.   The document was
printed for the first time in the Bulletin de la Société de l'histoire du Protestantisme français, i. 41–46.   Previously to this time, even so excellent and conscientious a historian as Schlosser, in his life of Beza (Heidelberg, 1809), p.
272, had represented the reformer as so free from blind fanaticism that, instead of lamenting the king's abjuration, he regarded it only as a necessary
step to heal the wounds of lacerated France.

[2] M. Charles Read has done good service to the cause of history by collecting and publishing, in the first volume of the Bulletin of the French Protestant Historical Society, not less than four important letters, three of them
till then inedited, directly bearing upon the abjuration.   Besides Beza's letter
above referred to, these comprise the " Discours au Roy par un sien sujet et
serviteur " (i. 105–112, 155–158), the letter of Jean de l'Espine (i. 449–456),
and that of Gabriel d'Amours (i. 280–285).

[3] "La belle Gabrielle d'Estrée, Maîtresse du Roy, prenoit part à ces intrigues.
Elle ne haïssoit pas les Reformez, qu'elle estimoit fidelles et gens de bien ; et

"I have ever had this honor from God," he wrote, " and this good fortune, to see you always prosper; and if you listened to

Appeal of
Gabriel
d'Amours.

Gabriel d'Amours, your minister, as you listen to Gabrielle your mistress, I should still see you a generous king and triumphant over your enemies.[1] How did you act lately, when I was near your majesty at Saint Denis and Chartres? Did I not remind you, in a sermon at Saint Denis, what Delilah did to Samson, who rendered him miserable and contemptible in the eyes of the Philistines? If you should act as did David after the prophet Nathan's remonstrance—as your majesty knows that God has graciously suffered me to have the boldness several times to address remonstrances to you which you have taken in very good part, as coming from your very humble and faithful subject and a pastor whom you love —I am sure that God will show you grace and mercy. But you keep on your way, as we are told by all who come to us from court. When God wrought such miracles through you, you did not live thus. We are told in these regions that you are about to imitate Solomon, who turned aside to idolatry; women were the cause of it. It is said that you have promised to go to mass, which I in no wise credit, and I shall ever fight in single combat to maintain the contrary. What! Can it be that the greatest captain in the world has become so cowardly as to go to mass for fear of men? Where would be that great magnanimity, that faith so rare, so great, which I so often beheld in you when, according to men, you saw nothing but desperate straits? What have you accomplished in all your life with a majority? On the contrary, what have you not achieved

---

même elle en avoit plusieurs au nombre de ses domestiques. Mais les Seigneurs de la Religion n'avoient pas beaucoup de complaisance pour elle : et jamais ils n'eussent favorisé ses ambitieux desseins. Au contraire, on luy faisoit esperer que si le Roy changeoit de Religion, elle auroit plus de lieu de pretendre à l'épouser ; parce qu'il pourroit faire casser par le Pape son mariage avec Marguerite de Valois, et se mettre en liberté d'en contracter un autre." Benoist, Histoire de l'édit de Nantes, i. 93.

[1] The play upon the words in the original cannot be imitated in the translation : "Si vous escoutiez *Gabriel Damours* v^{tre} [votre] *ministre,* comme vous escoutes *Gabriele* v^{tre} [votre] *amoureuse,* je vous verroy tousjours Roy genereux et triomphant de vos ennemis."

in conjunction with the small number of the true Israelites? Do you wish me to predict your misfortune—me, respecting whom you have many times said before your nobles that I always predicted you good fortune? I cannot do it. I will believe good until I shall have seen evil; sufficient unto the day the evil thereof, says Jesus Christ. You wish to be instructed by the bishops of the Romish Church, we are told. O, you are not the king that needs to be instructed! You are a greater theologian than am I, who am your minister. You have no lack of science (knowledge); but you have a little lack of conscience."[1]

Such remonstrances came from one who maintained that he would indeed ever pray to God in behalf of his misguided king,[2] and that, should that king forget himself so far as to attend mass, he would go and serve him in person, if not as his minister, yet as a soldier, having always been near him upon the battle-field when he still had the sword unsheathed and bloody.[3]

True it is that, in the midst of the universal cry of honest protest that arose from his old fellows in arms, as well as from his spiritual advisers, against Henry's projected disloyalty to his convictions, there were a few insidious voices of nominal Protestants speaking to him in the secrecy of his bedchamber, and counselling or justifying the step he was about to take. A knot of two or three ministers of the religion which he still professed, whether sincerely holding the latitudinarian views they expressed, or actuated, as was commonly reported, and as seems not improbable, by mercenary motives, whispered in his ear a theory of the relations of Roman Catholicism and the Reformation little calculated to strengthen the king's moral courage and resolution.

The "ministres courtisans."

---

[1] "Vous n'aves faulte de science, mais vous avez ung peu faulte de conscience."

[2] "Priez Dieu. Nous prierons incessament pour vous. Quand je vous remonstre, vous me respondès cela ordinairement, Que vous prierès de vostre costé et me commandès de prier Dieu pour vous. Je ne combas pas seulement par prières envers Dieu pour vous, mais contre tous ceux qui parlent mal de vous."

[3] Gabriel d'Amours to Henry IV., June 20, 1593, ubi supra.

The Romish body they conceded to be a church, and, indeed, not only a church, but the most ancient church, and consequently the only church that could lay claim to the name without further necessity of qualification. In some sense, and in spite of certain errors, it was the Church of Christ. A person might, therefore, certainly be saved within it. The fathers of the Reformation had erred in creating a schism, instead of correcting the existing faults.[1] The doctrine was a pleasing one to Henry, as it has always proved, in times of pressure and persecution, to a considerable number of men and women of somewhat shallow convictions. But whether the arguments of the recreant Huguenot ministers had any weight with Henry or not, certain it is that those who conversed with him, about this time, found him imbued with the very comfortable opinion, that the differences between the two religions were great only in consequence of the passionate representation of rival preachers.[2]

Among his Protestant courtiers, the future Duke of Sully distinguished himself by the encouragement he gave to his master's abjuration. A Huguenot by birth, but a soldier, not a theologian, much less a religious man in his feelings *Rosny encour-* and principles, the great noble had no inclination *ages Henry to abjure.* himself to abandon the profession of a faith uniting him to the party with which all his interests were identified. But he had no hesitation in declaring that in the king's conversion to Roman Catholicism lay the quickest, if not, indeed, the only, road to undisputed possession of the throne, and he has manifested no shame in recording on the pages of his Mémoires the part he took in the disgraceful proceeding.[3] Henry sum-

---

[1] Agrippa d'Aubigné, iii. (book 3, ch. 22) 290. The Mémoires de Sully, chap. 40, have something to say of "les connivences pleines d'artifice de quelques ministres et Huguenots du cabinet, qui vouloient profiter du temps à quelque prix, et par quelque voye que ce pût être."

[2] "Est certain aussy qu'il [Duplessis] le trouva imbeu d'une opinion, qui luy sembloit alleger sa faulte ; que le differend des relligions n'estoit grant que par l'animosité des prescheurs, et qu'ung jour, par son auctorité, il le pouvoit composer." Mémoires de Charlotte Arbaleste sur la vie de Duplessis Mornay, son Mari, i. 261.   [3] Œconomies royales, c. 38 (Ed. of 1663, i. 351-358).

moned him to his bedside one morning before he had risen, with the view of leading Sully to advise him to do the very thing he was already determined to do. Nor did the worldly-wise states-man decline to fall in with the plan. When Henry, in well-feigned perplexity, spread before him the difficulties and the perils of his situation—the growing restlessness of the royalists of his suite, the ingratitude of those whom he had imagined that he had bound to his cause by favors conferred, and the probable dangers to his state, if not to his life, from conspiracies already hatched against him—Rosny, seated by his command on the edge of his couch, calmly told him that he saw but two methods by which safety might be secured. The one was to accede to the desires of those of whom he stood in suspicion. The other was to arrest the richest and most powerful of these enemies, place them in some spot where they could do him no harm, and employ their abundant resources in the prosecution of the war. With the presentation of the alternative, Rosny modestly pro-posed to stop ; " for," said he, " to counsel you to go to mass is a thing which, it seems to me, you ought not to expect from me, seeing I belong to 'the religion.' Yet I will tell you frankly that this is the most prompt and easy means of thwarting all these intrigues and making all the shrewdest projects of your enemies end in smoke." When his majesty, however, pressed him to state frankly what he would do were he in his place, the courtier ceased to measure his words with well-affected hesita-tion. Not more distinctly did Vice depict to the youthful Her-cules at the cross-roads the sweets he might expect upon the path to which she allured him, in contrast with the hardships attending the path which Virtue was about to urge him to enter, than did Maximilien de Béthune portray the ease and comfort upon which Henry, when once converted, might count, as opposed to the misery to which he might regard himself condemned for the remainder of his days, should he prefer principle to interest, a clear conscience to luxurious repose. If, of the only two prac-ticable courses Henry should choose the resort to force, his wily adviser saw nothing before him but difficulties, fatigue, pain, annoyance, perils, and labors. He would be continually in the saddle, encased in his corselet, with his helmet on his head, with his pistol in his hand, with his sword at his side. What was more, he would have to bid adieu to rest, pleasures, pastimes, love, mistresses, games, dogs, birds, and plans for building ; for he could never extricate himself from his troubles but by numerous captures of cities, by multiplied combats, signal victories, and a great effusion of blood. "Instead of which," said he, "by the other road, which is that you accommodate yourself, touching religion, to the wishes of the greater number of your subjects, you will not encounter so many vexations, pains, and difficulties in this world. As to the other world," he added with a laugh, "I do not answer for that. But then it is your majesty's function to come to a final determination by yourself, without deriving it from another, and least of all from me, knowing that I am a Protestant, and that you keep me near you not as a theologian or an ecclesiastical counsellor, but as a man for action and a state counsellor."

If Rosny was no professed theologian, he took good care to give a very clear expression to his views on the question of the day, and found his royal listener in nowise inclined to cavil at them. The duke held it to be an undoubted truth, that, whatever religion men may externally profess, they cannot fail to be saved if they die in the observance of the Decalogue, and the belief in the Apostles' Creed, if they love God with all their heart, have charity toward their neighbor, hope in the mercy of God, and look for salvation through the meritorious death and righteousness of Jesus Christ. Nay, applying his opinion to the case in hand, he declared his own conviction that, should Henry put this theory into practice, he would attain eternal blessedness, whatever outward profession he might make of the Roman Catholic Church, while, by his equitable treatment of the Protestants, he would secure their love and loyal obedience. The conclusion of the whole matter was, that Sully deemed it impossible for Henry ever to reign peaceably so long as he should openly adhere to a religion to which the majority of his subjects, both great and small, had so strong an aversion; and that, without general tranquillity, it was idle to expect the prosperity of France, much less the realization of the king's magnificent design of the establishment of a universal Christian republic, composed of all the kings and potentates of Europe professing the name of Christ.

Henry dismissed Rosny with the promise that he would think over what he had heard, and with the quiet suggestion that Rosny, on his side, should communicate his hopes to as many of his intimate friends as he knew to be likely to favor them.[1]

Before two other distinguished Huguenots Henry the Fourth laid his perplexities, enlarging upon the alleged perils that environed him, and hinting even at plots to seize his person at Mantes and betray him to the Duke of Mayenne. But from these he obtained no such counsel as Rosny had given.

Agrippa d'Aubigné.   Agrippa d'Aubigné, using the familiarity bred of long association in arms, endeavored to prove to the king, in a private interview, that the condition of the realm was in nowise so critical as his majesty's distempered imagination fancied it. The old soldier was one of those that were very sceptical respecting the influence of the much-vaunted "third party" (tiers parti), believing in it no more than they did in the " third place " —purgatory—by means of whose terrors the Romish Church drove a profitable traffic.[2] He tried to remove Henry's apprehension of the election of a new king by the League, showing him that the choice of the Infanta's husband by the Paris states general would be the signal for all the disappointed candidates to come over to the side of the legitimate monarch and to give him their undivided support. The disgust of many of the staunch advocates of the League and the discontent, verging upon revolt, of the Parisian populace, were among the many elements in his favor. Nor did D'Aubigné fail to set before the wavering prince the blessings he had received at God's hands, and the curses sure to follow ingratitude; assuring him that better were it to reign over a mere corner of France while

---

[1] Sully, ubi supra, chap. 38, i. pp. 354–358.

[2] "Le roi n'avoit faute de Refformez qui se moquoient de ce tiers parti, lequel ils croioient aussi peu que le troisiesme lieu, qui est le Purgatoire, et en parloient au roi avec grand mespris." Histoire universelle, iii. 290 (book 3, c. 22).

serving the Almighty, than to obtain a precarious rule over the whole country, trampled upon by the victorious pope, and exposed to the insolence of his own subjects who had compelled him by threats to change his religion.[1]

Although the eyes of Duplessis Mornay had been slow to open to the true state of the case, he now took in clearly its opportunities and its perils. A month before, he had written the melancholy and significant words: "Our king is still himself, in the matter of religion; himself, on the other hand, as respects his pleasures. The one circumstance consoles me, when I see that he is not ashamed of the gospel of Christ; the other afflicts me when I see that he brings shame upon the profession of that gospel."[2] And now, more in sadness than with any real hope of preventing a foregone conclusion, he addressed to Henry a letter of remonstrance. "Sire," he said, "I have learned something of what took place on the fifteenth at Mantes, and I am only waiting the arrival of M. de Vicose to go to your majesty, thinking that I may be able to be of some service to you there. I am confident, Sire, in spite of whatever may be said, that your majesty cannot forget the favors God has showered on you; and I have a still stronger confidence that God, who was minded of you before you were born, will not forget you. If you hold this conference with the intention that the Truth shall be made known, you will wish her to be defended, and you will accordingly summon persons competent to do this. If you do not summon them, Sire, it will be asserted that you are only seeking an observance of forms, being already resolved to make a surrender. This is not credible in the case of the greatest prince of our times, still less of one who has so often experienced the intervention of the arm of God in his behalf. Think, Sire, that all those who have heretofore been wont to be in arms for you against your enemies, are to-day marshalled in the host before God, praying Him to strengthen

Marginal note: Duplessis Mornay.

---

[1] Agrippa d'Aubigné, iii. 292 (book 3, c. 22).

[2] "L'un me console quand je vois qu'il n'est poinct honteux de l'Evangile du Christ ; l'aultre m'afflige quand je vois qu'il faict honte à la profession de cest Evangile." Duplessis to La Fontaine, April 20, 1593, Mémoires, v. 400.

you, and to fulfil in you the saying, that His gifts and calling
are without repentance.   For myself, I maintain the point with
assurance against all comers ; and I very humbly entreat the
Almighty, Sire, that He may impart His Spirit to you according to the measure of your temptations, and may make you
victorious, to His own glory, to your salvation, and to the instruction of your people." [1]

That Henry was unmoved by these and other appeals from the
ministers of religion whom he venerated, and from the lords and
gentlemen with whom he had made common cause during so
many years, there is no reason to suppose.   On the
contrary, there are many things which indicate that
the final triumph of expediency over moral sentiment was not
effected without a painful conflict, a struggle in which the better nature at times asserted itself.   Nor is it doubtful that to
the king there seemed no other way out of his present perplexities than that of sacrificing his own religious belief to the creed
of the overwhelming majority of his people.   There were
many in his own times, as there have been many since
then, even to our day, who regarded the election of a king
by the pretended states general of the League as a calamity involving the inevitable ruin of the State.   The pretender, recognized by the pope, supported by the great majority of the French
people, assisted by a foreign king reputed to have greater resources of men and money than any other contemporary prince,
a king ready to expend the wealth of the Indies in the accomplishment of his designs, would gather to him even those Roman
Catholics who, in hope of their master's ultimate conversion,
had thus far remained loyal.   There seemed to be force even
in a brutal statement of the case made by the blunt and profane
Monsieur d'O, which the king could find no weapons to parry. [2]
It may even have appeared to Henry that, in a sense, when consenting to hear the Romish mass, he was consulting the safety
of his fellow Protestants.   For would not the ruin of his own

The king's
attitude.

[1] Duplessis Mornay to Henry IV., Saumur, May 25, 1593, Mémoires, v. 426,
427.

[2] See Monsieur d'O's address in Agrippa d'Aubigné, iii. 291, 292.

prospects, involving, as it seemed probable, the complete subjection of France to Spain, and the introduction of the intolerant and persecuting policy which had reigned supreme in Spain and the Spanish Netherlands, with all the horrors of the Inquisition, bring about the utter destruction of French Protestantism ? He did not, therefore, probably stand in his own eyes altogether as a hypocrite, when he went so far as to assure the Protestants whom he was forsaking, that he was sacrificing himself in their behalf, and that his Huguenot faith would always continue to be the real religion of his heart and soul.[1] None the less must he who would read aright the history of the Abjuration regard these sentiments only as the flimsy pretexts with which, while attempting to impose upon others, he may at times have imposed upon himself. A stranger to deep religious convictions, he had exhibited in his life no evidence that his actions were, or that he desired them to be, moulded after the pattern of a lofty morality. The profession of a few doctrines held by all Christendom, the intellectual acceptance of the distinctive tenets of the Reformed Church, the scoffing rejection of as many dogmas of the Romish Church—the papal supremacy, transubstantiation, purgatory, and the like—this constituted, apparently, the meagre fund of his religion. An attendance, more or less patient, upon the Huguenot " prêche," a listening, more or less deferential, to the exhortation or reproof of his Huguenot chaplains, a few cheap phrases of acknowledgment of Divine aid vouchsafed in his deliverances on the battle-field or elsewhere, were the scanty evidence of his piety. But his daily conduct was little affected either by his theological opinions or by his devotions; and for a score of years the epochs of his life had been as distinctly marked by the succession of his mistresses, as by the striking political events of the period. If there was any change, as time elapsed,

---

[1] "Lors commença le roi . . . à descouvrir par ses emissaires avec les Refformez, leur faire pitié jusques à ces termes : 'Mes amis, priez Dieu pour moi ; s'il faut que je me perde pour vous, au moins vous ferai-je ce bien, que je ne souffrirai aucune forme d'instruction, pour ne faire point de plaie à la Religion, qui sera toute ma vie celle de mon ame et de mon cœur ; et ainsi je ferai voir à tout le monde que je n'ai esté persuadé par autre théologie que la necessité de l'Estat.'" Agrippa d'Aubigné, iii. 293, 294.

it was a change for the worse.   The story of Henry's amours
was varied by accounts of the distress of his cast-off favorites,
and of his ingratitude.   Only a few months before the Abjuration, one such unfortunate had painfully reached Saint Denis
and the royal court only to end her miserable existence.[1]

In the case of a man whose life was so irregular, whose conduct
was evidently so little influenced by any motives derived from
the sanctions of religion—however gay and cheery he may have
been, however brave and patient, however well qualified to discharge the functions of a prince struggling to rescue his own
possessions and defend the lives and the rights of conscience of
his followers, however kingly in all his bearing—in such a case, it
would seem almost an absurdity to speak of conversion from one
religion to another.   The change involved no renunciation of
old principles, no adoption of new ones.   It was little more than
the parting from associates of long standing, the severing of external ties such as even the most thoughtless cannot altogether
regard as indifferent.   And, with all his faults, Henry was not
thoughtless or inconsiderate.   He had carefully weighed the temporal consequences of the step he was about to take, balancing
the possible dangers of a Huguenot combination and the institution of a new protectorate, against the more real and immediate
perils likely to follow from a further delay in abjuring the Protestant faith.   If his decision was quickly made, and so suddenly
announced to the world as to wear the appearance of precipi-
tancy, it was none the less the deliberate result of a long period
of calm and quiet observation of the necessary drift of political
events.   Certain it is that the fear lest the states of the League
might be on the eve of electing a rival king—a fear which the
spirit exhibited by the Archbishop of Lyons and his associates in
the opening sessions of the Conference of Suresnes transformed
from a remote apprehension into a conviction of impending dis-

---

[1] It is Lestoile, in his journal, under date of the end of 1592 (ii. 107),
that records the death of Madame Esther, a discarded mistress of Henry IV. at
La Rochelle, who, when her child had died, came to Saint Denis in the vain
hope of touching the king's pity.   He refused even to see her.   She scarcely
obtained a "Huguenot" burial.

aster—led him to carry out his purpose, long since formed, with
as much rapidity as ever he had executed a manœuvre at a critical moment on the fields of Coutras or Ivry. But if he seemed
surprised or hurried by the course of events, as his old friends
charitably supposed him to be,[1] the haste was rather apparent
than actual. Read in the light of the actual Abjuration, the
repeated professions so ostentatiously made by Henry at intervals, both before and since his accession to the throne of France,
of his readiness to be instructed, and his reiterations of the statement that he was not obstinate, point but too distinctly to a
matured plan of which only the time of the fulfilment was anticipated.

Meanwhile the King was anxious lest, in conciliating his former
enemies, he might alienate his former friends to such a degree
as to compel them to plan measures of defence, possibly even
to elect a protector of their churches, in place of him who was
deserting them. For this reason he listened to the suggestion
of the Duke of Bouillon, and authorized the Roman Catholic
nobles and gentlemen of his council to publish a formal statement that, pending the arrival of the time for the king's "instruction," no measures should be adopted to the prejudice of
the rights granted to the Protestants by the edicts of Henry
the Third, or of the good union and friendship existing between
the loyal Roman Catholics and the Huguenots.[2] It was doubt-

---

[1] "Tellement que le roy, se trouvant surpris et comme opprimé de ce soub-
dain et inopiné changement, voyant les visaiges et les cœurs des siens alienez
de luy, adverty à toute heure des gouverneurs et des places, ou que l'on pra-
ticquoit, ou qui se divertissoient de luy, se rezoleut, tant pour eviter ces re-
muemens, que pour se rendre la voie plus facile à son establissement, de s'ac-
commoder, comme il feit quelques jours apres, à l'Eglize romaine." Mémoires
de Charlotte Arbaleste sur la vie de Duplessis Mornay, son Mari, i. 256.—
Yet even Madame Duplessis Mornay admits that it seemed to many, "par la
prompte conclusion qu'il en preit, qu'il ne falloit qu'une preignante occasion pour l'y jetter, et que pieça elle estoit deliberée."

[2] The "Declaration of Mantes," dated May 16, 1593, was signed by François d'Orléans, Count of St. Pol, Chancellor Hurault, Méru, Bellegarde, D'O,
and others. See the text in Mémoires de Duplessis Mornay, v. 416, 417. Compare Madame Duplessis's remarks, Mémoires de Charlotte Arbaleste, i. 256,
and De Thou, viii. 259.

less with the same object in view that his majesty, about this time, sent again and again the most pressing letters to Du-plessis Mornay, begging, almost commanding him, to intrust to safe hands the City of Saumur, of which he was the vigilant governor, and come to court, if only for a few days. He had, he said, important matters concerning religion about which he needed his advice. Yet before the Abjuration, and for some weeks after, Duplessis declined to come. Had the king been wavering and in need of moral or religious support, nothing would have detained him an instant. But Henry had evidently made up his mind fully to the consummation of his disloyal act, and the sturdy Huguenot refused to become a witness, and, in some sense, an abettor of the disgraceful proceeding. Nothing, indeed, more clearly demonstrates the sincere respect entertained for Duplessis Mornay by the king, even at this moment of meditated treachery to his convictions, than do his reiterated messages. Henry even appealed to him as a soldier, and, when a battle seemed imminent before Dreux, summoned him to take horse on receipt of his letter, and come diligently with his company and with all the friends he could muster, lest he should be among the last. "Remember," said he, "that at the battle of Ivry you only arrived just in time. What annoyance would you have experienced if, when still three or four leagues distant, you had had tidings of the battle gained without you. Besides, I have need of you and of your counsel on some matters which present themselves. Therefore, without more excuses or delay, come and use diligence."[1] Six weeks later he wrote: "Monsieur Duplessis, I have written you so often to come, and you have not done it. I will write you but this once, to see if I shall be obeyed. Come, therefore, immediately after having provided for the safety of your post during your absence. Come! come! come! You will not have to stay here long."[2] In two days he again wrote with his own hand: "I

Henry entreats Duplessis Mornay to come to him.

---

[1] Henry IV. to Duplessis Mornay, Dreux, June 25, 1593, Mémoires, v. 465, 466.

[2] The same to the same, St. Denis, August 5, 1593, ibid., v. 505.

find it very strange that a number of persons who have seen you have reported to me that you complained of me, and I find this more strange in you than in any one else; for, besides the fact that I have never given you any occasion, and have loved you more than any other gentleman of my kingdom, I have always talked with you so freely, that, if you had any ground of complaint, you ought to let me know, or come to tell me yourself, without mentioning it to anybody else. I have many times written to you to come to me, but in vain. I see what is the reason. You love the general interests [of the Protestants] more than you love me. Still I shall always be both your good master and your king. Give me this satisfaction of seeing you, come by post or otherwise, and do not seek further excuses."[1] When a week had passed, he again wrote to the same effect;[2] and when a fortnight more had elapsed without Duplessis Mornay's arrival, he penned another autograph missive. "Monsieur Duplessis, I am wearied with constantly writing to you one and the same thing. I desire infinitely to see you, even before the coming of the deputies, who are to come with Vicose, and for whom I have sent by him. Come! I have so much need of your presence that I cannot do without it, for reasons which I cannot state in writing. Come, yet again! Your tarrying with me will be but a few days. I shall be glad should you have taken steps to satisfy the Swiss; but let not that so tie you down there as to be longer in coming." And the postscript again was: "Come! come! come! if you love me."[3]

If, however, Duplessis was resolute in declining the king's invitations, there was one point upon which he insisted much in his letters to Henry, and which he secured. The Protestant ministers were not to be asked to be present at an unequal combat. Henry yielded to the entreaties of Duplessis Mornay that, if his majesty was resolved to change his religion, and was only observing an empty form in such a conference as was proposed between the

The Protestants not to be invited to the "instruction."

[1] Same to same, Monceaux, August 7, 1593, ibid., v. 505, 506.
[2] Same to same, St. Denis, August 15, 1593, ibid., v. 514.
[3] Same to same, Melun, August 28, 1593, ibid., v. 527, 528.

ministers of the two faiths, he should not add the load of this fresh crime to the burden his conscience already bore. For, if he should surrender himself to idolatry, after such a combat in which truth could not be overcome, the king would, said Duplessis Mornay, become the author of a scandal to the entire Christian Church, and give the impression that he had yielded or succumbed inasmuch as he had seen the religion which he professed fairly refuted.[1] None the less did the Huguenot express his own determination never to despair of his master's recovery so long as a breath or pulse continued ;[2] and, writing to M. de Loménie, not many days after the king's conversion, he begged him to say to Henry : " If ever the desire shall seize his majesty to escape from the spiritual and temporal thraldom in which he now is, I cannot indeed grow in fidelity to his service, but certainly I shall redouble my courage, for the just pain I feel. They do not give him the peace of state, and they take away his peace of conscience. They do not reconcile the rebels, and they chill his most faithful servants. They do not restore to him his kingdom (for it is God and not the devil that can give it), and, so far as in them lies, they make him renounce the kingdom of heaven. I groan within me to see him thus served, thus cheated, thus betrayed, and I see no man of worth, even among the Catholics in these parts, that does not say the same thing." [3]

The single-minded and pious Huguenot had not lost all hope that his master might yet be extricated from the false position which he had voluntarily assumed. And it was not otherwise with good Catharine of Bourbon, a princess as like in steadfastness of character to her mother, Jeanne d'Albret, and her grandmother, Margaret of Angoulême, as was her brother in some less desirable traits to his male progenitors. Upon her the arguments used with Henry were thrown away. " I am very glad," she wrote to Duplessis

Catharine of Bourbon.

---

[1] Mémoires de Charlotte Arbaleste, i. 258.

[2] " Si estime je de nostre debvoir, comme des medecins, de l'assister de ce que Dieu a mis en nous, tant que le pouls lui bat." Lettre de M. Duplessis à plusieurs ministres, Saumur, June 9, 1593, Mémoires, v. 448.

[3] Duplessis Mornay to Loménie, August 11, 1593, Mémoires, v. 511.

Mornay, "that you have so good an opinion of my constancy, in
which I intend so to persevere that neither you nor any of those
that profess the same faith shall be disappointed. It is the subject of my prayers to God ; and you may well believe that I
employ in them the best hours of the day and the night. I
doubt not that the change of which you hear has saddened you.
As to myself, I am more annoyed than I can describe. But I
hope that God, who until now has shown us so many evidences
of His goodness, will not forsake us, and particularly will not
forsake him who, for the welfare of his people, does not fear to
abate something from his conscience, which I assure myself God
will restore to him, when these confusions are ended, as sound
and entire as ever it was." [1]

Meanwhile the last scene in the disgraceful drama was at
hand. The French prelates, convened to take part in the " instruction " of the king, had decided, not without the passionate
opposition of the Cardinal of Bourbon, that they were competent to admit his majesty into the communion of the Roman
Catholic Church, upon profession of his faith and repentance,
without waiting for the pope's absolution. [2] Friday, the twenty-
third of July, had been appointed by Henry as the
day upon which, in his quarters at Saint Denis, he
would listen to the arguments of his ghostly advisers.

Henry's "in-
struction."
July 23, 1593.

He had signified his desire that to four or five prelates, whom he
named, might be committed the honorable task of solving his
doubts—the Archbishop of Bourges, the Bishops of Nantes,
Chartres, and Mans, and the Bishop-elect of Evreux. The last
named was the ingenious and eloquent Du Perron ; the Bishop
of Chartres was the moderate Nicholas de Thou. The Cardinal
of Bourbon had sought to be included in the select company,
but Henry would not have him. On that point he was firm,
having no desire to have a spy of the League as one of his instructors. And as he had little compunction in improving any
occasion that offered for ridiculing the pretensions of his igno-

---

[1] Catharine de Navarre to Duplessis, July, 1593, Mémoires de Duplessis
Mornay, vi. 77.

[2] De Thou, viii. (bk. 107) 304–307.

rant but ambitious cousin, he even took pains to inform him
that, though his own acquaintance with theological subjects was
but slight, yet, were the controversy to be decided by Bourbon
and himself alone, he would have no trouble in securing the
victory over so incompetent an opponent.[1]   In truth, however,
notwithstanding his disclaimer, Henry was no contemptible dis-
putant on such subjects.   He had not listened to so many Huguenot sermons without carrying away some of the strong
doctrine upon which he had been fed.   He had not been an
altogether uninterested auditor of those sturdy Huguenot ministers, as fearless in debate as upon the battlefield, with whom
he had long consorted.   Gabriel d'Amours scarcely used hyperbole when he rated him above himself in theological attainments.

So the prelates discovered, in the course of their five hours'
interview with his majesty ; one of them admitting, the next
day, that he had never seen a heretic better instructed in his
error, or better able to defend it.[2]   Yet, truth to say, Henry
made no great effort.   He had little desire either to parade his
knowledge or to conceal the fact that he was yielding not to
the acuteness of reasoning of his opponents, but to the fancied
logic of events.   We may even give him credit for so much
of lingering loyalty to his Protestant convictions as that he
desired that the truths he had hitherto held should not seem,
to any intelligent man who could read below the surface, to
have been worsted in a fair and honorable fight.   The fencer
could not resist the temptation to make so rapid and accurate a use of his practised rapier as to reveal the fact that he
was, after all, making but a feint of defence, and to warn all
comers not to press him overmuch.   He was willing to submit
to the authority of the Roman Catholic Church, but evidently
that was all.   For a positive statement of belief in doctrines
which he deemed absurd, he plainly intimated he was not yet
prepared.   In some cases he parried a thrust with an apparently
careless jest.   When the prelates came to the matter of prayers
for the dead, he exclaimed, with quiet irony : " Let us drop

---

[1] De Thou, viii. (bk. 107) 308.   [2] Lestoile, ii. 160.

the ' *Requiem.*' I am not yet dead, and, what is more, I have no inclination to die." He said that he accepted the doctrine of Purgatory, not as an article of faith, but as a belief of the Church whose son he was, and to please his instructors, knowing it to be the very bread upon which the priests subsist. As the discussion went on, however, the tone of banter, in which he occasionally indulged, was dropped, and the pathos lurking beneath revealed itself. The cardinal doctrine of transubstantiation and the adoration of the wafer were reached. Here the delay was long. At last Henry yielded, but not without visible emotion. "You do not content me fully on this point," he said. "You do not satisfy me as I desired, and as I had promised myself that I should be satisfied by your instruction. Here, then, I place my soul this day in your hands. I pray you, take good care ; for where you make me enter, thence I shall go out only through death. This I swear and protest." As he said it, tears came to his eyes.[1] Presently he became calmer. He thanked the prelates for their pains, he professed to have had many difficulties cleared away, and intimated his readiness to accept their conclusions.[2] But when, taking advantage of his favorable inclinations, the archbishop and his associates presented to him a confession of faith in which he was to declare his belief in every particular dogma of the Roman Catholic Church,[3] the king warned them that they were in danger of going farther and faring worse. The next day he sent again for them, and again remonstrated with them. Emphasizing the doctrine of Purgatory in particular, he declared that most of

---

[1] Lestoile, ubi supra.

[2] See the "Procès-verbal de la cérémonie de l'abjuration d'Henry IV," authenticated by the signature of the Dean of Beauvais, appointed secretary by the prelates. It is reprinted in Cimber et Anjou, Archives curieuses, xiii. 343–351. "Discours des ceremonies observees à la conversion du tres-grand et tres-belliqueux Prince, Henry IV, Roy de France et de Navarre, à la religion Catholique, Apostolique et Romaine." Reprinted in Mémoires de la Ligue, v. 403.

[3] Sully, Œconomies royales, c. 40 (i. 387). With regard to the form of this paper, see the judicious note of a writer who has made the most satisfactory study of the abjuration in all its bearings, E. Stähelin, Uebertritt König Heinrichs IV., 610–612.

them did not themselves believe it.   Indeed, he pointedly asked
them: " Do you believe that there is such a place ? "   The
question received no answer, the prelates conveniently turning
the conversation to another topic.[1]   But the king's warning
took effect.   Henry was only required to express his assent to
a shorter formulary of a more general character.   It was quite
enough.   All the prelates really needed was his majesty's submission to the Roman Catholic Church.   Why be more particular in exacting from the new-comer a profession of positive
faith in every detail of doctrine, than in requiring such a definite avowal from the Church's ancient followers ?   Sincerity was
the exception, not the rule, with the latter; could the proselyte
who virtually confessed that political circumstances had done
more than all the arguments of the doctors in bringing him
over, be expected to do better than the native-born Romanist ?
It was sufficient for Henry to accept in the simplest form the
yoke which the loyal Roman Catholics of his suite wished to
place upon his neck, to sign a short paragraph or two, to be
seen at mass—meanwhile believing just as much or as little of
the Romish system of faith as he pleased.   No chaplain or
confessor would be likely to trouble his august penitent in future years by attempting to pry very narrowly into the tenets
actually held in the inner sanctuary of his breast.   On such
subjects, as well as in the domain of private morals, Henry
would henceforth enjoy greater immunity from reproof than
he had hitherto enjoyed when a D'Amours, among the ministers, or a Duplessis Mornay, among laymen, had, with the
characteristic Huguenot boldness, held up his sins before his
eyes.   The scantiness of the king's actual profession might,
moreover, be compensated for by a more ample paper, meant
for foreign circulation, and, if not actually signed by Henry, yet
authenticated by his secretary, Loménie, an adept in imitating
his master's handwriting.[2]   So early did Henry the Fourth be-

---

[1] Lestoile, ubi supra.

[2] " Man weiss, dass der König dem Papste bewilligte, was er den Bischöfen
versagte, und dass eben die zurückgewiesene Schrift als das Glaubensbe-
kenntniss Heinrichs IV. nach Rom abging—freilich nicht von ihm selber

gin to imitate the example of his Very Christian and Very
Catholic predecessors, and attempt to palm off upon a Curia,
itself not altogether inexperienced in such devices, a fraudulent
document which might satisfy the demands of the pontiff.

Even to the last moment the king was uneasy, restless, apprehensive. "On Sunday I shall take the perilous leap!" he
wrote, late on Friday, to his mistress, Gabrielle d'Estrées.[1] On
Saturday he took pains to gather about him all the prominent
men of his court, and, in a speech of studied calmness, announced his intentions and threw himself upon the support
of his loyal subjects.[2] Again, that very day, he renewed his
promise to some Protestant ministers to continue their friend,
and again asked them to pray for him; while, upon the very
morning of the day that was to witness his public reception into
the communion of the Roman Catholic Church, the Huguenot
minister La Faye was admitted into the bedchamber before
the king's rising, and had a private conference with his majesty,
whose tears and frequent embraces betrayed the perturbed condition of his mind.[3]

It was eight or nine o'clock, on the morning of Sunday, the
twenty-fifth of July, 1593, when Henry the Fourth left his

Henry abjures
Protestantism.
Saint Denis.
July 25, 1593.

lodgings at Saint Denis for the ancient abbey church
where his "reconciliation" was to be formally effected. He wore a white-satin doublet and white-satin
hose; his hat and the cloak thrown over his shoulders were
black. His escort was a crowd of nobles, officers of the crown,
and simple gentlemen who had flocked to witness the welcome
sight. Before him marched his Swiss, Scotch, and French
guards, with beating drum, while twelve trumpeters announced
his coming with loud and piercing notes. The streets were full
of people frantic with joy and filling the air with shouts of
"Long life to the King!" The inhabitants of the little town of

---

unterschrieben, sondern nach einer *pia fraus* nur durch seiner Sekretär de
Loménie, der die Handschrift der Königs auf das Beste nachzuahmen ver-
stand." Stähelin, 611.

[1] "Ce sera dimanche que je ferai le sault périlleus." Lestoile, ii. 160.

[2] Mémoires de Claude Groulart, 559, 560.

[3] Lestoile, ii. 161.

Saint Denis were outnumbered by the Parisians of every rank, who, in defiance of the express orders given by the heads of the League, had come out to see the event with their own eyes. Flowers strewn in the way, tapestry hung from the walls, gave the scene the appearance of a triumphal march. The abbey church itself was similarly decorated. Within the portal, seated in a chair of white damask, embroidered with the combined arms of France and Navarre, sat the Archbishop of Bourges awaiting the king's arrival. Cardinal Bourbon, a number of other prelates, and all the monks of Saint Denis attended him —the cardinal with a cross and a copy of the Holy Gospel in his hands. "Who are you?" asked the archbishop of the approaching monarch. "I am the king," was the reply. "What do you desire?" again asked the archbishop. "I desire," said Henry, "to be received within the pale of the Roman, Catholic, and Apostolic Church." "Do you so wish?" pursued the prelate. "Yes," answered the king, "I so wish and desire." And kneeling down at that instant he pronounced these words: "I protest and swear, in the presence of Almighty God, that I will live and die in the Roman, Catholic, and Apostolic religion, that I will protect and defend it against all persons, at the risk of my blood and life, renouncing all heresies contrary to the doctrines of the said Roman, Catholic, and Apostolic Church." The archbishop had advanced a step or two. The king handed him his profession of faith, kissed the ring upon the prelate's hand, and then and there received the church's absolution and blessing. This over, the royal penitent was helped to rise from his knees, and, not without difficulty for the press, proceeded to the grand altar of the church. Again kneeling before it, he repeated a second time, upon the Holy Gospels, the oath he had taken at the portal. Amid deafening cries of "Vive le roi!" incessantly ringing through the sacred edifice, he again rose, ascended the steps, crossed himself, and kissed the altar. Then came the swelling music of the grand "Te Deum laudamus." Behind the altar, the king was heard in confession by the archbishop; next he returned into the presence of the people to take part in the solemnities of the mass, beating upon his breast and prostrating himself at the elevation of the host. The service over and the royal largesse made, according to custom, within the church, Henry was escorted home with blare of trumpets and with salvos of artillery which were heard, to the consternation of the League, in Paris itself.[1] The people had seen the king at the mass. The only Huguenot who ever sat upon the throne of France had denied his convictions, and outwardly embraced a religion which, in his heart, he neither loved nor respected. It remained to be seen, whether to the king who had made the ignoble purchase, or to the nation whose representative nobles had exacted the price and connived at the sacrifice of truth and honor, the City of Paris, soon to open its gates, was in reality worth the costly mass paid for it.

The news of the abjuration produced in the minds of honest men, far and near, the most painful impression. Politicians might applaud an act intended to conciliate the favor of the great majority of the nation, and extol the astuteness of the king in choosing the most opportune moment for his change of religion—the moment when he would secure the support of the Roman Catholics, fatigued by the length of the war and too eager for peace to question very closely the sincerity of the king's motives, without forfeiting the support of the Huguenots. But men of conscience, judging Henry's conduct by a standard of morality immutable and eternal, passed a severe sentence of condemnation upon the most flagrant instance of a betrayal of moral convictions which the age had known. It was a Roman Catholic and a persistent royalist who, on hearing of the strange event of Saint Denis, exclaimed to another of the same religious and political sentiments: "Ah, my friend! The king is lost! Now he is deserving of death, which he never was before." It was a bishop

Public opinion respecting the abjuration.

---

[1] The contemporary pamphlet entitled "Discours des ceremonies observees à la conversion du tres-grand et tres-belliqueux Prince, Henry IV, Roy de France et de Navarre, à la Religion Catholique, Apostolique et Romaine," to which I have already referred, may be considered the best authority for this portion of the history of the abjuration. De Thou, Davila, the Recueil des choses mémorables, Lestoile, the official account signed by the Dean of Beauvais (reprinted in Cimber et Danjou, Archives curieuses, xiii. 343–351), etc., may also be consulted to advantage.

of the established church who deplored the abjuration in these words: "I am a Catholic in life and in profession, and the king's very faithful subject and servant. Such I shall ever live, such I shall die. Yet I should have deemed it quite as good, nay, better, that the king had remained in his religion, rather than change it as he has done. In the matter of conscience we have a God above who is our Judge. Regard for Him alone ought to influence the conscience of kings, not regard for kingdoms, and crowns, and the forces of men. I look only for disaster as the consequence of this." [1]

From across the Channel, Henry's faithful ally added a voice of frank, though affectionate, remonstrance. Queen Elizabeth, in the first transports of her indignation, had been disposed summarily to recall from France every soldier she had sent thither, and to withhold from the French king all aid for the future. [2] In a calmer moment, when less incensed but not less deeply grieved, she wrote the following letter, with her own hand, in acknowledgment of a message received through Henry's special envoy, M. de Morlas:

Letter of Queen Elizabeth.

"Ah! what sorrow, what regrets, and what groans have I felt in my soul, at the sound of the tidings which Morlas has brought me! My God! Is it possible that any worldly consideration can have effaced the terror denounced by the Divine wrath? Can we, even according to reason, look for a good sequel to so iniquitous an act?

"Can you imagine that He who has sustained and preserved you by His hand would permit you to walk alone in your greatest need? It is a perilous thing to do evil that good may come. Still I hope that a more healthy inspiration may come to you. Meanwhile, I shall not cease to place you in the foremost rank of my devotions, in order that the hands of Esau may not spoil the blessings of Jacob. Whereas you promise me all friendship and faithfulness, I confess that I have dearly merited them, nor shall I repent, provided you do not change your Father

[1] Lestoile, ii. 164.

[2] See the correspondence of Beauvoir la Nocle, French ambassador in England, MSS., State Paper Office, apud Motley, United Netherlands, iii. 253.

(otherwise I shall be to you but a bastard sister on the Father's side) ; for I shall always love the natural better than the adopted. God knows it is so, and may He guide you in the right way. Your very confident sister, sire, if it be after the old fashion ; with the new I will have nothing to do.   ELIZABETH R." [1]

" It is a perilous thing to do evil that good may come!" The English queen could not have expressed more tersely her warning to Henry the Fourth ; she could not have enunciated more distinctly a principle of such uniform application that one need go no farther than to Henry himself to find, in his own person, in his posterity, and in the country over which he reigned, sufficient illustration of its truth.

The abjuration has not been without its apologists from the date of its occurrence down to our own days.   There will probably be no lack of them in time to come.   In France herself it is one of the most disastrous results of the act that it has lowered the tone of political morality, by substituting for the inflexible rule of duty a more convenient and variable standard of temporary expediency.   Doubtless Henry veiled from his own eyes, and, so far as he could, from the eyes of others, the deformity of the deed he committed, by investing it with the garb of a signal advantage to be derived, not so much by himself as by his kingdom.   And ever since there have been those who have not wearied of exalting his conduct, when, forsooth, he sacrificed personal religious belief upon the altar of national unity, into a brilliant exhibition of the virtue of self-abnegation.   It may, however, well be questioned whether the king was mainly inspired by any such elevated patriotism as is here supposed, and

---

[1] This striking letter, which I translate, is a proof that, if Queen Elizabeth's French accent was so odd as to expose her to some ridicule, she wrote the language forcibly and well.   See Read, Henri IV et le ministre Chamier, 93. Copies of the letter are to be found in the Colbert MSS. of the National Library of Paris, vol. 16 ; in the Dupuy MSS., vol. 121, in the Archives of the Council of State, Geneva, No. 2183, and in the Cottonian MSS., British Museum, Titus C. 7, 161.   This last gives the date as November 12, 1593.   M. Read (ubi supra, and in the Bulletin de la Société de l'histoire du Protestantisme français, vii. 263, 264) has given a more correct transcript of the original than M. Capefigue.

whether a monarch with whom cool calculation of private advantage was a constant trait of character really entertained views so disinterested. "It is the usual artifice of bad passions," an eminent historian of our own times has aptly remarked, when writing on another but a kindred theme, "to ascribe the cruel gratifications in which they indulge themselves either to some great idea whose accomplishment they are pursuing or to the absolute necessity of success." But he justly adds, "History would dishonor herself did␣she accept these lying excuses. It is her duty to refer the evil to its source, and to restore to the vices of men what belongs to them." [1]

If there be any who, after a dispassionate perusal of the story of Henry's renunciation of the faith of his childhood, still hold to the opinion that the insincere action was, under the circumstances, deserving of approbation rather than censure, the historian may well doubt his ability to move them from their position. He might, indeed, point out the unhappy consequences evidencing themselves in the gradual but sure degeneracy of the king, and in the disasters that overtook the dynasty of which he was the founder ; he might draw upon his fancy to construct a picture of what France would possibly have been, had the monarch but been true to himself and to his real belief. But, after all, the question in hand is not so much a historical inquiry as a problem of ethics from whose unalterable decisions there is no appeal. In the estimation of the just, however, enlightened by the lessons of experience, the path of truth and fidelity to principle is not only the path of duty ; it is always the course of true safety.[2]

---

[1] Guizot, Histoire de la République d'Angleterre et de Cromwell, i. 95.

[2] 'Ορθὸν ἀλήθει' ἀεί., Soph. Ant., 1195. Sir James Stephen has thoughtfully discussed the abjuration of Henry IV. in the sixteenth of his Lectures on the History of France. No impartial student of the past will hesitate to conclude, with the Cambridge professor, that the day of the king's "impious, because pretended, conversion was among the *dies nefasti* of his country."

CHAPTER XIV.

THE EDICT OF NANTES.

THE events that occurred at Saint Denis, as recorded in the preceding chapter, render it proper that the history should, from this point forward, assume a somewhat different type.

Change in character of the history.

Until the Abjuration the fortunes of the Huguenots had been inseparably connected with the personal successes and reverses of Henry the Fourth. However imperfect an exponent the king was of the moral and religious life of the French Protestants, however fickle and selfish his zeal, however prone his disposition to subordinate Huguenot interests to his own, he was still the nominal head of the party, the solemnly elected Protector of the Reformed Churches, as, during previous reigns, he had been the recognized mouth-piece of their complaints and their demands. A prince of the blood, the apparently remote prospect that he might one day be summoned to the throne had been a sufficient pretext for the institution of the most formidable conspiracy against the established order ever set on foot in France; and this merely because of the fact that he was a Protestant who, after his compulsory renunciation of his religion, at the time of the massacre of St. Bartholomew's Day, had, when left to himself, resumed its profession. The circumstance that the desperate struggle, which he had waged for four years previous to his accession, was forced upon him because of his Protestant creed has made the record of his victories and defeats germane to the story of those more truly religious men whom similar reasons led to fight shoulder to shoulder with him.

His abjuration alters the situation essentially. The historian of Huguenot affairs may now be excused from the attempt to chronicle all the remaining incidents of the reign of a king who has become a stranger to Protestantism, and may be allowed to refer the curious to the pages of works more general in their scope.

It is true that Henry himself failed, at first, to comprehend the full import of the change he had made. He still claimed to be a Huguenot; though what a Roman Catholic Huguenot might be, he did not explain. He denied that he had changed his faith. When a courtier informed him of the fact that a certain person had been of the religion which his majesty formerly held and had recently abjured, the king took him up sharply. "What religion do you say I held ? I have never known, nor do I now know, any but one Catholic religion ! I am not a Jew !" [1] He did not even take care to hide his affection for certain things which served as badges of Huguenot belief. Passing through his sister's rooms, and finding the company engaged in singing the psalms of Marot and Beza, he did not hesitate to join in with his own voice.[2] No wonder that the inconsistency was eagerly laid hold of by unfriendly preachers in the interest of the League, and paraded before the eyes of the people as proof positive of his majesty's hypocrisy. "Is it not notorious," exclaimed the gray friar Guarinus, "that although Henry of Bourbon goes to mass, he nevertheless is accustomed to sing,

Henry still claims to be a Huguenot.

'Quiconque se fie en Dieu jamais ne périra ?'" [3]

---

[1] Lestoile, ii. 212.

[2] Ibid., under date of Sunday, March 2, 1597, ii. 281. Vaumesnil and others were singing Psalm 79, "Les gens entrez sont en ton heritage." Madame de Monceaux (Gabrielle d'Estrées) begged the monarch to stop, and placed her hand on his mouth. This led some of those present to exclaim in a low voice : "Do you see that wretched woman (cette vilaine) who wants to prevent the king from singing God's praises ?"

[3] Ibid., ii. 191. The last lines of Theodore Beza's version of the thirty-fourth psalm are intended, which, however, more correctly are,

"Quiconque espère au Dieu vivant
Jamais ne périra."

If we may believe Lestoile, Friar Guarinus, when discovered at the time of the surrender of Paris (March, 1594), in his place of concealment, a garret, fell down on his knees and humbly promised his captor that, if spared, he would preach as zealously for the king as he had hitherto preached against him.

Nor was this the only indication of the king's lingering fondness for the church he had left. Whenever he met one of his sister's Huguenot ministers, he made it his practice to take him apart and whisper in his ear such requests as, "Pray to God in my behalf! Do not forget me in your prayers." [1]

It cannot, however, be denied that, as time advanced, such manifestations diminished in frequency, and Henry came more and more to a conscious recognition of the gulf which had opened between his Huguenot subjects and himself.

His occasional anxiety of mind.

Sometimes the enormity of the crime he had committed in sacrificing his religious convictions impressed him deeply, and he became the victim of deep dejection. This was particularly the case when, having fallen ill at the time of the prolonged siege of La Fère, he summoned to his bedside a Huguenot nobleman whose bluntness of speech had more than once given him deep offence. It was the same Agrippa d'Aubigné who, not long before, after his majesty had been wounded in the lip by the misdirected knife of Jean Chastel, gave him the significant warning: "Sire, God, whom you have as yet abandoned only with your lips, has contented Himself with piercing your lips. But when the heart shall have renounced Him, He will pierce the heart." [2] The Huguenot on the present occasion found his old captain agitated by a strange solicitude. Having shut himself in with Agrippa alone, and after shedding many tears and more than once kneeling in prayer to God Almighty, Henry adjured him, in view of the many caustic but useful truths he had heard from his mouth, to answer him frankly this momentous question: Whether he believed that by his change of religion he had committed the sin against the Holy Ghost? In vain D'Aubigné excused him-

---

[1] Lestoile (under date of May, 1595), ii. 263.

[2] "Sire, Dieu que vous n'avez encores delaissé que des levres, s'est contenté de les percer ; mais quand le cœur le renoncera il percera le cœur." Agrippa d'Aubigné, Histoire universelle, iii. 377. In his Mémoires (Edition Panthéon, 502), Agrippa repeats the incident with slight variations. He adds that, while Henry seemed not to take the remark amiss, his mistress, the fair Gabrielle, exclaimed: "What fine words, but badly employed!" "Yes, madam," he replied, "because they will be of no use."

self from undertaking to answer, and begged permission to call
in a minister to solve his master's scruples.   Henry insisted
upon an immediate reply, which D'Aubigné made as best he
could, setting forth in a simple manner the four elements which
he deemed essential characteristics of the unpardonable sin,
and leaving to the king the sole responsibility of determining
for himself whether the description applied to him.[1]   The interview lasted full four hours, and was frequently interrupted
by fervent prayers uttered by the monarch in his own behalf.
But nothing came of it.   On the morrow Henry's indisposi-
tion was relieved, and he never alluded to the subject again.[2]

But Henry had become a Roman Catholic, and only those
events of his subsequent history are entitled to a place here
that are necessary to a complete understanding of the difficulties and delays still besetting the Huguenot struggle for some
measure of religious liberty, if not for an unattainable equality
in the sight of the law.

The opposition of the League to the king's claims had lost
its only specious pretext when the king forsook his alleged
heresy; yet that opposition still continued.   In fact, the desperation engendered by the conviction that sooner or later a
Roman Catholic prince of undoubted legitimacy must prevail
led to excesses even greater than had hitherto been
witnessed.   Such preachers as Boucher grew more
outrageous in the use of scurrilous language from the
pulpit.   Henry of Bourbon fared little better at their hands
than Henry of Valois had fared.   They proclaimed his con-

*Continued
virulence of
the clergy.*

---

[1] They were, 1st, a knowledge of the sin when committing it; 2d, having
extended a hand to the spirit of error and repelled with the other hand the
spirit of truth; 3d, the absence of repentance; and, 4th, despair of God's
mercy.

[2] There seems, at first sight, to be a serious discrepancy between the two accounts given of this interview by Agrippa d'Aubigné; for, whereas the Histoire universelle states that it was at Travecy that Henry fell dangerously ill,
and by implication places the scene of the conversation at this village, the
Mémoires make him to have been at death's door at Monceaux when visited
by the Huguenot captain.   But Travecy is a village just north of La Fère, and
by the Monceaux in question is undoubtedly meant the place now known
as Monceau-lès-Leups, somewhat farther toward the east.   Both villages are

version a feigned one, the absolution he had received invalid. One of their number called upon his hearers to pray Almighty God not to permit the pope, who was always guided by the Holy Ghost and could not err in the faith, to be so persuaded by the prayers of the Béarnais as to grant him his favor. As for the redoutable Boucher himself, who a few months since had not scrupled, at the fifth anniversary of the Parisian Barricades, to say that Henry was a miscreant, good for nothing else than to be thrown into a tumbrel and hung on the gallows, he still continued to preach the startling doctrine that it was out of the power of the pope, nay, of God himself, to absolve so desperate a sinner as Henry of Navarre![1]

Whatever he may have thought of his own ability, Pope Clement showed no disposition to exercise in the king's behalf any of the resources that might lurk in the apostolic treasuries of grace. When the monarch sent the Duke of Nevers to Rome to endeavor to placate the pontiff, Clement stoutly refused to recognize Henry the Fourth, or Navarre (for so he affected to style him), as King of France, or to receive the duke in any capacity save as a private individual. Even then he treated him with little courtesy, while the ecclesiastics who accompanied Nevers were told that they must purge themselves of the fault of their participation in the recent events at Saint Denis in the presence of the Cardinal of Santa Severina, Grand Inquisitor and Grand Penitentiary, before they could be admitted to the honor of kissing the feet of his holiness. In the sequel this degrading condition was observed, slightly modified, indeed, in consequence of the duke's earnest remonstrance against the indignity placed upon him and his suite by making the French prelates appear to be fit subjects for the action of the Inquisition; but the Cardinal of Aragon, whom the pontiff proposed to substitute for the

Pope Clement intractable.

Mission of Nevers to Rome.

---

within the bounds of the present commune of La Fère, and were occupied during the siege by the royalists. It is not improbable that the house occupied by the king was on the confines of the two villages; or, the historian may accidentally have used the name of one village for that of the other. They are barely six miles distant from each other.

[1] De Thou, viii. (bk. 107) 311; Lestoile, ii. 135, 212.

Grand Inquisitor, was notoriously devoted to Spanish interests and hostile to France. In the object of his mission Nevers utterly failed. Clement was deaf to all argument. He was resolved to deny the king the desired absolution. Without waiting for the ambassador to broach the subject, he exclaimed : " Do not tell me that your king is a Catholic. I shall never believe that he is really converted unless an angel come from heaven to assure me that he is. As for the Catholics that have followed his party, I do not hold them to be disobedient and deserters of religion and of the crown; but they are only bastard children and sons of the bondwoman. On the contrary, those of the League are the true legitimate children, the true mainstays, and even the true pillars of the Catholic religion." [1] He explained his resolute attitude toward the French king, when, a little later, he declared that Henry had not given a single mark of Catholicity, except that he used the sign of the Cross; he persevered in his attempts to reduce a kingdom to which he had forfeited his rights, and this, too, in spite of the papal excommunication ; he had not restored the Roman Catholic religion in Béarn ; he still treated with the Protestant princes of Germany and with Queen Elizabeth ; he even tolerated Huguenot preaching within his palace, for the benefit of his sister.[2] In the end the Duke of Nevers made his way out of the pontifical capital rather in the fashion of an escaping enemy than with the formalities of an ambassador returning from a mission. Receiving the information, as he was departing through the Porta del Popolo, that Clement had instructed officers to serve upon the ecclesiastics who accompanied him a citation to appear before the Inquisition, upon pain of excommunication in case of disobedience, the duke bade them ride at

---

[1] "Ayant reconneu vostre Sainteté, en toutes les trois audiences precedentes, fort resolue de n'absoudre mon Roy ; me disant d'elle-mesme, sans que je luy parlasse de ce fait, qu'elle ne vouloit croire qu'il fust bien converty, si un ange du ciel ne venoit le luy dire à l'aureille." Discours de la legation de M. le duc de Nevers, in the Mémoires de Nevers, ii. 463. I have used in the text the more extended report of Clement's words in the Discours de ce que fit Monsieur de Nevers à son voyage   Rome en l'année 1593, ibid., ii. 414.

[2] De Thou, viii. (bk. 108) 361.

his side; meanwhile giving out that he would not hesitate to kill on the spot any person presumptuous enough to undertake the execution of the pope's command. And so he left Rome.[1]

It was about eighteen months later that negotiations were renewed with the head of the Roman Catholic Church. We shall not be uncharitable if we suppose that the marked successes of Henry the Fourth, to which reference must soon be made, were the chief cause of the entertainment, on the part of Clement, of proposals which he had at first rejected. D'Ossat, later cardinal, and Du Perron, Bishop of Evreux, were now the French agents. Their exertions, if not more strenuous or more skilful, were attended with better success than those of the duke. The pope and the ultramontane party at first endeavored to exact the hardest conditions from the king, as the price of reconciliation. They talked of requiring Henry to repeal the tolerant Edict of 1577, to exclude all Protestants from offices of trust and dignity, to proscribe all religious liberty, so soon as the present war should be at an end, to restore to the adherents of the League all their forfeited honors, to renounce alliance with the Protestant Powers, and to do other things alike repugnant to the royal plans and impossible of execution. But, now that success had perched on the royal banners, it was a matter of comparative ease for the envoys to show the absurdity of expecting such measures. They refused absolutely to take any steps which might appear to place the crown of France at the disposal of the pope, or be construed as a rehabilitation of his majesty. This much of humiliation Henry was spared throughout a transaction in itself sufficiently humbling to a monarch possessed of ordinary self-respect. The envoys consented to abjure in the king's name any Calvinistic or other heretical doc-

Efforts of D'Ossat and Du Perron.

---

[1] De Thou, viii. 355. The "Discours de la legation de M. le duc de Nevers" is the most authentic account of this embassy, being penned by the duke in the form of a letter to Pope Clement VIII. himself, under date of January 14, 1594. It occupies pp. 437–489 of the second volume of the Mémoires de Nevers. Another and shorter account which the duke gave to the world, under the name of a third person, is contained in the same Mémoires (ii. 405–433). It gives some details not found in the fuller statement.

trines which he might once have held, and to swear submission to the Roman See.   They took the trouble to engage that their master would go at least four times a year to the confessional, and approach at least four times a year the holy communion. Not only so, but, unless prevented by sufficient reasons, he would say his chaplet every day, recite the litanies every Wednesday, and repeat the rosary of the blessed Virgin every Friday.   He would take the Virgin to be his protectress, would observe all the fasts of the church, would hear mass daily.   He would re-establish Roman Catholicism in his ancestral states of Béarn, and would bring up the young Prince of Condé, presumptive heir to the throne, in the Roman Catholic religion.   Indeed, the envoys were reluctantly brought to promise in Henry's behalf, that he would publish and execute in France the Decrees of the Council of Trent.   They took good care, however, to stipulate that exception should be made of those articles, should there be any such, that could not be carried into effect without disturbing the quiet of the State.[1]

These points having been virtually agreed upon, the pope was as well satisfied as circumstances would allow him to be.

The pope sat-   However, he went through the form of consulting
isfied.   the "sacred college," which took more than a fort-
night for the expression of the opinions of its members.   More than three-fourths of the cardinals declared themselves in favor of granting the absolution.   Nor could the edifying spectacle of the "supreme pontiff" publicly seeking divine illumination be spared.   Twice did Clement, with a very small company of ecclesiastics, his servants, proceed at dawn of day from the Quirinal palace to the basilica of Santa Maria Maggiore, there to engage in protracted supplications at the shrine of the Virgin.   The pope walked barefooted, as did also his attendants. He looked neither to the right nor to the left, but fixed his eyes upon the ground.   He wept continually, and refrained from giving his customary benediction to the passers-by.[2]

---

[1] I refer the reader, curious in such matters, to the summary of sixteen articles in De Thou, viii. (book 113) 640.

[2] Letter of D'Ossat to Villeroy, Rome, August 30, 1595, in Lettres du Cardinal d'Ossat, i. 165.

The pompous ceremonial of the absolution took place on Sunday, the seventeenth of September, 1595, upon the square in front of St. Peter's. Here, in the presence of an immense concourse of people, the two Frenchmen who represented the King of France knelt and swore, with their hands resting upon the Holy Gospels, that the monarch, their master, would persevere in the Roman, Catholic and Apostolic religion, and that he would observe all the conditions previously agreed upon and now publicly read. Here, too, the same envoys of the Very Christian King kneeled a second time before Clement, while the words of the Fifty-first Psalm were solemnly sung by the papal choir. As each successive verse was repeated, the pope, with a rod which he held in his hand, lightly smote the shoulders of the representatives of the most prominent monarchy of Europe, in token that the Church emancipated Henry of Navarre from the censures which bound him. The ceremony might be explained as a mere relic of Roman law which had passed over into the usage of the primitive Christian discipline. Most men, however, listened with impatience to the strains of the Miserere, and murmured that the pope had inflicted a disgraceful stain upon the fair escutcheon of France—or, as the caustic Agrippa d'Aubigné well expresses himself, " que la pantoufle par-là se décrottoit sur les fleurs de lis."[1]

Ceremony of the king's absolution.

Meanwhile, if Henry's abjuration had not instantly conciliated the friendship and favor of the occupant of the papal chair, neither did it protect the king's person from conspiracies aimed at his life. The plot of Pierre Barrière followed closely upon the monarch's change of religious profession. Happily, the culprit's imprudence in communicating his design to several ecclesiastics led to his arrest before he had a chance to attempt the execution. A Carmelite, a Capuchin, and one or two fanatical priests kept his secret, but a Dominican monk from Florence proved more loyal to the country where he was domiciled than they had been

Conspiracies against Henry's life. Pierre Barrière.

---

[1] Histoire universelle, iii. 431. See, in addition to De Thou, viii. 635–643, the important letters of D'Ossat, in the work already mentioned.

to the land of their birth.[1]   The execution of Barrière, who was broken upon the wheel before being suffered to die, did not deter Jean Chastel, a lad of only nineteen years, but a precocious pupil in a college of the Jesuits, from renewing the attempt before eighteen months had passed.   This time the machinations of Henry's enemies were more nearly successful.   The puny boy—for such he was in stature—insinuated himself into the royal apartments, where the monarch, who had just returned from Picardy, and was still booted, was receiving the greetings of his nobles.   The king was leaning forward courteously to raise Ragny and Montigny from their knees, when Chastel, who had approached unperceived, struck at him with a knife.   The blow was aimed at Henry's throat, but only cut his upper lip and loosened one of his teeth.   There was no possibility of mistaking the school where Chastel had learned his lesson all too well.   He admitted that he had studied three years with the Jesuits, and on his person were tokens of his motive and of his design.   He wore a shirt which had hung at the famous shrine of the Virgin "paritura" at Chartres, with the words "Henrico quarto" inscribed thereon.   He was provided with some strings of beads blessed by priestly hands, with an "agnus Dei," and with scraps of paper on which the significant prayer was written: "Lord, vouchsafe me strength to execute (my purpose) against Henry of Bourbon!"[2]

In Barrière's attempt the inspiration of the crime by the

Jean Chastel.

---

[1] Recueil des choses mémorables, 766, 767 ; Lestoile, ii. 174 ; De Thou, viii. (bk. 107) 321–324; " Brief discours du procès criminel faict à Pierre Barrière, dict la Barre, natif d'Orleans, accusé de l'horrible et execrable parricide par lui entrepris et attenté contre la personne du Roi," reprinted in Mémoires de la Ligue, v. 450–457, and in Cimber et Danjou, Archives curieuses, xiii. 362–370.

[2] Henry IV. to Duplessis Mornay, December 27, 1594, in Mémoires de Duplessis Mornay, vi. 128, 129 (a circular letter, of which a copy was addressed to the municipality of Lyons, etc.); Loménie to the same, December 28, 1594, ibid., vi. 130, 131 ; Mémoires de la Ligue, vi. 249, etc.; De Thou, viii. (bk. iii.) 532, etc.; Recueil, 781, 782 ; Lestoile, ii. 252.   The most copious source of information on the subject of Jean Chastel, his crime his trial, and his punishment is, however, the sixth or supplementary volume of the Mémoires de Condé (London, 1743), which devotes nearly two hundred pages to documents bearing upon the subject.   The most remarkable of these is, undoubtedly, the audacious defence of the assassin published in 1595, under the title of "Apologie pour Je-

Society of Jesus had been suspected; in the attempt of Chastel the hand of that society and of the King of Spain, whose ready tool the organization had long been, was all but caught in the act. No wonder that the execution of Chastel was accompanied by the expulsion of the Jesuits—"the Society of *Judas*," the people nicknamed them [1]—and closely followed by a declaration of war on the part of the king against the gray-headed monarch of Spain, Philip the Second, now tottering on the verge of the grave, to whom the employment of the assassin's dagger to accomplish his ends had long been congenial occupation. [2]

Expulsion of the Jesuits.

Despite papal opposition and Spanish or Jesuit daggers, however, Henry had been making steady progress in his struggle to attain universal recognition. In January, 1594, the city of Meaux made its submission. In February, Lyons copied the example of Meaux; then followed Péronne, Mondidier, Roye, and Orleans. On the twenty-seventh day of the same month the impressible people beheld the spectacle of the solemn anointing of Henry. Rheims being in the hands of the enemy, Chartres was chosen to be the scene of the great pageant. The sacred "ampoule," wherein the holy oil had been carefully kept in store for such occasions in the cathedral of Rheims, was, of course, quite out of reach; but fortunately there was discovered an escape from what might have proved an insuperable difficulty. It was ascertained that a vial, whose contents possessed equal virtue for the consecration of kings, was to be found in the abbey of Marmoutier. Like the more famous "ampoule" of Rheims, this vessel

Henry's successes.

He is anointed at Chartres.

---

han Chastel, Parisien, exécuté à mort, et pour les Pères et Escolliers de la Société de Jesus, bannis du Royaume de France." The real author of the treatise was, it is said, Jean Boucher, the same furious preacher who had from his pulpit for years denounced in unmeasured terms Henry III. and his successor, and who wrote a famous book on the "feigned conversion" of the latter.

[1] Mémoires de la Ligue, vi. 275.

[2] Henry IV.'s declaration of war is dated January 17, 1595, just three weeks after Chastel's attempt. It is published in Mémoires de la Ligue, vi. 297-300. The document refers particularly to the miraculous deliverance of the king from "le coup effroyable, tiré de la main d'un François . . . mais poussé d'un esprit tres-inhumain et vrayement Espagnol."

with its precious contents was reported to have been miraculously sent from heaven for the express purpose of being used in the ceremonial of the coronation of kings. Besides, the ampoule of Marmoutier had this in its favor, that the custodians asserted it had been the means of operating a wonderful cure in the case of St. Martin of Tours himself.[1] Moreover, said the ecclesiastics, it had been almost miraculously preserved from the fury of the Huguenots in the year 1562, when most of the sacred relics of Chartres had been consigned to the flames and the rich reliquaries had been melted up.[2] Still easier was it to find a substitute for the Archbishop of Rheims, the traditional celebrant. The worthy Nicholas de Thou, Bishop of Chartres, figured in his place, but care was taken throughout the official account of the ceremonial to designate him, not by his own proper name, but by that of the prelate whose functions he was discharging.[3]

The minor advantages gained by the king were followed by the recovery of his capital. On the twenty-second of March, 1594, Henry made his entry into Paris, to the great satisfaction of all good and patriotic citizens, to the deep mortification of the League and of Philip the Second, who could no longer gratify his self-complacence by calling it, as he had lately done, "his good city." Though the time had evidently come for the submission of the rebellious capital, it was money, after all, that had decided the governor, M. de Brissac, to open the gates ; and Henry had good reason to correct a speaker who referred to the surrender of Paris as a rendering to Cæsar the things that are Cæsar's, even as one must render to God the things that are God's. "Ventre saint-gris," said the monarch, using his ordinary exclamation and playing

Entry into
Paris March
22, 1594.

----

[1] See the contemporary pamphlet, "L'ordre des cérémonies du Sacre et Couronnement du tres chrestien roy de France et de Navarre, Henry IV " (reprinted in Cimber et Danjou, Archives curieuses, xiii. 399–431), which describes the vase as " la sainte ampoulle, précieusement gardée en l'abbaye de Marmoustier, lez la ville de Tours, depuis la guerison que miraculeusement elle apporta à saint Martin." The " ampoule " is mentioned in the curious itinerary of Jodocus Sincerus, x. 97.

[2] Cayet, Chronologie novenaire, 554.

[3] L'ordre des cérémonies du Sacre, ubi supra, xiii. 405.   See De Thou, viii. 376, etc.; Agrippa d'Aubigné, iii. 333.

upon the similarity of the words in French, "I have not been treated like Cæsar; it has not been rendered, it has been vended to me!"[1] And now were the acts of the League one by one undone, so far as resolutions on paper, and solemn declarations, and pompous ceremonies and Te Deums over the king's triumphs could undo them. A parliament, most of whose members had lately been the determined enemies of the prince whom they recognized only as King of Navarre, re-enforced by the judges who had been sitting at Tours, passed the most loyal of decisions. The Parisian counsellors, who had made haste to order a sacred procession to be made annually on the anniversary of the massacre of St. Bartholomew's Day, and had assiduously commemorated the Day of the Barricades by another yearly pilgrimage to the shrines of the city, now exhibited equal eagerness in putting an end to "all processions and solemnities ordered during, or on occasion of, the late troubles," and in establishing in perpetuity a new procession in honor of the happy reduction of Paris to the king's obedience, wherein all the members of parliament were to take part attired in red gowns.[2] The university followed in the footsteps of the parliamentary judges. The doctors who for years had been denouncing Henry as an apostate from the faith, with no claims to the throne which he had not forfeited by his persistent heresy, and who had entertained doubts whether the pope himself could absolve him of his guilt, were now quite clear in the belief that obedience to constituted authority is the duty of every Christian, took an oath not only to submit to him with all loyal devotion, but to spare neither their blood nor their prayers in his behalf, and declared that any of their number who might refuse to follow their example were rebels, guilty of treason, public enemies, and disturbers of the peace.[3]

The example of Paris was copied, within a few months, by Rouen and Havre, by Troyes and Sens and Riom, by Agen

---

[1] "On ne me l'a rendu à moy : on me l'a bien vendu." Lestoile, ii. 218.

[2] "Arrest de la cour de parlement de Paris, du trentiesme jour de Mars, 1594." Mémoires de la Ligue, vi. 95-97.

[3] See " Acte public et instrument de l'obeissance rendue, jurée et signée au roy tres-chrestien Henry IV, par M. les recteurs, docteurs et supposts de l'u-

and Villeneuve and Poitiers.   The Duke of Elbeuf, also, made
his submission, and secured the retention of the governorship of Poitiers; while the Duke of Guise, who
yielded later in the year, managed to extort from
the king such extravagant concessions that the very
courtiers, a greedy set, blamed the royal complaisance, and
Chancellor Chiverny not only remonstrated, but obtained from
Henry an official statement of the objections which he interposed.[1]   The scene was repeated with still greater intensity
when, by the Edict of Folembray, the very chief of the culprits
of the League, the Duke of Mayenne, secured even greater advantages than had fallen to the lot of his nephew.   The courageous Diana of Montmorency made strenuous opposition to the
edict in his favor, protesting against it in the name of Queen
Louise, widow of Henry the Third, because the edict cleared
the duke of all responsibility for the murder of her late husband; and the Parliament of Paris attempted again and again
to insert some saving clauses, but was in the end compelled to
enter the obnoxious paper upon its records without modification.[2]
Under Henry the Fourth, in his determined effort to become
undisputed master of France, nothing prospered more than an
enmity which held out persistently against his invitations and
his arms.   Only unflinching loyalty was little esteemed and remained unrewarded.

In all the numerous edicts published by Henry for the reduction of the rebellious cities of his kingdom, there
was, so far as the Huguenots were concerned, a dreary
uniformity.   However they might differ in other respects, they agreed in one thing: the worship of the Protestants
was formally excluded from the municipal limits, and even from

Submission of cities and leaders.

The Huguenots excluded from many places.

niversité de Paris," dated April 22, 1594, with the form of the oath, etc.,
in Mémoires de la Ligue, vi. 98, etc.   It should be noted that Boucher,
Guarinus, Feuardent, and a few others of the most prominent Leaguers did
not sign, and consulted their safety by flight.   On the surrender of Paris, De
Thou, viii. 382–392, the Recueil des choses mémorables, 774–776, Pasquier,
Œuvres choisies, ii. 345, etc., may be consulted.

[1] See De Thou, viii. 399–401, 510–512; Agrippa d'Aubigné, iii. 338, etc.

[2] De Thou, viii. 737–742; Agrippa d'Aubigné, iii. 374, 375; Mémoires de la
Ligue, vi. 376–390.

the suburbs.   Nor was the enactment which discriminated in
so humiliating a manner against the exercises of their faith
consigned to an inconspicuous place in the statute, where its
presence might be less glaringly offensive.   Everywhere it occupied the most prominent position, so as not to be overlooked
even by the most careless reader.   The very first of the articles
of capitulation granted to Vitry, Governor of Meaux, when he
made his submission, was a promise of his majesty that he
would maintain all the inhabitants in the Roman, Catholic, and
Apostolic religion, without allowing the exercise of any other
worship.[1]   This was on the fourth of January, 1594.   The next
month Orleans and Bourges opened their gates to Henry, and
in the initial article of the edicts registered in the Parliament
at Tours in favor of each of the cities was a solemn provision
that, in the entire bailiwick and in all the towns within the jurisdiction of the "presidial" court, there should henceforth be no
other worship than that of the Roman, Catholic, and Apostolic
religion, save in the places and in the manner permitted by the
Edict of Pacification of 1577, and by the declarations and articles
since published for its execution.[2]   In the edict by which the
monarch magnanimously[3] took his rebellious capital back into
his good favor, in the month of March following, he began by
re-enacting the exclusion of all other religious exercises than
those of the Romish Church from the city and suburbs of Paris,
and its neighborhood to the distance of ten leagues.[4]   April
witnessed similar royal edicts, containing similar provisions
unfriendly to Protestantism, in favor of Rouen, Havre and

[1] "Sans qu'il y soit faict autre exercice de religion."   Articles accordez par
le Roy aux habitants de la ville de Meaux, in Recueil des Edicts et Articles accordez par le Roy Henry IV pour la réunion de ses subjets.   Imprimé l'An
de Grace 1604.   Fol. 4.

[2] Ibid., fols. 9, 14.

[3] "Recognoissant qu'il n'y a rien qui nous donne plus de tesmoignage que
nous sommes faits à la ressemblance de Dieu, que la clemence et debonnaireté,
oubliant d'un franc courage les offenses et fautes passées, avons declare," etc.
Ibid., fols. 22, 23.

[4] Ibid., ubi supra.   Duplessis Mornay, while rejoicing over the capture of
Paris, may be pardoned for having entertained the fear that it might here fare
with Henry as with the Englishman who, at the battle of Poitiers, is said to
have caught a Frenchman *who carried him off*.   Mémoires, vi. 47.

Verneuil in Normandy, of Troyes in Champagne, and of Sens. In May the Roman Catholics were assured by a solemn compact that there should be no Huguenot prêche in Lyons; in July, not only that there should be none in Poitiers, but that the services of the mass should be re-established in Niort, Fontenay, La Rochelle, and all other places of the district of Poitou where it had been intermitted. So fared it likewise with Château-Thierry, Laon, Amiens, and Beauvais, in the north; with Agen, Villeneuve, and Marmande, in the south; with St. Malo, in the west. When the Duke of Guise made his peace, in the last month of the year, his reconciliation brought with it the interdiction of the Reformed rites at Rheims, Rocroy, St. Dizier, Guise, Joinville, Fismes, and Montcornet; just as when the Sieur de Bois-Dauphin, in the following year, saw fit to come to terms with his liege, he secured a similar proscription of Protestantism from Mans and all the other places which he brought with him to the king's service. Mayenne's submission was conditioned upon the concession of the cities of Châlons, Seurre, and Soissons to him as places of security, for the space of six years; and, for that term, neither was Protestant worship to be held there, nor was any Protestant to be appointed to an office of trust or emolument. So it was that Protestant worship was, a little later, expelled from a distance of four leagues about Toulouse; and, shortly before the promulgation of the great edict of which I am shortly to speak, from Rochefort on the Loire, from Craon, and, in the compact with the Duke of Mercœur, the last of the Leaguers to hold out, from the city of Nantes itself and for a distance of three leagues all around—this last by a "perpetual and irrevocable" edict.[1]

In the midst of all these provisions for the sole occupancy
No provisions
favorable to
them.
of all the great points of influence in the kingdom by the Roman Catholic Church, there was not a sentence in behalf of the king's former associates, those who continued to profess the religious faith he had once held, the men whose valor and self-sacrifice had triumphantly

---

[1] All these edicts are contained in the "Recueil des Edicts et Articles accordez par le Roy Henry IV pour la reunion de ses subjets," fols. 1–136.

carried him, through many a bloody conflict, to the throne.
Each new proclamation contained a reiteration of his majesty's
purpose to maintain the Romish priests, in their persons, in
their ecclesiastical functions, in their revenues. There was
not a syllable about any possible rights to which the Protestant
minister of the Gospel might himself be imagined to be entitled, not a syllable asserting that the Protestant laity merited
some scanty return of gratitude for their unswerving loyalty.
Instead of this, in each successive edict made to secure the adhesion of mercenary traitors, wearied of their rebellion, and
anxious to drive the best possible bargain with the king, the
Huguenots saw themselves excluded from one or more new
cities. It became evident at length that, if the process were
continued much longer, Protestantism would presently find no
place for the sole of its foot between the British Channel and
the Mediterranean Sea.

It is time that we should return to the Huguenots, grieved
but not dismayed at the king's defection. Certainly they were
not so much surprised as they might have been, had
Henry's attitude from the moment of his accession
been a more generous one. With his first public
declaration at St. Cloud, the late chief of the Huguenots clearly
assumed a neutral position as between Roman Catholicism and
Protestantism. Yet this was the moment which a man of deep
religious sympathies—or, indeed, even a man of shallow convictions, but loyally grateful to the companions associated with
him for long years—would have chosen to identify himself
more completely than ever before with the adherents of the
same faith. Henry's course as king was from the beginning an
acknowledgment of his selfishness—an admission that he had
now come to regard the religion which he had hitherto professed only as the scaffolding by which he had climbed to his
present elevation, but for which he had little concern, regarding
the perpetuity of the structure as essential neither to his happiness nor to his security. A Gaspard de Coligny would have
shrunk from putting such an indignity upon his creed or upon
his fellow-believers.

The outlook was certainly discouraging. The Huguenots

Marginal note: The Huguenots not dis-
mayed.

knew the king too well to believe that he was of himself disposed
to persecute his old associates in arms.   And yet who could say
Possibility of   whither the course of blind submission upon which he
persecution.   had started would lead?   Had he not already gone
far beyond his own expectations?   He had been urged to enter the Roman Catholic Church with the purpose of purify-
it of its admitted abuses; and he had from the very first
been compelled to sanction by his example the most flagrant of
those abuses.   Most remarkable of all, those very counsellors
who were commonly supposed to deny the existence of a God
were the persons who insisted most upon Henry's swearing that
Duplessis   he had implicit belief in images and relics, in purga-
Mornay's ex-   tory and indulgences.   Duplessis Mornay graphically
postulation.   described the king's unhappy plight in a letter of ex-
postulation addressed to the monarch himself.   "'Sire,' you
were told, 'give your people the satisfaction they desire; you
may afterward believe what you will.   Hear as little of the
mass as you please, provided you are seen to be present at its
celebration.'   Where, on the contrary, is the rigor that has not
been observed?   Have you not been called upon to swear contrary to your conscience, and to abjure your creed in the most
precise, the least justifiable, terms—a thing which they would
not have required of a Turk or a Jew?   These gentlemen, in
short, have taken pleasure in triumphing over your faith—a
faith heretofore triumphant over so many temptations, over so
many assaults.   You were assured that your abjuration was the
veritable method of destroying the papal authority in France;
and you have been made to swear to maintain that authority!
Nor is this all.   You will be called on to do penance for having been a Huguenot, and the pope will impose that penance
upon you in the form of a war to be waged against 'heretics'
—in other words, upon the best Christians, the most loyal of
Frenchmen, the most sincere among your subjects.   At first
the proposition will shock your native kindliness.   You will
exclaim, 'How shall I wage war against my servants whose
blood I drank in my necessity!'   Nevertheless you will have to
come to it.   You will be entrapped into undertaking hostilities
merely for a few months.   'Prove to us that yours is not a

simulated conversion,' will be the cry of the League. The Roman pontiff will add his authority and exact the price of his absolution. Meanwhile He who of yore defended you will arm Himself against you, and against such an adversary there is neither counsel nor might."

" Sire," said the Protestant champion, in conclusion, "do you indeed wish to remove from the Huguenots the desire to have a Protector? Then take away the need of one. Be yourself their protector. Continue to them that former care, that former affection. Anticipate their supplications by your free action, their just demands by a voluntary gift of such things as are necessary. When they shall recognize the fact that you have a care for them, they will cease to have it for themselves. But pardon him who tells you that they doubt whether you have enough care of yourself. You know what injures, what pleases them. Present to yourself the petitions which you used to present to the kings, your predecessors, for the liberty, the security, the dignity of the Huguenots. Those petitions have certainly not since then abated aught of their equity; nay, the Protestants have added thereto by subsequent good services, and they must have gained by your accession to power. For you may both now set forth and grant their just complaints; you may be, without other deputies, and with more good-will, the judge, if you choose, and the advocate, and the grantor, all together." [1]

It is not improbable that, as the biographer of Duplessis Mornay asserts, the frank and noble appeal marvellously touched the king, who perceived both its reasonableness and its truth. At any rate, Henry was more than ever urgent that his old Huguenot adviser should come promptly to court. And when, in September, 1593, Duplessis Mornay at last arrived at Chartres, where the court was temporarily staying, his majesty received him with marked favor. At once he took him apart, and assured him that he had been constrained by the necessi-

---

[1] I have quoted, partly only in substance, one of the most remarkable letters ever addressed by Duplessis Mornay to Henry IV. It may be read entire both in the Mémoires of that nobleman, v. 535–544, and in his life, published in Leyden in 1647, pp. 201–207. It is not dated, but must have been written in August or in the early part of September, 1593.

ties of his situation to sacrifice himself for his subjects, that
he aimed in particular to be able more easily to give rest to the
Protestants. He told him that he saw plainly from
his letter that Duplessis Mornay supposed him to
have made an abjuration which he had not made,
and he proceeded to narrate the events of Saint Denis after his
own fashion. " Yes," said the Huguenot, " but I know that
your abjuration has been sent to the pope." The king did not
deny the fact—it was useless to do so, as he found that Duplessis Mornay was well informed of the truth—but he had an
answer ready. " I did not write nor sign the abjuration in
question. It was written and signed by M. de Loménie, my
secretary, who ordinarily imitates my handwriting." " Sire,"
replied the fearless Protestant, " the document was presented
to the pope with your consent, by your command, as your own.
You wish it to be believed such, otherwise the paper is useless.
Let your conscience flatter itself with this subtle device, but,
sire, do you think that God can be deceived by such sophis-
tries ? " Henry had much to say with regard to his hopes of
reforming the church by means of national and universal councils, or of some good pope whose election he thought he had
fair reason to look for. But Duplessis Mornay met him at
every point, and showed him the futility of his expectations.
A good pope, he maintained, was a contradiction in terms.
Pontiffs who, like Pius the Second, made great professions of
reformatory projects became, upon their accession, the worst
advocates of corrupt measures. Cardinal du Bellay expressed
the truth when justifying his conduct in refusing to be exalted to
the Roman See. " God forbid," he said, " that I should become
the son of perdition ! There is, my friend, such a pestilence
attaching to that chair, that no sooner is a man seated thereon
than he is infected by it, even though he belonged to the class
of those who previously seemed the most excellent men in the
world. It is a chair of pestilence—*cathedra pestilentiæ*—from
which may God save me ! " [1]

The wisest among the Huguenots had been as unwilling that

The king tries to justify his abjuration.

---

[1] Vie de Duplessis Mornay, 207.

the deputies of the churches should be present at the pretended "Instruction" of Henry as they were anxious that those depu-

Huguenot deputies at Mantes. ties should accept his majesty's invitation to come and discuss with him—and, possibly, with represent- atives of the other faith—the terms upon which the adherents of both religions might live peaceably together in France. To consent to witness the "Instruction" would have been to condemn themselves in advance to become absurd spec- tators of the preparations made for a triumph over the truth and its professors. In acceding to the proposed conference, however, they were following the instinct of self-preservation. Among the Protestant leaders the Duke of Bouillon was almost the only person who deemed it imprudent for the delegates of the church to go to Mantes. It was October when these repre- sentatives, numbering about sixty persons, reached the spot, but several weeks elapsed before his majesty, purposely detained by his Roman Catholic counsellors, we are told, in the neigh- borhood of Dieppe and Fécamp, arrived. Nor was it until the Protestants had sent to remonstrate with him, and to remind him that it was solely in obedience to his command that they had come from so great distances and in such numbers, that Henry returned to the banks of the Seine.[1] Meanwhile the deputies had improved their enforced delay by putting in shape the documents containing their demands and their com- plaints—the latter forming, unfortunately, a large and formida- ble budget. These papers they placed in Henry's hands when, on the twelfth of December, he admitted them to an audi- ence in his private cabinet. Their spokesman, M. Feydeau, lately member of the Parliament of Bordeaux, delivered an address not less remarkable for the care of its composition than for the mingled frankness and boldness of its thought or the dignity of the delivery.[2] The king's reply was gracious and conciliatory; for he declared one of his objects in calling them together to be to prove that his "conversion" had in no- wise diminished his affection for them, and another, that, since

---

[1] Ibid., 209. Mémoires de Charlotte Arbaleste, etc., i. 263.
[2] Mémoires de Charlotte Arbaleste, etc., ubi supra.

his rebellious subjects showed signs of an inclination to peace, pacification might not be concluded without the intervention of the Huguenots.[1]

But it soon appeared that his majesty was more lavish of words than of deeds. For a time it looked as though the deputies would be dismissed with vague assurances that justice would be done them in the course of three months, the king being Unsatisfactory unable to attend to the matter at present because negotiations. of his pressing engagements. The absurdity of this policy, however, was soon demonstrated. If the king was waiting to hear from Rome of the success of the negotiation of the Duke of Nevers, it was idle to expect that the fit time for satisfying the just demands of the Huguenots would ever come. If Nevers should fail, it would never do to add to the difficulties already standing in the way of obtaining the papal absolution. If Nevers should succeed, it would never do to disturb so soon the pope's good humor. Besides, to disappoint the deputies by sending them away without an answer would be to exasperate the very men of influence among the Huguenots whom it had been Henry's purpose, in convening them at Mantes, to propitiate. In the end, the Huguenot memorial was referred to a commission composed of six or seven persons, all Roman Catholics (in order to avoid giving umbrage to the more violent men of the royalist party)—Chancellor Chiverny, the privy councillors D'O, Bellièvre, Schomberg, Pontcarré and Chandon, and Forget, one of the secretaries of state.[2] Nor did even

---

[1] "Pource que mes sujets rebelles faisoyent contenance de vouloir entendre à quelque paix, je n'ai voulu que ce fust sans vous appeller, afin que rien ne se fist à vostre prejudice : comme vous en avez esté asseurés par la promesse que firent lors les princes et officiers de ma couronne, lesquels jurerent en ma presence, qu'il ne seroit rien traitté en la conference de paix contre ceux de la religion." Account of the interview in Mémoires de la Ligue, v. 780.

[2] Mémoires de Charlotte Arbaleste, etc., i. 264 ; Vie de Duplessis Mornay, ii. 210. M. Anquez (Histoire des Assemblées politiques des Réformés de France, 58), is mistaken in speaking of "le chancelier de Bellièvre." Pomponne de Bellièvre, the illustrious negotiator, did not reach the chancellorship until 1599, upon the death of Philippe Hurault, Count of Chiverny, brother-in-law of the historian De Thou. Chiverny had held the office for sixteen years, having himself, in 1583, succeeded Cardinal Birague. He had been

this body find it a matter altogether easy to solve the question of Huguenot rights, and were fain to have recourse, by the king's permission, to the advice of some members of the Protestant party. Bouillon and Duplessis Mornay were requested to confer with them. Day after day the subject was carefully considered, in the apartments of the latter, by two earnest men on either side. But when the fruit of so much consultation was at last brought forth, in the form of an announcement to the deputies of what the monarch could grant them, the terms were scarcely such as to satisfy even so patient a people as the Reformed, accustomed through a whole generation to the denial of their natural rights.

The Huguenots were again offered the full advantage of the Edict of 1577, with its corollary in the shape of the articles agreed upon later at Nérac and Fleix. This edict was to be verified anew in all the parliaments of the realm, without restriction or modification, and the intolerant edicts of 1585 and 1588 were once more to be declared null and void. Inasmuch, however, as changes had been rendered necessary by the recent troubles, it was provided that a special ordinance should be drawn up—not, indeed, to be published to the world (lest new favor might seem to be shown to the Huguenots), but to be placed in the hands of the chancellor and the secretaries of state for their guidance, and to be intimated by his majesty to parliaments, governors, and lieutenant-governors of provinces as necessity might dictate.

Proposed ordinance of Mantes.

The ordinance thus to be held in reserve was not given with precision, but was stated to be substantially as follows: The Roman Catholic religion was to be re-established in all places from which it had been excluded during the late disturbances; but the Protestant religion was to remain as heretofore. Since the open country afforded no safety for the exercise of the Reformed rites, the king would provide the Protestants with places for worship in the cities obedient to him, according to the circumstances of each. In the royal court Protestant worship might

---

master of the seals for the five years previous, during the cardinal's old age. See De Thou, vi. (bk. 78) 311; ix. (bk. 123) 315.

be held freely so long as the queen's sister was there; in her absence it might still be held, but with more caution, without psalm-singing, in the houses of such noblemen as the Dukes of Bouillon, La Trémouille, and Rohan, and Duplessis Mornay. Under similar restrictions the Protestants might worship in the army, in the quarters of the captains of the men-at-arms and others. In view of the approaching ceremonials of his coronation and the convocation of the order "du Saint Esprit," and the promise there to be given to exterminate heresy, the king would, through no oath made or to be made, hold himself bound to wage war against or persecute the Protestants.

Nor, it may be observed, was this last assurance a superfluous precaution. For in the engagement which Henry entered into at Chartres, before his investiture and coronation, with hands resting upon the gospel, and kissing the sacred volume, were these words: "Moreover, I shall endeavor, according to my ability, in good faith, to drive from my jurisdiction and from the lands subject to me all heretics denounced by the church, promising on oath to keep all that has been said. So help me God and these holy gospels of God!"[1] And at the subsequent convocation of the order of the Holy Ghost he swore, on the wood of the Holy Cross, to observe, even to the minutest particular, all the statutes of that intolerant institution, whose very foundation had been laid in the determination to root out of France the enemies of the Roman Catholic and Apostolic religion.[2]

The king's coronation oath.

In order to meet the complaint of the Huguenots that, while compelled, like the rest of the inhabitants of the kingdom, to bear the burden of the support of the Roman Catholic Church, they had in addition to defray the expenses of their own worship, provision was made for the establishment of a fund in the royal treasury, in the name of madame, the queen's sister, for the purpose of paying the salaries of the Huguenot ministers.[3]

---

[1] Cayet, Chronologie novenaire, 557.   [2] Ibid., ubi supra, 562.

[3] " Qu'il seroit faict fondz en l'espargne d'une somme pour l'entretenement des ministres, dont le roolle seroit baillé, deuement certifié par les provinces." Mémoires de Charlotte Arbaleste sur la vie de Duplessis Mornay son mari,

There were other articles—allowing Protestants to make bequests to their churches and to other religious purposes, guaranteeing the education of children in the faith of their parents, and permitting the erection of Protestant colleges for the instruction of the youth wherever it might be deemed advisable. With regard to the last point, however, the king's counsellors displayed a remarkable degree of apprehension lest it might cause trouble ; for they begged that it should not be reduced to writing.[1]

So it was that, despite all their efforts to convince the king that they deserved better at his hands, the deputies were compelled to leave Mantes with a reply which they could not take the responsibility of either accepting or declining, but must refer to the churches for their decision. It is a noteworthy circumstance, however, that, while engaged in the fruitless struggle to obtain justice, they did not confine themselves to a discussion "Union of of their grievances ; but, at Mantes, in the very presence of the court, they solemnly renewed the ancient union of the Huguenots, confirmed, at various intervals of time, at Nismes, at Milhau, at Montauban, and at La Rochelle, and again swore to live and die united in the confession of faith heretofore presented to the kings of France. Not only did Henry, though notified of their intention, express no disapproval of their action, but he is even said to have urged its

---

i. 266. The inaccuracy of the edition of Duplessis Mornay's mémoires, of which this work of his wife is the first volume, was pointed out in a report made to the French Government, in 1850, by M. Avenel (reprinted in Bulletin de la Société de l'histoire du Prot. français, ii. 101–107). In the passage above cited, the editor has read " l'Espagne " for " l'espargne " (l'épargne) ; and, strange to say, M. Anquez, in his extremely valuable " Histoire des Assemblées politiques," to the ability and general thoroughness of which I wish here to bear witness, has perpetuated the mistake (p. 109). In view of the relations between the two neighboring kingdoms of France and Spain, not to speak of the ultra Roman Catholic sentiments of Philip II., the idea of establishing in Spain a fund for the maintenance of the Protestant ministers of France is scarcely less ludicrous than would have been a proposal to place the money at Rome with the request that Pope Clement should act as honorary treasurer.

[1] Mémoires de Charlotte Arbaleste, etc., i. 265–267 ; Vie de Duplessis Mornay, 210, 211.

necessity.[1] The National Synod of Montauban, meeting a few months later, enjoined upon all the churches of the realm to swear to sustain the union formed in the assembly of Mantes. For this purpose the Protestants were to meet either in their churches or, where they constituted the entire population, as in some parts of Languedoc, in the municipal halls.[2]

The assembly of Mantes concluded its sessions on the twenty-third of January, 1594. The four years that intervened between this date and the enactment of the Edict of Nantes, in April, 1598, were occupied by an unintermitted struggle on the part of the Protestant churches of France, through their representatives, to secure the definite recognition of their rights. Nor can it be said that Henry seemed to be averse to granting them, at some future time, such guarantees as they might require for their safety and comfort. More keenly alive, however, to the difficulties of his own position than to the intolerable load of oppression beneath which they were staggering, his majesty was more than willing that they should wait uncomplainingly until such time as he had arranged his temporal affairs quite to his satisfaction. And in the successive arrangements which he entered into for the reduction of the rebellious leaders and cities of the League, he scouted the idea that his old allies ought any further to be called in for consultation, despite the fact that, as has been seen, each pacificatory edict trenched very materially upon the Edict of 1577, to whose integrity and maintenance he had repeatedly bound himself. He did, indeed, again send the edict in question to the parliaments for renewed registry, and he exerted his powers of persuasion to induce the refractory judges to proceed at once to the distasteful act.[3] Yet his efforts were to so little

Protracted struggle to secure Protestant rights.

---

[1] Mémoires de Charlotte Arbaleste, etc., i. 268 ; Vie de Duplessis Mornay, 211, 212 ; Anquez, 59, 60. Benoist, Histoire de l'édit de Nantes, i. 111, 112, has some judicious observations on this important circumstance.

[2] Article XXIII. of the National Synod of Montauban (matières générales), Aymon, i. 181.

[3] "J'estois present," wrote M. d'Esmery (A. De Thou), March 15, 1594, "quand il en parla à Messieurs les presidens et deputés de la court. Il ne se peult rien adjouster à l'affection qu'il monstra avoir en cest affaire." Mémoires de Duplessis Mornay, vi. 25.

purpose that the Parliament of Paris, the only one of the sovereign courts that obeyed the royal injunction, scarcely ratified it by a majority of six votes; whereas at Tours it had, a few years before, been unanimously approved, while yet unaffected by the concessions made to the League.[1]

Meanwhile the Huguenots were not secure against the perils arising from the presence of false or timid brethren. At Mantes, during the sessions of the political assembly, a public discussion was set on foot between the famous Roman Catholic controvertialist Du Perron and a prominent Protestant, Jean Baptiste Rotan, pastor and doctor of theology from La Rochelle, in which it is said to have been previously arranged that the latter should betray his cause by an insufficient defence. Whether the story was true or false, whether Rotan broke down at the last moment through sudden fright or remorse, or really fell sick, certain it is that he yielded his post to Michel Bérauld, of Montauban, a man alike proof against corruption and impervious to fear. With such an antagonist the Roman Catholic clergy saw that they had nothing to gain, and consequently managed to have the discussion given up.[2] On the other hand, the resolute front which the Huguenots determined to maintain, as against the acceptance of the unsatisfactory edict of 1577, threatened to be broken by the timidity or worldly wisdom of some of their own number, in and about the capital, who weakly petitioned for the simple verification of that edict, and so called down upon their heads

Dangers from weak brethren.

---

[1] " Bref discours par lequel chacung peult estre esclairci des justes procedures de ceulx de la relligion reformée," in Mémoires de Duplessis Mornay, vii. 284.

[2] Agrippa d'Aubigné, iii. 365, 366, affirms the treachery of Rotan, which Benoist, Histoire de l'édit de Nantes, i. 112, inclines apparently to believe, and Aymon, Tous les Synodes, i. 211, 212, repeats without comment. I confess that the testimony inculpating Rotan is, in my judgment, more than outweighed by the marks of continued confidence reposed in him by the National Synod of Montauban, which, while electing Bérauld moderator, made Rotan adjunct or assistant moderator; and not only (by Article L. of its proceedings, "matières générales") thanked him for the part he had taken in the controversy at Mantes, but appointed him the first of twenty-one theologians to take part in the discussion should it be resumed. Aymon, ubi supra, i. 185, 186.

the censure of the National Synod of Montauban.[1]   There was certainly some color for the suspicion that the proximity of the court had not been without its influence in obscuring the perception of propriety, if not in corrupting the simplicity, of the Huguenots of Paris and of the Île de France, when this province gravely submitted to the same synod the question, Whether it would be well to take politic action in conjunction with the Roman Catholics of the kingdom against the pope for the maintenance of the liberties of the Gallican Church.   No wonder that the synod—fully aware of the fact that the Gallican party was scarcely less hostile to the Reformation and its adherents than were the ultramontanes, that in the bloody persecutions of which the Protestants had been the victims for the past three-quarters of a century they had suffered about as much from the advocates of the Pragmatic Sanction as from the friends of the Concordat—flatly informed the proponents that their suggestion was deemed unworthy of being submitted for deliberation.[2]

The Huguenots held a political assembly at Sainte Foy, on the Dordogne, by permission of the king, on the fifteenth of July, 1594.[3]   The deputies, who had waited upon the king at Mantes, had carried to the provinces the offers of the court; and their constituents, without exception, declared the terms inadmissible.   It was one great object of the new convocation again to urge upon his majesty the redress of their wrongs, of which the catalogue had meantime rather increased than diminished.   New treaties had been made with cities of the League, involving fresh instances of exclusion for the Huguenots.   The agents

Political assembly of Sainte Foy, July, 1594.

Grievances.

---

[1] See Article XXII., Aymon, i. 181 ; also, Benoist, i. 124.

[2] See Article IV. (matières particulières), Aymon, i. 190.

[3] Not the middle of May, as Agrippa d'Aubigné, and Anquez, following him, say.   The acts of the Synod of Montauban (held June 15–28) refer to the assembly as about to be convened.   Anquez's slurring remark that Duplessis Mornay is possibly less sincere, when he says that the assembly came together "under his majesty's authority and command," than D'Aubigné, who speaks of the king's permission as being couched "in general and not in express terms," seems to be uncalled for.   The correspondence of Duplessis Mornay refers to this permission in many places besides that cited by Anquez, and, in particular, in Duplessis Mornay's letter to Henry IV., of April 4, 1594.

whom they despatched to the north had grievances to narrate in
abundance—how at Paris itself a " lieutenant-civil " had issued
an order to compel all persons, on pain of imprisonment, to
salute pictures of the saints, crosses, banners, and reliquaries,
when carried through the public streets ; how at Lyons all that
refused to profess the Romish faith were banished the city and
province on pain of death ; how at Rennes, in Brittany, an ordinance of the provincial parliament forbade the reading, sell-
ing, or possessing of Protestant books; how at Bordeaux the
foulest of outrages had been perpetrated when, in open session,
a president of the Parliament of Guyenne and its oldest counsellor—the same envenomed enemy of the Reformed religion
who wrote a famous " History of the Rise, Progress, and Overthrow of the Heresies of this Century," to which I have had
frequent occasion to refer in treating of the earlier fortunes
of the Huguenots [1]—not only ordered the disinterment of a
child buried in the cemetery of Ozillac, in Saintonge, but took
occasion to extend the inhuman prescription to the bodies of
all Protestants consigned to holy ground within the past ten
years.[2] The same envoys had no lack of complaints to pour
into the king's ear respecting the funds for the support of Protestant ministers withheld by the financial officers of the crown,
respecting the " chambres mi-parties " nowhere established, respecting the danger to the security of the Huguenots from the
fact that the League now held the chief places in the royal
council, in the army, in the administration, rich in means, formidable to the monarch himself, still more formidable to the
adherents of the Protestant faith.[3]

---

[1] Rise of the Huguenots, i. 373, et al.

[2] "Mémoire pour l'assemblée de ceux de la relligion, teneue à Saincte Foy
dressé par M. Duplessis baillé à M. de Chouppes," in Mémoires de Duplessis
Mornay, vi. 66–72. The incident respecting Florimond de Ræmond is more
fully told in the celebrated pamphlet, issued two or three years later, under
the title of "Plaintes des églises reformées de France sur les violences et injustices qui leur sont faites en plusieurs endroicts du royaume, et pour lesquelles elles se sont en toute humilité à diverses fois addressées à sa majesté."
It is reprinted in the sixth volume of the Mémoires de la Ligue, 463–530. See
p. 522.

[3] "Mémoire pour l'assemblée," ubi supra.

But the representations made to his majesty by the political assembly of Sainte Foy were as fruitless as those of the conference of Mantes. The delegates, Chouppes and Tixier, were first put off for three months, to receive an answer at Saint Germain en Laye. When the court condescended to reply, it was only to offer terms even more unsatisfactory than before—the Edict of 1577 mutilated, if possible, more than ever, since a greater number of its provisions were infringed by recent compacts; the articles respecting the exercise of worship at court and in the army, the maintenance of the ministry, and the cities of refuge, purposely omitted ; other articles restricted, rendered obscure, entirely changed. Even these paltry offers could not be obtained in writing; they must be placed in care of some Protestant gentleman of the royal council, signed, indeed, by the king and countersigned by a secretary of state, but not to be published until some future time when verified by parliament.[1]

Before adjourning to reassemble at Saumur, on the return of the deputies to court, the assembly of Sainte Foy had not been idle. It had taken in hand and remodelled the political organization of the Huguenots to suit the altered condition of things. Twenty-eight public and eight secret articles attest the zeal with which it applied itself to a difficult task. The articles provide for a general assembly of the Reformed churches, to meet once or twice a year and to consist of ten members. One member was to be elected by Brittany and Normandy ; a second by Picardy, Champagne, the principality of Sedan, and the district of Metz; the third by Île de France, the Pays Chartrain, Dunois, Berry, and Orleanois; the fourth by Touraine, Anjou, Maine, Perche, Vendomois, and Loudunois. Saintonge, Aunis, La Rochelle, and Angoumois were to send the fifth ; Poitou and Châtellerault the sixth ; Burgundy, Lyonnais, Provence, and Dauphiny the seventh ; Lower Languedoc and Auvergne, with Vivarais, the. eighth ; Lower Guyenne and Gascony, with Périgord and Limousin, the ninth ; and Upper Languedoc, Auvergne, and

Political organization of the Huguenots.

---

[1] " Bref discours," ubi supra, vii. 282.

Guyenne, with Quercy, etc., the tenth. Of the members, four were to be taken from the noblesse and tiers état respectively, and two were to be ministers chosen in rotation by the provinces. Each of the ten ecclesiastical provinces was also to have its own particular assembly, composed of a nobleman, a minister, and a magistrate from each of the "colloques" within its geographical limits, and its particular council, of from five to seven members, whose duty would be to watch for the defence of the province, to appoint the governors of the places of surety within its bounds, and to discharge such other trusts as might naturally fall to it. The provincial assemblies were empowered to select the members both of the provincial councils and of the general assemblies.[1] Such, in brief, was the plan of government instituted by the Huguenots for their own protection at this juncture, when the defection of their former head, the present king, and the apathy of the court in redressing their wrongs seemed to make it incumbent upon them to stand on their guard and not suffer themselves to be taken at unawares and overwhelmed by their sleepless enemies. As to electing a new protector in place of Henry, the idea was virtually abandoned about this time. The Duke of Bouillon would, indeed, have been pleased to see the elector palatine chosen to fill the office once held by the King of Navarre; but the proposal met with little favor in any quarter.[2] It was well known that Henry looked upon the selection of a successor to himself with such jealousy that it would have been likely to go ill with any one so foolhardy as to accept the perilous distinction. It was equally notorious that a great number, if not indeed the majority, of the Huguenots felt that they had had quite enough of what they styled familiarly the "Protectoral Tyranny," and, having gotten rid of one somewhat arbitrary and self-willed chief, were in no haste to replace him by another respecting whom it was by no means certain that he would not prove even more obnoxious.

---

[1] Agrippa d'Aubigné devotes an entire chapter of his history to the articles adopted at Sainte Foy (iii. 367–374). See, also, Anquez, 62–66.

[2] Benoist, Histoire de l'édit de Nantes, i. 123.

Disappointed, but not having abated a whit of their determination to maintain their rights, the Huguenots again met

Assembly of
Saumur, Feb-
ruary, 1595. in political assembly—at Saumur, which, under the
governorship of Duplessis Mornay, had in a sense
become their central point. Although the convocation
was appointed for December, 1594, it was not until the twenty-
fourth of February, 1595, that the return of Chouppes and
Tixier from their long detention at court permitted the sessions
to open. But if the two deputies had tarried long, they brought
back little to satisfy the impatience of the Protestant churches.
His majesty would concede nothing beyond his previous offers.
The assembly then resolved, as a last resort, to try the virtue of
a brief petition, which they hoped might touch the king's heart,
and sent it by such men as La Noue and La Primaudaye. This,
too, proved an abortive attempt. The Huguenots were gravely
asked to content themselves with the remaining shreds of the
Edict of 1577, a law which in its integrity they had, as we have
seen, pronounced unsatisfactory, but which now, shorn of pretty
much everything it may have contained of advantage to Protestantism, was desired by their opponents more than by the
Huguenots. If anything could add to the annoyance of the
churches, it was the fact that the court still made a mystery of
its dealings with them, as if ashamed to have it known that it
would do anything for them. At the very moment when edicts
in favor of the League were at once concluded by the royal
council, registered promptly by the parliaments, published amid
popular applause in every city, and carried into immediate execution, the paltry responses which the government deigned to
send to the Huguenots, after long and provoking delays, were
conveyed in most ungracious forms. In the present instance,
as a great favor, the king's reply to the petition forwarded
through La Noue and his companion was indeed given to the
former in writing, but he was instructed merely to read it to the
assembly of his brethren in the faith, and that, too, not until
three months after its receipt. Even then the document was
not in any proper and authentic form.[1]

---

[1] "Bref discours," ubi supra, vii. 284, 285.

It was under such circumstances that the fourth political assembly held by the Protestants since Henry's abjuration opened its sessions at Loudun, on the first of April, 1596. It was an important convocation, meeting at a momentous epoch in Huguenot history in particular, as well as in the history of France entire. On the seventeenth of January, 1595, just three weeks after the dastardly attempt of Jean Chastel upon the king's life, Henry signed his formal declaration of war against Philip the Second of Spain, a monarch who, not content with the butchery of his own subjects, boldly resorted to the assassin's knife that he might rid himself of powerful or dangerous rivals. Much as, against such an enemy, open warfare might be preferable to a deadly conflict under the forms of peace, it was no child's play that Henry of Bourbon should throw down the gauntlet for Philip the Second to pick up. There were in France itself elements that favored the Spaniard. Not to speak of the Spanish troops actually upon the soil of Brittany, the Duke of Mercœur, who had invited them there, still held a great part of that important province in the name of the League. This treacherous and defiant nobleman, though indebted for his greatness to the blind favor of Henry the Third and to the marriage by which he had been permitted to become Henry's brother-in-law, had, as we have seen, the unspeakable meanness to join his kinsmen in a conspiracy directed against the authority, if not indeed against the life, of his benefactor. Upon that benefactor's assassination his malignity, far from abating, led him openly to approve the murderous deed. He suffered a book to be published in his province, and with his ducal "privilege," wherein the author, Bishop Le Bossu, a creature of his whom he had raised to the see of Nantes, denounced the deceased monarch as worse than Nero, or Herod, or Judas, as a tyrant, as traitor to humankind and to the Church; while his assassination was approved as proceeding from an inspiration of the Holy Ghost, his murderer enrolled as a martyr worthy of canonization, the very knife which Jacques Clément had used declared to be a precious relic that ought to be carefully preserved for the edification of future genera-

Assembly of Loudun, April, 1596.

War declared against Spain.

Mercœur in Brittany.

tions.[1] Since the accession of Henry the Fourth the duke had
become still more insolent, hoping, in the dismemberment of
France, to secure for himself some independent kingdom or
principality on the coast of the Atlantic ocean. While other
chieftains of the League submitted, he still expected to maintain
himself against his lawful superior, or, at least, to extort, as was
the case in the end, very favorable terms as the price of return
to his allegiance. Nor was it alone in Brittany that treason
lurked. The very generals of Henry were not all above suspicion, and many of those who had reluctantly abandoned the
League were but half-hearted in their support of a king still suspected of Huguenot leanings, as against the Spanish monarch
who had figured for more than a generation as the champion
of the Roman Catholic cause.

The first year of the war with Spain had, therefore, been
marked less by victories than by reverses; for the gains in
Burgundy made by no means so deep an impression upon the
world as the loss by the French of Cambray, in October, 1595,
and the fall of Calais, in April, 1596.[2]

Engrossed in the prosecution of this war, the king was more
than ever indisposed to deal with the Huguenot question otherwise than by temporizing expedients. Meantime, what little
hope the Protestants had hitherto cherished had wellnigh vanished. The king had indeed fulfilled his promise so far as to
renew by public proclamation the edict given at Poitiers in
1577, and since then already twice re-enacted;[3] but that was
all that had been done for the protection of the Huguenots.
They had now new grounds for anxiety. A part of the west
was in commotion. The oppressive conduct of the Duke of

---

[1] "Manifeste contre M. de Mercœur, duquel le roy suspendit la publication
cause du traicté qui intervint, sa majesté s'approchant de Bretaigne, 1595."
In Mémoires de Duplessis Mornay, vi. 391, 392.

[2] See De Thou, Agrippa d'Aubigné, etc.

[3] At Mantes, after Henry the Third's death, in 1589; again in 1591; and,
now for the third time, in November, 1594. Registered by the Parliament
of Paris, January 31, 1595, after a continuous deliberation of twelve days,
and, as we have seen, by a scanty majority of six votes. De Thou, viii. 512;
Lestoile, ii. 257–259.

Épernon had caused an armed uprising of the nobles of both religions in defence of the tiers état of Saintonge. Five hundred horse and six thousand foot soldiers were either in the field or ready to take it; castles were captured, and cities of the neighborhood were summoned to join the struggle for the common good.[1] A barbarous massacre had been perpetrated near La Chataigneraie,[2] much after the fashion of that ill-fated carnage at Vassy, a third of a century before, which kindled the flames of the first civil war. Here, too, the Protestants were attacked when engaged in their public services. The troops of the garrison of Rochefort had been specially invited by the bloodthirsty Lady de la Chataigneraie to come and put an end to the indignity which she and her children felt to be put upon them by the Huguenots, in celebrating their worship close to her lands on those of a gentleman friendly to the Protestant religion. Full well did they execute their commission, sparing neither man nor woman, neither decrepit age nor innocent childhood. Among the slain was a babe that had been brought to be baptized at the " prêche," and a boy so tender in years and so unsuspicious in nature that he tried to save his life by offering his murderer the insignificant sum of eight sous for his ransom.[3]

The massacre near La Chataigneraie.

Exasperated by this savage butchery, the Huguenots of Poitou promptly summoned a provincial assembly at Fontenay, not far from the scene of the incident, to deliberate upon the measures to be adopted for the purpose of securing the punishment of the guilty, and to urge his majesty by no means to grant an amnesty under the provisions of any subsequent treaty.[4]

Such were the circumstances in which the deputies of the Huguenots of the whole kingdom convened at Loudun, to hear from the mouth of La Noue and La Primaudaye the report

---

[1] Duplessis Mornay to Loménie, September 16, 1595, Mémoires, vi. 353.

[2] Now a village of about eighteen hundred inhabitants, in the department of Vendée.

[3] Mémoires de Charlotte Arbaleste, etc., i. 292, 293. See, especially, the account in " Plaintes des Églises Réformées de France " (1597), reprinted in Mémoires de la Ligue, vi. 477.

[4] Duplessis Mornay to Loménie, September 27, 1595, in Mémoires, vi. 358.

of their ill success. No wonder that the conclusion reached, after listening to the report, was that it was a vain thing to entertain any further hopes from deputations to the court. What was to be done? On mature deliberation the prevalent opinion was that, since no peace would be granted them, the Huguenots must fall back upon the truce into which Henry of Navarre, as their representative, had entered with Henry the Third. Certainly, it was argued, the present monarch is bound by the engagements made by his predecessor. Moreover, at his accession his majesty declared it to be his will to have the articles of the truce executed in all points, until such time as a free council, whether universal or national, and a meeting of the states general of the kingdom should devise a permanent settlement. The Huguenots have, therefore, the declarations of two monarchs in their favor. Possessing no other sufficient law to defend their lives, they ought at once to have recourse to the protection which they had an indefeasible right to claim.

The truce to be revived.

Even now, however, the desire for peace led the assembly of Loudun to send a final messenger to the king. M. de Vulson found Henry engaged in the long siege of La Fère, and still more reluctant than before to notice his importunate petitioners. Not only did he somewhat summarily dismiss Vulson with the same offers that had so often been rejected by the Protestants, but Vulson was also the bearer of a peremptory command to the members of the Loudun assembly at once to break up their meeting and return each to his province. Accepting the decision as final, " the deputies prepared themselves, after supplication to Almighty God, to obey his majesty's commands, and, retiring to their distant homes, there to provide for their safety, according to the tenor of the truce, in as orderly a manner as possible, and with as little damage to the king's interests as might be." [1]

It is worth while here to inquire more particularly into the spirit and intentions of the Huguenots at this important junct-

---

[1] " Bref discours," ubi supra, vii. 286, 287 ; Mémoires de Charlotte Arbaleste, etc., i. 300, 301.

ure ; when even the most friendly of their Roman Catholic contemporaries seem to have condemned their persistence as ill-timed. So true is it that the just demands of the weaker party, if urged in a time of public quiet, are wont to be treated with coldness or contempt ; if brought forward during a season of calamitous reverses, are stigmatized as the unpatriotic utterances of men who take advantage of the common disasters to secure private ends.

<small>Attitude of the Huguenots.</small>

The Protestants were advancing no fresh and novel requests. When Henry found fault with them for their inopportune clamors, and suggested that they wait until after the conclusion of the war with Spain, he well knew that they claimed no more than they had asked at the date of his accession and in every succeeding year. The fact was that the king and those about him had been trading upon the well-known Huguenot endurance. The Protestants had borne so much, that they might be expected to bear more ; they had so long submitted to injustice, that they were counted upon as certain to continue to furnish the edifying spectacle of a body of men whom nothing could provoke to resistance. It was forgotten that the most exemplary patience has its bounds. It was forgotten that the Huguenots, who were so loath to resent the neglect of their interests on the part of one from whom they had least expected it, were, after all, the same men that had waged war for an entire generation against their oppressors. It was certainly a bitter disappointment that the leader who had stood at their head for so great a part of the conflict should have gone over to the side of the enemy, and should now betray more anxiety to conciliate his new partisans than desire to reward the fidelity of the old comrades to whom he owed his life and crown. But the Huguenots and their representatives at Loudun had accustomed themselves to the posture of their affairs, and were resolved to make the best of it. At least they would not consent, while favors of every kind were showered upon the former adherents of the League, to act as slaves whom no amount of oppression could goad to manly resistance.

"I have written to you," said Duplessis Mornay in a letter to a friend across the Channel, "respecting our assembly of Lou-

dun. Every one there desires peace, but every one is weary of
the uncertainty of our condition, resulting especially from the
rigor of the parliaments and of all the courts of justice
of the kingdom, which still put into execution the
edicts of the League. It is vain to preach patience to
them. They reply that they have had patience, but to no purpose. The king has been reigning for seven years, and their
condition daily grows worse. Everything that it wishes is done
for the League. Neither the court nor the tribunals refuse anything to its adherents. The story of the Prodigal Son does not
compare with their treatment. At least, say the Huguenots,
after having killed for them the fatted calf, let not the rope be
left about our necks as the reward of our fidelity." [1]

Views of Duplessis Mor-nay.

But there was danger in the air. There was such a thing as
presuming too much on Huguenot patience. [2] The scales were
held with too unequal a hand. Men asked themselves involun-
tarily: "What would the result have been, had it been some
poor Huguenot that lost a Calais or a Cambray intrusted to
him for safe-keeping?" [3]

Duplessis Mornay was not alone in his sombre prognostications. Odet de la Noue, worthy son of the redoubtable knight
of the Iron Arm, warned the king of danger in admirable letters, models of a respectful frankness which
does not flinch from speaking unpalatable truths even in the
ears of royalty. The Huguenots, he told him, loved peace and
desired no other protector than Henry of Navarre. Their preservation was a matter of importance to him; for he would find
in his kingdom no more faithful, obedient, and courageous men
than they. Yet they were treated throughout France as the
very dregs of the people, as men without standing in the eye
of the law. These grievances, not in one province, but in all
the provinces, had brought them to the resolution to support
themselves so as to stand erect, without waiting for the hope

Of Odet de la Noue.

---

[1] Duplessis Mornay to La Fontaine, May 3, 1596, Mémoires, vi. 468.

[2] "On se fonde trop sur nostre patience, laquelle par tant d'injustices et de
desnis de justice pourroit changer." Ibid., ubi supra.

[3] "Que seroit-ce si ung povre huguenot avoit perdeu ou ung Calais ou ung
Cambray, qui luy eust esté baillé en garde?" Ibid., vi. 467.

of rising again when once they might have fallen to the ground. The truce, made with Henry the Third in 1589, authorized the Huguenots to retain for this purpose all the places they then held.　The promise made by his present majesty to the Protestant deputies at Sainte Foy invited them to retain them.　In addition to this the Huguenots had a very strong reason for pursuing such a course, in that they would be lost and become the prey of their enemies if they should give the cities up. "I will therefore tell you frankly," said La Noue, "that we are determined not to relax our hold upon a single one of them, but to keep and maintain them at any cost, until by some written edict such provision shall be made for our grievances that we shall have no further occasion for fear.　We shall be met with reference to the edict of 1577; but that edict is in no wise appropriate to the present time, even did the law still possess the arms and legs which have been cut off by the treaties of the League."

So spoke an honest Huguenot and a true and loyal Frenchman.　Without security, without greater religious liberty, without "chambres mi-parties," in place of parliaments notoriously prejudiced against them, it was impossible to satisfy the Protestants, and, unless they should be satisfied, all other remedies would amount to nothing.　"Here, Sire," said La Noue, "is a general but accurate account of what is going at this place, which I will set forth once more in still fewer words.　Just as it is our determination to persist until death in the obedience we owe you, to live in peace and not to seek war in any fashion whatsoever; so are we resolved rather to undergo a thousand wars and a thousand disasters than relinquish a single point of what is absolutely necessary to the conservation of the churches. I believe, Sire, that you will not condemn so holy a desire, for the realization of which you formerly took so great pains and encountered so many dangers with us. . . . As for myself, I am your very humble and obedient subject, and shall never be other. Yet you would esteem me cowardly and wicked if, professing the religion I do, I did not desire and seek the welfare of those who make a similar profession.　This is not incompatible with your service.　Finally, Sire, I beg you, in God's name, give us

some secure position.   The attempt needs but to be made.   It
is not a difficult matter.   Everything will go well, provided
there be no procrastination." [1]

It was at the critical juncture, when the assembly of Loudun
was on the point of breaking up, to carry throughout France
the seeds of a war engendered by the despair of ever obtaining
redress, that the wise counsels of a man of known moderation
and prudence served to avert a calamity threatening disaster to
the kingdom, possibly to the Huguenots also.   So long as it
was practicable, Duplessis Mornay had restrained his fellow-
Protestants, assuring them of his own conviction of Henry's
rectitude of purpose.   But now he had written to the king
himself, and signified the impossibility of feeding his subjects
of "the religion" upon vain and delusive hopes.   "I recognize," he wrote, "the magnitude of the matters your majesty has
in hand ; and yet I venture to tell you, Sire, that the affair here
is not one to be neglected." [2]   And he had urged him, as the best
method to be pursued, to send some good man, be he Roman
Catholic or Protestant, to hear and report upon the oppression
of which the Huguenots had but too much reason to complain.

Happily, if Henry was not much given to making sudden
changes in his plans, his was not a nature that hardens itself
Concession of against the dictates of prudence and persists, to its
the king.   own ruin, in a pernicious course.   Apprehending at
length the peril which further delay might entail, he promptly
replied to Duplessis Mornay that his intentions had been mis-
understood, and begged that nobleman to induce his fellow-
Protestants to remain at Loudun until the arrival of some leading men of his privy council, whom he promised to despatch
at the earliest moment, with the view of satisfying his subjects
of the Reformed faith. [3]   Half apologetically, he wrote about

---

[1] Odet de la Noue to Henry IV., Loudun, June 26, 1596, MS. belonging to
M. Lesens, printed in Bulletin de la Société de l'histoire du Protestantisme
français, xxxii. (1883) 401–404.   Another letter of La Noue, of August 16,
1596, printed ibid., xxxii. 405–407, from the MS. in the Collection Dupuy,
National Library, Paris, is of almost equal interest.

[2] Duplessis Mornay to Henry IV., Saumur, May 11, 1596, Mémoires, vi. 473.

[3] "Bref discours," ubi supra, vii. 287, 288.

the same time to Duplessis Mornay: "I doubt not that there is a great deal that is wrong in the quarters where you are, seeing that here there is so much that I do not know what remedy to apply, although, believe me, I spare myself in no wise in the quest."[1]

The intimation of the royal intentions reached the assembly before it had broken up—whether in obedience to the king's previous commands, or in accordance with the plan of carrying to the scattered Huguenots of France the determination to stand by the terms of the truce of Henry the Third. The members, we are told, received the intelligence with great demonstrations of joy, and of thankfulness to Almighty God for so inclining his majesty's heart and the hearts of his advisers.[2] The king's deputies soon followed—Vic and Calignon, both of them men of recognized probity and skill. But now again difficulties at once arose ; the powers with which Vic and Calignon had been invested were too limited to be of practical use, resolving themselves into little more than offering what had been so often rejected—the Edict of Poitiers, with some insufficient compensation for what that edict had lost through the successive treaties made with cities and chieftains of the League.

The end was not yet. However, the king seemed to be thoroughly in earnest, and was listening to better advisers. Instead of insisting upon the dispersal of the assembly, he was anxious not only to have it continue in session, but to bring it nearer to the capital ; possibly not without the hope that the blandishments of the court might make some impression even upon men so resolute. The delegates accepted the proposal ; but only with a distinct understanding that they should not be invited, as before, merely to be again dismissed with complaints scarcely heard, and with a few vague notes hurriedly written on the margin of the several articles of their carefully prepared pe-

---

[1] Henry IV. to Duplessis Mornay, Abbeville, June 2, 1596, Mémoires, vi. 488.

[2] "Bref discours," ubi supra, vii. 288 ; Mémoires de Charlotte Arbaleste, etc., i. 300, 301.

titions.[1]   On the tenth of November the Huguenots, who for
seven months and over had been sitting at Loudun, transported

The assembly   themselves to the little town of Vendôme, on Henry's
removes to
Vendôme and   patrimonial estates.   A little later they thought it
Saumur.   prudent to retire to safer quarters at Saumur, on the
Loire, where Duplessis Mornay was governor.

Meantime the king's deputies continued to come and go between the Huguenot assembly and the court, but the old year
closed leaving the matters in dispute as unsettled as ever.   The
first three months of the year 1597 did not pass before the
monarch fancied that, in the fresh complications of civil affairs,
he had additional and stronger grounds for adjourning to a more
favorable season the legislation necessary to give to Protestantism a standing in the state, and to its adherents some measure
of security for life, property, and religious worship.

As if previous reverses had not been sufficient, there came to
the court, plunged, at the time, in extraordinary festivities and

Fall of Amiens,   gayeties and masquerades, the startling intelligence
March 11, 1597.   that the city of Amiens, key to the situation in the
north of the kingdom, had, on the eleventh of March, been
surprised and taken by the Spaniards.   The sense of disgrace
connected with its capture was felt even more than the possible danger.   A few soldiers disguised as peasants had effected
one of those daring surprises of which the century had seen so
many.   A loaded wagon breaking down at the gate of Amiens
had prevented the portcullis from falling to its place.   The score
of soldiers had facilitated the entrance of two hundred, the two
hundred had opened the way for the whole Spanish army.   A
city boasting the possession of more than fifteen thousand burgesses capable of bearing arms was taken and plundered, its
men maltreated and its women outraged, by an insignificant
force of three thousand of the enemy.   The blow was a cruel
one; Henry felt it to the quick, and the smart reminded him of
the more glorious days of the past, when, fighting with his small
following of Huguenot soldiers, he had been a match for all

---

[1] "Des apostilles faicts à la haste sur leurs requestes."   "Bref discours,"
ubi supra, vii. 289.

the armies which had in vain been hurled against him. "I have been long enough playing the King of France," he exclaimed. "Now I must play the King of Navarre."[1]

How should the Huguenots act in this emergency? This was the question that instantly confronted them, both as individuals and as a body of religionists of similar views and interests. Denied the rights for which they had so long been contending, enjoying—under a king until lately professing their faith and certainly elevated to the throne more by their valor and self-devotion than by the adhesion of any other persons—less freedom of action than they had possessed under monarchs who were their avowed enemies, baffled at every step in their attempt to secure justice by the persistent unwillingness of a royal council which had more than once frustrated even the monarch's own kindly disposition and definite concessions—must they, notwithstanding all, flock to his support, not only forgetting all past disappointments, but renouncing present claims? So very naturally thought Henry; so thought his Roman Catholic courtiers, one and all; so, deceived by the glamour of the doctrine of the divine right of kings, and of the unqualified duty of passive obedience on the part of subjects, thought even the fairest men of the opposite party; so thought a few of the Huguenots themselves. The majority were of a different mind, and the more just appreciation of the rights of man now entertained will lead us to side with them. The Huguenots were willing, and more than willing, to pour out their life's blood for the defence of king and country. They had no desire to take advantage of the time to exact conditions, still less to require hard or unjust conditions. But they must know, once for all, where they stood, what was going to become of them. If they were to suffer and die for king and country, they must at least be certain that that king and that country were theirs. The time for quibbling

Side note: What ought the Huguenots to do?

---

[1] "C'est assés faire le roy de France; il est temps de faire le roy de Navarre." Lestoile, ii. 282. See De Thou, ix. 79-81; Mémoires de la Ligue, vi. 530-532; Agrippa d'Aubigné, iii. 387, 388; and Motley, United Netherlands, iii. 435, etc.

and shuffling and prevaricating and procrastinating, if there
ever was a time for such unworthy actions, had long gone by.
The government must give a categorical answer to this question : " Are the adherents of the Reformed Church entitled to
equal rights, to something more solid than mere sufferance at
the hands of Roman Catholics ? " No reply but " Yes " or
" No " was admissible. If they were Christians, if they were
Frenchmen, if they had proved themselves loyal subjects, let
them be treated as such. It required no time, no slow and painful deliberation, for king and council to decide whether they
would accord the Huguenots their inalienable rights.[1] It was
high time that all Frenchmen should learn from necessity what,
to their great misfortune, they had hitherto failed to learn
from reason and from experience—that they must accustom
themselves, whatever their religious opinions might be, to live
harmoniously together.[2]

The king had lost no time in notifying the Protestant assembly of Saumur of the disaster that had befallen him, and in
begging them to postpone their demands and hasten to the assistance of their sovereign in this his hour of need. The answer which the Huguenots returned to the royal summons is
an important document, exhibiting clearly the principles which,
according as they were just or erroneous, must lead us to admire
or reprehend the conduct of the Protestants.

" Sire," they said, in a letter dated on the twenty-fifth of
March, 1597, and signed by Clermont, as president, and by
Chamier, as secretary, "we have received, through
Monsieur de Montglat, the epistle which it has pleased
your majesty to write us. From this we learn both
of the loss of Amiens and of the displeasure your majesty has
experienced thereat. We sympathize in your grief, as true
members of the body of which you are the head, being unable

The assembly's answer to the king.

---

[1] The extended correspondence of Duplessis Mornay is a mine of information respecting the attitude of the Huguenots. It should be read entire, so
far as these years are concerned, by any one who wishes to obtain an accurate
idea of their religious principles and unflinching patriotism.

[2] Duplessis Mornay to Henry IV., Saumur, March 25, 1597, Mémoires, vii.
175. See, also, the letter of June 2, 1596, ibid., vi. 490.

to see you afflicted without being ourselves afflicted. It is just and reasonable that all should unite and hasten to the public defence, and we hold unworthy of the French name, yea, of the Christian name, all who may purpose to be wanting in this their bounden duty. As such we declare accursed that remnant of rebels and disobedient leaguers who, instead of upholding the freedom of their native land, traitorously subject it to the yoke of foreign slavery.

" But, Sire, we cannot notice that your majesty exhorts us to this union, and that he asks us to divest ourselves of prejudice, without complaining of the unfavorable judgment you seem to pass upon us. For we are charged with a crime of which we are innocent—we who have no other aim but to live together as true Frenchmen, bound by mutual friendship and concord ; we who have so little regard for our personal interests that we have no life, no possessions, but such as we are ready to use for the public weal, as we have ever done. To admonish us to be content with what has been accorded us, is a thing not less strange than prejudicial to the object which your majesty desires of us. It is strange, because you formerly bore us such good will that it is almost impossible that you can now desire our hurt. It is prejudicial, in that while intending to persuade us to serve you against your enemies, you persuade us at the same time to render ourselves incapable of doing you service. We cannot do service to your majesty unless we subsist. Now, we can neither be nor continue to subsist, if we remain bound to the hard conditions which we are asked to accept. We shall be told that heretofore we have subsisted with a great deal less. That is true ; but the disease is now at its crisis. For, on the one hand, having borne as large a share as we were able of the disasters of the state, and sacrificed all our interests in order to aid and re-establish it, we cherished the hope that when the state might fare better we also should enjoy greater prosperity. On the other hand, our enemies will overwhelm us without delay, unless the matters needed for our preservation be provided for by your majesty. Therefore it is that we remain firm, Sire, and purpose to remain firm, with no intention of keeping men's minds in suspense by our fresh demands.

"Are we not Christians, Sire? Why do men wish to deprive us of liberty to pray to God? Shall the pope suffer the Jews to deny our Lord in the city of Rome, and will he not suffer us to adore Him publicly in France? Tithes have from all antiquity been instituted for the support of the pastors of the people; we are compelled to pay tithes to our mortal enemies.

"There are two things which prevent us from now giving up, in view of the state of affairs, the demands we have so much reason to urge, or from adjourning them to another season. The one is that they are so absolutely needful to us that we shall perish if deprived of them; the other, that whatever we might defer would be so much lost. . . .

"Let your majesty give us a law under which we may be able to live with honor, and we will boldly answer for all ' those of the religion ' that they will never prove recreant to the loyalty and obedience they owe you, that they will never have anything more at heart than to hasten to lay down their lives at your majesty's feet, resisting the common enemy of this state. This is the goal of our aspirations, for whose attainment we now have greater reason to hope, since it has pleased your majesty, for the purpose of enabling us to secure it, to appoint members of his council who ardently desire the prosperity and quiet of the realm. We very humbly beg you to be pleased once more to command them to surmount all difficulties in order to grant us the things that are necessary. Having these, we protest that we shall be satisfied; as also we protest that we shall never consent to be deprived of them, lest we be suicides, authors of our own ruin. Against that ruin we entreat your majesty to oppose yourself, in conjunction with us, as courageously and as zealously as you did in former days." [1]

---

[1] The full text of the letter is published in the appendix to M. Charles Read's Daniel Chamier (Paris, 1858), pp. 214, 215. The learned author of this very valuable work (the first president of the French Protestant Historical Society) supposes that the letter was the production of Daniel Chamier, who signed it in the capacity of secretary. I think that this is a mistake, and that here again we have a paper from the pen of Duplessis Mornay. The reference made by the writer to the toleration of the Jews by the pope in the city of Rome may be compared with the sentences respecting the same circum-

Meanwhile, to the original negotiators on the part of the king had happily been added, at the suggestion of the Protestants, Schomberg and De Thou. two men of tried fidelity to principle and of marked ability, recently commissioned by his majesty to treat with that troublesome rebel, the Duke of Mercœur. With the help of such men as Schomberg, Count of Nanteuil, and Jacques Auguste de Thou, it was hoped that a pacific settlement might soon be reached. Nor was this anticipation disappointed. Under their patient and skilful management the crude outline of a contract between the Roman Catholics and the Protestants was gradually fashioned into the notable edict which, for the greater part of a century, was to constitute the charter of Huguenot rights.

Of the difficulties that stood in the way we can best form a notion from a consideration of the radical differences in the positions occupied by the opposing parties on the question of religious toleration. To the Roman Catholic, the existence of Protestantism in France was a fact indeed, but a fact militating against the unity of the kingdom, a misfortune not only to be deplored, but to be cured as speedily as possible. "Une foi, une loi, un roi," was still a favorite motto. To the Huguenot, Protestantism in France was an establishedfact, a permanent condition of French jurisprudence.

The Roman Catholic sought to relegate the Reformed worship to distant parts of the country, to exclude it from the cities, to compel it to forego all external marks of its presence, to prevent its convocations from meeting the eye, the singing of its psalms from offending the ear of the faithful masses of the people. He insisted that its adherents be rigidly banished from all offices of honor, trust, or emolument, that its ministers receive no official recognition. The tithes must, as heretofore, be reserved for the clergy of the established church. If the adherents of the Reformed Church must have ministers of their own,

---

stance contained in a "Remonstrance to the States of Blois," drawn up by Duplessis Mornay, in 1576. See the document in his Mémoires, ii. 40–78, and especially pp. 49–51.

let them pay for their maintenance; let them expect no relief from bearing a proportionate share in the expense of supporting an ecclesiastical order of which it was their fault or their misfortune that they did not reap the advantage.

On the other hand, the Huguenot claimed an equality with the Roman Catholic in all pertaining to citizenship—an equal right to worship God according to his own convictions of duty and propriety, and without discrimination of time and place; equal protection of person and goods by means of courts impartial because constituted of a bench of judges equally divided between the two communions; equal admission to all offices in the civil administration, in the army, in the judiciary; equal participation in the funds for the support of the ministry to which he or his fathers had contributed; finally, since it was vain, in view of the numerical preponderance of the Roman Catholics, to expect that even the monarch himself, however equitably disposed, would be able to defend the Protestant minority from oppression, if indeed from exposure to bloody attack and massacre, cities of refuge to be left in Huguenot hands, but with garrisons paid from the royal treasury, to serve both as a means of protection and as a pledge of future peace.

To adjust views so diametrically opposed would have been a hopeless task. Happily for the negotiators, they were not called upon to make an entirely new settlement. With the Edict of Poitiers and the conclusions of the Conference of Nérac and the Peace of Fleix as the basis, they had but to enlarge the concessions of Henry the Third to the extent at which they would in some measure satisfy the Protestants, while not offending the Roman Catholics so far as to prevent them from accepting the results of their work. It may, indeed, be urged that they would have done far better had they cast aside the trammels of the Edict of 1577 and arranged the relations of the Protestants to the state on the broad foundation of natural law, conceding to the partisans of the Reformation all the inalienable prerogatives of man as a rational being responsible to God alone for his religious belief. But, not to say that Schomberg and De Thou were intrusted with no ample powers to enable them to establish the principle of religious equality, the age itself was unprepared for the assertion of that principle. Every country of Europe had its own state religion, from which if dissent was tolerated at all, the toleration carried with it no acknowledged claim to impartial protection and support.   It was a marvel to contemporaries, as it is a marvel to the candid student of history in our times, that, in the face of obstacles so formidable, the ingenuity of Vic and Calignon, of Schomberg and De Thou, on the side of the court, and of Duplessis Mornay, of Clairville, and of others scarcely less worthy of individual mention, from among the Huguenots, was successful in devising a law so skilfully and so justly framed in all its parts that, under its benign provisions, the partisans of the two religions had every prospect of being able to live together in mutual amity and in quietness for centuries, if not for all time, had not the fatal resolution been formed in the mind of Louis the Fourteenth to secure by his arbitrary authority the complete religious unity of the kingdom.

The pressure of the court upon the assembled deputies at Saumur to make, in view of the fall of Amiens and the unpromising state of the king's affairs, concessions which they were expressly forbidden from making by their instructions, led to yet another change, both of place and of form, in the political gathering.   With the monarch's consent, the Huguenots took a brief recess, that they might have time to visit their constituents and then reassemble in the city of Châtellerault, on The assembly the sixteenth of June, with larger numbers and better at Châtelle able to express the sentiments of the masses of the rault, June, 1597. Protestant people.   It was a goodly company that convened.   Each province was represented by a nobleman, a minister of the Gospel, and a member of the third estate.   To these members were added, according to the regulations adopted at Sainte Foy, several high lords of the party, among whom Claude de la Trémouille exerted the greatest influence and was elected to the important position of presiding officer of the assembly.[1]

If the royal council and Henry himself had hoped for any abatement of the Protestant demands from the delegates fresh

---

[1] Benoist, Histoire de l'édit de Nantes, i. 188, 189.

from intercourse with the Huguenots of the provinces, they were utterly disappointed. Far from being weaker, their tone It abates none was only the more determined. On the essential of its claims. point of the security to be accorded to the Protestants, almost the only point of importance where substantial agreement had not been reached, the deputies were inflexible in defence of the rights of which they were the appointed guardians. If Duplessis Mornay had previously descried peril, he now realized how imminent it was. Some of the Huguenot leaders refused to rally to the king's standard until his majesty should be pleased to give them some satisfaction. La Trémouille himself had raised troops in the king's name, but remained in Poitou and would not hasten northward to Picardy ; just as the Duke of Bouillon from Limousin turned his arms eastward into Auvergne and Gévaudan to meet the insurrectionary force of Montmorency Fosseuse, instead of crossing swords with the Spaniards.[1] The majority of the members of the assembly of Châtellerault, indeed almost all, stood in the same attitude. They insisted that the little account which the king's council made of the importance of satisfying the demands of the Protestants, even as to necessary things, was a sufficient reason that the Protestants should persist in their demands for things not necessary—nay, that they should even take advantage of the public affliction of the kingdom, inasmuch as their enemies preferred to refuse their just demands rather than avail themselves of the services of the Huguenots by granting those demands.[2]

Nor ought severe censure to be directed against the Huguenots, so often disappointed, so heart-sick because of hope long deferred, if they exhibited to the world a considerable amount of irritation. They were, indeed, on the eve of securing an edict by whose provisions all their most essential wants would be met ; but they were gifted with no supernatural prescience, and their course must be judged not by what we now know, but by what they knew. And they only knew that years of earnest discussion and humble petition, years crowded with

---

[1] Mémoires de la vie de J. A. de Thou, pp. 188, 189.
[2] Mémoires de Charlotte Arbaleste, etc., i. 313, 314.

fruitless journeyings to and from court and with repulses from indifferent or hostile councillors, years in which their laboriously prepared statements of grievances and exhibits of the things they must have in order to maintain a bare existence had received little attention, had been negligently read, and had called forth for all reply only a few vague assurances hurriedly dashed off with the pen and amounting in truth to nothing at all—they only knew that all these years of tedious waiting had not bettered their actual condition in the slightest degree.

It may indeed be that the cool-headed Duplessis Mornay was more nearly right than were most of his fellow-believers, when he urged that some concessions on their part at this juncture would insure the immediate enactment of a law in favor of the Protestants, who might then go at once to the help of the king before the walls of Amiens. Such a law would, in the present emergency, be instantly registered by the Parliament of Paris, and the reproach now heaped upon the Protestants for their tardiness would be turned into congratulation for the opportune service they rendered. On the other hand, if Amiens should be permanently lost to France, the Protestants would share in the disaster experienced by the whole realm; whereas, if Amiens should be retaken by Henry without their participation, in the exploit, their condition would only become the worse. As a consequence of the peace between him and Philip which would soon ensue, the crown would be more redoubtable and the French king's Roman Catholic councillors would feel themselves relieved of all necessity of granting Protestant demands.

This moderate and prudent advice, however, met with the pertinent rejoinder that, however specious the arguments might be, experience had demonstrated their fallacy. The circumstance that the Huguenots had gone to the rescue of Henry of Valois, in his extremity, led to no such exhibition of gratitude as the advocates of concession now maintained would certainly result from the disinterested subordination of their needs to the exigencies of Henry of Bourbon. In the end, all that Duplessis Mornay could boast to have effected was that, by his patriotic and ingenious diplomacy, he forestalled an outbreak which might have been the prelude of another disastrous civil war.[1]

It must not, however, be inferred from the invectives which it became the fashion among Roman Catholic historians, even of the fairer kind, to pour out upon the heads of the Protestants, for their supposed lack of loyalty, that

Huguenot
support in
arms.

Henry found himself altogether unsupported by Huguenot troops or captains in the hour of his extremity. He was still surrounded by noblemen and officers of the Reformed faith. Some of his best troops belonged to Protestant families. Calvinists constituted almost the whole of the regiment of Navarre, which was among the corps that suffered most severely in the field. The lists of the dead and of the wounded were an unimpeachable testimony to the extent to which the king's success was due to Protestant co-operation. Among the great nobles, Rohan, future hero of the last Huguenot struggles under the reign of Louis the Thirteenth, signalized himself as having made his first experiment of war in the campaign for the recovery of Amiens.[2]

And yet the general fact remained that, uncertain both of their present condition and of their future prospects, the Huguenots exhibited no such ardor in flocking to the standard of their old leader as they had shown in previous contests, and that his exhortations, accompanied by no acts of friendship, remained as powerless to stir their enthusiasm as his covert threats of injury were impotent to excite their fears.[3] They were fully resolved not to be drawn by cajolery, not to be driven by menaces, into any abandonment of their rights. They even took steps dis-

---

[1] Mémoires de Charlotte Arbaleste, etc., i. 314, 315.

[2] Benoist, ubi supra, i. 192.

[3] See, for example, Henry's letter to Schomberg, dated March 31, 1597—by no means one of his most manly effusions—in which he writes: "Car je ne me porte pas bien de ma personne et suis assailly de tant de necessitez et de faix que je ne sçay quasy plus à quel sainct me vouer, pour sortir de ce malheureux passage, et si ceux de la dicte Religion continuent à demander choses que je ne leur puisse accorder sans diviser mes subjects plus que devant, ils augmenteront tellement ma peine et ma douleur, que je m'asseure qu'à la fin ils y auront regret. Car ils m'accableront d'ennuy et m'osteront tout moyen de remedier au mal qui nous consomme." Lettres missives, iv. 726.

tinctly looking to a vindication of those rights by arms. Certain cities and strongholds left in their hands as pledges of security seemed about to fall into their enemies' possession through lack of means to pay the garrisons. In some cases the appropriation had been altogether withheld. Elsewhere it had been in great part diverted into other channels, and the financial officers of the crown had received orders to pay to the Protestants no more than would suffice to meet the wages of the soldiers for the first four months of the year. The object of the king's crafty councillors was only too evident. The Huguenot assembly, however, forestalled it by such prompt action as the crisis demanded; for it authorized a seizure of the moneys in the hands of the royal collectors of taxes sufficient to provide for these crying needs.[1]

Of this persistency on the part of the Protestants there was the more need, because of the disappointments to which they were again subjected. No sooner had the assembly accepted the propositions which Schomberg declared himself empowered by the king to make, than De Thou, Vic, and Calignon arrived from court with later instructions and essential modifications of what Schomberg had conceded. Convinced that they were trifled with, the Huguenot delegates could scarcely be prevented from at once returning to their homes in disgust. A new and strange impatience seized them. They would not brook delay. If they expected a messenger from the king, they were indignant that he tarried, were it but a part of a week. "Four days in themselves are not much," said one; "but four days added on to upward of four years of procrastination drive the deputies beyond the bounds of endurance."[2]

---

[1] Letter of the assembly of Châtellerault to Duplessis Mornay, November 22, 1597, in Mémoires de Duplessis Mornay, vii. 396, 397. After rehearsing the grounds of their action, the assembly proceeds: "Nous avons esté contraincts, à la requisition des gouverneurs, d'ordonner au conseil de Poictou de faire payer lesdictes garnisons, suivant ce qu'il avoit esté convenu. Et nous serons aussi contraincts de faire de mesmes ailleurs, s'il n'y est aultrement pourveu; car la conservation de nos places nous est en singuliere recommendation. Et c'est aussi l'intention du roy que les garnisons soient payées."

[2] Duplessis Mornay to Schomberg, August 11, 1597, Mémoires, vii. 313.

So the autumn and winter of this eventful year wore away. In September the city of Amiens again fell into the hands of its rightful monarch. The prospect of an early ter-

Amiens re-taken. September, 1597.

mination of the war with Spain was bright. Henry's mind could now be relieved of the fear that in making concessions he might seem to have been constrained. None the less was he determined that the Protestants, whom he accused of a desire to dictate terms to him, should appear to have accepted only what he was pleased to grant.[1] He insisted that the assembly of Châtellerault should send deputies of its own to court, there to lay before him what difficulties might still remain, and receive his ultimate decision. It was with this commission, appointed on the twenty-fourth of February, 1598, and consisting of four Protestant members, and with the Duke of Bouillon, whom the assembly requested to assist them, that the final arrangements were made which were promulgated, two months later, in the Edict of Nantes.[2] The commission, like the assembly of which it was an emanation, stood its ground firmly. The four Huguenots were shrewd negotiators, who, much to the disgust of those with whom they treated, would not abate a jot of their demands. Yet wise men among the Roman Catholics were fully convinced that even thus—if only the Protestants would act prudently and make due acknowledgments to the king for his goodness—the court had made an excellent bargain for France.[3]

In reality, however, France owes a deeper debt of gratitude for the great charter of Huguenot liberties, which was about to be conceded, to the political assembly of the Huguenots which

---

[1] Agrippa d'Aubigné, iii. 460, 461 ; Mémoires de De Thou, 188.

[2] See Anquez, 78, 79.

[3] Villeroy, Secretary of State, wrote to Bellièvre and Sillery, who were treating with Philip II.'s ambassadors at Vervins, March 7, 1598 : "L'assemblée de Chastellerault a aussi envoyé quatre deputés pour conclure et achever du tout les affaires qui les concernent, si bien que j'estime que nous en pourrons sortir à Angers où nous allons aujourd'hui ; mais vous sçavés à quel prix ce sera, car ils n'ont rien rabatteu de leur compte ; et pourveu qu'ils soient sages et qu'ils recognoissent comme ils doibvent la bonté de sa majesté, encores n'en serons nous que bons marchands."

closed its eventful sessions on the eleventh of June, about two months after the date of the royal signature, than to Henry the Fourth himself.[1] It is true that the king must be credited with an honest desire that the Protestants of France should obtain such a standing in the sight of the law as would enable them to live in peace and comfort. He was doubtless sincere in the declaration that he would deeply regret any disturbance of amicable relations with old associates in creed and in arms, whom he averred that he loved even more than they loved themselves.[2] Nor is it unlikely that, in the course of the many years during which he had been forced to contemplate the subject, first as a subject and a Protestant, later as a professed Roman Catholic and a monarch, Henry had matured a scheme according to which the adherents of the two prevalent religions might live together in France with mutual forbearance and toleration. But, whatever that scheme may have been, it is equally undeniable that the plan actually adopted and incorporated in the famous edict, so far as it differed from the methods of previous edicts and was not a mere indorsement of their provisions, emanated not from the sovereign, but from the resolute band of men who, month after month and year after year, stood together without flinching, without for a moment harboring the thought of the surrender of a single one of the interests for whose defence they had been convened. The brilliant king, with his sparkling wit and his affable manners, may make a more conspicuous figure upon the stage of history; but the quiet and tireless assembly which sat at Loudun, at Vendôme, at Saumur, at Châtellerault, and would have gone to the ends of the earth if only it might secure the rights of its constituents, is better entitled to the rank of protagonist, since it was the true author of the system

Honor due to the Huguenot assembly.

---

[1] This is also the view of Léonce Anquez (Histoire des assemblées politiques des Réformés de France, 79), a Roman Catholic historian of extraordinary fairness and impartiality.

[2] " Ceulx que je puis dire aimer plus qu'ils ne s'aiment eulx mesmes." Autograph letter of Henry IV. to Duplessis Mornay, Monceaux, January 18, 1598, Mémoires, vii. 522, and Lettres missives, iv. 898.

under whose successful operation the kingdom enjoyed for long years a peace founded upon justice and equity.

It was in the month of March and in the city of Angers that Henry signed the edict by which he took into his favor that last and most treacherous of the adherents of the League, the Duke of Mercœur.[1]   Then proceeding down the Loire, to receive the submission of the province in which the duke had for nine years maintained himself with almost regal authority, his majesty reached the capital of Brittany, the commercial city of Nantes, on the eleventh of April, 1598.   Two days later he signed the edict which has come to be known as the Edict of Nantes.   It was a remarkable circumstance, noticed even at the time as a singular coincidence, that the great law establishing the civil rights of the Huguenots was issued at the very place where, thirty-eight years earlier, on the first of February, 1560, in the reign of Francis the Second, and in the midst of the most violent persecution, the first assembly of the malcontents, soon to be known as Huguenots, was brought together by the incredible diligence of Godefroy de la Reynaudie.[2]   By one of the strange revenges of history, the same Breton port that witnessed the stealthy convocation of a few patriots resolved to attempt against great odds the overthrow of a tyrannical usurpation of power, was destined to behold the promulgation of one of the most illustrious of laws ever enacted in behalf of religious liberty, given in answer to the petition of the successors of those patriots who had now become an important element of the French population.[3]

The Edict of Nantes signed, April 13, 1598.

---

[1] This document brings to a close the long series of humiliating concessions to the rebels of the League contained in the "Recueil des edicts et articles accordez par le roy Henry III pour la réunion de ses subjects.   Imprimé l'an de Grace, MDCIIII."   See, also, Mémoires de la Ligue, vi. 625–640.   Arrangements were contemporaneously made for the marriage of Henry's bastard son Cæsar to the duke's only daughter, a girl of only six years.   De Thou, ix. 152.

[2] Rise of the Huguenots, i. 380.

[3] De Thou, ix. 155.   It seems strange, at first sight, that this historian should make the interval between 1560 and 1598 amount to thirty-nine years; but the error is probably due to the fact that, occurring before Easter, the date of the famous meeting at Nantes, which preceded the "Tumult of Amboise," fell within the bounds of the year 1559 old style.

The Edict of Nantes is a long and somewhat complicated document. Besides the edict proper, contained in ninety-five public articles, there is a further series of fifty-six " secret " articles, and a " brevet " or patent of the king, all of which were signed on the thirteenth of April ; and these documents are supplemented by a second set of twenty-three " secret " articles, dated on the last day of the same month. The first of these four papers is expressly declared to be a " perpetual and irrevocable edict." It is this portion of the law that specially demands a careful examination.

The preamble begins with a statement of the " frightful troubles, confusions, and disorders " to which Henry, at his accession, found France a prey, and the complete success which had at length attended his labors, put forth even at the risk of his own life, to restore peace and quiet to the kingdom. Among the matters which he has been obliged to postpone until this moment, and chief among these matters, are, on the one hand, the complaints which he has received from many cities and provinces that the Catholic religion has not been universally reestablished, according to the edicts heretofore given for the pacification of the realm; and, on the other, the petitions and remonstrances of his subjects of the " pretended Reformed religion," both touching the fact that what has been conceded to them by those edicts remains unexecuted, and respecting the additional provisions which they desire for the exercise of their religion, the liberty of their consciences, and the security of their persons and fortunes, in view of their just apprehensions caused by the recent troubles of which the chief object has been their overthrow. " But now," writes the king, " that it hath pleased God to begin to grant us the enjoyment of some better quiet, we have judged that we cannot better employ that quiet than by attending to what may concern the glory of His holy name and service, and providing that He may be worshipped and adored by all our subjects ; and if it hath not pleased Him to permit that this be done as yet in one and the same form of religion, that it be, at least, with one and the same intention, and with such order that there be not, for that reason, any trouble and tumult amongst them, and that we and this kingdom may always merit and retain the glorious title of 'Very Christian,' a title which was acquired long since by many meritorious actions, and by the same means remove the cause of the disaster and trouble that may arise on the question of religion, which is always the most delicate and far-reaching of all questions. Recognizing, therefore, this matter to be of very great importance, and worthy of very careful consideration, having taken up the memorials of the complaints of our Catholic subjects, having also permitted our subjects of the pretended Reformed religion to assemble by deputies to draw up their complaints, and to collect all the aforesaid remonstrances, and having conferred with them divers times respecting this question, and having reviewed the preceding decrees, we judge it necessary now to give respecting the whole matter, to all our said subjects a general, clear, definite, and absolute law, by which they may regulate their conduct as to all the differences which have heretofore arisen among them or may hereafter arise— a law wherewith both may have reason to be satisfied, as far as the nature of the times may permit." In thus acting, the monarch declares further that he is moved simply by zeal to the service of God, and by a desire that a lasting peace may reign among his subjects. He prays that the same divine goodness which has ever watched over France may give grace to all Frenchmen to comprehend well that in the maintenance of the law now given consists, next to their duty to the Almighty and to their king, the principal foundation of their union and concord, tranquillity and quiet, and of the re-establishment of the entire state in its pristine splendor, opulence, and power. The king on his part promises to enforce the exact observance of the edict, which has been drawn up after mature deliberation and consultation of the princes of the blood and the great officers and dignitaries of the state.

Our chief concern being with the fortunes of the Huguenots, the provisions for the re-establishment of the Roman Catholic

Liberty of consience.

worship, wherever in the course of the events of the last thirty years that worship had been interfered with or banished, need not claim our attention. For the benefit of the Protestants the cardinal concession was liberty to dwell anywhere in the royal dominions, without being subjected to inquiry, vexed, molested, or constrained to do anything contrary to their conscience. As respects public worship, while perfect equality was not established, the dispositions were such

Religious worship.

as to bring it within the power of a Protestant in any part of the kingdom to meet his fellow-believers for the holiest of acts, at least from time to time. To every Protestant nobleman enjoying that extensive authority known as "haute justice," and to noblemen in Normandy distinguished as possessors of "fiefs de haubert," the permission was granted to have religious services on all occasions and for all comers at their principal residence, as well as on other lands whenever they themselves were present. Noblemen of inferior jurisdiction were allowed to have worship on their estates, but only for themselves and their families. In addition to these seigniorial rights, the Protestant *people* received considerable accessions to the cities where they might meet for public religious purposes. The exercise of their worship was authorized in all cities and places where such worship had been held on several occasions in the years 1596 and 1597, up to the month of August; and in all places in which worship had been, or ought to have been, established in accordance with the Edict of 1577, as interpreted by the Conference of Nérac and the Peace of Fleix. But in addition to these, a fresh gift of a second city in every bailiwick and sénéchaussée of the kingdom greatly increased the facilities enjoyed by the scattered Huguenots for reaching the assemblies of their fellow-believers.

In the matter of education and of public charity, the provisions of the edict were large enough to satisfy the natural aspirations of the Protestants both to afford their children

Education and charity.

and their needy members all the advantages enjoyed by the rest of the community, and to give that religious culture upon which the reformers had always laid great stress. Scholars of both religions were to be admitted without distinction of religion to all universities, colleges, and schools throughout France. The same impartiality was to extend to the reception of the sick in the hospitals, and to the poor in the provision made for their relief. More than this, the Protestants were permitted to establish schools of their own in all places where their worship was authorized, and the grants already made by Henry the Fourth for the erection of Protestant universities at La Rochelle, Nismes, and Montélimart were duly confirmed. The right of Protestants to endow scholastic or eleemosynary institutions by testamentary bequests, and the right of Protestant fathers to prescribe, during their lifetime or by will after their death, the teachers of their children, were fully recognized.

The scandal and inhumanity exhibited in the refusal of burial to the Protestant dead, as well as in the disinterment of such bodies as had been placed in consecrated ground, Cemeteries. was henceforth precluded by the assignment of portions of the public cemeteries or of new cemeteries of their own to the Protestants.

The civil equality of the Protestants was assured by an article which declared them to be admissible to all public positions, dignities, offices, and charges, and forbade any Civil equality. other examination into their qualifications, conduct, and morals than those to which their Roman Catholic brethren were subjected.

Recognizing the disadvantages under which the Protestants suffered in the ordinary courts of justice, and their inability to Courts of justice. obtain an impartial hearing and an equitable decision from the majority of Roman Catholic judges, the Edict of Nantes developed still further the exceptional legislation instituted by previous edicts of pacification. Provision was made for the establishment of a " chamber of the edict," as it was styled,[1] in the Parliament of Paris, with six Protestants among its sixteen counsellors, to take cognizance of cases in which Protestants were concerned. A similar chamber was promised in each of the parliaments of Rouen and Rennes. In

---

[1] " Laquelle sera appellée et intitulée la chambre de l'édit." In point of fact, however, it must be remembered that the clamor of the parliament prevented the establishment of a distinct chamber, the six Protestant judges being distributed among the various existing chambers in such a manner that their influence was practically reduced to a minimum.

Southern France three "chambres mi-parties" were either continued or created, with an equal number of Roman Catholic and Protestant judges—the first at Castres, for the province of Languedoc; the second at Bordeaux or Nérac, as should thereafter be determined, for Guyenne; and the third at Gap, for Dauphiny. These chambers were regarded as belonging respectively to the parliaments of Toulouse, or Languedoc, of Bordeaux, or Guyenne, and of Grenoble, or Dauphiny.

The two most delicate matters, in view of the relation of the Protestants to the crown, yet remain to be mentioned. The first, which was the support of the Protestant ministers of the Gospel, was provided for in the "brevet" or patent bearing even date with the edict itself. In this document his majesty, while careful to avoid the slightest reference to a theme distasteful to his Roman Catholic subjects, declares his desire to help his Protestant subjects "to meet sundry great expenses which they have to sustain," and thereupon appropriates to their use from the royal treasury the sum of forty-five thousand crowns annually, to be employed " in certain secret affairs that concern them, which his majesty does not wish to be specified or declared." Not less thorny was the settlement of the matter of the cautionary cities still held by the Protestants in various parts of the kingdom, and of the payment of the wages of the garrisons defending them. This settlement was made in the second series of secret articles already referred to, whereby the Protestants were formally authorized to retain possession of these places for the term of eight years from the date of the publication of the edict, and the annual sum of one hundred and eighty thousand crowns was set apart to defray the expense of their maintenance.[1]

Support of Protestant ministers.

Of the garrisons of places of refuge.

---

[1] The Edict of Nantes has frequently been printed with more or less exactness and completeness. Professor Anquez has printed, I believe for the first time, the four documents constituting the entire settlement in their original form. Benoist, in the appendix to the first volume of his Histoire de l'édit de Nantes, and Weiss, in the appendix to his Histoire des réfugiés protestants, have given them in the form in which they were registered by the Parliament of Paris. The "Recueil concernant les religionnaires (Edicts, déclarations et

Such are the main features of a law whose enactment marks an important epoch in the history of jurisprudence. If the supreme aim of the state should be the prosperity of every citizen under the kindly sway of laws extending their protection indifferently to the adherents of every religious creed, and securing to all an equal measure of quiet and safety, then the Edict of Nantes deserves to rank among the grandest monuments of European civilization ; then were the assiduous and persevering sessions of the Assembly of Loudun, Saumur, and Châtellerault, the toil of De Thou and Schomberg and Duplessis Mornay, and the solicitude of Henry the Fourth himself not labor lost. Of persecution fierce and bloody the world had seen quite enough, among Christians as well as among Moslems and pagans. Of toleration dictated by political necessity there had been not a little, as well as of a species of contemptuous toleration such as that which the followers of the Arabian prophet extended with supreme disdain to "dogs of unbelievers," whose persons they loathed and whose conflicting tenets they despised. But of religious liberty, based upon any notion, even approximate, of equality, there had been a great dearth ; and it was precisely this doctrine of complete religious liberty which was enunciated in the Edict of Nantes with a precision remarkable for the time of its publication. True, a candid examination will not justify us in denying the assertion that the great achievement of Henry the Fourth's reign was of the character of a compromise between natural justice and social necessity ;[1] but it is to the glory of its authors that the concessions were mostly in the interests of the indefeasible rights of man.

An epoch in modern civilization.

The Edict of Nantes was not at once presented to the parliaments ; nor was it, indeed, until early in the following year that the Parliament of Paris formally entered the document upon

---

arrests, etc.) "—reprint of 1885—gives only the edict proper and the first set of secret articles. The "Inventaire général de l'histoire de France " (Geneva, 1613) contains the edict proper alone, without the preamble.

[1] " Cette transaction dernière entre la justice naturelle et la nécessité sociale." Essai sur l'histoire du tiers-état, par Augustin Thierry (Paris, 1853), i. 183.

its registers. The cause of this delay was the desire felt by the royal council that the papal legate, Alexander de' Medici, Cardinal of Ferrara, should have the opportunity of leaving the kingdom before the occurrence of an event which the estimable prelate—for truly estimable is he represented as having been—might have regarded as a personal affront.[1]

Meanwhile, on the second of May, 1598, the war between France and Spain had been happily brought to an end by a treaty of peace signed at Vervins, and a month later the capital and all France rejoiced over the solemn ratification of the conditions which restored quietness to a land long a prey to the devastations of the sword.[2] The only drawback to the universal satisfaction lay in the fact that England and the Netherlands, faithful allies of France, had not been included in the compact, and that Henry had broken his explicit engagement to make no arrangements with Philip in which Queen Elizabeth was not included. By no class of Frenchmen was this more regretted than by the Huguenots, who had lately recurred to the queen and to Prince Maurice of Orange, and had enjoyed the great advantage of their intercessions with Henry. However, as the virgin queen was pretty well used to be treated after this fashion by her continental associates, and as the King of France, while plighting his word that he would henceforth be a firm friend of Philip, had secretly as-

The Peace of Vervins. May, 1598.

---

[1] De Thou, ix. 155. "Je ne désire le retour du legat à Rome," wrote Henry IV. to the Duke of Luxemburg, "sinon pour s'esclaircir et consoler aux occasions qui se presentent à nostre commun bien et contentement, et je fais retarder la publication de l'Edict avec les Huguenots à cause de sa presence." Letter of August 17, 1598, Lettres missives, v. 15, 16, and Bulletin, ii. 30.

[2] On the treaty of Vervins, see the text of the articles in Mémoires de Duplessis Mornay, viii. 431–450 ; on the public rejoicings, " Les pompes et ceremonies faites à l'acte solemnel, auquel le roy jura publiquement la paix, en la presence des deputez d'Espagne, 1598 " (reprinted in Mémoires de la Ligue, vi. 680–686). The Mémoires de Duplessis Mornay contain a great number of letters, etc., respecting the negotiation of this peace. In a letter written on the day the treaty was signed, Bellièvre and Sillery notify Villeroy, French minister of state, that "my lord the legate has told us that the pope will derive so great satisfaction from this peace, that he esteems that should the king apply to him for one additional cardinal, the pope will gratify him with one." Mémoires, viii. 429.

sured the Dutch that he would give them, underhand, such aid as would prevent them from being overwhelmed by the Spaniard, the breach of faith produced less astonishment or commotion than might have been expected.

And now had Henry the Fourth the opportunity of demonstrating to the world whether the edict in favor of the Protestants was in truth a law extorted from him by force, as the apologists for its revocation by his grandson averred, making use of this statement to prove the justice of repealing privileges iniquitously secured. The question is not, indeed, of any great ethical importance. The Great Charter granted by Henry of Bourbon to his Huguenot subjects, like that other charter granted by John Lackland to his British barons, must stand upon its own intrinsic merits, and the only point of real moment in the eye of impartial history is, whether its provisions coincide with the dictates of natural equity, whether the document as a whole is an approximate and somewhat faithful exponent of the relations which the state ought to recognize as subsisting between different forms of religion enjoying the joint protection of the civil power.

The charter in which free England glories, even in the nineteenth century, was secured at Runnymede, nearly seven hundred years ago, by armed men encamped in menacing attitude over against their monarch. If the Huguenot noblemen and burgesses had, in a similar manner, compelled the King of France, at the point of the lance, to concede to them an edict incorporating the principles of religious liberty more perfectly than had been done in any previous enactment, the fact would not have diminished in the least our legitimate admiration of the document, nor afforded even a plausible pretext for its subsequent recall.

In point of fact, however, there are few historical truths more distinctly established than that, while Henry had been dilatory in granting the privileges demanded by the Huguenots, his delays had been due to no aversion to them or unwillingness to reward their patriotic and loyal services, but solely to the opposition, actual or apprehended, of his council. He might regard as ill-timed the persistence of the Huguenots; he might not agree with them in each of the points deemed by them essential to their security; he might even, on occasion, indulge in a little petulant remonstrance; but never did he seriously contemplate a settlement very different from that at which the deputies finally arrived, and no one in the kingdom, perhaps, was better pleased when that settlement was actually reached. Four months after signing the edict, Henry justified his action to the Duke of Luxemburg by pointing to the necessity of satisfying a great and powerful part of his subjects, but did not fail to emphasize especially the debt of gratitude he owed the Huguenots. "I have been too well served and helped by them in my need," said he, "to neglect their interests; and were I to neglect them, I should introduce into my kingdom troubles more dangerous than those of the past." [1]

But the king's zeal for his edict did not stop with private utterances. There were obstacles from many different quarters to be overcome. The clergy, the parliaments, the university raised up difficulty after difficulty. Nothing was too absurd to be used as an instrument of resistance. All the faculties of the University of Paris manifested their hatred of the Protestants, and refused to admit them either to the benches of the students or to chairs of instruction. Such enmity was natural enough when it came from the Theological Faculty, or Sorbonne; but it was scarcely to be expected that the Medical Faculty should distinguish itself by its greater rancor and more determined opposition. Again the pulpits resounded in denunciation of the new compact to the advantage of heresy, and several bishops went so far as to order public prayers to be said throughout their dioceses imploring Almighty God that the edict might not become the law of the land. In fact, amid the excitement of the prelates the great moderation of the papal nuncio, who remained after the legate's

Opposition of the clergy and the university.

---

[1] Henry's words are significant: "Je ne puis reculer les Huguenots des charges sans hazarder le repos de mon Estat ; car la partie de ceux de contraire religion est encore trop enracinée en iceluy, et trop forte et puissante dedans et dehors pour estre mise à nonchaloir. J'en ay esté trop bien servy et assisté en ma nécessité ; je remettrois des troubles en mon Royaulme plus dangereux que par le passé." Henry IV. to the Duke of Luxemburg, August 17, 1598, Lettres missives, v. 15, and Bulletin, ii. 30.

departure, was remarked as not less singular than creditable to his good sense and charity.[1]

With all these opponents Henry displayed his accustomed tact and discernment. If any preacher was particularly vehement, he summoned him and administered a severe reprimand. To the deputies of the clergy he gave an answer cleverly combining conciliation with firmness. The prelates might even interpret his words as implying that he intended by and by to bring about religious uniformity. "During the war," he said, "I used to run to the quarter where the fire burned most fiercely, to put it out; now that peace has come back, I shall do what I ought to do in time of peace. I know that Religion and Justice are the columns and support of this kingdom, which is preserved by righteousness and piety; and were they not, I should wish to establish them, but step by step, as I shall do in all things. I shall act in such wise, God helping me, that the church will be as well off as she was a hundred years ago. I hope to clear my conscience on this point, and to satisfy you. This will be done little by little. Paris was not built in a day. Bring it to pass by your good examples that the people be as strongly incited to right action as they have heretofore been deterred from it. You have exhorted me to do my duty; I exhort you to do yours. Let us both act aright. Go by one way and let me go by the other, and if we meet, the thing will be quickly done. My predecessors have given you words with much pomp; and I, in my gray jacket, will give you results. I wear but a gray jacket. I am gray on the outside, but all gilt within." [2]

But it was upon the Parliament of Paris in particular that

Henry's address to the clergy.

---

[1] Benoist, Histoire de l'édit de Nantes, i. 271–273 ; Lestoile, ii. 296.

[2] "Je n'ay qu'une jaquette grise; je suis gris par le dehors, mais tout doré au dedans." Réponse de Henri IV aux députés du clergé, 28 Septembre, 1598, MSS. Du Puy, National Library, printed in Bulletin de la Société de l'histoire du Prot. français, ii. 28, and Lettres missives, v. 33, 34. Two months later La Noue writes : "Quant à nostre edict, le roy opiniastre pour nous le faire verifier, et a sur ce poinct vaincu les ecclesiastiques de haute lutte, et les a fort menacés et gourmandés." La Noue to Duplessis Mornay, November 28, 1598, Mémoires de Duplessis Mornay, ix. 188..

Henry found it necessary to exert the most direct and steady pressure. On a few points, indeed, he was willing to introduce modifications in the edict. He thought it not unreasonable that the Protestants should be required to obtain the royal per-

Modifications made in a few points.

mission to hold their synods and other ecclesiastical bodies, and that they should be debarred from themselves sitting in synods held outside of the kingdom or from receiving foreign Protestants into their own synods. And, indeed, the Duke of Sully and others of the same religion regarded it as for the advantage óf the Huguenots that a privilege should be denied them which would have exposed them to the charge of foreign intrigue.[1] But, while accepting such suggestions, the king insisted upon the reception and registry of the edict without essential change. The delay of the judges to comply with his wishes led him at last to summon the presidents and chief members of the court before him, and to address to them a speech of more than ordinary historical importance.

The judges found Henry in his cabinet, where he had been telling Marshal la Chastre that famous story of a marvel which

The king's determined speech to the Parliament of Paris.

happened just after the massacre of Saint Bartholomew's Day—how that, when playing at dice with the late Duke of Guise and two others, he had seen drops of blood appear upon the table; that twice he had wiped them off, but that when they came to light for a third time he had declined to continue the game, with the exclamation that the augury was a bad one for those who had spilled blood.

Not without a purpose did the king preface his remarks to

---

[1] Mémoires de Sully, ch. 89 (ed. of 1663, ii. 241, etc.) ; Inventaire général, ii. 771; Benoist, i. 274. It is to be noted, and the circumstance is characteristic of the diplomacy of the times, that while Henry added to the 34th of the secret articles, respecting the holding of synods, etc., the words " par la permission de sa majesté," and subsequently denied the request of the Protestants to strike the clause out, he agreed to give them special letters patent, " according to which they shall be able, notwithstanding the aforesaid article, to use, in respect to the holding of consistories, colloquies, synods, etc., the same forms and liberties as heretofore." See Anquez, 191. Other concessions to the parliament related to the " Chamber of the Edict," at Paris, and the promise of Henry to appoint no Protestants to judicial offices in the provinces. De Thou, ix. 279.

the judges by repeating the story to them.   Then turning to
the object of the interview, he told them that he met them,
not like his predecessors, in royal habit or with sword and
cape, but dressed in a simple doublet, like a father speaking
familiarly to his children.   He wished to beg them to verify
the edict he had given to "those of the religion."   It was for
the good of peace, which he had made without the kingdom,
and now wished to establish within it.   He reminded them of
their obligations to him for their very possessions.   If obedience was due to his predecessors, much more was it due to him,
for he had re-established the state.   He knew of the intrigues
set on foot in parliament, at the instigation of factious preachers;
but he would himself deal with these men, and would not wait
for the action of the judges.   It was the same path that had
been taken leading to the Barricades, and by degrees to the assassination of the late king.   He would cut the root of all that,
and put an end to seditious preaching and to those who pro-
moted it.   "I have leaped the walls of cities," said he; "I shall
have no trouble in vaulting over the barricades."   He declared
that, as to the Catholic religion, he was a better Catholic than
they were, and the eldest son of the church, which none of
them could ever be.   As to influence with the pope, he assured
them he had more of it than they had, and that he could, at
pleasure, have them all declared heretics, should they refuse
to obey him.   Nay, he added jocosely, not a thing they could
say or do escaped him, for he had a familiar spirit which revealed all to him.   Those who desired that his edict should
not pass wished him to have a war upon his hands.   Very
well, he would declare it to-morrow against the Protestants,
but he had not any intention of waging it himself.   No; he
would leave that to his hearers, the judges of parliament, who
should go to it marching in their gowns, and would resemble
that famous procession of the Capuchin monks in the time of
the siege of Paris, when each of them carried a musket over
his monastic dress.   A fine sight would they present![1]

---

[1] "Ceux qui ne désirent que mon édict passe me veulent la guerre; je la dé-
clareray demain à ceulx de la Religion, mais je ne la leur feray pas; vous irés

He had formerly played the soldier; there had been murmurs, and he had not seemed to hear. Now he was king, and spoke as a king; he was resolved to be obeyed. The judiciary was indeed his right arm; but when the gangrene attacked the right arm, the left arm must cut it off. When one of his regiments did not serve him, he broke it up; should parliament fail to verify the edict, it would gain nothing—the edict would pass nevertheless. He referred to the action of other parliaments, and declared that their failure to execute his commands had been the occasion of new requests on the part of the Protestants; he did not want the refusal of the Parliament of Paris, on the present occasion, to lead to fresh demands. He spoke with contempt of the men who were now so loud in their professions of devotion to the church and to catholicism. Let him but give to this man a benefice worth two thousand crowns, to that man an income of four thousand livres, their lips would instantly be sealed. He reminded them that the Edict of Nantes was in reality the edict of Henry the Third given in 1577. It was also his own, for Henry the Third had made it with him.[1] Now that he confirmed it, he did not approve of intending to do one thing and writing another. If others had done so, he would not follow their example. Deceit is hateful everywhere, but especially hateful in princes, whose word ought to be immutable. "Concede to my prayers," said Henry, in conclusion, "what you would not like to have conceded to my threats; you will have none from me. Do, I beg you, as speedily as possible what I command you. You will do this not only for me, but also for yourselves, and in the interests of peace."[2]

---

tous, avec vos robes, et ressemblerés la procession des Capucins, qui portoient le mousquet sur leurs habits. Il vous feroit beau voir."

[1] "Considérés que l'edict dont je vous parle c'est l'edict du feu Roy. Il est aussy le mien, car il a esté faict avec moy."

[2] The words of Henry are given with very slight variations in a MS. of the National Library, under the heading " Les paroles que le roy a teneues à Messieurs de la Cour de Parlement le vii février 1599 " (printed in Bulletin de la Société de l'histoire du Protestantisme français, ii. 128–131), and in the Inventaire général de l'histoire de France, ii. 774–776. See, also, De Thou, ix. 276–279; Agrippa d'Aubigné, iii. 461.

These were not the words of one who was constrained, of a prince from whom an obnoxious law was wrung by fears or by threats. They were the earnest expostulations of a king who heartily approved the edict the registration of which he urged, recognizing in it the only basis of lasting peace between his subjects of differing creeds. And it is particularly deserving of notice that, overlooking minor differences, he regarded it as essentially the same edict with that of Poitiers, signed by Henry the Third in September, 1577; an edict which, therefore, Henry of Bourbon, then leader of the Huguenots, had himself sought for, and which he so highly approved that, to use the words of the contemporary historian, Agrippa d'Aubigné, he had adopted it as his own, styling the peace his peace, and displaying great zeal in its observance.[1]

It was useless to make further resistance. On the twenty-fifth of February, 1599, the Edict of Nantes was formally The edict verified by the Parliament of Paris, and was accepted as the law of the land. On the seventeenth of March Henry took steps for its complete execution throughout France, by the appointment of commissioners —a nobleman and a magistrate from each province—to attend to the work.[2]

The edict registered, February 25, 1599.

Not far from a year had been spent in the consideration of the edict by the public; many weeks had the edict been under the minute examination of the highest judicature. But the time had not been lost. The very modifications that had been made in the original document, much as the Huguenots might deplore them, strengthened the law. The delay, the changes, whether for the better or for the worse, made it henceforth impossible for any one to allege, with even a show of truth, that the Edict of Nantes had been passed otherwise than after mature deliberation and with full knowledge of the case. From this time forward the settlement by Henry the Fourth would hold the

---

[1] "Le roi de Navarre avoit fait son propre du traitté, et nommé cette paix sienne, se passionnant à l'observation." Histoire universelle, ii. 328 (bk. iii., ch. 23). See above, vol. i., ch. ii., p. 167.

[2] De Thou, ix. 284.

place of a just and necessary law, and could not honestly be mistaken for a violent compromise framed to put an end to a state trouble.[1]

To judicious men on all sides the Edict of Nantes appeared a measure as opportune as it was just. By none was it welcomed with greater satisfaction than by those candid and reasonable Roman Catholics who, free from jealousy of the inestimable boon of religious liberty which the new law confirmed to the Protestants, thoughtfully considered the immense advantages it conferred upon the adherents of the other creed. In La Rochelle and in more than a hundred other walled towns and cities, and in a thousand parish churches or monasteries, scattered through the provinces of Poitou, Angoumois, Saintonge, Aunis, Dauphiny, Languedoc, and Provence, the celebration of the mass was restored, after having been intermitted for a period of about fifteen years.[2] "Thus is it," observes a historian writing a few years later, "that both Roman Catholics and Protestants, living henceforth under the favor and blessing of the Edict, confess that they owe an undying obligation to his majesty for having, with such admirable wisdom and constancy, removed the cause of civil divisions resulting from difference of religion."[3]

It is welcomed by all reasonable men.

Accordingly the Edict of Nantes was, in the course of time, accepted, not as a temporary expedient, similar to any one of the preceding pacificatory ordinances, not as a law which either the reigning monarch himself or his successors might alter or repeal at will, but as a fundamental law of the state, which, being the result of the mature deliberation and consent of all orders of the kingdom, could be

The Edict of Nantes a fundamental law.

[1] This is the weighty verdict of Duplessis Mornay in his important communication of March 9, 1599, to the new political assembly which, with the king's approval, had succeeded the old assembly at Châtellerault. (See Anquez, 172.) "On ne pourra dire desormais que cest edict n'ait passé avec meure deliberation, et grande cognoissance de cause, pour tenir, d'ici en avant, lieu de loi juste et necessaire, et non plus de transaction violente pour terminer ung trouble d'estat." Mémoires, ix. 247.

[2] Cayet, Chronologie septenaire, 48. The Inventaire général, ii. 808, increases these figures to over 250 walled towns and 2,000 parishes and monasteries. [3] Inventaire général, ubi supra.

abrogated only by the united action of all the parties concerned. This was not a view likely to commend itself to the approval of the courtiers of Louis the Fourteenth, or of any who held the slavish doctrine of the omnipotence of kings; but it was the view of the liberty-loving Huguenots, and, doubtless, of the majority of fair-minded men of whatever religious creed. The doctrine was distinctly propounded by the great orator and preacher, Jean Claude, when the "Grand Monarque" undertook to overthrow the great work of his sire. "It was not," he said, "the sole authority of Henry the Great that established the Edict. We have seen that the Edict is a decree of his justice rendered after both sides had been heard; we have seen that it is an agreement, and, as it were, a compromise made between the Catholics and the Reformed, authorized by the public faith of the entire state, sealed with the seal of the oath, and ratified by the execution. Now this is what renders the Edict inviolable, and places it beyond the reach of Henry's successors. In this respect they can only be the guardians and executors, and not the masters on whose good pleasure it depends. Henry the Great never employed the force of arms to compel the Roman Catholics to consent to it, and, although since his death the states general were held, under the minority of Louis the Thirteenth the Edict remained in force. It is therefore, as we have said, a fundamental law of the kingdom, which the kings cannot touch. But even were it a result of the sole authority of Henry, which is evidently false, it would not follow that the king at present reigning could revoke it. Why? Because there are many things that depend upon one's good pleasure to do, but not upon one's good pleasure to undo; and of this nature is the Edict. It is a royal promise which Henry the Great made to the Reformed of his kingdom, as well for himself as for his successors forever, and consequently it is a condition, or, if you will, an encumbrance, which he has laid upon his inheritance, and from which his heirs are no longer at liberty to divest themselves."[1]

---

[1] Jean Claude, Les Plaintes des Protestans cruellement opprimez dans le Royaume de France, 145–147.

It is of interest to note how the edict that gave such satisfaction to all the best men of both religions throughout France,

Displeasure of Pope Clement the Eighth. the edict that was to render it possible for Huguenots and Roman Catholics to live in peace and amity, as citizens of the same commonwealth, regardful of one
another's rights while mindful each of his own, was received at
Rome.

On Saturday, the twenty-seventh of March, 1599, soon after
the news of the registration of the Edict of Nantes by the Parliament of Paris reached the Eternal City, Clement the Eighth
summoned the French envoys to an audience, of which Cardinal
d'Ossat has left us a lengthy and precise report.

"I am the most grieved and disconsolate person in the
world," said the pope, "because of the edict which the King of
France has made in favor of the heretics, and to the prejudice
of the Catholic religion. This edict has at last passed and has
been published, contrary to the hope I had always entertained
since it was spoken of. I had always believed that the king
made it merely to satisfy the Huguenots in appearance, and that
he would have been very glad to have the clergy oppose it and
parliament refuse to pass it in order to use this excuse subsequently with the Huguenots. Now I see quite the opposite of
what I had expected of the king. First, I see an edict the most
accursed that can be imagined, whereby liberty of conscience is
granted to every one, which is the worst thing in the world.[1] In
addition to this, the worship of that damnable sect is permitted
throughout the whole kingdom ; the heretics are introduced into
the courts of parliament, and admitted to all charges, honors, and
dignities, so that they will henceforth oppose everything that
may turn to the advantage of the Catholic religion, and will pro-
mote and further heresy. Moreover, I see that the king has
made this edict at a time when he is at peace both within and

---

[1] " Premierement, il voioit un Edit le plus maudit qui se pouvoit imaginer
(ce sont ses mots, que nous vous reciterons ici, et tout le long de cete letre,
sans y rien mêler du nôtre), par lequel Edit étoit permise liberté de conscience
à tout chacun, qui étoit la pire chose du monde." Cardinal d'Ossat to Henry
IV., Rome, March 28, 1599, Lettres, ii. 44.

without his realm ; so that it cannot be said that he has been
forced to make it.   When the other kings made similar edicts, it
was clearly seen that they were compelled to do so, because there
were armies of heretics in the field and open war.   Besides, the
other kings were Catholics, and were grievously offended by the
heretics ; so that they could not be suspected of having any
inclination toward those people, whatever they might be seen
doing.   In the third place, I take it as a very evil augury, and
it grieves me extremely, that his majesty has exhibited such
zeal and ardor to have this edict pass.   In all other civil affairs
he has ever shown great moderation, but in this he has betrayed
extraordinary vehemence.   The clergy opposed it, parliament
refused it ; but the king, instead of using this as an excuse against
the Huguenots, became greatly incensed against the Catholics,
set them at defiance, threatened them, and finally constrained
them by force to submit to an edict pernicious to the Catholic
religion.   He was even indignant with the Archbishop of Tours
for having caused prayers to be said to God that this edict
might not be passed and that He would give the king His inspiration.   There can be no good reason or cause for his majesty's fearing or esteeming the heretics, who are the worse, the
less numerous, and the feebler part of the kingdom, more than
he does the Catholics, who are the better part and the more
considerable in numbers, quality, and power.   It is a very bad
sign that, when it is proposed to secure the passage of an edict
in favor of the heretics and against the Catholics, he takes offence, speaks authoritatively, says that he will be obeyed ; and
yet, that to secure the reception and publication of the decrees
of the Council of Trent, which is a thing holy in itself, and one
that he has promised and sworn to do, he has never once spoken
of it to parliament, which is said to be less inclined toward it
than it ought to be.   It alarms me that he so takes to heart the
interests of the heretics, and is so lukewarm in what concerns
the Catholic religion, the fulfilment of his promise and oath,
and his conscience.   I no longer know what to hope for, or
what to think.   I absolved him and recognized him as king
contrary to the advice of the greatest and most powerful princes
of Christendom, who predicted at the time that I should find

myself cheated. Yet I did not fail to do all that I could for the king's contentment and for his greatness; nor did I stop until I had given him peace both within and without his realm. And now the return I am to receive for all this is that I shall become the laughing-stock of the whole world."

Such were some of the complaints of the pope, who added much more to the same purpose, and wrought himself up to so high a pitch of excitement as even to inform Cardinal d'Ossat that, as he had not hesitated to leap the ditch one way to give the king his absolution, so he would not shrink from crossing the chasm once more in an opposite direction were it necessary to do so.[1]

---

[1] Ibid., ubi supra. Needless to say that the shrewd ambassador did not fail to use his opportunity to mollify the angry pontiff, going to the length of endeavoring to convince him that he was grossly misinformed respecting the contents of the edict, and boldly averring that his majesty had never made the speech to the parliament which had been published to the world under his name. " Que nous connoissions bien, que Sa Sainteté avoit veu un certain écrit, qu'on avoit fait courir sous le nom et titre de réponse, que Votre Majesté eût faite à ceux de ladite Cour de Parlement ; et voulions avertir Sa Sainteté que c'étoit un écrit faux et suposé, contenant plusieurs choses que Votre Majesté n'avoit jamais dites ; et que Sa Sainteté n'y devoit point ajoûter foi, comme nous en avions été avertis par ceux qui étoient auprès de Votre Majesté."

CHAPTER XV.

AFTER THE EDICT.

THE twelve years which intervened between the promulgation of the Edict of Nantes and the death of Henry the Fourth constitute the halcyon days of the Huguenots of France. No such period of comparative peace and prosperity had preceded the adoption of the great law for their protection. Behind the Protestants were three-quarters of a century characterized by persecutions, wars, and massacres, with intervals of tranquillity scarcely sufficiently long to enable them to recover breath and prepare for the advent of new severities. Before them, though happily they knew it not as yet, there lay another term of three-quarters of a century, of which, if a considerable portion was to be peaceful and pros-perous, the later years would be mainly notable for the gradual infringement of the provisions of their cherished edict, and would end in the formal abrogation of that edict under circumstances of peculiar disregard of the dictates of natural justice ; while, still beyond, there stretched more than one hundred years of pro-scription, a whole century during which all worship of Almighty God, all administration of the sacraments of Baptism and the Lord's Supper, the singing of the old Huguenot psalms, the very possession of the Huguenot Bible, would be forbidden—during which the galleys would be the punishment meted out to such laymen as ventured to frequent the religious assemblies held on the bleak Cévennes, and death upon the wheel would await the venturesome minister of the Gospel whom the love of the souls of his brethren in the faith might attract to the sunny but dan-gerous plains of Languedoc.

The story of the interval during which the Protestants could claim the protection of a monarch not ill-disposed toward them,

A period of comparative quiet.

while less crowded with stirring events than the previous period, possesses its own peculiar interest. The Huguenots began at once to enjoy their well-earned peace. Not, indeed, that their opponents made haste to concede the rights which the law of Henry had granted or confirmed. If the Parliament of Paris had, in this regard, been slow, the other sovereign courts were still more dilatory. The judges of Grenoble waited until September, 1599 ; those of Dijon, Toulouse, and Bordeaux until January, 1600, before they could be induced to give the edict official recognition. At Rennes, the Parliament of Brittany took a year to make up its mind to submit to the king's command, registering the law on the twenty-third of August, 1600. The Parliament of Aix-en-Provence had done likewise earlier in the same month ; while the refractory Parliament of Normandy, in session at Rouen, did, indeed, enter the obnoxious law upon its records within three months from the time of its reception, but accompanied it with modifications and saving clauses, calculated to rob it of much of its usefulness to the Protestants, which it declined, for a period of not less than ten years, to erase. Only on the fifth of August, 1609, did these stubborn magistrates consent to receive the edict in its official shape, at the same time making a minute of the fact that they accepted the law " on the very express command of the king, several times repeated, both by word of mouth and in writing." [1]

Dilatoriness of the parliaments.

It may not be amiss to refer briefly to the conduct of two or three of these judicial bodies. After deliberating upon the edict for more than three weeks, the Parliament of Bordeaux resolved to send a deputation to the king with a budget of complaints, which might be summed up under three heads, according as they were directed against the extension given to Protestant worship, the admission of Protestants to all offices, and the re-establishment of the hated " chambres mi-parties " and " tri-parties." The deputies were instructed to inform his majesty that, unless these points

The Parliament of Bordeaux.

---

[1] See Anquez, Histoire des assemblées politiques des Réformés de France, 177–180.

should be remedied, the parliament would never receive the edict of its own accord, preferring that the king should do everything of his sovereign authority rather than submit to voluntary degradation. But the envoys returned home with the unwelcome intelligence that Henry not only blamed the judges severely for their remonstrances, but threatened them with suspension or removal.

President Chessac and counsellor Jessac had surprised King Henry while he was frolicking with his children in the great hall of the castle of Saint Germain-en-Laye, but his majesty was not at all disconcerted by their unexpected apparition. "Do not think it strange," said he, "that you see me sporting with these little children. I can beget children, and I know how to undo men. I have just been playing the fool with my children ; now I am going to play the wise man with you and give you audience." So saying he led the way into an adjoining chamber, where for a whole hour and a quarter he listened attentively to what the president had to say. At the conclusion he had the good grace to congratulate the orator upon his harangue, declaring that never in all his life had he heard anything better spoken. " But," said he, "I would that the body corresponded with the garment in which it is arrayed ; for I see clearly that your maxims and your proposals are precisely the same as those which the late Cardinal of Lorraine set forth before the late king, in the city of Lyons, when his majesty was on his return from Poland, tending to the commotion in the state which we have witnessed. Thank God, we have obtained the peace we so longed for. It has cost us too much that we should endanger it by troubles. I mean to continue that peace, and to inflict exemplary chastisement upon any man that may undertake to introduce change. I am your lawful king, your head." Then alluding to the orator's boast that, alone among the parliaments of France, the court he represented had remained steadfast in its loyalty, he remarked with biting sarcasm : " Assuredly, you were very fortunate in that. Yet, after God, we must ascribe the praise not merely to you, who never lacked the evil disposition to create a disturbance like the rest, but to the late Marshal Matignon, who held a tight rein over you and prevented

Henry's address to the judges.

you from doing so. Long ago, when only King of Navarre, I
understood your complaint full well, but had not the remedies
at hand. Now that I am King of France I comprehend it still
better, and I have the medicines to cure it and to cause those to
repent who would oppose my commands. I have made an edict.
I intend that it shall be observed. Whatever may happen, I
mean to be obeyed. It will be well for you if you do so." [1]

Nor were Henry's menaces all. Chancellor Bellièvre and
Marshal Ornano wrote letters directly to the judges, and counselled submission to the royal will, assuring them "that the
king had given the edict to the Huguenots by treaty and, as it
were, by contract, and that so his faith was pledged." [2] The
judges of Bordeaux thereupon registered the edict " by the very
express command of the king, and without approval of any
other religion than the Roman Catholic." But their perverse
opposition did not end here. Unable to annul, they attempted
to thwart. In no case was the letter, much less the spirit, of
the provisions admitting Protestants to office duly observed.
True, the Protestant members of the Chamber of Nérac were
by letters patent accorded the same salaries, honors, authority,
and rank as their Roman Catholic associates; but the parliament registered that document only upon condition that they
be styled " counsellors in the court and chamber of the edict,"
and be not reckoned as forming part of the parliamentary body.
When, therefore, they presented themselves to take the customary oath, they were excused from doing so on the ground that
they had already been sworn in the presence of the chancellor.
Good care was taken not to inscribe their names on the tabular
statement made up at the beginning of each year, and, to facilitate the omission, the names of their Roman Catholic colleagues
were likewise left out. There was little prospect that a cham-

---

[1] "Reponse du Roy à messieurs les depputez de Bourdeaux, messieurs le
second président Chessac et conseiller Jessac et autres, faicte à Sainct Germain
en Laye, le 3e de nov. 1599, sur la verification de l'edict de Nantes." MSS.
Nat. Library. Lettres missives, v. 180, 181.

[2] "Que le roi avait baillé l'édit aux huguenots par traité et quasi par contrat,
et qu'ainsi sa foi était engagée." Boscheron des Portes, Histoire du parlement
de Bordeaux, i. 325.

ber so treated would prove to be of much practical utility, especially when the judges were themselves equally divided between the two opposing faiths.[1]

The king granted audience to the deputies from the Parliament of Toulouse upon the same day on which he met their colleagues of Bordeaux. His reply to their remonstrance was determined, almost angry. "It is strange," said he, "that you cannot cast out your ill-will. I perceive very well that you still have the Spaniard in your belly! Who would believe it, that those who have hazarded life, property, and honor for the defence and preservation of this kingdom are to be deemed unworthy of honorable and public trusts, like treacherous Leaguers who deserve to be set upon and driven from the kingdom? Meanwhile, the men that have left no stone unturned to ruin the state would be regarded as good Frenchmen, meriting and competent to hold offices! I am not blind; I see clearly. I mean that 'those of the Religion' shall live in peace in my kingdom, and be capable of taking office; not because they are of the 'Religion,' but inasmuch as they have been faithful servants of mine and of the French crown. I am determined to be obeyed. I am resolved that my edict be published throughout my kingdom. It is time that all of us, sated with war, should learn wisdom from our own experience."[2]

Henry and the Parliament of Toulouse.

These were not the words of a monarch upon whom an unwelcome law had been forced by rebellious subjects, and who was engaged in an unpalatable undertaking when striving to secure for it judicial recognition. The integrity and patriotism of the Huguenots could not have been more distinctly indorsed; their claim to grateful recognition on the part of the king, whom they had been mainly instrumental in placing upon the throne, could not have been more frankly admitted.

Nor did Henry's zeal cool down with the lapse of time. We have seen that the Edict of Nantes was not recorded in its in-

---

[1] Boscheron des Portes, Histoire du parlement de Bordeaux, i. 325–329.

[2] "La Réponse du Roy aux depputez de Tholose touchant la verification de l'edict de Nantes." MSS. Nat. Library. Lettres missives, v. 181, 182.

tegrity upon the books of the Parliament of Normandy until
August, 1609, that is to say, less than a year before the monarch's death. If the judges were obstinate, if the con-

The Parlia-
ment of
Rouen.

test was, as has been suggested, the longest and most
determined in which a parliament of France is known
ever to have engaged, certainly Henry, though slow in coming to extreme measures, was not less resolute than they. He
had about reached the conclusion to send commissioners to execute the law at Rouen, even without a previous registration, to
grant the Protestants of Normandy the right to remove all their
cases from the supreme court of the province to the " Chamber
of the Edict" at Paris, possibly even to suspend the functions
of the Parliament of Rouen altogether, when the latter discovered its error and remedied it. If the last to come to terms,
this body was also the only one of the great judicial bodies that
ultimately recorded the edict without any modifications. It was
characteristic of Henry of Bourbon that, even through his justifiable irritation at the parliament's exasperating refusals, his native good-humor and kindliness of disposition did not fail to manifest themselves. He condescended to reason with the judges.
" Had you known the damage," said he, " which this delay in-
flicts upon my affairs, I will presume so much upon your affection as to believe that you would not have proved so intractable;
if only for the reason that you thus expose me to a ceaseless importunity, and leave me burdened by extraordinary expenses for
the maintenance of the garrisons in the cities which the Protestants retain and will not restore until after my edict shall have
been everywhere recorded. You must yield. I beg you to do so."[1]

Meanwhile, if the parliaments were stubborn in their resistance, the Huguenots were not wanting in urgent efforts to se-

Persistence of
the Hugue-
nots.

cure the full execution of the edict. Unwilling to
abandon the slightest point that had been granted to
them, many of the leaders insisted that the king should
restore to the edict even those features—referred to in the
last chapter of this history—of minor importance though they

---

[1] A full account is given in Floquet, Histoire du parlement de Normandie,
iv. 261–269.

might be, which had been removed for the purpose of breaking the force of their opponents' objections. The more judicious, however, were by no means disposed to endanger the permanence of the great boon which had been secured by ill-timed demands for more; and his majesty himself was firm in the refusal to reopen the matter. Doubtless, the objects which the Huguenots had in view were the most proper and just; but it required all the influence which could be exerted by Duplessis Mornay, and by other men of the same stamp, to impress upon their more excitable and impulsive, but not less conscientious, brethren the importance of distinguishing between what was necessary to the very existence of the churches and what was merely conducive to comfort and ease. The great man just named was no blind optimist, bent upon persuading himself and others that the perfect ideal of religious prosperity had been reached. But he saw in the present state of things clear grounds for joy and for gratitude to the Almighty.

"Our churches," he wrote to a friend across the Channel, "enjoy, by the grace of God, and under the blessing of the king's edicts, a condition which they are not disposed to change. The Gospel is freely preached, and not without prog- Hopeful condition of the churches. ress. Justice is dispensed to us. We have towns in which we can take shelter from the storm. If any infraction of the law occurs, our complaints are listened to; frequently reparation is made. We might wish that in many localities our places of worship were nearer or more convenient; that we had a greater share in the distribution of honors and offices; and, possibly, this would be neither without its advantages nor unmerited by our past services. But these are things to be desired, not to be exacted; matters for complaint either emanating from Christians who are too delicate, or based on purely human considerations. To set the world in commotion for this, even in the slightest degree, we are not at all inclined. God knows the progress that He wishes to grant to His Church, and He has the means in His own hand. To us it belongs not to rush forward, but to draw back from passing the bounds of piety and justice. Only, may it please God to preserve our king for us, to maintain him in his present disposition to avert

all contrary counsels. I deny not, however, that our churches
have apprehensions—fears which, as says the jurisconsult, fall
even upon constant men—when they hear that the Jesuits,
those firebrands of Christendom, take possession of his ears;
when, from time to time, that society proposes the establishment of the decrees of the Council of Trent." [1]

The fact was the condition of the Huguenots was one in which
hope and fear were mingled, but in which hope preponderated
over fear. The malice of their enemies had not been removed,
and a watchful clergy was ever ready to take advantage of prejudices long rife among the people. Yet that malice was well
kept in check by a government generally inclined to be cautious,
often to be conspicuously fair. At times the magistrates even
went to the length of prohibiting popular songs which, because

Seditious
songs pro-
scribed.
insulting to the Protestants, might at any moment become the cause of sedition. So it fared with a frivolous ditty entitled " La vache à Colas," which, Lestoile
tells us, had attained such wide currency that, at Paris and in all
the towns and villages of France, scarcely anything else was

"La vache à
Colas."
heard. Great and small vied with one another, and
delighted themselves, above all, in singing it at every
Huguenot door, to provoke the inmates, until such time as the
authorities made proclamation, at the sound of the trumpet (on
the tenth of September, 1605), forbidding its repetition in the
streets. Yet the production, which occasioned much scandal
and some bloodshed, was as silly as it was weak; having for
subject the misfortune of poor Nicolas or Colas, whose cow was
said to have found her way into a Protestant "prêche," at
Orleans or Chartres, during the time of service, and had been
killed by the terrified attendants. [2]

Occasionally, but, it is to be feared, not very often, the Protestant and Roman Catholic communities lived together in a charity well worthy of being called Christian. The little town of
Castelmoron, in the very centre of the modern department of

---

[1] Duplessis Mornay to M. de la Fontaine, March 26, 1604, Mémoires, v. 539,
540.

[2] Lestoile, ii. 387.

Lot-et-Garonne, presented a signal instance, which, but for the fortunate preservation of a stray legal document, might never have been known to posterity. This is nothing less than a compact, solemnly attested, between the adherents of the two religions, to continue to use in common the parish cemetery, as well as the belfry and the bell, and more especially to contribute, each according to his means, as determined by the tax-roll, to the repairs to the belfry, now in a dangerous condition. Castelmoron was situated in the midst of a region formerly the scene of Blaise de Montluc's barbarous exploits ; yet this document vouches for the fact that, "since the rise of the troubles in France resulting from diversity of religions, the inhabitants of this town, parish, and jurisdiction, by God's blessing, have deported themselves so kindly to one another, under the tolerance of the king's edicts, that they have had no debates or contentions on account of religion, whether for its worship, for the burial of the deceased of either religion, for the use of bell and belfry, or for other matters which have caused many contests elsewhere. On the contrary, the inhabitants of both religions have buried their dead in the parish cemetery, and in the tombs of their ancestors, without distinction of persons, and have made use of the bell to call the people to divine worship, to hear the 'prêches' and sermons, and to celebrate baptisms, marriages, and other exercises of God's service."[1]

Castelmoron, a model of Christian charity.

Of the condition and prospects of the Huguenots at this epoch in their history we have a quaint account in the treatise of Sir Edwin Sandys, entitled "Europæ Speculum," written in Paris itself, just after the verification of the Edict of Nantes by the Parliament of Paris. "Of France," says the author, "how much the better it is known unto us at home, so much the less shall I need to speak much in this place. Neither is it very easy to proportion the parties, by reason they of the Religion are so scattered in all places. Yet in Poitou they have almost all ; in Gascoignie, an half ; in Languedoc,

Sir Edwin Sandys' view.

---

[1] "Accord entre les catholiques et les protestants de Castelmoron, en Agenais, 13 septembre, 1609." Bulletin de la Société de l'histoire du Protestantisme français, ii. 502–505.

Normandy, and other west-maritime provinces, a reasonable strong part; as likewise in sundry Mediterranean, of which Delphinat (Dauphiny) the chief. But whatsoever be the proportion of their number to their opposites, which is manifoldly inferior—not one in twenty—their strength is such as their wars have witnessed; and especially that at this day, after such massacring them, so general a rising of the whole realm against them, by the utmost extremity of fire and sword to exterminate them, they are esteemed to be stronger than at any time heretofore—in sum, so strong that neither have their adversaries, I trow, any great hope and themselves no fear to be borne down by war. That the practices of peace by partiality and injustice in their suits litigious (which hath already sorely bitten and afflicted their estates), by depriving them of place of office and honor in the realm, by confining the exercise of their religion into chambers or remote corners, did not impoverish, abase, and dishearten their party, and so withdraw those from them which would otherwise stick to them—this is that which they have misdoubted, and which by the edict now passed and verified they have sought to remedy.

" But, looking a little more attentively into this party, I find that, as conscience in what religion soever doth, even in the mists of error, breed an honestness of mind and integrity of life and actions in whom it settleth (of so divine and pure virtue is the love of the Creator, which is the ground of all that merit the· name of religious), so also that in them which affect the greatest singleness, and, in a manner, a very careless simplicity in their religion, as contenting themselves with the possession of the rich treasure of truth, and for the preserving of it or themselves recommending those cases to God only, yet tract of affliction, much misery, often overreaching by subtlety of adversaries, doth finally purge out those gross-witted humors and engender a very curious and advantageous wariness in all their proceedings; having learned by experience the wisdom of that aphorism, that a small error in the foundation and beginning of all things doth prove in the proceeding and end of them a great mischief. As hath fallen out in these men, who do as far here outgo their opposites in all civil policies as in other places they of their religion are lightly outgone by them. Which, next unto the divine blessing which accompanieth good causes, where wickedness or wilful witlessness does not bar against it, I account the chief reason of their present strength and assurance. By their providence in their capitulations, by their resoluteness in their executions, by their industry and dexterity in all occasions presented, they have possessed themselves of an exceeding great number of towns and places. There is scant any office or estate can fall void but they lay in by all means to get into it. They have their synods for their church affairs, their conventions and councils for their civil. Their people is warlike, and so will they continue them. Their only want is of a prince of the blood to grace them; for as for leaders, a matter of main importance, they are still above their adversaries, having, besides those three of principal and known name, sundry other in Gascoignie of less place and degree, but in skill and prowess not inferior to the best. In fine, they have learned the wisdom of *Spes sibi quisque* and μέμνησο ἀπιστεῖν, the contrary whereof before brought them so near to their ruin." [1]

The difficulty experienced by Sir Edwin in estimating the number of the adherents of the Protestant religion in France still invests the subject; not, indeed, that all data are wanting, but because of the somewhat vague and contradictory statements

---

[1] Europæ Speculum; or, a View or Survey of the State of Religion in the Westerne parts of the World (Hagæ-Comitis, 1629), 176–179. This interesting production, the fruit of extended travels and personal observation in different countries of Europe, is in the form of a letter of about two hundred and fifty pages, addressed to John Whitgift, Archbishop of Canterbury, and dated Paris, April 9, 1599. The object of the learned author (son and namesake of the distinguished reforming Archbishop of York) was not merely to inquire into the condition of Christendom, but to discover "what possibility and good means there may be of uniting at leastwise the several branches of the Reformed professors, if unity universal be more to be desired than hoped." The Europæ Speculum was not published, except in a garbled form, until thirty years after its composition; but the garbled edition in question had already been translated into Italian, and had been honored with a place in the "Index librorum prohibitorum," where it still figures: "Sandis, Edoino, Relatione dello stato della Religione, etc.," condemned by decree of February 4, 1627.

that have come down to us. It would seem, however, that Sandys, in reducing the Huguenots to less than a twentieth part of the population of France, has fallen into almost as great an error as those other writers who represent them as constituting a full third of the kingdom. According to a writer whose accuracy is unfortunately as open to suspicion as his honesty is
Protestant statistics. above reproach, Henry the Fourth instituted a census of his Protestant subjects, in part to gratify the curiosity of Queen Elizabeth of England. Upon its completion, in March, 1598, it was found that the Huguenot community consisted of two hundred and seventy-four thousand families, or one million and a quarter of souls. Of these families, two thousand four hundred and sixty-eight ranked as noble. Of churches there were nine hundred and fifty-one ; six hundred and ninety-four being public, and two hundred and fifty-seven attached to fiefs. The ministers of the Gospel were said to number two thousand eight hundred, and the "proposants," or candidates for the ministry, four hundred.[1] Implicit confidence cannot be reposed in these statistics. The number of ministers, which may be an error of the pen for eight hundred, is greatly overstated. The number of churches exceeds considerably the seven hundred and sixty-three reported by the Synod of Montpellier, in the month of May, 1598,[2] the seven hundred and fifty-three reported by the Synod of Jargeaux, in 1601,[3] the seven hundred and fifty-eight reported by the Synod of La Rochelle, in 1607,[4] and the eight hundred and seven reported by the Synod of Alençon, in 1637.[5] It may, however, be concluded with safety

---

[1] Gregorio Leti, in his Italian life of Queen Elizabeth, ii. 348, apud Bulletin de la Société de l'histoire du Protestantisme français,.i. 123, 124, where M. Eugène Haag has briefly discussed these figures.

[2] Aymon, Tous les Synodes, i. 226.

[3] Ibid., i. 252, 253.

[4] Ibid., i. 340, 341.

[5] Ibid., i. 291–306 (of Introduction). This last list is particularly valuable, both because of its detail and of the fact that it was the last drawn up before the suppression of the national synods of the Reformed churches. The considerable increase in the number of individual churches is due to the circumstance that those of Béarn, not previously included in the enumeration, and amounting to forty-seven in all, are added to the list.

that the Protestants of France, including Henry's hereditary
kingdom of Navarre, at the end of the sixteenth and in the beginning of the seventeenth century, constituted a body of one
million or one million and a quarter of souls—possibly one-
twelfth or one-fifteenth of the entire population—and boasting
between eight hundred and one thousand churches, large and
small, where divine worship was conducted by a somewhat
smaller number of ordained ministers, never, perhaps, exceeding
seven or eight hundred.[1]

One matter seemed likely to furnish subject for contention
between the crown and the adherents of the Reformed faith.
Their "political assemblies" had too long proved serviceable
to the Protestants that they should be willing to renounce the
liberty to convene them. It was the misfortune of
the position into which the malice of their foes, and
especially the League, had driven them, that the Huguenots
seemed to occupy the attitude of an armed force compelled ever
to be on the alert to ward off the hostile attacks to which they
were exposed. Under such circumstances, deprived, as they
were, of that protection which, under a more stable and equitable government, they might have invoked from the laws, and
liable to the additional peril of finding in unfriendly governors
and prejudiced judges their most formidable enemies—since
the former might defy the edict, the latter render its provisions
of no avail by chicanery—the Huguenots set a high price
upon the unity of action afforded to them by their representative bodies, and particularly by those that had to do with the
more secular concerns of the churches. Through the political
assemblies, provincial and national, the sense of the Reformed
community could at any time be quickly and certainly ascertained, measures of self-defence be prudently concerted, a har-
monious plan of action be adopted. To the monarch, for the
very same reason, these gatherings were suspicious; and the
prince who, before his accession to the throne, had seen in them
a very legitimate and very acceptable means of advancing his

*Political as-
semblies.*

---

[1] On the list last named there are six hundred and forty-seven names of
pastors. See the remarks of Benoist, i. 257.

interests, now frowned upon them as tending to form or per-
petuate an ecclesiastical republic within the bounds of the civil
commonwealth.[1]

Henry did, indeed, grant permission to the political assembly
of Châtellerault, before its adjournment in June, 1598, to make
provision for another similar body to convene at Saumur and
remain together until the formal publication of the Edict of
Nantes by the Parliament of Paris. It may be that his majesty
entertained less apprehension that this body might procure him
annoyance, from the fact that it had been stipulated that the
selection of its members should virtually be left to him. Each
of the provinces did, indeed, nominate three candidates to
represent it, but to the crown was left the designation of
the one who should go to Saumur.[2] In the unsettled condition of their affairs, it appeared only reasonable, even to the
king, that the Protestants, whose interests were so vitally concerned, should be able to act in a corporate capacity, in case
of any sudden emergency. Subsequently his majesty interposed no considerable objection to the prolongation of the
existence of the assembly until the establishment of the
"chambre mi-partie" at Nérac. But when this had been
effected (September, 1600), and the assembly of
Saumur still continued its sessions, the king exhibited his displeasure and called for the dispersion of the members.[3]

Assembly of
Saumur, 1600.

Some Protestants, among them Duke Claude de la Trémouille, remonstrated with the assembly against what they
considered an abuse of the royal patience. But the members

---

[1] "Le roy a congédié l'assemblée de Saumur," wrote the Duke of Bouillon,
"monstrant avoir quelque jalousie que cela formast un corps dans son estat."
Bouillon to Bongars, apud Anquez, 186.

[2] Anquez, 172. This author says (p. 208) that in 1601 the Protestants counted fifteen provinces. His list, however, includes only fourteen. There was a
considerable fluctuation in the designation.

[3] See especially the letter of Fresnes-Forget, Secretary of State, to Duplessis
Mornay, St. Germain, March 27, 1601, in Mémoires, ix. 408-409. The secretary
asked Duplessis Mornay to use his influence in persuading the assembly to
disband. If there should be any opposition to the king's will, he told him,
"without doubt you will be credited with it."

saw in the horizon such signs of danger as seemed to justify their remaining together.[1] They consequently asked for the intercession of the National Synod, then in session at Jargeaux, and that body appointed the eminent pastor and professor Daniel Chamier, together with the sieur Maravat, to go to court and beg his majesty to be pleased to grant the prolongation of the assembly of Saumur. But Henry was inflexible.[2] All that he would consent to was that the Protestants should be permitted to have one or two deputies at court, to present such petitions and complaints as their fellow religionists might wish to make to the king, and that they should hold an assembly for the purpose of appointing these deputies.[3] The assembly of Saumur consequently broke up on the thirty-first of May, 1601, and on the sixteenth of October of the same year the assembly of Sainte Foy met. That very day the delegates performed the duty which had called them together, by electing two deputies general to reside at Paris and watch over the interests of the Protestant cause throughout the whole kingdom. Both were to hold office for twelve months, but were to spend an additional month in instructing their successors in the matters which it was essential that they should know.

Assembly of
Sainte Foy,
October, 1601.

---

[1] It would appear from a document in the Mémoires de Duplessis Mornay, ix. 398–400—"Lettre de messieurs de l'assemblée generale, estant lors à Saulmur, à M. de la Trémouille," January 4, 1601—that the king's Roman Catholic advisers, prompted by the Jesuits, were endeavoring to overset the "brevet"—one of the four documents together constituting the compact of Nantes. The effort was the more likely to be successful, as the "brevet" bore only the signature of the king and the indorsement of one of the secretaries of state; although Henry, when granting it, had promised to secure it as complete validity as if it had been given under the great seal and verified by the parliaments. From another paper in the same collection, ix. 406— "Advis de M. Duplessis pour Messieurs Saincte Chaste et Burnier, allant en court," February 27, 1601—we learn of a scheme to take the government of the Huguenot cities of security from the hands of their exclusively Protestant magistrates and divide it equally between the adherents of the two opposing creeds.

[2] Henri IV. à l'assemblée de Saumur, May 1, 1601. Anquez, appendice, 509–510.

[3] Article XXXII., Matiéres particuliéres, Synode de Gergeau (May 9–25, 1601), in Aymon, i. 250 ; Soulier, Histoire des édits de pacification, 240, 241 ; Letter of Bouillon to Bongars, ubi supra.

Although it would seem that no distinction was drawn between their powers, a discrimination was made in favor of the deputy chosen from the nobles in respect of salary; he was to receive six thousand livres, while the member from the "third estate" was paid one-quarter less.

This step was an important one. For the first time the Huguenots were permitted official representation at court, in the person of one or two men of tried fidelity and ability, expressly chosen that they might be present to notice and remonstrate against any infraction of the edict, now become a fundamental law of the realm, as well as to urge upon the king any measure which might be necessary for the defence of their brethren in the faith. Receiving a salary, liberal in amount for the times, and thus raised above the necessity, if not the temptation, of receiving bribes, they were sworn not to accept any office, money, or benefice during their term of service, and to exact from government the appropriation promised for the support of the Protestant ministers of the Gospel, as well as the sums for the maintenance of the garrisons in the cities placed in Protestant hands.[1] Scarcely could a better plan have been devised for preserving the rights of the churches and for reducing the probability of disruption. To use the figure of a contemporary, the deputies general were the two eyes of the Huguenot churches, without which they must have groped their way and lived in darkness, but possessing which they were able to keep themselves well advised respecting the designs of their enemies, and defer, if they could not ultimately dissipate, the storms to which they were exposed.[2]

From Messrs. de Saint Germain and Desbordes-Mercier, the first persons elected to this responsible position, to the Marquis

The deputies general.

---

[1] Anquez, 208, 209.

[2] "La présence des députés généraux auprès du roi a de grandes utilités, en ce qu'ils entretiennent la liaison avec notre prince, sollicitent l'exécution des choses promises, observent la bonne ou mauvaise foi dont on y procéde et en donnent avis partout, reçoivent et font retentir les griefs qui peuvent survenir d'heure à autre, et, ès cas inopinés, ont seuls vocation de donner conseil à toutes nos Eglises en général, lesquelles, sans ces deux yeux, ne peuvent marcher qu'à tâtons et vivre en ténèbres." Duplessis Mornay, May 21, 1620, apud Anquez, 226.

of Ruvigny and his son, the later Earl of Galway, who successively held office in the reign of Louis the Fourteenth, the deputies general of the Huguenots, with scarcely an exception, deserved well of their constituents, by reason of their faithfulness, integrity, and enlightened zeal for the interests of Protestantism.

The assembly of Sainte Foy had intended that another assembly, to be held the next year, should select the successors of the deputies general whom it had chosen; but Henry had no notion of establishing a precedent for such annual convocations. For two years he was deaf to all the solicitations that were addressed to him, insisting that the present deputies should continue their functions without a re-election. When, at last, he consented that a political assembly of the Protestants should be held at Châtellerault, he burdened the grant with unwel-
The assembly of Châtellerault, July, 1606. come conditions. This was to be the last gathering of the kind; its numbers were to be limited to two members from each province; it must concern itself only with the election of the deputies general, and take the place of the National Synod appointed for La Rochelle; worst of all, it must admit to its sessions a royal commissioner, with very evident designs upon the independence of the debates. And when, late in July, 1606, the assembly opened, M. de Rosny, known later as the Duke of Sully, appeared as such commissioner, with instructions that revealed fully the monarch's attitude toward his Protestant subjects. They would be permitted to make no new demands, to elect no protector of their churches—the king claimed that title as his own exclusive right. As to their deputies general, the assembly might either choose twelve candidates, of whom the king would take six, two by two, to reside near his person successively for two years; or, each province might choose the two deputies general in succession; or, if neither plan pleased them, they might elect six persons at once, of whom the king would take two to fill the places of the present incumbents.

Meanwhile, Rosny was allowed to hold forth hopes to the Protestants that, if they were moderate in their claims for money, his majesty would prolong the term during which they

might retain their cautionary cities beyond the eight years stipulated at Nantes.[1]

The assembly of Châtellerault, fearful lest the king might
remain constant in his resolution not to bring his Huguenot
subjects together again in a similar convocation, took good care
before adjourning to provide against that contingency by ordering that, unless an assembly should be called for the year 1607,
the National Synod be charged with the duty of electing the
deputies general and with the consideration of the other external interests of the churches. The plan was not displeasing to
the king, who, accordingly, when the eighteenth of the French
Protestant National Synods met in La Rochelle (March and
April, 1607), ordered it to make choice of six persons for the
office of deputy general, from whom he would himself select
two to serve for three years.[2] But true to the Huguenot traditions, which drew a clear line of demarcation between the
prerogatives of the national synod and those of the political
assembly, the Synod of La Rochelle showed no inclination to
intrude of its own accord, or to be forced by others,
to encroach upon the functions of the sister body. It
did indeed make choice of deputies general, but only
two in number, alleging that the instructions of none of its
members made mention of more. It declined to take the responsibility of prolonging their term of office, and begged the
king to authorize the convocation of a political assembly, as
being the only body which could lawfully take cognizance of
any modification either in the number or in the term of service
of the deputies.[3]

The Synod of La Rochelle, 1607.

This was the old Huguenot spirit, keen in its sense of justice,
too conscientious in the defence of right, too frank in speech,
too republican, if we may say so, to please a king who was disposed to have his own way, or courtiers who were well inclined

---

[1] See the royal instructions to Rosny, dated July 3 and 4, 1605, in the
Mémoires de Sully (Œconomies royales), iv. c. 52, pp. 424-432, of the edition
of 1663. Also, Anquez, 214-217.

[2] "Brevet du Roi," December 29, 1606, in Aymon, Tous les Synodes, i.
343, 344.

[3] Acts of the National Synod of La Rochelle, ibid., i. 342-350.

to let him have it.   No wonder that Henry positively declined
to accept Villarnoul, son-in-law of Duplessis Mornay, and
Mirande, the synod's candidates, and declared that he would
continue to recognize the late deputies general, Odet de La
Noue, son of the champion of the Iron Arm, and Ducros. But
neither of the gentlemen whom the king thus honored considered himself to be authorized to act for his fellow religionists.
Meanwhile the great body of the Protestants asserted the validity of the election of their successors, and called for the convocation of a political assembly to solve the knotty matter.   In
the end such an assembly was summoned to meet at
Jargeaux in the autumn of the year 1608. It consented to meet the views of the monarch by the selection of six candidates, and of these Henry had the good grace
to choose the very same men for deputies general whom he had
declined when their names were presented to him alone.[1]

Assembly of
Jargeaux,
1608.

The assembly of Jargeaux was the last of the political convocations of the Huguenots during this reign.

Meanwhile the more strictly ecclesiastical activity of the
French Protestants had never been greater than during the period now under consideration. Of the nineteen national synods held by the Huguenots up to the date of the death of
Henry the Fourth, not less than seven fell within the compass
of this monarch's reign ; and of these, five belong to the portion
of that reign which was subsequent to the enactment of the
Edict of Nantes.   During the preceding reigns the highest
representative body of the Reformed churches had of necessity
been convened rarely and at irregular intervals.   The commotion consequent upon the massacre of St. Bartholomew's Day
compelled the persecuted Huguenots to abstain from holding
a national synod for nearly six years ; while the wars of the
League introduced a break of over eleven years between the
first Synod of Vitré, in May, 1583, and the Synod of Montauban, in June, 1594.   Now, for the first time, the desire,
long cherished, of regular and frequent periodical convocations
was nearly realized.   The national synods successively met, at

---

[1] Anquez, 222, etc.

Montpellier, on the twenty-fifth of May, 1598; at Jargeaux, on the ninth of May, 1601 ; at Gap, on the first of October, 1603 ; at La Rochelle, on the first of March, 1607 ; and at Saint Maixent, on the twenty-fifth of May, 1609.

Much as the proceedings of these assemblies contain which might concern the theologian or the ecclesiastical antiquary, there is little in the records that need detain the general reader. He may, however, be interested in noticing the prominence given to the support of the educational establishments—to which our attention will shortly be turned—and find a proof of the zeal of the Huguenots in behalf of higher institutions of learning in the fact that, of the forty-three thousand and three hundred crowns granted by Henry the Fourth for the maintenance of the Reformed churches, they instantly appropriated one-thirteenth part to their universities.[1] He may still further notice, as characteristic of the times, that the Synod of Gap gave no uncertain sound as to the doctrine of the Protestant churches respecting the papacy, by solemnly reaffirming their belief—a belief in attestation of which many of their martyrs had suffered a violent death—that the Pope of Rome was properly identified with the Antichrist of the Holy Scriptures. Not only so, but the same assembly formally resolved to append to the thirty-first article of the Confession of Faith a very explicit declaration to the same effect, wherein the church professed its conviction that the Roman Pontiff was the Son of Perdition, predicted in the Word of God under the emblem of the Harlot clothed in scarlet, seated on the seven hills of the great city, and reigning over the kings of the earth, and uttered its confident expectation that the Lord would consume him with the spirit of His mouth and finally destroy him with the brightness of His coming.[2] The Synod of La Rochelle, in one of its earlier sessions, indorsed these views, and fully sanctioned the addition to the Confession of Faith.[3] Subsequently, however, learning that their action was highly displeasing to the king, and deferring to the judgment

---

[1] Acts of the Synod of Montpellier, in Aymon, Tous les Synodes, i. 225.
[2] Acts of the Synod of Gap, ibid., i. 258, 272.
[3] Acts of the Synod of La Rochelle, ibid., i. 303.

of Duplessis Mornay, who urged a more moderate course,[1] the synod receded in part from its action.   It consented to suspend the publication of the obnoxious statement; but it took good care to accompany the concession with the express condition that no person be molested or brought to trial for maintaining the doctrine in question, whether from the pulpit or in written or oral discussion.   It stipulated, furthermore, that his majesty be petitioned to take measures that no person be held to account for having printed the article referred to, or for having in his possession copies of it already issued.[2]

While consenting to leave out of their compendious statement of doctrine a declaration which might be regarded as unessential, and therefore unnecessary, the Huguenots evidently saw no prospect in the near future of relief from the necessity of defending by controversy the doctrines of the Reformation. So it was that, acting on a suggestion coming from the churches of Anjou, the Synod of Saint Maixent determined that it was expedient that certain persons be selected in each province whose special duty it should be to prepare themselves upon certain particular doctrines.   Accordingly the entire field of theological controversy was mapped out and distributed geographically, with a precision which was probably never surpassed elsewhere.   To Poitou, for instance, was assigned the task of discussing " The Word of God, Written and Unwritten;" Saintonge was to qualify itself to treat of "The Church and the Councils;" Upper Languedoc was intrusted with the settlement of "The Sacraments in general, and the True Sacraments in particular." To each of fourteen ecclesiastical provinces its own theme was assigned; in each, suitable persons, carefully selected,

---

[1] "Et à la vérité messieurs, nous estant libre d'en dire ce que nous en sentons, et en nos presches et en nos livres, je ne sçais quelle utilité nous peult revenir de rechercher quelque chose plus oultre, et estime que sans aulcung prejudice de nostre profession et doctrine, nous pouvions nous abstenir d'en imprimer et publier l'article en nostre confession, et en ceste chose indifferente de soi, donner contentement à sa majesté, puis mesme qu'au regard des affaires elle y recognoist de la difference." Mémoires de Duplessis Mornay, x. 198–200.

[2] Acts of the Synod of La Rochelle, Aymon, i. 314.

were to hold themselves ready to combat for the views of
the Reformed Churches, within a restricted circle of doctrine,
whensoever they might be called upon to enter into dispute
with their adversaries.[1]

Of the disputes within the bosom of the Reformed Church,
the less conspicuous controversy of Piscator, and the nas-
cent controversy respecting the views promulgated by Arminius, soon to assume far wider importance, I shall not speak
here.   Slight as were the proportions which these discussions
had as yet attained, they were sufficient to awaken the apprehension of Duplessis Mornay, a firm believer in the propriety
of sinking all minor questions, in view of the great struggle
confronting Protestantism entire.   "I beg you," he wrote to
La Noue, "employ here your own prudence and the authority
of the Duke of Bouillon, that there be not engendered a difference among us for a doctrine which is either identical or but
little different.   You see where we already are in the matter of
Arminius.   Our [Roman Catholic] adversaries concede us substantial matters in order to draw us to them, but we cannot give
up matters that are immaterial in order to remain united with
one another.   Would to God that we were willing to know
nothing save Christ crucified for us, rejecting everything opposed to this and having no curiosity respecting what is beyond
it."[2]

Meanwhile some theological discussions had arisen of more
than usual interest, even to the general reader.   In one of these
the character of Henry the Fourth had shown to little
advantage.   Having made his peace with Rome, the
king was indisposed to forfeit, or even to endanger, the
rewards of his abjuration by tolerating in France any attacks
upon the Roman Church or its pontiff, which might furnish
subject for complaint to the Jesuits, to Clement the Eighth,
or to his successor, Paul the Fifth.   He therefore entered upon a course of conciliation, including the recall of the Jesuits

Papal and Jesuit influence.

---

[1] Acts of the National Synod of Saint Maixent, Aymon, i. 376, 377.

[2] Letter to La Noue, February 22, 1608, Mémoires de Duplessis Mornay, x.
222.

to France, the choice of Father Cotton, of that order, as royal confessor, and the overthrow, through the joint influence of the confessor and of other members of the same order, of the stately monument, or pyramid, erected in front of the main entrance to the Palais de Justice, and on the ruins of the house of the miscreant's father, to the everlasting execration of the crime of Jean Chastel.[1]

In 1600 Henry was particularly sensitive, because of the fact that the plans he had for some time been pursuing in respect to his marriage were well under way to realization. His efforts to obtain a divorce from Margaret of Valois, the hated bride whose nuptials had been graced by the massacre of St. Bartholomew's Day, had been crowned with success. The commission appointed by the pope had pronounced the marriage, contracted twenty-eight years before, void from the beginning, upon such grounds as the Roman curia has rarely been at a loss to discover whenever policy or interest has rendered it advisable so to do.[2]

The king's divorce and marriage.

The king was in the midst of his preparations for his marriage with Maria de' Medici, daughter of the late Grand Duke of Tuscany. It was at this inopportune time that the king's notice was particularly directed to the recent publication of a work composed by Duplessis Mornay, as the result of no little labor and research, having for its title " The Institution, Usage, and Doctrine of the Holy Sacrament of the Eucharist in the Ancient

---

[1] The curious may find, in the tenth volume of the translation of De Thou, published at the Hague in 1740, pp. 26 and following, a full description of the monument, with its inscriptions, and a large and authentic representation of its appearance. The "pyramid," in point of fact, was only an obelisk constituting the uppermost part of the structure.

[2] For the reasons, see De Thou, ix. (bk. 123) 317, and the correspondence of Cardinal d'Ossat from Rome, in vol. ii. of his Mémoires. Not to speak of the circumstance that there was *natural* relationship between the parties—they were second cousins, for Margaret of Angoulême, Henry's grandmother, was the sister of Francis I., Margaret of Valois' grandfather—there was *spiritual* relationship also, inasmuch as Henry II., the bride's father, had acted as godfather to the groom at his baptism. True, Gregory XIII. had granted a dispensation *after* the marriage had taken place, but Margaret of Valois declared that she had never willingly accepted it.

Church; as well as how, when, and by what degrees the Mass was introduced in its place." The general theme was no novel Duplessis Mornay's book on the Eucharist. one; for the question regarding the Lord's Supper and the Roman Catholic doctrine of Transubstantiation had been a favorite article of controversy for not much less than a century. But the book attracted special attention at this time, first, because it was written with uncommon elegance of style; next, because it transferred the ground of dispute from the Holy Scriptures, where it was currently supposed that the papal party had been worsted, to the writings of the Fathers, where that party flattered itself that its position was impregnable; and, most of all, because the work emanated from the very neighborhood of the throne.[1] The author, disdaining to take refuge under a pseudonym, or to attempt even partial concealment of his identity behind the thin veil of initials, had boldly announced himself as "Messire Philippe de Mornay, Lord of Plessis-Marly, Councillor of the King in his Council of State." The beauties of the style might have been ignored; churchmen might have affected to look another way when an inconvenient appeal was made to patristic authority; but some notice must perforce be taken of the audacious champion of the Reformation, who had so distinctly proclaimed the fact that he stood high in favor with Henry the Fourth some years after his abjuration. The denunciation of the writer and of his work from the pulpits of Paris and the provinces, the censures of the Sorbonne, and the order that the book should be consigned to the flames, concern us here as little as do the attempts made in print to refute its statements. The capital point was that Duplessis Mornay had committed the un- Henry's annoyance. pardonable sin against the king of attacking the Roman See at a moment when it was particularly important for Henry to have the support of the Roman See. His majesty was as furious againt Duplessis Mornay as he was indignant

---

[1] " La beauté du stile," says De Thou, ix. (bk. 123) 326, " le faisoit rechercher de tout le monde, et lire avec d'autant plus d'avidité, que l'auteur appuyoit son sentiment de l'autorité des peres grecs et latins, et même de quelques théologiens scholastiques."

with the National Synod of Gap for having ventured to declare that the pope was Antichrist and the Man of Sin. It availed nothing to the synod that Henry had himself, when simple king of Navarre, subscribed, if not actually composed, letters to be carried by Ségur to the Protestant monarchs of the North, wherein the Roman pontiff was expressly designated by the former of these uncomplimentary appellations. Henry's memory of letters written fifteen or eighteen years before was as conveniently faulty as his knowledge of the fact that the Reformed Churches of France had always held and proclaimed the view he now chose to reprobate. It availed as little to Duplessis Mornay that, to use the king's own words uttered immediately after the incidents next to be related, his majesty "had never had a better or greater servant;" that "through his conduct" the king, "after being, as it were, banished to the Pyrenees, had attained the kingdom;" that Duplessis Mornay "had had a chief part in this great and glorious fortune."[1] Past favors counted for nothing in Henry's estimation, as compared with present advantage. The pope must be vindicated, the papal honor must be avenged, even at the expense of the most faithful, trusty, and useful statesman that had ever sat at the king's council board. Nor did Henry attempt to hide his resentment from its object. With a countenance very different from the benignant visage he had been used to turn upon him, he told Duplessis: "You could not have done me a greater displeasure than to attack the pope, to whom I am more obliged than to my own father."[2] He made no account of Duplessis Mornay's reply that he had attacked, not the pope, but the papal system; that this was permitted by the royal edicts; indeed, that there was nothing more common than this in all the states that suffered two different religions to exist side by side.[3] Henry was resolved to punish the Huguenot nobleman in a signal manner, and the opportunity soon came, or, rather, was made.

Informed that the king had more than once asserted that all that Duplessis Mornay alleged on the authority of the Fathers

[1] Vie de Duplessis Mornay, 272.
[2] Ibid., 265.   [3] Ibid., ubi supra.

was false, the latter replied by declaring that his majesty could
not confer a greater obligation upon him than by appointing
commissioners before whom he would be called upon to verify
all the quotations from one end to the other of his book.   This
was all that was wanted.   The king summoned to him David
du Perron, Bishop of Evreux, and that versatile controversialist
promptly took up the gauntlet Duplessis had thrown down,
promising that he would point out five hundred flagrant

The Bishop
of Evreux's
charge.

falsifications, by actual count and without exaggeration,
and of such a kind as to be detected by a simple in-
spection, on opening the book, and without entering upon the
determination of the meaning.[1]   Alarmed at the prospect of
another religious conference, which might, for aught he knew,
be as pernicious to the cause he represented as had been the
Colloquy of Poissy, under the reign of Charles the Ninth, the
papal nuncio came in much consternation to Henry and entreated him to avoid a dangerous experiment.   He might have
spared himself the trouble.   The king had no intention of allowing the discussion to enter into the merits of the respective
doctrines of Roman Catholicism and Protestantism, and his assurances removed the prelate's uneasiness.

The conference was appointed for the royal palace at Fontainebleau.   On his arrival Duplessis Mornay was not left long
in doubt respecting the treatment he might expect.   His overthrow seemed to be a foregone conclusion.   The bishop had
been consulted on every point, and already occupied the attitude
of a prospective victor.   The place, the time, the mode of the
conference, the very commissioners to whom the decision was
to be referred, all had been settled; but the man most nearly
interested in the matter had not been requested to give his
opinion respecting the arrangements.   Henry showed no inclination to allow his old Huguenot servant any opportunity to
speak to him in private, and when at last he could not avoid
granting him audience, did not attempt to conceal his animosity.

---

[1] " Cinq cens faussetés enormes, de conte fait et sans hyperbole, telles
qu'elles se pouvoient juger par la seule vue, à l'ouverture du livre, sans entrer
au jugement du sens."

Duplessis Mornay addressed him with his accustomed frankness. " Time was, Sire," said he, " when you talked of reforming the Church, in case God should place you in peaceable pos-
Duplessis and session of this state, and you commanded me to medi-
the king.   tate upon the means of reforming it.   I thought of
none more appropriate than to portray in the eyes of your people the ancient form and belief of the Christian Church.   To
accomplish this has been the sole end of my book on the Eucharist. It was not ambition. I had known the world too well
to imagine that I should succeed by any such way.   Yet, Sire, I
am so unfortunate that the enemies of truth and my enemies
have persuaded you that my book is full of falsifications.   I had
promised myself that the straightforwardness of my actions,
during twenty years and upward of faithful service, must be a
warrant with your majesty for the truth of my words.   This
just grief therefore stung my heart to the quick, and led me to
request your majesty to appoint commissioners to examine from
one end to the other, and leaf by leaf, the passages alleged by
me from the holy Fathers.   Now, Sire, had the Bishop of Evreux had the same object as I, he also would have pursued the
same plan.   This examination might have been carried on both
noiselessly and advantageously ; since your majesty would have
had no other interest than the truth itself, and would consequently have apportioned the sun equally between us.   As for
the wind's being more favorable for him, I care little for that.[1]
Now that the bishop has made a public matter of it, and has interested the papal nuncio and the entire Romish Church, it is
no longer the same thing.   Your majesty, on the contrary, is
interested on behalf of his state to make this action succeed to
their satisfaction, at whatever price it may be.   And thus it is
my misfortune to have my master no longer as an umpire, but
as a party to the suit.   Now, Sire, were my life, or even my honor
alone, at stake, I would gladly lay them down for your service.[2]

---

[1] It will occur to every reader that, even so late as in the warfare of the sixteenth and seventeenth centuries, great stress was laid upon the double advantage of having the sun's rays and the wind in the faces of antagonists.

[2] " J'en feroy littière pour vostre service."

But since I am bound to the defence of the truth, where the honor of God is at stake, I very humbly beseech your majesty to pardon me if I seek for the just and reasonable means of guaranteeing it against those measures which are proposed to you for the purpose of supplanting it."[1] How warmly the king responded to these generous words, by openly espousing the pope's quarrel, and resenting Duplessis Mornay's alleged attack upon him, we saw but a moment ago. Henry even declined to read the petition handed to him by the Huguenot, wherein were set forth his view of what would be a just procedure, and turned it over to the chancellor, with the direction to bring the parties face to face as soon as possible. "Very well, Sire," exclaimed Duplessis Mornay, "since so it pleases God, I see that the game is settled. You will be made to condemn the Truth within four walls, and God will give me the grace, if I live, to make it resound to the four corners of the world."[2]

It is needless to rehearse every step in an incident so iniquitous and so disgraceful to the king, so honorable to the victim of his spite. The bishop who had promised to point out five hundred falsified passages in the book on the Eucharist was permitted to narrow down the number to be examined to

The sixty "errors." sixty. One night, at an hour past midnight, the list was handed to Duplessis Mornay, with the references as briefly noted as decency would allow. At two o'clock the copies of the Fathers belonging to the Bishop of Evreux were brought to the Huguenot in his room. At six o'clock the bishop sent for them to be returned. In those four hours Duplessis Mornay was expected, with his feeble eyesight, to examine and verify the whole sixty passages, in editions of the ancient authors, in some cases different from those which he had made use of in writing his book. In point of fact he had only time to compare nineteen out of the sixty. At eight o'clock, apparently for no other reason than lest he might have too much leisure to prepare his

[1] Vie de Duplessis Mornay, 264, 265.
[2] "Et bien, Sire, puisqu'il plaist ainsi à Dieu, je voy la partie faite ; on vous fera condamner la Verité entre quatre murailles, et Dieu me fera la grace, si je vis, de la faire retentir aux quatre coins du monde." Ibid., 266.

vindication, he was summoned into the king's presence. The conference was not to be held until after noon. His majesty had lost none of his determination to break down his Huguenot follower. He said Duplessis Mornay ought to have examined the whole sixty passages; it might be he had selected the nineteen that were most advantageous to him.

So it was that, harassed and robbed of his rest, Duplessis Mornay was to enter into the conference. Truth to say, there was another person also who had passed a sleepless night. So uneasy was Henry lest, after all, the result might be different from what he had promised the pope that he scarcely closed his eyes. M. de Loménie, who slept in his majesty's room, observed the circumstance. "It must be," said he, "that your majesty has this matter strangely at heart. On the eve of Coutras, of Arques, and of Ivry, three battles in which our all was at stake, your majesty was not so anxious." The king admitted that it was so.

On Thursday, the fourth of May, 1600, at one o'clock in the afternoon, the conference took place, in the " Salle du Bain " of the castle of Fontainebleau. The king and his entire court were present. The commissioners had been chosen, three as Roman Catholics—De Thou, Pithou, and Martin—and two as Protestants—Casaubon and Du Frêne Canaye. Chancellor Bellièvre was to preside. Much has been said of the unfairness of the selection. Martin, the king's physician, is reported to have been a man distinguished for violence rather than moderation; Du Frêne Canaye to have been a Protestant only in name, since he had already promised to be " converted," and having come to court for that purpose was naturally anxious to distinguish himself by some good service done to the cause he was about to espouse; and Casaubon, eminent humanist as he was, had as little experience in the matters he was to be called upon to decide, as practice in the ways of courts.[1] As to the estimable De Thou, and his no

The Fontainebleau conference, May 4, 1600.

The commissioners.

---

[1] The suggestion of Benoist that Casaubon was wavering in his attachment to his religion appears to be based upon cruel suspicion, and to be an unwarrantable deduction from the well-known moderation and irenic tendencies of the

less respectable friend Pithou, both of them men of probity, their office was not of their seeking, and De Thou, in particular, had begged to be excused from its discharge. But he had been informed, on the king's behalf, that he must remember that he was already looked upon with suspicion by many because he had had a hand in drawing up the provisions of the Edict of Nantes, and that, if he declined on the present occasion to act as a commissioner, he must expect never again to be invited to discharge any important function. It matters little, however, how far these statements are true or false. The conduct of the commissioners may be fully explained by the timidity or servility of gownsmen—lawyers, judges, and professors—which evidenced itself on many occasions during the reigns of the last Valois kings and during the reign now under consideration, and which was to reappear far too often under succeeding monarchs down to the time of the Revolution. There were few men on the bench who dared to make a determined resistance to the expressed or implied will of the king. The majority were overawed; they bowed their heads to the royal mandate, reluctantly, perhaps, and blaming him in their hearts, but none the less obediently. Parliament might indeed show strenuous resistance when its privileges were endangered, or when the Roman Catholic supremacy was threatened, or when so insidious a body as the Society of Jesus attempted to entrench itself in France to the prejudice of University not less than episcopal authority. But of an honest resistance made by a judicial body to the condemnation of any man whom the

Pliancy of judges.

---

scholar. His "Ephemerides," of which the Bulletin de la Société de l'histoire du Protestantisme français, has given some extracts in translation, are an unimpeachable evidence of his simple and unaffected piety. It is an interesting coincidence that an entry in this private diary, made on Sunday the 16th of April, a little over a fortnight before he took part in the conference of Fontainebleau, testifies to his admiration for Duplessis Mornay and for the very book upon which he was to pass judgment. "16th day before the Calends of May. To-day, Sunday, I did not attend divine worship, unhappy man that I am! But I spent a part of the day in reading, for my edification, the book written by Monsieur Duplessis on the Lord's Supper and the Mass; I even passed a good part of the day with this great man. May God preserve him to us, as well as such men as resemble him." Bulletin, ii. 257.

crown desired to crush, there seems not to be an example that
can be alleged in France during the sixteenth century.   Chris-
topher de Thou, father of the historian and the commissioner at
Fontainebleau, was not worse than his associate judges; yet not
only did he vote to condemn the Prince of Condé to death in
the last days of Francis the Second, in obedience to the known
desire of the government,[1] but in the reign of Charles the Ninth
he went to the length of congratulating the king on his dissimulation at the massacre of Saint Bartholomew's Day, and laud-
ing the royal prudence in bearing long with insults and at
last crushing a dangerous conspiracy.[2]   As for the chancellor,
Chancellor   Pomponne de Bellièvre, he was the same man, who,
Bellièvre.   though he had fawned upon Admiral Gaspard de Coligny when alive,[3] had the effrontery, immediately after the hero's
assassination, to declare to the Swiss, to whom he had been sent
on a mission of falsehood and deception, that the admiral was a
vile conspirator, a man " who notoriously supported in his suite
and at his call more murderers than were to be found in all the
rest of the kingdom," [4] a man who attracted strangers to him by
a simulation of probity, honesty, and justice, but in himself was
only a compound of " malice, rapine, avarice, and injustice."
Needless to say that the assassin, Maurevel, who shot at Coligny
from behind a lattice, was a high-spirited gentleman, driven to
the verge of desperation by the admiral's repeated acts of in-
iquity, a much-injured hero who was resolved to sell his life as
dear as possible.[5]

With so pliable a chancellor to preside, there was little

---

[1] Rise of the Huguenots, i. 438–440.

[2] Ibid., ii. 483.

[3] See Mémoires de l'estat de France soubs Charles IX., apud Delaborde,
François de Chastillon, 397, etc.

[4] "Ledit feu admiral, lequel, comme chacun sçait avoit tousjours plus de
meurtriers entretenus à sa suite et à son commandement, qu'il n'en demeuroit
en tout le reste du roïaume." Infra, 393.

[5] Remonstrances faites par le sieur de Bellièvre, conseiller au conseil d'Estat
et privé du roy aux ambassadeurs de messieurs les treize cantons des anciennes
Ligues des haultes Allemagnes, en la journée à Baden en Argonne, le 8ᵉ jour
de décembre, 1572. MS. Nat. Lib., apud Delaborde, François de Chastillon,
391–397.

prospect that any other result would be reached than such as his majesty might choose to indicate to be pleasing to him.

The chancellor's introductory words once over, the Bishop of Evreux congratulated the king upon the intention he had

The confer-
ence opened. clearly announced, not to trench upon the prerogatives of the church. Then Duplessis Mornay was permitted to speak. He professed his want of solicitude respecting a book which he had written solely to further that reformation of the church which was so earnestly desired by all good people. If the volume was useless for that purpose, he was not so much attached to it but that he would burn it with his own hands. He hoped, however, that it would be fairly examined, and that his good faith and diligence would be recognized. Still, it would not be strange if among five or six thousand passages quoted from the Fathers, there should be found some wherein his eye, or his memory, or even his judgment might have erred. Let the Doctors of the Roman Catholic Church be examined with such rigor; which one of them could be found to stand the test? Lastly, let it be well understood that whatever might be the issue, it concerned him alone, and could in nowise work damage to the truth of the doctrine of the Reformed Church, "which," said he, "has existed before me, will exist after me, and, by the grace of God, shall ever exist."

Then came the examination of the particular passages of Duplessis Mornay's book, a task in which the historian may well be excused from attempting to follow; for, in the place of the multitude of flagrant falsifications which Du Perron had boastfully declared himself able to point out, he had come down to the dreary and trifling business of noting paltry errors, for the most part unworthy of serious consideration, such as even the most careful and conscientious of men might easily have fallen into. Two passages respecting the doctrine of transubstantiation, taken from Duns Scotus and Durand, were first brought up, in which Du Perron alleged that Duplessis Mornay had, from want of familiarity with scholastic writers, taken the "objection" for the "answer." The judges themselves were at fault; they had decided that the matter called for further examination in one of the cases, and were about to say the same of the other, when the king, approaching them, told them they must decide; whereupon they declared that Duplessis Mornay had mistaken the objection for the answer. In two passages from St. Chrysostom and St. Jerome, the bishop maintained that the Huguenot ought to have included some lines more in his quotations. Duplessis Mornay replied that it would have made no difference in the sense; but the judges gave the somewhat tame verdict that "it would have been well to add them." In all, nine passages were examined, with similar results, before the approach of night interrupted the conference. It was to have been resumed the next morning, but Duplessis Mornay,

The conference interrupted.

worn out by his anxiety and enforced loss of sleep, and ill, besides, was in no condition to go on. In fact, for one reason and another, the disputation was never renewed. No one was very eager for its resumption. The judges were heartily disgusted with their ungrateful task. Duplessis Mornay could hope for no justice at the hands of a tribunal so dominated by a prince resolved upon the humiliation of his faithful follower. The bishop had gained all the éclat his cheap victory could procure him. The king had secured his point. He had done the pope a service for which he

Henry's elation.

was entitled to a suitable reward. That night he bade to be served in the Salle du Bain; he would sup, he said, on the battle-field. The conceit was certainly unworthy of a great monarch, but more despicable was the note which he wrote, immediately after the conference, to the Duke of Épernon, for the purpose of making capital with the Jesuits out of his recent encounter. "My friend," he wrote to the man whom he cordially hated, "the diocese of Evreux has got the better of the diocese of Saumur, and the gentleness with which we have proceeded has taken away the opportunity for any Huguenot to say that anything had force but truth. The bearer, who was present, will relate to you how I did wonders. Assuredly this is one of the greatest blows struck for the church of God in a long time. Treading in these footsteps, we shall bring back more wanderers from the church in a sin-

gle year, than by another way in fifty years." [1]   In the midst
of his elation, however, Henry took good care to let the
triumphant Du Perron understand that it was not the bishop's
dialectical skill that had won the day.   " Let us confess the
truth," said he to him, " that the good cause had good need of
help." [2]   As for Duplessis Mornay, the victim of a prearranged
plot for his overthrow, he wrote calmly, though feelingly, of
the event : " I do not see that, in the case of Luther, the Emperor Charles resorted to such a procedure, though his cause
was then, if at any time, odious and altogether new and unsupported by public edict.   Yet Luther was listened to with kindness, and was admitted to confer without fraud.   Albeit he was
a man who had done no service to the emperor, but, on the
contrary, appeared to be doing him many ill offices ; whereas,
of the fifty years I have attained, I have given my king the
twenty-five best years, and in these twenty-five, fifty lives." [3]
The Huguenot statesman may have been betrayed into some
mistakes in the composition of his book ; he may very likely, as
Sully would have us believe, have made a weak defence, harassed by his enemies, and, most of all, oppressed by a keen sense
of the ingratitude with which his long and loyal service was
requited.   Yet, in the eyes of all fair men of his own times, as
in the view of posterity, he occupied a more enviable position
than either the King of France or the ambitious prelate for
whom, to use Sully's witty expression, Duplessis Mornay had
secured a cardinal's hat. [4]

---

[1] Henry to the Duke of Épernon, Fontainebleau, May 5, 1600, in the Mémoires de Sully (edition of 1663), iv. 8, and in Lettres missives, x. 230, 231 ;
also in Vie de Duplessis Mornay, 271, etc.   If Henry himself was not ashamed,
some of his Roman Catholic followers must have blushed for him, inasmuch
as they quietly changed the expression " j'y ay faict merveilles " into "il s'y
est faict merveilles."   The discreditable letter was scattered broadcast through
France, and indeed throughout Europe.

[2] " J'ai voulleu, dict-il, soupper au champ de bataille (sçavoir en la salle du
baing, où elle avoit esté teneue), mais dictes verité, Monsieur d'Evreux, bon
droict a eu bon besoing d'ayde."   Mémoires de Charlotte Arbaleste, i. 367.

[3] Duplessis Mornay to Loménie, July 24, 1600, Mémoires, ix. 381.

[4] " Et bien, que vous en semble de vostre pape ? "   Henry the Fourth had
asked Sully.   To which the latter replied : " Il me semble, Sire, qu'il est plus

If Henry, led by political considerations to identify himself
more and more with the church which political considerations
Catharine of alone had influenced him in joining, seemed at times
Bourbon.   to have lost all the memories of his Huguenot training, it was otherwise with his brave sister. Both before and
after her marriage with the Duke of Bar, son of the Duke of
Lorraine, she remained constant to her early convictions. Her
husband, a man as susceptible to priestly menaces as the most
ambitious of churchmen could desire to have for a penitent,
having once married her, was easily persuaded by his ghostly
advisers that he had committed a mortal sin in wedding a
woman who was not only a Protestant, but also a distant relation of his own. None but the pope, whose absolution he
secretly went to Rome to solicit, could liberate his soul from
the apprehension that it was doomed to eternal pains. The
poor man was in the deepest dejection, and begged his unfortunate bride to do the only thing that would melt the pontiff's
heart, by embracing Roman Catholicism. He insisted on her
listening to the arguments of one Commolet, a member of
the order of Jesus; but after two interviews with him she declared that she had learned to be still more of a Huguenot and
less of a Jesuit than before.[1] So resolute a character offered
little encouragement to Roman Catholic proselytism. The
duchess maintained her religious practices, regularly attended
and partook of the Lord's Supper according to the Reformed
rites, and was as steadfast as she had been years before, when
she playfully assured her correspondent, Duplessis Mornay, that
she had never been to mass either in deed or in thought, hav-

---

pape que vous ne pensez ; car voyez-vous pas qu'il donne un chapeau rouge à
Monsieur d'Evreux." In addition to this, he volunteered the remark that,
if Protestantism had no better support than Duplessis Mornay had given it,
he would renounce it to-day, rather than wait until to-morrow. Mémoires de
Sully, c. 95 (ii. 318). On the conference of Fontainebleau, see De Thou, ix.
(book 123) 326–329 ; Vie de Duplessis Mornay (Leyden, 1647), 262–272 ;
Mémoires de Charlotte Arbaleste (Madame Duplessis Mornay), i. 365–369 ; the
correspondence in M. Duplessis Mornay's Mémoires, ix. 370–389, etc.; Benoist,
Histoire de l'édit de Nantes, i. 340–355 ; Lestoile, ii. 311–317.

[1] Letters of Catharine of Bourbon, May, 1599, and November, 1599, Mémoires de Duplessis Mornay, ix. 269, 298, 299.

ing reserved her conversion to such time as he should be elected pope.[1]

In truth, however, Henry the Fourth himself was loath to be esteemed estranged from his old associates in faith and arms. He showed himself very sensitive to certain speeches of indiscreet Protestants, which seemed to imply that he had become a persecutor, and maintained that, in the midst of many difficulties he was doing what he could for them.[2]

Meanwhile, to the Protestants outside the kingdom he was very gracious. In the course of the war with Savoy, which, in his inability to obtain from Charles Emmanuel any satisfaction for the marquisate of Saluces, he entered upon in 1600, he succeeded in reducing almost the whole of the district of Bresse, and approached the city of Geneva. Here a deputation waited upon him, headed by the octogenarian, Theodore Beza, whose laudatory speech, full of thanks for the benefits the king had conferred upon the cause of true religion in France, was graciously received. In reply Henry promised the little republic his continued protection, in token of which he did them the good service of reducing the fort of Sainte Cathérine, a formidable stronghold which in the Duke of Savoy's hands was a perpetual menace to the city. He was even invited to visit Geneva, where the honest burghers entertained him and his suite of nobles with princely hospitality. The next year peace was concluded, according to the terms of which Fort Sainte Cathérine was to be restored to the Duke of Savoy; but, before leaving, the king secretly gave the Genevese permission to tear down the walls—a task upon the accomplishment of which the entire population entered with such instant alacrity, and which they accomplished so thoroughly, as to leave no vestige of the hated work to be turned over to their dangerous neighbor. Great was the anger of the duke. The ambassador of Spain threatened that his master would take sides with Savoy.

Henry's kindness to the Genevese.

---

[1] Letter of the same, ubi supra, 1594, vi. 81.

[2] See the account given by M. Le Macon, of an interview he had recently had with the king in a gallery of the palace of Fontainebleau, in a letter dated June 18, 1601, Mémoires de Duplessis Mornay, ix. 419.

Most of all was Cardinal Aldobrandini, the papal legate, indignant that the Very Christian King should so insult his holiness by openly taking under his protection the interests of a city not only heretical, but the very citadel of heresy.[1]

The incident just mentioned is among the last of the striking events in the life of the aged reformer, who, more than forty years before, had won renown at the Colloquy of Poissy; although that life was protracted a few years longer.[2] During the whole of the period intervening, most eventful for French Protestantism, his name had been a tower of strength. There was no one whose eloquence the opponents of the Huguenots feared more, no one whom they would more gladly have gained over by any means within their reach. And, as false rumors that the brilliant young orator had been vanquished in debate by the Cardinal of Lorraine were circulated at the time of the colloquy, so stories of the conversion of the aged divine were deliberately manufactured and sown broadcast throughout Europe a few years before his death. Sir Edwin Sandys, when in Italy, was informed—the news came from Rome, where such news was systematically invented —"that Beza, the arch-heretic, Calvin's successor, drawing toward his death, had in full senate at Geneva recanted his religion, exhorting them, if they had any care to save their souls, to seek reconciliation with the Catholic Church, and to send for the Jesuits to instruct them ; whereupon both himself, by special order from the pope, was absolved by the Bishop of Geneva ere he died, and the city had sent to Rome an ambassage of submission." " A beginning of which news," adds Sir Edwin, " it was my chance to hear, as being whispered among the Jesuits, two months ere it brake out; but when it was once advertised so solemnly from Rome, it ran all over Christendom, and in Italy it was so verily believed to be true that there were,

Marginal note: Rumored conversion of Theodore Beza.

---

[1] Mémoires de Sully, c. 97 (ii. 367, etc.) ; De Thou, ix. (book 125) 395, etc.; Agrippa d'Aubigné, iii. 483. Fort Sainte Cathérine had been erected by the duke about two or three leagues south east of Geneva. Henry IV. and Beza met at the little village of Luiset, within a short distance of the fort.

[2] Beza died in October, 1605.

as is said, who rode on very purpose to see those ambassadors of
Geneva, yet invisible." [1] The truth was that François de Sales,
the future saint, relieved the monotony of his labors for the
conversion of the district of Chablais (1594 to 1598) by sundry
visits to Theodore Beza at Geneva.   It might indeed
François de
Sales attempts have seemed somewhat presumptuous for a young
to bribe him. ecclesiastic of scarcely thirty years to hope to convert
by arguments, whether drawn from biblical or patristic theology,
a master in dialectics his senior by nearly a half century.   But
courtesy was a native virtue with the polished reformer, and he
heard with consideration, and refuted with respect, the words
of François de Sales, until, in his final interview, the latter, de-
spairing of success by the unaided force of reason, condescended
to an appeal to lower motives.   But when the future saint proceeded to offer Beza, in the name of the pope, a yearly pension
of four thousand gold crowns, as well as a sum double in amount
the value of all his personal effects, whatever they might be
worth, the reformer repudiated with honest scorn the dishonorable proposal to sell his integrity and a reputation the fruit of
nearly fourscore years of disinterested service to the cause of
truth for so paltry a bribe.   He merely pointed to the empty
shelves of his bookcases, whose treasured volumes he had but
recently sold that he might apply the proceeds to the relief of
the poor, and turned his back upon his astonished visitor with
the words: "Get thee behind me, Satan!"   Others will have it
that, in gentler, but not less positive, terms, he said: " Go, sir!
I am too old and too deaf to be able to hear such words." [2]
And that was the reason the men of Sienna and of Rome waited
in vain at their gates for the coming of Beza to receive the
apostolic absolution.

If the efforts of St. François de Sales to convert the Protestants of the district of Chablais were attended with greater suc-

---

[1] Europæ Speculum, 101. About the middle of September, 1597, a crowd
lingered at the gates of the city of Sienna, expecting to see Beza himself on
his way to Rome, and were sadly disappointed that he did not arrive. Heppe,
Theodor Beza, 314.

[2] See the full account in Gaberel, Histoire de l'Église de Genève, ii. 640,
etc.; Heppe, Theodor Beza, 311–316.

cess, the reason will be found neither in the superior cogency
of his arguments, nor in the greater readiness of the inhabitants
to be impressed by them, but solely in the material aid

His method
of converting
Chablais.

wherewith the missionary was abundantly supplied.
The people of that division of the modern department of Haute Savoie which lies upon the southern side of Lake
Leman—anciently known as the Bailiwick of Chablais—had,
during the twenty-eight years of Bernese occupation (1536–
1564), become strongly Protestant, and their religious liberty
was guaranteed by the treaty of Nyon, under which they again
became subjects of the ducal crown of Savoy. They consequently turned a deaf ear to François de Sales's preaching, so
long as he resorted to persuasion alone. When, however, after
two years of discouragement, he succeeded in prevailing upon
the duke to banish the Protestant minister and schoolmaster, to
deprive all Protestants of office, " to sow terror among the
inhabitants by good edicts," and to be " liberal to the new con-
verts ; " when the regiment of Martinengo [1] was quartered upon
the inhabitants ; especially, when the duke came in person, declaring that he had brought his sword to second the holy enterprises of François de Sales—then, indeed, conversions, such as
they were, multiplied apace. Such devices as gathering all the
chief citizens of Thonon, the principal place of the district, in

---

[1] " The Martinengo regiment was a name that had only to be whispered in
all that region to make the blood run cold with horror. It was a regiment of
Spanish mercenaries that had been trained in the American wars to an ex-
quisite delight and ingenuity in human torture. Seven years before, in the
provinces neighboring the Chablais, it had been let loose like a ferocious beast
by the duke upon his own unarmed Protestant subjects, and day after day
had revelled in ingenious torture, murder, and destruction. The simple procès-verbal containing the catalogue of these atrocities is one of the most awful
pages in history. . . . To violate, to torture, to maim, to murder by slow degrees, were not enough ; the bodies of the murdered must be mutilated and
obscenely exposed." L. W. Bacon, ubi infra. The horrible details, too foul
for modern eyes to read, for modern ears to hear, are given, village for village,
and in part, name by name, in the contemporary pamphlet " Bref et vrai recueil des horribles carnages perpetrés de froid sang par les troupes du Duc de
Savoye, à leurs entrées tant du balliage de Gez, que du mandement de Gaillard,
ès environs de Geneve, sur les povres paysans et sujects dudit Duc," etc. Reprinted in Mémoires de la Ligue, iv. 743, etc., and in Gaberel, ii. 235–242.

the town-hall, where the obstinate Protestants were roughly
ordered by the duke to step to one side of the room, worked
satisfactorily ; for the recalcitrants were driven into banishment
within three days, while the rest submitted, and were converted.
In short, the scenes of the times of the Revocation of the Edict
of Nantes were anticipated by eighty-seven years. Evidently
St. Francois de Sales is entitled to a distinction, which his pane-
gyrists have not thought fit to place to his credit, as, if not absolutely the author of that ingenious instrument of conversion
known as the "mission bottée," yet one of the first to appreciate and turn to account its latent capabilities ; for the "dragon-
nades" of 1598 differed from those of 1685 only in that the
troopers were in the service of the Duke of Savoy, instead of
receiving their pay from the coffers of Louis the Fourteenth.[1]

Meanwhile the Protestants of France were long to be free
from the cruelty practised upon their brethren in the district of
Chablais. Averse to needless commotion, not even
the attempt of Biron, heir both to his father's military skill and to his father's treachery, was successful
in luring them into a rebellion ; and the Duke of Bouillon was,
perhaps, the only Protestant leader of prominence who was
strongly suspected of complicity in the abortive plot, and who
consulted safety by flight.[2] Nor were the Huguenots moved

Marshal Bi-
ron's con-
spiracy.

---

[1] The proof of the responsibility of St. François de Sales for all the atrocious
persecution to which Chablais was subjected is incontrovertible.   The original
documents are mostly preserved in the Turin Archives.   M. Gaberel made
excellent use of them in his history of the Church of Geneva, published in 1855,
already referred to, ii. 583–639 ; and more recently, the Rev. Leonard W.
Bacon, D.D., has analyzed and set forth the evidence in a convincing form
in an article in Macmillan's Magazine for September, 1878, under the title
"Two Sides to a Saint."—Meanwhile the most flattering representations of the
canonized Bishop of Geneva continue to be current.   "To the last moment of
his life," says Mrs. Jameson, "love, in its scriptural sense of a tender, all-em-
bracing charity, was the element in which he existed. . . .   He is celebrated
for his devotional writings, which are almost as much admired by Protestants as
by Catholics for their eloquence and Christian spirit ; he is yet more interesting for his benign and tolerant character ; his zeal, so tempered by gentleness."   Legends of the Monastic Orders, 467.

[2] D'Aubigné, one of the Huguenots whose opinion Bouillon sought, scouted
the idea that his party should throw in their lot with the marshal, and carried

even by the new favor shown the Jesuits, and by the introduction of that order into Béarn.

True, the city of La Rochelle again distinguished itself for its almost republican independence.   One Séguiran, a Jesuit, made bold to seek admission to the old Protestant stronghold, and, unknown to Henry, procured from two of the royal secretaries a letter in his majesty's name, commanding the city to receive him.   But the Rochellois had lost neither their caution nor their readiness in repartee.   When Séguiran presented himself at the gates, announcing himself as a companion of the Order of Jesus and the bearer of letters from the king, the quick-witted porter at once declined to recognize him in either capacity.   "The Lord Jesus," he said, "has no companions, and I do not believe that you have any letters from the king." [1]   And Henry, though, when informed of the occurrence, he felt compelled to assume the appearance of anger at the audacity of the Rochellois, was secretly well pleased.   Firmly believing that in no way could he guard his life from their conspiracies but by granting to the Jesuits extraordinary favors, his majesty did indeed go to the length of urging upon the pope the canonization of Ignatius Loyola and Francis Xavier; [2] but it was policy, not love, that led him to assume a part so little consistent with his past history.

The Jesuit at the gates of La Rochelle.

The comparative peace enjoyed under the Edict of Nantes, during the last years of the reign of Henry the Fourth, enabled the Huguenots to carry more fully into execution the plans they had long since formed respecting education.

In few respects was the history of the Protestant party in France more remarkable than in the evidence of an unfaltering determination to provide for the youth a system of instruction at once excellent in itself and unobjectionable in its moral and religious tendencies.   It was no accident that, even amid the fires of persecution, during a period in which

Protestant education.

with him the entire company that was present. Histoire universelle, iii. (bk. v. chapters x. and xi.) 486, etc.   [1] Benoist, i. 439.
  [2] See the letter of Henry IV. to the pope, of July, 1609, Lettres missives, vii. 747, 748.

the Huguenots were denied those rights of conscience at present esteemed to be of the common heritage of man, when their
public exercises of worship were alternately restricted within narrow limits and utterly proscribed, their ministers forbidden the
kingdom or made liable to imprisonment and death at the gallows, this devoted people should have pondered long and to so
good purpose over the general subject of popular education. A
creed that exalts the authority of the written word of God and
pays little attention to human tradition, that vindicates the
right of every Christian to read and judge for himself respecting the truths which the Divine Author intended to convey in
the pages of that word, and makes little of priestly interpreta-
tion—such a creed demands of necessity the intellectual elevation of the masses of the people to a plane far higher than that
which will answer the requirements of other creeds, based upon
unquestioning obedience on the part of the laity to the prescriptions of the sacerdotal class. It was natural, therefore, that the
Huguenots of France should make it their first care to provide
the people with that primary instruction which the Roman Catholic clergy had failed to furnish to their flocks. In the kingdom of the Very Christian King it was as true as throughout the
rest of Western Europe, that "popular instruction was the child
of Protestantism." Not a city, not a town or village, was conquered by the "new doctrines," but a Protestant school followed
closely upon the newly instituted church, and the teacher was
esteemed a scarcely less essential officer in the' ecclesiastical pol-
ity than the preacher of the gospel himself. It was not long
before every child of a Huguenot family was acquiring not only
the arts of reading and writing, but the rudiments of religious
doctrine as contained in the catechism of John Calvin. The
enemies of the Protestants observed, with feelings akin to despair, that, throughout great tracts of country, "the children were learning religion only in the catechism brought from
Geneva, and all knew it by heart."[1] In some places where the
Protestants were in power, education was not only gratuitous

---

[1] Villars to the Guises, October, 1560, in Négociations sous François II., 671.
See Rise of the Huguenots, i. 429.

but compulsory; and the parents or guardians of all children under fourteen years of age who neglected to send them daily to school were subjected to a fine.[1]

But this was not enough. The wants of those who aspired to a higher education must be met, and for them a training esteemed by the Protestants to be truly Christian must be provided. France in the middle of the sixteenth century had its colleges and universities, some of them already dating from a hoary antiquity. Including the University of Paris, whose au-

The state universities. thority and attendance threw all the rest into the shade, there were fifteen universities within the bounds of the kingdom. Paris claimed to date from the close of the twelfth century, if not earlier. Toulouse and Montpellier traced their origin back to the thirteenth century; Orleans and Cahors, Angers and Orange to the fourteenth; Aix, Dôle, Poitiers, Caen, Nantes, Bourges, and Bordeaux to the fifteenth; Rheims alone belonged to the sixteenth. The colleges, below but affiliated with these, numbered about forty.[2] This educational system, suited as it might be to the Roman Catholic majority of the kingdom, was in great part useless to the Protestant minority. The Huguenot student of medicine might, it is true, safely frequent the lecture-rooms of the celebrated faculty of Montpellier, the Huguenot student of jurisprudence the halls of the no less noted Faculty of Law, chief ornament of the University of Orleans—so long, at least, as the body of their Roman Catholic fellow-students would tolerate the presence of reputed heretics among them. But the candidate for the Reformed ministry could not hope to obtain the teaching he needed in the halls of the Sorbonne and at the hands of professors to whom the very notion of a biblical training was an offence. Nor could the more general training preparatory to all professional education be safely sought in the existing colleges, even had their standard of learning been higher than it was.

The Huguenots felt at once that they must have their own

---

[1] Minutes of the Council of the city of Castres, April 17, 1577, in Mémoires de Gaches, 491.

[2] D. Bourchenin, Étude sur les Académies Protestantes en France au XVI° et au XVII° siècle, 19.

universities and colleges, and nobly did they apply themselves
to the task of securing them. For, whereas, at other times and
in other countries, the chief impediment has been the lack of
pecuniary resources for the establishment and maintenance of
these higher schools, among the Huguenots of France, from the
time they came into existence down to the moment when their
religion was proscribed by Louis the Fourteenth, a yet more
formidable and well-nigh insurmountable obstacle was found
in the sleepless activity of the hostile clergy of the established church. Nor did that activity cease when the Protestant
college or university was once set on foot. It continued, in the
form of vexatious interference, down to the day when the ill-
will of the monarch and the subserviency of the courts of justice
permitted the execution of a determined, and, in the end, successful effort to close the doors of every Protestant school in
France.

Meantime the Huguenots gradually provided themselves with
not less than thirty colleges and eight "académies," or universities.[1] Over against the venerable seats of learning
already named they established the Protestant universities of Nismes, Orthez, Orange, Sédan, Montpellier, Montauban (later removed to Puylaurens),
Saumur, and Die—youthful institutions, full of vitality and
promise of usefulness, for which they had no reason to blush

The eight
Protestant
"académies"
or universi-
ties.

---

[1] It is to be noticed, however, that the national synods of the reign of Henry
the Fourth, whose zeal for the maintenance of these institutions has been
already spoken of, do not mention all the académies whose names appear in the
text. Orthez was in Béarn, and Orange in the principality of that name, neither
district being as yet incorporated in France. The National Synod of Montpellier makes an appropriation for the maintenance of the existing " universities "
at Saumur and Montauban, and grants a smaller sum to help in the organization of the "académies" of Montpellier and Nismes. The Synod of Jargeaux
continues the support of these schools of learning, and orders a further sum
of 500 crowns to be given annually "for the advancement of that of Sédan,
which is very convenient for the neighboring provinces." These are the only
five académies provided for in the succeeding synods, held at Gap and La
Rochelle. The Synod of Gap declined, in view of the pecuniary burdens
already weighing upon the churches, and for other reasons, to undertake the
expense of founding the " académie " at Die. See Aymon, Tous les Synodes,
i. 225, 251, 273, 339.

when a contrast was drawn between these newer seminaries and their elder sisters and rivals. The story of their scientific and theological achievements belongs chiefly to a period subsequent to the date of the assassination of Henry the Fourth; nor could it be treated in such detail as might be desirable, save in a work specially devoted to the consideration of this theme. Moreover, it must not be forgotten that, besides these institutions within the boundaries of France proper, there existed other schools of learning, immediately outside of the kingdom, which were not less potent in their influence upon the educational elevation of the Huguenots. At Montbéliard, at Strasbourg, and especially at Geneva, the Protestant youth of France might find the opportunity to gain the priceless advantage of a liberal education at the feet of competent Christian teachers, even when persecution raged most fiercely against the adherents of the Reformation at home. Under the venerable Theodore Beza the Académie of Geneva continued to enjoy high repute for the breadth of its course of instruction and the ability of the men whom it had sent out as graduates from its halls. Not, indeed, that either the department of law or the department of medicine at once attained the prominence reached, from the very nature of the case, by the department of theology almost at the start. But the names of Ennemond Bonnefoy and his eminent colleague, François Hotman, a master of Roman law, were glorious enough to illustrate any university; and if the students of medicine were never numerous, they were, at least, taught to rise above the current prejudices of the age. It is no insignificant fact that, in 1564, an ordinance was secured from the government of the little republic, permitting the dissection of the bodies of malefactors executed by order of the law, and even of persons dying in the hospitals.[1]

Under the beneficent edict for their protection the Hugue-

---

[1] Bourchenin, Étude sur les Académies Protestantes, 91. On this general subject the reader may consult Professor Michel Nicolas's recently published Histoire de l'ancienne Académie protestante de Montauban (1598–1659) et de Puylaurens (1660–1685), and the same author's contributions to the Bulletin de la Société de l'histoire du Protestantisme français, vols. ii., iv., and vi. The venerable professor's decease is announced as these pages are passing through the press.

nots began, wherever their worship was tolerated, to provide
themselves with large and commodious buildings, such as for
many years they had not even dreamed of erecting.
Erection of
spacious Hu-
guenot "tem-
ples."
True, forty years earlier, in the first glow attending the wonderful expansion of the reformatory
movement in the reign of Francis the Second, some spacious
edifices had been hastily constructed to meet the sudden
demand. Of such a character was the great Protestant structure which M. de Vieilleville (in August, 1560) found in the
very centre of the city of Dieppe, and which that estimable
man, with great regret, felt himself compelled to tear down—a
very handsome structure, described in his Mémoires as closely
resembling the Coliseum of Rome or the ruined amphitheatre
at Nismes, and as requiring three days for its demolition.[1] Since
that period the Huguenots had frequently enjoyed the opportunity of taking possession of parish churches, in places in
which the Protestants constituted the large majority of the
population, and when the fortunes of war threw cities into their
hands. But now they were compelled to restore the churches
to the adherents of the established form of religion. Besides,
the churches in question were at best but poorly adapted to the
purposes of Protestant worship. Admirably suited as they
were for spectacular effects, their acoustic properties were not
good. The priest officiating at the altar could easily be seen,
but his voice was imperfectly heard. To the Roman Catholics
this was of little moment. The priest's sermons were few; he
made no attempts to expound the Sacred Scriptures; and the
occasional harangues of some friar in Advent or Lententide
were all that the people were called upon to follow. But to
the Protestants the sermons were all-important. Catharine
de' Medici had not been far out of the way when she said that
all the Huguenots wanted to be perfectly satisfied was " to have
their fill of preaching "—" leur saoule de presches." It was
of the utmost consequence that each worshipper should be able
to hear with distinctness every syllable uttered by the minister,
beginning with the text, through all the heads of his discourse,

---

[1] Mémoires de Vieilleville, ii. 448; Rise of the Huguenots, i. 408.

down to the practical application at the end. At the same time, since it was not in every town or village that Protestant preaching was permitted, since the Huguenots could assemble only in two places in a bailiwick or sénéchaussée, or upon some property of a nobleman possessing the prerogative of administering " haute justice," and since they must therefore come from considerable distances round about, the church edifices—or " temples," as they were wont to call them—must be so constructed as to seat congregations vastly exceeding in size those which are wont to frequent divine service in countries where houses of worship may be multiplied indefinitely. A new art was called into existence—the art of rearing great structures, having little that would strike the eye of the beholder as strictly ecclesiastical in pattern or association, but furnishing sitting or standing room for an incredible number of persons; and all this without taxing beyond measure the slender purses of men who had for a generation been withstanding the most relentless of attacks. There were places, like commercial Dieppe, where at one time the Protestants claimed almost the entire population. The few Roman Catholics that remained were

Dieppe.

men of no standing or influence. The Protestants believed themselves in good faith to be entitled to the parish churches, which their own ancestors had built and endowed ; especially as the smallest of the existing chapels would easily contain all the congregation which the priests could gather.[1] Frustrated in expectations deemed by them most reasonable, they set themselves to build anew. On the Sunday after Pente-

---

[1] In a petition addressed by the Protestants of Dieppe to M. de la Curée, governor of the city, in April, 1563, they applied for permission to retain the church of St. Jacques, leaving the other church of St. Remy "à ceux quy voudront vivre en la religion de l'esglise Romaine, quy sont tous gens de basse condition, et en sy petit nombre, que le dit temple de St. Remy est beaucoup plus grand qu'il ne leur faut. C'est pourquoy la plus grande partye des habitans quy doit emporter l'autre, et dont les predecesseurs ont fondé, edifié, donné, et augmenté le dit temple . . . sera dedommagée des frais qu'il conviendroit faire pour batir autre lieu." So in a letter to the Prince of Condé, of April 20, 1563, they speak of their Roman Catholic fellow-citizens as " en sy petit nombre et de sy viles personnes, qu'ils n'aparoissent ny ne se mettent aucunement en effet de paroistre." Daval, Histoire de la Réformation à Dieppe, i. 50, 52.

cost, the twenty-second of June, 1601, they had the satisfaction of worshipping for the first time in a "temple" just finished, which measured ninety feet in length by seventy-four feet in breadth. Six or seven years later, the walls were overthrown in a great storm that swept over the place. The Protestants of Dieppe were not discouraged. The temple that arose from the ruins, in 1608, was oval in shape, and measured one hundred and ten feet across the greater diameter and eighty feet across the shorter. Its cost was about twenty thousand livres.[1] We need not follow the faithful chronicler, who describes with loving minuteness all the architectural features of this marvel of convenience and compactness, but we may be well assured that, as its vast auditorium re-echoed to the strains of the psalms, or the great body of worshippers listened with devout attention to the reading and exposition of the gospel in their mother-tongue, the hearts of many were raised in thankfulness to Almighty God for having deigned to confer upon them the inestimable blessings guaranteed by the Edict of Nantes. Our informant has unfortunately neglected to tell us how many persons could gather within the sacred walls. The number could scarcely have been less than five or six thousand, and may easily have exceeded those figures; but whatever it was, the place was found too crowded. Within four years the structure was enlarged by taking into the audience-room some parts of the building previously destined to another purpose.[2]

The Protestants of the capital were, in one respect, at a peculiar disadvantage. The Roman Catholic counsellors of Henry the Fourth would hear of no edict in favor of the Huguenots, unless the services of Protestant worship should be banished to a distance of at least five leagues from Notre Dame; and the negotiators had been compelled to yield the point. After the publication of the Edict of Nantes, the little village of Ablon, situated on the left bank of the winding river Seine, at about the required distance above Paris, was selected as a proper site. Even this poor concession was greeted with delight by the Huguenots of the city, long accustomed to such

Ablon.

---

[1] Ibid., ubi supra, i. 174, 175.   [2] Ibid., ubi supra, i. 196.

poor and occasional privileges as a favored few alone could enjoy, in the apartments of the king's sister or in the quarters of
some foreign embassy.   But the hardships to be endured in
reaching Ablon were great enough to discourage less devout worshippers.   In bad weather, to row fifteen miles up the river
before service, and fifteen miles back in the evening, was a formidable undertaking.   The exposure was fatal to many a man
and woman,[1] not to speak of accidents by collision, such as that
which, at a subsequent time, occurred to the eminent Isaac
Casaubon, when going even the short distance to Charenton,
and which came near ending his life and the lives of the members of his family that accompanied him.   Most disastrous,
however, was the journey to the infants whom Protestant parents were obliged to carry this great distance to be baptized,
since the discipline of the Reformed Church, as we have seen,
permitted the initial ordinance to be performed only in connection with public worship and preaching.   Within a single year
forty children succumbed to disease brought on by their unfortunate exposure.[2]   For several years the king was deaf to the remonstrances of his Huguenot subjects, but at length, in 1606, he
consented to relieve them of the necessity of going so far.   Of
his own authority, and almost without consulting any one else,
he fixed upon a place destined to become famous in
Charenton.   connection with later Protestant history.   Charenton,
then little more than a hamlet, stood on the northern bank of
the Seine, just below its junction with the Marne.   The selec-

---

[1] The Ephemerides of Casaubon are full of references to these sad experiences.   In his own family a nephew lost his life as the direct consequence of
a trip to Ablon by boat on Palm-Sunday, 1602.   Bulletin de la Soc. de l'hist.
du Prot. français, ii. 272.

[2] The "Cahier des plaintes et remonstrances pour ceux de la religion," presented to the king in 1601, says that the children were in evident danger of
their lives, "tant pour la longueur et incommodité du chemin que à cause des
grandes froidures de l'hyver et chaleurs de l'esté, dont il est advenu que
plusieurs desdits enfans jusques au nombre de quarante, ont esté l'hyver passé
miserablement esteints et suffoqués."   Bulletin, etc., ii. 253, 254.   Henry IV.,
in his letters-patent of August 1, 1606, granting the change of place from
Ablon to Charenton, speaks of the inability of Protestant parents to carry their
children to the former place for baptism, "sans péril, en les exposant à l'in-
jure de l'air par un si grand chemin."   Ibid., iii. 421.

tion of this spot almost caused a riot among the bigoted Parisians, who did not fail to call the king's attention to the fact that,
in bringing the hated Protestant services so near to the capital,
he was violating one of the prescriptions of his edict. Having
once made up his mind, Henry was not easily moved from his
purpose; but instead of an angry retort he preferred to close
the mouths of the objectors by an unanswerable jest. "In order
not to break my word," he said, with a smile, "we shall have
henceforth to count five leagues from Paris to Charenton!" [1]
No surveyor other than a king could have made the distance
above a league and a half, or two leagues at most.

Of the first "temple" of Charenton, erected as soon as the royal
permission was obtained, the notices are few and unsatisfactory.
Of the second, which arose after the destruction of the former
by fire, we have a fuller description. This was the building
that remained down to the period of the Revocation, and whose
overthrow, accomplished by order of Louis the Fourteenth, was
as much a source of rejoicing to the clergy and to the order of
the Jesuits, as an occasion of lamentation to the Protestants.
Its lofty roof, as ancient prints show, a conspicuous object for
a great distance around, was the beacon by which the devout
Protestants of Paris shaped their course every Lord's Day
morning, as, with singing of the melodies of Bourgeois or the
more intricate harmonies of Goudimel, they wended their way
by boat to the quay, among a throng of other boats bound for
the same destination. On the floor of the sacred edifice, and in
the two galleries surrounding it, there was said to be space for
fourteen thousand worshippers, and recent calculations seem to
show that the estimate was not exaggerated. [2] Even this structure was not spacious enough to hold the congregations at Easter and on the other occasions when the Sacrament of the Lord's

---

[1] "Elle les contenta d'une réplique prompte qu'elle leur fist en sousriant,
que, pour ne pas manquer à ses promesses, il falloit désormais compter cinq
lieues de Paris à Charenton." Bulletin, etc., iii 429.

[2] Bulletin, etc., v. 171, 172. In connection with the admirable monograph
on the early "temples" of the church of Paris, published in this periodical,
there are given views of the second "temple" of Charenton, as well as a plan
and sections of the building. Ibid., v. 174, 177, 178.

Supper was administered to the crowds that poured out from
Paris. At these great solemnities there was erected, in another
part of the grounds attached to the " temple," a great tent, under
which communion services, including public preaching, went
on contemporaneously with those observed within the edifice.
At such seasons the approach to the Protestant " temple "
was lined on both sides with the stalls of booksellers, much as
they graced the entrance to the college of the Sorbonne in the
city itself, and every controversial work as it appeared, from
the ponderous tome down to the trifling pamphlet or handbill,
could be purchased by such of the throng as might be so inclined.[1]

It was a favorite thought of the early reformers of France
that their new principle of life might and ought to exhibit
its reality and its power in every action and in every place—
that their words, their manners, and morals, even their
very dwellings, could become the vehicles of conveying
to others a notion of the lively hopes that animated

Writing on the posts and the gates.

them. Thus it was that, not content with causing the interior
of their houses to resound with the words and the music of
their cherished psalms, they were fond of decorating the outside with short inscriptions, drawing their sentiments from
the sacred volume. The practice would doubtless have become
more wide-spread, had not the same repressive hand that strove
to silence the singing within the doors been extended to prevent the Huguenot from placing any distinctive badge of his
religion upon the outer walls of his house. It was, therefore,
only where the Protestants were relatively numerous, and chiefly where they constituted the great mass of the population, that
they ventured to indulge in this beautiful usage. No Huguenot inscription must be looked for upon the old edifices of Paris,
or Tours, or Orleans. More appropriate for them would be
some persecuting device, such as still stands on the frontal of
the Palazzo della Ragione of Milan, perpetuating the memory of
the zeal of the founder, Podestà Oldrado Grosso, in the destruc-

---

[1] See the plan of the temple and its surroundings, Bulletin, etc., iii. 436,
437.

tion of those mediæval reformers who may be regarded as the
forerunners of the later Huguenots,

> " Qui solium struxit, Catharos, ut debuit, uxit."

In fact, the line or two drawn from Clément Marot or Theodore Beza would have seemed strangely out of place when the
gaudy drapery was annually hung out of window and wound
about column on the great feast of Fête Dieu, or Corpus Christi.

While many of the inscriptions have certainly been destroyed
by the Roman Catholic successors of the Huguenot
proprietors, a number have survived, especially in the
western part of France. At Coulonges sur l'Autize,
on the stone support of a window, may still be read the lines,

Some Huguenot inscriptions.

> " Quiconque espère au Dieu vivant,
> Jamais ne périra "—

" Whoever hopes in the living God never shall perish "—being
the end of the thirty-fourth Psalm in the metrical paraphrase.
An inscription upon the lintel of the door of a farm-house, in a
village hard by, declares :

> " On a beau sa maison bâtir ;
> Si le Seigneur n'y met sa main,
> Cela n'est que bâtir en vain "—

" Except the Lord build the house, they labor in vain that
build it "—from the beginning of the one hundred and twenty-
seventh Psalm.

Often short and pithy precepts find their place upon the
stone. Over an old portal in the Rue du Minage, at La Rochelle,
there are several couplets. One is,

> " Vaincre le mal en bien faisant
> Est à notre Dieu fort plaisant "—

" To overcome evil with good is well-pleasing to our God."
Another,

> " A parler tardif,
> A ouïr hâtif "—

" Slow to speak, quick to hear." A third,

> " Vaut mieux sagesse,
> Que posséder richesse "—

" Better is wisdom than the possession of riches."

But the thought upon which the pious builders dwelt with most satisfaction would appear to have been the contrast between the earthly and temporary, and the heavenly or eternal, home. So at Marsilly, a village a few leagues from La Rochelle, immediately below the Latin words "Soli Deo" one can yet read the French couplet,

"Ici bas n'avons un manoir éternel,
Mais eu cerchons (cherchons) un tout perpétuel"—

"Here below we have no eternal abode, but we seek for one that is everlasting." And, in La Rochelle itself, the most suggestive device of all, the more beautiful for its concise and simple grandeur, consists only of the words, cut over the door of a house,

"En attendant une meilleure"—

"While waiting for a better one."[1]

A day of permanent peace, an era of established tranquillity, seemed at length to have dawned upon the Huguenots, under the kindly rule of the former "protector" of their churches, and beneath the safeguard of the perpetual and ir-

Assassination of Henry the Fourth.

revocable law enacted for their benefit. The most cautious recognized the signs of continued growth. The sanguine anticipated an advance of Protestantism in France unexampled for rapidity during the previous years of persecution. All had brilliant visions of a long career of uninterrupted prosperity. A blow, sudden and brutal, awakened them rudely from their dream.

The spring of the year 1610 found Henry the Fourth about

---

[1] See the interesting contributions, by P. P. and L. de Richemond fils, to the Bulletin de la Société de l'histoire du Protestantisme français, x. 4, 113, 114.—"The former guild-house of the French Tanners' Guild in Berlin, where, after the Revocation of the Edict of Nantes, they had been welcomed by the Elector Frederick William the Great and given a house, now No. 2 Belle Alliance Place, has still the old insignia carved over the door: an eagle, covering by his wings a number of small birds ; and, underneath, the second verse of the fifty-seventh Psalm in French: 'Sous l'ombre de tes ailes nous avons trouvé asile.'" Communicated by B. Fernow, Esq., Department of MSS., State Library, Albany.

to enter upon a great and important war. The decease of John William, Duke of Juliers (Jülich) and Cleves, without male offspring, had left his extensive possessions on the lower Rhine to be a bone of contention between the Protestants and Roman Catholics of the German Empire. Solicited by the former, and not averse to avenge the insults and injuries he had received at the hands of the Habsburgs, the French monarch definitely resolved to espouse the cause of his former allies, and to support the claim of the Margrave of Brandenburg to the disputed succession. Meanwhile he secured by treaty the co-operation of Charles Emmanuel, of Savoy, whose friendship was to be still further cemented by the marriage of the king's eldest daughter to the Prince of Piedmont, eldest son and heir of the duke. Besides the motives of policy hurrying Henry into war with the house of Austria, other and less creditable considerations are said to have been equally potent. Henry was anxious to punish the states that had harbored a fugitive whose escape from Paris caused him extreme annoyance. The son of the murdered Henry of Condé, the infant about whose legitimacy there hung so dark a cloud of uncertainty,[1] had grown to be a youth of some twenty-two years of age. Educated, in defiance of his father's well-known wishes, at the royal court and in the Roman Catholic faith, the prince had, within a few months, been married to Charlotte Marguerite of Montmorency, daughter of the constable, a woman not less remarkable for beauty than illustrious in descent. It was not long, however, before the youthful bridegroom discovered, or believed that he had discovered, that, in so dissolute a court, neither his own honor nor the virtue of his wife could long be secure. A subject, even if a prince of the blood, might scarcely hope to shield his consort from the dangerous solicitation of a king with whom advancing years had not increased respect for conjugal fidelity. The Prince of Condé fled from the kingdom, and placed the princess, his wife, in a sure refuge at Brussels, under protection of the Austrian archduke, while he himself went on as far south as Milan. Unsuccessful in his attempts to induce his cousin to

---

[1] See above, chapter viii., pages 20-22.

return to France, Henry the Fourth found in this episode new grounds for hastening the preparations he was already making to measure his strength against that of the " Holy Roman Empire."

Before setting out upon the campaign which he fondly expected to be the most brilliant of his life, the king was persuaded to confer the regency during his prospective absence upon his queen, Maria de' Medici, now the mother of several young princes whom she had borne him. Her coronation took place on Thursday, the thirteenth of May, in the abbey church of Saint Denis. The Cardinal of Joyeuse was the chief officiating ecclesiastic, and no circumstance that could contribute dignity and impressiveness to the august occasion was wanting. Another pageant was reserved for the ensuing Sunday, when the queen regent was to make her pompous entry into the capital. Already the citizens of Paris were busy with preparations in view of that event. Statues, triumphal columns, inscriptions, paintings, were rising at every point upon the intended route of the procession. Meantime Henry did not suffer his attention to be diverted from his martial project. Lest a moment of precious time might be lost, he superintended in person the preparations for the coming campaign. So it was that, between three and four o'clock in the afternoon of Friday, the fourteenth of May, he rode out of the courtyard of the Louvre, intending to see with his own eyes the progress of the workmen, and to encourage them by his presence. He bade his customary guard not to escort him. Into the capacious carriage he entered with about half a dozen noblemen of rank. He gave the Duke of Épernon a seat by him on his right; his first squire, Liancourt, and Marquis Mirabeau were in front and opposite; Marshal Lavardin and Roquelaure were in the boot at one door of the carriage, the Duke of Montbazon and Marquis La Force in the boot at the other door. The king had ordered all the curtains to be raised, and was soon engaged in earnest conversation with his companions. An assassin, François Ravaillac, of Angoulême, had been lingering at the palace gate. hoping to find an opportunity to do his bloody work when the king should emerge from the portal. He was disappointed.

Épernon occupied the place in which he had expected Henry to be, and the victim he sought was beyond his reach. But the favorable moment, which Ravaillac thought had escaped him, came only too soon. The royal carriage in a few minutes reached the Rue de la Féronnerie, a thoroughfare narrow at best, and long since rendered still more contracted by the wooden stores or stalls which had been erected on the left-hand side, attached to the stone wall of the Cimetière des Innocents. Here two heavily laden wagons, one with hay, the other with casks of wine, blocked the way, causing the horses to stop again and again. The lackeys had left the carriage to take a shorter or less impeded path through the cemetery, the gentlemen in waiting had become separated and were following as best they could. The single footman, who might have warded off the murderous blow from his master, had stopped to fasten his garter, which had become detached. Ravaillac, elbowing his way in the crowd, reached the spot, heated and panting for breath, and found that his time had come. The king was opposite to him, his cloak thrown off, his right arm leaning on the neck of Épernon, to whom he had given a paper to read, his other arm resting on Montbazon's shoulder, his left side altogether unprotected. The stealthy assassin had but to take a single step to reach over the carriage-wheel, to draw his well-sharpened knife from beneath his cloak, to make one swift thrust, then a second, and all was over. The weapon was carefully directed to the king's heart, and had accomplished the miscreant's purpose. Before the noblemen with whom Henry was conversing knew that he had received a wound, he was already bathed in blood and unconscious. In an instant more he was dead.

Thus perished the foremost prince of Europe, the monarch who, of all the kings that ever sat on the throne of France, is perhaps most deservedly held in grateful remembrance by posterity.

The character of Henry the Fourth can best be gathered from the record of his life. Those who have carefully followed each step of his course, from his birth in the castle of Pau, as far removed from any prospect of the crown of France as his home at the foot of the Pyrenees was distant from the splendors of the Louvre, may be safely left to paint the portrait of his virtues and vices for themselves. His had been a checkered life, full of changes, full of surprises; and his personal qualities were scarcely less marked by inconsistencies and contradictions. His Appearance appearance was prepossessing. Though he was not and character of Henry of above the middle height his bearing was dignified Navarre. and commanding. A high, broad forehead; eyes keen, restless, and penetrating; a complexion fresh and ruddy; a long, aquiline nose; a mouth expressive of mingled gentleness and decision—these combined to make up an aspect which affected the beholder favorably. When he opened his lips the grace and sprightliness of his speech, the mirthfulness of his tone, his vivacity, his quickness at repartee, not less than his affability and courtesy, deepened the impression already made, winning admiration, and transforming kindly dispositions into firm friendship and devoted affection. Yet the same mouth that could gain the hearts of men by the honeyed sweetness of its words, gave vent occasionally to biting sarcasm; and the nearest and most attached of associates could testify, from personal experience, that if Henry of Navarre was a master of the art of judicious encouragement to valiant action, he was certainly also an adept in the use of the power of derision, caring little what might be the past services of the unfortunate victims of his scornful laughter. Some maintained that the king readily forgave and forgot the injuries done him. On this point there was a difference of opinion. But there was no difference as to the facility with which Henry banished from mind all recollection of the good offices of his followers. In the domain of private morals the conflict of warring tendencies in Henry's nature was most sharply defined. Noble aspirations, elevating him above the plane reached by the majority of the men of his day, wrestled with grovelling tastes which tended to degrade him to the lowest depths of a purely sensual existence. Thus he often seemed likely to prove in turn the glory and the shame of his age.

Such was Henry of Navarre, Henry the Fourth of France— Henry the Great, as his admiring subjects not improperly surnamed him—so grand a man, in some aspects, that we wonder

that his character should have been marred by such blemishes—
so faulty a man, from other points of view, that we marvel that
he could ever have been esteemed magnanimous; an enigma to
his contemporaries, scarcely less an enigma to succeeding gener-
ations; a man of singular strength and of singular weakness; a
compound of rare virtues and extraordinary vices; keen of perception, acute, persevering, patient of fatigue, buoyant, courageous, affable, witty, a cheery companion, impetuous, forgetful of
danger, a leader in perilous enterprises, with a jest for every
emergency, with an encouraging word or look for each of his
followers—a general, in short, for whom not one of his Huguenot soldiers but would have deemed it a privilege to lay down
life; a man, on the other hand, of excessive fondness for pleasure, a very Samson, who more than once allowed his locks to
be shorn, who more than once suffered himself to be robbed of
his strength to gratify a Delilah; selfish, even where he was
most liberal; calculating, where he appeared most disinterested;
fickle in his love, whether to man or to woman; not incapable
of suffering a discarded mistress, and the mother of his child, to
die of want and neglect within a stone's throw of his castle, or
of arranging beforehand for the unmerited discomfiture in unequal controversy of a brave and loyal Duplessis Mornay, when
the discomfiture would inure to some fancied advantage of the
king.

Yet neither the patriot nor the lover of religious freedom can
be oblivious of the claims of the first Bourbon king of France
to the gratitude of posterity. His was the sagacious intellect,
his the unfaltering courage, his the steady hand that brought
order out of the confusion into which the civil wars of the latter
half of the sixteenth century had plunged his country. It was
Henry of Navarre who never despaired of the commonwealth,
even in the darkest hour of the conflict with the League. It
was he who restored to France her rightful position among the
leading states of western Europe. It was this intrepid and
adventurous king who, had his life been spared, might have
undertaken, with more hope of success than any monarch of
his age, to realize the fanciful but brilliant dream of a universal Christian Republic, ever pacific because ever settling

the controversies that might arise by peaceful arbitration—a Christian Republic formed by the union of fifteen states, as nearly equal in power as possible, which should bury their mutual animosities the better to wage war against the infidel.[1]   The expectation that the adherents of the Lutheran, the Reformed, and the Roman Catholic religions, renouncing the insane endeavor to obtain exclusive sway throughout the world, would agree to dwell together in charity and tolerate each other as members of one Christian communion, might be chimerical when applied to the whole of Europe.   Yet it was but the expansion of that which Henry had undertaken to do, by means of the Edict of Nantes, for the single kingdom of France of that which he had succeeded in accomplishing, so far as mere legislation can effect anything.   For this the Huguenots—and not the Huguenots alone, but every well-wisher of his country, and every believer in the sacred right of liberty of conscience—owed the murdered king so great a debt of gratitude that they freely forgot every foible of his character, even to his recreancy to the faith in which he was brought up and which he had insincerely abjured, and remembered him only as the greatest benefactor of France.

Of the military designs which Henry cherished, of the victories he hoped to win at the head of the main body of his army in Germany, of the blows he expected Lesdiguières to strike at the supremacy of the house of Habsburg in Italy, of contemplated achievements in the interest of nations long oppressed by the dread of a Spanish world-empire, this is not the place to

---

[1] The reader need scarcely be reminded that the fifteen sovereign "dominations" in question were to be, first, the six hereditary monarchies of France, Spain, Great Britain, Denmark, Sweden, and Savoy, or Northern Italy ; second, the six elective monarchies of the Empire, Poland, Hungary, Venice, Bohemia, and the States of the Church, or Southern Italy ; and, third, the three consolidated republics of the Low Countries, Switzerland, and Italy.   It would appear that the matter formed the subject of frequent conversation and discussion between Henry IV. and the Duke of Sully, and was broached by the latter when sent on an embassy to Queen Elizabeth, in 1601.   The queen's death retarded, the assassination of the king put an end to, the prosecution of the scheme.   See Mémoires de Sully (edition of 1663), ii. 8, 399, 400 ; iii. 45, 46, 453 ; iv. 752, etc.

speak. Whatever were his designs—whether practicable or visionary, whether their realization might have conduced to the pacific settlement of those great questions which were to convulse Christendom in the succeeding century, or would but have served to precipitate the inevitable catastrophe—the blade of a single obscure enthusiast sufficed in an instant to frustrate them all. From the hands of a monarch of wonderful quickness and grasp of intellect, a man of singular vitality and in the flower of his manly vigor, the sceptre slipped into those of a son, a minor, the child of a queen of Italian parentage, and, as well by instinct as by education, inimical to the enterprises of her husband. Maria de' Medici might be guiltless of complicity in the assassination of Henry of Navarre, but that her sympathies were altogether with those who profited by its perpetration there can be no doubt.

The deed of Ravaillac has remained a mystery even down to the present time, and will probably remain a mystery for all time. The murderer was not, indeed, at once despatched by the indignant bystanders, as had been the case with Jacques Clément. There was, therefore, a better prospect of success in discovering the instigators of the murder of Henry the Fourth than there had been of ascertaining the authors of the murder of Henry the Third. But the frightful tortures to which Ravaillac was subjected were ineffectual to compel him to disclose the truth, and, whether the judges were too clumsy or too timid, his secret seems to have died with him, when he was at last put to death, torn asunder by four horses, less than a fortnight after the commission of his crime. The guilt was laid at the door of Spain, whose exploits in the matter of assassination had been notorious both before and since the time when Balthazar Gérard shot William of Orange on the staircase at Delft; or at the door of the Duke of Épernon, who sat on Henry's right in the carriage when Ravaillac stabbed him—Épernon, from whom no deed of treachery was unlooked for, a deadly enemy of the king, albeit that king had condescended to call him "my friend," when gleefully announcing to him Duplessis Mornay's discomfiture, just ten years before; or at the door of the Jesuits, who, despite the

Ravaillac's crime a mystery.

past favors of the monarch, and despite the fact that Father Cotton, a member of their order, was the royal confessor, never forgot their inherited allegiance to the crown once worn by Gondy's certificate of the innocence of the Jesuits. Philip the Second. The Bishop of Paris, Cardinal Gondy, it is true, was at the pains to clear the reverend fathers of the aspersion in a formal document, solemnly attested and given under his hand and seal, on the twenty-sixth of June, whereby he declared that the rumors afloat were impostures, calumnies, and malicious fabrications, to the disadvantage of the Roman Catholic and Apostolic religion. Not only were the Jesuits altogether free from blame, but their Order was, according to the writer, as well for its doctrine as for the good life of its members, exceedingly useful to the Church of God and profitable to the State.[1] So far as it had any influence, however, the certificate of the bishop tended rather to draw attention to the probability that the intriguing society founded by Loyola had been concerned in the misdeed, than to remove suspicion from the breast of any impartial man. The reputation of the apologists of the Jesuits for strict veracity did not rank among the best; and the Huguenots from the first held them responsible. "It is a great pity," wrote Duplessis Mornay, only a day or two after hearing the fatal intelligence, "that the horror of our age has reached such a point as to reduce to an art the method of assassinating princes, and that, in place of the hell which awaits such execrable murderers, men have been able systematically to persuade them that the highest rank of paradise is reserved for them. Since the Jesuits are, next to the Mohammedans, the first restorers of this training, it will be a great marvel if this blow has been struck without their intervention."[2]

The grief of the Huguenots was intense, their solicitude respecting the future too deep to be wholly allayed, even by

---

[1] The attestation of the Bishop of Paris is a brief but interesting production, worthy a place among the curiosities of literature. It is reprinted, together with a number of other important documents relative to the trial of Ravaillac, in the third part of the sixth or supplementary volume of the Mémoires de Condé, published at the Hague in 1743, page 246.

[2] Duplessis Mornay to J. A. de Thou, May 18, 1610, Mémoires, xi. 29.

prompt assurances, offered in the young dauphin's name, that the existing laws for their protection would be conscientiously observed. They knew, indeed, that the best interests of the commonwealth were bound up with their safety, and that in no way could the peace of France be better conserved than by respecting the sanction which the Edict of Nantes had received both from the monarch and from the highest courts of judicature. But they also knew that powerful and sleepless enemies were only biding the time when a determined attempt to annul the tolerant legislation of Henry the Fourth might be undertaken with reasonable hope of success. Whether the perils environing them would ultimately be dissipated, or the catastrophe prove inevitable, was a question the answer to which was beyond the bounds of human prescience.

INDEX.

INDEX.

A.

514

INDEX.

Orléans, Louis d', a Leaguer, his pamphlet, i. 313.
Ornano, Alphonso, "the Corsican," colonel of the Italian infantry, a minor favorite of Henry III., i. 228; advises the king to put Guise out of the way, ii. 38; ii. 44, 97, 122, 189, 437.
Orthez, i. 258; its university, ib., note; ii. 477.
Ossat, Cardinal, his remarks respecting the absence of any attempts at regicide among the Huguenots, ii. 160, 161; his efforts to obtain the absolution of Henry IV., ii. 365.
Ourcamp, Abbey of, i. 405.
Ozillac, ii. 387.

P.

Paillez, Viscount of, i. 259.
Palatine, Count, i. 253.
Palatine, Elector. See Frederick the Pious; Casimir, John, etc.
Palissy, Bernard, the potter, his history, ii. 7, seq.; visited in the Bastile by Henry III., ii. 8; his intrepid reply to the king's solicitations, ib.
Pamiers, i. 258.
Panat, Viscount of, i. 259.
Paris, fright of, i. 93; Huguenots attacked at, i. 113; opposition to signing the League, i. 149, 166; the plague at, i. 208; the League at, i. 274, seq.; growth of the League according to the narrative of Nicholas Poulain, i. 291, seq.; the city searched by the king's orders, i. 319; refuses money to the king, i. 355; Henry of Navarre's letter to the city, i. 388; the citizens beg Guise to come, ii. 33; day of the barricades at, ii. 41, seq.; its municipal officers removed by the League, ii. 47; how it might be punished by the king, ii. 51; its delight at the publication of the Edict of Union, ii. 58, which the citizens flock to sign, ii. 59; fury of the Parisians at the murder of the Guises, ii. 124; attack of Henry IV. on the faubourgs of the city, ii. 185; it is besieged by Henry IV., ii. 211; its preparations for a siege, ii. 212; census of, ii. 213; progress of famine, ii. 214; the besieged have recourse to strange food, ii. 216; Gondy, Bishop of Paris, and Espinac, Archbishop of Lyons, sent to confer with Henry IV. respecting peace, ii. 217, seq.; the city makes no sorties, ii. 222, 223; failure of a nocturnal attack upon, ii. 230; the city is provisioned, ii. 231; the "jour des farines," January 20, 1591, ii. 244; retaliatory action of the rebel parliament, ii. 268, 269; the citizens urgent

for peace, ii. 314, 331; it surrenders to Henry IV., ii. 370.
Paris, the Bishop of, on Huguenot arbitration, i. 5.
Parliament of Paris, the, remonstrates against the proscriptive legislation of Henry III. and the papal bull, i. 370, seq.; its plea for liberty of conscience, ib.; it is reprimanded by Henry III., ii. 6; it registers the Edict of Union, ii. 58; its dignified conduct when President Le Maistre is arrested, ii. 126; declaration of January 30, 1589, in support of the Roman Catholic religion, ii. 128, seq.; its retaliatory acts, ii. 268, 269, 308, 309; it declares null and void any compact contrary to the Salic law, ii. 325; dilatoriness in registering the Edict of Nantes, ii. 424–428; its pliancy, ii. 463.
Parma, Alexander Farnese, Duke and Prince of, i. 292; ii. 32; he comes to the relief of Paris, ii. 224, seq.; he takes Lagny in the teeth of Henry IV., ii. 229; his retreat, ii. 233; he again invades France to relieve the city of Rouen, ii. 286; his help dispensed with, ii. 288; he is again begged to return, ii. 289; he is wounded, but makes a masterly retreat, ii. 290, 291; his death, ii. 293.
Parry, William, i. 285.
Pasquier, Étienne, on "la reine blanche," i. 10, 450.
Pasquin on the ruin of the "Invincible Armada," ii. 82.
Patriarchate, French, proposed, ii. 271.
Patris, Guillaume de, i. 184.
Pau, i. 258, 437.
Paulin, Viscount, i. 48, 259.
Peace conference proposed, ii. 316; invitation of the royalist nobles, ii. 317, seq.
Peace negotiations of April, 1575, i. 48, etc.; end of, i. 64; peace of Monsieur, May, 1576, i. 93, seq.; its unpopularity, i. 97; peace of Bergerac (Poitiers), 1577, i. 167; peace of Fleix, 1580, i. 210, seq.; peace of Vervins, May, 1598 (with Spain), ii. 421.
Pellevé, Cardinal, ii. 320, 323, 324.
Penitents, the, i. 38.
People. See Tiers État.
Périgord, county of, i. 259.
Périgueux, i. 94, 224, 259.
Péronne, i. 94; league of, i. 103; manifesto of, i. 107; declaration of, i. 314, seq.; ii. 369.
Perouse, valley of, ii. 298.
Perplexity of the persecuting clergy, i. 385.
Perron, du, Bishop and Cardinal, his efforts to secure the papal absolution of Henry IV., ii. 265, 385; he charges Duplessis Mornay with having made

Date Due